SELECTIONS FROM PLATO

SELECTIONS

FROM

PLATO

WITH INTRODUCTION AND NOTES

BY

LEWIS LEAMING FORMAN

FOREWORD BY

ALEXANDER TULIN

UNIVERSITY OF OKLAHOMA PRESS
NORMAN

Library of Congress Cataloging-in-Publication Data

Plato.
[Selections. English. 2006]
Selections from Plato / with introduction and notes by Lewis Leaming Forman ; foreword by Alexander Tulin.
p. cm.
Originally published: 1st ed. London : Macmillan, 1911, in series: Classical series. With new foreword.
Includes bibliographical references and indexes.
ISBN 0-8061-3776-2 (pbk. : alk. paper)
1. Philosophy, Ancient. I. Forman, Lewis Leaming. II. Title.

B358.F64 2006
184—dc22

2005046672

The paper in this book meets the guidelines for permanence and durability of the Committee on Production Guidelines for Book Longevity of the Council on Library Resources, Inc.∞

Published by MacMillan and Co., Limited 1900. University of Oklahoma Press edition published 2006.

TO

MY MOTHER

AND OUR PAST

L. L. F.

TABLE OF SELECTIONS

III. Plato—Socrates

IV. Briefer Extracts

FOREWORD

Lewis Leaming Forman's *Selections from Plato* is (as school commentaries go) quite unique, for it contains an analysis of Platonic syntax, diction, and idiom so original and intimate that, if one studies it carefully, one will never again look at Plato's Greek with quite the same eyes. It is my hope that this re-publication of Forman's *Selections* will call attention to a useful and valuable work that has been all but forgotten by students and scholars of Greek.

Forman was born in Romney, Indiana, in 1857, and died in Ithaca, New York, in 1933. In 1894 he took his Ph.D. at The Johns Hopkins University, and immediately began his teaching career at Cornell, where he served three separate stints (1894–1900, 1902–11, 1921–24), all in a junior capacity. In addition to his dissertation on certain uses of the genitive and dative (Baltimore, 1894), which was supervised by Basil Gildersleeve, and *Selections From Plato* (London, 1900), he published an *Index Andocideus, Lycurgeus, Dinarcheus* (Oxford, 1897), *A First Greek Book* (New York and London, 1899), and a school edition of Aristophanes' *Clouds* (New York, 1915). He also left an elementary Latin book in manuscript form among his papers.[1]

Forman's *Selections* contains the whole of the *Apology* and *Crito*, together with selected passages from other dialogues. It includes an introduction and Greek text, followed by detailed grammatical notes, valuable appendices to these notes, and three analytical indices that allow the book to be used for reference purposes.[2]

The book was written for freshmen—but that was at a time when incoming freshmen generally had four years of secondary Greek under their belts. Today the book is best suited for intermediate and advanced undergraduates, though it can also be studied profitably by graduate students at all levels as well as by scholars and translators working with Greek prose authors generally (see, by way of example, pp. 410–11).

The reader should begin by working through the line-by-line grammatical notes that form the bulk of the commentary—starting either with the *Crito* and a few of the easier selections, or else directly with the *Apology*. If the reader then follows up on Forman's many references and cross-references, both to the commentary and to the appendices, one will find remarkably clear and insightful discussions of many of the essential points of Greek. For instance:

• sundry comments and observations on particles and particle collocations, many of them attaining to the status of a small essay;

• discussions of various prepositions, negatives, and idioms;

• detailed analyses of the (often commonsense) principles underlying Greek word order, of the structures apparent in complex conditionals, and of the important logical pattern known as the *argumentum ex contrario*—a pattern of thought, as Forman notes, that can be found on nearly every page of Plato.

In sum, there is a veritable wealth of material in this volume to repay careful study, and students and scholars of Plato and the orators will be much the richer for it.

ALEXANDER TULIN
Howard University

NOTES

1. For biographical details, see W. W. Briggs, Jr. (ed.), *Biographical Dictionary of North American Classicists* (Westport and London, 1994), 191 [Briggs]; also G. Kirkwood, *The Classics at Cornell: The First Century* (Ithaca, 2000), 27–37, who adds a number of interesting and revealing vignettes.

2. The introduction is not without interest, but shows its age. The text, based largely on the vulgate (which at that time was Hermann's Teubner), shows no familiarity with Burnet's great Oxford edition, the first volume of which also appeared in 1900. A review of *Selections,* by R. D. Archer-Hind, appeared in *Classical Review* 15 (1901), 230.

PREFACE

THE following Selections have not been edited as an Introduction to Platonic Philosophy, still less to offer initiation into the question of its evolution (dialogue-chronology, etc.). Nor does the editor discuss, or even tabulate, the various readings of the manuscripts. The aim of the book is a far more humble one, viz. to offer an introduction, 1st to Plato's language, with the constant aid of grammar and dictionary, 2nd to the noble figure of Socrates as presented in Plato's pages. These two considerations have controlled both the selection of the passages and the writing of the notes. All else has been rigorously excluded. It would indeed have been pleasant to quote the poets here and there, to cite modern instances, to illustrate the usages of the language from other writers, etc. etc. But the editor's sad experience has been that such notes are not read and, to be frank, are of little value to the ordinary Freshman. *He* is still wrestling with the principal parts of the simpler verbs, his vocabulary chiefly military, and as for particles! He either ignores them all, or translates all the γάρ's by 'for' and all the rest by 'indeed.' Philosophical and literary notes, therefore, he does not want, and will not read. No more will he read or be aided by learned references to *B.B.*, *A.J.P.*, *Zeitschr. f. d. oest. Gymn.*, *Meisterhans*, and other hieroglyphic literature. He skips them all and buys a "crib." There he finds practical aid. Who will blame him?

It may be objected that no student should be permitted to open Plato until he knows his grammar. Perfectly true. And the editor wishes to be the first to declare that the notes here offered on Plato are by no means the kind that should be offered—that it is a "base use" he makes of Plato, taking his words as texts for instruction on *μέντοι, γάρ*, prolepsis, etc.—that *of course* Plato should be studied in conjunction with Euripides, Pindar, Greek religion, and Greek life. But all that is as it ought to be, not as it is. For who does not know that beginners *are* permitted to open Plato often after a bare two years' interval from their induction into the Greek alphabet?—a chaotic two years, spent in dimly learning to distinguish a few forms, to guess at the rest, to feel for the syntax, and to prepare for a so-called "examination" on about 250 pages of mixed epic and Xenophontese. After which—college and Plato. Now nobody knows better than the Freshman himself how little he knows (for he is ordinarily a quite reasonable being). He is therefore quite willing to work with grammar and dictionary, if aid be given him. But this he must have. For in truth Liddell & Scott's dictionary is rather formidable to one who has hitherto worked with mere vocabularies. The articles are often long; and he does not know where to look for his wants. And the grammar is no less of an enigma. The aid therefore which such conscientious students need in the preparation of a lesson, this book tries to give. It is hoped that thus it will free the teacher from bothering details in construction, and allow him time within his hour for whatever form of supplementary exegesis he may find advisable in the broader fields of philosophy, literature, and antiquities.

A further set of notes has been added in an Appendix containing information chiefly on various syntactic habits of the Greek language, but in no wise necessary to a correct understanding of the text. It matters little, for example, to the sense of a passage, whether *περί* is used with genitive or dative. Nor is one apt to miss the sense, though he be ignorant of the limitations of *παρά* with the dative. All such matters, consequently, are relegated to the Appendix for the use of those who study the language fundamentally.

As regards the selections—they were chosen, as already said, rather to introduce the student to Socrates than to Plato. Though we perhaps come to know neither of them till we have ourselves reached middle life, yet in youth we can more easily *think* we know Socrates than Plato. At all events we are humanly touched at his death, our indignation is righteous and healthy, and we love Socrates.

Not till we have walked "upon the back of heaven" can we fall down to revere our divine guide Plato.

The editor's best thanks are due to Professor George Prentice Bristol for his constant encouragement and advice on the work, as well as for that best proof of friendship—proof-reading. It is needless for him to add that as the book leaves his hands the feeling arises which probably comes to all those who issue a book—that this creature before him is not that which it was to be, not by leagues. His only consolation is that the purchaser has not wholly lost his money. For has he not 275 pages of Plato?

NOTE ON THE TEXT. After having proceeded a long way in the construction of a text showing all the modern improvements (ἦ for ἦν, contract optat. in -οίην, and so on), together with many readings from the *Phaedo*-papyrus, implications from the Armenian version, and emendations from the philological journals, the editor at last found himself on such slippery ground that he retraced his steps and decided to follow closely the best manuscripts—in the conventional fashion, however, and not venturing to restore δαί, αἰεί, and the like. In the matter of orthography it is true, ὑός has been admitted. But a year has passed since the text was put into the publishers' hands, and so swiftly does each year add to a man's conservatism that if the printing were to be done again, the editor would perhaps restore υἱός. As for deviations from the ordinary text and interpretation, the following are the only ones worth mentioning:

P. 30, li. 19 (*Apol.* 34 D) αὖ τό for αὐτὸ τό (Adam)
121,1 (*Gorg.* 474 B) οὔκουν for οὐκοῦν (Editor)
132,1 (,, 479 C) καλῶς for ἄλλως (Editor)
136,6 (,, 483 A) πάναισχρον for πᾶν αἴσχιον (Editor)
148,28 (,, 524 C) κατεαγότ' αὖ for κατεαγότα (Editor)
171,1 (*Theaet.* 173 D) εἰ δὲ εὖ for εὖ δέ (Badham)
211,16 (*Rep.* 408 A) ἐκμύζησάν τ' for ἐκμυζήσαντ' (Adam)

212,23 (*Rep.* 414 D) ἔτι. ἤδη for ἐπειδή (Adam)
222,31 (,, 493 D) ὅτι μὲν γὰρ ἄν for ὅτι μὲν γάρ, ἐάν (Adam)
238,1 (,, 562 B) ὑπὲρ πλούτου for ὑπέρπλουτος (Madvig)
240,10 (,, 563 D) τισί for τὶς (Adam)
244,29 (,, 590 D) οἰκείως for οἰκεῖον (Editor).

Further, a transposition of words has been made in 144,28 (*Gorg.* 522 A), οἴεσθαί γε χρή being assigned to Socrates rather than to Callicles; and in 211,10 (*Rep.* 407 E), ὅτι τοιοῦτος ἦν being put after ἦν δ' ἐγώ rather than after παῖδες αὐτοῦ (as Schneider long ago suggested).—Also, a new interpretation has been offered on the μή πως ἐγώ κτλ. of *Apol.* 19 C (see n. on 4,31), and, with considerable misgiving, on *Phaedr* 229 C ἀλλ' εἰ ἀπιστοίην κτλ. (259,11).

CORNELL UNIVERSITY
ITHACA, NEW YORK
May 23, 1900.

INTRODUCTION

THE LIFE OF SOCRATES

The outer Socrates

As far as it is known, the life [1] of Socrates in its merely outward bodily incident may be told in a paragraph:—A very poor,[2] very ugly,[3] humble,[4] citizen of Athens—of strong *physique*, wonderful powers of endurance and perfect self-control,[5] yet by no means an ascetic [6]—of the greatest good sense, yet "queer" withal, given to fits of abstraction [7] and of dancing by himself [8]—of no pretensions to learning,[9] yet called σοφος [10]—possessing many friends, but more enemies [11]—with no means of livelihood known to us,[12] though responsible for the maintenance of a family, leaving at his death a wife and three sons [13]—fond of city-life beyond measure, passing out of its gates only at the rarest intervals [14] (thrice to serve his country as a soldier [15])—abstaining wholly from politics (a course peculiar and reprehensible in Athens) because held back by a strange inward monitor, a 'something divine' [16]—loafing his whole life through, day after day from early dawn, in the marketplace, in the gymnasia, in the promenades, wherever he found the busiest throng [17]—questioning, disputing, talking, talking, talking,[18] with any and all who would (rich or poor, low or high, stranger or foreigner, young or old)[19]—forever engaging them in conversation only to trip them in their logic like a wrestler,[20] to numb them like a torpedo-fish,[21] to sting them like a gadfly,[22] to prove they were using terms of which they did not know the meaning, to convict them of ignorance in general,[23] though ever declaring and with honest conviction[24] that he himself knew no more nor as much as they —still ever returning to the question of the definition of those terms so glibly used by all, still asking "what anyhow *is* piety, impiety, beauty, cowardice, justice, State, Government"[25]—always followed by an admiring crowd of for the most part rich young men, who enjoyed the sport of the confutations[26]—ridiculed and bitterly assailed for all this by the poets of comedy—but still loafing on busily and seriously (consecrated to it, as he thought, by the oracle of Apollo) forty, fifty, sixty, seventy years (born c. 469 B.C.) through the grand days of highest Athenian achievement and empire, through the dragging years of the long Peloponnesian War (431–404), till finally, the bitter mixed animosities of a generation gathering head against him (political, personal, religious), he was accused of introducing strange gods and doctrine, was condemned and put to death in the year 399 B.C. at seventy years of age —this is the life of Socrates the Athenian.

His Failure

2

Evidently a failure! It is bitter enough to forfeit the greeting of a single fellowbeing (even the wag of a dog's tail may save a man from suicide); but who can think the thoughts of despair and humiliation that come to a man condemned by his fellows to death, told that he is unfit to live, that there is no foothold for him on the upper earth? Yet we read that Socrates was not cast down. In perfect equanimity he passed the days between his condemnation and the execution of the sentence, in perfect equanimity he drank the hemlock, watched its slow numbness creep from feet to limbs, from limbs towards heart, then covered his head and died.[27] What did it mean? This was not the death of a guilty man. Some justifying thought must have sustained him at the last. And that we must discover, if we would know the real Socrates. Thousands of men have been put to death and forgotten. Yet this man we still hear of, study about, and regard as one of the great heroes and honours of the race. Is there anything heroic in the details of the above epitome? Is it heroic to be a "hoary old loafer" in the midst of splendid achievement and tensest life?

The Search for the true Socrates

Evidently, so far, we have got only the shell of **3**
the man. The halo about the heads of saints should teach us by symbol that a man is not contained within the periphery of his body, that his soul is larger than his skull, that his *ef-fluence* is the essence of him. It is this effluence of Socrates that we seek. But the liquid soul of a man is not easy to re-collect, when the vessel has been broken two thousand years. For, first, we should know the influxes that have formed him. To write the life of Socrates would be to write that of all Greece down to his time with all its religion, philosophy, sea, air, and mountain. We mortals are for an instant "struck from the float

forever held in solution," and like absorbent jelly-fish consume into ourselves all we greedily can from environment temporal and spatial, remote as well as near. No star so distant but that we lay it under contribution to make up the bundle we call "I." And how many of us can disengage our own identity from this inpouring flux of *Nicht-ich* Not-I?

The Greatness of Contemporary Athens

4 Yet we may indicate some of those nearer and stronger pulsations of influence that must have beaten in upon him. There was the huge contemporary life of Athens itself. Recall its energy and fierce young pulse-beat when Socrates was born (c. 469 B.C.). Ten years earlier, the battle of Plataea had cleared Greek soil of the Persian host, or rather buried the most of them in it. Out of the Persian Wars Athens had emerged supreme among the Greeks at sea, winning the headship (ἡγεμονία) of the great Delian Confederacy. Themistocles, Aristeides, Cimon, were the magical names of the period. Persians yet remained to be dislodged from the islands and Thrace; the Phoenician fleets und Persian pay had to be barred from the Aegean sea. The work was begun with splendid zeal—discipline and strength developed—victories won. From the Delian League, in which Athens was but a member, rose the Athenian Empire, under which former allies appeared as subject states. Those were the days when Athenian triremes manned by Athenian citizen-sailors swept the Aegēan, collecting tribute (if need be, by force), besieging recalcitrant cities, and thrusting the Persians finally back into the East (battle of Eurymedon c. 465 B.C.). Nor was this sufficient field for the exercise of Athens'

fullgrown powers. In 460 an expedition was dispatched to Egypt to aid the insurgent Inaros against the Persians. And battles must be fought in behalf of the Greek states that had preferred her lead also by land to that of Sparta—battles fought sometimes by old men and boys (the others being abroad on duty) and yet proving victories. Then came the building of the Long Walls (c. 456 B.C.), that Socrates, now a boy of thirteen, must have watched with wonder, as they rose swiftly and tall, to connect Athens with its port-town Peiraeus 4½ miles distant. The mighty days of Pericles had come. The treasure of the Delian League was conveyed from the little island of Delos to imperial Athens; and the lawsuits of the subject-cities were also transferred thither, bringing crowds of strangers of many dialects. Sophocles at that time was the glory of the poets, Myron and Phidias the contemporary sculptors, Polygnōtus the painter. The fair Odeion or music-hall was built; and the Propylaea or Portals of the acropolis; and (crowning glory of all—still standing, like the Propylaea, in ruined beauty) the Parthenon.

Socrates in the Midst—Abstracted

In the midst of all this activity and creation, 5
Socrates grew up. He was thirty-one years of age when the Parthenon was completed (438 B.C.). What part had he taken in it all? What contribution had he made? He had led no λόχος, commanded no trireme, won no name in the state (democratic as the state had become), had taken no prizes at the athletic games, executed no famous work as sculptor, composed no tragedy, no lyric, no history, offered no system of philosophy—and, worse

than all, gave no promise of doing any of these things. Men of thirty-one should be in their prime, or at least their potency ready to bursting. Can it be that Socrates was not open to impressions from this tremendous fiery Athenian spirit that consumed all else about him? Was he stockish? Either this he must have been—*or* some equally tremendous fiery spirit within him was counteracting that outer one and holding him there abstracted and inactive. That he could have won a name, had he chosen, among the immortals in that active world, no one can doubt. With his constitutional health, his self-control, his unparalleled power of winning whatever man he would, he could feel assured of leadership. What inner demon, then, impelled him to utter words that turned men from him, made them fear and hate him? Clearly, the influx from the brimming life about him was not an assimilating but a repelling one. He drank from other sources. He was in the throng, but not of it, was a foreigner in his native city.

The true Socrates not in Contemporary Literature

6 Before seeking further the inflowing elements, let us go to his contemporaries for the effluence of the man. What was their impression from him? The first mention he obtains is from the comedians. In 423 B.C. he suddenly emerges as the central figure in the *Clouds* of Aristophanes—proving that he was at that time well known. He is here attacked as a clever, thievish, ragged, shoeless keeper of a φροντιστήριον ('Reflectory'), where youth are taught physics, atheism, disrespect for their parents, and how to win a case by argument, be the cause just or unjust. Other

Not in Comedy.

comedians too had only bad flings for him, as Eupolis, who makes him a beggarly chatterer and a thief. But of course the comic stage cannot be looked to for true portraiture. A few lineaments of fact are all it requires, the rest is pure fiction, poetry (*ficto* = ποιέω, *fictio* = ποίησις). For the Socratic essence therefore we must look elsewhere.

Nothing else seems to have been written about 7
him, barring occasional jokes in the comedies, until after his death, when, in the course of not many years, an extensive literature sprang up from the pens of friends and enemies alike, due primarily to the tragic circumstances of his end. Defamatory speeches were written by display-orators, apologies and "Socratic dialogues" by many of his faithful companion-pupils. But from all this only the dialogues by Plato and the *Memorabilia* with three shorter pieces by Xenophon remain. These, with the fragmentary remarks by Aristotle, who belonged to the next generation, and was the pupil in turn of Plato, are all that deserve attention for the establishment of the first truths concerning the real Socrates. (I say "first" truths, because, a basis being once obtained, some truth may be deduced from even the caricature by Aristophanes.)

Is he in Plato and Xenophon?

Now it would seem to be a simple matter to 8
learn the master's teaching and beliefs from two such disciples as were Plato and Xenophon. For the writings of Plato are voluminous, those of Xenophon apparently circumstantial. Yet in fact, it is a difficult and almost insoluble problem. For in the first place, the *aim* of their form of literary presentation was not, at that period, to set down literal objective fact as it actually occurred,—was not to make a mere historic record such as is required of the modern biographer,

The question is not easy to answer.

because, in the second place, the Greeks of that period were probably incapable of so reporting fact. The standards of human testimony have all changed.

9 And first, as regards the *intention* of the literary form chosen by Plato and Xenophon, viz. the dialogue-form. In the first chapter of Aristotle's *Poetics*, that philosopher complains that there is no term which on the one hand *in*-cludes what is known as poetry and also such productions as the Socratic dialogues (οἱ Σωκρατικοὶ λόγοι), yet on the other hand *ex*-cludes such works as those of Empedocles on physics, which, though written in hexameter, are *not* poetry. The term "poetry," he says (from ποιέω 'to make-up'), is the proper designation; but this word is applied to works of metrical form only, without regard to content. Certainly it is clear from this remark of Aristotle's, that the Greeks were entirely aware of the fictitious character of the Socratic dialogues—that they no more took them for literal truth than we do the modern "historical" novel or drama. They were creations, products of outline-fact and constructive imagination,—as much so as the caricatures of the comedians. No deception was intended, none was possible. A literal acceptance of them in modern times, like the literal acceptance of the Old Testament, lands us in much confusion and only proves that we have lost the ancient point of view, their imaginative freedom, and that we prefer item-fact for characteristic truth. Even Thucydides, the greatest of their historians, holding a position wholly unique in his period for telling the truth, states that in recording speeches, though he follows the general tenor of what was said, yet writes "what would have been best said to the purpose" (I 22). What historian, now, would enter the lists with a

All writing was more or less fiction.

free pen, to tilt against stenographers? And congressional records!

Indeed—passing on to the second point, that the 10
Greeks of that creative period were not *capable* of reporting outward fact as such—not merely was this the case because antiquity was always looking for the miraculous, with not even a presentiment of the sweep of the law of causation, and hence finding a fact wherever they expected it, not where it occurred,—but also because they saw instinctively and unconsciously the general in the particular, they went past the fact to the truth, assimilated and then created by natural unreflective process. The sculptor saw not *the* model before him, with it may be too long a head, too short an arm, too full a muscle here, too thin there,—he saw *a* model and reproduced it—the ideal human form, suppressing the defects of the accidental before him, supplying the perfections of the universal in his own mind. So worked the genius of Plato on the model Socrates,—filling out inchoate thought, suppressing perhaps roughness of diction and manner, sharpening to delicate keenness the native irony, idealizing to the highest degree, carving out with a hand of love the god's image in his master.

The reasons for this.

That Plato so wrought has long been known. 11
Much doctrine he puts into the mouth of Socrates that is properly his own. The situation is singular. Remembering that, had there been no Socrates, there would have been no Plato, each seems to have created the other; a fusion has taken place. They are like double stars. And the attempt to disengage them is the labour and delight of every young Platonist.

But that Xenophon also carved with idealizing 12
hand is not so widely admitted. The inclination is, to find in his report the true Socrates, the moralizing,

Xenophon, no less than Plato, a "maker."

utilitarian Socrates, that brought philosophy down from heaven [28] for common men, as Prometheus brought fire. *For*, Xenophon was a soldier, a man of affairs, a man who could report as he heard and saw, even though at times he did not catch the import; because, in brief Xenophon was a prosaic modern soul, who had not the poetic or making faculty—now regarded as only another name for the faculty of lying.

13 But it has been clearly enough seen in recent years [29] that Xenophon also was not destitute of the characteristic faculty of his period—that he too could "create," though not in Plato's brilliant skilful fashion. For if his *Cyropaedia* is, as every one knows, a fictitious history, if his *Hiero* is a fictitious dialogue (and who will care to deny it?), if his *Agesilaus* is rhetorical encomium rather than sober chronicle, and his *Lacedaemonian State* is likewise a panegyric of Lycurgus, is it not at least possible that his Socratic pieces should be tinctured with a poetic element? Nay more, is he not convicted of it in his *Oeconomicus*? For in his opening sentence he says he once heard Socrates "in the following conversation"—in the course of which (4, 18–19) Socrates talks about the death of the younger Cyrus and the behaviour on that occasion of Ariaeus. But when, pray, could Xenophon have heard Socrates so discoursing? Socrates had been dead five years before Xenophon returned from the famous ἀνάβασις. Xenophon is merely writing his *Reminiscences* as all wrote them in his day—with a strong poetic (manufacturing) instinct. And no better in his case than in Plato's can we estimate the amount of his subjectivity. Plato's Socrates is an idealist, and we reject the portrait as flattered. Xenophon's Socrates is a moralist, an exhorter, and somewhat given to consulting and

upholding oracles, and we accept it. This is unreasonable. In truth, we could better trust Plato. For *his* portraitures are all sharply outlined and distinct—the complacent old Professor Gorgias, the frisky young sophist Polus, Cephalus of mellowed age, Euthydēmus and Thrasymachus two howling scoffers though wholly distinct. But why name them? Each clear-cut one of them is more characteristically true than any photography could make them. Whereas, Xenophon's heroes are all hopelessly alike and fall together—all perhaps hopelessly Xenophon. For though he had the poetic impulse of his age, he had not the poetic power of its great geniuses. His Cyrus the Elder, his Agesilaus, his Hiero or Simonides (for it makes no difference), his Socrates, his Ischomachus, and the rest, are always talking on the same subjects, constantly enjoying good cheer, forever moralizing, forever taking omens—and (fatal coincidence!) so does Xenophon in the *Anabasis.* Briefly, he exemplifies well the lawyer's truism that a man's testimony is chiefly valuable as offering information about the man himself, not about the matter in hand. It can *not* be certain that Socrates was a proverbial philosopher because Xenophon makes him so. A man so eternally a homilist and little else, as Xenophon's Socrates, could never have held together the band of intellects the real Socrates did.[30] By his mere approach he would have cleared the market-place more effectually than the policemen with their coloured rope. That he could have been allowed to reach the age of seventy would seem incredible.

The result is—that the real Socrates has eluded 14
us again. His inspiration, we found, was not imperial Athens. Neither could he have been the idealist he is in Plato; nor yet is it probable that all

his aims were those of a moralizer and utilitarian as he appears in Xenophon. Aristotle's report we postpone awhile.

15 Shall we once more turn to the influxes? If the near, brilliant, sensuous life about him fired him not with ambition, left him cold and insensible, to what invisible world was he responsive? In what thought-world was he wrapped, when he stood in long abstraction motionless? Let us this time take a wider sweep.

A new search for Socrates proposed.

Pre-Socratic Philosophy[31]

16 To realize the beliefs of the earliest Greeks, let us recall our own microcosmic reproduction of them. For also our childhood, like that of the Greek race, was animated in every part, and saturated with *personality*. We said "Tree go bye-bye" to the trees, "Chair hit baby" to the chairs—we fed and talked to dolls, and tended them in illness—we rode broomsticks as wild horses, readily supplying voice and heels from our own anatomy—we held long colloquy with people invisible to sceptics—if we stumbled over the door-step, we kicked it in wrath "to teach it better"—horse-tail hairs, we were convinced, became water-snakes—Santa Claus, we held, came down the chimney (for how else could he come?)—thunder and rain betokened a scouring-day in heaven—whether trees walked in the night, we could not say with certainty, though the thing was likely. In short, we were young Greeks of four thousand years ago. Nothing was dead. Anything could happen. There was no supernatural. One event was no more surprising than another. Things were what they seemed. There was an incipience within us, which, with slight

To the child, the outer world is sentient and personal.

encouragement, would have repeopled mountain, river, and wood with satyrs, dryads, nymphs, and all the rest of the fair Greek host. We kept no record of time, we were easily confused between yesterday, to-day, and to-morrow, we had no sharp lines of distinction between the outer and the inner world, between fact and fancy, reality and dream. In later years we come to see that the child-life personified —though often the old child within us cries out in protest that it is the adult life which (to use Grote's term) *rei-fies.*

Be that as it may, the Greeks who fought the 17
Trojan War were of the same mental status that we as children were. And to the like Greeks Homer later sang of the Trojan War. In that period, as in our child-life, neither war nor peace nor any other part of life was possible without a permeating divinity. An event must have a cause. If men did not bring it about, the gods must have wrought it. Therefore the record of the Trojan War and of all those other exploits of gods and men—the Argonautic Expedition, the sieges of Thebes, the labours of Hercules, the lives of the gods themselves, of Earth, Heaven, Ocean, Zeus, Ares, and the rest—all that record of Homer, Hesiod, and others, was not to Greek ears poetry, but history ; not fiction, but fact. And such it was bound to remain, and into such fact all new events were bound to be converted, until men should learn to record the lapse of time, to write annals, discover that things are not what they seem, detect the unfailing sequences of nature, and obtain control of events that to earlier men seemed the direct act of the gods,—all which gradually came about.[32]

To the early Greek, the same.

They knew not poetry, but history.

The change came, as does the adolescence of the 18

individual—imperceptibly, simultaneous in all its parts—political, moral, intellectual,—first the few leading the way, then the many, —first the tentative effort, then a stronger, then the custom. For example, in the matter of these gods: —They had been conceived and fashioned in times anterior to the moral sense, when violence, theft, and the gratification of every passion were the natural right of the stronger, when lying and treachery were the cunning resource of the weaker. They had been projected into the sky like huge Brocken shadows, an expansion and glorification of the old Greek man entire, with all his appetites and sins, a deification of all he fain would be. To them men prayed for aid in every undertaking, whether (by the later standards) good or bad. It was not, for the early Greek, a question of good or bad. All desires were good to him who felt them. The gods were strong and he was weak; and he wished them on his side. But with the growth of the feeling for right and wrong, the badness of these gods, made in man's earlier image, emerged to view. What had seemed pure gold now proved spotted metal. Maleficence in divinity was shocking. For the gods should be good, while these gods were wicked. Such light, however, came not to the many. Before the Persian Wars we hear of but few who had come to such conclusions—for instance, the poet Xenophanes, who denounced and repudiated these anthropomorphic creations and their creators the poets (as he thought),—preaching instead a single unchangeable impersonal god. But from others we catch but a protest now and then, an apology, an allegorizing explanation, or perhaps a doubt of the records, as from Pindar. Thus much for the incipience of a moral change previous to the Persian Wars.

Incipient adolescence.

Again, an intellectual change was taking place. 19
The vivid child-power of personification faded out, as those of observation grew. Ocean, Air, Heaven, were stripped of their masks. Oceanus perhaps was not a god, but merely water—a liquid—a material substance. It may be true, as Homer had said, that he was the original of the gods and of all things (*θεῶν γένεσις, γένεσις πάντεσσι*), but true only in the sense that all life begins in liquid form. **ὕδωρ**, then, was the *ἀρχή* ('beginning,' 'first principle') of all, and not Father Ocean. So taught THALES of Milētus (born c. 640 B.C.), the first of the Ionian "physical" philosophers and the first, of whom we have record, to break with the old religious view. But reifying once begun, the search for a *thing-ἀρχή* once proposed, other groping guesses quickly followed. Not water, said a second Milesian ANAXIMANDER, can be the *ἀρχή*, nor any other stuff of definite properties—which could act but as a bar to opposite properties; it must contain the potency of all qualities, but none actually; it must also be inexhaustible, indestructible, and infinite or without limit (*ἄ-πειρον*). And so he named it **τὸ ἄπειρον**—a conception that after all merely pours matter into Hesiod's old religious *χάος* ('chaos,' 'void'; *χά-σκω* 'to yawn,' 'be open') and remained for Anaximander a semi-religious thing, since he called it *θεῖον*. Again, to a third Milesian, ANAXIMENES, *ἀήρ* 'air' seemed a sufficiently indeterminate element, lying midway between subtlety and solidity. For from it, by rarefaction, spring fire and aether; while by condensation, it gives rise to cloud, water, earth, stone in progressive order. Histories of philosophy next tell of the famous PYTHAGORAS of Samos, the traveller and pupil to ancient Egypt, the mathe-

Reification (science) begins.

The Ionian philosophers.

matician, the believer in *μετ-εμ-ψύχωσις* or transmigration of soul between men and animals, the founder of a secret brotherhood at Crotōna in Magna Graecia. For him, the *ἀρχή* of all things was NUMBER—not our incorporeal abstraction, but a real stuff or matter, having magnitude. What he meant by it, is not easy for us to conceive. A good deal of mysticism hangs about his speculation, as also of mystery about the man himself. His authority over the brotherhood was complete. With them arose that saying which settled all discussion, *αὐτὸς ἔφᾱ* (= *ἔφη*) 'himself (the master) said it' *ipse dixit*.

20 A younger contemporary of his was the poet mentioned above, XENOPHANES. He and his follower PARMENIDES had the poet's sense for the universal (still sometimes born into abstracted solitary men), which liquefies solid matter, solidifies aether, loses all lines of demarcation, cannot (try as it will) maintain distinctions in either outer or inner world, fuses all together, is conscious only of a huge full universe of BEING, that never was nor will be, but always *is*, that never had *ἀρχή*, will never have an end, was uncreated of any God, but is itself the one all-embracing God, which "sees and thinks and hears." This is Pan-theism—a deep sub-mergence of all the differences generated by our fleeting senses (all sights and sounds and contacts) into the absolute, unconditioned ocean of Being, God. To those who have attained to this vision, all the activities of our little days and nights, our wars, our nations, the storms, floods, and earthquakes of the globe—all are but a non-appreciable quiver in the huge immovable One, the solid jelly of Being. There are no chinks of non-Being. There is no Motion, no generation, no decay; these are only appearances (*φαινόμενα*), con-

The Eleatic school.

ditioned, and relative to the senses. There is no Many; that too belongs to the show-world of our senses. ALL IS ONE. To the poet's abstracting soul, to Xenophanes or to Parmenides, this thought, by its very sweep and grandeur, carried conviction and needed no proof. But for those who lived the life of the senses and believed in a Many and in Motion, ZENO, the pupil of Parmenides and a very lawyer for subtlety, devised four arguments [33] against this Many and four against Motion, which to this day require a professional logician to answer. They may be full of fallacy, reducing reason to unreason (e.g. showing that swift-footed Achilles will never overtake a tortoise, if the tortoise have the start), but they captivated the Greek mind and had a lasting influence.

Heraclītus.

Perhaps contemporary with Xenophanes lived 21
HERACLITUS of Ephesus, surnamed the *Dark* (ὁ σκοτεινός); for he spoke in ungrammatic riddles that did not deal with this fixed and ordinary life. Like the philosophers of Being, he too recognized no single element as the ἀρχή of things, such as water, air, or an infinite mass (τὸ ἄπειρον). But no more could he conceive a motionless Being. On the contrary, there was no Being. For him (as sometimes yet for sad and wistful men) all was "becoming," ever a motion, a change and a flux of φαινόμενα. BECOMING is the *only* reality. These φαινόμενα are ceaselessly passing up and down into their opposites—day into night, night into day; hunger into satiety and back again; youth and age, sleeping and waking, life and death, generation and decay, with never a pause in the busy silent flow. Life *is* motion. Only the dead have quiet. πάντα ῥεῖ ποταμοῦ δίκην 'all things flow as a river.' 'War is the father of all things' πόλεμος πατὴρ πάντων.

And the symbol of all this *becoming* was Fire (πῦρ)—the restless lambent destructive fire, the generating heat. (Strange prophetic speculation in his eyes! It is the developed doctrine of Heraclītus that we learn in the modern phrases "heat as a mode of motion," "vortex-motion the ultimate analysis of the atom and the material world," "Evolution the widest generalization of the human mind.")

The atomists and others.

22 Again another poet-scientist was EMPEDOCLES (born c. 500 B.C.) with his Four Elements (earth, air, fire, water), and LOVE and HATE as the mixers. ANAXAGORAS his contemporary contended not for four elements, but for as many as there were different kinds of things (flesh, bone, blood, fire, gold, etc. etc.), with MIND (νοῦς) to classify them out of an original chaotic mass. Still later came DEMOCRITUS (born c. 460 B.C.—*after* Socrates), the expounder of the atomic theory (αἱ ἄ-τομοι 'the uncuttable' substances, sc. οὐσίαι). Out of the collision of these storming atoms in their everlasting downpour, springs the world.

The beginnings of the modern sciences.

23 The present space and occasion admit no more than the enunciation of the Principle of each of these philosophers. But most of them developed a cosmogony (κοσμογονία) of greater or less detail, explaining the motions and form of the earth, the constitution of the sun and stars, the reason of night and day, the action of our senses, digestion, procreation, etc. In short, nearly all the sciences may be found in embryo at this period of Greek philosophy—astronomy, geology, zoology, physics, physiology, medicine, and the rest. It is easily seen how such studies *reified* the world. The personality of the gods had, for these investigators at least, faded, as the Brocken shadows on the mist fade at sunset. To be sure

their explanations were crude; their observation, though often acute, was unaided by instruments of precision; patient experiment was unknown; their theories were the veriest guesswork; their scientific imagination was only the fertile old theistic imagination on a new line (what is that mighty word Evolution but a capitalized abstraction?); they felt little need as yet of thick strata of solid facts to support their fancies. *But* the immensely important fact of that period is, that the point of view had changed. No longer did supernaturalism with its incoherent lapses, its lawless freakish outbreaks, reign supreme, unforetokening and unforetellable. A sense of order in the universe, of a κόσμος, of the invariable sequence of events—the so-called Laws of Nature, had arisen.

But not for a long period did such a sense come 24
to the many. All this activity of speculation had been confined to the few. The masses prayed on to their gods with ingratiating offerings to help them return good for good and evil for evil (by the old Greek code of morals), and to send them personally and particularly their heart's desire, whatever it happened to be.—Thus much for the slow adolescence of the intellect.

The people remain religious.

But along with the moral and the intellectual 25
adolescence came also political advance. Gradually, for all Greek states save Sparta, the ancient stagnant days of king and obedient subject had passed by. No longer was custom, and the ruler's mandate, the sole regulator of all the life of the serf. Kings had given way to oligarchies, they in turn to despots (seated in the first instance by espousal of the people's cause against the nobility), the despots again to democracy, which at first gave restricted but soon ever-widening rights

Political advance.

to all. In Athenian history, recall the liberating archonship of Solon and later the reforms of Cleisthenes. Then followed the Persian Wars, that most decisive event in Greek history, which broke down the cell-walls of the narrow life of Greece, merged local cults, dissolved local prejudice, fused local interests, into a new protoplasm for a larger national life, which was to be the people's life. Kings and isolation were past.—The activity, the hope, and the fulness of that outer visible life as it streamed in Athens have been described above.

The Sophists [34]

26 Not long were the people in discovering who won the prizes, whose the headship was, in this hot and open competition. It fell to the men of native insight (σύνεσις 'power of putting together') sharpened by *technique* and cleverness (σοφία), and facile of speech (δεινοὶ λέγειν). If the fiat-power of the old nobility had passed, and the young aristocrat would maintain the pre-eminence of his ancestors, it must be no longer by command but by persuasion. He must compete with the lively wit of an awakened people; and the people as well had to defend themselves against each other. The old education did not suffice. It was not enough to learn the rudiments with a little music and poetry, and the rest of youth spent in training the body in the gymnasium. Contests in future were to be won by wit and word. A new learning was needed for the new life. And the need was practical and pressing, as it had been a few years earlier in Sicily, where democracy had swept away privilege and every man had to see to his own safety of property and person.—The demand

The need of rhetoric in democracy.

created the supply. Rhetoricians appeared, who (for a consideration) taught not only effective speech (Zeno's art of refutation, and how to make the weaker cause win), but artistic speech, such as should delight and even dazzle an audience. For in that flood of contemporary art-life (sculpture, drama, architecture), natural eloquence did not suffice, even though sharpened by logic. There must be rhythm, balance, antithesis, studied effect.

Yet not merely in oratory, whether for artistic 27
display, for political ends, or for use in the law-courts, was felt the need of a higher, broader learning. Expansion was in the air. The Spirit of Democracy was the Spirit of Empire. After levelling rich and poor, ignoble and noble before the law and in the government, it was now adding city after city to its list of subject-states, nor would it longer brook exclusiveness in the domain of wisdom. What wise men had discovered, all must know. If there was any New Learning under the sun, imperial Athens, "the Prytaneum of Wisdom," must have it. Curious hints had been dropped that Achilles the swift could not overtake tortoise the slow, and (what was more serious) that the god Ηλιος, the Sun, was a stone, nay even that there were (Zeus save the mark!) no gods at all! What did this mean?—Here too imperial Athens, mistress of the world's marts, could obtain what she would. Teachers flocked to her from East and West, from Sicily, from Thrace, from Peloponnesus, from everywhere, to tell her what it all meant, to instruct her in these new branches—astronomy, mathematics, grammar, ethics, true interpretation of the poets—what you will—any and all (for a consideration).

The need of general culture.

These, with the rhetoricians, were the famous 28
Sophists (οἱ σοφισταί) of antiquity—men who (always

The Sophists defined.

for a consideration) offered to make you wise (σοφίζειν), professional teachers of higher learning, popularizers of knowledge, purveyors (aye, "hucksters," Plato called them) of useful education that would help one to get on in the world. They did *not* teach those physical or metaphysical speculations of their predecessors concerning the first principles of things (the ἀρχαί), nor did they offer speculations of their own on that subject. Their audiences and pupils were, to be sure, drawn chiefly from the cultured class of wealth, yet, like most popular audiences, they had little interest in speculations. They wished results.

29 And what indeed of all that previous speculation had been the results? As dishearteningly negative as well could be. The philosophers had disagreed with each other and proved mutually destructive. Even the clever Zeno, though able to confute all opponents, could not with certainty make good his own position. The basis of them all had been unsound. From Parmenides and Heraclītus down, it had been known and often enough set forth that things are not what they seem, that our senses deceive us, that their report of the outer world cannot be trusted. And yet what had been the procedure of them all, including even those whose ἀρχή had not been a thing of the senses (as water or air) but an abstraction such as Becoming or Mind? Why, although their ἀρχαί had been the product of reflection, yet the elements, material, *object* of that reflection had been *the outer world*—which they apprehended and could apprehend only through those lying senses. (A few to be sure had speculated on the nature of the soul. But all save Anaxagoras had made it a corporeal thing or wholly dependent upon corporeal things. Nor did

The negative results of speculation.

Anaxagoras, after hitting on the thought of an immaterial νοῦς, know what to do with it.) Reflection, therefore, mind, was no more trustworthy, rose no higher, than its origin the senses. In truth, Mind and the Senses were identical. Perception was the only knowledge. The philosophers had built on sand. No wonder their theories fell. The fact is, speculation had had its day. The only thing for a sensible man to do was to pitch the whole quest for an ultimate explanation of the world over the world's back fence. And so the sophists did. For after all, argued PROTAGORAS of Abdēra, one of the earliest of the sophists (born c. 480 B.C.), after all, men can get along *without* an ultimate basis. We cannot hope for a vision of the reality of things—their true essence—the final underlying Absolute, that Parmenides wrote poetry about. All is fleeting appearance (φαινόμενα), as Heraclītus said. As for truth? That is relative and personal. What appears to you, is true for you; what to me, for me. That is as near truth as we can get. "Man is the measure of all things" πάντων χρημάτων μέτρον ἄνθρωπος. In short, Protagoras was a despairing sceptic—yet quite content withal, quite self-complacent, and, on the assumed basis, quite hopeful (for a consideration) of furthering humanity's progress by teaching rhetoric and what he called Knockdown Arguments (καταβάλλοντες λόγοι). Sophists who taught aught else, as Hippias, he rather derided. Indeed Rhetoric and Refutation (with some tricks for evading the same at the hands of your adversary) were the principal content of sophistic endeavour, the chief desire of their Athenian audience. For Athens had gone mad over contests of any sort. Just as they had had a mighty ἀγών ('contest') with the Persians, and now were

Protagoras the first sophist.

in the midst of one for supremacy among the Greeks, just as they had always witnessed them at the great games, so had they established them between the poets of tragedy, between the poets of comedy, so must they have them even *in* tragedy and comedy, and between citizen and citizen in the courts of law, and between these clever sophists, aye between cocks in the cock-pit. What buffoonery and utter scoffing levity it led to in the hands of little sophists, may be seen in Plato's *Euthydēmus.*[35]

30 The other greatest sophist after Protagoras was GORGIAS the entrancing orator from Leontīni in Sicily, who first came to Athens, already an old man, in 427 B.C. on an embassy from his native city. Scepticism in him became dogmatism. He denied Being or Reality altogether. "*Nothing* is; even assuming it, it cannot be known; or, assuming it could, it cannot be communicated." This is mocking nihilism. Trained to formal dexterity, despising all earnest science and pursuing only his art of speaking, he "indulged in the jest of satirizing as empty the entire labour of philosophy. . . But the facts that he did this and that his work found applause show how, among the men who occupied themselves in instructing the people, and in the circles of scientific culture itself, faith in science was becoming lost at just the time when the mass of the people was seeking its welfare in it" (Windelband's *Hist. of Philos.* Tufts' transl. p. 90). And so his life passed, a long and happily balanced period of artistic, poetic, metaphoric, antithetic, paromoeic oratory (full of μέν . . δέ)—his feet never once touching any of Carlyle's "eternal verities"—enormously admired and of exemplary conduct, as was also Protagoras.

The dogmatic agnosticism of Gorgias.

31 Of exemplary character were all the early sophists.

For among their other pretensions was also that of teaching virtue and of turning out good men and citizens. Protagoras had composed a pretty myth concerning the equal distribution of justice and reverence to all men by the gods[36]; so too Prodicus, a famous story about the Choice of Heracles at the fork of the path of Virtue and the path of Vice.[37] And all this, despite their scepticism on the possibility of knowledge and their boast of the ability to make the weaker cause win. Did they fancy that outward life and inner conviction can be thus severed? that it matters not what men think, if their deeds be right? Foolish wise men! How long will the deeds remain right? As if life *could* be unbased from an ultimate κόσμος and, with its convictions torn away, become anything but a chaos—a silliness, sound, and fury! But their pupils were not so foolish. Youthful blood may draw a straight deduction. "If there is no *truth* of universal validity, there can be no universally valid *law*; if man in his *opinions* is the measure of all things, he is so also in his *actions*; if, for each man, that is true which appears to him true, then that which seems to each right and good must be right and good" (Zeller, *Pre-Socrat. Philos.* Alleyne's transl. II p. 475). Such was the quick logic of the pupils, and such the doctrine of lesser sophists.[38] Scepticism concerning knowledge was transferred to morality. And the barriers once down, the flood came. Why obey laws that are valid only by human convention (θέσει)? (And convention it is, as witness the fickle change of them by this rampant democracy.[39]) Let us obey rather the laws given by nature (φύσει). Now a man's *natural* right is to satisfy his desires as completely as he can. If therefore convention oppose nature (θέσις vs. φύσις)—

Unbased morality and its outcome.

away with your θέσις. *Might* is right. Your "good" man is simply stupid or a coward. (See infra, pp. 135, 198.)

32 It happens that this doctrine of the right of might, the outcome of the teaching of negative sophistic, was the one actually then being practised by the Greeks in the Peloponnesian war. One has but to read of the murder of the innocent Plataeans by the Spartans or of the neutral Melians by the Athenians to realize it.[40] But not alone in this doctrine (for which some excuse might be found in the passions of war) did contemporary life coincide with sophistic theory. The whole social fabric seems to have become corrupt and disorganized. Never has a state sped through a meteoric path of glory so swiftly as the Athenian — in one and the same century rising to the zenith and sinking to the lowest horizon. The terrible presentation of the situation found in Thucydides[41] almost inclines one to take Aristophanes' tirades on the degeneracy of his times not as jest but in sober earnest. In truth, that the Athenians could regard as comic rather than tragic such tableaux of their own lives as those shown them by Aristophanes, is just the most deplorable element in the situation. It was bad enough that they should lose religious faith and throw morality and honour to the winds, but to lack also all sense of shame at their naked wickedness was infinitely worse.

Greek morality during the Peloponnesian war.

33 Yet it will not do to hold the sophists alone responsible for the outcome, as did those Athenians who seized on Socrates as a sophist and put him to death. Rather forgetfulness of their simple past and their fathers' gods, pride in their present greatness, cruelty and

Interdependence of thought and life.

selfishness and the other traits of the period may well have been engendered by their position and the necessities of their position as an imperial state. Hence it may be fairer to regard the sophists rather as the product of their period, or as a reflection of it,[42] acted upon as well as reacting, effect as well as cause. Be that as it may and without attempting to adjudge the blame, the contemporaneous facts for the last years of the fifth century were these: the acme of Athens' greatness and power had passed; the days of moderate democracy were past; supernaturalism, the essence of their ancient religion (scoffed at by the cultured, uneasily suspected by the common people) was as good as past; morality and reverence for the law and custom were passing with it; the attempts of the physical philosophers to find in the outer world either an ἀρχή of things or an absolute, unconditioned Reality had been all exploded and passed by the dialectic of Zeno and the sophists;—there remained, masquerading in the cloak of philosophy, the grinning chattering skeleton of rhetoric—a thing of polished periods, but, within, the Spirit of Negation.

The true Socrates at last[43]

Now at length we may at least suspect what 34
those thoughts could well have been that held Socrates motionless a day and night, and idle for life in the midst of turbulent activity. The problem working in the head of the ugly stonecutter was, how to save and reconcile Athens, morality, and philosophy—how to connect and unify them as they lay unhinged—where to find an eternal verity on which to base man's life, a something universally valid from which to start afresh?

The riddle of the Sphinx.

Was the problem any less important than those of practical statesmen, as Themistocles, Pericles, Demosthenes? As if states were possible at all, without these searchers after the eternal verities upon which states must be founded—these Anointed Ones, the founders of religions. "Professor" Protagoras could live comfortably on the assumed basis of φαινόμενα—the basis of a butterfly over an abyss—but not Socrates.

35 The true life of this man therefore was spent in the subterranean depths of the world-problem: What is the eternal verity? A true biography of him would lead us through the various adits, shafts, and galleries of thought blasted out by the old sapper—which, as we have seen, is impossible, the roof being fallen, the ways choked, Plato and Xenophon having countermined him in accordance with the literary freedom of their times and each in the direction of his own predilection—Plato the idealist driving deeper into philosophy, Xenophon, the good man, constantly opening up shafts to utilitarian surface-morality. The original mine therefore seems past ascertainment.

36 But not yet. There is yet the sober Aristotle to consult—that greatest "dry light" (*lumen siccum*) of the world, whether the facts he shines upon were objective or subjective—were past, present, or to come. What manner of man is *his* Socrates? We turn to him as a last resort. Alas, suspicious outcome! *His* Socrates is —a logician! the thing above all others that Aristotle was himself. This chameleon Socrates—thus to change his colour! This ocean-surface—to reflect whatever cloud sailed by! Will he elude us again? At length perhaps not. For, assuming him to be Aristotle's logician, we have an hypothesis that better than any other reconciles the many facts of the case

Aristotle's report on Socrates.

and shows how in the manifold terrible cross-currents of the age Socrates was caught and sucked down. For the logician stands midway between the mere moralizer (who, logic or no logic, will make men good for here and now) and the soaring Platonic idealist (who, working through and transcending logic, will reach the lofty goal of ultimate Being—this world and logic left sightlessly below). Looking back therefore to the problem in its entirety that confronted Socrates, viz. how to hinge together again and unify Athenian life with religion and morality, and these in turn with philosophy, it seems at least a probable hypothesis that initially his heart's desire was a moral one—to save Athens for right living (this being the Socrates of honest Xenophon); that next, failing to distinguish the various uses of the word ἀρετή (which meant not only moral but every kind of goodness or excellence), he made the mistake of conditioning all the virtues upon knowledge,[44] nay even went so far as to *identify* virtue with knowledge;[45] that thereafter he found himself involved in what proved to be his life's work, viz. *to determine knowledge*, as the basis of the whole, and the primary thing to be established; that in his attempt at this determination he came upon principles, which, working upon the imaginative Plato, created the Platonic Socrates, but, when worked upon by Aristotle, proved to be those of not possibly any one but a logical Socrates.—Certainly the hypothesis is not to be condemned because it starts Socrates with chiefly a moral aim and brings him out with chiefly an intellectual result. Is it so rare for a man to find the road longer than he thought—to become interested by the way and fail of the summit—to mistake a means for the end? And the road was long indeed. After deciding that he must reach

The steps of his thought.

right living (moralizing) by the way of right thinking (knowledge), let us see the forest he entered upon.

37 No man can I find, he says, who has real knowledge. On test—and these sophists are clever and right in their test by analyzing cross-examining dialectic or discussion—on test I find men's knowledge to be sham-knowledge—a fancying they know when they do not know.[46] But alas, I find that I myself know nothing. And yet in *knowing* that I do not know, I am wiser than they.[47] Again, the sophists are right to reject all those contradictory theories concerning the origin of things;[48] it is futile to peer into the outer world for truth through senses that we know are lying. Yet surely the sophists are wrong in despairing, on that account, of ultimate truth. We need not look without. We must look within. Not nature, but man himself contains the truth. *Γνῶθι σαυτόν* 'know thyself'—so reads the motto at Delphi. Not outward things, but our *notions* of them must be studied. These we must clarify and define. The terms we use must have a fixed meaning. The word *bravery*,[49] for example, must not signify to one man one thing, to another another, nor yet to the same man now one thing, now another. What *is* "bravery" (*τί ἔστιν*)?[50] What do we mean by it, and how are we to find its meaning? Why, by gathering up (*ἐπάγειν*) all the various uses of the word and abstracting the meaning common to all. That shall be our definition of "bravery." Not till we thus qualify and quantify our notions, have we the right to talk of knowledge. Knowledge forsooth! We are not ripe for it. We must first learn the method of knowledge—INDUCTION and DEFINITION.[51]

His quest for knowledge.

38 And so it came about that on this method of knowledge—general concepts obtained by induction

—he spent his life. Perhaps he never completely lost sight of his youthful moral aim. It is certain that the concepts he preferably worked on were moral. "What is Justice, Piety, Goodness, and the rest?" He may to the last have hoped thereby to make Athens just, pious, and good. If so, deluded hope! Athens remained *in statu quo*. And the general concepts he had quarried out to be granite stepping-stones to practical goodness proved more useful for other purposes. From them it was that Plato, his spiritual son, mounted by invisible ladders to his own eternal changeless Visions (ἰδέαι, Ideas); while Aristotle later found them invaluable doorsteps to his formal logic! (Humble stonecutter to the Valhalla of all the Wise!)

He finds, not knowledge, but its method.

Socrates was consequently neither a philosopher **39**
with a system nor a moralist with a finished code. Rather he gave others intellectual impulse, was yeast for others' bread, or (as he put it) a midwife[52] to others' thoughts. Indeed had he himself got past the peirastic stage (πειράομαι 'I try') or the protoplastic fluid, it would be hard to account for the diversity of doctrine held by the various Socratic schools—doctrines diametrically opposed one to another, yet all claiming to be Socratic. On the hypothesis, however, that what he gave them was a method and not a result, their diversity is natural enough. They applied his logic, but as each started from his own premises, they readily arrived at different conclusions—hence the Realist and Nominalist, the Moralist and Immoralist, side by side, Socratic pupils.

He moved and helped others to think.

Again, on the supposition that his strength lay in **40**
his rationalizing rather than in moralizing or mysticism, it may easily be seen why he was classed by plain people with

Why he was identified with the sophists.

the sophists, indeed, why he was held by Aristophanes in his *Clouds* to be the arch-sophist of them all. We, of course, who are not under the slings and arrows of his outrageous dialectic, can clearly see that he was separated from them by a heaven-wide distance. Seriousness and sincerity of purpose were his: levity was theirs. Discontent with the present and buoyant hope for the future marked him: contented pessimism them. They taught for a living: he tried to make life worth living. But at the same time it must be admitted that he too was a child of his age, that the resemblances between him and them were more numerous and striking than the differences—nay even that Aristophanes had some reason for choosing him as their representative.

41 For he too had broken with the old religion, though apparently he does not care to ask himself how far the dissent had gone.[53] True, he observed the rites[54] conscientiously (though perhaps not so sedulously as Xenophon represents); yet he recommended, as Xenophon admits,[55] a large reduction in omen-taking and other dependence on the gods, and would substitute for it self-dependent knowledge.

He agreed with them in the matter of religion,

42 And in morals it was he, with the younger sophists, who would incite to open rebellion. The older sophists might divest themselves of worn-out habits of thought, but in outward life they conformed to custom. Socrates went further; it was slavish, he said, to follow a custom one could not justify by reason.

in morals,

43 In his relations to the state, though it is true that he punctiliously obeyed the laws of the recognized government[56] and discharged well whatever duties fell upon him, yet from politics he held aloof because of his warning δαιμόνιόν τι,

in politics,

making himself a foreigner with the sophists. Like them, too, he believed that intending statesmen should receive a special training [57] (though not that offered by the sophists); and he criticized the folly of a democracy that elected its rulers by lot.[58] *He* would have an "aristocracy of intellect."

And as for that peculiar sophist-art of confutation 44
—not to speak of unfortunate laymen that fell into his hands, the very sophists themselves must acknowledge him past-master. It is on record that no man ever confuted him,[59] that all were helpless in his hands.

in the art of confutation.

But still further, and worse than all—he was not 45
only spreading this disputatious business in the common walks of life, but introducing a pestilent new method of enucleating the "what is it" out of words that (before he began) were perfectly clear what they were.[60] He could obfuscate the most sensible people and prove them no better than idiots. Like the wizards of legerdemain, he could produce the most unreasonable things out of their mental pockets. Now the older sophists, after exploding the theories of the physical philosophers with their dialectic, were quite content to live the life of *φαινόμενα*, frankly admitting that the thing was pure assumption, but willing to make the best of it. Socrates however was not content. Applying his rationalistic dialectic fuse to all alike, whether smith or shoemaker, sophist, politician or poet, he was for stopping all this foolish activity of theirs—whether in the line of traditional custom or of original creation (think of it! the age of Pericles!), stopping it until it defined its terms and justified itself before reason. They should not undertake the music of life, till they had mastered the *τέχνη*, the five-finger exercises of thinking, reflec-

He went beyond them in sophisticating the common people.

tion, dialectic. To be sure, he did not himself know what was to come after the exercise. That he frankly confessed. *He* knew nothing. But he hoped, if they practised the method well, music might come of it. (Pathetic hopeful Socrates! Is there any preparatory method to life? Is it not a reading at sight, for the most cautious of us? And is not the sweetest music full of discord?)

46 And so, in his eager optimism, he applied his rationalistic fuse and—was himself landed in a better world. The truth is, Socrates committed the error (natural to discoverers) of carrying his principle too far. As the Ionian philosophers had taken one element (e.g. air or water) to be the only element in the material world, so in the mental world Socrates took reason. He undertook to rationalize the whole of life—to substitute conscious action not merely for conventional but for creative as well. Now the first is anarchic enough.[61] For not by nine-tenths can the tent of reason be stretched to cover all the φαινόμενα (the side-shows) of life. Nothing is harder than reasoning. There is little occasion for it in the side-shows. Yet each man likes to think he thinks. And for most men it is more unendurable to be proved a fool than to be proved wicked. But to be proved both these things at once ("Virtue *is* knowledge," insisted Socrates)—away with him![62]

Results.

47 But in catechizing the poets, Socrates surely showed himself utterly un-Greek, utterly unaware of the direct, unconscious, intuitive workings of a creative mind. (Did he fancy *any* creation could justify itself as rational? Would he eradicate instinct?) *He* preferred, among the poets, Euripides, the unspontaneous, the rationalist. Can we imagine Aeschylus composing under the guidance of Socrates?

Irresistibly, one is reminded of the short episode between the frog and the centipede (I quote from memory):

> The Centipede was happy quite
> Until the Frog for fun
> Asked: "Pray, which leg comes after which?"
> This worked her mind to such a pitch,
> She lay exhausted in the ditch,
> Considering how to run.

Taking the world as it runs and whether we will or no, we must admit that conscious action is a fine thing in its own place, but nowhere else; that logic confutes well, but does not therefore convert; that it is good for the world, as for the individual, to have had the experience of rationalizing, but that after all it is a rather youthful disciplinary stage. Preceding it are the days of the *gratus puellae risus ab angulo, lenesque sub noctem susurri;* after it, comes the period of the old men who sat on the walls of Troy and chirped like grasshoppers, liking to have fair Helen by. But we may be pretty sure they did not chirp by the syllogism.

Conclusion.

We conclude, therefore, that the condemnation of 48
Socrates was the most natural event in the world. Daily human life will hold in solution so much reason, and no more. Society may admit a modicum of rationalizing and find it harmless; but a large and undiluted quantity injected into its system, it will throw off energetically and spontaneously, as poison. Socrates failed to see the logical cogency of that fine old motto of all conservatism: Whatever is, is right. In his practice certainly, he came dangerously near to identifying himself (and his enemies did identify him) with that other party, the party of "progress," which proclaims: Whatever is, is wrong. The war between

them will ever go on, will ever be truceless, *πόλεμος πατὴρ πάντων.* Victory is now to the one, now to the other. In the case of Socrates, one is mournfully reminded of the fate of Camarīna, a coast-town in Sicily. Its progressive party were for draining the back marshes. An oracle forbade it:

Μὴ κίνει Καμάρῖναν· ἀκίνητος γὰρ ἀμείνων
Do not disturb Camarīna; for undisturbed she is stronger.

The progressive party persisted and the marshes were drained. Assault by land was made possible. The enemy came. And Camarīna fell.

49 But none the less for these reflections is Socrates one of the world's heroes. For in the long run the world is fair, and measures a man not by his results but by his intentions. Even with martyrdom at the end, an enthusiast's life, a lover's life, is the glorious one. Happy was Socrates in having a cause, heroic he was in dying for it.—The only truly tragic thing about martyrdom is, not that the *man* dies, but that after a while his cause does.

NOTES TO THE INTRODUCTION

1. Among the books most available for the ordinary reader perhaps the best on the life of Socrates are: Grote, *Hist. of Greece*, ch. 68. Curtius, *Hist. of Greece* (translated by Ward), bk. 5, ch. 2. Zeller, *Socrates and the Socratic Schools* (transl. by Reichel, 3rd edit.), ch. 3; or the same in German *Die Philosophie der Griechen* II 1 (4th edit.), p. 44. There may also be mentioned (but not for its value) the Greek life by Diogenes Laertius living c. 200 A.D.

2. On the voluntary poverty of Socrates, see infra 11,20 *ἐν πενίᾳ μυρίᾳ εἰμί*. 36,6 'perhaps I could pay a fine of a mina' (c. $18.00). X. *Oec.* 2,3 *οἶμαι . . εὑρεῖν ἄν* ('would fetch') *μοι τὴν οἰκίαν καὶ τὰ ὄντα πάντα πάνυ ῥᾳδίως πέντε μνᾶς.* Socrates believed the easiest way to wealth and leisure was not by heaping up money to the height of his wants, but by reducing his wants to the amount of his money; see X. *Mem.* I 6,1–10 where he closes with the thought *τὸ μὲν μηδενὸς δεῖσθαι θεῖον εἶναι, τὸ δ' ὡς ἐλαχίστων ἐγγυτάτω τοῦ θείου.*

3. He was as ugly as a satyr; see infra p. 96. In Xen. *Symp.* 5,5–7 he jestingly defends his features in detail, proving them to be more beautiful than those of the handsome Critobūlus "because more useful." His eyes were set out on the surface (*ἐπι-πόλαιοι*) like those of a crab (*καρκίνος*) and hence could see better sideways (*τὸ ἐκ πλαγίου*). His nostrils spread out (*οἱ μυκτῆρες ἀναπέπτανται*) and so could receive scents from all quarters (*πάντοθεν ὀσμὰς προσδέχεσθαι*). The flatness of his nose (*τὸ σιμὸν τῆς ῥινός*) offered no obstruction to his vision. (This feature is referred to also in *Theaet.* 143 E and hinted at infra 177,10 where he is compared in looks to the torpedo.) His mouth was large, the better to bite with (*τοῦ ἀποδάκνειν ἕνεκα*); his lips thick (*τὰ χείλη παχέα*), and so of softer kiss (*μαλακώτερον τὸ φίλημα*). He admits, however, that he is inconveniently rotund (*μείζω τοῦ καιροῦ τὴν γαστέρα ἔχων*). He had the gait of a *βρένθος* (Arist. *Nub.* 362, infra 101,2)—whatever kind of a bird that may be—pelican or duck—stalking or waddling.

4. He was a true-born Athenian (i.e. both his parents were Athenian), but Sophroniscus his father was a sculptor (a common calling, then and there), and his mother Phaenarete was a midwife; see Plat. *Theaet.* 149 A.

5. On his hardy health, endurance, and temperance, see infra p. 98 ff. and 258,9. From X. *Mem.* I 6,2 we learn how he lived on the poorest fare, wore the same poor cloak summer and winter, and went shoeless and shirtless: *σῖτά τε σιτεῖ καὶ ποτὰ πίνεις τὰ φαυλότατα, καὶ ἱμάτιον ἠμφίεσαι οὐ μόνον φαῦλον, ἀλλὰ τὸ αὐτὸ θέρους τε καὶ χειμῶνος, ἀνυπόδητός τε καὶ ἀχίτων διατελεῖς.*

6. He was genial, loved company, accepted the dinner-invitations of the rich, enjoyed their good things without envy, could drink more than other man present, yet never went to excess. For all this, one should read Xenophon's *Symposium* and Plato *Symp.* 176 C, 214 A, and infra 99,7.

7. See infra p. 94 and p. 99,23 ff.

8. X. *Symp.* 2,19 *Χαρμίδης οὑτοσὶ κατέλαβέ με ὀρχούμενον.*

9. It may be inferred from *Crito* 50 D (infra 56,25) that Socrates received the ordinary schooling of his day. Further instruction from books or teachers cannot be safely deduced from the few remaining passages bearing on the matter. In X. *Mem.* I 6,14 he is represented as unrolling and reading with his friends the writings of ancient wise men: *τοὺς θησαυροὺς τῶν πάλαι σοφῶν ἀνδρῶν, οὓς ἐκεῖνοι κατέλιπον ἐν βιβλίοις γράψαντες, ἀνελίττων κοινῇ σὺν τοῖς φίλοις διέρχομαι.* But it was not till after he had reached manhood that anything beyond elementary instruction was offered in systematic form, that, namely, by the sophists (see infra § 26). Hitherto the free and constant intercourse of citizen with citizen—the schooling of life itself—was thought sufficient.

10. For the appellation *σοφός*, see infra 3,7. 11,3. 36,17.

11. On his "many bitter enmities" see infra 10,28.

12. It may be true that he learned the sculptor's art from his father (so Diog. Laert. II 19). In the second century A.D., Pausanias saw some statuary (a Hermes and three Graces) attributed to his chisel, standing at the entrance to the acropolis (I 22,8. IX 35,7); but that they were indeed his work is doubtful (see Frazer's note *ad loc.*). Neither Xenophon nor Plato refer to him as a sculptor, and infra 11,18–21 and 24,27–30 he declares that he has no occupation but that of examining and confuting his fellow-mortals.

13. See Zeller, p. 54 (Engl. transl. p. 62) for the shadowy personality of the wife Myrto (if she ever existed) as well as for Xanthippe, even in antiquity famous and proverbial for the shrewish wife. It seems probable that Socrates married late in life, since no mention is made of Xanthippe in the *Clouds* of Aristophanes 423 B.C., when Socrates was forty-six years of age

—and we can hardly believe old Attic comedy would have spared the situation, had it then existed. Better evidence, however, is Plato's reference infra 30,23 to the eldest son as μειράκιον ἤδη at the time of his father's death. See further infra 68,25. 90,2. X. *Mem.* II 2; *Symp.* 2,10.

14. See infra 59,21–30. 60,30. 260,31. *Meno* 80 B.

15. Infra 20,30; and pp. 98 and 100. *Charm.* 153 A, 156 D, *Lach.* 181 B.

16. About this warning voice of Socrates much has been written—*how* much will be seen by a reference to Zeller's citations, p. 75 (Engl. transl. p. 83). In English, Riddell's Appendix A to the *Apology* should be read, or at least what Grote says concerning it in his 68th chapter. The monitor is spoken of by Plato and Xenophon as a σημεῖον, a φωνή, a θεῖόν τι καὶ δαιμόνιον (but never as a δαίμων or real spirit). It came frequently (τὸ εἰωθὸς σημεῖον), beginning from childhood (ἐκ παιδός). According to Plato it restrained but did not suggest action (ἀπο-τρέπει, προ-τρέπει δ' οὔποτε infra 25,23)—though of course from its failure to check, Socrates could infer its approval. Not alone in matters of great import did it restrain him (e.g. from the preparation of a speech for his trial, X. *Mem.* IV 8,5–6), but in quite trivial matters (πάνυ ἐπὶ σμικροῖς infra 39,9); Plato on one occasion makes it seat him again when rising to depart, and so cause for him a lucky meeting with two sophists (*Euthyd.* 272 E); at another time it gives him pause on the casual crossing of a river (*Phaedr.* 242 B).

It is clear from this that the monitor was not identical with our "conscience" (which speaks on matters of right and wrong only, not on indifferent matters), but was rather sometimes a "presentiment," sometimes an undefined sense of inconsistency or unfitness in the proposed act. It seems to have been a native (ἐκ παιδός) swiftness of judgment, reaching conclusions by unconscious and unanalyzable process—a sort of woman-instinct or tact, which Socrates called θεῖον or δαιμόνιον ('divine,' 'supernatural') just because, honest logician that he was, he could not tell how else the judgment got into his head, hence *must* have been sent, and for his welfare, and hence must be obeyed implicitly as a sort of private oracle. (Strange inconsistent Rationalist, dimly to recognize his limit!) His friends looked to him for guidance, as they would to a soothsayer or to their own omen-taking. *They* never had a whisper of such voice. "He never dwelt upon it himself as anything grand or awful . . but spoke of it often in his usual strain of familiar playfulness. . . To his enemies and to the Athenian public, it appeared in the light of an offensive heresy, an impious innovation on the orthodox creed, and a desertion of the recognized gods of Athens" (Grote)—to Meletus indeed it seemed no better than flat atheism (infra 16,31). See infra 25,19–25. 39,6–19.

Theaet. 151 A. X. *Mem.* I 1,2–5. IV 3,12–13. 8,1,5–6,11. X. *Symp.* 8,5.

17. Socrates was to be found ἐν ἀγορᾷ ἐπὶ τῶν τραπεζῶν, ἵνα . . ὑμῶν πολλοὶ ἀκηκόασι (infra 2,11). He was always ἐν τῷ φανερῷ· πρῴ τε γὰρ εἰς τοὺς περιπάτους καὶ τὰ γυμνάσια ᾔει, καὶ πληθούσης ἀγορᾶς ἐκεῖ φανερὸς ἦν, καὶ τὸ λοιπὸν ἀεὶ τῆς ἡμέρας ἦν ὅπου πλείστοις μέλλοι συνέσεσθαι (X. *Mem.* I 1,10). The Lycēum seems to have been his favourite gymnasium; the dialogues *Euthydemus* and *Lysis* are held there. See further *Euthyph.* init. and *Symp.* 223 D.

18. The cant name for these philosophers of ceaseless talk was ἀδολέσχαι 'chatterers,' 'prattlers,' perhaps 'button-holers.' See Aristoph. *Nub.* 1485. Plat. *Soph.* 225 D.

19. On his mission to all classes and conditions of men, see infra 11,15. 22,14,28. 23,4. 28,5. X. *Mem.* I 1,10 τοῖς δὲ βουλομένοις ἐξῆν ἀκούειν. In the third book of the *Memorabilia* visits are reported to painters, sculptors, armourers; and infra pp. 8 foll. to politicians, poets, and artisans.

20. See infra p. 103.

21. See infra p. 177.

22. See infra 24,13.

23. See infra pp. 8–11.

24. Undoubtedly, however, there was irony in this "ignorance" of his—and mixed with his humility on each occasion there could not but be a gloating certainty that here was another fly in his web. His professions of ignorance, his assurances that only a weak spider's web held them, merely enraged his victims the more at their confutation.

25. It may be well to set down a few points regarding Socrates' attitude towards various branches of learning:

(1) He thought it folly to theorize on the nature and ultimate causes of the universe. Were not human affairs of more importance and nearer home? And was it not plain that such questions were beyond man's ken? See too how the wise men disagreed! X. *Mem.* I 1,11 οὐδὲ γὰρ περὶ τῆς τῶν πάντων φύσεως ('nature of the universe'), ᾗπερ τῶν ἄλλων οἱ πλεῖστοι, διελέγετο, σκοπῶν ὅπως ὁ καλούμενος ὑπὸ τῶν σοφιστῶν κόσμος ('ordered world') ἔφυ, καὶ τίσιν ἀνάγκαις ἕκαστα γίγνεται τῶν οὐρανίων, ἀλλὰ καὶ τοὺς φροντίζοντας τὰ τοιαῦτα μωραίνοντας ἀπεδείκνυε. ‖ καὶ πρῶτον μὲν περὶ αὐτῶν ἐσκόπει πότερά ποτε νομίσαντες ἱκανῶς ἤδη τἀνθρώπεια εἰδέναι ἔρχονται ἐπὶ τὸ περὶ τῶν τοιούτων φροντίζειν, ἢ τὰ μὲν ἀνθρώπεια παρέντες, τὰ δαιμόνια δὲ σκοποῦντες ἡγοῦνται τὰ προσήκοντα πράττειν. ‖ ἐθαύμαζε δ' εἰ μὴ φανερὸν αὐτοῖς ἐστιν ὅτι ταῦτα οὐ δυνατόν ἐστιν ἀνθρώποις εὑρεῖν· ἐπεὶ καὶ τοὺς μέγιστον φρονοῦντας ('those who made the greatest pretensions') ἐπὶ τῷ περὶ τούτων λέγειν οὐ ταὐτὰ δοξάζειν ἀλλήλοις, ἀλλὰ τοῖς μαινομένοις ὁμοίως διακεῖσθαι πρὸς ἀλλήλους. See infra 4,30; 17,5 for his disclaimers to such knowledge of physics.

(2) Again, he thought that such branches as geometry might be carried too far into the merely theoretical. This he disapproved. X. *Mem.* IV 7,2 *γεωμετρίαν μέχρι μὲν τούτου ἔφη δεῖν μανθάνειν, ἕως ἱκανός τις γένοιτο, εἴ ποτε δεήσειε, γῆν μέτρῳ ὀρθῶς ἢ παραλαβεῖν ἢ παραδοῦναι ἢ διανεῖμαι ἢ ἔργον ἀποδείξασθαι* ('set apart as a field'). . . *τὸ δὲ μέχρι τῶν δυσσυνέτων διαγραμμάτων γεωμετρίαν μανθάνειν ἀπεδοκίμαζεν. ὅ τι μὲν γὰρ ὠφελοίη ταῦτα οὐκ ἔφη ὁρᾶν· καίτοι οὐκ ἄπειρός γε αὐτῶν ἦν. ἔφη δὲ ταῦτα ἱκανὰ εἶναι ἀνθρώπου βίον κατατρίβειν καὶ ἄλλων πολλῶν τε καὶ ὠφελίμων μαθημάτων ἀποκωλύειν.*—So too astronomy should be carried no further than was useful X. *Mem.* IV 7,4 *ἐκέλευε δὲ καὶ ἀστρονομίας ἐμπείρους γίγνεσθαι, καὶ ταύτης μέντοι μέχρι τοῦ νυκτός τε ὥραν καὶ μηνὸς καὶ ἐνιαυτοῦ δύνασθαι γιγνώσκειν ἕνεκα πορείας τε καὶ πλοῦ καὶ φυλακῆς, καὶ ὅσα ἄλλα ἢ νυκτὸς ἢ μηνὸς ἢ ἐνιαυτοῦ πράττεται, πρὸς ταῦτ' ἔχειν τεκμηρίοις χρῆσθαι, τὰς ὥρας τῶν εἰρημένων διαγιγνώσκοντας. . . τὸ δὲ μέχρι τούτου ἀστρονομίαν μανθάνειν, μέχρι τοῦ καὶ τὰ μὴ ἐν τῇ αὐτῇ περιφορᾷ ὄντα* (i.e. not in the same system with us) *καὶ τοὺς πλάνητάς τε καὶ ἀσταθμήτους ἀστέρας γνῶναι, καὶ τὰς ἀποστάσεις* ('distances') *αὐτῶν ἀπὸ τῆς γῆς καὶ τὰς περιόδους καὶ τὰς αἰτίας αὐτῶν ζητοῦντας κατατρίβεσθαι* ('wear their lives out'), *ἰσχυρῶς ἀπέτρεπεν. ὠφέλειαν μὲν γὰρ οὐδεμίαν οὐδ' ἐν τούτοις* (any more than in "unintelligible" geometry) *ἔφη ὁρᾶν· καίτοι οὐδὲ τούτων γε ἀνήκοος* ('ignorant') *ἦν· ἔφη δὲ καὶ ταῦτα ἱκανὰ εἶναι κατατρίβειν ἀνθρώπου βίον, καὶ πολλῶν καὶ ὠφελίμων ἀποκωλύειν.*

(3) Rather, the proper study of mankind, he thought, was man. X. *Mem.* I 1,16 *περὶ τῶν ἀνθρωπείων ἀεὶ διελέγετο, σκοπῶν τί εὐσεβές, τί ἀσεβές, τί καλόν, τί αἰσχρόν, τί δίκαιον, τί ἄδικον, τί σωφροσύνη, τί μανία, τί ἀνδρεία, τί δειλία, τί πόλις, τί πολιτικός, τί ἀρχὴ ἀνθρώπων, τί ἀρχικὸς ἀνθρώπων, καὶ περὶ τῶν ἄλλων, ἃ τοὺς μὲν εἰδότας ἡγεῖτο καλοὺς κἀγαθοὺς εἶναι, τοὺς δ' ἀγνοοῦντας ἀνδραποδώδεις ἂν δικαίως κεκλῆσθαι.* So Aristotle *Metaphys.* I 6 *Σωκράτους δὲ περὶ μὲν τὰ ἠθικὰ* ('ethics') *πραγματευομένου, περὶ δὲ τῆς ὅλης φύσεως οὐθέν* (=*οὐδέν*). So infra p. 261. See Zeller p. 134 (Engl. transl. p. 137).

26. See infra 11,22–24.

27. See infra pp. 92–93.

28. (§ 12) Cic. *Tusc. Disp.* v 4,10 Socrates autem primus philosophiam devocavit de caelo et in urbibus conlocavit et in domus etiam introduxit et coëgit de vita et moribus rebusque bonis et malis quaerere.

29. (§ 13) On the lack of creative power in Xenophon and his great amount of subjectivity, see Karl Joël's most interesting book *Der echte und der Xenophontische Sokrates*, Berlin 1893, to which I owe the position taken in this Introduction concerning Socrates' aim and results.

30. (§ 13) Joël, p. 209, points out how little testimony Zeller can cite from Plato for pure moralizing on the part of his

master. In Plato, whatever the virtue under consideration may be, it must have in it φρόνησις.

31. (§ 16) Among the briefer accounts of Pre-Socratic philosophy, that by Schwegler, in *Hist. of Philos.* §§ 3–10, is particularly good and clear.

32. (§ 17) See Grote's *Hist. of Greece*, part I, ch. 16.

33. (§ 20) See Zeller's *Pre-Socratic Philos.* I, p. 614 (Engl. transl.).

34. (§ 26) Consult Zeller's *Pre-Socrat. Phil.* II, p. 394 (Engl. transl.); Schwegler, § 11; Grote's *History*, ch. 67.

35. (§ 29) See infra p. 154.

36. (§ 31) See Plato's *Protag.* 320 C.

37. (§ 31) See X. *Mem.* II 1.

38. (§ 31) E.g. Critias, Polus, Thrasymachus.

39. (§ 31) See X. *Mem.* IV 4,14.

40. (§ 32) Thucyd. III 52 ff. V 116.

41. (§ 32) Thucyd. III 82–83.

42. (§ 33) See infra, p. 220, and espec. p. 222 top.

43. (§ 34) Schwegler, § 12.

44. (§ 36) Joël, *op. cit.*, p. 194.

45. (§ 36) VIRTUE IS KNOWLEDGE. On this (for us surprising) identification is based all the rest of Socratic doctrine. We may be sure that it is Socratic from the unanimity of the witnesses. Aristot. *Eth. Eud.* I 5 ἐπιστήμας ᾤετ' εἶναι πάσας τὰς ἀρετάς. X. *Mem.* III 9,5 ἔφη δὲ καὶ τὴν δικαιοσύνην καὶ τὴν ἄλλην πᾶσαν ἀρετὴν σοφίαν εἶναι. Plat. *Lach.* 194 D ταῦτα ἀγαθὸς ἕκαστος ἡμῶν, ἅπερ σοφός· ἃ δὲ ἀμαθής, ταῦτα δὲ κακός.

Plato, later, distinguished the ἄλογον μέρος ψυχῆς ('irrational part of soul'), the ἐπιθυμητικόν (the 'passionate part'); and St. Paul testifies to the struggle between flesh and spirit: οὐ γὰρ ὃ θέλω, τοῦτο πράσσω, ἀλλ' ὃ μισῶ, τοῦτο ποιῶ (*Rom.* 7,15). But Socrates did not at all recognize the will or the emotions as parts of soul-life. All was swallowed up in Reason (λόγος). That was the supreme and the only function. A conflict, therefore, between the will and the reason was for him impossible. So possessed was he by his discovery of the λόγος, that he denied there was any virtue without knowledge. There might be sham piety, justice, bravery, but "he only is pious who *knows* what is right towards God, he is just who *knows* what is right towards men, he is brave who *knows* how to treat dangers properly" (Zeller, p. 144; and see X. *Mem.* IV 6, §§ 4, 6, 11).

If virtue is knowledge, then vice is ignorance. Socrates accepted this result. Constantly he repeats that no one sins voluntarily, that a man does wrong only because he knows no better, that to err knowingly would be a voluntary choice of unhappiness — which is absurd. See infra 15,28 ff., *Meno*

77 B, *Prot.* 345 D οὐδεὶς τῶν σοφῶν ἀνδρῶν ἡγεῖται οὐδένα ἀνθρώπων ἑκόντα ἐξαμαρτάνειν. Cf. also Zeller, p. 141 (Engl. transl. p. 141). This onesided exaggeration of the thinking faculty, and blindness to all else, on the part of Socrates is soberly and frequently corrected by Aristotle (see Joël p. 214 ff. for the passages). But a newly-discovered truth *must* be over-accentuated, it seems, to obtain any hearing whatever; or again, truth must be born into (incarnated in) a body of error, to divest itself of which is its life-long struggle; and when, alas, the process is complete, it finds itself worn out and supplanted by a new truth in a new body of error.

46. (§ 37) Infra, pp. 8–10.

47. (§ 37) Infra, 8,27.

48. (§ 37) X. *Mem.* I 1,13.

49. (§ 37) *Lach.* 190 C ff.

50. (§ 37) X. *Mem.* IV 6,1. Zeller, p. 107.

51. (§ 37) *Definition by induction* is, therefore, according to Aristotle, Socrates' contribution to human advancement; *Metaphys.* XIII 4 δύο γάρ ἐστιν ἅ τις ἂν ἀποδοίη ('render') Σωκράτει δικαίως, τούς τ' ἐπακτικοὺς λόγους καὶ τὸ ὁρίζεσθαι καθόλου. Cf. Zeller p. 107 (Engl. transl. p. 111). Xenophon also refers to such activity of his master, but only in passing; e.g. *Mem.* IV 6,1 and 13. 5,12. For it is practical morality, not theory, that fills the *Memorabilia.* Joël (p. 208) can find but a hundredth part of the work that testifies to Socrates as a logician. Indeed its author forgets even this, when elsewhere he is developing his own principles, attributing them to Socrates. Joël opposes III 9,5 to IV 4.

52. (§ 39) *Theaetetus* 149 A f.

53. (§ 41) Zeller, pp. 136, 179 (Engl. transl., p. 140).

54. (§ 41) Infra 17,5 (when he indignantly denies that he thinks the sun a stone); 100,5 (where he prays to the sun). See too his beautiful little prayer at the close of *Phaedrus* 279 B.

55. (§ 41) *Mem.* I 1,9.

56. (§ 43) He did not, however, recognize the authority of the Thirty. Infra 26,31.

57. (§ 43) X. *Mem.* III 6. 9,10.

58. (§ 43) X. *Mem.* I 2,9.

59. (§ 44) *Symp.* 213 E. X. *Mem.* I 2,14.

60. (§ 45) Infra 177,17.

61. (§ 46) Grote thinks that in such a Republic as Plato constructs Socrates "would not have been allowed to pursue his vocation for a week" (*Hist.* VIII, p. 299).

62. (§ 46) The present account accentuates the personal animus that instigated the prosecution of Socrates. But it may well have been the charge of atheism that, before the common people, convicted him. Though their conduct might be corrupt, yet their creed was sound. And on that they were

quite intolerant. For atheism or impiety Anaxagoras had been banished, Protagoras compelled to flee, Diagoras of Melos to do likewise, Phidias to die in prison, while Aspasia barely escaped condemnation through the intercession of Pericles. Long afterwards too, Aristotle withdrew from Athens to avoid the same charge. Nor should the memorable outbreak of religious feeling be forgotten that occurred in 415 B.C. on the occasion of the mutilation of the Hermes-statues. See Holm, *Hist. of Greece* (Engl. transl.) II, p. 293.

THE APOLOGY OF SOCRATES

(*Entire*)

Socrates' Defence before his Judges

Socrates is no orator, but in a plain way will tell the truth. Let the Athenians have regard to that, and not his manner.

Ὅ τι μὲν ὑμεῖς, ὦ ἄνδρες Ἀθηναῖοι, πεπόν- 17 A
θατε ὑπὸ τῶν ἐμῶν κατηγόρων, οὐκ
οἶδα· ἐγὼ δ᾽ οὖν καὶ αὐτὸς ὑπ᾽ αὐτῶν
ὀλίγου ἐμαυτοῦ ἐπελαθόμην· οὕτω
πιθανῶς ἔλεγον. καίτοι ἀληθές γε,
ὡς ἔπος εἰπεῖν, οὐδὲν εἰρήκασιν.
μάλιστα δὲ αὐτῶν ἓν ἐθαύμασα τῶν
πολλῶν ὧν ἐψεύσαντο, τοῦτο ἐν ᾧ ἔλεγον ὡς
χρὴ ὑμᾶς εὐλαβεῖσθαι, μὴ ὑπ᾽ ἐμοῦ ἐξαπατη-
θῆτε, ὡς δεινοῦ | ὄντος λέγειν. τὸ γὰρ μὴ B
αἰσχυνθῆναι, ὅτι αὐτίκα ὑπ᾽ ἐμοῦ ἐξελεγχθή-
σονται ἔργῳ, ἐπειδὰν μηδ᾽ ὁπωστιοῦν φαίνωμαι
δεινὸς λέγειν, τοῦτό μοι ἔδοξεν αὐτῶν ἀναι-
σχυντότατον εἶναι, εἰ μὴ ἄρα δεινὸν καλοῦσιν
οὗτοι λέγειν τὸν τἀληθῆ λέγοντα· εἰ μὲν γὰρ
τοῦτο λέγουσιν, ὁμολογοίην ἂν ἔγωγε οὐ κατὰ
τούτους εἶναι ῥήτωρ. οὗτοι μὲν οὖν, ὥσπερ
ἐγὼ λέγω, ἤ τι ἢ οὐδὲν ἀληθὲς εἰρήκασιν·
ὑμεῖς δ᾽ ἐμοῦ ἀκούσεσθε πᾶσαν τὴν ἀλήθειαν—
οὐ μέντοι μὰ Δία, ὦ ἄνδρες Ἀθηναῖοι, κεκαλ-

17 λιεπημένους γε λόγους, ὥσπερ οἱ τούτων, ῥήμασί
C τε καὶ ὀνόμασιν, οὐδὲ κεκοσμημένους, | ἀλλὰ
ἀκούσεσθε εἰκῇ λεγόμενα τοῖς ἐπιτυχοῦσιν
ὀνόμασιν. πιστεύω γὰρ δίκαια εἶναι ἃ λέγω,
καὶ μηδεὶς ὑμῶν προσδοκησάτω ἄλλως· οὐδὲ
γὰρ ἂν δήπου πρέποι, ὦ ἄνδρες, τῇδε τῇ ἡλικίᾳ
ὥσπερ μειρακίῳ πλάττοντι λόγους εἰς ὑμᾶς
εἰσιέναι. καὶ μέντοι καὶ πάνυ, ὦ ἄνδρες
Ἀθηναῖοι, τοῦτο ὑμῶν δέομαι καὶ παρίεμαι·
ἐὰν διὰ τῶν αὐτῶν λόγων ἀκούητέ μου ἀπολο-
γουμένου, δι' ὧνπερ εἴωθα λέγειν καὶ ἐν ἀγορᾷ
ἐπὶ τῶν τραπεζῶν (ἵνα ὑμῶν πολλοὶ ἀκηκόασι),
D καὶ ἄλλοθι, μήτε θαυμάζειν | μήτε θορυβεῖν
τούτου ἕνεκα. ἔχει γὰρ οὑτωσί. νῦν ἐγὼ πρῶτον
ἐπὶ δικαστήριον ἀναβέβηκα, ἔτη γεγονὼς ἑβδομή-
κοντα· ἀτεχνῶς οὖν ξένως ἔχω τῆς ἐνθάδε λέξεως.
ὥσπερ οὖν ἄν, εἰ τῷ ὄντι ξένος ἐτύγχανον ὤν,
ξυνεγιγνώσκετε δήπου ἄν μοι, εἰ ἐν ἐκείνῃ τῇ
18 φωνῇ τε καὶ τῷ τρόπῳ ἔλεγον, ἐν | οἷσπερ ἐτε-
θράμμην, καὶ δὴ καὶ νῦν τοῦτο ὑμῶν δέομαι
δίκαιον, ὥς γέ μοι δοκῶ, τὸν μὲν τρόπον τῆς
λέξεως ἐᾶν (ἴσως μὲν γὰρ χείρων, ἴσως δὲ βελτίων
ἂν εἴη), αὐτὸ δὲ τοῦτο σκοπεῖν καὶ τούτῳ τὸν
νοῦν προσέχειν, εἰ δίκαια λέγω ἢ μή· δικαστοῦ
μὲν γὰρ αὕτη ἀρετή, ῥήτορος δὲ τἀληθῆ λέγειν.

He will answer his old accusers first. More formidable are they than the present three.

Πρῶτον μὲν οὖν δίκαιός εἰμι ἀπολογήσα-
σθαι, ὦ ἄνδρες Ἀθηναῖοι, πρὸς τὰ
πρῶτά μου ψευδῆ κατηγορημένα καὶ
τοὺς πρώτους κατηγόρους, ἔπειτα δὲ
πρὸς τὰ ὕστερα καὶ τοὺς ὑστέρους.
B | ἐμοῦ γὰρ πολλοὶ κατήγοροι γεγόνασι πρὸς

ὑμᾶς καὶ πάλαι πολλὰ ἤδη ἔτη καὶ οὐδὲν 18
ἀληθὲς λέγοντες, οὓς ἐγὼ μᾶλλον φοβοῦμαι
ἢ τοὺς ἀμφὶ Ἄνυτον, καίπερ ὄντας καὶ τούτους
δεινούς· ἀλλ' ἐκεῖνοι δεινότεροι, ὦ ἄνδρες, οἳ
ὑμῶν τοὺς πολλοὺς ἐκ παίδων παραλαμβά-
νοντες ἔπειθόν τε καὶ κατηγόρουν ἐμοῦ μᾶλλον
οὐδὲν ἀληθές, ὡς ἔστι τις Σωκράτης, σοφὸς
ἀνήρ, τά τε μετέωρα [φροντιστὴς] καὶ τὰ
ὑπὸ γῆς ἅπαντα ἀνεζητηκὼς καὶ τὸν ἥττω
λόγον κρείττω ποιῶν. οὗτοι, ὦ ἄνδρες Ἀθη-
ναῖοι, | ταύτην τὴν φήμην κατασκεδάσαντες, οἱ C
δεινοί εἰσίν μου κατήγοροι· οἱ γὰρ ἀκούοντες
ἡγοῦνται τοὺς ταῦτα ζητοῦντας οὐδὲ (The reasons for this.)
θεοὺς νομίζειν. ἔπειτά εἰσιν οὗτοι
οἱ κατήγοροι πολλοὶ καὶ πολὺν χρόνον ἤδη
κατηγορηκότες, ἔτι δὲ καὶ ἐν ταύτῃ τῇ ἡλικίᾳ
λέγοντες πρὸς ὑμᾶς, ἐν ᾗ ἂν μάλιστα ἐπιστεύ-
σατε παῖδες ὄντες (ἔνιοι δ' ὑμῶν καὶ μειράκια),
ἀτεχνῶς ἐρήμην κατηγοροῦντες ἀπολογουμένου
οὐδενός. ὃ δὲ πάντων ἀλογώτατον, ὅτι οὐδὲ
τὰ ὀνόματα οἷόντε αὐτῶν εἰδέναι καὶ εἰπεῖν, |
πλὴν εἴ τις κωμῳδοποιὸς τυγχάνει ὤν. ὅσοι D
δὲ φθόνῳ καὶ διαβολῇ χρώμενοι ὑμᾶς ἀνέπει-
θον, οἱ δὲ καὶ αὐτοὶ πεπεισμένοι ἄλλους πεί-
θοντες, οὗτοι πάντων ἀπορώτατοί εἰσιν· οὐδὲ
γὰρ ἀναβιβάσασθαι οἷόντ' ἐστὶν αὐτῶν ἐνταυ-
θοῖ οὐδ' ἐλέγξαι οὐδένα, ἀλλ' ἀνάγκη ἀτεχνῶς
ὥσπερ σκιαμαχεῖν ἀπολογούμενόν τε καὶ ἐλέγ-
χειν μηδενὸς ἀποκρινομένου. ἀξιώσατε οὖν
καὶ ὑμεῖς, ὥσπερ ἐγὼ λέγω, διττούς μου τοὺς
κατηγόρους γεγονέναι, ἑτέρους μὲν τοὺς ἄρτι

18 κατηγορήσαντας, ἑτέρους δὲ | τοὺς πάλαι, οὓς ἐγὼ
E λέγω, καὶ οἰήθητε δεῖν πρὸς ἐκείνους πρῶτόν με ἀπολογήσασθαι· καὶ γὰρ ὑμεῖς ἐκείνων πρότερον ἠκούσατε κατηγορούντων καὶ πολὺ μᾶλλον ἢ τῶνδε τῶν ὕστερον.

(The consequent difficulty for him.)

Εἶεν· ἀπολογητέον δή, ὦ ἄνδρες Ἀθηναῖοι,
19 καὶ ἐπιχειρητέον | ὑμῶν ἐξελέσθαι τὴν διαβολήν, ἣν ὑμεῖς ἐν πολλῷ χρόνῳ ἔσχετε, ταύτην ἐν οὕτως ὀλίγῳ χρόνῳ. βουλοίμην μὲν οὖν ἂν τοῦτο οὕτως γενέσθαι, εἴ τι ἄμεινον καὶ ὑμῖν καὶ ἐμοί, καὶ πλέον τί με ποιῆσαι ἀπολογούμενον· οἶμαι δὲ αὐτὸ χαλεπὸν εἶναι, καὶ οὐ πάνυ με λανθάνει οἷόν ἐστιν. ὅμως τοῦτο μὲν ἴτω ὅπῃ τῷ θεῷ φίλον, τῷ δὲ νόμῳ πειστέον καὶ ἀπολογητέον.

He was a wicked scientist, they said; and made the worse cause win; and taught others the same—all which is untrue.

Ἀναλάβωμεν οὖν ἐξ ἀρχῆς, τίς ἡ κατηγορία ἐστίν, ἐξ ἧς ἡ ἐμὴ διαβολὴ γέγονεν,
B ᾗ δὴ καὶ πιστεύων | Μέλητός με ἐγράψατο τὴν γραφὴν ταύτην. εἶεν· τί δὴ λέγοντες διέβαλλον οἱ διαβάλλοντες; ὥσπερ οὖν κατηγόρων τὴν ἀντωμοσίαν δεῖ ἀναγνῶναι αὐτῶν· Σωκράτης ἀδικεῖ καὶ περιεργάζεται ζητῶν τά τε ὑπὸ γῆς καὶ οὐράνια καὶ τὸν ἥττω λόγον κρείττω ποιῶν καὶ ἄλλους τὰ αὐτὰ
C ταῦτα διδάσκων. | τοιαύτη τίς ἐστι· ταῦτα γὰρ ἑωρᾶτε καὶ αὐτοὶ ἐν τῇ Ἀριστοφάνους κωμῳδίᾳ, Σωκράτη τινὰ ἐκεῖ περιφερόμενον, φάσκοντά τε ἀεροβατεῖν καὶ ἄλλην πολλὴν φλυαρίαν φλυαροῦντα, ὧν ἐγὼ οὐδὲν οὔτε μέγα οὔτε μικρὸν πέρι ἐπαΐω. καὶ οὐχ ὡς ἀτιμάζων

λέγω τὴν τοιαύτην ἐπιστήμην, εἴ τις περὶ τῶν 19
τοιούτων σοφός ἐστιν, μή πως ἐγὼ ὑπὸ Μελήτου
τοσαύτας δίκας φύγοιμι· ἀλλὰ γὰρ ἐμοὶ τού-
των, ὦ ἄνδρες Ἀθηναῖοι, οὐδὲν μέτεστιν. μάρ-
τυρας δὲ αὐτοὺς | ὑμῶν τοὺς πολλοὺς παρέχομαι, D
καὶ ἀξιῶ ὑμᾶς ἀλλήλους διδάσκειν τε καὶ φρά-
ζειν, ὅσοι ἐμοῦ πώποτε ἀκηκόατε διαλεγομένου·
πολλοὶ δὲ ὑμῶν οἱ τοιοῦτοί εἰσιν· φράζετε
οὖν ἀλλήλοις, εἰ πώποτε ἢ μικρὸν ἢ μέγα
ἤκουσέ τις ὑμῶν ἐμοῦ περὶ τῶν τοιούτων δια-
λεγομένου· καὶ ἐκ τούτων γνώσεσθε ὅτι τοιαῦτ᾽
ἐστὶ καὶ τἆλλα περὶ ἐμοῦ, ἃ οἱ πολλοὶ λέγουσιν.

Not true either, that he is a professor of knowledge—for a fee, as Gorgias, Prodicus, Hippias.

Ἀλλὰ γὰρ οὔτε τούτων οὐδέν ἐστιν, οὐδέ
γ᾽ εἴ τινος ἀκηκόατε ὡς ἐγὼ παι-
δεύειν ἐπιχειρῶ ἀνθρώπους καὶ χρή-
ματα πράττομαι, | οὐδὲ τοῦτο ἀληθές· E
ἐπεὶ καὶ τοῦτό γέ μοι δοκεῖ καλὸν
εἶναι, εἴ τις οἷόστ᾽ εἴη παιδεύειν
ἀνθρώπους ὥσπερ Γοργίας τε ὁ Λεοντῖνος καὶ
Πρόδικος ὁ Κεῖος καὶ Ἱππίας ὁ Ἠλεῖος.
τούτων γὰρ ἕκαστος, ὦ ἄνδρες, οἷόστ᾽ ἐστὶν,
ἰὼν εἰς ἑκάστην τῶν πόλεων τοὺς νέους, οἷς
ἔξεστι τῶν ἑαυτῶν πολιτῶν προῖκα ξυνεῖναι ᾧ
ἂν βούλωνται—τούτους πείθουσι τὰς ἐκείνων
ξυνουσίας | ἀπολιπόντας σφίσιν ξυνεῖναι χρή- 20
ματα διδόντας καὶ χάριν προσειδέναι. ἐπεὶ καὶ
ἄλλος ἀνήρ ἐστι Πάριος ἐνθάδε σοφός, ὃν ἐγὼ
ᾐσθόμην ἐπιδημοῦντα· ἔτυχον γὰρ προσελθὼν
ἀνδρί, ὃς τετέλεκε χρήματα σοφισταῖς πλείω
ἢ ξύμπαντες οἱ ἄλλοι, Καλλίᾳ τῷ Ἱππονίκου·
τοῦτον οὖν ἀνηρόμην (ἐστὸν γὰρ αὐτῷ δύο

20 ὑέε) Ὦ Καλλία, ἦν δ' ἐγώ, εἰ μέν σου τὼ
ὑέε πώλω ἢ μόσχω ἐγενέσθην, εἴχομεν ἂν
αὐτοῖν ἐπιστάτην λαβεῖν καὶ μισθώσασθαι, ὃς
B ἔμελλεν αὐτὼ καλώ τε κἀγαθὼ ποιήσειν | τὴν
προσήκουσαν ἀρετήν· ἦν δ' ἂν οὗτος ἢ τῶν
ἱππικῶν τις ἢ τῶν γεωργικῶν· νῦν δ' ἐπειδὴ
ἀνθρώπω ἐστόν, τίνα αὐτοῖν ἐν νῷ ἔχεις ἐπιστά-
την λαβεῖν; τίς τῆς τοιαύτης ἀρετῆς, τῆς ἀν-
θρωπίνης τε καὶ πολιτικῆς, ἐπιστήμων ἐστίν;
οἶμαι γάρ σε ἐσκέφθαι διὰ τὴν τῶν ὑέων κτῆσιν.
ἔστιν τις, ἔφην ἐγώ, ἢ οὔ; Πάνυ γε, ἦ δ' ὅς.
Τίς, ἦν δ' ἐγώ, καὶ ποδαπός, καὶ πόσου διδά-
σκει; Εὔηνος, ἔφη, ὦ Σώκρατες, Πάριος, πέντε
μνῶν. καὶ ἐγὼ τὸν Εὔηνον ἐμακάρισα, εἰ ὡς
C ἀληθῶς ἔχοι ταύτην τὴν | τέχνην καὶ οὕτως ἐμ-
μελῶς διδάσκει. ἐγὼ γοῦν καὶ αὐτὸς ἐκαλλυνό-
μην τε καὶ ἡβρυνόμην ἄν, εἰ ἠπιστάμην ταῦτα·
ἀλλ' οὐ γὰρ ἐπίσταμαι, ὦ ἄνδρες Ἀθηναῖοι.

Ὑπολάβοι ἂν οὖν τις ὑμῶν ἴσως· Ἀλλ', ὦ
Σώκρατες, τὸ σὸν τί ἐστι πρᾶγμα;
πόθεν αἱ διαβολαί σοι αὗται γεγό-
νασιν; οὐ γὰρ δήπου σοῦ γε οὐδὲν
τῶν ἄλλων περιττότερον πραγματευο-
μένου ἔπειτα τοσαύτη φήμη τε καὶ
λόγος γέγονεν, εἰ μή τι ἔπραττες
ἀλλοῖον ἢ οἱ πολλοί· λέγε οὖν ἡμῖν, τί ἐστιν,
D ἵνα μὴ ἡμεῖς περὶ σοῦ αὐτοσχεδιάζωμεν. | ταυτί
μοι δοκεῖ δίκαια λέγειν ὁ λέγων, κἀγὼ ὑμῖν
πειράσομαι ἀποδεῖξαι, τί ποτ' ἐστὶν τοῦτο ὃ
ἐμοὶ πεποίηκεν τό τε ὄνομα καὶ τὴν διαβολήν.
ἀκούετε δή. καὶ ἴσως μὲν δόξω τισὶν ὑμῶν

Whence then this prejudice, and the name σοφός? Because he is indeed wise, as the Delphic oracle once said;

παίζειν, εὖ μέντοι ἴστε, πᾶσαν ὑμῖν τὴν ἀλήθειαν 20
ἐρῶ. ἐγὼ γάρ, ὦ ἄνδρες Ἀθηναῖοι, δι᾽ οὐδὲν
ἀλλ᾽ ἢ διὰ σοφίαν τινὰ τοῦτο τὸ ὄνομα ἔσχηκα.
ποίαν δὴ σοφίαν ταύτην; ἥπερ ἐστὶν ἴσως
ἀνθρωπίνη σοφία. τῷ ὄντι γὰρ κινδυνεύω
ταύτην εἶναι σοφός· οὗτοι δὲ τάχ᾽ ἄν, οὓς
ἄρτι ἔλεγον, μείζω τινὰ ἢ | κατ᾽ ἄνθρωπον E
σοφίαν σοφοὶ εἶεν, ἢ οὐκ ἔχω τί λέγω· οὐ
γὰρ δὴ ἔγωγε αὐτὴν ἐπίσταμαι, ἀλλ᾽ ὅστις
φησὶ ψεύδεταί τε καὶ ἐπὶ διαβολῇ τῇ ἐμῇ
λέγει. καί μοι, ὦ ἄνδρες Ἀθηναῖοι, μὴ θορυ-
βήσητε, μηδὲ ἂν δόξω τι ὑμῖν μέγα λέγειν· οὐ
γὰρ ἐμὸν ἐρῶ τὸν λόγον, ὃν ἂν λέγω, ἀλλ᾽ εἰς
ἀξιόχρεων ὑμῖν τὸν λέγοντα ἀνοίσω. τῆς γὰρ
ἐμῆς, εἰ δή τίς ἐστιν σοφία καὶ οἵα, μάρτυρα
ὑμῖν παρέξομαι τὸν θεὸν τὸν ἐν Δελφοῖς.
Χαιρεφῶντα γὰρ ἴστε που. οὗτος | ἐμός τε 21
ἑταῖρος ἦν ἐκ νέου καὶ ὑμῶν τῷ πλήθει ἑταῖρός
τε καὶ ξυνέφυγε τὴν φυγὴν ταύτην καὶ μεθ᾽
ὑμῶν κατῆλθε. καὶ ἴστε δὴ οἷος ἦν Χαιρεφῶν,
ὡς σφοδρὸς ἐφ᾽ ὅ τι ὁρμήσειεν. καὶ δή ποτε
καὶ εἰς Δελφοὺς ἐλθὼν ἐτόλμησε τοῦτο μαντεύ-
σασθαι· καί, ὅπερ λέγω, μὴ θορυβεῖτε, ὦ
ἄνδρες· ἤρετο γὰρ δή, εἴ τις ἐμοῦ εἴη σοφώ-
τερος. ἀνεῖλεν οὖν ἡ Πυθία μηδένα σοφώτερον
εἶναι. καὶ τούτων πέρι ὁ ἀδελφὸς ὑμῖν αὐτοῦ
οὑτοσὶ μαρτυρήσει, ἐπειδὴ ἐκεῖνος τετελεύτηκεν.

Σκέψασθε δέ, ὧν ἕνεκα | ταῦτα λέγω· μέλλω B
γὰρ ὑμᾶς διδάξειν, ὅθεν μοι ἡ διαβολὴ
γέγονε. ταῦτα γὰρ ἐγὼ ἀκούσας ἐνε-
θυμούμην οὑτωσί· Τί ποτε λέγει ὁ

though what the oracle meant, he was long in doubt.

21 θεός, καὶ τί ποτε αἰνίττεται; ἐγὼ γὰρ δὴ οὔτε μέγα οὔτε σμικρὸν ξύνοιδα ἐμαυτῷ σοφὸς ὤν· τί οὖν ποτε λέγει φάσκων ἐμὲ σοφώτατον εἶναι; οὐ γὰρ δήπου ψεύδεταί γε· οὐ γὰρ θέμις αὐτῷ. καὶ πολὺν μὲν χρόνον ἠπόρουν, τί ποτε λέγει, ἔπειτα μόγις πάνυ ἐπὶ ζήτησιν αὐτοῦ τοιαύτην τινὰ ἐτραπόμην. ἦλθον ἐπί τινα τῶν δοκούντων σοφῶν εἶναι, ὡς ἐνταῦθα, |
C εἴπερ που, ἐλέγξων τὸ μαντεῖον καὶ ἀποφανῶν τῷ χρησμῷ ὅτι Οὑτοσὶ ἐμοῦ σοφώτερός ἐστι, σὺ δ' ἐμὲ ἔφησθα. διασκοπῶν οὖν τοῦτον (ὀνόματι γὰρ οὐδὲν δέομαι λέγειν, ἦν δέ τις τῶν πολιτικῶν, πρὸς ὃν ἐγὼ σκοπῶν τοιοῦτόν τι ἔπαθον, ὦ ἄνδρες Ἀθηναῖοι), καὶ διαλεγόμενος αὐτῷ, ἔδοξέ μοι οὗτος ὁ ἀνὴρ δοκεῖν μὲν εἶναι σοφὸς ἄλλοις τε πολλοῖς ἀνθρώποις καὶ μάλιστα ἑαυτῷ, εἶναι δ' οὔ· κἄπειτα ἐπειρώμην αὐτῷ δεικνύναι ὅτι οἴοιτο μὲν εἶναι
D σοφός, εἴη δ' οὔ. | ἐντεῦθεν οὖν τούτῳ τε ἀπηχθόμην καὶ πολλοῖς τῶν παρόντων, πρὸς ἐμαυτὸν δ' οὖν ἀπιὼν ἐλογιζόμην ὅτι τούτου μὲν τοῦ ἀνθρώπου ἐγὼ σοφώτερός εἰμι· κινδυνεύει μὲν γὰρ ἡμῶν οὐδέτερος οὐδὲν καλὸν κἀγαθὸν εἰδέναι, ἀλλ' οὗτος μὲν οἴεταί τι εἰδέναι οὐκ εἰδώς, ἐγὼ δέ, ὥσπερ οὖν οὐκ οἶδα, οὐδὲ οἴομαι· ἔοικα γ' οὖν τούτου γε σμικρῷ τινι αὐτῷ τούτῳ σοφώτερος εἶναι, ὅτι ἃ μὴ οἶδα οὐδὲ οἴομαι εἰδέναι. ἐντεῦθεν ἐπ' ἄλλον ᾖα τῶν ἐκείνου δοκούντων σοφωτέρων εἶναι, καί
E μοι | ταὐτὰ ταῦτα ἔδοξε· καὶ ἐνταῦθα κἀκείνῳ

But on questioning men in public life he found himself wiser than they, in that he knew his ignorance, while they did not.

For pointing this out, he got their ill-will.

καὶ ἄλλοις πολλοῖς ἀπηχθόμην. μετὰ 21 ταῦτ᾽ οὖν ἤδη ἐφεξῆς ᾖα, αἰσθανόμενος μὲν (καὶ λυπούμενος καὶ δεδιὼς) ὅτι ἀπηχθανόμην, ὅμως δὲ ἀναγκαῖον ἐδόκει εἶναι τὸ τοῦ θεοῦ περὶ πλείστου ποιεῖσθαι· ἰτέον οὖν σκοποῦντι τὸν χρησμόν, τί λέγει, ἐπὶ ἅπαντας τούς τι δοκοῦντας εἰδέναι. καὶ νὴ τὸν κύνα, ὦ ἄνδρες | Ἀθηναῖοι (δεῖ γὰρ πρὸς ὑμᾶς τἀληθῆ 22 λέγειν), ἦ μὴν ἐγὼ ἔπαθόν τι τοιοῦτον· οἱ μὲν μάλιστα εὐδοκιμοῦντες, ἔδοξάν μοι ὀλίγου δεῖν τοῦ πλείστου ἐνδεεῖς εἶναι ζητοῦντι κατὰ τὸν θεόν, ἄλλοι δὲ δοκοῦντες φαυλότεροι ἐπιεικέστεροι εἶναι ἄνδρες πρὸς τὸ φρονίμως ἔχειν. δεῖ δὴ ὑμῖν τὴν ἐμὴν πλάνην ἐπιδεῖξαι ὥσπερ πόνους τινὰς πονοῦντος, ἵνα <μή> μοι καὶ ἀνέλεγκτος ἡ μαντεία γένοιτο. μετὰ γὰρ τοὺς πολιτικοὺς ᾖα ἐπὶ τοὺς ποιητὰς τούς τε τῶν τραγῳδιῶν καὶ τοὺς τῶν διθυράμβων καὶ τοὺς | ἄλλους, ὡς ἐνταῦθα ἐπ᾽ αὐτοφώρῳ B καταληψόμενος ἐμαυτὸν ἀμαθέστερον ἐκείνων ὄντα. ἀναλαμβάνων οὖν αὐτῶν τὰ ποιήματα, ἅ μοι ἐδόκει μάλιστα πεπραγματεῦσθαι αὐτοῖς, διηρώτων ἂν αὐτούς, τί λέγοιεν, ἵν᾽ ἅμα τι καὶ μανθάνοιμι παρ᾽ αὐτῶν. αἰσχύνομαι οὖν ὑμῖν εἰπεῖν, ὦ ἄνδρες, τἀληθῆ· ὅμως δὲ ῥητέον. ὡς ἔπος γὰρ εἰπεῖν ὀλίγου αὐτῶν ἅπαντες οἱ παρόντες ἂν βέλτιον ἔλεγον περὶ ὧν αὐτοὶ ἐπεποιήκεσαν. ἔγνων οὖν καὶ περὶ τῶν ποιητῶν ἐν ὀλίγῳ τοῦτο, ὅτι οὐ σοφίᾳ | ποιοῖεν ἃ ποιοῖεν, ἀλλὰ φύσει τινὶ καὶ ἐνθουσιάζοντες, C ὥσπερ οἱ θεομάντεις καὶ οἱ χρη-

Poets also knew not their limitations,

22 σμῳδοί· καὶ γὰρ οὗτοι λέγουσι μὲν πολλὰ καὶ καλά, ἴσασιν δὲ οὐδὲν ὧν λέγουσι. τοιοῦτόν τί μοι ἐφάνησαν πάθος καὶ οἱ ποιηταὶ πεπονθότες· καὶ ἅμα ᾐσθόμην αὐτῶν διὰ τὴν ποίησιν οἰομένων καὶ τἆλλα σοφωτάτων εἶναι ἀνθρώπων, ἃ οὐκ ἦσαν. ἀπῇα οὖν καὶ ἐντεῦθεν τῷ αὐτῷ οἰόμενος περιγεγονέναι ᾧπερ καὶ τῶν πολιτικῶν.

nor yet did good artisans.

Τελευτῶν οὖν ἐπὶ τοὺς χειροτέχνας ᾖα· ἐμαυτῷ
D γὰρ ξυνῄδη οὐδὲν ἐπισταμένῳ, | ὡς ἔπος εἰπεῖν, τούτους δέ γ' ᾔδη ὅτι εὑρήσοιμι πολλὰ καὶ καλὰ ἐπισταμένους. καὶ τούτου μὲν οὐκ ἐψεύσθην, ἀλλ' ἠπίσταντο ἃ ἐγὼ οὐκ ἠπιστάμην καί μου ταύτῃ σοφώτεροι ἦσαν. ἀλλ', ὦ ἄνδρες Ἀθηναῖοι, ταὐτόν μοι ἔδοξαν ἔχειν ἁμάρτημα, ὅπερ καὶ οἱ ποιηταί, καὶ οἱ ἀγαθοὶ δημιουργοί· διὰ τὸ τὴν τέχνην καλῶς ἐξεργάζεσθαι ἕκαστος ἠξίου καὶ τἆλλα τὰ μέγιστα σοφώτατος εἶναι, καὶ αὐτῶν αὕτη ἡ πλημμέλεια ἐκείνην τὴν σοφίαν ἀπέκρυπτεν·
E ὥστε με ἐμαυτὸν ἀνερωτᾶν | ὑπὲρ τοῦ χρησμοῦ, πότερα δεξαίμην ἂν οὕτως ὥσπερ ἔχω ἔχειν, μήτε τι σοφὸς ὢν τὴν ἐκείνων σοφίαν μήτε ἀμαθὴς τὴν ἀμαθίαν, ἢ ἀμφότερα ἃ ἐκεῖνοι ἔχουσιν ἔχειν. ἀπεκρινάμην οὖν ἐμαυτῷ καὶ τῷ χρησμῷ ὅτι μοι λυσιτελοῖ ὥσπερ ἔχω ἔχειν.

Hence their common hatred of this "wise man," who spends his life in confuting

Ἐκ ταυτησὶ δὴ τῆς ἐξετάσεως, ὦ ἄνδρες Ἀθηναῖοι, πολλαὶ μὲν ἀπέχθειαί μοι
23 γεγόνασι | καὶ οἷαι χαλεπώταται καὶ βαρύταται, ὥστε πολλὰς διαβολὰς ἀπ' αὐτῶν γεγονέναι, ὄνομα δὲ τοῦτο

them. (Hence too his own poverty.)

λέγεσθαι, σοφὸς εἶναι. οἴονται γάρ 23 με ἑκάστοτε οἱ παρόντες ταῦτα αὐτὸν εἶναι σοφόν, ἃ ἂν ἄλλον ἐξελέγξω· τὸ δὲ κινδυνεύει, ὦ ἄνδρες, τῷ ὄντι ὁ θεὸς σοφὸς εἶναι, καὶ ἐν τῷ χρησμῷ τούτῳ τοῦτο λέγειν, ὅτι ἡ ἀνθρωπίνη σοφία ὀλίγου τινὸς ἀξία ἐστὶν καὶ οὐδενός. καὶ φαίνεται τοῦτον λέγειν τὸν Σωκράτη, προσκεχρῆσθαι δὲ τῷ ἐμῷ ὀνόματι, ἐμὲ παράδειγμα ποιούμενος, | ὥσπερ ἂν εἰ εἴποι ὅτι Οὗτος ὑμῶν, ὦ ἄνθρω- B ποι, σοφώτατός ἐστιν, ὅστις ὥσπερ Σωκράτης ἔγνωκεν ὅτι οὐδενὸς ἄξιός ἐστι τῇ ἀληθείᾳ πρὸς σοφίαν. ταῦτ᾽ οὖν ἐγὼ μὲν ἔτι καὶ νῦν περιιὼν ζητῶ καὶ ἐρευνῶ κατὰ τὸν θεόν, καὶ τῶν ἀστῶν καὶ ξένων ἄν τινα οἴωμαι σοφὸν εἶναι· καὶ ἐπειδάν μοι μὴ δοκῇ, τῷ θεῷ βοηθῶν ἐνδείκνυμαι ὅτι οὐκ ἔστι σοφός. καὶ ὑπὸ ταύτης τῆς ἀσχολίας οὔτε τι τῶν τῆς πόλεως πρᾶξαί μοι σχολὴ γέγονεν ἄξιον λόγου οὔτε τῶν οἰκείων, ἀλλ᾽ ἐν | πενίᾳ μυρίᾳ εἰμὶ C διὰ τὴν τοῦ θεοῦ λατρείαν.

And the youth who imitated his confutations were thought to be "corrupted."

Πρὸς δὲ τούτοις οἱ νέοι μοι ἐπακολουθοῦντες, οἷς μάλιστα σχολή ἐστιν, οἱ τῶν πλουσιωτάτων, αὐτόματοι χαίρουσιν ἀκούοντες ἐξεταζομένων τῶν ἀνθρώπων, καὶ αὐτοὶ πολλάκις ἐμὲ μιμοῦνται, εἶτα ἐπιχειροῦσιν ἄλλους ἐξετάζειν· κἄπειτα, οἶμαι, εὑρίσκουσι πολλὴν ἀφθονίαν οἰομένων μὲν εἰδέναι τι ἀνθρώπων, εἰδότων δὲ ὀλίγα ἢ οὐδέν. ἐντεῦθεν οὖν οἱ ὑπ᾽ αὐτῶν ἐξεταζόμενοι ἐμοὶ ὀργίζονται, ἀλλ᾽ οὐχ αὐτοῖς,

23 καὶ λέγουσιν ὡς | Σωκράτης τίς ἐστι μιαρώ-
D τατος καὶ διαφθείρει τοὺς νέους· καὶ ἐπειδάν τις αὐτοὺς ἐρωτᾷ, ὅ τι ποιῶν καὶ ὅ τι διδάσκων, ἔχουσι μὲν οὐδὲν εἰπεῖν, ἀλλ᾽ ἀγνοοῦσιν, ἵνα δὲ μὴ δοκῶσιν ἀπορεῖν, τὰ κατὰ πάντων τῶν φιλοσοφούντων πρόχειρα ταῦτα λέγουσιν, ὅτι τὰ μετέωρα καὶ τὰ ὑπὸ γῆς, καὶ θεοὺς μὴ νομίζειν, καὶ τὸν ἥττω λόγον κρείττω ποιεῖν. τὰ γὰρ ἀληθῆ, οἴομαι, οὐκ ἂν ἐθέλοιεν λέγειν, ὅτι κατάδηλοι γίγνονται προσποιούμενοι μὲν εἰδέναι, εἰδότες δὲ οὐδέν. ἅτε οὖν, οἶμαι,
E φιλότιμοι | ὄντες καὶ σφοδροὶ καὶ πολλοί, καὶ ξυντεταμένως καὶ πιθανῶς λέγοντες περὶ ἐμοῦ, ἐμπεπλήκασιν ὑμῶν τὰ ὦτα καὶ πάλαι καὶ σφοδρῶς διαβάλλοντες. ἐκ τούτων καὶ Μέλητός μοι ἐπέθετο καὶ Ἄνυτος καὶ Λύκων, Μέλητος μὲν ὑπὲρ τῶν ποιητῶν ἀχθόμενος, Ἄνυτος δὲ ὑπὲρ τῶν δημιουργῶν [καὶ τῶν πολιτικῶν], Λύκων |
24 δὲ ὑπὲρ τῶν ῥητόρων· ὥστε, ὅπερ ἀρχόμενος ἐγὼ ἔλεγον, θαυμάζοιμ᾽ ἄν, εἰ οἷός τ᾽ εἴην ἐγὼ ὑμῶν ταύτην τὴν διαβολὴν ἐξελέσθαι ἐν οὕτως ὀλίγῳ χρόνῳ οὕτω πολλὴν γεγονυῖαν. ταῦτ᾽ ἔστιν ὑμῖν, ὦ ἄνδρες Ἀθηναῖοι, τἀληθῆ, καὶ ὑμᾶς οὔτε μέγα οὔτε μικρὸν ἀποκρυψάμενος ἐγὼ λέγω οὐδ᾽ ὑποστειλάμενος. καίτοι οἶδα σχεδὸν ὅτι τούτοις αὐτοῖς ἀπεχθάνομαι· ὃ καὶ τεκμήριον ὅτι ἀληθῆ λέγω καὶ ὅτι αὕτη ἐστὶν ἡ διαβολὴ ἡ ἐμὴ καὶ τὰ αἴτια ταῦτά ἐστιν. καὶ ἐάντε νῦν ἐάντε
B | αὖθις ζητήσητε ταῦτα, οὕτως εὑρήσετε.

This old prejudice it is that I now face and can hardly hope to remove.

Περὶ μὲν οὖν ὧν οἱ πρῶτοί μου κατήγοροι

24

But now, let us examine in detail the formal charge of this good Meletus. "He corrupts the youth," and "he introduces new divinities."

κατηγόρουν, αὕτη ἐστὶν ἱκανὴ ἀπολογία πρὸς ὑμᾶς· πρὸς δὲ Μέλητον τὸν ἀγαθόν τε καὶ φιλόπολιν, ὥς φησι, καὶ τοὺς ὑστέρους μετὰ ταῦτα πειράσομαι ἀπολογεῖσθαι. αὖθις γὰρ δή, ὥσπερ ἑτέρων τούτων ὄντων κατηγόρων, λάβωμεν αὖ τὴν τούτων ἀντωμοσίαν. ἔχει δέ πως ὧδε· Σωκράτη φησὶν ἀδικεῖν τούς τε νέους διαφθείροντα καὶ θεοὺς οὓς ἡ πόλις νομίζει οὐ νομίζοντα, ἕτερα δὲ δαιμόνια | C καινά. τὸ μὲν δὴ ἔγκλημα τοιοῦτόν ἐστιν· τούτου δὲ τοῦ ἐγκλήματος ἓν ἕκαστον ἐξετάσωμεν. φησὶ γὰρ δὴ τοὺς νέους ἀδικεῖν με διαφθείροντα. ἐγὼ δέ γε, ὦ ἄνδρες Ἀθηναῖοι, ἀδικεῖν φημι Μέλητον, ὅτι σπουδῇ χαριεντίζεται, ῥᾳδίως εἰς ἀγῶνα καθιστὰς ἀνθρώπους, περὶ πραγμάτων προσποιούμενος σπουδάζειν καὶ κήδεσθαι, ὧν οὐδὲν τούτῳ πώποτε ἐμέλησεν. ὡς δὲ τοῦτο οὕτως ἔχει, πειράσομαι καὶ ὑμῖν ἐπιδεῖξαι.

(On the first count, Meletus, when cross-examined, is reduced to an absurdity;

Καί μοι δεῦρο, ὦ Μέλητε, εἰπέ· ἄλλο τι ἢ περὶ πολλοῦ ποιεῖ, | D ὅπως ὡς βέλτιστοι οἱ νεώτεροι ἔσονται; Ἔγωγε. Ἴθι δή νυν εἰπὲ τούτοις, τίς αὐτοὺς βελτίους ποιεῖ; δῆλον γὰρ ὅτι οἶσθα, μέλον γέ σοι. τὸν μὲν γὰρ διαφθείροντα ἐξευρών, ὥς φῄς, ἐμὲ εἰσάγεις τουτοισὶ καὶ κατηγορεῖς· τὸν δὲ δὴ βελτίους ποιοῦντα ἴθι εἰπὲ καὶ μήνυσον αὐτοῖς, τίς ἐστιν. ὁρᾷς, ὦ Μέλητε, ὅτι σιγᾷς καὶ οὐκ ἔχεις εἰπεῖν; καίτοι οὐκ αἰσχρόν σοι δοκεῖ

24 εἶναι καὶ ἱκανὸν τεκμήριον οὗ δὴ ἐγὼ λέγω,
ὅτι σοι οὐδὲν μεμέληκεν; ἀλλ' εἰπέ, ὠγαθέ,
τίς αὐτοὺς ἀμείνους ποιεῖ; Οἱ νόμοι. Ἀλλ'
E οὐ | τοῦτο ἐρωτῶ, ὦ βέλτιστε, ἀλλὰ τίς ἄνθρω-
πος, ὅστις πρῶτον καὶ αὐτὸ τοῦτο οἶδε, τοὺς
νόμους. Οὗτοι, ὦ Σώκρατες, οἱ δικασταί.
Πῶς λέγεις, ὦ Μέλητε; οἵδε τοὺς νέους παι-
δεύειν οἷοίτε εἰσὶ καὶ βελτιους ποιοῦσιν;
Μάλιστα. Πότερον ἅπαντες, ἢ οἱ μὲν αὐτῶν,
οἱ δ' οὔ; Ἅπαντες. Εὖ γε νὴ τὴν Ἥραν
λέγεις, καὶ πολλὴν ἀφθονίαν τῶν ὠφελούντων.
τί δὲ δή; οἵδε οἱ ἀκροαταὶ βελτίους ποιοῦσιν
25 | ἢ οὔ; Καὶ οὗτοι. Τί δὲ οἱ βουλευταί;
Καὶ οἱ βουλευταί. Ἀλλ' ἄρα, ὦ Μέλητε, μὴ
οἱ ἐν τῇ ἐκκλησίᾳ, οἱ ἐκκλησιασταί, διαφθεί-
ρουσι τοὺς νεωτέρους; ἢ κἀκεῖνοι βελτίους
ποιοῦσιν ἅπαντες; Κἀκεῖνοι. Πάντες ἄρα, ὡς
ἔοικεν, Ἀθηναῖοι καλοὺς κἀγαθοὺς ποιοῦσι
πλὴν ἐμοῦ, ἐγὼ δὲ μόνος διαφθείρω. οὕτω
λέγεις; Πάνυ σφόδρα ταῦτα λέγω. Πολλήν γέ
μου κατέγνωκας δυστυχίαν. καί μοι ἀπόκριναι·
ἦ καὶ περὶ ἵππους οὕτω σοι δοκεῖ ἔχειν—οἱ
B μὲν βελτίους | ποιοῦντες αὐτοὺς πάντες ἄνθρωποι
εἶναι, εἷς δέ τις ὁ διαφθείρων; ἢ (τοὐναντίον
τούτου πᾶν) εἷς μέν τις ὁ βελτίους οἷόστ' ὢν
ποιεῖν ἢ πάνυ ὀλίγοι (οἱ ἱππικοί), οἱ δὲ πολλοὶ
ἐάνπερ ξυνῶσι καὶ χρῶνται ἵπποις, διαφθείρου-
σιν; οὐχ οὕτως ἔχει, ὦ Μέλητε, καὶ περὶ
ἵππων καὶ τῶν ἄλλων ἁπάντων ζῴων; πάντως
δήπου, ἐάντε σὺ καὶ Ἄνυτος οὐ φῆτε ἐάντε
φῆτε· πολλὴ γὰρ ἄν τις εὐδαιμονία εἴη περὶ

τοὺς νέους, εἰ εἷς μὲν μόνος αὐτοὺς διαφθείρει, 25
οἱ δ' ἄλλοι ὠφελοῦσιν. ἀλλὰ | γάρ, ὦ Μέλητε, C
ἱκανῶς ἐπιδείκνυσαι ὅτι οὐδεπώποτε ἐφρόντισας
τῶν νέων, καὶ σαφῶς ἀποφαίνεις τὴν σαυτοῦ
ἀμέλειαν, ὅτι οὐδέν σοι μεμέληκεν περὶ ὧν
ἐμὲ εἰσάγεις.

Ἔτι δὲ ἡμῖν εἰπέ, ὦ πρὸς Διὸς Μέλητε,
πότερον ἔστιν οἰκεῖν ἄμεινον ἐν πολίταις χρη-
στοῖς ἢ πονηροῖς; ὦταν, ἀπόκριναι· οὐδὲν γάρ
τοι χαλεπὸν ἐρωτῶ. οὐχ οἱ μὲν πονηροὶ
κακόν τι ἐργάζονται τοὺς ἀεὶ ἐγγυτάτω ἑαυτῶν
ὄντας, οἱ δ' ἀγαθοὶ ἀγαθόν τι; Πάνυ γε.
Ἔστιν οὖν ὅστις βούλεται ὑπὸ τῶν ξυνόντων
| βλάπτεσθαι μᾶλλον ἢ ὠφελεῖσθαι; ἀποκρίνου, D
ὦ ἀγαθέ· καὶ γὰρ ὁ νόμος κελεύει ἀποκρίνε-
σθαι. ἔσθ' ὅστις βούλεται βλάπτεσθαι; Οὐ
δῆτα. Φέρε δή, πότερον ἐμὲ εἰσάγεις δεῦρο
ὡς διαφθείροντα τοὺς νεωτέρους καὶ πονηροτέ-
ρους ποιοῦντα ἑκόντα ἢ ἄκοντα; Ἑκόντα
ἔγωγε. Τί δῆτα, ὦ Μέλητε; τοσοῦτον σὺ ἐμοῦ
σοφώτερος εἶ τηλικούτου ὄντος τηλικόσδε ὤν,
ὥστε σὺ μὲν ἔγνωκας ὅτι οἱ μὲν κακοὶ κακόν τι
ἐργάζονται ἀεὶ τοὺς μάλιστα πλησίον | ἑαυτῶν, E
οἱ δὲ ἀγαθοὶ ἀγαθόν· ἐγὼ δὲ δὴ εἰς τοσοῦτον
ἀμαθίας ἥκω, ὥστε καὶ τοῦτ' ἀγνοῶ, ὅτι, ἐάν
τινα μοχθηρὸν ποιήσω τῶν ξυνόντων, κινδυ-
νεύσω κακόν τι λαβεῖν ἀπ' αὐτοῦ, ὥστε τοῦτο
<τὸ> τοσοῦτον κακὸν ἑκὼν ποιῶ, ὡς φῂς σύ;
ταῦτα ἐγώ σοι οὐ πείθομαι, ὦ Μέλητε, οἶμαι
δὲ οὐδὲ ἄλλον ἀνθρώπων οὐδένα· ἀλλ' ἢ οὐ
διαφθείρω, ἤ, εἰ διαφθείρω, | ἄκων· ὥστε σύ 26

26 γε κατ᾽ ἀμφότερα ψεύδει. εἰ δὲ ἄκων διαφθείρω, τῶν τοιούτων [καὶ ἀκουσίων] ἁμαρτημάτων οὐ δεῦρο νόμος εἰσάγειν ἐστίν, ἀλλὰ ἰδίᾳ λαβόντα διδάσκειν καὶ νουθετεῖν· δῆλον γὰρ ὅτι, ἐὰν μάθω, παύσομαι ὅ γε ἄκων ποιῶ. σὺ δὲ ξυγγενέσθαι μέν μοι καὶ διδάξαι ἔφυγες καὶ οὐκ ἠθέλησας, δεῦρο δὲ εἰσάγεις, οἷ νόμος ἐστὶν εἰσάγειν τοὺς κολάσεως δεομένους, ἀλλ᾽ οὐ μαθήσεως.

Ἀλλὰ γάρ, ὦ ἄνδρες Ἀθηναῖοι, τοῦτο μὲν δῆλον ἤδη ἐστίν, ὃ ἐγὼ ἔλεγον, ὅτι Μελήτῳ |
B τούτων οὔτε μέγα οὔτε μικρὸν πώποτε ἐμέλησεν. ὅμως δὲ δὴ λέγε ἡμῖν, πῶς με φῂς διαφθείρειν, ὦ Μέλητε, τοὺς νεωτέρους; ἢ δῆλον δὴ ὅτι κατὰ τὴν γραφήν, ἣν ἐγράψω, θεοὺς διδάσκοντα μὴ νομίζειν οὓς ἡ πόλις νομίζει, ἕτερα δὲ δαιμόνια καινά; οὐ ταῦτα λέγεις, ὅτι διδάσκων διαφθείρω; Πάνυ μὲν οὖν σφόδρα ταῦτα λέγω. Πρὸς αὐτῶν τοίνυν, ὦ Μέλητε, τούτων τῶν θεῶν, ὧν νῦν ὁ λόγος ἐστίν, εἰπὲ ἔτι σαφέστερον καὶ ἐμοὶ καὶ τοῖς ἀνδράσιν τούτοις.

and in the matter of the second, contradicts himself; for he now declares Socrates to be an atheist).

C ἐγὼ γὰρ οὐ | δύναμαι μαθεῖν, πότερον λέγεις διδάσκειν με νομίζειν εἶναί τινας θεοὺς (καὶ αὐτὸς ἄρα νομίζω εἶναι θεούς, καὶ οὐκ εἰμὶ τὸ παράπαν ἄθεος οὐδὲ ταύτῃ ἀδικῶ, οὐ μέντοι οὕσπερ γε ἡ πόλις, ἀλλὰ ἑτέρους, καὶ τοῦτ᾽ ἔστιν ὅ μοι ἐγκαλεῖς, ὅτι ἑτέρους), ἢ παντάπασί με φῂς οὔτε αὐτὸν νομίζειν θεοὺς τούς τε ἄλλους ταῦτα διδάσκειν. Ταῦτα λέγω, ὡς τὸ παράπαν οὐ νομίζεις θεούς. Ὦ

θαυμάσιε Μέλητε, *ἵνα τί ταῦτα λέγεις; οὐδὲ* 26
| *ἥλιον οὐδὲ σελήνην ἄρα νομίζω θεοὺς εἶναι,* D
ὥσπερ οἱ ἄλλοι ἄνθρωποι; Μὰ Δί', *ὦ ἄνδρες*
δικασταί, ἐπεὶ τὸν μὲν ἥλιον λίθον φησὶν εἶναι,
τὴν δὲ σελήνην γῆν. Ἀναξαγόρου *οἴει κατ-*
ηγορεῖν, ὦ φίλε Μέλητε, *καὶ οὕτω καταφρονεῖς*
τῶνδε καὶ οἴει αὐτοὺς ἀπείρους γραμμάτων
εἶναι, ὥστε οὐκ εἰδέναι, ὅτι τὰ Ἀναξαγόρου
βιβλία τοῦ Κλαζομενίου *γέμει τούτων τῶν*
λόγων; καὶ δὴ καὶ οἱ νέοι ταῦτα παρ' ἐμοῦ
μανθάνουσιν, ἃ ἔξεστιν ἐνίοτε, εἰ πάνυ πολλοῦ,
δραχμῆς | *ἐκ τῆς ὀρχήστρας πριαμένοις* Σωκρά- E
τους καταγελᾶν, ἐὰν προσποιῆται ἑαυτοῦ εἶναι,
ἄλλως τε καὶ οὕτως ἄτοπα ὄντα; ἀλλ', ὦ
πρὸς Διός, *οὑτωσί σοι δοκῶ οὐδένα νομίζειν*
θεὸν εἶναι; Οὐ *μέντοι μὰ* Δία *οὐδ' ὁπωστιοῦν.*
Ἄπιστός *γ' εἶ, ὦ* Μέλητε, *καὶ ταῦτα μέντοι,*
ὡς ἐμοὶ δοκεῖς, σαυτῷ. ἐμοὶ γὰρ δοκεῖ οὑτοσί,
ὦ ἄνδρες Ἀθηναῖοι, *πάνυ εἶναι ὑβριστὴς καὶ*
ἀκόλαστος, καὶ ἀτεχνῶς τὴν γραφὴν ταύτην
ὕβρει τινὶ καὶ ἀκολασίᾳ καὶ νεότητι γράψασθαι.
ἔοικεν γὰρ ὥσπερ | *αἴνιγμα ξυντιθέντι δια-* 27
πειρωμένῳ· Ἆρα *γνώσεται* Σωκράτης *ὁ σοφὸς*
δὴ ἐμοῦ χαριεντιζομένου καὶ ἐναντί' ἐμαυτῷ
λέγοντος, ἢ ἐξαπατήσω αὐτὸν καὶ τοὺς ἄλλους
τοὺς ἀκούοντας; οὗτος γὰρ ἐμοὶ φαίνεται τὰ
ἐναντία λέγειν αὐτὸς ἑαυτῷ ἐν τῇ γραφῇ, ὥσπερ
ἂν εἰ εἴποι· ἀδικεῖ Σωκράτης *θεοὺς οὐ νομίζων,*
ἀλλὰ θεοὺς νομίζων. καίτοι τοῦτό ἐστι παί-
ζοντος.

Ξυνεπισκέψασθε *δή, ὦ ἄνδρες, ᾗ μοι φαίνεται*

27 ταῦτα λέγειν· σὺ δὲ ἡμῖν ἀπόκριναι, ὦ Μέλητε·
ὑμεῖς δέ, ὅπερ κατ' ἀρχὰς ὑμᾶς παρῃτησάμην, |
B μέμνησθέ μοι μὴ θορυβεῖν, ἐὰν ἐν τῷ εἰωθότι
τρόπῳ τοὺς λόγους ποιῶμαι. ἔστιν ὅστις
ἀνθρώπων, ὦ Μέλητε, ἀνθρώπεια μὲν νομίζει
πράγματ' εἶναι, ἀνθρώπους δὲ οὐ νομίζει; ἀπο-
κρινέσθω, ὦ ἄνδρες, καὶ μὴ ἄλλα καὶ ἄλλα
θορυβείτω· ἔσθ' ὅστις ἵππους μὲν οὐ νομίζει,
ἱππικὰ δὲ πράγματα; ἢ αὐλητὰς μὲν οὐ νομίζει
εἶναι, αὐλητικὰ δὲ πράγματα; οὐκ ἔστιν, ὦ
ἄριστε ἀνδρῶν· εἰ μὴ σὺ βούλει ἀποκρίνασθαι,
ἐγώ σοι λέγω καὶ τοῖς ἄλλοις τουτοισί. ἀλλὰ
C τὸ ἐπὶ τούτῳ γε ἀπόκριναι· ἔσθ' ὅστις | δαιμόνια
μὲν νομίζει πράγματ' εἶναι, δαίμονας δὲ οὐ
νομίζει; Οὐκ ἔστιν. Ὡς ὤνησας, ὅτι μόγις
ἀπεκρίνω ὑπὸ τουτωνὶ ἀναγκαζόμενος. οὐκοῦν
δαιμόνια μὲν φῄς με καὶ νομίζειν καὶ διδάσκειν
—εἴτ' οὖν καινὰ εἴτε παλαιά, ἀλλ' οὖν δαιμόνιά
γε νομίζω κατὰ τὸν σὸν λόγον, καὶ ταῦτα καὶ
διωμόσω ἐν τῇ ἀντιγραφῇ· εἰ δὲ δαιμόνια
νομίζω, καὶ δαίμονας δήπου πολλὴ ἀνάγκη
νομίζειν μέ ἐστιν. οὐχ οὕτως ἔχει; ἔχει δή·
τίθημι γάρ σε ὁμολογοῦντα, ἐπειδὴ οὐκ ἀποκρίνει.
D τοὺς δὲ δαίμονας οὐχὶ ἤτοι θεούς | γε ἡγούμεθα
ἢ θεῶν παῖδας; φῂς ἢ οὔ; Πάνυ γε. Οὐκοῦν
εἴπερ δαίμονας ἡγοῦμαι, ὡς σὺ φῄς, εἰ μὲν θεοί
τινές εἰσιν οἱ δαίμονες, τοῦτ' ἂν εἴη ὃ ἐγώ φημί
σε αἰνίττεσθαι καὶ χαριεντίζεσθαι, θεοὺς οὐχ
ἡγούμενον φάναι ἐμὲ θεοὺς αὖ ἡγεῖσθαι πάλιν,
ἐπειδήπερ γε δαίμονας ἡγοῦμαι· εἰ δ' αὖ οἱ
δαίμονες θεῶν παῖδές εἰσιν (νόθοι τινὲς ἢ ἐκ

νυμφῶν ἢ ἔκ τινων ἄλλων, ὧν δὴ καὶ λέγονται), 27
τίς ἂν ἀνθρώπων θεῶν μὲν παῖδας ἡγοῖτο εἶναι,
θεοὺς δὲ μή; ὁμοίως γὰρ ἂν ἄτοπον εἴη, ὥσπερ
ἂν εἴ τις ἵππων μὲν | παῖδας ἡγοῖτο ἢ καὶ ὄνων E
[τοὺς ἡμιόνους], ἵππους δὲ καὶ ὄνους μὴ ἡγοῖτο
εἶναι. ἀλλ', ὦ Μέλητε, οὐκ ἔστιν ὅπως σὺ
ταῦτα οὐχὶ ἀποπειρώμενος ἡμῶν ἐγράψω τὴν
γραφὴν ταύτην, ἢ ἀπορῶν ὅ τι ἐγκαλοῖς ἐμοὶ
ἀληθὲς ἀδίκημα· ὅπως δὲ σύ τινα πείθοις ἂν καὶ
σμικρὸν νοῦν ἔχοντα ἀνθρώπων, ὡς [οὐ] τοῦ
αὐτοῦ ἐστιν καὶ δαιμόνια καὶ θεῖα ἡγεῖσθαι, καὶ
αὖ τοῦ αὐτοῦ μήτε δαίμονας μήτε θεοὺς μήτε |
ἥρωας, οὐδεμία μηχανή ἐστιν. 28

Enough of this farce. Not in it, but in the popular prejudice lies my danger, as I always knew.

Ἀλλὰ γάρ, ὦ ἄνδρες Ἀθηναῖοι, ὡς μὲν ἐγὼ
οὐκ ἀδικῶ κατὰ τὴν Μελήτου γραφήν,
οὐ πολλῆς μοι δοκεῖ εἶναι ἀπολογίας,
ἀλλὰ ἱκανὰ καὶ ταῦτα· ὃ δὲ καὶ ἐν
τοῖς ἔμπροσθεν ἔλεγον, ὅτι πολλή μοι
ἀπέχθεια γέγονεν καὶ πρὸς πολλούς,
εὖ ἴστε ὅτι ἀληθές ἐστιν. καὶ τοῦτ' ἔστιν ὃ ἐμὲ
αἱρήσει, ἐάνπερ αἱρῇ, οὐ Μέλητος οὐδὲ Ἄνυτος,
ἀλλ' ἡ τῶν πολλῶν διαβολή τε καὶ φθόνος. ἃ
δὴ πολλοὺς καὶ ἄλλους καὶ ἀγαθοὺς ἄνδρας
ᾕρηκεν, οἶμαι δὲ καὶ αἱρήσειν· οὐδὲν | δὲ δεινόν, B
μὴ ἐν ἐμοὶ στῇ.

But a man recks of duty, not of danger.

Ἴσως δ' ἂν οὖν εἴποι τις· Εἶτ' οὐκ αἰσχύνει,
ὦ Σώκρατες, τοιοῦτον ἐπιτήδευμα ἐπιτηδεύσας,
ἐξ οὗ κινδυνεύεις νυνὶ ἀποθανεῖν; ἐγὼ δὲ τούτῳ
ἂν δίκαιον λόγον ἀντείποιμι, ὅτι Οὐ καλῶς
λέγεις, ὦ ἄνθρωπε, εἰ οἴει δεῖν κίνδυ-
νον ὑπολογίζεσθαι τοῦ ζῆν ἢ τεθνάναι

28 ἄνδρα, ὅτου τι καὶ σμικρὸν ὄφελός ἐστιν,
ἀλλ' οὐκ ἐκεῖνο μόνον σκοπεῖν, ὅταν πράττῃ,
πότερα δίκαια ἢ ἄδικα πράττει, καὶ ἀνδρὸς
ἀγαθοῦ ἔργα ἢ κακοῦ. φαῦλοι γὰρ ἂν τῷ
C γε σῷ λόγῳ εἶεν τῶν | ἡμιθέων ὅσοι ἐν
Τροίᾳ τετελευτήκασιν, οἵ τε ἄλλοι καὶ ὁ τῆς
Θέτιδος ὑός, ὃς τοσοῦτον τοῦ κινδύνου κατεφρό-
νησεν παρὰ τὸ αἰσχρόν τι ὑπομεῖναι, ὥστε
ἐπειδὴ εἶπεν ἡ μήτηρ αὐτῷ προθυμουμένῳ
Ἕκτορα ἀποκτεῖναι, θεὸς οὖσα, οὑτωσί πως, ὡς
ἐγὼ οἶμαι· Ὦ παῖ, εἰ τιμωρήσεις Πατρόκλῳ τῷ
ἑταίρῳ τὸν φόνον καὶ Ἕκτορα ἀποκτενεῖς, αὐτὸς
ἀποθανεῖ· αὐτίκα γάρ τοι, φησί, μεθ' Ἕκτορα
πότμος ἑτοῖμος· ὁ δὲ ταῦτα ἀκούσας τοῦ μὲν
θανάτου καὶ τοῦ κινδύνου ὠλιγώρησε, πολὺ δὲ
D μᾶλλον | δείσας τὸ ζῆν κακὸς ὢν καὶ τοῖς φίλοις
μὴ τιμωρεῖν, αὐτίκα, φησί, τεθναίην δίκην
ἐπιθεὶς τῷ ἀδικοῦντι, ἵνα μὴ ἐνθάδε μένω καταγέ-
λαστος παρὰ νηυσὶ κορωνίσιν ἄχθος ἀρούρης.
μὴ αὐτὸν οἴει φροντίσαι θανάτου καὶ κινδύνου;
οὕτω γὰρ ἔχει, ὦ ἄνδρες Ἀθηναῖοι, τῇ ἀληθείᾳ·
οὗ ἄν τις ἑαυτὸν τάξῃ ἡγησάμενος βέλτιστον
εἶναι ἢ ὑπ' ἄρχοντος ταχθῇ, ἐνταῦθα δεῖ, ὡς
ἐμοὶ δοκεῖ, μένοντα κινδυνεύειν, μηδὲν ὑπολογιζό-
μενον μήτε θάνατον μήτε ἄλλο μηδὲν πρὸ τοῦ
αἰσχροῦ.

As in battles, so in life, I stand where posted. Why fear death? Who knows it is an evil?

Ἐγὼ οὖν δεινὰ ἂν εἴην εἰργασμένος, ὦ ἄνδρες
E Ἀθηναῖοι, εἰ, ὅτε μέν με | οἱ ἄρχοντες
ἔταττον, οὓς ὑμεῖς εἵλεσθε ἄρχειν μου,
καὶ ἐν Ποτειδαίᾳ καὶ ἐν Ἀμφιπόλει
καὶ ἐπὶ Δηλίῳ, τότε μὲν οὗ ἐκεῖνοι

ἔταττον ἔμενον ὥσπερ καὶ ἄλλος τις καὶ 28
ἐκινδύνευον ἀποθανεῖν, τοῦ δὲ θεοῦ τάττοντος,
ὡς ἐγὼ ᾠήθην τε καὶ ὑπέλαβον, φιλοσοφοῦντά
με δεῖν ζῆν καὶ ἐξετάζοντα ἐμαυτὸν καὶ τοὺς
ἄλλους, ἐνταῦθα δὲ φοβηθεὶς ἢ θάνατον ἢ
ἄλλο | ὁτιοῦν πρᾶγμα λίποιμι τὴν τάξιν. δεινὸν 29
τἂν εἴη, καὶ ὡς ἀληθῶς τότ' ἄν με δικαίως
εἰσάγοι τις εἰς δικαστήριον, ὅτι οὐ νομίζω
θεοὺς εἶναι ἀπειθῶν τῇ μαντείᾳ καὶ δεδιὼς
θάνατον καὶ οἰόμενος σοφὸς εἶναι οὐκ ὤν. τὸ
γάρ τοι θάνατον δεδιέναι, ὦ ἄνδρες, οὐδὲν ἄλλο
ἐστὶν ἢ δοκεῖν σοφὸν εἶναι μὴ ὄντα· δοκεῖν γὰρ
εἰδέναι ἐστὶν ἃ οὐκ οἶδεν. οἶδε μὲν γὰρ οὐδεὶς
τὸν θάνατον οὐδ' εἰ τυγχάνει τῷ ἀνθρώπῳ
πάντων μέγιστον ὂν τῶν ἀγαθῶν, δεδίασι δ' ὡς
εὖ εἰδότες ὅτι μέγιστον τῶν κακῶν ἐστι. καὶ
τοῦτο πῶς οὐκ | ἀμαθία ἐστὶν αὕτη ἡ ἐπονεί- B
διστος, ἡ τοῦ οἴεσθαι εἰδέναι ἃ οὐκ οἶδεν; ἐγὼ
δ', ὦ ἄνδρες, τούτῳ καὶ ἐνταῦθα ἴσως διαφέρω
τῶν πολλῶν ἀνθρώπων, καὶ εἰ δή τῳ σοφώτερός
του φαίην εἶναι, τούτῳ ἄν, ὅτι οὐκ εἰδὼς ἱκανῶς
περὶ τῶν ἐν Ἅιδου οὕτω καὶ οἴομαι οὐκ εἰδέναι·
τὸ δὲ ἀδικεῖν καὶ ἀπειθεῖν τῷ βελτίονι,
καὶ θεῷ καὶ ἀνθρώπῳ, ὅτι κακὸν καὶ
αἰσχρόν ἐστιν οἶδα. πρὸ οὖν τῶν
κακῶν, ὧν οἶδα ὅτι κακά ἐστιν, ἃ μὴ
οἶδα εἰ ἀγαθὰ ὄντα τυγχάνει οὐδέποτε
φοβήσομαι οὐδὲ φεύξομαι· ὥστε οὐδ' εἴ με νῦν
ὑμεῖς ἀφίετε Ἀνύτῳ | ἀπιστήσαντες, ὃς ἔφη ἢ C
τὴν ἀρχὴν οὐ δεῖν ἐμὲ δεῦρο εἰσελθεῖν ἤ, ἐπειδὴ
εἰσῆλθον, οὐχ οἷόντ' εἶναι τὸ μὴ ἀποκτεῖναί με,

But disobedience is indeed evil. Hence, slay me or not, I will always obey God and confute ignorance.

29 λέγων πρὸς ὑμᾶς ὡς, εἰ διαφευξοίμην, ἤδη ἂν
ὑμῶν οἱ ὑεῖς, ἐπιτηδεύοντες ἃ Σωκράτης διδά-
σκει, πάντες παντάπασι διαφθαρήσονται,—εἴ
μοι πρὸς ταῦτα εἴποιτε· Ὦ Σώκρατες, νῦν μὲν
Ἀνύτῳ οὐ πεισόμεθα, ἀλλ' ἀφίεμέν σε, ἐπὶ
τούτῳ μέντοι, ἐφ' ᾧτε μηκέτι ἐν ταύτῃ τῇ
ζητήσει διατρίβειν μηδὲ φιλοσοφεῖν· ἐὰν δὲ
D ἁλῷς ἔτι τοῦτο πράττων, ἀποθανεῖ· εἰ οὖν | με,
ὅπερ εἶπον, ἐπὶ τούτοις ἀφίοιτε, εἴποιμ' ἂν ὑμῖν
ὅτι Ἐγὼ ὑμᾶς, ἄνδρες Ἀθηναῖοι, ἀσπάζομαι μὲν
καὶ φιλῶ, πείσομαι δὲ μᾶλλον τῷ θεῷ ἢ ὑμῖν,
καὶ ἕωσπερ ἂν ἐμπνέω καὶ οἷόστε ὦ, οὐ μὴ
παύσωμαι φιλοσοφῶν καὶ ὑμῖν παρακελευόμενός
τε καὶ ἐνδεικνύμενος ὅτῳ ἂν ἀεὶ ἐντυγχάνω
ὑμῶν, λέγων οἷάπερ εἴωθα, ὅτι Ὦ ἄριστε
ἀνδρῶν, Ἀθηναῖος ὤν, πόλεως τῆς μεγίστης
καὶ εὐδοκιμωτάτης εἰς σοφίαν καὶ ἰσχύν,
χρημάτων μὲν οὐκ αἰσχύνει ἐπιμελούμενος,
E ὅπως σοι ἔσται ὡς πλεῖστα, καὶ δόξης | καὶ
τιμῆς, φρονήσεως δὲ καὶ ἀληθείας καὶ τῆς
ψυχῆς, ὅπως ὡς βελτίστη ἔσται, οὐκ ἐπιμελεῖ
οὐδὲ φροντίζεις; καὶ ἐάν τις ὑμῶν ἀμφισβητῇ
καὶ φῇ ἐπιμελεῖσθαι, οὐκ εὐθὺς ἀφήσω αὐτὸν
οὐδ' ἄπειμι, ἀλλ' ἐρήσομαι αὐτὸν καὶ ἐξετάσω
καὶ ἐλέγξω, καὶ ἐάν μοι μὴ δοκῇ κεκτῆσθαι
ἀρετήν, φάναι δέ, ὀνειδιῶ ὅτι τὰ πλείστου ἄξια
30 περὶ | ἐλαχίστου ποιεῖται, τὰ δὲ φαυλότερα περὶ
πλείονος. ταῦτα καὶ νεωτέρῳ καὶ πρεσβυτέρῳ,
ὅτῳ ἂν ἐντυγχάνω, ποιήσω, καὶ ξένῳ καὶ ἀστῷ,
μᾶλλον δὲ τοῖς ἀστοῖς, ὅσῳ μου ἐγγυτέρω ἐστὲ
γένει. ταῦτα γὰρ κελεύει ὁ θεός, εὖ ἴστε, καὶ ἐγὼ

οἴομαι οὐδέν πω ὑμῖν μεῖζον ἀγαθὸν γενέσθαι 30 ἐν τῇ πόλει ἢ τὴν ἐμὴν τῷ θεῷ ὑπηρεσίαν. οὐδὲν γὰρ ἄλλο πράττων ἐγὼ περιέρχομαι ἢ πείθων ὑμῶν καὶ νεωτέρους καὶ πρεσβυτέρους μήτε σωμάτων ἐπιμελεῖσθαι μήτε χρημάτων πρότερον μηδὲ οὕτω | σφόδρα ὡς τῆς ψυχῆς, B ὅπως ὡς ἀρίστη ἔσται, λέγων· Οὐκ ἐκ χρημάτων ἀρετὴ γίγνεται, ἀλλ᾿ ἐξ ἀρετῆς χρήματα καὶ τὰ ἄλλα ἀγαθὰ τοῖς ἀνθρώποις ἅπαντα καὶ ἰδίᾳ καὶ δημοσίᾳ. εἰ μὲν οὖν ταῦτα λέγων διαφθείρω τοὺς νέους, ταῦτ᾿ ἂν εἴη βλαβερά· εἰ δέ τίς μέ φησιν ἄλλα λέγειν ἢ ταῦτα, οὐδὲν λέγει. πρὸς ταῦτα, φαίην ἄν, ὦ Ἀθηναῖοι, ἢ πείθεσθε Ἀνύτῳ ἢ μή, καὶ ἢ ἀφίετε ἢ μὴ ἀφίετε, ὡς ἐμοῦ οὐκ ἂν ποιήσοντος ἄλλα, οὐδ᾿ εἰ μέλλω | πολλάκις τεθνάναι. C

Slay me—and you hurt yourselves. For I am your better conscience—

Μὴ θορυβεῖτε, ἄνδρες Ἀθηναῖοι, ἀλλ᾿ ἐμμείνατέ μοι οἷς ἐδεήθην ὑμῶν, μὴ θορυβεῖν ἐφ᾿ οἷς ἂν λέγω, ἀλλ᾿ ἀκούειν· καὶ γάρ, ὡς ἐγὼ οἶμαι, ὀνήσεσθε ἀκούοντες. μέλλω γὰρ οὖν ἄττα ὑμῖν ἐρεῖν καὶ ἄλλα, ἐφ᾿ οἷς ἴσως βοήσεσθε· ἀλλὰ μηδαμῶς ποιεῖτε τοῦτο. εὖ γὰρ ἴστε, ἐὰν ἐμὲ ἀποκτείνητε τοιοῦτον ὄντα, οἷον ἐγὼ λέγω, οὐκ ἐμὲ μείζω βλάψετε ἢ ὑμᾶς αὐτούς. ἐμὲ μὲν γὰρ οὐδὲν ἂν βλάψειεν οὔτε Μέλητος οὔτε Ἄνυτος· οὐδὲ γὰρ ἂν δύναιτο· οὐ γὰρ οἴομαι θεμιτὸν | εἶναι ἀμείνονι D ἀνδρὶ ὑπὸ χείρονος βλάπτεσθαι. ἀποκτείνειε μεντἂν ἴσως ἢ ἐξελάσειεν ἢ ἀτιμώσειεν· ἀλλὰ ταῦτα οὗτος μὲν ἴσως οἴεται καὶ ἄλλος τίς

30 που μεγάλα κακά, ἐγὼ δ' οὐκ οἴομαι, ἀλλὰ πολὺ μᾶλλον ποιεῖν ἃ οὗτος νυνὶ ποιεῖ, ἄνδρα ἀδίκως ἐπιχειρεῖν ἀποκτιννύναι. νῦν οὖν, ὦ ἄνδρες Ἀθηναῖοι, πολλοῦ δέω ἐγὼ ὑπὲρ ἐμαυτοῦ ἀπολογεῖσθαι, ὥς τις ἂν οἴοιτο, ἀλλὰ ὑπὲρ ὑμῶν, μή τι ἐξαμάρτητε περὶ τὴν τοῦ θεοῦ δόσιν ὑμῖν ἐμοῦ καταψηφισάμενοι. ἐὰν γὰρ
E ἐμὲ | ἀποκτείνητε, οὐ ῥᾳδίως ἄλλον τοιοῦτον εὑρήσετε, ἀτεχνῶς, εἰ καὶ γελοιότερον εἰπεῖν, προσκείμενον τῇ πόλει ὑπὸ τοῦ θεοῦ, ὥσπερ ἵππῳ μεγάλῳ μὲν καὶ γενναίῳ ὑπὸ μεγέθους δὲ νωθεστέρῳ καὶ δεομένῳ ἐγείρεσθαι ὑπὸ μύωπός τινος· οἷον δή μοι δοκεῖ ὁ θεὸς ἐμὲ τῇ πόλει προστεθηκέναι—τοιοῦτόν τινα, ὃς ὑμᾶς ἐγείρων καὶ πείθων καὶ ὀνειδίζων ἕνα
31 ἕκαστον οὐδὲν παύομαι | τὴν ἡμέραν ὅλην πανταχοῦ προσκαθίζων. τοιοῦτος οὖν ἄλλος οὐ ῥᾳδίως ὑμῖν γενήσεται, ὦ ἄνδρες, ἀλλ' ἐὰν ἐμοὶ πείθησθε, φείσεσθέ μου· ὑμεῖς δ' ἴσως τάχ' ἂν ἀχθόμενοι, ὥσπερ οἱ νυστάζοντες ἐγειρόμενοι, κρούσαντες ἄν με, πειθόμενοι Ἀνύτῳ, ῥᾳδίως ἂν ἀποκτείναιτε, εἶτα τὸν λοιπὸν βίον καθεύδοντες διατελοῖτε ἄν, εἰ μή τινα ἄλλον ὁ θεὸς ὑμῖν ἐπιπέμψειεν κηδόμενος ὑμῶν. ὅτι δ' ἐγὼ τυγχάνω ὢν τοιοῦτος, οἷος ὑπὸ τοῦ θεοῦ τῇ πόλει δεδόσθαι, ἐνθένδε ἂν |
B κατανοήσαιτε· οὐ γὰρ ἀνθρωπίνῳ ἔοικε τὸ ἐμὲ τῶν μὲν ἐμαυτοῦ ἁπάντων ἠμεληκέναι καὶ ἀνέχεσθαι τῶν οἰκείων ἀμελουμένων τοσαῦτα ἤδη ἔτη, τὸ δὲ ὑμέτερον πράττειν ἀεί, ἰδίᾳ ἑκάστῳ προσιόντα ὥσπερ πατέρα ἢ ἀδελφὸν

the small voice—to each separately,

πρεσβύτερον, πείθοντα ἐπιμελεῖσθαι 31
ἀρετῆς. καίτοι εἰ μέν τι ἀπὸ τούτων
ἀπέλαυον καὶ μισθὸν λαμβάνων ταῦτα παρεκε-
λευόμην, εἶχον ἄν τινα λόγον· νῦν δὲ ὁρᾶτε
δὴ καὶ αὐτοὶ ὅτι οἱ κατήγοροι, τἆλλα πάντα
ἀναισχύντως οὕτω κατηγοροῦντες, τοῦτό γε
οὐχ οἷοίτε ἐγένοντο ἀπαναισχυντῆσαι παρα-
σχόμενοι | μάρτυρα, ὡς ἐγώ ποτέ τινα ἢ ἐπρα- C
ξάμην μισθὸν ἢ ᾔτησα. ἱκανὸν γάρ, οἶμαι, ἐγὼ
παρέχομαι τὸν μάρτυρα ὡς ἀληθῆ λέγω—τὴν
πενίαν.

but not to the city at large. My divine sign forbids me politics; else long since I had perished.

Ἴσως ἂν οὖν δόξειεν ἄτοπον εἶναι, ὅτι δὴ
ἐγὼ ἰδίᾳ μὲν ταῦτα ξυμβουλεύω
περιιὼν καὶ πολυπραγμονῶ, δημοσίᾳ
δὲ οὐ τολμῶ ἀναβαίνων εἰς τὸ
πλῆθος τὸ ὑμέτερον ξυμβουλεύειν
τῇ πόλει. τούτου δὲ αἴτιόν ἐστιν ὃ
ὑμεῖς ἐμοῦ πολλάκις ἀκηκόατε πολλαχοῦ λέγον-
τος, ὅτι μοι θεῖόν τι | καὶ δαιμόνιον γίγνεται, D
ὃ δὴ καὶ ἐν τῇ γραφῇ ἐπικωμῳδῶν Μέλητος
ἐγράψατο· ἐμοὶ δὲ τοῦτ' ἔστιν ἐκ παιδὸς ἀρξά-
μενον, φωνή τις γιγνομένη, ἥ, ὅταν γένηται,
ἀεὶ ἀποτρέπει με τοῦτο ὃ ἂν μέλλω πράττειν,
προτρέπει δὲ οὔποτε· τοῦτ' ἔστιν ὅ μοι ἐναν-
τιοῦται τὰ πολιτικὰ πράττειν. καὶ παγκάλως
γέ μοι δοκεῖ ἐναντιοῦσθαι· εὖ γὰρ ἴστε, ὦ
ἄνδρες Ἀθηναῖοι, εἰ ἐγὼ πάλαι ἐπεχείρησα
πράττειν τὰ πολιτικὰ πράγματα, πάλαι ἂν
ἀπωλώλη καὶ οὔτ' ἂν ὑμᾶς ὠφελήκη | οὐδὲν E
οὔτ' ἂν ἐμαυτόν. καί μοι μὴ ἄχθεσθε λέγοντι
τἀληθῆ· οὐ γὰρ ἔστιν ὅστις ἀνθρώπων σωθή-

31 σεται οὔτε ὑμῖν οὔτε ἄλλῳ πλήθει οὐδενὶ
γνησίως ἐναντιούμενος καὶ διακωλύων πολλὰ
ἄδικα καὶ παράνομα ἐν τῇ πόλει γίγνεσθαι, |
32 ἀλλ' ἀναγκαῖόν ἐστι τὸν τῷ ὄντι μαχούμενον
ὑπὲρ τοῦ δικαίου, καὶ εἰ μέλλει ὀλίγον χρόνον
σωθήσεσθαι, ἰδιωτεύειν, ἀλλὰ μὴ δημοσιεύειν.

Yet for justice' sake, I publicly opposed both the democracy (in the case of the generals),

Μεγάλα δ' ἔγωγε ὑμῖν τεκμήρια παρέξομαι
τούτων, οὐ λόγους, ἀλλ' ὃ ὑμεῖς
τιμᾶτε, ἔργα. ἀκούσατε δή μου τὰ
ἐμοὶ ξυμβεβηκότα, ἵνα εἰδῆτε ὅτι
οὐδ' ἂν ἑνὶ ὑπεικάθοιμι παρὰ τὸ
δίκαιον δείσας θάνατον, μὴ ὑπείκων
δὲ ἅμ' ἂν καὶ ἀπολοίμην. ἐρῶ δὲ ὑμῖν φορτικὰ
μὲν καὶ δικανικά, ἀληθῆ δέ. ἐγὼ γάρ, ὦ
B Ἀθηναῖοι, ἄλλην μὲν ἀρχὴν οὐδεμίαν | πώ-
ποτε ἦρξα ἐν τῇ πόλει, ἐβούλευσα δέ· καὶ
ἔτυχεν ἡμῶν ἡ φυλὴ [Ἀντιοχὶς] πρυτανεύουσα,
ὅτε ὑμεῖς τοὺς δέκα στρατηγοὺς τοὺς οὐκ
ἀνελομένους τοὺς ἐκ τῆς ναυμαχίας ἐβούλεσθε
ἀθρόους κρίνειν—παρανόμως, ὡς ἐν τῷ ὑστέρῳ
χρόνῳ πᾶσιν ὑμῖν ἔδοξε. τότ' ἐγὼ μόνος τῶν
πρυτάνεων ἠναντιώθην μηδὲν ποιεῖν παρὰ τοὺς
νόμους καὶ ἐναντία ἐψηφισάμην· καὶ ἑτοίμων
ὄντων ἐνδεικνύναι με καὶ ἀπάγειν τῶν ῥητόρων,
καὶ ὑμῶν κελευόντων καὶ βοώντων, μετὰ τοῦ
C νόμου καὶ τοῦ | δικαίου ᾤμην μᾶλλόν με δεῖν
διακινδυνεύειν ἢ μεθ' ὑμῶν γενέσθαι μὴ δίκαια
βουλευομένων, φοβηθέντα δεσμὸν ἢ θάνατον.
καὶ ταῦτα μὲν ἦν ἔτι δημοκρατουμένης τῆς

and the oligarchy (in Leon's arrest),

πόλεως· ἐπειδὴ δὲ ὀλιγαρχία ἐγέ-
νετο, οἱ τριάκοντα αὖ μεταπεμψά-

μενοί με πέμπτον αὐτὸν εἰς τὴν θόλον προσ- 32
έταξαν ἀγαγεῖν ἐκ Σαλαμῖνος Λέοντα τὸν Σαλαμί-
νιον, ἵνα ἀποθάνοι—οἷα δὴ καὶ ἄλλοις ἐκεῖνοι
πολλοῖς πολλὰ προσέταττον, βουλόμενοι ὡς
πλείστους ἀναπλῆσαι αἰτιῶν· τότε μέντοι ἐγὼ
οὐ | λόγῳ ἀλλ' ἔργῳ αὖ ἐνεδειξάμην ὅτι ἐμοὶ D
θανάτου μὲν μέλει (εἰ μὴ ἀγροικότερον ἦν
εἰπεῖν) οὐδ' ὁτιοῦν, τοῦ δὲ μηδὲν ἄδικον μηδ'
ἀνόσιον ἐργάζεσθαι, τούτου δὲ τὸ πᾶν μέλει.
ἐμὲ γὰρ ἐκείνη ἡ ἀρχὴ οὐκ ἐξέπληξεν, οὕτως
ἰσχυρὰ οὖσα, ὥστε ἄδικόν τι ἐργάσασθαι, ἀλλ'
ἐπειδὴ ἐκ τῆς θόλου ἐξήλθομεν, οἱ μὲν τέτταρες
ᾤχοντο εἰς Σαλαμῖνα καὶ ἤγαγον Λέοντα, ἐγὼ
δὲ ᾠχόμην ἀπιὼν οἴκαδε. καὶ ἴσως ἂν διὰ
ταῦτα ἀπέθανον, εἰ μὴ ἡ ἀρχὴ διὰ ταχέων
κατελύθη· καὶ τούτων | ὑμῖν ἔσονται πολλοὶ E
μάρτυρες.

Ἆρ' οὖν ἄν με οἴεσθε τοσάδε ἔτη διαγε-
νέσθαι, εἰ ἔπραττον τὰ δημόσια, καὶ πράττων
ἀξίως ἀνδρὸς ἀγαθοῦ ἐβοήθουν τοῖς δικαίοις
καί, ὥσπερ χρή, τοῦτο περὶ πλείστου ἐποιού-
μην; πολλοῦ γε δεῖ, ὦ ἄνδρες Ἀθηναῖοι.
οὐδὲ γὰρ ἂν ἄλλος ἀνθρώπων οὐδείς. | ἀλλ' 33
ἐγὼ διὰ παντὸς τοῦ βίου δημοσίᾳ τε, εἴ πού
τι ἔπραξα, τοιοῦτος φανοῦμαι, καὶ
ἰδίᾳ ὁ αὐτὸς οὗτος, οὐδενὶ πώποτε
ξυγχωρήσας οὐδὲν παρὰ τὸ δίκαιον
οὔτε ἄλλῳ οὔτε τούτων οὐδενί, οὓς
οἱ διαβάλλοντες ἐμέ φασιν ἐμοὺς
μαθητὰς εἶναι. ἐγὼ δὲ διδάσκαλος μὲν οὐδενὸς
πώποτ' ἐγενόμην· εἰ δέ τίς μου λέγοντος καὶ

and, privately, my so-called pupils—though I am no teacher, and take no fee.

33 τὰ ἐμαυτοῦ πράττοντος ἐπιθυμεῖ ἀκούειν, εἴτε
νεώτερος εἴτε πρεσβύτερος, οὐδενὶ πώποτε
ἐφθόνησα, οὐδὲ χρήματα μὲν λαμβάνων διαλέ-
B γομαι, μὴ λαμβάνων | δὲ οὔ, ἀλλ' ὁμοίως καὶ
πλουσίῳ καὶ πένητι παρέχω ἐμαυτὸν ἐρωτᾶν,
καὶ ἐάν τις βούληται ἀποκρινόμενος ἀκούειν
ὧν ἂν λέγω. καὶ τούτων ἐγὼ εἴτε τις χρηστὸς
γίγνεται εἴτε μή, οὐκ ἂν δικαίως τὴν αἰτίαν
ὑπέχοιμι, ὧν μήτε ὑπεσχόμην μηδενὶ μηδὲν
πώποτε μάθημα μήτε ἐδίδαξα· εἰ δέ τίς φησι
παρ' ἐμοῦ πώποτέ τι μαθεῖν ἢ ἀκοῦσαι ἰδίᾳ ὅ
τι μὴ καὶ οἱ ἄλλοι πάντες, εὖ ἴστε ὅτι οὐκ
ἀληθῆ λέγει.

'Αλλὰ διὰ τί δή ποτε μετ' ἐμοῦ χαίρουσί
C τινες πολὺν χρόνον διατρίβοντες; | ἀκηκόατε,
ὦ ἄνδρες 'Αθηναῖοι· πᾶσαν ὑμῖν τὴν ἀλήθειαν
ἐγὼ εἶπον,—ὅτι ἀκούοντες χαίρουσιν ἐξεταζο-
μένοις τοῖς οἰομένοις μὲν εἶναι σοφοῖς οὖσι δ' οὔ·
ἔστι γὰρ οὐκ ἀηδές. ἐμοὶ δὲ τοῦτο, ὡς ἐγώ
φημι, προστέτακται ὑπὸ τοῦ θεοῦ πράττειν καὶ
ἐκ μαντείων καὶ ἐξ ἐνυπνίων καὶ παντὶ τρόπῳ,
ᾧπερ τινί ποτε καὶ ἄλλῳ θεία μοῖρα ἀνθρώπῳ
καὶ ὁτιοῦν προσέταξε πράττειν. ταῦτα, ὦ 'Αθη-
ναῖοι, καὶ ἀληθῆ ἐστιν καὶ εὐέλεγκτα. εἰ γὰρ δὴ
D ἔγωγε τῶν νέων τοὺς μὲν διαφθείρω, | τοὺς δὲ διέ-
φθαρκα, χρῆν δήπου, εἴτε τινὲς αὐτῶν
πρεσβύτεροι γενόμενοι ἔγνωσαν ὅτι
νέοις οὖσιν αὐτοῖς ἐγὼ κακὸν πώποτέ
τι ξυνεβούλευσα, νυνὶ αὐτοὺς ἀναβαί-
νοντας ἐμοῦ κατηγορεῖν καὶ τιμωρεῖ-
σθαι· εἰ δὲ μὴ αὐτοὶ ἤθελον, τῶν οἰκείων τινὰς

If indeed I corrupted the youth, why do neither they nor their relatives appear against me?

τῶν ἐκείνων, πατέρας καὶ ἀδελφοὺς καὶ ἄλλους 33
τοὺς προσήκοντας, εἴπερ ὑπ' ἐμοῦ τι κακὸν
ἐπεπόνθεσαν αὐτῶν οἱ οἰκεῖοι, νῦν μεμνῆσθαι
καὶ τιμωρεῖσθαι. πάντως δὲ πάρεισιν αὐτῶν
πολλοὶ ἐνταυθοῖ, οὓς ἐγὼ ὁρῶ, πρῶτον μὲν
Κρίτων οὑτοσί, ἐμὸς ἡλικιώτης καὶ δημότης,
Κριτοβούλου | τοῦδε πατήρ, ἔπειτα Λυσανίας E
ὁ Σφήττιος, Αἰσχίνου τοῦδε πατήρ· ἔτι Ἀντιφῶν
ὁ Κηφισιεὺς οὑτοσί, Ἐπιγένους πατήρ· ἄλλοι
τοίνυν οὗτοι, ὧν οἱ ἀδελφοὶ ἐν ταύτῃ τῇ δια-
τριβῇ γεγόνασιν, Νικόστρατος Θεοζοτίδου, ἀδελ-
φὸς Θεοδότου (καὶ ὁ μὲν Θεόδοτος τετελεύτηκεν,
ὥστε οὐκ ἂν ἐκεῖνός γε αὐτοῦ καταδεηθείη),
καὶ Πάραλος ὅδε ὁ Δημοδόκου, οὗ ἦν Θεάγης
ἀδελφός· ὅδε δὲ | Ἀδείμαντος ὁ Ἀρίστωνος, 34
οὗ ἀδελφὸς οὑτοσὶ Πλάτων, καὶ Αἰαντόδωρος,
οὗ Ἀπολλόδωρος ὅδε ἀδελφός. καὶ ἄλλους
πολλοὺς ἐγὼ ἔχω ὑμῖν εἰπεῖν, ὧν τινα ἐχρῆν
μάλιστα μὲν ἐν τῷ ἑαυτοῦ λόγῳ παρασχέσθαι
Μέλητον μάρτυρα· εἰ δὲ τότε ἐπελάθετο, νῦν
παρασχέσθω (ἐγὼ παραχωρῶ) καὶ λεγέτω, εἴ
τι ἔχει τοιοῦτον. ἀλλὰ (τούτου πᾶν τοὐναντίον)
εὑρήσετε, ὦ ἄνδρες, πάντας ἐμοὶ βοηθεῖν ἑτοί-
μους τῷ διαφθείροντι, τῷ κακὰ ἐργαζομένῳ
τοὺς οἰκείους αὐτῶν, ὥς φασι Μέλητος καὶ |
Ἄνυτος. αὐτοὶ μὲν γὰρ οἱ διεφθαρμένοι τάχ' B
ἂν λόγον ἔχοιεν βοηθοῦντες· οἱ δὲ ἀδιάφθαρτοι,
πρεσβύτεροι ἤδη ἄνδρες, οἱ τούτων προσήκοντες,
τίνα ἄλλον ἔχουσι λόγον βοηθοῦντες ἐμοὶ ἀλλ'
ἢ τὸν ὀρθόν τε καὶ δίκαιον, ὅτι ξυνίσασι
Μελήτῳ μὲν ψευδομένῳ, ἐμοὶ δὲ ἀληθεύοντι;

Enough! No tears nor children's prayers in my behalf! I am not wilful; but such appeals disgrace the city, pervert justice, and are impious.

34 Εἶεν δή, ὦ ἄνδρες· ἃ μὲν ἐγὼ ἔχοιμ' ἂν
ἀπολογεῖσθαι, σχεδόν ἐστι ταῦτα καὶ
ἄλλα ἴσως τοιαῦτα. τάχα δ' ἄν τις
ὑμῶν ἀγανακτήσειεν ἀναμνησθεὶς |
C ἑαυτοῦ, εἰ ὁ μὲν καὶ ἐλάττω τουτουὶ
τοῦ ἀγῶνος ἀγῶνα ἀγωνιζόμενος ἐδεήθη
τε καὶ ἱκέτευσε τοὺς δικαστὰς μετὰ
πολλῶν δακρύων, παιδία τε αὑτοῦ
ἀναβιβασάμενος, ἵνα ὅτι μάλιστα ἐλεηθείη, καὶ
ἄλλους τῶν οἰκείων καὶ φίλων πολλούς, ἐγὼ
δὲ οὐδὲν ἄρα τούτων ποιήσω, καὶ ταῦτα κινδυ-
νεύων, ὡς ἂν δόξαιμι, τὸν ἔσχατον κίνδυνον.
τάχ' οὖν τις ταῦτα ἐννοήσας αὐθαδέστερον ἂν
πρός με σχοίη, καὶ ὀργισθεὶς αὐτοῖς τούτοις
θεῖτο ἂν μετ' ὀργῆς τὴν ψῆφον. εἰ δή τις
D ὑμῶν οὕτως ἔχει — | οὐκ ἀξιῶ μὲν γὰρ ἔγωγε,
εἰ δ' οὖν, ἐπιεικῆ ἄν μοι δοκῶ πρὸς τοῦτον
λέγειν λέγων ὅτι Ἐμοί, ὦ ἄριστε, εἰσὶν μέν
πού τινες καὶ οἰκεῖοι· καὶ γὰρ τοῦτο αὖ τὸ
τοῦ Ὁμήρου, οὐδ' ἐγὼ ἀπὸ δρυὸς οὐδ' ἀπὸ
πέτρης πέφυκα, ἀλλ' ἐξ ἀνθρώπων, ὥστε καὶ
οἰκεῖοί μοί εἰσι καὶ υἱεῖς, ὦ ἄνδρες Ἀθηναῖοι,
τρεῖς, εἷς μὲν μειράκιον ἤδη, δύο δὲ παιδία·
ἀλλ' ὅμως οὐδένα αὐτῶν δεῦρο ἀναβιβασάμενος
δεήσομαι ὑμῶν ἀποψηφίσασθαι. τί δὴ οὖν οὐδὲν
τούτων ποιήσω; οὐκ αὐθαδιζόμενος, ὦ Ἀθηναῖοι,
E οὐδ' ὑμᾶς | ἀτιμάζων, ἀλλ'—εἰ μὲν θαρραλέως
ἐγὼ ἔχω πρὸς θάνατον ἢ μή, ἄλλος λόγος,
πρὸς δ' οὖν δόξαν καὶ ἐμοὶ καὶ ὑμῖν καὶ ὅλῃ
τῇ πόλει οὔ μοι δοκεῖ καλὸν εἶναι ἐμὲ τούτων
οὐδὲν ποιεῖν καὶ τηλικόνδε ὄντα καὶ τοῦτο

τοὔνομα ἔχοντα, εἴτ' οὖν ἀληθὲς εἴτ' οὖν ψεῦδος· 34
ἀλλ' οὖν δεδογμένον γέ ἐστι τὸν Σωκράτη διαφέ-
ρειν τινὶ τῶν πολλῶν | ἀνθρώπων. εἰ οὖν ὑμῶν 35
οἱ δοκοῦντες διαφέρειν εἴτε σοφίᾳ εἴτε ἀνδρείᾳ
εἴτε ἄλλῃ ᾑτινιοῦν ἀρετῇ τοιοῦτοι ἔσονται,
αἰσχρὸν ἂν εἴη· οἵουσπερ ἐγὼ πολλάκις ἑώρακά
τινας, ὅταν κρίνωνται, δοκοῦντας μέν τι εἶναι,
θαυμάσια δὲ ἐργαζομένους, ὡς δεινόν τι οἰομένους
πείσεσθαι, εἰ ἀποθανοῦνται, ὥσπερ ἀθανάτων
ἐσομένων, ἂν ὑμεῖς αὐτοὺς μὴ ἀποκτείνητε· οἱ
ἐμοὶ δοκοῦσιν αἰσχύνην τῇ πόλει περιάπτειν,
ὥστ' ἄν τινα καὶ τῶν ξένων ὑπολαβεῖν ὅτι οἱ
διαφέροντες Ἀθηναίων εἰς ἀρετήν, | οὓς αὐτοὶ B
ἑαυτῶν ἔν τε ταῖς ἀρχαῖς καὶ ταῖς ἄλλαις
τιμαῖς προκρίνουσιν, οὗτοι γυναικῶν οὐδὲν δια-
φέρουσι. ταῦτα γάρ, ὦ ἄνδρες Ἀθηναῖοι, οὔτε
ὑμᾶς χρὴ ποιεῖν τοὺς δοκοῦντας καὶ ὁπῃοῦν τι
εἶναι, οὔτ', ἂν ἡμεῖς ποιῶμεν, ὑμᾶς ἐπιτρέπειν,
ἀλλὰ τοῦτο αὐτὸ ἐνδείκνυσθαι, ὅτι πολὺ μᾶλλον
καταψηφιεῖσθε τοῦ τὰ ἐλεεινὰ ταῦτα δράματα
εἰσάγοντος καὶ καταγέλαστον τὴν πόλιν ποι-
οῦντος ἢ τοῦ ἡσυχίαν ἄγοντος.

Χωρὶς δὲ τῆς δόξης, ὦ ἄνδρες, οὐδὲ δίκαιόν
μοι δοκεῖ εἶναι δεῖσθαι τοῦ δικαστοῦ | οὐδὲ C
δεόμενον ἀποφεύγειν, ἀλλὰ διδάσκειν καὶ πείθειν.
οὐ γὰρ ἐπὶ τούτῳ κάθηται ὁ δικαστής, ἐπὶ τῷ
καταχαρίζεσθαι τὰ δίκαια, ἀλλ' ἐπὶ τῷ κρίνειν
ταῦτα· καὶ ὀμώμοκεν οὐ χαριεῖσθαι οἷς ἂν δοκῇ
αὐτῷ, ἀλλὰ δικάσειν κατὰ τοὺς νόμους. οὔκουν
χρὴ οὔτε ἡμᾶς ἐθίζειν ὑμᾶς ἐπιορκεῖν οὔθ' ὑμᾶς
ἐθίζεσθαι· οὐδέτεροι γὰρ ἂν ἡμῶν εὐσεβοῖεν.

35 μὴ οὖν ἀξιοῦτέ με, ὦ ἄνδρες Ἀθηναῖοι, τοιαῦτα
δεῖν πρὸς ὑμᾶς πράττειν, ἃ μήτε ἡγοῦμαι καλὰ
D εἶναι μήτε δίκαια μήτε ὅσια, ἄλλως τε μέντοι | νὴ
Δία [πάντως] καὶ ἀσεβείας φεύγοντα ὑπὸ Μελήτου
τουτουΐ. σαφῶς γὰρ ἄν, εἰ πείθοιμι ὑμᾶς καὶ
τῷ δεῖσθαι βιαζοίμην ὀμωμοκότας, θεοὺς ἂν
διδάσκοιμι μὴ ἡγεῖσθαι ὑμᾶς εἶναι, καὶ ἀτεχνῶς
ἀπολογούμενος κατηγοροίην ἂν ἐμαυτοῦ ὡς θεοὺς
οὐ νομίζω. ἀλλὰ πολλοῦ δεῖ οὕτως ἔχειν·
νομίζω τε γάρ, ὦ ἄνδρες Ἀθηναῖοι, ὡς οὐδεὶς
τῶν ἐμῶν κατηγόρων, καὶ ὑμῖν ἐπιτρέπω καὶ
τῷ θεῷ κρῖναι περὶ ἐμοῦ ὅπῃ μέλλει ἐμοί τε
ἄριστα εἶναι καὶ ὑμῖν.

After the Verdict "Guilty."

E | Τὸ μὲν μὴ ἀγανακτεῖν, ὦ ἄνδρες Ἀθηναῖοι,
ἐπὶ τούτῳ τῷ γεγονότι, ὅτι μου κατ-
36 εψηφίσασθε, | ἄλλα τέ μοι πολλὰ
ξυμβάλλεται, καὶ οὐκ ἀνέλπιστόν μοι
γέγονεν τὸ γεγονὸς τοῦτο, ἀλλὰ πολὺ μᾶλλον
θαυμάζω ἑκατέρων τῶν ψήφων τὸν γεγονότα
ἀριθμόν. οὐ γὰρ ᾤόμην ἔγωγε οὕτω παρ'
ὀλίγον ἔσεσθαι, ἀλλὰ παρὰ πολύ· νῦν δέ, ὡς
ἔοικεν, εἰ τριάκοντα μόναι μετέπεσον τῶν ψήφων,
ἀπεπεφεύγη ἄν. Μέλητον μὲν οὖν, ὡς ἐμοὶ
δοκῶ, καὶ νῦν ἀποπέφευγα, καὶ οὐ μόνον
ἀποπέφευγα, ἀλλὰ παντὶ δῆλον τοῦτό γε, ὅτι,
εἰ μὴ ἀνέβη Ἄνυτος καὶ Λύκων κατηγορήσοντες
B ἐμοῦ, κἂν ὦφλε χιλίας δραχμάς, | οὐ μεταλαβὼν
τὸ πέμπτον μέρος τῶν ψήφων.

This verdict I expected, but not by so small a majority.

> My counter-penalty? Justly—maintenance in the Prytaneum. For imprisonment, exile, etc. I do not deserve,

Τιμᾶται δ' οὖν μοι ὁ ἀνὴρ θανάτου. εἶεν· 36
ἐγὼ δὲ δὴ τίνος ὑμῖν ἀντιτιμήσομαι, ὦ ἄνδρες Ἀθηναῖοι; ἢ δῆλον ὅτι τῆς ἀξίας; τί οὖν; τί ἄξιός εἰμι παθεῖν ἢ ἀποτεῖσαι, ὅ τι μαθὼν ἐν τῷ βίῳ οὐχ ἡσυχίαν ἦγον, ἀλλ' ἀμελήσας ὧνπερ οἱ πολλοί, χρηματισμοῦ τε καὶ οἰκονομίας καὶ στρατηγιῶν καὶ δημηγοριῶν καὶ τῶν ἄλλων ἀρχῶν καὶ ξυνωμοσιῶν καὶ στάσεων τῶν ἐν τῇ πόλει γιγνομένων, ἡγησάμενος ἐμαυτὸν τῷ ὄντι ἐπιεικέστερον εἶναι ἢ ὥστε εἰς ταῦτ' | ἰόντα σῴζεσθαι, C
ἐνταῦθα μὲν οὐκ ᾖα, οἷ ἐλθὼν μήτε ὑμῖν μήτε ἐμαυτῷ ἔμελλον μηδὲν ὄφελος εἶναι, ἐπὶ δὲ τὸ ἰδίᾳ ἕκαστον [ἰὼν] εὐεργετεῖν τὴν μεγίστην εὐεργεσίαν, ὡς ἐγώ φημι, ἐνταῦθα ᾖα, ἐπιχειρῶν ἕκαστον ὑμῶν πείθειν μὴ πρότερον μήτε τῶν ἑαυτοῦ μηδενὸς ἐπιμελεῖσθαι, πρὶν ἑαυτοῦ ἐπιμεληθείη, ὅπως ὡς βέλτιστος καὶ φρονιμώτατος ἔσοιτο, μήτε τῶν τῆς πόλεως, πρὶν αὐτῆς τῆς πόλεως, τῶν τε ἄλλων οὕτω κατὰ τὸν αὐτὸν τρόπον ἐπιμελεῖσθαι· τί οὖν εἰμι ἄξιος παθεῖν | τοιοῦτος D
ὤν; ἀγαθόν τι, ὦ ἄνδρες Ἀθηναῖοι, εἰ δεῖ γε κατὰ τὴν ἀξίαν τῇ ἀληθείᾳ τιμᾶσθαι· καὶ ταῦτά γε ἀγαθὸν τοιοῦτον, ὅ τι ἂν πρέποι ἐμοί. τί οὖν πρέπει ἀνδρὶ πένητι εὐεργέτῃ, δεομένῳ ἄγειν σχολὴν ἐπὶ τῇ ὑμετέρᾳ παρακελεύσει; οὐκ ἔσθ' ὅ τι μᾶλλον, ὦ ἄνδρες Ἀθηναῖοι, πρέπει οὕτως, ὡς τὸν τοιοῦτον ἄνδρα ἐν πρυτανείῳ σιτεῖσθαι, πολύ γε μᾶλλον ἢ εἴ τις ὑμῶν ἵππῳ ἢ ξυνωρίδι ἢ ζεύγει νενίκηκεν Ὀλυμπίασιν. ὁ μὲν γὰρ ὑμᾶς ποιεῖ εὐδαίμονας δοκεῖν εἶναι,

E ἐγὼ δὲ εἶναι· καὶ ὁ | μὲν τροφῆς οὐδὲν δεῖται,
ἐγὼ δὲ δέομαι. εἰ οὖν δεῖ με κατὰ τὸ δίκαιον
37 τῆς ἀξίας τιμᾶσθαι, τούτου | τιμῶμαι, ἐν πρυτα-
νείῳ σιτήσεως.

Ἴσως οὖν ὑμῖν καὶ ταυτὶ λέγων παραπλησίως
δοκῶ λέγειν ὥσπερ περὶ τοῦ οἴκτου καὶ τῆς
ἀντιβολήσεως, ἀπαυθαδιζόμενος· τὸ δὲ οὐκ ἔστιν,
ὦ Ἀθηναῖοι, τοιοῦτον, ἀλλὰ τοιόνδε μᾶλλον.
πέπεισμαι ἐγὼ ἑκὼν εἶναι μηδένα ἀδικεῖν ἀνθρώ-
πων. (ἀλλὰ ὑμᾶς τοῦτο οὐ πείθω· ὀλίγον γὰρ
χρόνον ἀλλήλοις διειλέγμεθα· ἐπεί, ὡς ἐγᾦμαι,
εἰ ἦν ὑμῖν νόμος, ὥσπερ καὶ ἄλλοις ἀνθρώποις,
B περὶ θανάτου μὴ μίαν ἡμέραν μόνον | κρίνειν,
ἀλλὰ πολλάς, ἐπείσθητε ἄν· νῦν δ' οὐ ῥᾴδιον
ἐν χρόνῳ ὀλίγῳ μεγάλας διαβολὰς ἀπολύεσθαι.)
πεπεισμένος δὴ ἐγὼ μηδένα ἀδικεῖν, πολλοῦ
δέω ἐμαυτόν γε ἀδικήσειν καὶ κατ' ἐμαυτοῦ
ἐρεῖν αὐτὸς ὡς ἄξιός εἰμί του κακοῦ, καὶ
τιμήσεσθαι τοιούτου τινὸς ἐμαυτῷ, τί δείσας;
ἢ μὴ πάθω τοῦτο, οὗ Μέλητός μοι τιμᾶται, ὅ
φημι οὐκ εἰδέναι οὔτ' εἰ ἀγαθὸν οὔτ' εἰ κακόν
ἐστιν; ἀντὶ τούτου δὴ ἕλωμαι ὧν εὖ οἶδ' ὅτι
κακῶν ὄντων; τοῦ τιμησάμενος; πότερον δε-
C σμοῦ; καὶ τί | με δεῖ ζῆν ἐν δεσμωτηρίῳ,
δουλεύοντα τῇ ἀεὶ καθισταμένῃ ἀρχῇ [, τοῖς
ἕνδεκα]; ἀλλὰ χρημάτων, καὶ δεδέσθαι, ἕως
ἂν ἐκτείσω; ἀλλὰ ταὐτόν μοί ἐστιν, ὅπερ νῦν
δὴ ἔλεγον· οὐ γὰρ ἔστι μοι χρήματα, ὁπόθεν
ἐκτείσω. ἀλλὰ δὴ φυγῆς τιμήσωμαι; ἴσως
γὰρ ἄν μοι τούτου τιμήσαιτε. πολλὴ μεντἂν
με φιλοψυχία ἔχοι, εἰ οὕτως ἀλόγιστός εἰμι,

ὥστε μὴ δύνασθαι λογίζεσθαι ὅτι ὑμεῖς μὲν 37
ὄντες πολῖταί μου οὐχ οἷοίτε ἐγένεσθε ἐνεγκεῖν
τὰς ἐμὰς διατριβὰς | καὶ τοὺς λόγους, ἀλλ' D
ὑμῖν βαρύτεραι γεγόνασιν καὶ ἐπιφθονώτεραι,
ὥστε ζητεῖτε αὐτῶν νυνὶ ἀπαλλαγῆναι,—ἄλλοι
δὲ ἄρα αὐτὰς οἴσουσι ῥᾳδίως; πολλοῦ γε δεῖ,
ὦ Ἀθηναῖοι. καλὸς οὖν ἄν μοι ὁ βίος εἴη
ἐξελθόντι τηλικῷδε ἀνθρώπῳ ἄλλην ἐξ ἄλλης
πόλεως ἀμειβομένῳ καὶ ἐξελαυνομένῳ ζῆν. εὖ
γὰρ οἶδ' ὅτι, ὅποι ἂν ἔλθω, λέγοντος ἐμοῦ
ἀκροάσονται οἱ νέοι ὥσπερ ἐνθάδε· κἂν μὲν
τούτους ἀπελαύνω, οὗτοι ἐμὲ αὐτοὶ ἐξελῶσι,
πείθοντες τοὺς πρεσβυτέρους· ἐὰν δὲ μὴ |
ἀπελαύνω, οἱ τούτων πατέρες τε καὶ οἰκεῖοι δι' E
αὐτοὺς τούτους. ——

Ἴσως οὖν ἄν τις εἴποι· σιγῶν δὲ καὶ ἡσυχίαν
ἄγων, ὦ Σώκρατες, οὐχ οἷόστ' ἔσει
ἡμῖν ἐξελθὼν ζῆν; τουτὶ δή ἐστι
πάντων χαλεπώτατον πεῖσαί τινας
ὑμῶν. ἐάντε γὰρ λέγω ὅτι τῷ θεῷ
ἀπειθεῖν τοῦτ' ἔστιν καὶ διὰ τοῦτο
ἀδύνατον ἡσυχίαν ἄγειν, οὐ πείσεσθέ μοι ὡς
εἰρωνευομένῳ· | ἐάντ' αὖ λέγω ὅτι καὶ τυγχάνει 38
μέγιστον ἀγαθὸν ὂν ἀνθρώπῳ τοῦτο, ἑκάστης
ἡμέρας περὶ ἀρετῆς τοὺς λόγους ποιεῖσθαι καὶ
τῶν ἄλλων, περὶ ὧν ὑμεῖς ἐμοῦ ἀκούετε δια-
λεγομένου καὶ ἐμαυτὸν καὶ ἄλλους ἐξετάζοντος,
ὁ δὲ ἀνεξέταστος βίος οὐ βιωτὸς ἀνθρώπῳ,
ταῦτα δ' ἔτι ἧττον πείσεσθέ μοι λέγοντι. τὰ
δὲ ἔχει μὲν οὕτως, ὡς ἐγώ φημι, ὦ ἄνδρες,
πείθειν δὲ οὐ ῥᾴδιον. καὶ ἐγὼ ἅμα οὐκ εἴθι-

nor could I change my life. But my friends here offer to pay a fine of thirty minae.

38 σμαι ἐμαυτὸν ἀξιοῦν κακοῦ οὐδενός. εἰ μὲν
B γὰρ ἦν μοι χρήματα, ἐτιμησάμην | ἂν χρημάτων ὅσα ἔμελλον ἐκτείσειν· οὐδὲν γὰρ ἂν ἐβλάβην· νῦν δὲ οὐ γὰρ ἔστιν, εἰ μὴ ἄρα ὅσον ἂν ἐγὼ δυναίμην ἐκτεῖσαι, τοσούτου βούλεσθέ μοι τιμῆσαι. ἴσως δ' ἂν δυναίμην ἐκτεῖσαι ὑμῖν μνᾶν ἀργυρίου· τοσούτου οὖν τιμῶμαι. Πλάτων δὲ ὅδε, ὦ ἄνδρες Ἀθηναῖοι, καὶ Κρίτων καὶ Κριτόβουλος καὶ Ἀπολλόδωρος κελεύουσί με τριάκοντα μνῶν τιμήσασθαι, αὐτοὶ δ' ἐγγυᾶσθαι· τιμῶμαι οὖν τοσούτου, ἐγγυηταὶ δὲ ὑμῖν ἔσονται τοῦ ἀργυρίου οὗτοι ἀξιόχρεῳ.

After the Sentence "Death."

You who have condemned me will win disgrace cheaply —Death would soon have come to an old man.

C | Οὐ πολλοῦ γ' ἕνεκα χρόνου, ὦ ἄνδρες Ἀθηναῖοι, ὄνομα ἕξετε καὶ αἰτίαν ὑπὸ τῶν βουλομένων τὴν πόλιν λοιδορεῖν, ὡς Σωκράτη ἀπεκτόνατε, ἄνδρα σοφόν· φήσουσι γὰρ δή με σοφὸν εἶναι, εἰ καὶ μή εἰμι, οἱ βουλόμενοι ὑμῖν ὀνειδίζειν. εἰ οὖν περιεμείνατε ὀλίγον χρόνον, ἀπὸ τοῦ αὐτομάτου ἂν ὑμῖν τοῦτο ἐγένετο· ὁρᾶτε γὰρ δὴ τὴν ἡλικίαν, ὅτι πόρρω ἤδη ἐστὶ τοῦ βίου, θανάτου δὲ ἐγγύς. λέγω δὲ τοῦτο
D οὐ πρὸς πάντας ὑμᾶς, ἀλλὰ πρὸς τοὺς | ἐμοῦ καταψηφισαμένους θάνατον. λέγω δὲ καὶ τόδε πρὸς τοὺς αὐτοὺς τούτους. ἴσως με οἴεσθε, ὦ ἄνδρες, ἀπορίᾳ λόγων ἑαλωκέναι τοιούτων, οἷς ἂν ὑμᾶς ἔπεισα, εἰ ᾤμην δεῖν ἅπαντα ποιεῖν καὶ λέγειν, ὥστε ἀποφυγεῖν τὴν δίκην. πολλοῦ

γε δεῖ. ἀλλ' ἀπορίᾳ μὲν ἑάλωκα, οὐ μέντοι 38
λόγων, ἀλλὰ τόλμης καὶ ἀναισχυντίας καὶ τοῦ
ἐθέλειν λέγειν πρὸς ὑμᾶς τοιαῦτα, οἷ' ἂν ὑμῖν
ἥδιστα ἦν ἀκούειν, θρηνοῦντός τέ μου καὶ ὀδυρο-
μένου καὶ ἄλλα ποιοῦντος καὶ | λέγοντος πολλὰ E
καὶ ἀνάξια ἐμοῦ, ὡς ἐγώ φημι· οἷα δὴ καὶ
εἴθισθε ὑμεῖς τῶν ἄλλων ἀκούειν. ἀλλ' οὔτε
τότε ᾠήθην δεῖν ἕνεκα τοῦ κινδύνου πρᾶξαι οὐδὲν
ἀνελεύθερον, οὔτε νῦν μοι μεταμέλει
οὕτως ἀπολογησαμένῳ, ἀλλὰ πολὺ
μᾶλλον αἱροῦμαι ὧδε ἀπολογησάμενος τεθνάναι
ἢ ἐκείνως ζῆν. οὔτε γὰρ ἐν δίκῃ οὔτ' ἐν
πολέμῳ οὔτ' ἐμὲ οὔτ' ἄλλον οὐδένα δεῖ τοῦτο
| μηχανᾶσθαι, ὅπως ἀποφεύξεται πᾶν ποιῶν 39
θάνατον. καὶ γὰρ ἐν ταῖς μάχαις πολλάκις
δῆλον γίγνεται ὅτι τό γε ἀποθανεῖν ἄν τις
ἐκφύγοι καὶ ὅπλα ἀφεὶς καὶ ἐφ' ἱκετείαν
τραπόμενος τῶν διωκόντων· καὶ ἄλλαι μηχαναὶ
πολλαί εἰσιν ἐν ἑκάστοις τοῖς κινδύνοις, ὥστε
διαφεύγειν θάνατον, ἐάν τις τολμᾷ πᾶν ποιεῖν
καὶ λέγειν. ἀλλὰ μὴ οὐ τοῦτ' ᾖ χαλεπόν, ὦ
ἄνδρες, θάνατον ἐκφυγεῖν, ἀλλὰ πολὺ χαλεπώ-
τερον πονηρίαν· θᾶττον γὰρ θανάτου θεῖ. καὶ
| νῦν ἐγὼ μὲν ἅτε βραδὺς ὢν καὶ πρεσβύτης B
ὑπὸ τοῦ βραδυτέρου ἑάλων, οἱ δ' ἐμοὶ κατήγοροι
ἅτε δεινοὶ καὶ ὀξεῖς ὄντες ὑπὸ τοῦ θάττονος,
τῆς κακίας. καὶ νῦν ἐγὼ μὲν ἄπειμι ὑφ'
ὑμῶν θανάτου δίκην ὀφλών, οὗτοι δ' ὑπὸ
τῆς ἀληθείας ὠφληκότες μοχθηρίαν
καὶ ἀδικίαν. καὶ ἔγωγε τῷ τιμή-
ματι ἐμμένω—καὶ οὗτοι. ταῦτα μέν που ἴσως

I repent not of my words,

and I abide by the award.

39 οὕτως καὶ ἔδει σχεῖν, καὶ οἶμαι αὐτὰ μετρίως ἔχειν.

Τὸ δὲ δὴ μετὰ τοῦτο ἐπιθυμῶ ὑμῖν χρη-
C σμῳδῆσαι, | ὦ καταψηφισάμενοί μου· καὶ γάρ εἰμι ἤδη ἐνταῦθα, ἐν ᾧ μάλιστα ἄνθρωποι χρησμῳδοῦσιν, ὅταν μέλλωσιν ἀποθανεῖσθαι. φημὶ γάρ, ὦ ἄνδρες, οἳ ἐμὲ ἀπεκτόνατε, τιμωρίαν ὑμῖν ἥξειν εὐθὺς μετὰ τὸν ἐμὸν θάνατον πολὺ χαλεπωτέραν νὴ Δία ἢ οἵαν ἐμὲ ἀπεκτόνατε· νῦν γὰρ τοῦτο εἴργασασθε οἰόμενοι ἀπαλλάξεσθαι τοῦ διδόναι ἔλεγχον τοῦ βίου· τὸ δὲ ὑμῖν πολὺ ἐναντίον ἀποβήσεται, ὡς ἐγώ φημι. πλείους ἔσονται ὑμᾶς οἱ ἐλέγχοντες,
D οὓς νῦν ἐγὼ κατεῖχον, ὑμεῖς | δὲ οὐκ ᾐσθάνεσθε· καὶ χαλεπώτεροι ἔσονται ὅσῳ νεώτεροί εἰσιν, καὶ ὑμεῖς μᾶλλον ἀγανακτήσετε. εἰ γὰρ οἴεσθε ἀποκτείνοντες ἀνθρώπους ἐπισχήσειν τοῦ ὀνειδίζειν τινὰ ὑμῖν ὅτι οὐκ ὀρθῶς ζῆτε, οὐκ ὀρθῶς διανοεῖσθε· οὐ γάρ ἐσθ' αὕτη ἡ ἀπαλλαγὴ οὔτε πάνυ δυνατὴ οὔτε καλή, ἀλλ' ἐκείνη καὶ καλλίστη καὶ ῥᾴστη, μὴ τοὺς ἄλλους κολούειν, ἀλλ' ἑαυτὸν παρασκευάζειν, ὅπως ἔσται ὡς βέλτιστος. ταῦτα μὲν οὖν ὑμῖν τοῖς καταψηφισαμένοις μαντευσάμενος ἀπαλλάττομαι.

For you, I prophesy no escape, thus, from confutation. Others will succeed me.

E | Τοῖς δὲ ἀποψηφισαμένοις ἡδέως ἂν διαλεχθείην ὑπὲρ τοῦ γεγονότος τουτουῒ πράγματος, ἐν ᾧ οἱ ἄρχοντες ἀσχολίαν ἄγουσι καὶ οὔπω ἔρχομαι οἷ ἐλθόντα με δεῖ τεθνάναι. ἀλλά μοι, ὦ ἄνδρες, παραμείνατε τοσοῦτον

To you who would have freed me I say: The God's sign has been silent; hence all must be well.

χρόνον· οὐδὲν γὰρ κωλύει διαμυθολογῆσαι 39
πρὸς ἀλλήλους, ἕως ἔξεστιν. ὑμῖν γὰρ ὡς
| φίλοις οὖσιν ἐπιδεῖξαι ἐθέλω τὸ νυνί μοι 40
ξυμβεβηκὸς τί ποτε νοεῖ. ἐμοὶ γάρ, ὦ ἄνδρες
δικασταί (ὑμᾶς γὰρ δικαστὰς καλῶν ὀρθῶς ἂν
καλοίην), θαυμάσιόν τι γέγονεν. ἡ γὰρ εἰωθυῖά
μοι μαντικὴ [ἡ τοῦ δαιμονίου] ἐν μὲν τῷ
πρόσθεν χρόνῳ παντὶ πάνυ πυκνὴ ἀεὶ ἦν καὶ
πάνυ ἐπὶ σμικροῖς ἐναντιουμένη, εἴ τι μέλλοιμι
μὴ ὀρθῶς πράξειν· νυνὶ δὲ ξυμβέβηκέ μοι,
ἅπερ ὁρᾶτε καὶ αὐτοί, ταυτὶ ἅ γε δὴ οἰηθείη
ἄν τις καὶ νομίζεται ἔσχατα κακῶν εἶναι.
ἐμοὶ δὲ οὔτε ἐξιόντι ἕωθεν οἴκοθεν | ἠναντιώθη B
τὸ τοῦ θεοῦ σημεῖον, οὔτε ἡνίκα ἀνέβαινον
ἐνταυθοῖ ἐπὶ τὸ δικαστήριον, οὔτε ἐν τῷ λόγῳ
οὐδαμοῦ μέλλοντί τι ἐρεῖν. καίτοι ἐν ἄλλοις
λόγοις πολλαχοῦ δή με ἐπέσχε λέγοντα μεταξύ·
νῦν δὲ οὐδαμοῦ περὶ ταύτην τὴν πρᾶξιν οὔτ'
ἐν ἔργῳ οὐδενὶ οὔτ' ἐν λόγῳ ἠναντίωταί μοι.
τί οὖν αἴτιον εἶναι ὑπολαμβάνω; ἐγὼ ὑμῖν
ἐρῶ· κινδυνεύει γάρ μοι τὸ ξυμβεβηκὸς τοῦτο
ἀγαθὸν γεγονέναι, καὶ οὐκ ἔσθ' ὅπως ἡμεῖς
ὀρθῶς ὑπολαμβάνομεν, ὅσοι οἰόμεθα | κακὸν C
εἶναι τὸ τεθνάναι. μέγα μοι τεκμήριον τούτου
γέγονεν· οὐ γὰρ ἔσθ' ὅπως οὐκ ἠναντιώθη ἄν
μοι τὸ εἰωθὸς σημεῖον, εἰ μή τι ἔμελλον ἐγὼ
ἀγαθὸν πράξειν.

Ἐννοήσωμεν δὲ καὶ τῇδε, ὡς πολλὴ ἐλπίς
ἐστιν ἀγαθὸν αὐτὸ εἶναι. δυοῖν γὰρ
θάτερόν ἐστιν τὸ τεθνάναι· ἢ γὰρ
οἷον μηδὲν εἶναι μηδὲ αἴσθησιν

Death is no evil, whether unconsciousness or a

40 joining elsewhere those already dead.

μηδεμίαν μηδενὸς ἔχειν τὸν τεθνεῶτα, ἢ κατὰ τὰ λεγόμενα μεταβολή τις τυγχάνει οὖσα καὶ μετοίκησις τῇ ψυχῇ τοῦ τόπου τοῦ ἐνθένδε εἰς ἄλλον τόπον. καὶ εἴτε
D μηδεμία αἴσθησίς ἐστιν, ἀλλ' | οἷον ὕπνος, ἐπειδάν τις καθεύδων μηδ' ὄναρ μηδὲν ὁρᾷ, θαυμάσιον κέρδος ἂν εἴη ὁ θάνατος. ἐγὼ γὰρ ἂν οἶμαι, εἴ τινα ἐκλεξάμενον δέοι ταύτην τὴν νύκτα, ἐν ᾗ οὕτω κατέδαρθεν, ὥστε μηδὲ ὄναρ ἰδεῖν, καὶ τὰς ἄλλας νύκτας τε καὶ ἡμέρας τὰς τοῦ βίου τοῦ ἑαυτοῦ ἀντιπαραθέντα ταύτῃ τῇ νυκτί—δέοι σκεψάμενον εἰπεῖν, πόσας ἄμεινον καὶ ἥδιον ἡμέρας καὶ νύκτας ταύτης τῆς νυκτὸς βεβίωκεν ἐν τῷ ἑαυτοῦ βίῳ, οἶμαι ἂν μὴ ὅτι ἰδιώτην τινά, ἀλλὰ τὸν μέγαν βασιλέα εὐαριθ-
E μήτους | ἂν εὑρεῖν αὐτὸν ταύτας πρὸς τὰς ἄλλας ἡμέρας καὶ νύκτας. εἰ οὖν τοιοῦτον ὁ θάνατός ἐστιν, κέρδος ἔγωγε λέγω· καὶ γὰρ οὐδὲν πλείων ὁ πᾶς χρόνος φαίνεται οὕτω δὴ εἶναι ἢ μία νύξ. εἰ δ' αὖ οἷον ἀποδημῆσαί ἐστιν ὁ θάνατος ἐνθένδε εἰς ἄλλον τόπον, καὶ ἀληθῆ ἐστιν τὰ λεγόμενα, ὡς ἄρα ἐκεῖ εἰσιν ἅπαντες οἱ τεθνεῶτες, τί μεῖζον ἀγαθὸν τούτου εἴη ἄν, ὦ ἄνδρες δικασταί; εἰ γάρ τις ἀφικό-
41 μενος εἰς Ἅιδου, ἀπαλλαγεὶς τούτων | τῶν φασκόντων δικαστῶν εἶναι, εὑρήσει τοὺς ἀληθῶς δικαστάς, οἵπερ καὶ λέγονται ἐκεῖ δικάζειν, Μίνως τε καὶ Ῥαδάμανθυς καὶ Αἰακὸς καὶ Τριπτόλεμος καὶ ἄλλοι ὅσοι τῶν ἡμιθέων δίκαιοι ἐγένοντο ἐν τῷ ἑαυτῶν βίῳ, ἆρα φαύλη ἂν εἴη ἡ ἀποδημία; ἢ αὖ Ὀρφεῖ ξυγγενέσθαι

καὶ Μουσαίῳ καὶ Ἡσιόδῳ καὶ Ὁμήρῳ ἐπὶ 41 πόσῳ ἄν τις δέξαιτ' ἂν ὑμῶν; ἐγὼ μὲν γὰρ πολλάκις ἐθέλω τεθνάναι, εἰ ταῦτ' ἔστιν ἀληθῆ· ἐπεὶ ἔμοιγε καὶ αὐτῷ θαυμαστὴ ἂν εἴη ἡ διατριβὴ αὐτόθι, | ὁπότε ἐντύχοιμι Παλαμήδει B καὶ Αἴαντι τῷ Τελαμῶνος καὶ εἴ τις ἄλλος τῶν παλαιῶν διὰ κρίσιν ἄδικον τέθνηκεν, ἀντιπαραβάλλοντι τὰ ἐμαυτοῦ πάθη πρὸς τὰ ἐκείνων, ὡς ἐγὼ οἶμαι,—οὐκ ἂν ἀηδὴς εἴη. καὶ δὴ τὸ μέγιστον, τοὺς ἐκεῖ ἐξετάζοντα καὶ ἐρευνῶντα ὥσπερ τοὺς ἐνταῦθα διάγειν, τίς αὐτῶν σοφός ἐστιν καὶ τίς οἴεται μέν, ἔστιν δ' οὔ— ἐπὶ πόσῳ δἄν τις, ὦ ἄνδρες δικασταί, δέξαιτο ἐξετάσαι τὸν ἐπὶ Τροίαν ἀγαγόντα τὴν πολλὴν στρατιὰν ἢ Ὀδυσσέα ἢ | Σίσυφον, ἢ—ἄλλους C μυρίους ἄν τις εἴποι καὶ ἄνδρας καὶ γυναῖκας; οἷς ἐκεῖ διαλέγεσθαι καὶ ξυνεῖναι καὶ ἐξετάζειν ἀμήχανον ἂν εἴη εὐδαιμονίας. πάντως οὐ δήπου τούτου γε ἕνεκα οἱ ἐκεῖ ἀποκτείνουσι· τά τε γὰρ ἄλλα εὐδαιμονέστεροί εἰσιν οἱ ἐκεῖ τῶν ἐνθάδε, καὶ ἤδη τὸν λοιπὸν χρόνον ἀθάνατοί εἰσιν, εἴπερ γε τὰ λεγόμενα ἀληθῆ ἐστιν.

Be of good hope. No harm befalls the good man.

Ἀλλὰ καὶ ὑμᾶς χρή, ὦ ἄνδρες δικασταί, εὐέλπιδας εἶναι πρὸς τὸν θάνατον, καὶ ἕν τι τοῦτο διανοεῖσθαι ἀληθές, ὅτι οὐκ ἔστιν ἀνδρὶ ἀγαθῷ | κακὸν D οὐδὲν οὔτε ζῶντι οὔτε τελευτήσαντι, οὐδὲ ἀμελεῖται ὑπὸ θεῶν τὰ τούτου πράγματα· οὐδὲ τὰ ἐμὰ νῦν ἀπὸ τοῦ αὐτομάτου γέγονεν, ἀλλά μοι δῆλόν ἐστι τοῦτο, ὅτι ἤδη τεθνάναι καὶ ἀπηλλάχθαι πραγμάτων βέλτιον ἦν μοι. διὰ

41 τοῦτο καὶ ἐμὲ οὐδαμοῦ ἀπέτρεψεν · τὸ σημεῖον,
καὶ ἔγωγε τοῖς καταψηφισαμένοις μου καὶ τοῖς
κατηγόροις οὐ πάνυ χαλεπαίνω. καίτοι οὐ
ταύτῃ τῇ διανοίᾳ κατεψηφίζοντό μου καὶ
κατηγόρουν, ἀλλ' οἰόμενοι βλάπτειν· τοῦτο
E αὐτοῖς | ἄξιον μέμφεσθαι. τοσόνδε
μέντοι αὐτῶν δέομαι· τοὺς ὑεῖς μου,
ἐπειδὰν ἡβήσωσι, τιμωρήσασθε, ὦ
ἄνδρες, ταὐτὰ ταῦτα λυποῦντες, ἅπερ
ἐγὼ ὑμᾶς ἐλύπουν· ἐὰν ὑμῖν δοκῶσιν ἢ χρημά-
των ἢ ἄλλου του πρότερον ἐπιμελεῖσθαι ἢ
ἀρετῆς, καὶ ἐὰν δοκῶσί τι εἶναι μηδὲν ὄντες,
ὀνειδίζετε αὐτοῖς, ὥσπερ ἐγὼ ὑμῖν, ὅτι οὐκ
ἐπιμελοῦνται ὧν δεῖ, καὶ οἴονταί τι εἶναι ὄντες
οὐδενὸς ἄξιοι. καὶ ἐὰν ταῦτα ποιῆτε, δίκαια |
42 πεπονθὼς ἐγὼ ἔσομαι ὑφ' ὑμῶν, αὐτός τε καὶ
οἱ ὑεῖς. ἀλλὰ γὰρ ἤδη ὥρα ἀπιέναι, ἐμοὶ μὲν
ἀποθανουμένῳ, ὑμῖν δὲ βιωσομένοις· ὁπότεροι
δὲ ἡμῶν ἔρχονται ἐπὶ ἄμεινον πρᾶγμα, ἄδηλον
παντὶ πλὴν εἰ τῷ θεῷ.

Reprove my sons, as I have you, if they are wise in their own conceit. Adieu.

CRITO

(*Entire*)

Socrates in Prison refuses all means of Escape.

SOCRATES. CRITO.

43
A ΣΩ. Τί τηνικάδε ἀφῖξαι, ὦ Κρίτων; ἢ οὐ πρῲ ἔτι ἐστίν;

ΚΡ. Πάνυ μὲν οὖν.

Crito comes at dawn. For the mission-ship has been sighted, and Socrates must now die.

ΣΩ. Πηνίκα μάλιστα; 43

ΚΡ. Ὄρθρος βαθύς.

ΣΩ. Θαυμάζω ὅπως ἠθέλησέ σοι ὁ τοῦ δεσμωτηρίου φύλαξ ὑπακοῦσαι.

ΚΡ. Ξυνήθης ἤδη μοί ἐστιν, ὦ Σώκρατες, διὰ τὸ πολλάκις δεῦρο φοιτᾶν, καί τι καὶ εὐεργέτηται ὑπ' ἐμοῦ.

ΣΩ. Ἄρτι δὲ ἥκεις ἢ πάλαι;

ΚΡ. Ἐπιεικῶς πάλαι.

ΣΩ. Εἶτα πῶς | οὐκ εὐθὺς ἐπήγειράς με, B ἀλλὰ σιγῇ παρακάθησαι;

ΚΡ. Οὐ μὰ τὸν Δία, ὦ Σώκρατες, οὐδ' ἂν αὐτὸς ἤθελον ἐν τοσαύτῃ τε ἀγρυπνίᾳ καὶ λύπῃ εἶναι. ἀλλὰ καὶ σοῦ πάλαι θαυμάζω, αἰσθανόμενος ὡς ἡδέως καθεύδεις· καὶ ἐπίτηδές σε οὐκ ἤγειρον, ἵνα ὡς ἥδιστα διάγῃς. καὶ πολλάκις μὲν δή σε καὶ πρότερον ἐν παντὶ τῷ βίῳ ηὐδαιμόνισα τοῦ τρόπου, πολὺ δὲ μάλιστα ἐν τῇ νῦν παρεστώσῃ ξυμφορᾷ, ὡς ῥᾳδίως αὐτὴν καὶ πρᾴως φέρεις.

ΣΩ. Καὶ γὰρ ἄν, ὦ Κρίτων, πλημμελὲς εἴη ἀγανακτεῖν τηλικοῦτον ὄντα, εἰ δεῖ ἤδη τελευτᾶν.

ΚΡ. | Καὶ ἄλλοι, ὦ Σώκρατες, τηλικοῦτοι ἐν C τοιαύταις ξυμφοραῖς ἁλίσκονται, ἀλλ' οὐδὲν αὐτοὺς ἐπιλύεται ἡ ἡλικία τὸ μὴ οὐχὶ ἀγανακτεῖν τῇ παρούσῃ τύχῃ.

ΣΩ. Ἔστι ταῦτα. ἀλλὰ τί δὴ οὕτω πρῴ ἀφῖξαι;

ΚΡ. Ἀγγελίαν, ὦ Σώκρατες, φέρων χαλεπήν, οὐ σοί, ὡς ἐμοὶ φαίνεται, ἀλλ' ἐμοὶ καὶ τοῖς

43 σοῖς ἐπιτηδείοις πᾶσιν καὶ χαλεπὴν καὶ βαρεῖαν, ἣν ἐγώ, ὡς ἐμοὶ δοκῶ, ἐν τοῖς βαρυτατ' ἂν ἐνέγκαιμι.

ΣΩ. Τίνα ταύτην; ἢ τὸ πλοῖον ἀφῖκται ἐκ
D Δήλου, οὗ δεῖ ἀφικομένου | τεθνάναι με;

ΚΡ. Οὔτοι δὴ ἀφῖκται, ἀλλὰ δοκεῖ μέν μοι ἥξειν τήμερον ἐξ ὧν ἀπαγγέλλουσιν ἥκοντές τινες ἀπὸ Σουνίου καὶ καταλιπόντες ἐκεῖ αὐτό. δῆλον οὖν ἐκ τούτων τῶν ἀγγέλων ὅτι ἥξει τήμερον, καὶ ἀνάγκη δὴ εἰς αὔριον ἔσται, ὦ Σώκρατες, τὸν βίον σε τελευτᾶν.

ΣΩ. Ἀλλ', ὦ Κρίτων, τύχῃ ἀγαθῇ. εἰ ταύτῃ τοῖς θεοῖς φίλον, ταύτῃ ἔστω. οὐ μέντοι οἶμαι ἥξειν αὐτὸ τήμερον.

44 ΚΡ. | Πόθεν τοῦτο τεκμαίρει;

ΣΩ. Ἐγώ σοι ἐρῶ. τῇ γάρ που ὑστεραίᾳ δεῖ με ἀποθνῄσκειν ἢ ᾗ ἂν ἔλθῃ τὸ πλοῖον.

ΚΡ. Φασί γέ τοι δὴ οἱ τούτων κύριοι.

ΣΩ. Οὐ τοίνυν τῆς ἐπιούσης ἡμέρας οἶμαι αὐτὸ ἥξειν, ἀλλὰ τῆς ἑτέρας. τεκμαίρομαι δὲ ἔκ τινος ἐνυπνίου, ὃ ἑώρακα ὀλίγον πρότερον ταύτης τῆς νυκτός· καὶ κινδυνεύεις ἐν καιρῷ τινι οὐκ ἐγεῖραί με.

ΚΡ. Ἦν δὲ δὴ τί τὸ ἐνύπνιον;

ΣΩ. Ἐδόκει τίς μοι γυνὴ προσελθοῦσα καλὴ καὶ εὐειδής, λευκὰ ἱμάτια ἔχουσα, καλέσαι με |
B καὶ εἰπεῖν· Ὦ Σώκρατες, ἤματί κεν τριτάτῳ Φθίην ἐρίβωλον ἵκοιο.

ΚΡ. Ἄτοπον τὸ ἐνύπνιον, ὦ Σώκρατες.

ΣΩ. Ἐναργὲς μὲν οὖν, ὥς γέ μοι δοκεῖ, ὦ Κρίτων.

Crito urges him yet to fly: First, what will men think of us your friends, if we let you perish?

ΚΡ. Λίαν γε, ὡς ἔοικεν. ἀλλ᾽, ὦ δαιμόνιε 44 Σώκρατες, ἔτι καὶ νῦν ἐμοὶ πείθου καὶ σώθητι· ὡς ἐμοί, ἐὰν σὺ ἀποθάνῃς, οὐ μία ξυμφορά ἐστιν, ἀλλὰ χωρὶς μὲν σοῦ ἐστερῆσθαι, τοιούτου ἐπιτηδείου οἷον ἐγὼ οὐδένα μήποτε εὑρήσω, ἔτι δὲ καὶ πολλοῖς δόξω, οἳ ἐμὲ καὶ σὲ μὴ σαφῶς ἴσασιν, ὡς οἷόστ᾽ | C ὢν σε σῴζειν, εἰ ἤθελον ἀναλίσκειν χρήματα, ἀμελῆσαι. καίτοι τίς ἂν αἰσχίων εἴη ταύτης δόξα—ἢ δοκεῖν χρήματα περὶ πλείονος ποιεῖσθαι ἢ φίλους; οὐ γὰρ πείσονται οἱ πολλοὶ ὡς σὺ αὐτὸς οὐκ ἠθέλησας ἀπιέναι ἐνθένδε, ἡμῶν προθυμουμένων.

ΣΩ. Ἀλλὰ τί ἡμῖν, ὦ μακάριε Κρίτων, οὕτω τῆς τῶν πολλῶν δόξης μέλει; οἱ γὰρ ἐπιεικέστατοι, ὧν μᾶλλον ἄξιον φροντίζειν, ἡγήσονται αὐτὰ οὕτω πεπρᾶχθαι, ὥσπερ ἂν πραχθῇ.

ΚΡ. Ἀλλ᾽ ὁρᾷς δὴ ὅτι ἀνάγκη, ὦ Σώκρατες, | D καὶ τῆς τῶν πολλῶν δόξης μέλειν. αὐτὰ δὲ δῆλα τὰ παρόντα νυνί, ὅτι οἷοίτ᾽ εἰσὶν οἱ πολλοὶ οὐ τὰ σμικρότατα τῶν κακῶν ἐξεργάζεσθαι, ἀλλὰ τὰ μέγιστα σχεδόν, ἐάν τις ἐν αὐτοῖς διαβεβλημένος ᾖ.

ΣΩ. Εἰ γὰρ ὤφελον, ὦ Κρίτων, οἷοίτ᾽ εἶναι οἱ πολλοὶ τὰ μέγιστα κακὰ ἐργάζεσθαι, ἵνα οἷοίτ᾽ ἦσαν καὶ ἀγαθὰ τὰ μέγιστα, καὶ καλῶς ἂν εἶχεν· νῦν δὲ οὐδέτερα οἷοίτε· οὔτε γὰρ φρόνιμον οὔτε ἄφρονα δυνατοὶ ποιῆσαι, ποιοῦσι δὲ τοῦτο ὅ τι ἂν τύχωσι.

44 ΚΡ. Ταῦτα μὲν δὴ οὕτως | ἐχέτω· τάδε δέ,
E ὦ Σώκρατες, εἰπέ μοι. ἆρά γε μὴ ἐμοῦ προμηθεῖ καὶ τῶν ἄλλων ἐπιτηδείων, μή, ἐὰν σὺ ἐνθένδε ἐξέλθῃς, οἱ συκοφάνται ἡμῖν πράγματα παρέχωσιν ὡς σε ἐνθένδε ἐκκλέψασιν, καὶ ἀναγκασθῶμεν ἢ καὶ πᾶσαν τὴν οὐσίαν ἀποβαλεῖν ἢ συχνὰ χρήματα, ἢ καὶ ἄλλο τι πρὸς τούτοις
45 παθεῖν; εἰ γάρ τι τοιοῦτον | φοβεῖ, ἔασον αὐτὸ χαίρειν· ἡμεῖς γάρ που δίκαιοί ἐσμεν σώσαντές σε κινδυνεύειν τοῦτον τὸν κίνδυνον καί, ἐὰν δέῃ, ἔτι τούτου μείζω. ἀλλ' ἐμοὶ πείθου καὶ μὴ ἄλλως ποίει.

Second be not concerned on our account. Bribery is cheap, and we are many.

ΣΩ. Καὶ ταῦτα προμηθοῦμαι, ὦ Κρίτων, καὶ ἄλλα πολλά.

ΚΡ. Μήτε τοίνυν ταῦτα φοβοῦ· καὶ γὰρ οὐδὲ πολὺ τἀργύριόν ἐστιν, ὃ 'θέλουσι λαβόντες τινὲς σῶσαί σε καὶ ἐξαγαγεῖν ἐνθένδε. ἔπειτα οὐχ ὁρᾷς τούτους τοὺς συκοφάντας ὡς εὐτελεῖς, καὶ οὐδὲν ἂν δέοι ἐπ' αὐτοὺς πολλοῦ ἀργυρίου;
B σοὶ δὲ ὑπάρχει μὲν | τὰ ἐμὰ χρήματα, ὡς ἐγὼ οἶμαι, ἱκανά· ἔπειτα καὶ εἴ τι ἐμοῦ κηδόμενος οὐκ οἴει δεῖν ἀναλίσκειν τἀμά, ξένοι αὖ τοι ἐνθάδε ἕτοιμοι ἀναλίσκειν· εἷς δὲ καὶ κεκόμικεν ἐπ' αὐτὸ τοῦτο ἀργύριον ἱκανόν, Σιμμίας ὁ Θηβαῖος· ἕτοιμος δὲ καὶ Κέβης καὶ ἄλλοι πολλοὶ πάνυ. ὥστε, ὅπερ λέγω, μήτε ταῦτα φοβούμενος ἀποκάμῃς σαυτὸν σῶσαι, μήτε ὃ ἔλεγες ἐν τῷ δικαστηρίῳ δυσχερές σοι γενέσθω, ὅτι οὐκ ἂν ἔχοις ἐξελθὼν ὅ τι χρῷο σαυτῷ· πολλαχοῦ μὲν γὰρ καὶ ἄλλοσε ὅποι ἂν ἀφίκῃ

ἀγαπήσουσί | σε· ἐὰν δὲ βούλῃ εἰς Θετταλίαν 45
ἰέναι, εἰσὶν ἐμοὶ ἐκεῖ ξένοι, οἵ σε περὶ πολλοῦ C
ποιήσονται καὶ ἀσφάλειάν σοι παρέξονται, ὥστε
σε μηδένα λυπεῖν τῶν κατὰ Θετταλίαν.
Ἔτι δέ, ὦ Σώκρατες, οὐδὲ δίκαιόν μοι
δοκεῖς ἐπιχειρεῖν πρᾶγμα, σαυτὸν
προδοῦναι, ἐξὸν σωθῆναι· καὶ τοιαῦτα
σπεύδεις περὶ σαυτὸν γενέσθαι, ἅπερ
ἂν καὶ οἱ ἐχθροί σου σπεύσαιέν τε
καὶ ἔσπευσάν σε διαφθεῖραι βουλό-
μενοι. πρὸς δὲ τούτοις καὶ τοὺς ὑεῖς τοὺς σαυτοῦ
ἔμοιγε δοκεῖς προδιδόναι, οὕς σοι ἐξὸν καὶ
ἐκθρέψαι | καὶ ἐκπαιδεῦσαι οἰχήσει καταλιπών, D
καὶ τὸ σὸν μέρος, ὅ τι ἂν τύχωσι, τοῦτο πρά-
ξουσιν· τεύξονται δέ, ὡς τὸ εἰκός, τοιούτων
οἷάπερ εἴωθεν γίγνεσθαι ἐν ταῖς ὀρφανίαις
περὶ τοὺς ὀρφανούς. ἢ γὰρ οὐ χρὴ ποιεῖσθαι
παῖδας ἢ ξυνδιαταλαιπωρεῖν καὶ τρέφοντα καὶ
παιδεύοντα· σὺ δέ μοι δοκεῖς τὰ ῥᾳθυμότατα
αἱρεῖσθαι· χρὴ δέ, ἅπερ ἂν ἀνὴρ ἀγαθὸς καὶ
ἀνδρεῖος ἕλοιτο, ταῦτα αἱρεῖσθαι, φάσκοντά γε
δὴ ἀρετῆς διὰ παντὸς τοῦ βίου ἐπιμελεῖσθαι·
ὡς ἔγωγε καὶ ὑπὲρ σοῦ καὶ ὑπὲρ | ἡμῶν τῶν E
σῶν ἐπιτηδείων αἰσχύνομαι, μὴ δόξῃ ἅπαν τὸ
πρᾶγμα τὸ περὶ σὲ ἀνανδρίᾳ τινὶ τῇ ἡμετέρᾳ
πεπρᾶχθαι—καὶ ἡ εἴσοδος τῆς δίκης εἰς τὸ
δικαστήριον, ὡς εἰσῆλθεν ἐξὸν μὴ εἰσελθεῖν,
καὶ αὐτὸς ὁ ἀγὼν τῆς δίκης, ὡς ἐγένετο, καὶ
τὸ τελευταῖον δὴ τουτί, ὥσπερ κατάγελως
τῆς πράξεως, κακίᾳ τινὶ καὶ ἀνανδρίᾳ τῇ
ἡμετέρᾳ διαπεφευγέναι | ἡμᾶς δοκεῖν, οἵτινές 46

Besides, it is not right to throw away life, desert your children, and expose us to ridicule.

46 σε οὐχὶ ἐσώσαμεν οὐδὲ σύ σαυτόν, οἷόντε ὂν καὶ δυνατόν, εἴ τι καὶ μικρὸν ἡμῶν ὄφελος ἦν. ταῦτα οὖν, ὦ Σώκρατες, ὅρα μὴ ἅμα τῷ κακῷ καὶ αἰσχρὰ ᾖ σοί τε καὶ ἡμῖν. ἀλλὰ βουλεύου, μᾶλλον δὲ οὐδὲ βουλεύεσθαι ἔτι ὥρα, ἀλλὰ βεβουλεῦσθαι. μία δὲ βουλή· τῆς γὰρ ἐπιούσης νυκτὸς πάντα ταῦτα δεῖ πεπρᾶχθαι. εἰ δ' ἔτι περιμενοῦμεν, ἀδύνατον καὶ οὐκέτι οἷόντε. ἀλλὰ παντὶ τρόπῳ, ὦ Σώκρατες, πείθου μοι καὶ μηδαμῶς ἄλλως ποίει.

B ΣΩ. Ὦ | φίλε Κρίτων, ἡ προθυμία σου πολλοῦ ἀξία, εἰ μετά τινος ὀρθότητος εἴη· εἰ δὲ μή, ὅσῳ μείζων, τοσούτῳ χαλεπωτέρα. σκοπεῖσθαι οὖν χρὴ ἡμᾶς, εἴτε ταῦτα πρακτέον εἴτε μή· ὡς ἐγὼ οὐ μόνον νῦν ἀλλὰ καὶ ἀεὶ τοιοῦτος, οἷος τῶν ἐμῶν μηδενὶ ἄλλῳ πείθεσθαι ἢ τῷ λόγῳ, ὃς ἄν μοι λογιζομένῳ βέλτιστος φαίνηται. τοὺς δὲ λόγους, οὓς ἐν τῷ ἔμπροσθεν ἔλεγον, οὐ δύναμαι νῦν ἐκβαλεῖν, ἐπειδή μοι ἥδε ἡ τύχη γέγονεν, ἀλλὰ σχεδόν τι ὅμοιοι φαίνονταί μοι, καὶ τοὺς αὐτοὺς πρεσβεύω |

But, Crito, what of all our fine reasoning heretofore? Were we not to disregard the opinion of the many,

C καὶ τιμῶ οὕσπερ καὶ πρότερον· ὧν ἐὰν μὴ βελτίω ἔχωμεν λέγειν ἐν τῷ παρόντι, εὖ ἴσθι ὅτι οὐ μή σοι ξυγχωρήσω, οὐδ' ἂν πλείω τῶν νῦν παρόντων ἡ τῶν πολλῶν δύναμις ὥσπερ παῖδας ἡμᾶς μορμολύττηται, δεσμοὺς καὶ θανάτους ἐπιπέμπουσα καὶ χρημάτων ἀφαιρέσεις. πῶς οὖν ἂν μετριώτατα σκοποίμεθα αὐτά; εἰ πρῶτον μὲν τοῦτον τὸν λόγον ἀναλάβοιμεν, ὃν σὺ λέγεις περὶ τῶν δοξῶν, πότερον καλῶς ἐλέγετο ἑκάστοτε ἢ οὔ, ὅτι ταῖς μὲν δεῖ τῶν 46 δοξῶν προσέχειν τὸν | νοῦν, ταῖς δὲ οὔ· ἢ D πρὶν μὲν ἐμὲ δεῖν ἀποθνῄσκειν καλῶς ἐλέγετο, νῦν δὲ κατάδηλος ἄρα ἐγένετο, ὅτι ἄλλως ἕνεκα λόγου ἐλέγετο, ἦν δὲ παιδιὰ καὶ φλυαρία ὡς ἀληθῶς; ἐπιθυμῶ δ' ἔγωγ' ἐπισκέψασθαι, ὦ Κρίτων, κοινῇ μετὰ σοῦ, εἴ τί μοι ἀλλοιότερος φανεῖται, ἐπειδὴ ὧδε ἔχω, ἢ ὁ αὐτός, καὶ ἐάσομεν χαίρειν ἢ πεισόμεθα αὐτῷ. ἐλέγετο δέ πως, ὡς ἐγᾦμαι, ἑκάστοτε ὧδε ὑπὸ τῶν οἰομένων τι λέγειν, ὥσπερ νῦν δὴ ἐγὼ ἔλεγον, ὅτι τῶν δοξῶν, ἃς οἱ ἄνθρωποι δοξάζουσιν, δέοι τὰς μὲν | περὶ πολλοῦ ποιεῖσθαι, τὰς δὲ E μή. τοῦτο πρὸς θεῶν, ὦ Κρίτων, οὐ δοκεῖ καλῶς σοι λέγεσθαι; σὺ γάρ (ὅσα γε τἀνθρώπεια) ἐκτὸς εἶ τοῦ μέλλειν ἀποθνῄσκειν | αὔριον, 47 καὶ οὐκ ἄν σε παρακρούοι ἡ παροῦσα ξυμφορά. σκόπει δή· οὐχ ἱκανῶς δοκεῖ σοι λέγεσθαι, ὅτι οὐ πάσας χρὴ τὰς δόξας τῶν ἀνθρώπων τιμᾶν, ἀλλὰ τὰς μέν, τὰς δ' οὔ; τί φῄς; ταῦτα οὐχὶ καλῶς λέγεται;

ΚΡ. Καλῶς.

ΣΩ. Οὐκοῦν τὰς μὲν χρηστὰς τιμᾶν, τὰς δὲ πονηρὰς μή;

ΚΡ. Ναί.

ΣΩ. Χρησταὶ δὲ οὐχ αἱ τῶν φρονίμων, πονηραὶ δὲ αἱ τῶν ἀφρόνων;

ΚΡ. Πῶς δ' οὔ;

ΣΩ. Φέρε δή, πῶς αὖ τὰ τοιαῦτα ἐλέγετο; γυμναζόμενος | ἀνὴρ καὶ τοῦτο πράττων πότερον B παντὸς ἀνδρὸς ἐπαίνῳ καὶ ψόγῳ καὶ δόξῃ τὸν

47 *as in matters of the body, so in those of the soul—i.e. right and wrong?*

νοῦν προσέχει, ἢ ἑνὸς μόνου ἐκείνου, ὃς ἂν τυγχάνῃ ἰατρὸς ἢ παιδοτρίβης ὤν;

ΚΡ. Ἑνὸς μόνου.

ΣΩ. Οὐκοῦν φοβεῖσθαι χρὴ τοὺς ψόγους καὶ ἀσπάζεσθαι τοὺς ἐπαίνους τοὺς τοῦ ἑνὸς ἐκείνου, ἀλλὰ μὴ τοὺς τῶν πολλῶν.

ΚΡ. Δῆλα δή.

ΣΩ. Ταύτῃ ἄρα αὐτῷ πρακτέον καὶ γυμναστέον καὶ ἐδεστέον γε καὶ ποτέον, ᾗ ἂν τῷ ἑνὶ δοκῇ, τῷ ἐπιστάτῃ καὶ ἐπαΐοντι, μᾶλλον ἢ ᾗ ξύμπασι τοῖς ἄλλοις.

ΚΡ. Ἔστι ταῦτα.

ΣΩ. Εἶεν. ἀπειθήσας δὲ τῷ ἑνὶ καὶ ἀτιμάσας C | αὐτοῦ τὴν δόξαν καὶ τοὺς ἐπαίνους, τιμήσας δὲ τοὺς τῶν πολλῶν λόγους καὶ μηδὲν ἐπαϊόντων, ἆρα οὐδὲν κακὸν πείσεται;

ΚΡ. Πῶς γὰρ οὔ;

ΣΩ. Τί δ' ἔστι τὸ κακὸν τοῦτο; καὶ ποῖ τείνει, καὶ εἰς τί τῶν τοῦ ἀπειθοῦντος;

ΚΡ. Δῆλον ὅτι εἰς τὸ σῶμα· τοῦτο γὰρ διόλλυσι.

ΣΩ. Καλῶς λέγεις. οὐκοῦν καὶ τἆλλα, ὦ Κρίτων, οὕτως (ἵνα μὴ πάντα διίωμεν), καὶ δὴ καὶ περὶ τῶν δικαίων καὶ ἀδίκων καὶ αἰσχρῶν καὶ καλῶν καὶ ἀγαθῶν καὶ κακῶν, περὶ ὧν νῦν ἡ βουλὴ ἡμῖν ἐστιν—πότερον τῇ τῶν D πολλῶν δόξῃ δεῖ ἡμᾶς | ἕπεσθαι καὶ φοβεῖσθαι αὐτὴν ἢ τῇ τοῦ ἑνός, εἴ τίς ἐστιν ἐπαΐων, ὃν δεῖ καὶ αἰσχύνεσθαι καὶ φοβεῖσθαι μᾶλλον ἢ ξύμπαντας τοὺς ἄλλους; ᾧ εἰ μὴ ἀκολου-

θήσομεν, διαφθεροῦμεν ἐκεῖνο καὶ λωβησόμεθα, 47
ὃ τῷ μὲν δικαίῳ βέλτιον ἐγίγνετο, τῷ δὲ ἀδίκῳ ἀπώλλυτο. ἢ οὐδέν ἐστι τοῦτο;

ΚΡ. Οἶμαι ἔγωγε, ὦ Σώκρατες.

ΣΩ. Φέρε δή, ἐὰν τὸ ὑπὸ τοῦ ὑγιεινοῦ μὲν βέλτιον γιγνόμενον ὑπὸ τοῦ νοσώδους δὲ διαφθειρόμενον διολέσωμεν πειθόμενοι μὴ τῇ τῶν ἐπαϊόντων δόξῃ, ἆρα βιωτὸν ἡμῖν ἐστιν | διεφθαρμένου E
αὐτοῦ; ἔστι δέ που τοῦτο τὸ σῶμα· ἢ οὐχί;

Life is not livable with either corrupted body, or corrupted soul;

ΚΡ. Ναί.

ΣΩ. Ἆρ' οὖν βιωτὸν ἡμῖν ἐστιν μετὰ μοχθηροῦ καὶ διεφθαρμένου σώματος;

ΚΡ. Οὐδαμῶς.

ΣΩ. Ἀλλὰ μετ' ἐκείνου ἆρ' ἡμῖν βιωτὸν διεφθαρμένου, ᾧ τὸ ἄδικον μὲν λωβᾶται, τὸ δὲ δίκαιον ὀνίνησιν; ἢ φαυλότερον ἡγούμεθα εἶναι τοῦ σώματος ἐκεῖνο, ὅ τι ποτ' ἐστὶ τῶν |
ἡμετέρων, περὶ ὃ ἥ τε ἀδικία καὶ ἡ δικαιοσύνη 48
ἐστίν;

ΚΡ. Οὐδαμῶς.

ΣΩ. Ἀλλὰ τιμιώτερον;

ΚΡ. Πολύ γε.

ΣΩ. Οὐκ ἄρα, ὦ βέλτιστε, πάνυ ἡμῖν οὕτω φροντιστέον, τί ἐροῦσιν οἱ πολλοὶ ἡμᾶς, ἀλλ' ὅ τι ὁ ἐπαΐων περὶ τῶν δικαίων καὶ ἀδίκων, ὁ εἷς, καὶ αὐτὴ ἡ ἀλήθεια. ὥστε πρῶτον μὲν ταύτῃ οὐκ ὀρθῶς εἰσηγεῖ, εἰσηγούμενος τῆς τῶν πολλῶν δόξης δεῖν ἡμᾶς φροντίζειν περὶ τῶν δικαίων καὶ καλῶν καὶ ἀγαθῶν καὶ τῶν ἐναντίων.—ἀλλὰ μὲν δή, φαίη

for, granted that the many can kill us, yet

48 γ' ἂν τις, οἷοίτε εἰσὶν ἡμᾶς οἱ πολλοὶ ἀποκτιννύναι.

we agreed (did we not?) that not mere living is the main thing, but *right* living.

B | ΚΡ. Δῆλα δὴ καὶ ταῦτα· φαίη γὰρ ἄν, ὦ Σώκρατες.

ΣΩ. Ἀληθῆ λέγεις· ἀλλ', ὦ θαυμάσιε, οὗτός τε ὁ λόγος, ὃν διεληλύθαμεν, ἔμοιγε δοκεῖ ἔτι ὅμοιος εἶναι [τῷ] καὶ πρότερον· καὶ τόνδε αὖ σκόπει, εἰ ἔτι μένει ἡμῖν ἢ οὔ, ὅτι οὐ τὸ ζῆν περὶ πλείστου ποιητέον, ἀλλὰ τὸ εὖ ζῆν.

ΚΡ. Ἀλλὰ μένει.

ΣΩ. Τὸ δὲ εὖ καὶ καλῶς καὶ δικαίως ὅτι ταὐτόν ἐστιν, μένει ἢ οὐ μένει;

ΚΡ. Μένει.

ΣΩ. Οὐκοῦν ἐκ τῶν ὁμολογουμένων τοῦτο σκεπτέον, πότερον δίκαιον ἐμὲ ἐνθένδε πειρᾶσθαι ἐξιέναι μὴ ἀφιέντων | C Ἀθηναίων ἢ οὐ δίκαιον· καὶ ἐὰν μὲν φαίνηται δίκαιον, πειρώμεθα, εἰ δὲ μή, ἐῶμεν. ἃς δὲ σὺ λέγεις τὰς σκέψεις περί τε ἀναλώσεως χρημάτων καὶ δόξης καὶ παίδων τροφῆς, μὴ ὡς ἀληθῶς ταῦτα, ὦ Κρίτων, σκέμματα ᾖ τῶν ῥᾳδίως ἀποκτιννύντων καὶ ἀναβιωσκομένων γ' ἄν, εἰ οἷοίτ' ἦσαν, οὐδενὶ ξὺν νῷ, τούτων τῶν πολλῶν. ἡμῖν δ', ἐπειδὴ ὁ λόγος οὕτως αἱρεῖ, μὴ οὐδὲν ἄλλο σκεπτέον ᾖ ἢ ὅπερ νῦν δὴ ἐλέγομεν, πότερον δίκαια πράξομεν καὶ χρήματα τελοῦντες

Is it *right* then (that is the only question) for me to try to escape?

D τούτοις τοῖς ἐμὲ ἐνθένδε | ἐξάξουσι καὶ χάριτας, καὶ αὐτοὶ ἐξάγοντές τε καὶ ἐξαγόμενοι, ἢ τῇ ἀληθείᾳ ἀδικήσομεν πάντα ταῦτα ποιοῦντες·

κἂν φαινώμεθα ἄδικα αὐτὰ ἐργαζόμενοι, μὴ οὐ 48
δέῃ ὑπολογίζεσθαι οὔτ' εἰ ἀποθνῄσκειν δεῖ
παραμένοντας καὶ ἡσυχίαν ἄγοντας, οὔτε ἄλλο
ὁτιοῦν πάσχειν πρὸ τοῦ ἀδικεῖν.

ΚΡ. Καλῶς μέν μοι δοκεῖς λέγειν, ὦ Σώκρατες. ὅρα δέ, τί δρῶμεν.

ΣΩ. Σκοπῶμεν, ὦ ἀγαθέ, κοινῇ, καὶ εἴ πῃ
ἔχεις ἀντιλέγειν ἐμοῦ λέγοντος, ἀντίλεγε, καί
σοι πείσομαι· εἰ δὲ | μή, παῦσαι ἤδη, ὦ E
μακάριε, πολλάκις μοι λέγων τὸν αὐτὸν λόγον,
ὡς χρὴ ἐνθένδε ἀκόντων Ἀθηναίων ἐμὲ ἀπιέναι·
ὡς ἐγὼ περὶ πολλοῦ ποιοῦμαι πείσας σε ταῦτα
πράττειν, ἀλλὰ μὴ ἄκοντος. ὅρα δὲ δὴ τῆς
σκέψεως τὴν ἀρχήν, ἐάν σοι ἱκανῶς λέγηται,
καὶ πειρῶ ἀποκρίνεσθαι τὸ | ἐρωτώμενον, ᾗ ἂν 49
μάλιστα οἴῃ.

ΚΡ. Ἀλλὰ πειράσομαι.

ΣΩ. Οὐδενὶ τρόπῳ φαμὲν ἑκόντας ἀδικητέον εἶναι, ἢ τινὶ μὲν ἀδικητέον τρόπῳ, τινὶ δὲ οὔ; ἢ οὐδαμῶς τό γε ἀδικεῖν οὔτε ἀγαθὸν οὔτε καλόν, ὡς πολλάκις ἡμῖν καὶ ἐν τῷ ἔμπροσθεν χρόνῳ ὡμολογήθη; [ὅπερ καὶ ἄρτι ἐλέγετο·]

But first, do you still admit, as you once did, that we must do no wrong even in retaliation,

ἢ πᾶσαι ἡμῖν ἐκεῖναι αἱ πρόσθεν ὁμολογίαι ἐν
ταῖσδε ταῖς ὀλίγαις ἡμέραις ἐκκεχυμέναι εἰσίν,
καὶ πάλαι, ὦ Κρίτων, ἄρα τηλικοίδε γέροντες
ἄνδρες πρὸς ἀλλήλους σπουδῇ διαλεγόμενοι |
ἐλάθομεν ἡμᾶς αὐτοὺς παίδων οὐδὲν δια- B
φέροντες; ἢ παντὸς μᾶλλον οὕτως ἔχει, ὥσπερ
τότε ἐλέγετο, ἡμῖν—εἴτε φασὶν οἱ πολλοὶ εἴτε
μή, καὶ εἴτε δεῖ ἡμᾶς ἔτι τῶνδε χαλεπώτερα

49 πάσχειν εἴτε καὶ πραότερα, ὅμως τό γε ἀδικεῖν τῷ ἀδικοῦντι καὶ κακὸν καὶ αἰσχρὸν τυγχάνει ὂν παντὶ τρόπῳ; φαμὲν ἢ οὔ;

ΚΡ. Φαμέν.

ΣΩ. Οὐδαμῶς ἄρα δεῖ ἀδικεῖν.

ΚΡ. Οὐ δῆτα.

ΣΩ. Οὐδὲ ἀδικούμενον ἄρα ἀνταδικεῖν, ὡς οἱ πολλοὶ οἴονται, ἐπειδή γε οὐδαμῶς δεῖ ἀδικεῖν.

C ΚΡ. | Οὐ φαίνεται.

ΣΩ. Τί δὲ δή; κακουργεῖν δεῖ, ὦ Κρίτων, ἢ οὔ;

ΚΡ. Οὐ δεῖ δήπου, ὦ Σώκρατες.

ΣΩ. Τί δέ; ἀντικακουργεῖν κακῶς πάσχοντα, ὡς οἱ πολλοί φασιν, δίκαιον ἢ οὐ δίκαιον;

ΚΡ. Οὐδαμῶς.

ΣΩ. Τὸ γάρ που κακῶς ποιεῖν ἀνθρώπους τοῦ ἀδικεῖν οὐδὲν διαφέρει.

ΚΡ. Ἀληθῆ λέγεις.

ΣΩ. Οὔτε ἄρα ἀνταδικεῖν δεῖ οὔτε κακῶς ποιεῖν οὐδένα ἀνθρώπων, οὐδ' ἂν ὁτιοῦν πάσχῃ ὑπ' αὐτῶν. καὶ ὅρα, ὦ Κρίτων, ταῦτα καθ-
D ομολογῶν, ὅπως μὴ παρὰ | δόξαν ὁμολογῇς. οἶδα γὰρ ὅτι ὀλίγοις τισὶ ταῦτα καὶ δοκεῖ καὶ δόξει. οἷς οὖν οὕτω δέδοκται καὶ οἷς μή, τούτοις οὐκ ἔστι κοινὴ βουλή, ἀλλὰ ἀνάγκη τούτους ἀλλήλων καταφρονεῖν, ὁρῶντας τὰ ἀλλήλων βουλεύματα. σκόπει δὴ οὖν καὶ σὺ εὖ μάλα, πότερον κοινωνεῖς καὶ ξυνδοκεῖ σοι καὶ ἀρχώμεθα ἐντεῦθεν βουλευόμενοι, ὡς οὐδέ-

ποτε ὀρθῶς ἔχοντος οὔτε τοῦ ἀδικεῖν οὔτε τοῦ 49
ἀνταδικεῖν οὔτε κακῶς πάσχοντα ἀμύνεσθαι ἀντιδρῶντα κακῶς, ἢ ἀφίστασαι καὶ οὐ κοινωνεῖς τῆς ἀρχῆς; ἐμοὶ μὲν | γὰρ καὶ πάλαι E
οὕτω καὶ νῦν ἔτι δοκεῖ, σοὶ δὲ εἴ πῃ ἄλλῃ δέδοκται, λέγε καὶ δίδασκε. εἰ δ' ἐμμένεις τοῖς πρόσθε, τὸ μετὰ τοῦτο ἄκουε.

ΚΡ. Ἀλλ' ἐμμένω τε καὶ ξυνδοκεῖ μοι· ἀλλὰ λέγε.

ΣΩ. Λέγω δὴ αὖ τὸ μετὰ τοῦτο, μᾶλλον δ' ἐρωτῶ· πότερον ἃ ἄν τις ὁμολογήσῃ τῳ δίκαια ὄντα ποιητέον ἢ ἐξαπατητέον;

and that a just compact must be kept?

ΚΡ. Ποιητέον.

ΣΩ. Ἐκ τούτων δὴ ἄθρει. ἀπιόντες ἐνθένδε ἡμεῖς μὴ πείσαντες τὴν πόλιν
| πότερον κακῶς τινας ποιοῦμεν, καὶ 50
ταῦτα οὓς ἥκιστα δεῖ, ἢ οὔ; καὶ ἐμμένομεν οἷς ὡμολογήσαμεν δικαίοις οὖσιν ἢ οὔ;

Yet would not flight be both a wrong to the State and a breaking of compact?

ΚΡ. Οὐκ ἔχω, ὦ Σώκρατες, ἀποκρίνασθαι πρὸς ὃ ἐρωτᾷς· οὐ γὰρ ἐννοῶ.

ΣΩ. Ἀλλ' ὧδε σκόπει. εἰ μέλλουσιν ἡμῖν ἐνθένδε εἴτε ἀποδιδράσκειν, εἴθ' ὅπως δεῖ ὀνομάσαι τοῦτο, ἐλθόντες οἱ νόμοι καὶ τὸ κοινὸν τῆς πόλεως ἐπιστάντες ἔροιντο· Εἰπέ μοι, ὦ Σώκρατες, τί ἐν νῷ ἔχεις ποιεῖν; ἄλλο τι ἢ τούτῳ τῷ ἔργῳ, ᾧ ἐπιχειρεῖς, διανοεῖ τούς τε νόμους ἡμᾶς | ἀπολέσαι καὶ ξύμπασαν τὴν πόλιν τὸ σὸν B
μέρος; ἢ δοκεῖ σοι οἷόν τε ἔτι ἐκείνην τὴν

What if the Laws should come and say: You undo the State.

50 πόλιν εἶναι καὶ μὴ ἀνατετράφθαι, ἐν ᾗ αἱ
γενόμεναι δίκαι μηδὲν ἰσχύουσιν, ἀλλὰ ὑπὸ
ἰδιωτῶν ἄκυροί τε γίγνονται καὶ διαφθείρονται;
τί ἐροῦμεν, ὦ Κρίτων, πρὸς ταῦτα καὶ ἄλλα
τοιαῦτα; πολλὰ γὰρ ἄν τις ἔχοι (ἄλλως τε
καὶ ῥήτωρ) εἰπεῖν ὑπὲρ τούτου τοῦ νόμου
ἀπολλυμένου, ὃς τὰς δίκας τὰς δικασθείσας
προστάττει κυρίας εἶναι. ἢ ἐροῦμεν πρὸς
C αὐτοὺς ὅτι Ἠδίκει | γὰρ ἡμᾶς ἡ πόλις καὶ οὐκ
ὀρθῶς τὴν δίκην ἔκρινεν; ταῦτα ἢ τί ἐροῦμεν;

ΚΡ. Ταῦτα νὴ Δία, ὦ Σώκρατες.

ΣΩ. Τί οὖν, ἂν εἴπωσιν οἱ νόμοι· Ὦ
Σώκρατες, ἦ καὶ ταῦτα ὡμολόγητο ἡμῖν τε
καὶ σοί, ἢ ἐμμένειν ταῖς δίκαις αἷς ἂν ἡ
πόλις δικάζῃ; εἰ οὖν αὐτῶν θαυμάζοιμεν
λεγόντων, ἴσως ἂν εἴποιεν ὅτι Ὦ Σώκρατες,
μὴ θαύμαζε τὰ λεγόμενα, ἀλλ' ἀποκρίνου,
ἐπειδὴ καὶ εἴωθας χρῆσθαι τῷ ἐρωτᾶν τε καὶ
ἀποκρίνεσθαι. φέρε γάρ, τί ἐγκαλῶν ἡμῖν |
D καὶ τῇ πόλει ἐπιχειρεῖς ἡμᾶς ἀπολλύναι; οὐ
πρῶτον μέν σε ἐγεννήσαμεν ἡμεῖς, καὶ δι'
ἡμῶν ἐλάμβανεν τὴν μητέρα σου ὁ πατὴρ
καὶ ἐφύτευσέν σε; φράσον οὖν, τούτοις ἡμῶν
τοῖς νόμοις τοῖς περὶ τοὺς γάμους μέμφει τι,
ὡς οὐ καλῶς ἔχουσιν; Οὐ μέμφομαι, φαίην
ἄν. Ἀλλὰ τοῖς περὶ τὴν τοῦ γενομένου
τροφήν τε καὶ παιδείαν, ἐν ᾗ καὶ σὺ
ἐπαιδεύθης; ἢ οὐ καλῶς προσέταττον ἡμῶν
οἱ ἐπὶ τούτοις τεταγμένοι νόμοι, παραγγέλ-
λοντες τῷ πατρὶ τῷ σῷ σε ἐν μουσικῇ καὶ
E γυμναστικῇ παιδεύειν; Καλῶς, | φαίην ἄν.

Under us you were born and reared, and us you must obey or persuade, but not treat with violence.

Εἶεν. ἐπειδὴ δὲ ἐγένου τε καὶ 50 ἐξετράφης καὶ ἐπαιδεύθης, ἔχοις ἂν εἰπεῖν πρῶτον μὲν ὡς οὐχὶ ἡμέτερος ἦσθα καὶ ἔκγονος καὶ δοῦλος, αὐτός τε καὶ οἱ σοὶ πρόγονοι; καὶ εἰ τοῦθ' οὕτως ἔχει, ἆρ' ἐξ ἴσου οἴει εἶναι σοὶ τὸ δίκαιον καὶ ἡμῖν, καὶ ἅττ' ἂν ἡμεῖς σε ἐπιχειρῶμεν ποιεῖν, καὶ σοὶ ταῦτα ἀντιποιεῖν οἴει δίκαιον εἶναι; ἢ πρὸς μὲν ἄρα σοι τὸν πατέρα οὐκ ἐξ ἴσου ἦν τὸ δίκαιον καὶ πρὸς τὸν δεσπότην (εἴ σοι ὢν ἐτύγχανεν) ὥστε, ἅπερ πάσχοις, ταῦτα καὶ ἀντιποιεῖν,—οὔτε κακῶς ἀκούοντα ἀντιλέγειν οὔτε τυπτόμενον | ἀντιτύπτειν οὔτε ἄλλα τοιαῦτα πολλά· πρὸς 51 δὲ τὴν πατρίδα ἄρα καὶ τοὺς νόμους ἐξέσται σοι, ὥστε, ἐὰν σὲ ἐπιχειρῶμεν ἡμεῖς ἀπολλύναι δίκαιον ἡγούμενοι εἶναι,—καὶ σὺ δὲ ἡμᾶς τοὺς νόμους καὶ τὴν πατρίδα (καθ' ὅσον δύνασαι) ἐπιχειρήσεις ἀνταπολλύναι, καὶ φήσεις ταῦτα ποιῶν δίκαια πράττειν, ὁ τῇ ἀληθείᾳ τῆς ἀρετῆς ἐπιμελόμενος; ἢ οὕτως εἶ σοφός, ὥστε λέληθέν σε ὅτι μητρός τε καὶ πατρὸς καὶ τῶν ἄλλων προγόνων ἁπάντων τιμιώτερόν ἐστιν ἡ πατρὶς καὶ σεμνότερον καὶ ἁγιώτερον καὶ ἐν μείζονι | μοίρᾳ καὶ παρὰ θεοῖς καὶ παρ' B ἀνθρώποις τοῖς νοῦν ἔχουσι, καὶ σέβεσθαι δεῖ καὶ μᾶλλον ὑπείκειν καὶ θωπεύειν πατρίδα χαλεπαίνουσαν ἢ πατέρα, καὶ ἢ πείθειν ἢ ποιεῖν ἃ ἂν κελεύῃ, καὶ πάσχειν, ἐάν τι προστάττῃ παθεῖν, ἡσυχίαν ἄγοντα, ἐάντε τύπτεσθαι ἐάντε δεῖσθαι, ἐάν τε εἰς πόλεμον

51 ἄγῃ τρωθησόμενον ἢ ἀποθανούμενον, ποιητέον ταῦτα, καὶ τὸ δίκαιον οὕτως ἔχει, καὶ οὐχὶ ὑπεικτέον οὐδὲ ἀναχωρητέον οὐδὲ λειπτέον τὴν τάξιν, ἀλλὰ καὶ ἐν πολέμῳ καὶ ἐν δικαστηρίῳ
C καὶ πανταχοῦ ποιητέον ἃ ἂν κελεύῃ ἡ | πόλις καὶ ἡ πατρίς, ἢ πείθειν αὐτὴν ᾗ τὸ δίκαιον πέφυκε, βιάζεσθαι δὲ οὐχ ὅσιον οὔτε μητέρα οὔτε πατέρα, πολὺ δὲ τούτων ἔτι ἧττον τὴν πατρίδα;—τί φήσομεν πρὸς ταῦτα, ὦ Κρίτων; ἀληθῆ λέγειν τοὺς νόμους ἢ οὔ;

ΚΡ. Ἔμοιγε δοκεῖ.

ΣΩ. Σκόπει τοίνυν, ὦ Σώκρατες, φαῖεν ἂν ἴσως οἱ νόμοι, εἰ ἡμεῖς ταῦτα ἀληθῆ λέγομεν, ὅτι οὐ δίκαια ἡμᾶς ἐπιχειρεῖς δρᾶν ἃ νῦν ἐπιχειρεῖς. ἡμεῖς γάρ σε γεννήσαντες, ἐκθρέψαντες, παιδεύσαντες, μεταδόντες ἁπάντων ὧν
D οἷοί τ' ἦμεν καλῶν σοὶ καὶ τοῖς ἄλλοις | πᾶσιν πολίταις, ὅμως προαγορεύομεν τῷ ἐξουσίαν πεποιηκέναι Ἀθηναίων τῷ βουλομένῳ, ἐπειδὰν δοκιμασθῇ καὶ ἴδῃ τὰ ἐν τῇ πόλει πράγματα καὶ ἡμᾶς τοὺς νόμους, ᾧ ἂν μὴ ἀρέσκωμεν ἡμεῖς, ἐξεῖναι λαβόντα τὰ αὑτοῦ ἀπιέναι ὅποι ἂν βούληται. καὶ οὐδεὶς ἡμῶν τῶν νόμων ἐμποδών ἐστιν οὐδ' ἀπαγορεύει, ἐάντε τις βούληται ὑμῶν εἰς ἀποικίαν ἰέναι, εἰ μὴ ἀρέσκοιμεν ἡμεῖς τε καὶ ἡ πόλις, ἐάντε μετοικεῖν ἄλλοσε ἐλθών, ἰέναι ἐκεῖσε ὅποι ἂν
E βούληται, ἔχοντα τὰ αὑτοῦ. ὃς δ' ἂν | ὑμῶν παραμείνῃ, ὁρῶν ὃν τρόπον ἡμεῖς τάς τε δίκας δικάζομεν καὶ τἆλλα τὴν πόλιν διοικοῦ-

You could have withdrawn from Athens, if we did not please you.

μεν, ἤδη φαμὲν τοῦτον ὡμολογηκέναι ἔργῳ 51
ἡμῖν, ἃ ἂν ἡμεῖς κελεύωμεν, ποιήσειν ταῦτα,
καὶ τὸν μὴ πειθόμενον τριχῇ φαμεν ἀδικεῖν,
ὅτι τε γεννηταῖς οὖσιν ἡμῖν οὐ πείθεται, καὶ
ὅτι τροφεῦσι, καὶ ὅτι ὁμολογήσας ἡμῖν πείθε-
σθαι οὔτε πείθεται οὔτε πείθει ἡμᾶς, εἰ μὴ
καλῶς τι ποιοῦμεν, προτιθέντων | ἡμῶν καὶ 52
οὐκ ἀγρίως ἐπιταττόντων ποιεῖν ἃ ἂν κελεύω-
μεν, ἀλλὰ ἐφιέντων δυοῖν θάτερα, ἢ πείθειν
ἡμᾶς ἢ ποιεῖν, τούτων οὐδέτερα ποιεῖ.

Yet you more constantly than all others have preferred residence here.

Ταύταις δή φαμεν καὶ σέ, Σώκρατες, ταῖς
αἰτίαις ἐνέξεσθαι, εἴπερ ποιήσεις ἃ
ἐπινοεῖς, καὶ οὐχ ἥκιστα Ἀθηναίων
σέ, ἀλλ᾽ ἐν τοῖς μάλιστα. εἰ οὖν
ἐγὼ εἴποιμι· Διὰ τί δή; ἴσως ἂν
μου δικαίως καθάπτοιντο λέγοντες ὅτι ἐν τοῖς
μάλιστα Ἀθηναίων ἐγὼ αὐτοῖς ὡμολογηκὼς
τυγχάνω ταύτην τὴν ὁμολογίαν. φαῖεν γὰρ
ἂν ὅτι Ὦ Σώκρατες, μεγάλα ἡμῖν | τούτων B
τεκμήριά ἐστιν, ὅτι σοι καὶ ἡμεῖς ἠρέσκομεν
καὶ ἡ πόλις· οὐ γὰρ ἄν ποτε τῶν ἄλλων
Ἀθηναίων ἁπάντων διαφερόντως ἐν αὐτῇ ἐπεδή-
μεις, εἰ μή σοι διαφερόντως ἤρεσκεν, καὶ οὔτ᾽
ἐπὶ θεωρίαν πώποτ᾽ ἐκ τῆς πόλεως ἐξῆλθες
οὔτε ἄλλοσε οὐδαμόσε, εἰ μή ποι στρατευ-
σόμενος, οὔτε ἄλλην ἀποδημίαν ἐποιήσω
πώποτε, ὥσπερ οἱ ἄλλοι ἄνθρωποι, οὐδ᾽
ἐπιθυμία σε ἄλλης πόλεως οὐδὲ ἄλλων νόμων
ἔλαβεν εἰδέναι, ἀλλὰ ἡμεῖς σοι ἱκανοὶ ἦμεν
καὶ ἡ ἡμετέρα πόλις· οὕτω | σφόδρα ἡμᾶς C
ᾑροῦ, καὶ ὡμολόγεις καθ᾽ ἡμᾶς πολιτεύσεσθαι,

52 τά τε ἄλλα καὶ παῖδας ἐν αὐτῇ ἐποιήσω, ὡς
ἀρεσκούσης σοι τῆς πόλεως. ἔτι τοίνυν ἐν
αὐτῇ τῇ δίκῃ ἐξῆν σοι φυγῆς τιμήσασθαι,
εἰ ἐβούλου, καὶ ὅπερ νῦν ἀκούσης τῆς πόλεως
ἐπιχειρεῖς, τότε ἑκούσης ποιῆσαι. σὺ δὲ τότε
μὲν ἐκαλλωπίζου ὡς οὐκ ἀγανακτῶν, εἰ δέοι
τεθνάναι σε, ἀλλὰ ᾑροῦ, ὡς ἔφησθα, πρὸ τῆς
φυγῆς θάνατον· νῦν δὲ οὔτ' ἐκείνους τοὺς
λόγους αἰσχύνει, οὔτε ἡμῶν τῶν νόμων ἐντρέπει,
D ἐπιχειρῶν διαφθεῖραι, πράττεις | τε ἅπερ ἂν
δοῦλος φαυλότατος πράξειεν, ἀποδιδράσκειν
ἐπιχειρῶν παρὰ τὰς ξυνθήκας τε καὶ τὰς ὁμο-
λογίας, καθ' ἃς ἡμῖν ξυνέθου πολιτεύεσθαι.

A proof of your compact with us.

πρῶτον μὲν οὖν ἡμῖν τοῦτ' αὐτὸ
ἀπόκριναι, εἰ ἀληθῆ λέγομεν φά-
σκοντές σε ὡμολογηκέναι πολιτεύεσθαι
καθ' ἡμᾶς ἔργῳ, ἀλλ' οὐ λόγῳ, ἢ οὐκ ἀληθῆ.
τί φῶμεν πρὸς ταῦτα, ὦ Κρίτων; ἄλλο τι ἢ
ὁμολογῶμεν;

ΚΡ. Ἀνάγκη, ὦ Σώκρατες.

ΣΩ. Ἄλλο τι οὖν ἂν φαῖεν ἢ ξυνθήκας
τὰς πρὸς ἡμᾶς αὐτοὺς καὶ ὁμολογίας παρα-
E βαίνεις, οὐχ ὑπὸ | ἀνάγκης ὁμολογήσας οὐδὲ
ἀπατηθεὶς οὐδὲ ἐν ὀλίγῳ χρόνῳ ἀναγκασθεὶς
βουλεύσασθαι, ἀλλ' ἐν ἔτεσιν ἑβδομήκοντα, ἐν
οἷς ἐξῆν σοι ἀπιέναι, εἰ μὴ ἠρέσκομεν ἡμεῖς
μηδὲ δίκαιαι ἐφαίνοντό σοι αἱ ὁμολογίαι εἶναι;
σὺ δὲ οὔτε Λακεδαίμονα προῃροῦ οὔτε Κρήτην,
ἃς δὴ ἑκάστοτε φῂς εὐνομεῖσθαι, οὔτε ἄλλην
οὐδεμίαν τῶν Ἑλληνίδων πόλεων οὐδὲ τῶν
53 βαρβαρικῶν, | ἀλλὰ ἐλάττω ἐξ αὐτῆς ἀπεδήμησας

ἢ οἱ χωλοί τε καὶ τυφλοὶ καὶ οἱ ἄλλοι 53
ἀνάπηροι· οὕτω σοι διαφερόντως τῶν ἄλλων Ἀθηναίων ἤρεσκεν ἡ πόλις τε καὶ ἡμεῖς οἱ νόμοι δῆλον ὅτι· τίνι γὰρ ἂν πόλις ἀρέσκοι ἄνευ νόμων; νῦν δὲ δὴ οὐκ ἐμμένεις τοῖς ὡμολογημένοις; ἐὰν ἡμῖν γε πείθῃ, ὦ Σώκρατες· καὶ οὐ καταγέλαστός γε ἔσει ἐκ τῆς πόλεως ἐξελθών.

Σκόπει γὰρ δή, ταῦτα παραβὰς καὶ ἐξαμαρτάνων τι τούτων, τί ἀγαθὸν ἐργάσει σαυτὸν ἢ τοὺς ἐπιτηδείους τοὺς | σαυτοῦ. ὅτι μὲν B
γὰρ κινδυνεύσουσί γέ σου οἱ ἐπιτήδειοι καὶ αὐτοὶ φεύγειν καὶ στερηθῆναι τῆς πόλεως ἢ τὴν οὐσίαν ἀπολέσαι, σχεδόν τι δῆλον· αὐτὸς δὲ πρῶτον μὲν ἐὰν εἰς τῶν ἐγγύτατά τινα πόλεων ἔλθῃς, ἢ Θήβαζε ἢ Μέγαράδε (εὐνομοῦνται γὰρ ἀμφότεραι), πολέμιος ἥξεις, ὦ Σώκρατες, τῇ τούτων πολιτείᾳ, καὶ ὅσοιπερ κήδονται τῶν αὐτῶν πόλεων ὑποβλέψονταί σε διαφθορέα ἡγούμενοι τῶν νόμων, καὶ βεβαιώσεις τοῖς δικασταῖς τὴν δόξαν, ὥστε δοκεῖν ὀρθῶς τὴν δίκην | δικάσαι· ὅστις γὰρ νόμων C
διαφθορεύς ἐστιν, σφόδρα που δόξειεν ἂν νέων γε καὶ ἀνοήτων ἀνθρώπων διαφθορεὺς εἶναι. πότερον οὖν φεύξει τάς τε εὐνομουμένας πόλεις καὶ τῶν ἀνδρῶν τοὺς κοσμιωτάτους; καὶ τοῦτο ποιοῦντι ἆρα ἄξιόν σοι ζῆν ἔσται; ἢ πλησιάσεις τούτοις καὶ ἀναισχυντήσεις διαλεγόμενος—τίνας λόγους, ὦ Σώκρατες; ἢ οὕσπερ ἐνθάδε, ὡς ἡ ἀρετὴ καὶ ἡ δικαιοσύνη πλείστου

And if you fly, how would Thebes or Megara receive the law-breaker and his teachings of justice?

53 ἄξιον τοῖς ἀνθρώποις καὶ τὰ νόμιμα καὶ οἱ νόμοι; καὶ οὐκ οἴει ἄσχημον ἂν φανεῖσθαι τὸ D τοῦ Σωκράτους | πρᾶγμα; οἴεσθαί γε χρή. ἀλλ᾽ ἐκ μὲν τούτων τῶν τόπων ἀπαρεῖς, ἥξεις δὲ εἰς Θετταλίαν παρὰ τοὺς ξένους τοὺς Κρίτωνος· ἐκεῖ γὰρ δὴ πλείστη ἀταξία καὶ ἀκολασία, καὶ ἴσως ἂν ἡδέως σου ἀκούοιεν, ὡς γελοίως ἐκ τοῦ δεσμωτηρίου ἀπεδίδρασκες σκευήν τέ τινα περιθέμενος, ἢ διφθέραν λαβὼν ἢ ἄλλα οἷα δὴ εἰώθασιν ἐνσκευάζεσθαι οἱ ἀποδιδράσκοντες, καὶ τὸ σχῆμα τὸ σαυτοῦ μεταλλάξας· ὅτι δὲ γέρων ἀνὴρ σμικροῦ χρόνου τῷ βίῳ λοιποῦ E ὄντος, ὡς τὸ εἰκός, | ἐτόλμησας οὕτω γλίσχρως ἐπιθυμεῖν ζῆν, νόμους τοὺς μεγίστους παραβάς, οὐδεὶς ὃς ἐρεῖ; ἴσως, ἂν μή τινα λυπῇς· εἰ δὲ μή, ἀκούσει, ὦ Σώκρατες, πολλὰ καὶ ἀνάξια σαυτοῦ. ὑπερχόμενος δὴ βιώσει πάντας ἀνθρώπους καὶ δουλεύων—τι ποιῶν; ἢ εὐωχούμενος ἐν Θετταλίᾳ, ὥσπερ ἐπὶ δεῖπνον ἀποδεδημηκὼς εἰς Θετταλίαν; λόγοι δὲ ἐκεῖνοι οἱ περὶ δικαιοσύνης τε καὶ τῆς ἄλλης ἀρετῆς ποῦ 54 ἡμῖν | ἔσονται; ἀλλὰ δὴ τῶν παίδων ἕνεκα βούλει ζῆν, ἵνα αὐτοὺς ἐκθρέψῃς καὶ παιδεύσῃς. τί δέ; εἰς Θετταλίαν αὐτοὺς ἀγαγὼν θρέψεις τε καὶ παιδεύσεις, ξένους ποιήσας, ἵνα καὶ τοῦτο ἀπολαύσωσιν; ἢ τοῦτο μὲν οὔ, αὐτοῦ δὲ τρεφόμενοι σοῦ ζῶντος βέλτιον θρέψονται καὶ παιδεύσονται, μὴ ξυνόντος σοῦ αὐτοῖς; οἱ γὰρ ἐπιτήδειοι, οἵ σοι ἐπιμελήσονται αὐτῶν, πότερον, ἐὰν εἰς Θετταλίαν

Or will you go to lawless Thessaly?

ἀποδημήσῃς, ἐπιμελήσονται, ἐὰν δὲ εἰς Ἅιδου 54
ἀποδημήσῃς, οὐχὶ ἐπιμελήσονται; εἴπερ γέ τι
ὄφελος αὐτῶν ἐστιν τῶν | σοι φασκόντων B
ἐπιτηδείων εἶναι, οἴεσθαί γε χρή.

Ἀλλ', ὦ Σώκρατες, πειθόμενος ἡμῖν τοῖς
σοῖς τροφεῦσι μήτε παῖδας περὶ
πλείονος ποιοῦ μήτε τὸ ζῆν μήτε
ἄλλο μηδὲν πρὸ τοῦ δικαίου, ἵνα
εἰς Ἅιδου ἐλθὼν ἔχῃς πάντα ταῦτα
ἀπολογήσασθαι τοῖς ἐκεῖ ἄρχουσιν· οὔτε γὰρ
ἐνθάδε σοι φαίνεται ταῦτα πράττοντι ἄμεινον
εἶναι οὐδὲ δικαιότερον οὐδὲ ὁσιώτερον, οὐδὲ
ἄλλῳ τῶν σῶν οὐδενί, οὔτε ἐκεῖσε ἀφικομένῳ
ἄμεινον ἔσται. ἀλλὰ νῦν μὲν ἠδικημένος
ἄπει, ἐὰν ἀπίῃς, οὐχ ὑφ' ἡμῶν τῶν νόμων |
ἀλλὰ ὑπ' ἀνθρώπων· ἐὰν δὲ ἐξέλθῃς οὕτως C
αἰσχρῶς ἀνταδικήσας τε καὶ ἀντικακουργήσας,
τὰς σαυτοῦ ὁμολογίας τε καὶ ξυνθήκας τὰς
πρὸς ἡμᾶς παραβὰς καὶ κακὰ ἐργασάμενος
τούτους οὓς ἥκιστα ἔδει, σαυτόν τε καὶ φίλους
καὶ πατρίδα καὶ ἡμᾶς, ἡμεῖς τέ σοι χαλεπανοῦμεν
ζῶντι, καὶ ἐκεῖ οἱ ἡμέτεροι ἀδελφοὶ
οἱ ἐν Ἅιδου νόμοι οὐκ εὐμενῶς σε ὑποδέξονται,
εἰδότες ὅτι καὶ ἡμᾶς ἐπεχείρησας ἀπολέσαι τὸ
σὸν μέρος. ἀλλὰ μή σε πείσῃ Κρίτων ποιεῖν
ἃ λέγει μᾶλλον | ἢ ἡμεῖς. D

Nay, Socrates, choose no thing before the right; listen not to Crito.

Ταῦτα, ὦ φίλε ἑταῖρε Κρίτων, εὖ ἴσθι ὅτι
ἐγὼ δοκῶ ἀκούειν, ὥσπερ οἱ κορυβαντιῶντες
τῶν αὐλῶν δοκοῦσιν
ἀκούειν, καὶ ἐν ἐμοὶ αὕτη ἡ ἠχὴ
τούτων τῶν λόγων βομβεῖ καὶ

This, Crito, rings in my ears. I can hear naught else. Let us follow God's lead.

54 ποιεῖ μὴ δύνασθαι τῶν ἄλλων ἀκούειν· ἀλλὰ
ἴσθι (ὅσα γε τὰ νῦν ἐμοὶ δοκοῦντα) ἐὰν λέγῃς
παρὰ ταῦτα, μάτην ἐρεῖς. ὅμως μέντοι, εἴ τι
οἴει πλέον ποιήσειν, λέγε.

ΚΡ. Ἀλλ', ὦ Σώκρατες, οὐκ ἔχω λέγειν.

E ΣΩ. Ἔα τοίνυν, ὦ Κρίτων, | καὶ πράττωμεν
ταύτῃ, ἐπειδὴ ταύτῃ ὁ θεὸς ὑφηγεῖται.

PHAEDO

(Beginning and end)

Socrates' Last Day.

ECHECRATES. PHAEDO.

Visiting Phlius, Phaedo is questioned about Socrates' death.

57 ΕΧ. Αὐτός, ὦ Φαίδων, παρεγένου Σωκράτει
A ἐκείνῃ τῇ ἡμέρᾳ ᾗ τὸ φάρμακον ἔπιεν
ἐν τῷ δεσμωτηρίῳ, ἢ ἄλλου του
ἤκουσας;

ΦΑΙΔ. Αὐτός, ὦ Ἐχέκρατες.

ΕΧ. Τί οὖν δή ἐστιν ἅττα εἶπεν
ὁ ἀνὴρ πρὸ τοῦ θανάτου; καὶ πῶς ἐτελεύτα;
ἡδέως γὰρ ἂν ἐγὼ ἀκούσαιμι. καὶ γὰρ οὔτε
τῶν πολιτῶν Φλειασίων οὐδεὶς πάνυ τι ἐπιχω-
ριάζει τὰ νῦν Ἀθήναζε, οὔτε τις ξένος ἀφῖκ-
B ται | χρόνου συχνοῦ ἐκεῖθεν, ὅστις ἂν ἡμῖν
σαφές τι ἀγγεῖλαι οἷός τ' ἦν περὶ τούτων,
πλήν γε δὴ ὅτι φάρμακον πιὼν ἀποθάνοι·
τῶν δὲ ἄλλων οὐδὲν εἶχεν φράζειν.

58 ΦΑΙΔ. Οὐδὲ τὰ περὶ τῆς δίκης | ἄρα ἐπύ-
θεσθε ὃν τρόπον ἐγένετο;

ΕΧ. Ναί, ταῦτα μὲν ἡμῖν ἤγγειλέ τις, 58
καὶ ἐθαυμάζομέν γε ὅτι πάλαι γενομένης αὐτῆς
πολλῷ ὕστερον φαίνεται ἀποθανών. τί οὖν ἦν
τοῦτο, ὦ Φαίδων;

ΦΑΙΔ. Τύχη τις αὐτῷ, ὦ Ἐχέκρατες,
συνέβη· ἔτυχεν γὰρ τῇ προτεραίᾳ
τῆς δίκης ἡ πρύμνα ἐστεμμένη τοῦ
πλοίου, ὃ εἰς Δῆλον Ἀθηναῖοι πέμ-
πουσιν.

He tells the cause of its long delay after condemnation,

ΕΧ. Τοῦτο δὲ δὴ τί ἐστιν;

ΦΑΙΔ. Τοῦτ' ἔστι τὸ πλοῖον, ὥς φασιν
Ἀθηναῖοι, ἐν ᾧ Θησεύς ποτε εἰς Κρήτην τοὺς
δὶς ἑπτὰ ἐκείνους ᾤχετο ἄγων | καὶ ἔσωσέ τε B
καὶ αὐτὸς ἐσώθη. τῷ οὖν Ἀπόλλωνι ηὔξαντο,
ὡς λέγεται, τότε, εἰ σωθεῖεν, ἑκάστου ἔτους
θεωρίαν ἀπάξειν εἰς Δῆλον· ἣν δὴ ἀεὶ καὶ νῦν
ἔτι ἐξ ἐκείνου κατ' ἐνιαυτὸν τῷ θεῷ πέμπουσιν.
ἐπειδὰν οὖν ἄρξωνται τῆς θεωρίας, νόμος ἐστὶν
αὐτοῖς ἐν τῷ χρόνῳ τούτῳ καθαρεύειν τὴν
πόλιν καὶ δημοσίᾳ μηδένα ἀποκτιννύναι, πρὶν
ἂν εἰς Δῆλόν τε ἀφίκηται τὸ πλοῖον καὶ πάλιν
δεῦρο· τοῦτο δ' ἐνίοτε ἐν πολλῷ χρόνῳ γίγνεται,
ὅταν τύχωσιν ἄνεμοι ἀπολαβόντες αὐτούς. ἀρχὴ
| δ' ἐστὶ τῆς θεωρίας, ἐπειδὰν ὁ ἱερεὺς τοῦ C
Ἀπόλλωνος στέψῃ τὴν πρύμναν τοῦ πλοίου·
τοῦτο δ' ἔτυχεν, ὥσπερ λέγω, τῇ προτεραίᾳ
τῆς δίκης γεγονός. διὰ ταῦτα καὶ πολὺς χρόνος
ἐγένετο τῷ Σωκράτει ἐν τῷ δεσμωτηρίῳ ὁ
μεταξὺ τῆς δίκης τε καὶ τοῦ θανάτου.

ΕΧ. Τί δὲ δὴ τὰ περὶ αὐτὸν τὸν θάνατον,
ὦ Φαίδων; τί ἦν τὰ λεχθέντα καὶ πραχθέντα,

58 καὶ τίνες οἱ παραγενόμενοι τῶν ἐπιτηδείων τῷ ἀνδρί; ἢ οὐκ εἴων οἱ ἄρχοντες παρεῖναι, ἀλλ' ἔρημος ἐτελεύτα φίλων;

D ΦΑΙΔ. | Οὐδαμῶς, ἀλλὰ παρῆσάν τινες, καὶ πολλοί γε.

ΕΧ. Ταῦτα δὴ πάντα προθυμήθητι ὡς σαφέστατα ἡμῖν ἀπαγγεῖλαι, εἰ μή τίς σοι ἀσχολία τυγχάνει οὖσα.

ΦΑΙΔ. Ἀλλὰ σχολάζω γε καὶ πειράσομαι ὑμῖν διηγήσασθαι· καὶ γὰρ τὸ μεμνῆσθαι Σωκράτους καὶ αὐτὸν λέγοντα καὶ ἄλλου ἀκούοντα ἔμοιγε ἀεὶ πάντων ἥδιστον.

ΕΧ. Ἀλλὰ μήν, ὦ Φαίδων, καὶ τοὺς ἀκουσομένους γε τοιούτους ἑτέρους ἔχεις· ἀλλὰ πειρῶ ὡς ἂν δύνῃ ἀκριβέστατα διεξελθεῖν πάντα.

E ΦΑΙΔ. Καὶ μὴν ἔγωγε θαυμάσια | ἔπαθον

of Socrates' calm,

παραγενόμενος. οὔτε γὰρ ὡς θανάτῳ παρόντα με ἀνδρὸς ἐπιτηδείου ἔλεος εἰσῄει· εὐδαίμων γάρ μοι ἁνὴρ ἐφαίνετο, ὦ Ἐχέκρατες, καὶ τοῦ τρόπου καὶ τῶν λόγων, ὡς ἀδεῶς καὶ γενναίως ἐτελεύτα, ὥστε μοι ἐκεῖνον παρίστασθαι μηδ' εἰς Ἅιδου ἰόντα ἄνευ θείας μοίρας ἰέναι, ἀλλὰ καὶ ἐκεῖσε ἀφικόμενον εὖ
59 πράξειν, εἴπερ τις πώποτε καὶ | ἄλλος. διὰ δὴ ταῦτα οὐδὲν πάνυ μοι ἐλεεινὸν εἰσῄει, ὡς εἰκὸς ἂν δόξειεν εἶναι παρόντι πένθει· οὔτε αὖ ἡδονὴ ὡς ἐν φιλοσοφίᾳ ἡμῶν ὄντων, ὥσπερ εἰώθεμεν (καὶ γὰρ οἱ λόγοι τοιοῦτοί τινες ἦσαν), ἀλλ' ἀτεχνῶς ἄτοπόν τί μοι πάθος παρῆν καί τις ἀήθης κρᾶσις ἀπό τε τῆς ἡδονῆς συγκεκραμένη ὁμοῦ καὶ ἀπὸ τῆς λύπης, ἐνθυμουμένῳ

ὅτι αὐτίκα ἐκεῖνος ἔμελλε τελευτᾶν. καὶ πάντες 59 οἱ παρόντες σχεδόν τι οὕτω διεκείμεθα, ὁτὲ μὲν γελῶντες, ἐνίοτε δὲ δακρύοντες, εἷς δὲ ἡμῶν καὶ διαφερόντως, Ἀπολλόδωρος· οἶσθα γάρ που τὸν ἄνδρα | καὶ τὸν τρόπον αὐτοῦ. B

ΕΧ. Πῶς γὰρ οὔ;

ΦΑΙΔ. Ἐκεῖνός τε τοίνυν παντάπασιν οὕτως εἶχεν, καὶ αὐτὸς ἔγωγε ἐτεταράγμην καὶ οἱ ἄλλοι.

ΕΧ. Ἔτυχον δέ, ὦ Φαίδων, τίνες παραγενόμενοι;

ΦΑΙΔ. Οὗτός τε δὴ ὁ Ἀπολλόδωρος τῶν ἐπιχωρίων παρῆν καὶ ὁ Κριτόβουλος καὶ ὁ πατὴρ αὐτοῦ [Κρίτων], καὶ ἔτι Ἑρμογένης καὶ Ἐπιγένης καὶ Αἰσχίνης καὶ Ἀντισθένης· ἦν δὲ καὶ Κτήσιππος ὁ Παιανιεὺς καὶ Μενέξενος καὶ ἄλλοι τινὲς τῶν ἐπιχωρίων· Πλάτων δέ, οἶμαι, ἠσθένει.

the names of the friends present,

ΕΧ. Ξένοι δέ τινες παρῆσαν;

ΦΑΙΔ. | Ναί, Σιμμίας τέ γε ὁ Θηβαῖος καὶ C Κέβης καὶ Φαιδωνίδης καὶ Μεγαρόθεν Εὐκλείδης τε καὶ Τερψίων.

ΕΧ. Τί δέ; Ἀρίστιππος καὶ Κλεόμβροτος <οὐ> παρεγένοντο;

ΦΑΙΔ. Οὐ δῆτα· ἐν Αἰγίνῃ γὰρ ἐλέγοντο εἶναι.

ΕΧ. Ἄλλος δέ τις παρῆν;

ΦΑΙΔ. Σχεδόν τι οἶμαι τούτους παραγενέσθαι.

ΕΧ. Τί οὖν δή; τίνες, φῄς, ἦσαν οἱ λόγοι;

59 ΦΑΙΔ. Ἐγώ σοι ἐξ ἀρχῆς πάντα πειράσομαι διηγήσασθαι. ἀεὶ γὰρ δὴ καὶ

of their daily visits to the prison, and of their last gathering.

D τὰς πρόσθεν ἡμέρας | εἰώθεμεν φοιτᾶν καὶ ἐγὼ καὶ οἱ ἄλλοι παρὰ τὸν Σωκράτη, συλλεγόμενοι ἕωθεν εἰς τὸ δικαστήριον, ἐν ᾧ καὶ ἡ δίκη ἐγένετο· πλησίον γὰρ ἦν τοῦ δεσμωτηρίου. περιεμένομεν οὖν ἑκάστοτε, ἕως ἀνοιχθείη τὸ δεσμωτήριον, διατρίβοντες μετ᾽ ἀλλήλων· ἀνεῴγετο γὰρ οὐ πρῴ· ἐπειδὴ δὲ ἀνοιχθείη, εἰσῇμεν παρὰ τὸν Σωκράτη καὶ τὰ πολλὰ διημερεύομεν μετ᾽ αὐτοῦ. καὶ δὴ καὶ τότε πρῳαίτερον συνελέγημεν. τῇ γὰρ προτεραίᾳ [ἡμέρᾳ] ἐπειδὴ

E ἐξήλθομεν ἐκ τοῦ δεσμωτηρίου | ἑσπέρας, ἐπυθόμεθα ὅτι τὸ πλοῖον ἐκ Δήλου ἀφιγμένον εἴη. παρηγγείλαμεν οὖν ἀλλήλοις ἥκειν ὡς πρῳαίτατα εἰς τὸ εἰωθός. καὶ ἥκομεν καὶ ἡμῖν ἐξελθὼν ὁ θυρωρός, ὅσπερ εἰώθει ὑπακούειν, εἶπεν περιμένειν καὶ μὴ πρότερον παριέναι, ἕως ἂν αὐτὸς κελεύσῃ. Λύουσι γάρ, ἔφη, οἱ ἕνδεκα Σωκράτη καὶ παραγγέλλουσιν ὅπως ἂν τῇδε τῇ ἡμέρᾳ τελευτήσῃ. οὐ πολὺν δ᾽ οὖν χρόνον ἐπισχὼν ἧκεν καὶ ἐκέλευεν ἡμᾶς εἰσιέναι. εἰσελθόντες

60 οὖν κατελαμβάνομεν | τὸν μὲν Σωκράτη ἄρτι λελυμένον, τὴν δὲ Ξανθίππην (γιγνώσκεις γάρ) ἔχουσάν τε τὸ παιδίον αὐτοῦ καὶ παρακαθημένην. ὡς οὖν εἶδεν ἡμᾶς ἡ Ξανθίππη, ἀνηυφήμησέ τε καὶ τοιαῦτ᾽ ἄττα εἶπεν, οἷα δὴ εἰώθασιν αἱ γυναῖκες, ὅτι Ὦ Σώκρατες, ὕστατον δή σε προσεροῦσι νῦν οἱ ἐπιτήδειοι καὶ σὺ τούτους. καὶ ὁ Σωκράτης βλέψας εἰς τὸν

Κρίτωνα· Ὦ Κρίτων, ἔφη, ἀπαγέτω τις αὐτὴν 60
οἴκαδε. καὶ ἐκείνην μὲν ἀπῆγόν τινες τῶν τοῦ
Κρίτωνος βοῶσάν τε καὶ κοπτομένην· | ὁ δὲ B
Σωκράτης ἀνακαθιζόμενος εἰς τὴν κλίνην συν-
έκαμψέ τε τὸ σκέλος καὶ ἐξέτριψε τῇ χειρί,
καὶ τρίβων ἅμα· Ὡς ἄτοπον, ἔφη,
ὦ ἄνδρες, ἔοικέ τι εἶναι τοῦτο, ὃ
καλοῦσιν οἱ ἄνθρωποι ἡδύ· ὡς θαυμα-
σίως πέφυκε πρὸς τὸ δοκοῦν ἐναντίον εἶναι, τὸ
λυπηρόν, τῷ ἅμα μὲν αὐτὼ μὴ ἐθέλειν παρα-
γίγνεσθαι τῷ ἀνθρώπῳ, ἐὰν δέ τις διώκῃ τὸ
ἕτερον καὶ λαμβάνῃ, σχεδόν τι ἀναγκάζεσθαι
λαμβάνειν καὶ τὸ ἕτερον, ὥσπερ ἐκ μιᾶς
κορυφῆς συνημμένω δύ' ὄντε. καί μοι δοκεῖ,
ἔφη, | εἰ ἐνενόησεν αὐτὰ Αἴσωπος, μῦθον ἂν C
συνθεῖναι, ὡς ὁ θεὸς βουλόμενος αὐτὰ διαλλάξαι
πολεμοῦντα, ἐπειδὴ οὐκ ἐδύνατο, συνῆψεν εἰς
ταὐτὸν αὐτοῖς τὰς κορυφάς, καὶ διὰ ταῦτα, ᾧ
ἂν τὸ ἕτερον παραγένηται, ἐπακολουθεῖ ὕστερον
καὶ τὸ ἕτερον. ὥσπερ οὖν καὶ αὐτῷ μοι
ἔοικεν· ἐπειδὴ ὑπὸ τοῦ δεσμοῦ ἦν ἐν τῷ σκέλει
τὸ ἀλγεινόν, ἥκειν δὴ φαίνεται ἐπακολουθοῦν
τὸ ἡδύ.

The pain of bonds, the pleasure of release.

Ὁ οὖν Κέβης ὑπολαβών· Νὴ τὸν Δία, ὦ
Σώκρατες, ἔφη, εὖ γ' ἐποίησας ἀνα-
μνήσας με. περὶ γάρ τοι τῶν ποιημά-
των | ὧν πεποίηκας, ἐντείνας τοὺς τοῦ D
Αἰσώπου λόγους καὶ τὸ εἰς τὸν Ἀπόλλω προοί-
μιον, καὶ ἄλλοι τινές με ἤδη ἤροντο, ἀτὰρ καὶ
Εὔηνος πρῴην, ὅ τι ποτὲ διανοηθείς, ἐπειδὴ
δεῦρο ἦλθες, ἐποίησας αὐτά, πρότερον οὐδὲν

Why Socrates composed verse in prison.

60 πώποτε ποιήσας. εἰ οὖν τί σοι μέλει τοῦ
ἔχειν ἐμὲ Εὐήνῳ ἀποκρίνασθαι, ὅταν με αὖθις
ἐρωτᾷ (εὖ οἶδα γὰρ ὅτι ἐρήσεται), εἰπέ, τί χρὴ
λέγειν. Λέγε τοίνυν, ἔφη, αὐτῷ, ὦ Κέβης,
τἀληθῆ, ὅτι οὐκ ἐκείνῳ βουλόμενος οὐδὲ τοῖς
ποιήμασιν αὐτοῦ ἀντίτεχνος εἶναι ἐποίησα
E ταῦτα (ᾔδη | γὰρ ὡς οὐ ῥᾴδιον εἴη), ἀλλ᾽
ἐνυπνίων τινῶν ἀποπειρώμενος, τί λέγει, καὶ
ἀφοσιούμενος, εἰ πολλάκις ταύτην τὴν μουσικήν
μοι ἐπιτάττοι ποιεῖν. ἦν γὰρ δὴ ἄττα τοιάδε·
πολλάκις μοι φοιτῶν τὸ αὐτὸ ἐνύπνιον ἐν τῷ
παρελθόντι βίῳ, ἄλλοτ᾽ ἐν ἄλλῃ ὄψει φαινό-
μενον, τὰ αὐτὰ δὲ λέγον· Ὦ Σώκρατες, ἔφη,
μουσικὴν ποίει καὶ ἐργάζου. καὶ ἐγὼ ἔν γε
τῷ πρόσθεν χρόνῳ, ὅπερ ἔπραττον, τοῦτο
ὑπελάμβανον αὐτό μοι παρακελεύεσθαί τε |
61 καὶ ἐπικελεύειν, ὥσπερ οἱ τοῖς θέουσι διακελευό-
μενοι, καὶ ἐμοὶ οὕτω τὸ ἐνύπνιον, ὅπερ ἔπραττον,
τοῦτο ἐπικελεύειν, μουσικὴν ποιεῖν, ὡς φιλοσο-
φίας μὲν οὔσης μεγίστης μουσικῆς, ἐμοῦ δὲ
τοῦτο πράττοντος· νῦν δ᾽ ἐπειδὴ ἥ τε δίκη
ἐγένετο καὶ ἡ τοῦ θεοῦ ἑορτὴ διεκώλυέ με
ἀποθνῄσκειν, ἔδοξε χρῆναι, εἰ ἄρα πολλάκις
μοι προστάττοι τὸ ἐνύπνιον ταύτην τὴν δημώδη
μουσικὴν ποιεῖν, μὴ ἀπειθῆσαι αὐτῷ, ἀλλὰ
ποιεῖν. ἀσφαλέστερον γὰρ εἶναι μὴ ἀπιέναι
B πρὶν ἀφοσιώσασθαι ποιήσαντα | ποιήματα καὶ
πειθόμενον τῷ ἐνυπνίῳ. οὕτω δὴ πρῶτον μὲν
εἰς τὸν θεὸν ἐποίησα, οὗ ἦν ἡ παροῦσα θυσία·
μετὰ δὲ τὸν θεόν, ἐννοήσας ὅτι τὸν ποιητὴν
δέοι, εἴπερ μέλλοι ποιητὴς εἶναι, ποιεῖν μύθους,

ἀλλ᾽ οὐ λόγους (καὶ αὐτὸς οὐκ ἦ μυθολογικός) 61 διὰ ταῦτα δὴ οὓς προχείρους εἶχον καὶ ἠπιστάμην μύθους τοὺς Αἰσώπου, τούτους ἐποίησα, οἷς πρώτοις ἐνέτυχον.

The philosopher is willing to die, but may not kill himself.

Ταῦτα οὖν, ὦ Κέβης, Εὐήνῳ φράζε, καὶ ἐρρῶσθαι καί, ἂν σωφρονῇ, ἐμὲ διώκειν ὡς τάχιστα. ἄπειμι δέ, ὡς ἔοικε, | τήμερον· κελεύουσι γὰρ C Ἀθηναῖοι. καὶ ὁ Σιμμίας· Οἷον παρακελεύει, ἔφη, τοῦτο, ὦ Σώκρατες, Εὐήνῳ. πολλὰ γὰρ ἤδη ἐντετύχηκα τῷ ἀνδρί· σχεδὸν οὖν, ἐξ ὧν ἐγὼ ᾔσθημαι, οὐδ᾽ ὁπωστιοῦν σοι ἑκὼν εἶναι πείσεται. Τί δέ; ἦ δ᾽ ὅς, οὐ φιλόσοφος Εὔηνος; Ἔμοιγε δοκεῖ, ἔφη ὁ Σιμμίας. Ἐθελήσει τοίνυν καὶ Εὔηνος καὶ πᾶς, ὅτῳ ἀξίως τούτου τοῦ πράγματος μέτεστιν. οὐ μέντοι ἴσως βιάσεται αὑτόν· οὐ γάρ φασι θεμιτὸν εἶναι. καὶ ἅμα λέγων ταῦτα καθῆκε τὰ σκέλη ἐπὶ | τὴν γῆν, καὶ καθεζόμενος οὕτως D ἤδη τὰ λοιπὰ διελέγετο. ἤρετο οὖν αὐτὸν ὁ Κέβης· Πῶς τοῦτο λέγεις, ὦ Σώκρατες, τὸ μὴ θεμιτὸν εἶναι ἑαυτὸν βιάζεσθαι, ἐθέλειν δ᾽ ἂν τῷ ἀποθνῄσκοντι τὸν φιλόσοφον ἕπεσθαι; Τί δέ, ὦ Κέβης; οὐκ ἀκηκόατε σύ τε καὶ Σιμμίας περὶ τῶν τοιούτων Φιλολάῳ συγγεγονότες; Οὐδέν γε σαφές, ὦ Σώκρατες. Ἀλλὰ μὴν καὶ ἐγὼ ἐξ ἀκοῆς περὶ αὐτῶν λέγω· ἃ μὲν οὖν τυγχάνω ἀκηκοώς, φθόνος οὐδεὶς λέγειν. καὶ γὰρ ἴσως καὶ μάλιστα πρέπει μέλλοντα ἐκεῖσε | ἀποδημεῖν διασκοπεῖν τε καὶ μυθολογεῖν περὶ E τῆς ἀποδημίας τῆς ἐκεῖ, ποίαν τινὰ αὐτὴν

61 οἰόμεθα εἶναι· τί γὰρ ἄν τις καὶ ποιοῖ ἄλλο ἐν τῷ μέχρι ἡλίου δυσμῶν χρόνῳ;

Κατὰ τί δὴ οὖν ποτε οὔ φασι θεμιτὸν εἶναι αὐτὸν ἑαυτὸν ἀποκτιννύναι, ὦ Σώκρατες; ἤδη γὰρ ἔγωγε, ὅπερ νῦν δὴ σὺ ἤρου, καὶ Φιλολάου ἤκουσα, ὅτε παρ' ἡμῖν διῃτᾶτο, ἤδη δὲ καὶ ἄλλων τινῶν, ὡς οὐ δέοι τοῦτο ποιεῖν· σαφὲς δὲ περὶ αὐτῶν οὐδενὸς πώποτε οὐδὲν ἀκήκοα. |

62 Ἀλλὰ προθυμεῖσθαι χρή, ἔφη· τάχα γὰρ ἂν καὶ ἀκούσαις. ἴσως μέντοι θαυμαστόν σοι φανεῖται, εἰ τοῦτο μόνον τῶν ἄλλων ἁπάντων ἁπλοῦν ἐστιν καὶ οὐδέποτε τυγχάνει τῷ ἀνθρώπῳ, ὥσπερ καὶ τἆλλα, ἔστιν ὅτε καὶ οἷς βέλτιον τεθνάναι ἢ ζῆν· οἷς δὲ βέλτιον τεθνάναι, θαυμαστὸν ἴσως σοι φαίνεται, εἰ τούτοις τοῖς ἀνθρώποις μὴ ὅσιον αὐτοὺς ἑαυτοὺς εὖ ποιεῖν, ἀλλὰ ἄλλον δεῖ περιμένειν εὐεργέτην. καὶ ὁ Κέβης ἠρέμα ἐπιγελάσας, Ἴττω Ζεύς, ἔφη τῇ αὑτοῦ φωνῇ εἰπών. Καὶ γὰρ ἂν δόξειεν, ἔφη

B ὁ Σωκράτης, | οὕτω γ' εἶναι ἄλογον· οὐ μέντοι ἀλλ' ἴσως γ' ἔχει τινὰ λόγον. ὁ μὲν οὖν ἐν ἀπορρήτοις λεγόμενος περὶ αὐτῶν λόγος, ὡς ἔν τινι φρουρᾷ ἐσμεν οἱ ἄνθρωποι καὶ οὐ δεῖ δὴ ἑαυτὸν ἐκ ταύτης λύειν οὐδ' ἀποδιδράσκειν, μέγας τέ τίς μοι φαίνεται καὶ οὐ ῥᾴδιος διιδεῖν· οὐ μέντοι ἀλλὰ τόδε γέ μοι δοκεῖ, ὦ Κέβης, εὖ λέγεσθαι, τὸ θεοὺς εἶναι ἡμῶν τοὺς ἐπιμελουμένους καὶ ἡμᾶς τοὺς ἀνθρώπους ἓν τῶν κτημάτων τοῖς θεοῖς εἶναι. ἢ σοὶ οὐ δοκεῖ οὕτως; Ἔμοιγε, φησὶν

For we live in the care of the gods.

C ὁ Κέβης. Οὐκοῦν, ἦ δ' ὅς, καὶ | σὺ ἂν τῶν

σαυτοῦ κτημάτων, εἴ τι αὐτὸ ἑαυτὸ ἀποκτιννύοι, 62
μὴ σημήναντός σου ὅτι βούλει αὐτὸ τεθνάναι,
χαλεπαίνοις ἂν αὐτῷ, καὶ εἴ τινα ἔχοις τιμω-
ρίαν, τιμωροῖο ἄν; Πάνυ γ', ἔφη. Ἴσως τοίνυν
ταύτῃ οὐκ ἄλογον, μὴ πρότερον αὐτὸν ἀποκτιν-
νύναι δεῖν, πρὶν ἀνάγκην τινὰ θεὸς ἐπιπέμψῃ,
ὥσπερ καὶ τὴν νῦν ἡμῖν παροῦσαν.

Ἀλλ' εἰκός, ἔφη ὁ Κέβης, τοῦτό γε φαίνεται.
ὃ μέντοι νῦν δὴ ἔλεγες, τὸ τοὺς φιλοσόφους
ῥᾳδίως ἂν ἐθέλειν ἀποθνῄσκειν, ἔοικεν τοῦτο,
ὦ Σώκρατες, ἀτόπῳ, | εἴπερ ὃ νῦν δὴ ἐλέγομεν D
εὐλόγως ἔχει, τὸ θεόν τε εἶναι τὸν ἐπιμελούμενον
ἡμῶν καὶ ἡμᾶς ἐκείνου κτήματα εἶναι. τὸ γὰρ
μὴ ἀγανακτεῖν τοὺς φρονιμωτάτους ἐκ ταύτης
τῆς θεραπείας ἀπιόντας, ἐν ᾗ ἐπι-
στατοῦσιν αὐτῶν οἵπερ ἄριστοί εἰσιν
τῶν ὄντων ἐπιστάται, θεοί, οὐκ ἔχει
λόγον. οὐ γάρ που αὐτός γε αὐτοῦ
οἴεται ἄμεινον ἐπιμελήσεσθαι ἐλεύθερος γενό-
μενος· ἀλλ' ἀνόητος μὲν ἄνθρωπος τάχ' ἂν
οἰηθείη ταῦτα, φευκτέον εἶναι ἀπὸ τοῦ δεσπότου,
καὶ οὐκ ἂν λογίζοιτο | ὅτι οὐ δεῖ ἀπό γε τοῦ E
ἀγαθοῦ φεύγειν, ἀλλ' ὅτι μάλιστα παραμένειν,
διὸ ἀλογίστως ἂν φεύγοι· ὁ δὲ νοῦν ἔχων ἐπι-
θυμοῖ που ἂν ἀεὶ εἶναι παρὰ τῷ αὐτοῦ βελτίονι.
καίτοι οὕτως, ὦ Σώκρατες, τοὐναντίον εἶναι εἰκὸς
ἢ ὃ νῦν δὴ ἐλέγετο· τοὺς μὲν γὰρ φρονίμους
ἀγανακτεῖν ἀποθνῄσκοντας πρέπει, τοὺς δ'
ἄφρονας χαίρειν. ἀκούσας οὖν ὁ Σωκράτης
ἡσθῆναί τέ μοι ἔδοξε τῇ τοῦ | Κέβητος πραγ- 63
ματείᾳ, καὶ ἐπιβλέψας εἰς ἡμᾶς· Ἀεί τοι, ἔφη,

Cebes: "Then why do you not rather repine at death?"

63 ὁ Κέβης λόγους τινὰς ἀνερευνᾷ, καὶ οὐ πάνυ εὐθέως ἐθέλει πείθεσθαι, ὅ τι ἄν τις εἴπῃ. καὶ ὁ Σιμμίας· Ἀλλὰ μήν, ἔφη, ὦ Σώκρατες, νῦν γέ μοι δοκεῖ τι καὶ αὐτῷ λέγειν Κέβης· τί γὰρ ἂν βουλόμενοι ἄνδρες σοφοὶ ὡς ἀληθῶς δεσπότας ἀμείνους αὑτῶν φεύγοιεν καὶ ῥᾳδίως ἀπαλλάττοιντο αὐτῶν; καί μοι δοκεῖ Κέβης εἰς σὲ τείνειν τὸν λόγον, ὅτι οὕτω ῥᾳδίως φέρεις καὶ ἡμᾶς ἀπολείπων καὶ ἄρχοντας ἀγαθούς, ὡς
B αὐτὸς ὁμολογεῖς, θεούς. | Δίκαια, ἔφη, λέγετε. οἶμαι γὰρ ὑμᾶς λέγειν ὅτι χρή με πρὸς ταῦτα ἀπολογήσασθαι ὥσπερ ἐν δικαστηρίῳ. Πάνυ μὲν οὖν, ἔφη ὁ Σιμμίας.

"Because I shall go to the abode of other wise and good gods, and perhaps of men."

Φέρε δή, ἦ δ' ὅς, πειραθῶ πιθανώτερον πρὸς ὑμᾶς ἀπολογήσασθαι ἢ πρὸς τοὺς δικαστάς. ἐγὼ γάρ, ἔφη, ὦ Σιμμία τε καὶ Κέβης, εἰ μὲν μὴ ᾤμην ἥξειν πρῶτον μὲν παρὰ θεοὺς ἄλλους σοφούς τε καὶ ἀγαθούς, ἔπειτα καὶ παρ' ἀνθρώπους τετελευτηκότας ἀμείνους τῶν ἐνθάδε, ἠδίκουν ἂν οὐκ ἀγανακτῶν τῷ θανάτῳ· νῦν δὲ εὖ
C ἴστε ὅτι | παρ' ἄνδρας τε ἐλπίζω ἀφίξεσθαι ἀγαθούς — καὶ τοῦτο μὲν οὐκ ἂν πάνυ διισχυρισαίμην· ὅτι μέντοι παρὰ θεοὺς δεσπότας πάνυ ἀγαθοὺς ἥξειν, εὖ ἴστε ὅτι, εἴπερ τι ἄλλο τῶν τοιούτων, διισχυρισαίμην ἂν καὶ τοῦτο. ὥστε διὰ ταῦτα οὐχ ὁμοίως ἀγανακτῶ, ἀλλ' εὔελπίς εἰμι εἶναί τι τοῖς τετελευτηκόσι καί, ὥσπερ γε καὶ πάλαι λέγεται, πολὺ ἄμεινον τοῖς ἀγαθοῖς ἢ τοῖς κακοῖς. Τί οὖν, ἔφη ὁ Σιμμίας, ὦ Σώκρατες; αὐτὸς ἔχων τὴν διάνοιαν ταύτην

ἐν νῷ ἔχεις ἀπιέναι, ἢ κἂν ἡμῖν 63
μεταδοίης; | κοινὸν γὰρ δὴ ἔμοιγε D
δοκεῖ καὶ ἡμῖν εἶναι ἀγαθὸν τοῦτο, καὶ
ἅμα σοι ἀπολογία ἐστίν, ἐὰν ἅπερ λέγεις ἡμᾶς
πείσῃς. Ἀλλὰ πειράσομαι, ἔφη. πρῶτον δὲ
Κρίτωνα τόνδε σκεψώμεθα, τί ἐστιν ὃ βούλε-
σθαί μοι δοκεῖ πάλαι εἰπεῖν. Τί, ὦ Σώκρατες,
ἔφη ὁ Κρίτων, ἄλλο γε ἢ πάλαι μοι
λέγει ὁ μέλλων σοι δώσειν τὸ φάρ-
μακον, ὅτι χρή σοι φράζειν ὡς
ἐλάχιστα διαλέγεσθαι; φησὶ γὰρ θερ-
μαίνεσθαι μᾶλλον διαλεγομένους, δεῖν δὲ οὐδὲν
τοιοῦτον προσφέρειν τῷ φαρμάκῳ· εἰ δὲ μή, |
ἐνίοτε ἀναγκάζεσθαι καὶ δὶς καὶ τρὶς πίνειν E
τούς τι τοιοῦτον ποιοῦντας. καὶ ὁ Σωκράτης·
Ἔα, ἔφη, χαίρειν αὐτόν· ἀλλὰ μόνον τὸ ἑαυτοῦ
παρασκευαζέτω ὡς καὶ δὶς δώσων, ἐὰν δὲ δέῃ,
καὶ τρίς. Ἀλλὰ σχεδὸν μέν τι ᾔδη, ἔφη ὁ
Κρίτων· ἀλλά μοι πάλαι πράγματα παρέχει.
Ἔα αὐτόν, ἔφη.

Simmias: "The grounds of your belief?"

After an interruption and warning from the executioner—

Ἀλλ' ὑμῖν δὴ τοῖς δικασταῖς βούλομαι ἤδη
τὸν λόγον ἀποδοῦναι, ὥς μοι φαίνεται εἰκότως
ἀνὴρ τῷ ὄντι ἐν φιλοσοφίᾳ διατρίψας τὸν
βίον θαρρεῖν μέλλων | ἀποθανεῖσθαι, καὶ 64
εὔελπις εἶναι ἐκεῖ μέγιστα οἴσεσθαι
ἀγαθά, ἐπειδὰν τελευτήσῃ· πῶς ἂν οὖν
δὴ τοῦθ' οὕτως ἔχοι, ὦ Σιμμία τε καὶ Κέβης,
ἐγὼ πειράσομαι φράσαι.

Κινδυνεύουσι γὰρ ὅσοι τυγχάνουσιν ὀρθῶς
ἁπτόμενοι φιλοσοφίας λεληθέναι τοὺς
ἄλλους, ὅτι οὐδὲν ἄλλο αὐτοὶ ἐπιτη-

Socrates: I believe the philosopher

64 *dies with courage and hope, because his life has been but an eager practice in dying, i.e.*

δεύουσιν ἢ ἀποθνῄσκειν τε καὶ τεθνάναι. εἰ οὖν τοῦτο ἀληθές, ἄτοπον δήπου ἂν εἴη προθυμεῖσθαι μὲν ἐν παντὶ τῷ βίῳ μηδὲν ἄλλο ἢ τοῦτο, ἥκοντος δὲ δὴ αὐτοῦ ἀγανακτεῖν, ὃ πάλαι προεθυμοῦντό τε καὶ ἐπετήδευον. καὶ ὁ Σιμμίας γελάσας· Νὴ τὸν Δία, ἔφη, ὦ

B Σώκρατες, | οὐ πάνυ γέ με νῦν γελασείοντα ἐποίησας γελάσαι. οἶμαι γὰρ ἂν τοὺς πολλοὺς αὐτὸ τοῦτο ἀκούσαντας δοκεῖν εὖ πάνυ εἰρῆσθαι εἰς τοὺς φιλοσοφοῦντας, καὶ ξυμφάναι ἂν τοὺς μὲν παρ' ἡμῖν ἀνθρώπους καὶ πάνυ ὅτι τῷ ὄντι οἱ φιλοσοφοῦντες θανατῶσι καὶ σφᾶς γε οὐ λελήθασιν ὅτι ἄξιοί εἰσιν τοῦτο πάσχειν. Καὶ ἀληθῆ γ' ἂν λέγοιεν, ὦ Σιμμία, πλήν γε τοῦ σφᾶς μὴ λεληθέναι. λέληθεν γὰρ αὐτοὺς ᾗ τε θανατῶσι καὶ ᾗ ἄξιοί εἰσιν θανάτου καὶ οἵου θανάτου οἱ ὡς ἀληθῶς φιλόσοφοι. εἴπωμεν

C γάρ, | ἔφη, πρὸς ἡμᾶς αὐτούς, χαίρειν εἰπόντες ἐκείνοις· ἡγούμεθά τι τὸν θάνατον εἶναι; Πάνυ γε, ἔφη ὑπολαβὼν ὁ Σιμμίας. Ἆρα μὴ ἄλλο

in separating soul from body.

τι ἢ τὴν τῆς ψυχῆς ἀπὸ τοῦ σώματος ἀπαλλαγήν; καὶ εἶναι τοῦτο τὸ τεθνάναι, χωρὶς μὲν ἀπὸ τῆς ψυχῆς ἀπαλλαγὲν αὐτὸ καθ' αὑτὸ τὸ σῶμα γεγονέναι, χωρὶς δὲ τὴν ψυχὴν ἀπὸ τοῦ σώματος ἀπαλλαγεῖσαν αὐτὴν καθ' αὑτὴν εἶναι; ἆρα μὴ ἄλλο τι ᾖ θάνατος ἢ τοῦτο; Οὔκ, ἀλλὰ τοῦτο, ἔφη. Σκέψαι δή, ὦ ἀγαθέ, ἐὰν ἄρα καὶ σοὶ ξυνδοκῇ ἅπερ ἐμοί. ἐκ γὰρ τούτων μᾶλ-

D λον | οἶμαι ἡμᾶς εἴσεσθαι περὶ ὧν σκοποῦμεν.

φαίνεταί σοι φιλοσόφου ἀνδρὸς εἶναι 64
ἐσπουδακέναι περὶ τὰς ἡδονὰς καλου-
μένας τὰς τοιάσδε, οἷον σίτων τε καὶ
ποτῶν; Ἥκιστα, ὦ Σώκρατες, ἔφη ὁ
Σιμμίας. Τί δέ; τὰς τῶν ἀφροδισίων; Οὐ-
δαμῶς. Τί δέ; τὰς ἄλλας τὰς περὶ τὸ σῶμα
θεραπείας δοκεῖ σοι ἐντίμους ἡγεῖσθαι ὁ τοιοῦ-
τος; οἷον ἱματίων διαφερόντων κτήσεις καὶ
ὑποδημάτων καὶ τοὺς ἄλλους καλλωπισμοὺς
τοὺς περὶ τὸ σῶμα πότερον τιμᾶν δοκεῖ σοι ἢ
ἀτιμάζειν, καθ' ὅσον μὴ πολλὴ | ἀνάγκη E
μετέχειν αὐτῶν; Ἀτιμάζειν ἔμοιγε δοκεῖ, ἔφη,
ὅ γε ὡς ἀληθῶς φιλόσοφος. Οὐκοῦν ὅλως
δοκεῖ σοι, ἔφη, ἡ τοῦ τοιούτου πραγματεία οὐ
περὶ τὸ σῶμα εἶναι, ἀλλὰ καθ' ὅσον δύναται
ἀφεστάναι αὐτοῦ, πρὸς δὲ τὴν ψυχὴν τετρά-
φθαι; Ἔμοιγε. Ἆρ' οὖν πρῶτον μὲν ἐν τοῖς
τοιούτοις δῆλός ἐστιν ὁ φιλόσοφος ἀπολύων
ὅτι μάλιστα | τὴν ψυχὴν ἀπὸ τῆς τοῦ σώματος 65
κοινωνίας διαφερόντως τῶν ἄλλων ἀνθρώπων;
Φαίνεται. Καὶ δοκεῖ γε δήπου, ὦ Σιμμία, τοῖς
πολλοῖς ἀνθρώποις, ᾧ μηδὲν ἡδὺ τῶν τοιούτων
μηδὲ μετέχει αὐτῶν, οὐκ ἄξιον εἶναι ζῆν, ἀλλ'
ἐγγύς τι τείνειν τοῦ τεθνάναι ὁ μηδὲν φροντί-
ζων τῶν ἡδονῶν, αἳ διὰ τοῦ σώματός εἰσιν.
πάνυ μὲν οὖν ἀληθῆ λέγεις.

For, since the body's pleasures he has not sought,

Τί δὲ δὴ περὶ αὐτὴν τὴν τῆς φρονήσεως
κτῆσιν; πότερον ἐμπόδιον τὸ σῶμα
ἢ οὔ, ἐάν τις αὐτὸ ἐν τῇ ζητήσει
κοινωνὸν συμπαραλαμβάνῃ; οἷον τὸ
τοιόνδε | λέγω· ἆρα ἔχει ἀλήθειάν B

and since with its dull senses it but deceives and hinders the pleasure of the Soul in

65 her perception of Right and Beauty,

τινα ὄψις τε καὶ ἀκοὴ τοῖς ἀνθρώποις, ἢ τά γε τοιαῦτα καὶ οἱ ποιηταὶ ἡμῖν ἀεὶ θρυλοῦσιν, ὅτι οὔτ᾽ ἀκούομεν ἀκριβὲς οὐδὲν οὔτε ὁρῶμεν; καίτοι εἰ αὗται τῶν περὶ τὸ σῶμα αἰσθήσεων μὴ ἀκριβεῖς εἰσιν μηδὲ σαφεῖς, σχολῇ αἵ γε ἄλλαι· πᾶσαι γάρ που τούτων φαυλότεραί εἰσιν· ἢ σοὶ οὐ δοκοῦσιν; Πάνυ μὲν οὖν, ἔφη. Πότε οὖν, ἦ δ᾽ ὅς, ἡ ψυχὴ τῆς ἀληθείας ἅπτεται; ὅταν μὲν γὰρ μετὰ τοῦ σώματος ἐπιχειρῇ τι σκοπεῖν, δῆλον

C ὅτι τότε ἐξαπατᾶται ὑπ᾽ αὐτοῦ. | Ἀληθῆ λέγεις. Ἆρ᾽ οὖν οὐκ ἐν τῷ λογίζεσθαι, εἴπερ που ἄλλοθι, κατάδηλον αὐτῇ γίγνεταί τι τῶν ὄντων; Ναί. Λογίζεται δέ γέ που τότε κάλλιστα, ὅταν αὐτὴν τούτων μηδὲν παραλυπῇ, μήτε ἀκοὴ μήτε ὄψις μήτε ἀλγηδὼν μηδέ τις ἡδονή, ἀλλ᾽ ὅτι μάλιστα αὐτὴ καθ᾽ αὑτὴν γίγνηται ἐῶσα χαίρειν τὸ σῶμα, καὶ (καθ᾽ ὅσον δύναται) μὴ κοινωνοῦσα αὐτῷ μηδ᾽ ἁπτομένη ὀρέγηται τοῦ ὄντος. Ἔστι ταῦτα. Οὐκοῦν καὶ ἐνταῦθα ἡ τοῦ φιλοσόφου ψυχὴ

D μάλιστα ἀτιμάζει | τὸ σῶμα καὶ φεύγει ἀπ᾽ αὐτοῦ, ζητεῖ δὲ αὐτὴ καθ᾽ αὑτὴν γίγνεσθαι; Φαίνεται. Τί δὲ δὴ τὰ τοιάδε, ὦ Σιμμία; φαμέν τι εἶναι δίκαιον αὐτὸ ἢ οὐδέν; Φαμὲν μέντοι νὴ Δία. Καὶ καλόν γέ τι καὶ ἀγαθόν; Πῶς δ᾽ οὔ; Ἤδη οὖν πώποτέ τι τῶν τοιούτων τοῖς ὀφθαλμοῖς εἶδες; Οὐδαμῶς, ἦ δ᾽ ὅς. Ἀλλ᾽ ἄλλῃ τινὶ αἰσθήσει τῶν διὰ τοῦ σώματος ἐφήψω αὐτῶν; λέγω δὲ περὶ πάντων, οἷον μεγέθους πέρι, ὑγιείας, ἰσχύος,

καὶ τῶν ἄλλων ἑνὶ λόγῳ ἁπάντων τῆς οὐσίας, 65
ὃ τυγχάνει | ἕκαστον ὄν· ἆρα διὰ τοῦ σώματος E
αὐτῶν τὸ ἀληθέστατον θεωρεῖται, ἢ ὧδε ἔχει·
ὃς ἂν μάλιστα ἡμῶν καὶ ἀκριβέστατα παρασκευάσηται αὐτὸ ἕκαστον διανοηθῆναι περὶ οὗ σκοπεῖ, οὗτος ἂν ἐγγύτατα ἴοι τοῦ γνῶναι ἕκαστον; Πάνυ μὲν οὖν. Ἆρ᾽ οὖν ἐκεῖνος ἂν τοῦτο ποιήσειε καθαρώτατα, ὅστις ὅτι μάλιστα αὐτῇ τῇ διανοίᾳ ἴοι ἐφ᾽ ἕκαστον, μήτε τὴν ὄψιν παρατιθέμενος ἐν τῷ διανοεῖσθαι μήτε τινὰ ἄλλην αἴσθησιν ἐφέλκων μηδεμίαν |
μετὰ τοῦ λογισμοῦ, ἀλλ᾽ αὐτῇ καθ᾽ αὑτὴν 66
εἰλικρινεῖ τῇ διανοίᾳ χρώμενος αὐτὸ καθ᾽ αὑτὸ εἰλικρινὲς ἕκαστον ἐπιχειροῖ θηρεύειν τῶν ὄντων, ἀπαλλαγεὶς ὅτι μάλιστα ὀφθαλμῶν τε καὶ ὤτων καὶ ὡς ἔπος εἰπεῖν ξύμπαντος τοῦ σώματος, ὡς ταράττοντος καὶ οὐκ ἐῶντος τὴν ψυχὴν κτήσασθαι ἀλήθειάν τε καὶ φρόνησιν, ὅταν κοινωνῇ; ἆρ᾽ οὐχ οὗτός ἐστιν, ὦ Σιμμία, εἴπερ τις καὶ ἄλλος, ὁ τευξόμενος τοῦ ὄντος; Ὑπερφυῶς, ἔφη ὁ Σιμμίας, ὡς ἀληθῆ λέγεις, ὦ Σώκρατες.

Οὐκοῦν ἀνάγκη, | ἔφη, ἐκ πάντων τούτων B

death can appear to him only as a road to his goal—away from the body, the source of all his woes.

παρίστασθαι δόξαν τοιάνδε τινὰ τοῖς γνησίως φιλοσόφοις, ὥστε καὶ πρὸς ἀλλήλους τοιαῦτα ἄττα λέγειν, ὅτι κινδυνεύει τοι ὥσπερ ἀτραπός τις ἐκφέρειν ἡμᾶς, ὅτι, ἕως ἂν τὸ σῶμα ἔχωμεν μετὰ τοῦ λόγου ἐν τῇ σκέψει, καὶ συμπεφυρμένη ᾖ ἡμῶν ἡ ψυχὴ μετὰ τοιούτου κακοῦ, οὐ μή ποτε κτησώμεθα ἱκανῶς οὗ ἐπι-

66 θυμοῦμεν· φαμὲν δὲ τοῦτο εἶναι τὸ ἀληθές.
μυρίας μὲν γὰρ ἡμῖν ἀσχολίας παρέχει τὸ
σῶμα διὰ τὴν ἀναγκαίαν τροφήν· ἔτι δέ, ἄν
C τινες | νόσοι προσπέσωσιν, ἐμποδίζουσιν ἡμῶν
τὴν τοῦ ὄντος θήραν. ἐρώτων δὲ καὶ ἐπι-
θυμιῶν καὶ φόβων καὶ εἰδώλων παντοδαπῶν
καὶ φλυαρίας ἐμπίμπλησιν ἡμᾶς πολλῆς, ὥστε
τὸ λεγόμενον ὡς ἀληθῶς τῷ ὄντι ὑπ᾽ αὐτοῦ
οὐδὲ φρονῆσαι ἡμῖν ἐγγίγνεται οὐδέποτε οὐδέν.
καὶ γὰρ πολέμους καὶ στάσεις καὶ μάχας
οὐδὲν ἄλλο παρέχει ἢ τὸ σῶμα καὶ αἱ τούτου
ἐπιθυμίαι. διὰ γὰρ τὴν τῶν χρημάτων κτῆσιν
πάντες οἱ πόλεμοι γίγνονται, τὰ δὲ χρήματα
D ἀναγκαζόμεθα κτᾶσθαι διὰ | τὸ σῶμα, δουλεύ-
οντες τῇ τούτου θεραπείᾳ· καὶ ἐκ τούτου
ἀσχολίαν ἄγομεν φιλοσοφίας πέρι διὰ πάντα
ταῦτα. τὸ δ᾽ ἔσχατον πάντων ὅτι, ἐάν τις ἡμῖν
καὶ σχολὴ γένηται ἀπ᾽ αὐτοῦ καὶ τραπώμεθα
πρὸς τὸ σκοπεῖν τι, ἐν ταῖς ζητήσεσιν αὖ
πανταχοῦ παραπῖπτον θόρυβον παρέχει καὶ
ταραχὴν καὶ ἐκπλήττει, ὥστε μὴ δύνασθαι ὑπ᾽
αὐτοῦ καθορᾶν τἀληθές, ἀλλὰ τῷ ὄντι ἡμῖν
δέδεικται ὅτι, εἰ μέλλομέν ποτε καθαρῶς τι
εἴσεσθαι, ἀπαλλακτέον αὐτοῦ καὶ αὐτῇ τῇ
E ψυχῇ θεατέον | αὐτὰ τὰ πράγματα· καὶ τότε,
ὡς ἔοικεν, ἡμῖν ἔσται οὗ ἐπιθυμοῦμέν τε καί
φαμεν ἐρασταὶ εἶναι, φρονήσεως, ἐπειδὰν
τελευτήσωμεν, ὡς ὁ λόγος σημαίνει, ζῶσιν δὲ
οὔ. εἰ γὰρ μὴ οἷόντε μετὰ τοῦ σώματος μηδὲν
καθαρῶς γνῶναι, δυοῖν θάτερον, ἢ οὐδαμοῦ
ἔστιν κτήσασθαι τὸ εἰδέναι ἢ τελευτήσασιν·

τότε γὰρ αὐτὴ καθ᾽ αὑτὴν ἡ ψυχὴ ἔσται
χωρὶς | τοῦ σώματος, πρότερον δ᾽ οὔ. καὶ ἐν 67
ᾧ ἂν ζῶμεν, οὕτως, ὡς ἔοικεν, ἐγγυτάτω
ἐσόμεθα τοῦ εἰδέναι, ἐὰν ὅτι μάλιστα μηδὲν
ὁμιλῶμεν τῷ σώματι μηδὲ κοινωνῶμεν, ὅτι μὴ
πᾶσα ἀνάγκη, μηδὲ ἀναπιμπλώμεθα τῆς τούτου
φύσεως, ἀλλὰ καθαρεύωμεν ἀπ᾽ αὐτοῦ, ἕως ἂν
ὁ θεὸς αὐτὸς ἀπολύσῃ ἡμᾶς· καὶ οὕτω μὲν
καθαροὶ ἀπαλλαττόμενοι τῆς τοῦ σώματος
ἀφροσύνης, ὡς τὸ εἰκός, μετὰ τοιούτων τε
ἐσόμεθα καὶ γνωσόμεθα δι᾽ ἡμῶν αὐτῶν πᾶν
τὸ εἰλικρινές· τοῦτο δ᾽ ἐστὶν ἴσως | τὸ ἀληθές. B
μὴ καθαρῷ γὰρ καθαροῦ ἐφάπτεσθαι μὴ οὐ
θεμιτὸν ᾖ. τοιαῦτα οἶμαι, ὦ Σιμμία, ἀναγκαῖον
εἶναι πρὸς ἀλλήλους λέγειν τε καὶ δοξάζειν
πάντας τοὺς ὀρθῶς φιλομαθεῖς. ἢ οὐ δοκεῖ
σοι οὕτως; Παντός γε μᾶλλον, ὦ Σώκρατες.

Οὐκοῦν, ἔφη ὁ Σωκράτης, εἰ ταῦτα ἀληθῆ,
ὦ ἑταῖρε, πολλὴ ἐλπὶς ἀφικομένῳ, οἷ ἐγὼ πορεύ-
ομαι, ἐκεῖ ἱκανῶς, εἴπερ που ἄλλοθι, κτήσασθαι
τοῦτο, οὗ ἕνεκα ἡ πολλὴ πραγματεία ἡμῖν ἐν
τῷ παρελθόντι βίῳ γέγονεν, ὥστε ἥ γε ἀποδημία
ἡ νῦν μοι | προστεταγμένη μετὰ ἀγαθῆς ἐλπίδος C
γίγνεται καὶ ἄλλῳ ἀνδρί, ὃς ἡγεῖταί οἱ παρ-
εσκευάσθαι τὴν διάνοιαν ὥσπερ κεκαθαρμένην.
Πάνυ μὲν οὖν, ἔφη ὁ Σιμμίας. Κάθαρσις δὲ εἶναι
ἆρα οὐ τοῦτο ξυμβαίνει, ὅπερ πάλαι
ἐν τῷ λόγῳ λέγεται, τὸ χωρίζειν ὅτι
μάλιστα ἀπὸ τοῦ σώματος τὴν ψυχὴν
καὶ ἐθίσαι αὐτὴν καθ᾽ αὑτὴν παντα-
χόθεν ἐκ τοῦ σώματος συναγείρεσθαί τε καὶ

Death then being a purification and a separation for his soul

67 ἀθροίζεσθαι, καὶ οἰκεῖν κατὰ τὸ δυνατὸν καὶ ἐν
τῷ νῦν παρόντι καὶ ἐν τῷ ἔπειτα μόνην καθ'
D αὐτήν, | ἐκλυομένην ὥσπερ ἐκ δεσμῶν ἐκ τοῦ
σώματος; Πάνυ μὲν οὖν, ἔφη. Οὐκοῦν τοῦτό
γε θάνατος ὀνομάζεται, λύσις καὶ χωρισμὸς
ψυχῆς ἀπὸ σώματος; Παντάπασί γε, ἦ δ' ὅς.
Λύειν δέ γε αὐτήν, ὥς φαμεν, προθυμοῦνται
ἀεὶ μάλιστα καὶ μόνοι οἱ φιλοσοφοῦντες ὀρθῶς,
καὶ τὸ μελέτημα αὐτὸ τοῦτό ἐστιν τῶν
φιλοσόφων, λύσις καὶ χωρισμὸς ψυχῆς ἀπὸ
σώματος, ἢ οὔ; Φαίνεται. Οὐκοῦν, ὅπερ ἐν
ἀρχῇ ἔλεγον, γελοῖον ἂν εἴη ἄνδρα
παρασκευάζονθ' ἑαυτὸν ἐν τῷ βίῳ
E ὅτι ἐγγυτάτω ὄντα | τοῦ τεθνάναι οὕτω
ζῆν, κἄπειθ' ἥκοντος αὐτῷ τούτου ἀγανακτεῖν;
οὐ γελοῖον; Πῶς δ' οὔ; Τῷ ὄντι ἄρα, ἔφη,
ὦ Σιμμία, οἱ ὀρθῶς φιλοσοφοῦντες ἀποθνῄσκειν
μελετῶσι, καὶ τὸ τεθνάναι ἥκιστα αὐτοῖς ἀνθρώ-
πων φοβερόν. ἐκ τῶνδε δὲ σκόπει. εἰ γὰρ
διαβέβληνται μὲν πανταχῇ τῷ σώματι, αὐτὴν
δὲ καθ' αὐτὴν ἐπιθυμοῦσι τὴν ψυχὴν ἔχειν,—
τούτου δὲ γιγνομένου εἰ φοβοῖντο καὶ ἀγανα-
κτοῖεν, οὐ πολλὴ ἂν ἀλογία εἴη, εἰ μὴ ἄσμενοι
68 ἐκεῖσε ἴοιεν, οἷ ἀφικομένοις ἐλπίς ἐστιν οὗ | διὰ
βίου ἤρων τυχεῖν (ἤρων δὲ φρονήσεως), ᾧ τε
διεβέβληντο, τούτου ἀπηλλάχθαι συνόντος
αὐτοῖς; ἢ ἀνθρωπίνων μὲν παιδικῶν καὶ γυναι-
κῶν καὶ ὑέων ἀποθανόντων πολλοὶ δὴ ἑκόντες
ἠθέλησαν εἰς Ἅιδου ἐλθεῖν, ὑπὸ ταύτης ἀγόμενοι
τῆς ἐλπίδος, τῆς τοῦ ὄψεσθαί τε ἐκεῖ ὧν
ἐπεθύμουν καὶ συνέσεσθαι· φρονήσεως δὲ ἄρα

is, as I said, the practice of the wise man's life.

τις τῷ ὄντι ἐρῶν, καὶ λαβὼν σφόδρα τὴν 68
αὐτὴν ταύτην ἐλπίδα, μηδαμοῦ ἄλλοθι ἐντεύξε-
σθαι αὐτῇ ἀξίως λόγου ἢ ἐν Ἅιδου, ἀγανακτήσει
τε ἀποθνῄσκων | καὶ οὐχ ἄσμενος εἶσιν αὐτόσε; B
οἴεσθαί γε χρή, ἐὰν τῷ ὄντι γε ᾖ, ὦ ἑταῖρε,
φιλόσοφος· σφόδρα γὰρ αὐτῷ ταῦτα δόξει,
μηδαμοῦ ἄλλοθι καθαρῶς ἐντεύξεσθαι φρονήσει
ἀλλ' ἢ ἐκεῖ. εἰ δὲ τοῦτο οὕτως ἔχει, ὅπερ
ἄρτι ἔλεγον, οὐ πολλὴ ἂν ἀλογία εἴη, εἰ
φοβοῖτο τὸν θάνατον ὁ τοιοῦτος; Πολλὴ μέντοι
νὴ Δία, ἦ δ' ὅς.

Οὐκοῦν ἱκανόν σοι τεκμήριον, ἔφη, τοῦτο
ἀνδρός, ὃν ἂν ἴδῃς ἀγανακτοῦντα
μέλλοντα ἀποθανεῖσθαι, ὅτι οὐκ ἄρ'
ἦν φιλόσοφος ἀλλά τις φιλοσώματος;

He who repines is no philosopher.

ὁ αὐτὸς δέ | που οὗτος τυγχάνει ὢν καὶ C
φιλοχρήματος καὶ φιλότιμος, ἤτοι τὰ ἕτερα
τούτων ἢ ἀμφότερα. Πάνυ, ἔφη, ἔχει οὕτως,
ὡς λέγεις. Ἆρ' οὖν, ἔφη, ὦ Σιμμία, οὐ καὶ
ἡ ὀνομαζομένη ἀνδρεία τοῖς οὕτω διακειμένοις
μάλιστα προσήκει; Πάντως δήπου, ἔφη. Οὐκοῦν
καὶ ἡ σωφροσύνη, ἣν καὶ οἱ πολλοὶ ὀνομάζουσι
σωφροσύνην, τὸ περὶ τὰς ἐπιθυμίας μὴ ἐπτοῆ-
σθαι, ἀλλ' ὀλιγώρως ἔχειν καὶ κοσμίως, ἆρ'
οὐ τούτοις μόνοις προσήκει τοῖς μάλιστα τοῦ
σώματος ὀλιγωροῦσίν τε καὶ ἐν φιλοσοφίᾳ
ζῶσιν; | Ἀνάγκη, ἔφη. Εἰ γὰρ ἐθέλεις, ἦ δ' D
ὅς, ἐννοῆσαι τήν γε τῶν ἄλλων
ἀνδρείαν τε καὶ σωφροσύνην, δόξει
σοι εἶναι ἄτοπος. Πῶς δή, ὦ
Σώκρατες; Οἶσθα, ἦ δ' ὅς, ὅτι τὸν

There is a false bravery which is fear, and a false temperance which is license,

68 θάνατον ἡγοῦνται πάντες οἱ ἄλλοι τῶν μεγάλων
κακῶν; Καὶ μάλ', ἔφη. Οὐκοῦν φόβῳ μειζόνων
κακῶν ὑπομένουσιν αὐτῶν οἱ ἀνδρεῖοι τὸν
θάνατον, ὅταν ὑπομένωσιν; Ἔστι ταῦτα. Τῷ
δεδιέναι ἄρα καὶ δέει ἀνδρεῖοί εἰσι πάντες πλὴν
οἱ φιλόσοφοι. καίτοι ἄλογόν γε δέει τινὰ καὶ
E δειλίᾳ ἀνδρεῖον εἶναι. Πάνυ | μὲν οὖν. Τί δὲ
οἱ κόσμιοι αὐτῶν; οὐ ταὐτὸν τοῦτο πεπόν-
θασιν—ἀκολασίᾳ τινὶ σώφρονές εἰσιν; καίτοι
φαμέν γε ἀδύνατον εἶναι, ἀλλ' ὅμως αὐτοῖς
συμβαίνει τούτῳ ὅμοιον τὸ πάθος τὸ περὶ
ταύτην τὴν εὐήθη σωφροσύνην· φοβούμενοι
γὰρ ἑτέρων ἡδονῶν στερηθῆναι καὶ ἐπιθυμοῦντες
ἐκείνων, ἄλλων ἀπέχονται ὑπ' ἄλλων κρατού-
μενοι. καίτοι καλοῦσί γε ἀκολασίαν τὸ ὑπὸ |
69 τῶν ἡδονῶν ἄρχεσθαι· ἀλλ' ὅμως συμβαίνει
αὐτοῖς κρατουμένοις ὑφ' ἡδονῶν κρατεῖν ἄλλων
ἡδονῶν. τοῦτο δ' ὅμοιόν ἐστιν ᾧ νῦν δὴ
ἐλέγετο, τῷ τρόπον τινὰ δι' ἀκολασίαν αὐτοὺς
σεσωφρονίσθαι. Ἔοικε γάρ. Ὦ μακάριε
Σιμμία, μὴ γὰρ οὐχ αὕτη ᾖ ἡ ὀρθὴ πρὸς
ἀρετὴν ἀλλαγή, ἡδονὰς πρὸς ἡδονὰς καὶ λύπας
πρὸς λύπας καὶ φόβον πρὸς φόβον καταλ-
λάττεσθαι, καὶ μείζω πρὸς ἐλάττω, ὥσπερ
νομίσματα, ἀλλ' ᾖ ἐκεῖνο μόνον τὸ νόμισμα
ὀρθόν, ἀντὶ οὗ δεῖ ἅπαντα ταῦτα καταλλάτ-
B τεσθαι, φρόνησις, | καὶ τούτου μὲν πάντα καὶ
μετὰ τούτου ὠνούμενά τε καὶ πιπρασκόμενα
τῷ ὄντι ᾖ καὶ ἀνδρεία καὶ σωφροσύνη καὶ
δικαιοσύνη καὶ ξυλλήβδην ἀληθὴς ἀρετὴ μετὰ
φρονήσεως, καὶ προσγιγνομένων καὶ ἀπογιγνο-

μένων καὶ ἡδονῶν καὶ φόβων καὶ τῶν ἄλλων 69
πάντων τῶν τοιούτων· χωριζόμενα δὲ φρονήσεως
ἀλλαττόμενα ἀντὶ ἀλλήλων μὴ σκιαγραφία τις
ᾖ ἡ τοιαύτη ἀρετὴ καὶ τῷ ὄντι ἀνδραποδώδης
τε καὶ οὐδὲν ὑγιὲς οὐδ' ἀληθὲς ἔχῃ, τὸ δ'
ἀληθὲς τῷ ὄντι ᾖ κάθαρσίς | τις τῶν τοιούτων C
πάντων, καὶ ἡ σωφροσύνη καὶ ἡ
δικαιοσύνη καὶ ἀνδρεία καὶ αὐτὴ ἡ
φρόνησις μὴ καθαρμός τις ᾖ. καὶ κινδυνεύουσι
καὶ οἱ τὰς τελετὰς ἡμῖν οὗτοι καταστήσαντες
οὐ φαῦλοι εἶναι, ἀλλὰ τῷ ὄντι πάλαι αἰνίτ-
τεσθαι ὅτι, ὃς ἂν ἀμύητος καὶ ἀτέλεστος εἰς
Ἅιδου ἀφίκηται, ἐν βορβόρῳ κείσεται, ὁ δὲ
κεκαθαρμένος τε καὶ τετελεσμένος ἐκεῖσε ἀφικό-
μενος μετὰ θεῶν οἰκήσει. εἰσὶν γὰρ δή, ὥς
φασιν οἱ περὶ τὰς τελετάς, πολλοὶ μὲν ναρθη-
κοφόροι, βάκχοι δέ τε παῦροι· οὗτοι δ' εἰσὶν |
κατὰ τὴν ἐμὴν δόξαν οὐκ ἄλλοι ἢ οἱ πεφιλο- D
σοφηκότες ὀρθῶς. ὧν δὴ καὶ ἐγὼ κατά γε τὸ
δυνατὸν οὐδὲν ἀπέλιπον ἐν τῷ βίῳ, ἀλλὰ
παντὶ τρόπῳ προυθυμήθην γενέσθαι· εἰ δ'
ὀρθῶς προυθυμήθην καί τι ἠνύσαμεν, ἐκεῖσε
ἐλθόντες τὸ σαφὲς εἰσόμεθα, ἂν θεὸς ἐθέλῃ,
ὀλίγον ὕστερον, ὡς ἐμοὶ δοκεῖ. ταῦτ' οὖν ἐγώ,
ἔφη, ὦ Σιμμία τε καὶ Κέβης, ἀπολογοῦμαι, ὡς
εἰκότως ὑμᾶς τε ἀπολείπων καὶ τοὺς
ἐνθάδε δεσπότας οὐ χαλεπῶς φέρω
οὐδ' ἀγανακτῶ, ἡγούμενος κἀκεῖ |
οὐδὲν ἧττον ἢ ἐνθάδε δεσπόταις τε E
ἀγαθοῖς ἐντεύξεσθαι καὶ ἑταίροις· [τοῖς δὲ
πολλοῖς ἀπιστίαν παρέχει·] εἴ τι οὖν ὑμῖν

but the true virtues purify.

This is the ground, friends, for my courage and hope.

69 πιθανώτερός εἰμι ἐν τῇ ἀπολογίᾳ ἢ τοῖς
Ἀθηναίων δικασταῖς, εὖ ἂν ἔχοι.

* * * * * * *

84 Καὶ ὁ Σιμμίας ἔφη. Καὶ μήν, ὦ Σώκρατες,
D τἀληθῆ σοι ἐρῶ. πάλαι γὰρ ἡμῶν
ἑκάτερος ἀπορῶν τὸν ἕτερον προωθεῖ
καὶ κελεύει ἐρέσθαι διὰ τὸ ἐπιθυμεῖν

The song of the dying swan.

μὲν ἀκοῦσαι ὀκνεῖν δὲ ὄχλον παρέχειν, μή σοι
ἀηδὲς ᾖ διὰ τὴν παροῦσαν συμφοράν. καὶ ὃς
ἀκούσας ἐγέλασέν τε ἠρέμα καί φησιν· Βαβαί,
ὦ Σιμμία· ἦ που χαλεπῶς ἂν τοὺς ἄλλους
E ἀνθρώπους | πείσαιμι ὡς οὐ συμφορὰν ἡγοῦμαι
τὴν παροῦσαν τύχην, ὅτε γε μηδ' ὑμᾶς δύναμαι
πείθειν, ἀλλὰ φοβεῖσθε, μὴ δυσκολώτερόν τι
νῦν διάκειμαι ἢ ἐν τῷ πρόσθεν βίῳ· καί, ὡς
ἔοικε, τῶν κύκνων δοκῶ φαυλότερος ὑμῖν εἶναι
τὴν μαντικήν, οἵ, ἐπειδὰν αἴσθωνται ὅτι δεῖ
αὐτοὺς ἀποθανεῖν, ᾄδοντες καὶ ἐν τῷ πρόσθεν
85 χρόνῳ, τότε δὴ πλεῖστα | καὶ μάλιστα ᾄδουσι,
γεγηθότες ὅτι μέλλουσι παρὰ τὸν θεὸν ἀπιέναι,
οὗπέρ εἰσι θεράποντες. οἱ δ' ἄνθρωποι διὰ τὸ
αὑτῶν δέος τοῦ θανάτου καὶ τῶν κύκνων
καταψεύδονται, καί φασιν αὐτοὺς θρηνοῦντας
τὸν θάνατον ὑπὸ λύπης ἐξᾴδειν, καὶ οὐ λογίζονται
ὅτι οὐδὲν ὄρνεον ᾄδει, ὅταν πεινῇ ἢ ῥιγῷ
ἤ τινα ἄλλην λύπην λυπῆται, οὐδὲ αὐτὴ ἥ τε
ἀηδὼν καὶ χελιδὼν καὶ ὁ ἔποψ, ἃ δή φασι
διὰ λύπην θρηνοῦντα ᾄδειν· ἀλλ' οὔτε ταῦτά
μοι φαίνεται λυπούμενα ᾄδειν οὔτε οἱ κύκνοι,
B ἀλλ' ἅτε, οἶμαι, | τοῦ Ἀπόλλωνος ὄντες μαντικοί

τέ εἰσι καὶ προειδότες τὰ ἐν Ἅιδου ἀγαθὰ 85
ᾄδουσι καὶ τέρπονται ἐκείνην τὴν ἡμέραν
διαφερόντως ἢ ἐν τῷ ἔμπροσθεν χρόνῳ. ἐγὼ
δὲ καὶ αὐτὸς ἡγοῦμαι ὁμόδουλός τε εἶναι τῶν
κύκνων καὶ ἱερὸς τοῦ αὐτοῦ θεοῦ, καὶ οὐ
χεῖρον ἐκείνων τὴν μαντικὴν ἔχειν παρὰ τοῦ
δεσπότου, οὐδὲ δυσθυμότερον αὐτῶν τοῦ βίου
ἀπαλλάττεσθαι. ἀλλὰ τούτου γε ἕνεκα λέγειν
τε χρὴ καὶ ἐρωτᾶν ὅ τι ἂν βούλησθε, ἕως
Ἀθηναίων ἐῶσιν ἄνδρες ἕνδεκα.

Socrates' Death.

Τὸ μὲν οὖν ταῦτα | διισχυρίσασθαι οὕτως 114
ἔχειν, ὡς ἐγὼ διελήλυθα, οὐ πρέπει D
νοῦν ἔχοντι ἀνδρί· ὅτι μέντοι ἢ ταῦτ'
ἐστὶν ἢ τοιαῦτ' ἄττα περὶ τὰς ψυχὰς

The good man therefore may have a fair hope.

ἡμῶν καὶ τὰς οἰκήσεις, ἐπείπερ ἀθάνατόν γε ἡ
ψυχὴ φαίνεται οὖσα, τοῦτο καὶ πρέπειν μοι δοκεῖ
καὶ ἄξιον κινδυνεῦσαι οἰομένῳ οὕτως ἔχειν· καλὸς
γὰρ ὁ κίνδυνος· καὶ χρὴ τὰ τοιαῦτα ὥσπερ
ἐπᾴδειν ἑαυτῷ, διὸ δὴ ἔγωγε καὶ πάλαι μηκύνω
τὸν μῦθον. ἀλλὰ τούτων δὴ ἕνεκα θαρρεῖν χρὴ
περὶ τῇ ἑαυτοῦ ψυχῇ ἄνδρα, ὅστις ἐν τῷ βίῳ
τὰς μὲν ἄλλας ἡδονὰς | τὰς περὶ τὸ σῶμα καὶ E
τοὺς κόσμους εἴασε χαίρειν, ὡς ἀλλοτρίους τε
ὄντας, καὶ πλέον θάτερον ἡγησάμενος ἀπεργά-
ζεσθαι, τὰς δὲ περὶ τὸ μανθάνειν ἐσπούδασέ
τε καὶ κοσμήσας τὴν ψυχὴν οὐκ ἀλλοτρίῳ
ἀλλὰ τῷ αὑτῆς κόσμῳ, σωφροσύνῃ τε καὶ
δικαιοσύνῃ καὶ ἀνδρείᾳ καὶ ἐλευθερίᾳ καὶ |

115 ἀληθείᾳ, οὕτω περιμένει τὴν εἰς Ἅιδου πορείαν, ὡς πορευσόμενος ὅταν ἡ εἱμαρμένη καλῇ. ὑμεῖς μὲν οὖν, ἔφη, ὦ Σιμμία τε καὶ Κέβης καὶ οἱ ἄλλοι, εἰς αὖθις ἔν τινι χρόνῳ ἕκαστοι πορεύσεσθε· ἐμὲ δὲ νῦν ἤδη καλεῖ, φαίη ἂν ἀνὴρ τραγικός, ἡ εἱμαρμένη, καὶ σχεδόν τί μοι ὥρα τραπέσθαι πρὸς τὸ λουτρόν· δοκεῖ γὰρ δὴ βέλτιον εἶναι λουσάμενον πιεῖν τὸ φάρμακον καὶ μὴ πράγματα ταῖς γυναιξὶ παρέχειν νεκρὸν λούειν.

Ταῦτα δὴ εἰπόντος αὐτοῦ ὁ Κρίτων· Εἶεν, | B ἔφη, ὦ Σώκρατες· τί δὲ τούτοις ἢ ἐμοὶ ἐπιστέλλεις ἢ περὶ τῶν παίδων ἢ περὶ ἄλλου του, ὅ τι ἄν σοι ποιοῦντες ἡμεῖς ἐν χάριτι μάλιστα ποιοῖμεν; Ἅπερ ἀεὶ λέγω, ἔφη, ὦ Κρίτων, οὐδὲν καινότερον—ὅτι ὑμῶν αὐτῶν ἐπιμελούμενοι ὑμεῖς καὶ ἐμοὶ καὶ τοῖς ἐμοῖς καὶ ὑμῖν αὐτοῖς ἐν χάριτι ποιήσετε ἅττ' ἂν ποιῆτε κἂν μὴ νῦν ὁμολογήσητε· ἐὰν δὲ ὑμῶν μὲν αὐτῶν ἀμελῆτε καὶ μὴ 'θέλητε ὥσπερ κατ' ἴχνη κατὰ τὰ νῦν τε εἰρημένα καὶ τὰ ἐν τῷ ἔμπροσθεν χρόνῳ ζῆν, οὐδὲ ἐὰν

Socrates last advice to his friends.

C πολλὰ ὁμολογήσητε | ἐν τῷ παρόντι καὶ σφόδρα, οὐδὲν πλέον ποιήσετε. Ταῦτα μὲν τοίνυν προθυμηθησόμεθα, ἔφη, οὕτω ποιεῖν· θάπτωμεν δέ σε τίνα τρόπον; Ὅπως ἄν, ἔφη, βούλησθε, ἐάνπερ γε λάβητέ με καὶ μὴ ἐκφύγω ὑμᾶς. γελάσας δὲ ἅμα ἡσυχῇ καὶ πρὸς ἡμᾶς ἀποβλέψας εἶπεν· Οὐ πείθω, ὦ ἄνδρες, Κρίτωνα, ὡς ἐγώ εἰμι οὗτος Σωκράτης, ὁ νυνὶ διαλεγόμενος καὶ διατάτ-

How to dispose of his body.

των ἕκαστον τῶν λεγομένων, ἀλλ' οἴεταί με 115
ἐκεῖνον εἶναι, ὃν ὄψεται ὀλίγον ὕστερον νεκρόν,
καὶ ἐρωτᾷ δή, | πῶς με θάπτῃ. ὅτι δὲ ἐγὼ D
πάλαι πολὺν λόγον πεποίημαι, ὡς, ἐπειδὰν
πίω τὸ φάρμακον, οὐκέτι ὑμῖν παραμενῶ, ἀλλ'
οἰχήσομαι ἀπιὼν εἰς μακάρων δή τινας εὐδαιμονίας, ταῦτά μοι δοκῶ αὐτῷ ἄλλως λέγειν,
παραμυθούμενος ἅμα μὲν ὑμᾶς, ἅμα δ' ἐμαυτόν.
ἐγγυήσασθε οὖν με πρὸς Κρίτωνα, ἔφη, τὴν
ἐναντίαν ἐγγύην ἢ ἣν οὗτος πρὸς τοὺς δικαστὰς
ἠγγυᾶτο. οὗτος μὲν γὰρ ἦ μὴν παραμενεῖν·
ὑμεῖς δὲ ἦ μὴν μὴ παραμενεῖν ἐγγυήσασθε,
ἐπειδὰν ἀποθάνω, ἀλλὰ οἰχήσεσθαι | ἀπιόντα, E
ἵνα Κρίτων ῥᾷον φέρῃ καὶ μὴ ὁρῶν μου τὸ
σῶμα ἢ καιόμενον ἢ κατορυττόμενον ἀγανακτῇ
ὑπὲρ ἐμοῦ ὡς δεινὰ πάσχοντος, μηδὲ λέγῃ ἐν
τῇ ταφῇ, ὡς ἢ προτίθεται Σωκράτη ἢ ἐκφέρει
ἢ κατορύττει. εὖ γὰρ ἴσθι, ἦ δ' ὅς, ὦ ἄριστε
Κρίτων, τὸ μὴ καλῶς λέγειν οὐ μόνον εἰς
αὐτὸ τοῦτο πλημμελές, ἀλλὰ καὶ κακόν τι
ἐμποιεῖ ταῖς ψυχαῖς. ἀλλὰ θαρρεῖν τε χρὴ
καὶ φάναι τοὐμὸν σῶμα θάπτειν, καὶ θάπτειν
οὕτως, | ὅπως ἄν σοι φίλον ᾖ καὶ μάλιστα 116
ἡγῇ νόμιμον εἶναι.

Ταῦτ' εἰπὼν ἐκεῖνος μὲν ἀνίστατο εἰς οἴκημά τι ὡς λουσόμενος, καὶ ὁ Κρίτων εἵπετο αὐτῷ, ἡμᾶς δ' ἐκέλευε περιμένειν. περιεμένομεν οὖν πρὸς ἡμᾶς αὐτοὺς διαλεγόμενοι περὶ τῶν εἰρημένων καὶ ἀνασκοποῦντες, τοτὲ δ' αὖ περὶ τῆς ξυμφορᾶς διεξιόντες, ὅση ἡμῖν γεγονυῖα εἴη, ἀτεχνῶς ἡγούμενοι ὥσπερ πατρὸς στερηθέντες

116 διάξειν ὀρφανοὶ τὸν ἔπειτα βίον. ἐπειδὴ δὲ
B ἐλούσατο | καὶ ἠνέχθη παρ' αὐτὸν τὰ παιδία
(δύο γὰρ αὐτῷ ὑεῖς σμικροὶ ἦσαν,
εἷς δὲ μέγας) καὶ αἱ οἰκεῖαι γυναῖκες
ἀφίκοντο, ἐκείναις ἐναντίον τοῦ
Κρίτωνος διαλεχθείς τε καὶ ἐπιστείλας ἅττα
ἐβούλετο, τὰς μὲν γυναῖκας καὶ τὰ παιδία
ἀπιέναι ἐκέλευσεν, αὐτὸς δὲ ἧκε παρ' ἡμᾶς.
καὶ ἦν ἤδη ἐγγὺς ἡλίου δυσμῶν· χρόνον γὰρ
πολὺν διέτριψεν ἔνδον. ἐλθὼν δ' ἐκαθέζετο
λελουμένος, καὶ οὐ πολλὰ μετὰ ταῦτα διελέχθη.
καὶ ἧκεν ὁ τῶν ἕνδεκα ὑπηρέτης καὶ στὰς
C παρ' αὐτόν· Ὦ Σώκρατες, | ἔφη, οὐ καταγνώ-
σομαι σοῦ ὅπερ ἄλλων καταγιγνώσκω,
ὅτι μοι χαλεπαίνουσι καὶ καταρῶν-
ται, ἐπειδὰν αὐτοῖς παραγγέλλω πίνειν τὸ
φάρμακον ἀναγκαζόντων τῶν ἀρχόντων. σὲ
δὲ ἐγὼ καὶ ἄλλως ἔγνωκα ἐν τούτῳ τῷ χρόνῳ
γενναιότατον καὶ πρᾳότατον καὶ ἄριστον ἄνδρα
ὄντα τῶν πώποτε δεῦρο ἀφικομένων, καὶ δὴ
καὶ νῦν εὖ οἶδ' ὅτι οὐκ ἐμοὶ χαλεπαίνεις
(γιγνώσκεις γὰρ τοὺς αἰτίους), ἀλλὰ ἐκείνοις.
νῦν, οἶσθα γὰρ ἃ ἦλθον ἀγγέλλων, χαῖρέ τε
D καὶ πειρῶ ὡς ῥᾷστα φέρειν | τὰ ἀναγκαῖα.
καὶ ἅμα δακρύσας μεταστρεφόμενος ἀπῄει. καὶ
ὁ Σωκράτης ἀναβλέψας πρὸς αὐτόν· Καὶ σύ,
ἔφη, χαῖρε, καὶ ἡμεῖς ταῦτα ποιήσομεν. καὶ
ἅμα πρὸς ἡμᾶς· Ὡς ἀστεῖος, ἔφη, ὁ ἄνθρωπος·
καὶ παρὰ πάντα μοι τὸν χρόνον προσῄει καὶ
διελέγετο ἐνίοτε καὶ ἦν ἀνδρῶν λῷστος, καὶ
νῦν ὡς γενναίως με ἀποδακρύει. ἀλλ' ἄγε δή,

His wife and children say farewell.

The executioner comes.

ὦ Κρίτων, πειθώμεθα αὐτῷ, καὶ ἐνεγκάτω τις 116
τὸ φάρμακον, εἰ τέτριπται· εἰ δὲ μή, τριψάτω
ὁ ἄνθρωπος. καὶ ὁ Κρίτων· Ἀλλ' οἶμαι, |
ἔφη, ἔγωγε, ὦ Σώκρατες, ἔτι ἥλιον εἶναι ἐπὶ E
τοῖς ὄρεσιν καὶ οὔπω δεδυκέναι. καὶ ἅμα ἐγὼ
οἶδα καὶ ἄλλους πάνυ ὀψὲ πίνοντας, ἐπειδὰν
παραγγελθῇ αὐτοῖς, δειπνήσαντάς τε καὶ
πιόντας εὖ μάλα, καὶ ξυγγενομένους γ' ἐνίους
ὧν ἂν τύχωσιν ἐπιθυμοῦντες. ἀλλὰ μηδὲν
ἐπείγου· ἔτι γὰρ ἐγχωρεῖ. καὶ ὁ Σωκράτης·
Εἰκότως γε, ἔφη, ὦ Κρίτων, ἐκεῖνοί τε ταῦτα
ποιοῦσιν, οὓς σὺ λέγεις (οἴονται γὰρ κερδανεῖν
ταῦτα ποιήσαντες), καὶ ἔγωγε ταῦτα εἰκότως
οὐ ποιήσω· οὐδὲν γὰρ οἶμαι κερδανεῖν | ὀλίγον 117
ὕστερον πιὼν ἄλλο γε ἢ γέλωτα ὀφλήσειν
παρ' ἐμαυτῷ, γλιχόμενος τοῦ ζῆν καὶ φειδό-
μενος οὐδενὸς ἔτι ἐνόντος. ἀλλ' ἴθι, ἔφη,
πιθοῦ καὶ μὴ ἄλλως ποίει.

The hemlock is brought.

Καὶ ὁ Κρίτων ἀκούσας ἔνευσε τῷ παιδὶ
πλησίον ἑστῶτι. καὶ ὁ παῖς ἐξελθὼν
καὶ συχνὸν χρόνον διατρίψας ἧκεν
ἄγων τὸν μέλλοντα διδόναι τὸ φάρμακον, ἐν
κύλικι φέροντα τετριμμένον· ἰδὼν δὲ ὁ Σωκρά-
της τὸν ἄνθρωπον· Εἶεν, ἔφη, ὦ βέλτιστε, σὺ
γὰρ τούτων ἐπιστήμων, τί χρὴ ποιεῖν; Οὐδὲν
ἄλλο, ἔφη, ἢ πιόντα περιιέναι, ἕως ἄν σου
βάρος ἐν τοῖς σκέλεσι γένηται, | ἔπειτα κατα- B
κεῖσθαι· καὶ οὕτως αὐτὸ ποιήσει. καὶ ἅμα
ὤρεξε τὴν κύλικα τῷ Σωκράτει· καὶ ὃς λαβὼν
καὶ μάλα ἵλεως, ὦ Ἐχέκρατες, οὐδὲν τρέσας
οὐδὲ διαφθείρας οὔτε τοῦ χρώματος οὔτε τοῦ

117 προσώπου, ἀλλ', ὥσπερ εἰώθει, ταυρηδὸν ὑποβλέψας πρὸς τὸν ἄνθρωπον· Τί λέγεις, ἔφη, περὶ τοῦδε τοῦ πώματος πρὸς τὸ ἀποσπεῖσαί τινι; ἔξεστιν ἢ οὔ; Τοσοῦτον, ἔφη, ὦ Σώκρατες, τρίβομεν, ὅσον οἰόμεθα μέτριον εἶναι πιεῖν. Μανθάνω, ἦ δ' ὅς· ἀλλ' εὔχεσθαί
C The final prayer. γέ που τοῖς | θεοῖς ἔξεστί τε καὶ χρή, τὴν μετοίκησιν τὴν ἐνθένδε ἐκεῖσε εὐτυχῆ γενέσθαι· ἃ δὴ καὶ ἐγὼ εὔχομαί τε καὶ γένοιτο ταύτῃ. καὶ ἅμ' εἰπὼν ταῦτα ἐπισχόμενος καὶ μάλα εὐχερῶς καὶ εὐκόλως ἐξέπιεν. καὶ ἡμῶν οἱ πολλοὶ τέως μὲν ἐπιεικῶς οἷοίτε ἦσαν κατέχειν τὸ μὴ δακρύειν, ὡς δὲ εἴδομεν πίνοντά τε καὶ πεπωκότα, οὐκέτι, ἀλλ' ἐμοῦ γε βίᾳ καὶ αὐτοῦ ἀστακτὶ ἐχώρει τὰ δάκρυα, ὥστε ἐγκαλυψάμενος ἀπέκλαιον ἐμαυτόν· οὐ γὰρ δὴ ἐκεῖνόν γε, ἀλλὰ τὴν ἐμαυτοῦ τύχην,
D οἵου ἀνδρὸς | ἑταίρου ἐστερημένος εἴην. ὁ δὲ Κρίτων ἔτι πρότερος ἐμοῦ, ἐπειδὴ οὐχ οἷόστ' ἦν κατέχειν τὰ δάκρυα, ἐξανέστη. Ἀπολλόδωρος δὲ καὶ ἐν τῷ ἔμπροσθεν χρόνῳ οὐδὲν ἐπαύετο δακρύων, καὶ δὴ καὶ τότε ἀναβρυχησάμενος κλαίων καὶ ἀγανακτῶν οὐδένα ὅντινα οὐ κατέκλασε τῶν παρόντων πλήν γε αὐτοῦ Σωκράτους. ἐκεῖνος δέ· Οἷα, ἔφη, ποιεῖτε, ὦ θαυμάσιοι. ἐγὼ μέντοι οὐχ ἥκιστα τούτου ἕνεκα τὰς γυναῖκας ἀπέπεμψα, ἵνα μὴ τοιαῦτα πλημμελοῖεν· καὶ γὰρ ἀκήκοα ὅτι ἐν εὐφημίᾳ |
E χρὴ τελευτᾶν. ἀλλ' ἡσυχίαν τε ἄγετε καὶ καρτερεῖτε. καὶ ἡμεῖς ἀκούσαντες ᾐσχύνθημέν τε καὶ ἐπέσχομεν τοῦ δακρύειν. ὁ δὲ περιελ-

θών, ἐπειδή οἱ βαρύνεσθαι ἔφη τὰ σκέλη, 117
κατεκλίνη ὕπτιος· οὕτω γὰρ ἐκέλευεν ὁ ἄνθρωπος· καὶ ἅμα ἐφαπτόμενος αὐτοῦ οὗτος ὁ δοὺς τὸ φάρμακον, διαλιπὼν χρόνον ἐπεσκόπει τοὺς πόδας καὶ τὰ σκέλη, κἄπειτα σφόδρα πιέσας αὐτοῦ τὸν πόδα ἤρετο, εἰ αἰσθάνοιτο· ὁ δ' οὐκ ἔφη· καὶ μετὰ τοῦτο αὖθις | τὰς 118
κνήμας· καὶ ἐπανιὼν οὕτως ἡμῖν ἐπεδείκνυτο, ὅτι ψύχοιτό τε καὶ πηγνῦτο. καὶ αὐτὸς ἥπτετο καὶ εἶπεν ὅτι, ἐπειδὰν πρὸς τῇ καρδίᾳ γένηται αὐτῷ, τότε οἰχήσεται. ἤδη οὖν σχεδόν τι αὐτοῦ ἦν τὰ περὶ τὸ ἦτρον ψυχόμενα, καὶ ἐκκαλυψάμενος (ἐνεκεκάλυπτο γάρ) εἶπεν, ὃ δὴ τελευταῖον ἐφθέγξατο· Ὦ Κρίτων, ἔφη, τῷ Ἀσκληπιῷ ὀφείλομεν ἀλεκτρυόνα· ἀλλὰ ἀπόδοτε καὶ μὴ ἀμελήσητε. Ἀλλὰ ταῦτα, ἔφη, ἔσται, ὁ Κρίτων· Ἀλλ' ὅρα, εἴ τι ἄλλο λέγεις. ταῦτα ἐρομένου αὐτοῦ οὐδὲν ἔτι ἀπεκρίνατο, ἀλλ' ὀλίγον χρόνον διαλιπὼν ἐκινήθη τε καὶ ὁ ἄνθρωπος ἐξεκάλυψεν αὐτόν, καὶ ὃς τὰ ὄμματα ἔστησεν· ἰδὼν δὲ ὁ Κρίτων συνέλαβε τὸ στόμα καὶ τοὺς ὀφθαλμούς.

The last charge—"a cock to Aesculapius."

Ἥδε ἡ τελευτή, ὦ Ἐχέκρατες, τοῦ ἑταίρου ἡμῖν ἐγένετο, ἀνδρός, ὡς ἡμεῖς φαῖμεν ἄν, τῶν τότε ὧν ἐπειράθημεν ἀρίστου καὶ ἄλλως φρονιμωτάτου καὶ δικαιοτάτου.

SYMPOSIUM

Socrates' Abstraction—Late to the Banquet.

174 D Τοιαῦτ' ἄττα σφᾶς ἔφη διαλεχθέντας ἰέναι. τὸν οὖν Σωκράτη ἑαυτῷ πως προσέχοντα τὸν νοῦν κατὰ τὴν ὁδὸν πορεύεσθαι ὑπολειπόμενον, καὶ περιμένοντος οὗ κελεύειν προϊέναι εἰς τὸ πρόσθεν. ἐπειδὴ δὲ γενέσθαι ἐπὶ τῇ οἰκίᾳ τῇ Ἀγάθωνος, ἀνεῳγμένην E καταλαμβάνειν τὴν θύραν, καί τι ἔφη αὐτόθι γελοῖον παθεῖν. οἷ μὲν γὰρ εὐθὺς παῖδά τινα ἔνδοθεν ἀπαντήσαντα ἄγειν οὗ κατέκειντο οἱ ἄλλοι, καὶ καταλαμβάνειν ἤδη μέλλοντας δειπνεῖν· εὐθὺς δ' οὖν ὡς ἰδεῖν τὸν Ἀγάθωνα, Ὦ, φάναι, Ἀριστόδημε, εἰς καλὸν ἥκεις, ὅπως συνδειπνήσῃς· εἰ δ' ἄλλου τινὸς ἕνεκα ἦλθες, εἰς αὖθις ἀναβαλοῦ, ὡς καὶ χθὲς ζητῶν σε, ἵνα καλέσαιμι, οὐχ οἷόστ' ἦ ἰδεῖν. ἀλλὰ Σωκράτη ἡμῖν πῶς οὐκ ἄγεις; καὶ ἐγώ, ἔφη, μεταστρεφόμενος οὐδαμοῦ ὁρῶ Σωκράτη ἑπόμενον· εἶπον οὖν ὅτι καὶ αὐτὸς μετὰ Σωκράτους ἥκοιμι, κληθεὶς ὑπ' ἐκείνου δεῦρ' ἐπὶ δεῖπνον. Καλῶς γ', ἔφη, ποιῶν σύ· ἀλλὰ ποῦ ἐστιν οὗτος; Ὄπισθεν 175 ἐμοῦ ἄρτι | εἰσῄει· ἀλλὰ θαυμάζω καὶ αὐτός, ποῦ ἂν εἴη. Οὐ σκέψει, ἔφη, παῖ, φάναι τὸν Ἀγάθωνα, καὶ εἰσάξεις Σωκράτη; σὺ δ', ἦ δ' ὅς, Ἀριστόδημε, παρ' Ἐρυξίμαχον κατακλίνου. καὶ ἓ μὲν ἔφη ἀπονίζειν τὸν παῖδα, ἵνα κατακέοιτο· ἄλλον δέ τινα τῶν παίδων ἥκειν ἀγγέλλοντα ὅτι Σωκράτης

Aristodemus tells the story.

Socrates is lost;

οὗτος ἀναχωρήσας ἐν τῷ τῶν γειτόνων προθύρῳ 175
ἕστηκεν καὶ οὗ καλοῦντος οὐκ ἐθέλει εἰσιέναι.
Ἄτοπόν γ', ἔφη, λέγεις· οὔκουν καλεῖς αὐτὸν
καὶ μὴ ἀφήσεις; | καὶ ὃς ἔφη εἰπεῖν Μηδαμῶς, B
ἀλλ' ἐᾶτε αὐτόν. ἔθος γάρ τι τοῦτ' ἔχει·
ἐνίοτε ἀποστὰς ὅποι ἂν τύχῃ ἕστηκεν. ἥξει
δ' αὐτίκα, ὡς ἐγὼ οἶμαι. μὴ οὖν κινεῖτε, ἀλλ'
ἐᾶτε. Ἀλλ' οὕτω χρὴ ποιεῖν, εἰ σοὶ δοκεῖ,
φάναι τὸν Ἀγάθωνα. ἀλλ' ἡμᾶς, ὦ παῖδες,
τοὺς ἄλλους ἑστιᾶτε. πάντως παρατίθετε ὅ τι
ἂν βούλησθε, ἐπειδάν τις ὑμῖν μὴ ἐφεστήκῃ·
ὃ ἐγὼ οὐδεπώποτε ἐποίησα· νῦν οὖν, νομίζοντες
καὶ ἐμὲ ὑφ' ὑμῶν κεκλῆσθαι ἐπὶ δεῖπνον καὶ
τούσδε | τοὺς ἄλλους, θεραπεύετε, ἵν' ὑμᾶς ἐπαι- C
νῶμεν.

Μετὰ ταῦτα ἔφη σφᾶς μὲν δειπνεῖν, τὸν δὲ
Σωκράτη οὐκ εἰσιέναι. τὸν οὖν Ἀγάθωνα
πολλάκις κελεύειν μεταπέμψασθαι τὸν Σωκράτη,
ἓ δὲ οὐκ ἐᾶν. ἥκειν οὖν αὐτὸν οὐ πολὺν
χρόνον, ὡς εἰώθει, διατρίψαντα, ἀλλὰ
μάλιστα σφᾶς μεσοῦν δειπνοῦντας.

but comes at last.

τὸν οὖν Ἀγάθωνα (τυγχάνειν γὰρ ἔσχατον
κατακείμενον μόνον), Δεῦρ', ἔφη φάναι, Σώ-
κρατες, παρ' ἐμὲ κατάκεισο, ἵνα καὶ τοῦ σοφοῦ
| ἀπολαύσω, ὅ σοι προσέστη ἐν τοῖς προθύροις. D
δῆλον γὰρ ὅτι ηὗρες αὐτὸ καὶ ἔχεις· οὐ γὰρ
ἂν προαπέστης. καὶ τὸν Σωκράτη καθίζεσθαι
καὶ εἰπεῖν ὅτι Εὖ ἂν ἔχοι, φάναι, ὦ Ἀγάθων,
εἰ τοιοῦτον εἴη ἡ σοφία, ὥστ' ἐκ τοῦ πληρε-
στέρου εἰς τὸν κενότερον ῥεῖν ἡμῶν, ἐὰν ἁπτώμεθα
ἀλλήλων, ὥσπερ τὸ ἐν ταῖς κύλιξιν ὕδωρ τὸ

175 διὰ τοῦ ἐρίου ῥέον ἐκ τῆς πληρεστέρας εἰς τὴν κενοτέραν. εἰ γὰρ οὕτως ἔχει καὶ ἡ σοφία,
E πολλοῦ τιμῶμαι τὴν παρὰ | σοὶ κατάκλισιν· οἶμαι γάρ με παρὰ σοῦ πολλῆς καὶ καλῆς σοφίας πληρωθήσεσθαι. ἡ μὲν γὰρ ἐμὴ φαύλη τις ἂν εἴη καὶ ἀμφισβητήσιμος, ὥσπερ ὄναρ οὖσα, ἡ δὲ σὴ λαμπρά τε καὶ πολλὴν ἐπίδοσιν ἔχουσα, ἥ γε παρὰ σοῦ νέου ὄντος οὕτω σφόδρα ἐξέλαμψεν καὶ ἐκφανὴς ἐγένετο πρῴην ἐν μάρτυσι τῶν Ἑλλήνων πλεῖν ἢ τρισμυρίοις. Ὑβριστὴς εἶ, ἔφη, ὦ Σώκρατες, ὁ Ἀγάθων. καὶ ταῦτα μὲν καὶ ὀλίγον ὕστερον διαδικασόμεθα ἐγώ τε καὶ σὺ περὶ τῆς σοφίας, δικαστῇ χρώμενοι τῷ Διονύσῳ· νῦν δὲ πρὸς τὸ δεῖπνον πρῶτα τρέπου.

Socrates' Ugliness—A Silenus.

ALCIBIADES

215 Σωκράτη δ' ἐγὼ ἐπαινεῖν, ὦ ἄνδρες, οὕτως
A ἐπιχειρήσω,—δι' εἰκόνων. οὗτος μὲν οὖν ἴσως οἰήσεται ἐπὶ τὰ γελοιότερα, ἔσται δ' ἡ εἰκὼν τοῦ ἀληθοῦς ἕνεκα, οὐ τοῦ γελοίου. φημὶ γὰρ
B δὴ ὁμοιότατον αὐτὸν εἶναι τοῖς σιληνοῖς τούτοις τοῖς ἐν τοῖς ἑρμογλυφείοις καθημένοις, οὕστινας ἐργάζονται οἱ δημιουργοὶ σύριγγας ἢ αὐλοὺς ἔχοντας, οἳ διχάδε διοιχθέντες φαίνονται ἔνδοθεν ἀγάλματα ἔχοντες θεῶν. καί φημι αὖ ἐοικέναι

A Satyr in form.

αὐτὸν τῷ σατύρῳ τῷ Μαρσύᾳ. ὅτι μὲν οὖν τό γε εἶδος ὅμοιος εἶ τούτοις, ὦ Σώκρατες, οὐδ' αὐτὸς ἄν που ἀμφισβητήσαις· ὡς δὲ καὶ τἆλλα ἔοικας, μετὰ τοῦτο ἄκουε.

ὑβριστὴς εἶ· ἢ οὔ; ἐὰν γὰρ μὴ ὁμολογῇς, 215
μάρτυρας παρέξομαι. ἀλλ' οὐκ αὐλητής; πολύ
γε θαυμασιώτερος ἐκείνου· ὁ μέν γε δι' ὀργάνων C
ἐκήλει τοὺς ἀνθρώπους τῇ ἀπὸ τοῦ στόματος
δυνάμει, καὶ ἔτι νυνὶ ὃς ἂν τὰ ἐκείνου αὐλῇ
(ἃ γὰρ Ὄλυμπος ηὔλει, Μαρσύου λέγω,—τούτου
διδάξαντος). τὰ οὖν ἐκείνου ἐάντε ἀγαθὸς
αὐλητὴς αὐλῇ ἐάντε φαύλη αὐλητρίς, μόνα
κατέχεσθαι ποιεῖ καὶ δηλοῖ τοὺς τῶν θεῶν τε
καὶ τελετῶν δεομένους διὰ τὸ θεῖα εἶναι. σὺ
δ' ἐκείνου τοσοῦτον μόνον διαφέρεις, ὅτι ἄνευ
ὀργάνων ψιλοῖς λόγοις ταὐτὸν τοῦτο
ποιεῖς. ἡμεῖς γοῦν ὅταν μέν του
ἄλλου ἀκούωμεν λέγοντος καὶ πάνυ ἀγαθοῦ D
ῥήτορος ἄλλους λόγους, οὐδὲν μέλει, ὡς ἔπος
εἰπεῖν, οὐδενί· ἐπειδὰν δὲ σοῦ τις ἀκούῃ ἢ τῶν
σῶν λόγων ἄλλου λέγοντος, κἂν πάνυ φαῦλος
ᾖ ὁ λέγων, ἐάντε γυνὴ ἀκούῃ ἐάντε ἀνὴρ ἐάντε
μειράκιον, ἐκπεπληγμένοι ἐσμὲν καὶ κατεχόμεθα.
ἐγὼ γοῦν, ὦ ἄνδρες, εἰ μὴ ἔμελλον κομιδῇ
δόξειν μεθύειν, εἶπον ὀμόσας ἂν ὑμῖν, οἷα δὴ
πέπονθα αὐτὸς ὑπὸ τῶν τούτου λόγων καὶ
πάσχω ἔτι καὶ νυνί. ὅταν γὰρ ἀκούω, πολύ E
μοι μᾶλλον ἢ τῶν κορυβαντιώντων ἥ τε καρδία
πηδᾷ καὶ δάκρυα ἐκχεῖται ὑπὸ τῶν λόγων
τούτου. ὁρῶ δὲ καὶ ἄλλους παμπόλλους τὰ
αὐτὰ πάσχοντας. Περικλέους δὲ ἀκούων καὶ
ἄλλων ἀγαθῶν ῥητόρων εὖ μὲν ἡγούμην
λέγειν, τοιοῦτον δ' οὐδὲν ἔπασχον, οὐδ'
ἐτεθορύβητό μου ἡ ψυχὴ οὐδ' ἠγανάκτει ὡς
ἀνδραποδωδῶς διακειμένου· ἀλλ' ὑπὸ τουτουῒ

But a charmer in speech.

None like him.

τοῦ Μαρσύου πολλάκις δὴ οὕτω διετέθην,
216 ὥστε μοι δόξαι μὴ βιωτὸν εἶναι ἔχοντι ὡς ἔχω. καὶ ταῦτα, Σώκρατες, οὐκ ἐρεῖς ὡς οὐκ ἀληθῆ. καὶ ἔτι γε νῦν ξύνοιδ' ἐμαυτῷ ὅτι εἰ ἐθέλοιμι παρέχειν τὰ ὦτα, οὐκ ἂν καρτερήσαιμι, ἀλλὰ ταὐτὰ ἂν πάσχοιμι. ἀναγκάζει γάρ με ὁμολογεῖν ὅτι πολλοῦ ἐνδεὴς ὢν αὐτὸς ἔτι ἐμαυτοῦ μὲν ἀμελῶ, τὰ δ' Ἀθηναίων πράττω. βίᾳ οὖν ὥσπερ ἀπὸ τῶν Σειρήνων ἐπισχόμενος τὰ ὦτα οἴχομαι φεύγων, ἵνα μὴ αὐτοῦ καθήμενος παρὰ τούτῳ καταγηράσω. πέπονθα δὲ
B πρὸς τοῦτον μόνον ἀνθρώπων, | ὃ οὐκ ἄν τις οἴοιτο ἐν ἐμοὶ ἐνεῖναι, τὸ αἰσχύνεσθαι ὁντινοῦν· ἐγὼ δὲ τοῦτον μόνον αἰσχύνομαι. ξύνοιδα γὰρ ἐμαυτῷ ἀντιλέγειν μὲν οὐ δυναμένῳ, ὡς οὐ δεῖ ποιεῖν ἃ οὗτος κελεύει, ἐπειδὰν δὲ ἀπέλθω, ἡττημένῳ τῆς τιμῆς τῆς ὑπὸ τῶν πολλῶν. δραπετεύω οὖν αὐτὸν καὶ φεύγω, καὶ ὅταν ἴδω, αἰσχύνομαι τὰ ὡμολογημένα. καὶ πολλάκις
C μὲν ἡδέως | ἂν ἴδοιμι αὐτὸν μὴ ὄντα ἐν ἀνθρώποις· εἰ δ' αὖ τοῦτο γένοιτο, εὖ οἶδα ὅτι πολὺ μεῖζον ἂν ἀχθοίμην· ὥστε οὐκ ἔχω ὅ τι χρήσωμαι τούτῳ τῷ ἀνθρώπῳ.

Socrates' Endurance and Bravery as a Soldier.

ALCIBIADES.

219 Καὶ μετὰ ταῦτα στρατεία ἡμῖν εἰς Ποτεί-
E δαιαν ἐγένετο κοινὴ καὶ συνεσιτοῦμεν ἐκεῖ. πρῶτον μὲν οὖν τοῖς πόνοις οὐ μόνον ἐμοῦ περιῆν, ἀλλὰ καὶ τῶν ἄλλων

In Poteidaea.

ἁπάντων—ὁπότ᾽ ἀναγκασθείημεν ἀποληφθέντες
που, οἷα δὴ | ἐπὶ στρατείας, ἀσιτεῖν, οὐδὲν 220
ἦσαν οἱ ἄλλοι πρὸς τὸ καρτερεῖν· ἔν τ᾽ αὖ
ταῖς εὐωχίαις μόνος ἀπολαύειν οἷόστ᾽ ἦν τά τ᾽
ἄλλα καὶ πίνειν (οὐκ ἐθέλων) ὁπότε ἀναγ-
κασθείη, πάντας ἐκράτει, καὶ ὃ πάντων θαυ-
μαστότατον, Σωκράτη μεθύοντα οὐδεὶς πώποτε
ἑώρακεν ἀνθρώπων. τούτου μὲν οὖν μοι δοκεῖ
καὶ αὐτίκα ὁ ἔλεγχος ἔσεσθαι· πρὸς δὲ αὖ
τὰς τοῦ χειμῶνος καρτερήσεις (δεινοὶ γὰρ
αὐτόθι χειμῶνες) θαυμάσια ἠργάζετο τά τε
ἄλλα, | καί ποτε ὄντος πάγου οἵου δεινοτάτου, B
καὶ πάντων ἢ οὐκ ἐξιόντων ἔνδοθεν ἤ, εἴ τις
ἐξίοι, ἠμφιεσμένων τε θαυμαστὰ δὴ ὅσα καὶ
ὑποδεδεμένων καὶ ἐνειλιγμένων τοὺς πόδας εἰς
πίλους καὶ ἀρνακίδας, οὗτος δ᾽ ἐν τούτοις ἐξῄει
ἔχων ἱμάτιον μὲν τοιοῦτον οἷόνπερ καὶ πρότερον
εἰώθει φορεῖν, ἀνυπόδητος δὲ διὰ τοῦ κρυστάλ-
λου ῥᾷον ἐπορεύετο ἢ οἱ ἄλλοι ὑποδεδέμενοι.
οἱ δὲ στρατιῶται ὑπέβλεπον αὐτὸν ὡς κατα-
φρονοῦντα σφῶν. Καὶ | ταῦτα μὲν δὴ ταῦτα· C

οἷον δ᾽ αὖ τόδ᾽ ἔρεξε καὶ ἔτλη καρτερὸς ἀνὴρ

ἐκεῖ ποτε ἐπὶ στρατείας, ἄξιον ἀκοῦσαι. ξυν-
νοήσας γὰρ αὐτόθι ἕωθέν τι εἱστήκει σκοπῶν,
καὶ ἐπειδὴ οὐ προὐχώρει αὐτῷ, οὐκ
ἀνίει ἀλλὰ εἱστήκει ζητῶν. καὶ ἤδη
ἦν μεσημβρία, καὶ ἄνθρωποι ᾐσθάνοντο, καὶ
θαυμάζοντες ἄλλος ἄλλῳ ἔλεγεν ὅτι Σωκράτης
ἐξ ἑωθινοῦ φροντίζων τι ἕστηκε. τελευτῶντες δέ
τινες τῶν νέων, ἐπειδὴ ἑσπέρα ἦν, δειπνήσαντες

His abstraction.

220 (καὶ γὰρ θέρος τότε γε ἦν) χαμεύνια ἐξενεγκά-
D μενοι ἅμα μὲν ἐν τῷ ψύχει καθηῦδον, ἅμα δ'
ἐφύλαττον αὐτὸν εἰ καὶ τὴν νύκτα ἑστήξοι. ὁ
δὲ εἱστήκει μέχρι ἕως ἐγένετο καὶ ἥλιος
ἀνέσχεν· ἔπειτα ᾤχετ' ἀπιὼν προσευξάμενος
τῷ ἡλίῳ. εἰ δὲ βούλεσθε ἐν ταῖς μάχαις
(τοῦτο γὰρ δὴ δίκαιόν γε αὐτῷ ἀποδοῦναι)·
ὅτε γὰρ ἡ μάχη ἦν, ἐξ ἧς ἐμοὶ καὶ τἀριστεῖα
ἔδοσαν οἱ στρατηγοί, οὐδεὶς ἄλλος ἐμὲ ἔσωσεν
ἀνθρώπων ἢ οὗτος, τετρωμένον οὐκ ἐθέλων |
E ἀπολιπεῖν, ἀλλὰ συνδιέσωσε καὶ τὰ ὅπλα καὶ
αὐτὸν ἐμέ. καὶ ἐγὼ μέν, ὦ Σώκρατες, καὶ
τότε ἐκέλευον σοὶ διδόναι τἀριστεῖα τοὺς
στρατηγούς—καὶ τοῦτό γέ μοι οὔτε μέμψει
οὔτε ἐρεῖς ὅτι ψεύδομαι· ἀλλὰ γὰρ τῶν
στρατηγῶν πρὸς τὸ ἐμὸν ἀξίωμα ἀποβλεπόντων
καὶ βουλομένων ἐμοὶ διδόναι τἀριστεῖα, αὐτὸς
προθυμότερος ἐγένου τῶν στρατηγῶν ἐμὲ
λαβεῖν ἢ σαυτόν. ἔτι τοίνυν, ὦ ἄνδρες,
221 ἄξιον ἦν θεάσασθαι Σωκράτη, ὅτε ἀπὸ | Δηλίου
At Delium. φυγῇ ἀνεχώρει τὸ στρατόπεδον·
ἔτυχον γὰρ παραγενόμενος ἵππον
ἔχων, οὗτος δὲ ὅπλα. ἀνεχώρει οὖν ἐσκεδα-
σμένων ἤδη τῶν ἀνθρώπων οὗτός τε ἅμα
καὶ Λάχης· καὶ ἐγὼ περιτυγχάνω, καὶ ἰδὼν
εὐθὺς παρακελεύομαί τε αὐτοῖν θαρρεῖν, καὶ
ἔλεγον ὅτι οὐκ ἀπολείψω αὐτώ. ἐνταῦθα δὴ
καὶ κάλλιον ἐθεασάμην Σωκράτη ἢ ἐν Ποτει-
δαίᾳ (αὐτὸς γὰρ ἧττον ἐν φόβῳ ἦ διὰ τὸ ἐφ'
ἵππου εἶναι) πρῶτον μὲν ὅσον περιῆν Λάχητος
B τῷ ἔμφρων | εἶναι· ἔπειτα ἔμοιγ' ἐδόκει, ὦ

Ἀριστόφανες, τὸ σὸν δὴ τοῦτο, καὶ ἐκεῖ 221
διαπορεύεσθαι ὥσπερ καὶ ἐνθάδε, βρενθυό-
μενος καὶ τὠφθαλμὼ παραβάλλων, ἠρέμα
παρασκοπῶν καὶ τοὺς φιλίους καὶ τοὺς
πολεμίους, δῆλος ὢν παντὶ καὶ πάνυ πόρρωθεν
ὅτι, εἴ τις ἅψεται τούτου τοῦ ἀνδρός, μάλα
ἐρρωμένως ἀμυνεῖται. διὸ καὶ ἀσφαλῶς ἀπῄει
καὶ οὗτος καὶ ὁ ἕτερος· σχεδὸν γάρ τι τῶν
οὕτω διακειμένων ἐν τῷ πολέμῳ οὐδὲ ἅπτονται,
ἀλλὰ τοὺς | προτροπάδην φεύγοντας διώκουσιν. C
πολλὰ μὲν οὖν ἄν τις καὶ ἄλλα ἔχοι Σωκράτη
ἐπαινέσαι καὶ θαυμάσια· ἀλλὰ τῶν μὲν ἄλλων
ἐπιτηδευμάτων τάχ᾽ ἄν τις καὶ περὶ ἄλλου
τοιαῦτα εἴποι, τὸ δὲ μηδενὶ ἀνθρώπων ὅμοιον
εἶναι, μήτε τῶν παλαιῶν μήτε τῶν
νῦν ὄντων, τοῦτο ἄξιον παντὸς
θαύματος. οἷος γὰρ Ἀχιλλεὺς ἐγένετο, ἀπεικά-
σειεν ἄν τις καὶ Βρασίδαν καὶ ἄλλους, καὶ
οἷος αὖ Περικλῆς, καὶ Νέστορα καὶ Ἀντήνορα,
εἰσὶ δὲ | καὶ ἕτεροι· καὶ τοὺς ἄλλους κατὰ D
ταὔτ᾽ ἄν τις ἀπεικάζοι· οἷος δὲ οὑτοσὶ γέγονεν
τὴν ἀτοπίαν ἄνθρωπος, καὶ αὐτὸς καὶ οἱ λόγοι
αὐτοῦ, οὐδ᾽ ἐγγὺς ἂν εὕροι τις ζητῶν, οὔτε
τῶν νῦν οὔτε τῶν παλαιῶν, εἰ μὴ ἄρα εἰ οἷς
ἐγὼ λέγω ἀπεικάζοι τις αὐτόν, ἀνθρώπων μὲν
μηδενί, τοῖς δὲ σιληνοῖς καὶ σατύροις, αὐτὸν
καὶ τοὺς λόγους. Καὶ γὰρ οὖν καὶ τοῦτο ἐν
τοῖς πρώτοις παρέλιπον, ὅτι καὶ οἱ λόγοι
αὐτοῦ ὁμοιότατοί εἰσι τοῖς σιληνοῖς τοῖς
διοιγομένοις. εἰ | γὰρ ἐθέλοι τις τῶν Σωκρά- E
τους ἀκούειν λόγων, φανεῖεν ἂν γελοῖοι τὸ

Unlike all other men.

221 πρῶτον· τοιαῦτα καὶ ὀνόματα καὶ ῥήματα
ἔξωθεν περιαμπέχονται, σατύρου τινα ὑβριστοῦ
δοράν. ὄνους γὰρ κανθηλίους λέγει καὶ χαλκέας
τινὰς καὶ σκυτοτόμους καὶ βυρσοδέψας, καὶ
ἀεὶ διὰ τῶν αὐτῶν τὰ αὐτὰ φαίνεται λέγειν,
ὥστε ἄπειρος καὶ ἀνόητος ἄνθρωπος πᾶς ἂν
222 τῶν λόγων καταγελάσειεν. | διοιγομένους δὲ
ἰδὼν δή τις καὶ ἐντὸς αὐτῶν γιγνόμενος πρῶτον
μὲν νοῦν ἔχοντας ἔνδον μόνους εὑρήσει τῶν
λόγων, ἔπειτα θειοτάτους καὶ πλεῖστα ἀγάλματ'
ἀρετῆς ἐν αὑτοῖς ἔχοντας καὶ ἐπὶ πλεῖστον
τείνοντας, μᾶλλον δὲ ἐπὶ πᾶν ὅσον προσήκει
σκοπεῖν τῷ μέλλοντι καλῷ κἀγαθῷ ἔσεσθαι.

LACHES

Socrates' Ruling Passion—Cross-Examination of all those he meets.

187 E Οὔ μοι δοκεῖς εἰδέναι ὅτι, ὃς ἂν ἐγγύτατα
Σωκράτους ᾖ λόγῳ, ὥσπερ γένει, καὶ
πλησιάζῃ διαλεγόμενος, ἀνάγκη αὐτῷ,
ἐὰν ἄρα καὶ περὶ ἄλλου του πρότερον ἄρξηται
διαλέγεσθαι, μὴ παύεσθαι ὑπὸ τούτου περιαγό-
μενον τῷ λόγῳ, πρὶν ἐμπέσῃ εἰς τὸ διδόναι
περὶ αὑτοῦ λόγον, ὅντινα τρόπον νῦν τε ζῇ
188 καὶ ὅντινα τὸν | παρεληλυθότα βίον βεβίωκεν·
ἐπειδὰν δ' ἐμπέσῃ, ὅτι οὐ πρότερον αὐτὸν
ἀφήσει Σωκράτης, πρὶν ἂν βασανίσῃ ταῦτα εὖ
τε καὶ καλῶς ἅπαντα. ἐγὼ δὲ συνήθης τέ
εἰμι τῷδε καὶ οἶδ' ὅτι ἀνάγκη ὑπὸ τούτου

Nicias speaks.

πάσχειν ταῦτα, καὶ ἔτι γε αὐτὸς ὅτι πείσομαι 188
ταῦτα εὖ οἶδα· χαίρω γάρ, ὦ Λυσίμαχε, τῷ
ἀνδρὶ πλησιάζων, καὶ οὐδὲν οἶμαι κακὸν εἶναι
τὸ ὑπομιμνῄσκεσθαι ὅ τι μὴ καλῶς ἢ πεποιή-
καμεν | ἢ ποιοῦμεν, ἀλλ' εἰς τὸν ἔπειτα βίον B
προμηθέστερον ἀνάγκη εἶναι τὸν ταῦτα μὴ
φεύγοντα ἀλλ' ἐθέλοντα κατὰ τὸ τοῦ Σόλωνος
καὶ ἀξιοῦντα μανθάνειν ἕωσπερ ἂν ζῇ, καὶ μὴ
οἰόμενον αὐτὸ τὸ γῆρας νοῦν ἔχον προσιέναι.
ἐμοὶ μὲν οὖν οὐδὲν ἄηθες οὐδ' αὖ ἀηδὲς ὑπὸ
Σωκράτους βασανίζεσθαι, ἀλλὰ καὶ πάλαι
σχεδόν τι ἠπιστάμην ὅτι οὐ περὶ τῶν μειρα-
κίων ἡμῖν ὁ λόγος ἔσοιτο Σωκράτους παρόντος,
ἀλλὰ περὶ ἡμῶν αὐτῶν. ὅπερ οὖν λέγω, | τὸ C
μὲν ἐμὸν οὐδὲν κωλύει Σωκράτει συνδιατρίβειν
ὅπως οὗτος βούλεται· Λάχητα δὲ τόνδε ὅρα
ὅπως ἔχει περὶ τοῦ τοιούτου.

THEAETETUS

Socrates is an Antaeus in Dialogue.

THEODORUS. SOCRATES.

ΘΕΟ. Οὐ ῥᾴδιον, ὦ Σώκρατες, σοὶ παρα- 169
καθήμενον μὴ διδόναι λόγον, ἀλλ' ἐγὼ ἄρτι A
παρελήρησα φάσκων σε ἐπιτρέψειν μοι μὴ
ἀποδύεσθαι, καὶ οὐχὶ ἀναγκάσειν καθάπερ
Λακεδαιμόνιοι· σὺ δέ μοι δοκεῖς πρὸς τὸν
Σκίρωνα μᾶλλον τείνειν. Λακεδαιμόνιοι μὲν |
γὰρ ἀπιέναι ἢ ἀποδύεσθαι κελεύουσι, σὺ δὲ B
κατ' Ἀνταῖόν τί μοι μᾶλλον δοκεῖς τὸ δρᾶμα

169 δρᾶν· τὸν γὰρ προσελθόντα οὐκ ἀνίης πρὶν ἀναγκάσῃς ἀποδύσας ἐν τοῖς λόγοις προσπαλαῖσαι.

ΣΩ. Ἄριστά γε, ὦ Θεόδωρε, τὴν νόσον μου ἀπῄκασας· ἰσχυρικώτερος μέντοι ἐγὼ ἐκείνων. μυρίοι γὰρ ἤδη μοι Ἡρακλέες τε καὶ Θησέες ἐντυγχάνοντες καρτεροὶ πρὸς τὸ λέγειν μάλ' εὖ συγκεκόφασιν, ἀλλ' ἐγὼ οὐδέν τι μᾶλλον ἀφίσταμαι· οὕτω τις ἔρως δεινὸς
C ἐνδέδυκε τῆς | περὶ ταῦτα γυμνασίας. μὴ οὖν μηδὲ σὺ φθονήσῃς προσανατριψάμενος σαυτόν τε ἅμα καὶ ἐμὲ ὀνῆσαι.

REPUBLIC VI

Socrates checkmates all Adversaries.

He narrates his talk with Adeimantus.

487 A Ἔστιν οὖν ὅπῃ μέμψει τοιοῦτον ἐπιτήδευμα, ὃ μήποτ' ἄν τις οἷόστε γένοιτο ἱκανῶς ἐπιτηδεῦσαι, εἰ μὴ φύσει εἴη μνήμων, εὐμαθής, μεγαλοπρεπής, εὔχαρις, φίλος τε καὶ ξυγγενὴς ἀληθείας, δικαιοσύνης, ἀνδρείας, σωφροσύνης; Οὐδ' ἂν ὁ Μῶμος, ἔφη, τό γε τοιοῦτον μέμψαιτο. Ἀλλ', ἦν δ' ἐγώ, τελειωθεῖσι τοῖς τοιούτοις παιδείᾳ τε καὶ ἡλικίᾳ ἆρα οὐ μόνοις ἂν τὴν πόλιν ἐπιτρέποις;

Καὶ ὁ Ἀδείμαντος, Ὦ Σώκρατες, ἔφη,
B πρὸς | μὲν ταῦτά σοι οὐδεὶς ἂν οἷόστ' εἴη ἀντειπεῖν· ἀλλὰ γὰρ τοιόνδε τι πάσχουσιν οἱ ἀκούοντες ἑκάστοτε ἃ νῦν λέγεις· ἡγοῦνται δι' ἀπειρίαν τοῦ ἐρωτᾶν καὶ ἀποκρίνεσθαι ὑπὸ

τοῦ λόγου παρ' ἕκαστον τὸ ἐρώτημα σμικρὸν 487
παραγόμενοι, ἀθροισθέντων τῶν σμικρῶν ἐπὶ
τελευτῆς τῶν λόγων μέγα τὸ σφάλμα καὶ
ἐναντίον τοῖς πρώτοις ἀναφαίνεσθαι, καὶ ὥσπερ
ὑπὸ τῶν πεττεύειν δεινῶν οἱ μή, τελευτῶντες,
| ἀποκλείονται καὶ οὐκ ἔχουσιν ὅ τι φέρωσιν, C
οὕτω καὶ σφεῖς τελευτῶντες ἀποκλείεσθαι, καὶ
οὐκ ἔχειν ὅ τι λέγωσιν ὑπὸ πεττείας αὖ
ταύτης τινὸς ἑτέρας, οὐκ ἐν ψήφοις ἀλλ' ἐν
λόγοις· ἐπεὶ τό γε ἀληθὲς οὐδέν τι μᾶλλον
ταύτῃ ἔχειν. λέγω δ' εἰς τὸ παρὸν ἀποβλέψας.
νῦν γὰρ φαίη ἄν τίς σοι λόγῳ μὲν οὐκ ἔχειν
καθ' ἕκαστον τὸ ἐρωτώμενον ἐναντιοῦσθαι,
ἔργῳ δὲ ὁρᾶν, ὅσοι ἂν ἐπὶ φιλοσοφίαν ὁρμή-
σαντες μὴ τοῦ πεπαιδεῦσθαι | ἕνεκα ἀψάμενοι D
νέοι ὄντες ἀπαλλάττωνται, ἀλλὰ μακρότερον
ἐνδιατρίψωσι, τοὺς μὲν πλείστους καὶ πάνυ
ἀλλοκότους γιγνομένους (ἵνα μὴ παμπονήρους
εἴπωμεν), τοὺς δ' ἐπιεικεστάτους δοκοῦντας
ὅμως τοῦτό γε ὑπὸ τοῦ ἐπιτηδεύματος οὗ σὺ
ἐπαινεῖς πάσχοντας, ἀχρήστους ταῖς πόλεσι
γιγνομένους. καὶ ἐγὼ ἀκούσας, Οἴει οὖν, εἶπον,
τοὺς ταῦτα λέγοντας ψεύδεσθαι; Οὐκ οἶδα, ἦ
δ' ὅς· ἀλλὰ τὸ σοὶ δοκοῦν ἡδέως ἂν ἀκούοιμι. |
Ἀκούοις ἂν ὅτι ἔμοιγε φαίνονται τἀληθῆ λέγειν. E
Πῶς οὖν, ἔφη, εὖ ἔχει λέγειν ὅτι οὐ πρό-
τερον κακῶν παύσονται αἱ πόλεις, πρὶν ἂν ἐν
αὐταῖς οἱ φιλόσοφοι ἄρξωσιν, οὓς ἀχρήστους
ὁμολογοῦμεν αὐταῖς εἶναι; Ἐρωτᾷς, ἦν δ'
ἐγώ, ἐρώτημα δεόμενον ἀποκρίσεως δι' εἰκόνος
λεγομένης.

PROTAGORAS

The Huckster Sophists.

SOCRATES NARRATES.

Hippocrates' early visit to him; Protagoras has arrived,

310 A Τῆς παρελθούσης νυκτὸς ταυτησί, ἔτι βαθέος ὄρθρου, Ἱπποκράτης ὁ Ἀπολλοδώρου ὑός, Φάσωνος δὲ ἀδελφός, τὴν θύραν τῇ βακτηρίᾳ πάνυ |
B σφόδρα ἔκρουε, καὶ ἐπειδὴ αὐτῷ ἀνέῳξέ τις, εὐθὺς εἴσω ᾔει ἐπειγόμενος, καὶ τῇ φωνῇ μέγα λέγων, Ὦ Σώκρατες, ἔφη, ἐγρήγορας ἢ καθεύδεις; καὶ ἐγὼ τὴν φωνὴν γνοὺς αὐτοῦ, Ἱπποκράτης, ἔφην, οὗτος· μή τι νεώτερον ἀγγέλλεις; Οὐδέν γ', ἦ δ' ὅς, εἰ μὴ ἀγαθά γε. Εὖ ἂν λέγοις, ἦν δ' ἐγώ· ἔστι δὲ τί, καὶ τοῦ ἕνεκα τηνικάδε ἀφίκου; Πρωταγόρας, ἔφη, ἥκει, στὰς παρ' ἐμοί. Πρῴην, ἔφην ἐγώ· σὺ δὲ ἄρτι πέπυσαι; Νὴ τοὺς θεούς, ἔφη, ἑσπέρας
C γε. καὶ | ἅμα ἐπιψηλαφήσας τοῦ σκίμποδος ἐκαθέζετο παρὰ τοὺς πόδας μου, καὶ εἶπεν· Ἑσπέρας δῆτα, μάλα γε ὀψὲ ἀφικόμενος ἐξ Οἰνόης. ὁ γάρ τοι παῖς με ὁ Σάτυρος ἀπέδρα· καὶ δῆτα μέλλων σοι φράζειν ὅτι διωξοίμην αὐτόν, ὑπό τινος ἄλλου ἐπελαθόμην· ἐπειδὴ δὲ ἦλθον καὶ δεδειπνηκότες ἦμεν καὶ ἐμέλλομεν ἀναπαύεσθαι, τότε μοι ἀδελφὸς λέγει ὅτι ἥκει Πρωταγόρας. καὶ ἔτι μὲν ἐνεχείρησα εὐθὺς παρὰ σὲ ἰέναι, ἔπειτά μοι λίαν πόρρω ἔδοξε
D τῶν νυκτῶν | εἶναι· ἐπειδὴ δὲ τάχιστά με ἐκ τοῦ κόπου ὁ ὕπνος ἀνῆκεν, εὐθὺς ἀναστὰς

οὕτω δεῦρο ἐπορευόμην. καὶ ἐγὼ γιγνώσκων 310
αὐτοῦ τὴν ἀνδρείαν καὶ τὴν πτοίησιν, Τί οὖν
σοι, ἦν δ' ἐγώ, τοῦτο; μῶν τί σε ἀδικεῖ
Πρωταγόρας; καὶ ὃς γελάσας, Νὴ τοὺς θεούς,
ἔφη, ὦ Σώκρατες, ὅτι γε μόνος ἐστὶ σοφός,
ἐμὲ δὲ οὐ ποιεῖ. Ἀλλὰ ναὶ μὰ Δία, ἔφην
ἐγώ, ἂν αὐτῷ διδῷς ἀργύριον καὶ πείθῃς ἐκεῖνον,
ποιήσει καὶ σὲ σοφόν. Εἰ γάρ, ἦ δ' ὅς, ὦ
Ζεῦ καὶ θεοί, ἐν τούτῳ εἴη· ὡς | οὔτ' ἂν τῶν E
ἐμῶν ἐπιλίποιμι οὐδὲν οὔτε τῶν φίλων· ἀλλ'
αὐτὰ ταῦτα καὶ νῦν ἥκω παρὰ σέ, ἵνα ὑπὲρ
ἐμοῦ διαλεχθῇς αὐτῷ. ἐγὼ γὰρ ἅμα
μὲν καὶ νεώτερός εἰμι, ἅμα δὲ οὐδὲ
ἑώρακα Πρωταγόραν πώποτε οὐδ'

and Hippocrates wishes to be taken to him as a pupil.

ἀκήκοα οὐδέν· ἔτι γὰρ παῖς ἦ, ὅτε τὸ πρότερον
ἐπεδήμησε. ἀλλὰ γάρ, ὦ Σώκρατες, πάντες
τὸν ἄνδρα ἐπαινοῦσιν καί φασιν σοφώτατον
εἶναι λέγειν· ἀλλὰ τί οὐ βαδίζομεν παρ' αὐτόν,
ἵνα ἔνδον καταλάβωμεν; | καταλύει δ', ὡς ἐγὼ 311
ἤκουσα, παρὰ Καλλίᾳ τῷ Ἱππονίκου· ἀλλ'
ἴωμεν. καὶ ἐγὼ εἶπον· Μήπω, ὠγαθέ, ἐκεῖσε
ἴωμεν· πρῲ γάρ ἐστιν· ἀλλὰ δεῦρο ἐξαναστῶμεν
εἰς τὴν αὐλήν, καὶ περιιόντες αὐτοῦ διατρίψω-
μεν, ἕως ἂν φῶς γένηται· εἶτα ἴωμεν. καὶ
γὰρ τὰ πολλὰ Πρωταγόρας ἔνδον διατρίβει,
ὥστε, θάρρει, καταληψόμεθα αὐτόν, ὡς τὸ
εἰκός, ἔνδον.

Μετὰ ταῦτα ἀναστάντες εἰς τὴν αὐλὴν
περιῇμεν. καὶ ἐγὼ ἀποπειρώμενος | τοῦ Ἱπ- B
ποκράτους τῆς ῥώμης διεσκόπουν αὐτὸν καὶ
ἠρώτων, Εἰπέ μοι, ἔφην ἐγώ, ὦ Ἱππόκρατες,

311 "To become what?" asks Socrates.

παρὰ Πρωταγόραν νῦν ἐπιχειρεῖς ἰέναι, ἀργύριον τελῶν ἐκείνῳ μισθὸν ὑπὲρ σεαυτοῦ, ὡς παρὰ τίνα ἀφιξόμενος καὶ τίς γενησόμενος; ὥσπερ ἂν εἰ ἐπενόεις παρὰ τὸν σαυτοῦ ὁμώνυμον ἐλθὼν Ἱπποκράτη τὸν Κῷον, τὸν τῶν Ἀσκληπιαδῶν, ἀργύριον τελεῖν ὑπὲρ σαυτοῦ μισθὸν ἐκείνῳ, εἴ τίς σε ἤρετο, Εἰπέ μοι, μέλλεις τελεῖν, ὦ

C Ἱππόκρατες, Ἱπποκράτει | μισθὸν ὡς τίνι ὄντι; τί ἂν ἀπεκρίνω; Εἶπον ἄν, ἔφη, ὅτι ὡς ἰατρῷ. Ὡς τίς γενησόμενος; Ὡς ἰατρός, ἔφη. Εἰ δὲ παρὰ Πολύκλειτον τὸν Ἀργεῖον ἢ Φειδίαν τὸν Ἀθηναῖον ἐπενόεις ἀφικόμενος μισθὸν ὑπὲρ σαυτοῦ τελεῖν ἐκείνοις, εἴ τίς σε ἤρετο, Τελεῖν τοῦτο τὸ ἀργύριον ὡς τίνι ὄντι ἐν νῷ ἔχεις Πολυκλείτῳ τε καὶ Φειδίᾳ; τί ἂν ἀπεκρίνω; Εἶπον ἂν ὡς ἀγαλματοποιοῖς. Ὡς τίς δὲ γενησόμενος αὐτός; Δῆλον ὅτι

D ἀγαλματοποιός. Εἶεν, ἦν δ' ἐγώ· παρὰ | δὲ δὴ Πρωταγόραν νῦν ἀφικόμενοι ἐγώ τε καὶ σὺ ἀργύριον ἐκείνῳ μισθὸν ἕτοιμοι ἐσόμεθα τελεῖν ὑπὲρ σοῦ, ἂν μὲν ἐξικνῆται τὰ ἡμέτερα χρήματα καὶ τούτοις πείθωμεν αὐτόν—· εἰ δὲ μή, καὶ τὰ τῶν φίλων προσαναλίσκοντες. εἰ οὖν τις ἡμᾶς περὶ ταῦτα οὕτω σφόδρα σπουδάζοντας ἔροιτο, Εἰπέ μοι, ὦ Σώκρατές τε καὶ Ἱππόκρατες, ὡς τίνι ὄντι τῷ Πρωταγόρᾳ ἐν νῷ ἔχετε χρήματα τελεῖν; τί ἂν αὐτῷ ἀποκριναίμεθα; τί ὄνομα ἄλλο γε λεγόμενον |

E περὶ Πρωταγόρου ἀκούομεν, ὥσπερ περὶ Φειδίου ἀγαλματοποιὸν καὶ περὶ Ὁμήρου ποιητήν, τί τοιοῦτον περὶ Πρωταγόρου ἀκούομεν; Σοφιστὴν 311 δή τοι ὀνομάζουσί γε, ὦ Σώκρατες, τὸν ἄνδρα εἶναι, ἔφη. Ὡς σοφιστῇ ἄρα ἐρχόμεθα τελοῦντες τὰ χρήματα; Μάλιστα. Εἰ οὖν καὶ τοῦτό τίς σε προσέροιτο, Αὐτὸς δὲ δὴ ὡς τίς γενησόμενος ἔρχει παρὰ | τὸν 312 Πρωταγόραν; καὶ ὃς εἶπεν ἐρυθριάσας (ἤδη γὰρ ὑπέφαινέν τι ἡμέρας, ὥστε καταφανῆ αὐτὸν γενέσθαι) Εἰ μέν τι τοῖς ἔμπροσθεν ἔοικεν, δῆλον ὅτι σοφιστὴς γενησόμενος. Σὺ δέ, ἦν δ' ἐγώ, πρὸς θεῶν, οὐκ ἂν αἰσχύνοιο εἰς τοὺς Ἕλληνας σαυτὸν σοφιστὴν παρέχων; Νὴ τὸν Δία, ὦ Σώκρατες, εἴπερ γε ἃ διανοοῦμαι χρὴ λέγειν. Ἀλλ' ἄρα, ὦ Ἱππόκρατες, μὴ οὐ τοιαύτην ὑπολαμβάνεις σου τὴν παρὰ Πρωταγόρου .μάθησιν ἔσεσθαι, ἀλλ' οἵαπερ | ἡ παρὰ τοῦ γραμματιστοῦ ἐγένετο καὶ κιθαριστοῦ B καὶ παιδοτρίβου; τούτων γὰρ σὺ ἑκάστην οὐκ ἐπὶ τέχνῃ ἔμαθες, ὡς δημιουργὸς ἐσόμενος, ἀλλ' ἐπὶ παιδείᾳ, ὡς τὸν ἰδιώτην καὶ τὸν ἐλεύθερον πρέπει. Πάνυ μὲν οὖν μοι δοκεῖ, ἔφη, τοιαύτη μᾶλλον εἶναι ἡ παρὰ Πρωταγόρου μάθησις.

"Not to become a sophist, but for general culture," thinks Hippocrates.

Οἶσθα οὖν ὃ μέλλεις νῦν πράττειν, ἤ σε λανθάνει; ἦν δ' ἐγώ. Τοῦ πέρι; Ὅτι μέλλεις τὴν ψυχὴν τὴν σαυτοῦ | παρασχεῖν θεραπεῦσαι C ἀνδρί, ὡς φῄς, σοφιστῇ· ὅ τι δέ ποτε ὁ σοφιστής ἐστιν, θαυμάζοιμ' ἂν εἰ οἶσθα. καίτοι εἰ τοῦτ' ἀγνοεῖς, οὐδὲ ὅτῳ παραδίδως τὴν ψυχὴν οἶσθα,

But what a sophist is he cannot tell.

312 οὔτ' εἰ ἀγαθῷ οὔτ' εἰ κακῷ πράγματι. Οἶμαί γ', ἔφη, εἰδέναι. Λέγε δή, τί ἡγεῖ εἶναι τὸν σοφιστήν; Ἐγὼ μέν, ἦ δ' ὅς, ὥσπερ τοὔνομα λέγει, τοῦτον εἶναι τὸν τῶν σοφῶν ἐπιστήμονα. Οὐκοῦν, ἦν δ' ἐγώ, τοῦτο μὲν ἔξεστι λέγειν καὶ περὶ ζωγράφων καὶ περὶ τεκτόνων, ὅτι

D οὗτοί εἰσιν οἱ τῶν σοφῶν ἐπιστήμονες· | ἀλλ' εἴ τις ἔροιτο ἡμᾶς, Τῶν τί σοφῶν εἰσιν οἱ ζωγράφοι ἐπιστήμονες, εἴποιμεν ἄν που αὐτῷ ὅτι τῶν πρὸς τὴν ἀπεργασίαν τὴν τῶν εἰκόνων, καὶ τἆλλα οὕτως. εἰ δέ τις ἐκεῖνο ἔροιτο, Ὁ δὲ σοφιστὴς τῶν τί σοφῶν ἐστιν; τί ἂν ἀποκρινοίμεθα αὐτῷ; ποίας ἐργασίας ἐπιστάτης; Τί ἄν, <εἰ> εἴποιμεν αὐτὸν εἶναι, ὦ Σώκρατες, ἐπιστάτην τοῦ ποιῆσαι δεινὸν λέγειν; Ἴσως ἄν, ἦν δ' ἐγώ, ἀληθῆ λέγοιμεν, οὐ μέντοι ἱκανῶς γε· ἐρωτήσεως γὰρ ἔτι ἡ ἀπόκρισις ἡμῖν δεῖται, περὶ ὅτου ὁ σοφιστὴς δεινὸν ποιεῖ λέγειν· ὥσπερ ὁ κιθαριστὴς

E δεινὸν δήπου | ποιεῖ λέγειν περὶ οὗπερ καὶ ἐπιστήμονα, περὶ κιθαρίσεως· ἦ γάρ; Ναί. Εἶεν· ὁ δὲ δὴ σοφιστὴς περὶ τίνος δεινὸν ποιεῖ λέγειν; Δῆλον ὅτι περὶ οὗπερ καὶ ἐπίσταται; Εἰκός γε· τί δή ἐστιν τοῦτο, περὶ οὗ αὐτός τε ἐπιστήμων ἐστὶν ὁ σοφιστὴς καὶ τὸν μαθητὴν ποιεῖ; Μὰ Δί', ἔφη, οὐκέτι ἔχω σοι λέγειν.

313 Καὶ ἐγὼ εἶπον | μετὰ τοῦτο· Τί οὖν; οἶσθα εἰς οἷόν τινα κίνδυνον ἔρχει ὑποθήσων τὴν ψυχήν; ἢ εἰ μὲν τὸ σῶμα ἐπιτρέπειν σε ἔδει τῳ,

The danger of entrusting one's soul to a stranger,

διακινδυνεύοντα ἢ χρηστὸν αὐτὸ γενέσθαι ἢ 313
πονηρόν, πολλὰ ἂν περιεσκέψω, εἴτ' ἐπιτρεπτέον εἴτε οὔ, καὶ εἰς συμβουλὴν τούς τε φίλους ἂν παρεκάλεις καὶ τοὺς οἰκείους, σκοπούμενος ἡμέρας συχνάς· ὃ δὲ περὶ πλείονος τοῦ σώματος ἡγεῖ, τὴν ψυχήν, καὶ ἐν ᾧ πάντ' ἐστὶν τὰ σὰ ἢ εὖ ἢ κακῶς πράττειν, χρηστοῦ ἢ πονηροῦ αὐτοῦ γενομένου, περὶ δὲ τούτου οὔτε τῷ πατρὶ οὔτε | τῷ ἀδελφῷ B
ἐπεκοινώσω οὔτε ἡμῶν τῶν ἑταίρων οὐδενί, εἴτ' ἐπιτρεπτέον εἴτε καὶ οὐ τῷ ἀφικομένῳ τούτῳ ξένῳ τὴν σὴν ψυχήν, ἀλλ' ἑσπέρας ἀκούσας, ὡς φῄς, ὄρθριος ἥκων περὶ μὲν τούτου οὐδένα λόγον οὐδὲ συμβουλὴν ποιεῖ, εἴτε χρὴ ἐπιτρέπειν σαυτὸν αὐτῷ εἴτε μή, ἕτοιμος δ' εἶ ἀναλίσκειν τά τε σαυτοῦ καὶ τὰ τῶν φίλων χρήματα, ὡς ἤδη διεγνωκὼς ὅτι πάντως συνεστέον Πρωταγόρᾳ, ὃν οὔτε γιγνώσκεις, ὡς φῄς, οὔτε διείλεξαι οὐδεπώποτε, σοφιστὴν δ' ὀνομάζεις, | τὸν δὲ σοφιστήν, ὅ τι C
ποτ' ἐστίν, φαίνει ἀγνοῶν, ᾧ μέλλεις σαυτὸν ἐπιτρέπειν; καὶ ὃς ἀκούσας, Ἔοικεν, ἔφη, ὦ Σώκρατες, ἐξ ὧν σὺ λέγεις. Ἆρ' οὖν, ὦ Ἱππόκρατες, ὁ σοφιστὴς τυγχάνει ὢν ἔμπορός τις ἢ κάπηλος τῶν ἀγωγίμων, ἀφ' ὧν ψυχὴ τρέφεται; Φαίνεται γὰρ ἔμοιγε τοιοῦτός τις· τρέφεται δέ, ὦ Σώκρατες, ψυχὴ τίνι; Μαθήμασιν δήπου, ἦν δ' ἐγώ. καὶ ὅπως γε μή, ὦ ἑταῖρε, ὁ σοφιστὴς ἐπαινῶν ἃ πωλεῖ ἐξαπατήσῃ ἡμᾶς, ὥσπερ οἱ περὶ τὴν τοῦ σώματος τροφήν, ὁ

a huckster of knowledge of dubious value.

313 ἔμπορός | τε καὶ κάπηλος. καὶ γὰρ οὗτοί που
D ὧν ἄγουσιν ἀγωγίμων οὔτε αὐτοὶ ἴσασιν ὅ τι
χρηστὸν ἢ πονηρὸν περὶ τὸ σῶμα, ἐπαινοῦσιν
δὲ πάντα πωλοῦντες, οὔτε οἱ ὠνούμενοι παρ'
αὐτῶν, ἐὰν μή τις τύχῃ γυμναστικὸς ἢ ἰατρὸς
ὤν. οὕτω δὲ καὶ οἱ τὰ μαθήματα περιάγοντες
κατὰ τὰς πόλεις καὶ πωλοῦντες καὶ καπη-
λεύοντες τῷ ἀεὶ ἐπιθυμοῦντι ἐπαινοῦσιν μὲν
πάντα ἃ πωλοῦσιν, τάχα δ' ἄν τινες, ὦ
ἄριστε, καὶ τούτων ἀγνοοῖεν ὧν πωλοῦσι ὅ τι
χρηστὸν ἢ πονηρὸν πρὸς τὴν ψυχήν· ὡς δ' |
E αὕτως καὶ οἱ ὠνούμενοι παρ' αὐτῶν, ἐὰν μή
τις τύχῃ περὶ τὴν ψυχὴν αὖ ἰατρικὸς ὤν.
εἰ μὲν οὖν σὺ τυγχάνεις ἐπιστήμων τούτων τί
χρηστὸν καὶ πονηρόν, ἀσφαλές σοι ὠνεῖσθαι
μαθήματα καὶ παρὰ Πρωταγόρου καὶ παρ'
ἄλλου ὁτουοῦν· εἰ δὲ μή, ὅρα, ὦ μακάριε,
314 μὴ περὶ τοῖς φιλτάτοις | κυβεύῃς τε καὶ
κινδυνεύῃς. καὶ γὰρ δὴ καὶ πολὺ μείζων
κίνδυνος ἐν τῇ τῶν μαθημάτων ὠνῇ ἢ ἐν τῇ
τῶν σιτίων. σιτία μὲν γὰρ καὶ ποτὰ πριά-
μενον παρὰ τοῦ καπήλου καὶ ἐμπόρου ἔξεστιν
ἐν ἄλλοις ἀγγείοις ἀποφέρειν, καὶ πρὶν δέ-
ξασθαι αὐτὰ εἰς τὸ σῶμα πιόντα ἢ φαγόντα,
καταθέμενον οἴκαδε ἔξεστιν συμβουλεύσασθαι,
παρακαλέσαντα τὸν ἐπαΐοντα, ὅ τι τε ἐδεστέον
ἢ ποτέον καὶ ὅ τι μή, καὶ ὁπόσον καὶ ὁπότε·
ὥστε ἐν τῇ ὠνῇ οὐ μέγας ὁ κίνδυνος. μαθή-
B ματα δὲ οὐκ | ἔστιν ἐν ἄλλῳ ἀγγείῳ ἀπενεγκεῖν,
ἀλλ' ἀνάγκη, καταθέντα τὴν τιμὴν τὸ μάθημα
ἐν αὐτῇ τῇ ψυχῇ λαβόντα καὶ μαθόντα ἀπιέναι

ἢ βεβλαμμένον ἢ ὠφελημένον. ταῦτα οὖν σκο- 314
πώμεθα καὶ μετὰ τῶν πρεσβυτέρων ἡμῶν· ἡμεῖς
γὰρ ἔτι νέοι ὥστε τοσοῦτο πρᾶγμα διελέσθαι.
νῦν μέντοι, ὥσπερ ὡρμήσαμεν, ἴωμεν καὶ ἀκού-
σωμεν τοῦ ἀνδρός, ἔπειτα ἀκούσαντες
καὶ ἄλλοις ἀνακοινωσώμεθα· καὶ γὰρ
οὐ μόνος Πρωταγόρας αὐτόθι ἐστίν,
ἀλλὰ καὶ Ἱππίας ὁ Ἠλεῖος· οἶμαι | δὲ καὶ C
Πρόδικον τὸν Κεῖον· καὶ ἄλλοι πολλοὶ καὶ σοφοί.

But let us go and hear the man.

Δόξαν ἡμῖν ταῦτα ἐπορευόμεθα· ἐπειδὴ δὲ
ἐν τῷ προθύρῳ ἐγενόμεθα, ἐπιστάντες περί
τινος λόγου διελεγόμεθα, ὃς ἡμῖν κατὰ τὴν
ὁδὸν ἐνέπεσεν· ἵν' οὖν μὴ ἀτελὴς γένοιτο,
ἀλλὰ διαπερανάμενοι οὕτως ἐσίοιμεν, στάντες
ἐν τῷ προθύρῳ διελεγόμεθα, ἕως συνωμολογή-
σαμεν ἀλλήλοις. δοκεῖ οὖν μοι, ὁ θυρωρός,
εὐνοῦχός τις, κατήκουεν ἡμῶν, κινδυνεύει δὲ
διὰ | τὸ πλῆθος τῶν σοφιστῶν ἄχθεσθαι τοῖς D
φοιτῶσιν εἰς τὴν οἰκίαν· ἐπειδὴ γοῦν
ἐκρούσαμεν τὴν θύραν, ἀνοίξας καὶ
ἰδὼν ἡμᾶς, Ἔα, ἔφη, σοφισταί τινες·
οὐ σχολὴ αὐτῷ. καὶ ἅμα ἀμφοῖν τοῖν χεροῖν
τὴν θύραν πάνυ προθύμως ὡς οἷός τ' ἦν
ἐπήραξεν. καὶ ἡμεῖς πάλιν ἐκρούομεν, καὶ ὃς
ἐγκεκλῃμένης τῆς θύρας ἀποκρινόμενος εἶπεν, Ὦ
ἄνθρωποι, ἔφη, οὐκ ἀκηκόατε ὅτι οὐ σχολὴ αὐτῷ;
Ἀλλ' ὠγαθέ, ἔφην ἐγώ, οὔτε παρὰ Καλλίαν ἥκο-
μεν οὔτε σοφισταί ἐσμεν· ἀλλὰ θάρρει· | Πρω- E
ταγόραν γάρ τοι δεόμενοι ἰδεῖν ἤλθομεν· εἰσάγ-
γειλον οὖν. μόγις οὖν ποτε ἡμῖν ἄνθρωπος
ἀνέῳξεν τὴν θύραν.

A difficult access at Callias' house.

The sophists there gathered.

314 Ἐπειδὴ δὲ εἰσήλθομεν, κατελάβομεν Πρωτα-
γόραν ἐν τῷ προστῴῳ περιπατοῦντα,
ἑξῆς δ᾽ αὐτῷ συμπεριεπάτουν ἐκ μὲν
τοῦ ἐπὶ θάτερα Καλλίας ὁ Ἱππονίκου καὶ ὁ
315 ἀδελφὸς αὐτοῦ ὁ ὁμομήτριος, Πάραλος | ὁ
Περικλέους, καὶ Χαρμίδης ὁ Γλαύκωνος, ἐκ
δὲ τοῦ ἐπὶ θάτερα ὁ ἕτερος τῶν Περικλέους
Ξάνθιππος καὶ Φιλιππίδης ὁ Φιλομήλου καὶ
Ἀντίμοιρος ὁ Μενδαῖος, ὅσπερ εὐδοκιμεῖ μάλιστα
τῶν Πρωταγόρου μαθητῶν καὶ ἐπὶ τέχνῃ μαν-
θάνει, ὡς σοφιστὴς ἐσόμενος. τούτων δὲ οἳ
ὄπισθεν ἠκολούθουν ἐπακούοντες τῶν λεγομέ-
νων, τὸ μὲν πολὺ ξένοι ἐφαίνοντο, οὓς ἄγει ἐξ
ἑκάστων τῶν πόλεων ὁ Πρωταγόρας, δι᾽ ὧν
διεξέρχεται, κηλῶν τῇ φωνῇ ὥσπερ Ὀρφεύς,
B οἱ δὲ κατὰ τὴν φωνὴν | ἕπονται κεκηλημένοι·
ἦσαν δέ τινες καὶ τῶν ἐπιχωρίων ἐν τῷ χορῷ.
τοῦτον τὸν χορὸν μάλιστα ἔγωγε ἰδὼν ἥσθην,
ὡς καλῶς ηὐλαβοῦντο μηδέποτε ἐμποδὼν ἐν τῷ
πρόσθεν εἶναι Πρωταγόρου, ἀλλ᾽ ἐπειδὴ αὐτὸς
ἀναστρέφοι καὶ οἱ μετ᾽ ἐκείνου, εὖ πως καὶ ἐν
κόσμῳ περιεσχίζοντο οὗτοι οἱ ἐπήκοοι ἔνθεν καὶ
ἔνθεν, καὶ ἐν κύκλῳ περιιόντες ἀεὶ εἰς τὸ ὄπισθεν
καθίσταντο κάλλιστα.

Τὸν δὲ μετ᾽ εἰσενόησα, ἔφη Ὅμηρος,
C Ἱππίαν τὸν Ἠλεῖον, | καθήμενον ἐν τῷ κατ᾽
ἀντικρὺ προστῴῳ ἐν θρόνῳ· περὶ αὐτὸν δ᾽ ἐκάθ-
ηντο ἐπὶ βάθρων Ἐρυξίμαχός τε ὁ Ἀκουμενοῦ
καὶ Φαῖδρος ὁ Μυρρινούσιος καὶ Ἄνδρων ὁ
Ἀνδροτίωνος καὶ τῶν ξένων πολῖταί τε αὐτοῦ
καὶ ἄλλοι τινές. ἐφαίνοντο δὲ περί φύσεώς τε

καὶ τῶν μετεώρων ἀστρονομικὰ ἄττα διερωτᾶν 315
τὸν Ἱππίαν, ὁ δ' ἐν θρόνῳ καθήμενος ἑκάστοις
αὐτῶν διέκρινεν καὶ διεξῄει τὰ ἐρωτώμενα.

Καὶ μὲν δὴ καὶ Τάνταλόν γε εἰσεῖδον.
ἐπεδήμει γὰρ ἄρα καὶ Πρόδικος ὁ | Κεῖος, ἦν δὲ D
ἐν οἰκήματί τινι, ᾧ πρὸ τοῦ μὲν ὡς ταμιείῳ
ἐχρῆτο Ἱππόνικος, νῦν δὲ ὑπὸ τοῦ πλήθους
τῶν καταλυόντων ὁ Καλλίας καὶ τοῦτο ἐκκενώ-
σας ξένοις κατάλυσιν πεποίηκεν. ὁ μὲν οὖν
Πρόδικος ἔτι κατέκειτο, ἐγκεκαλυμμένος ἐν
κῳδίοις τισὶν καὶ στρώμασιν καὶ μάλα πολ-
λοῖς, ὡς ἐφαίνετο· παρεκάθηντο δὲ αὐτῷ ἐπὶ
ταῖς πλησίον κλίναις Παυσανίας τε ὁ ἐκ
Κεραμέων καὶ μετὰ Παυσανίου νέον τι ἔτι
μειράκιον, ὡς μὲν ἐγᾦμαι, καλόν τε κἀγαθὸν
τὴν φύσιν, | τὴν δ' οὖν ἰδέαν πάνυ καλός. E
ἔδοξα ἀκοῦσαι ὄνομα αὐτῷ εἶναι Ἀγάθωνα, καὶ
οὐκ ἂν θαυμάζοιμι, εἰ παιδικὰ Παυσανίου τυγ-
χάνει ὤν. τοῦτ' ἦν τὸ μειράκιον, καὶ τὼ
Ἀδειμάντω ἀμφοτέρω, ὅ τε Κήπιδος καὶ ὁ
Λευκολοφίδου, καὶ ἄλλοι τινὲς ἐφαίνοντο· περὶ
δὲ ὧν διελέγοντο οὐκ ἐδυνάμην ἔγωγε μαθεῖν
ἔξωθεν, καίπερ λιπαρῶς ἔχων ἀκούειν τοῦ Προ-
δίκου (πάσσοφος γάρ μοι δοκεῖ ἀνὴρ εἶναι καὶ
θεῖος), | ἀλλὰ διὰ τὴν βαρύτητα τῆς φωνῆς 316
βόμβος τις ἐν τῷ οἰκήματι γιγνόμενος ἀσαφῆ
ἐποίει τὰ λεγόμενα.

GORGIAS

It is better to suffer Wrong than do Wrong.

SOCRATES. POLUS. CALLICLES.

469 ΠΩΛ. Σὺ ἄρα βούλοιο ἂν ἀδικεῖσθαι μᾶλλον
B ἢ ἀδικεῖν;

Socrates' choice;

C ΣΩ. βουλοίμην | μὲν ἂν ἔγωγε οὐδέτερα· εἰ δ' ἀναγκαῖον εἴη ἀδικεῖν ἢ ἀδικεῖσθαι, ἑλοίμην ἂν μᾶλλον ἀδικεῖσθαι ἢ ἀδικεῖν. * * *

the reason.

470 ΣΩ. Τὸν μὲν γὰρ καλὸν κἀγαθὸν ἄνδρα καὶ
E γυναῖκα εὐδαίμονα εἶναί φημι, τὸν δὲ ἄδικον καὶ πονηρὸν ἄθλιον. * * *

Lawyers confute by the testimony of many witnesses;

471 ΣΩ. Ὦ μακάριε, ῥητορικῶς γάρ με ἐπιχειρεῖς
E ἐλέγχειν, ὥσπερ οἱ ἐν τοῖς δικαστηρίοις ἡγούμενοι ἐλέγχειν. καὶ γὰρ ἐκεῖ οἱ ἕτεροι τοὺς ἑτέρους δοκοῦσιν ἐλέγχειν, ἐπειδὰν τῶν λόγων ὧν ἂν λέγωσι μάρτυρας πολλοὺς παρέχωνται καὶ εὐδοκίμους, ὁ δὲ τἀναντία λέγων ἕνα τινὰ παρέχηται ἢ μηδένα. οὗτος δὲ ὁ ἔλεγχος
472 οὐδενὸς ἄξιός ἐστιν πρὸς τὴν | ἀλήθειαν· ἐνίοτε γὰρ ἂν καὶ καταψευδομαρτυρηθείη τις ὑπὸ πολλῶν καὶ δοκούντων εἶναί τι. καὶ νῦν περὶ ὧν σὺ λέγεις ὀλίγου σοι πάντες συμφήσουσιν ταῦτα Ἀθηναῖοι καὶ οἱ ξένοι, ἐὰν βούλῃ κατ' ἐμοῦ μάρτυρας παρασχέσθαι, ὡς οὐκ ἀληθῆ λέγω· μαρτυρήσουσί σοι, ἐὰν μὲν βούλῃ, Νικίας ὁ Νικηράτου καὶ οἱ ἀδελφοὶ μετ' αὐτοῦ, ὧν οἱ τρίποδες οἱ ἐφεξῆς ἑστῶτές εἰσιν ἐν τῷ Διονυ-

σίῳ, ἐὰν δὲ βούλῃ, Ἀριστοκράτης ὁ Σκελλίου, 472
οὗ αὖ ἐστιν ἐν Πυθοῖ τοῦτο τὸ καλὸν | ἀνάθημα, B
ἐὰν δὲ βούλῃ, ἡ Περικλέους ὅλη οἰκία ἢ ἄλλη
συγγένεια, ἥντινα ἂν βούλῃ τῶν ἐνθάδε ἐκλέξα-
σθαι. ἀλλ' ἐγώ σοι εἷς ὢν οὐχ ὁμολογῶ· οὐ
γάρ με σὺ ἀναγκάζεις, ἀλλὰ ψευδομάρτυρας
πολλοὺς κατ' ἐμοῦ παρασχόμενος ἐπιχειρεῖς
ἐκβάλλειν με ἐκ τῆς οὐσίας καὶ τοῦ ἀληθοῦς.
ἐγὼ δέ, ἂν μὴ σὲ αὐτὸν ἕνα ὄντα
μάρτυρα παράσχωμαι ὁμολογοῦντα
περὶ ὧν λέγω, οὐδὲν οἶμαι ἄξιον λόγου
μοι πεπεράνθαι περὶ | ὧν ἂν ἡμῖν C
ὁ λόγος ᾖ· οἶμαι δὲ οὐδὲ σοί, ἐὰν μὴ ἐγώ σοι
μαρτυρῶ εἷς ὢν μόνος, τοὺς δ' ἄλλους πάντας
τούτους χαίρειν ἐᾷς. ἔστιν μὲν οὖν οὗτός τις
τρόπος ἐλέγχου, ὡς σύ τε οἴει καὶ ἄλλοι
πολλοί· ἔστιν δὲ καὶ ἄλλος, ὃν ἐγὼ αὖ οἶμαι.
παραβαλόντες οὖν παρ' ἀλλήλους σκεψώμεθα,
εἴ τι διοίσουσιν ἀλλήλων. καὶ γὰρ τυγχάνει
περὶ ὧν ἀμφισβητοῦμεν οὐ πάνυ σμικρὰ ὄντα,
ἀλλὰ σχεδόν τι ταῦτα, περὶ ὧν εἰδέναι τε
κάλλιστον μὴ εἰδέναι τε αἴσχιστον· τὸ γὰρ
κεφάλαιον αὐτῶν ἐστιν ἢ γιγνώσκειν ἢ
ἀγνοεῖν, ὅστις τε εὐδαίμων ἐστὶν καὶ ὅστις
| μή. αὐτίκα πρῶτον, περὶ οὗ νῦν ὁ λόγος D
ἐστίν, σὺ ἡγεῖ οἷόντε εἶναι μακάριον ἄνδρα
ἀδικοῦντά τε καὶ ἄδικον ὄντα, εἴπερ Ἀρχέλαον
ἄδικον μὲν ἡγεῖ εἶναι, εὐδαίμονα δέ· ἄλλο τι
ὡς οὕτω σου νομίζοντος διανοώμεθα;

but Socrates, by the admissions of the defendant himself.

ΠΩΛ. Πάνυ γε.

ΣΩ. Ἐγὼ δέ φημι ἀδύνατον. ἓν μὲν τουτὶ

472 ἀμφισβητοῦμεν. εἶεν· ἀδικῶν δὲ δὴ εὐδαίμων ἔσται ἆρ', ἂν τυγχάνῃ δίκης τε καὶ τιμωρίας;

ΠΩΛ. Ἥκιστά γε, ἐπεὶ οὕτω γ' ἂν ἀθλιώτατος εἴη.

E ΣΩ. Ἀλλ' ἐὰν ἄρα μὴ τυγχάνῃ | δίκης ὁ ἀδικῶν, κατὰ τὸν σὸν λόγον εὐδαίμων ἔσται;

ΠΩΛ. Φημί.

Socrates' Paradox: The wrong-doer is less wretched if punished.

ΣΩ. Κατὰ δέ γε τὴν ἐμὴν δόξαν, ὦ Πῶλε, ὁ ἀδικῶν τε καὶ ὁ ἄδικος πάντως μὲν ἄθλιος, ἀθλιώτερος μέντοι, ἐὰν μὴ διδῷ δίκην μηδὲ τυγχάνῃ τιμωρίας ἀδικῶν, ἧττον δὲ ἄθλιος, ἐὰν διδῷ δίκην καὶ τυγχάνῃ δίκης ὑπὸ θεῶν τε καὶ ἀνθρώπων.

473 ΠΩΛ. | Ἄτοπά γε, ὦ Σώκρατες, ἐπιχειρεῖς λέγειν.

ΣΩ. Πειράσομαι δέ γε καὶ σὲ ποιῆσαι, ὦ ἑταῖρε, ταὐτὰ ἐμοὶ λέγειν· φίλον γάρ σε ἡγοῦμαι. νῦν μὲν οὖν ἃ διαφερόμεθα ταῦτ' ἐστί· σκόπει δὲ καὶ σύ· εἶπον ἐγώ που ἐν τοῖς ἔμπροσθεν τὸ ἀδικεῖν τοῦ ἀδικεῖσθαι κάκιον εἶναι.

ΠΩΛ. Πάνυ γε.

ΣΩ. Σὺ δὲ τὸ ἀδικεῖσθαι.

ΠΩΛ. Ναί.

ΣΩ. Καὶ τοὺς ἀδικοῦντας ἀθλίους ἔφην εἶναι ἐγώ, καὶ ἐξηλέγχθην ὑπὸ σοῦ—

ΠΩΛ. Ναὶ μὰ Δία.

B ΣΩ. Ὡς | σὺ οἴει, ὦ Πῶλε.

ΠΩΛ. Ἀληθῆ γε οἰόμενος ἴσως.

ΣΩ. Σὺ δέ γε εὐδαίμονας αὖ τοὺς ἀδικοῦντας, ἐὰν μὴ διδῶσι δίκην.

473

ΠΩΛ. Πάνυ μὲν οὖν.

ΣΩ. Ἐγὼ δὲ αὐτοὺς ἀθλιωτάτους φημί, τοὺς δὲ διδόντας δίκην ἧττον. βούλει καὶ τοῦτο ἐλέγχειν;

ΠΩΛ. Ἀλλ' ἔτι τοῦτ' ἐκείνου χαλεπώτερόν ἐστιν, ὦ Σώκρατες, ἐξελέγξαι.

ΣΩ. Οὐ δῆτα, ὦ Πῶλε, ἀλλ' ἀδύνατον· τὸ γὰρ ἀληθὲς οὐδέποτε ἐλέγχεται.

Polus would refute by a rhetorical question,

ΠΩΛ. Πῶς λέγεις; ἐὰν ἀδικῶν ἄνθρωπος ληφθῇ τυραννίδι | C ἐπιβουλεύων, καὶ ληφθεὶς στρεβλῶται καὶ ἐκτέμνηται καὶ τοὺς ὀφθαλμοὺς ἐκκάηται, καὶ ἄλλας πολλὰς καὶ μεγάλας καὶ παντοδαπὰς λώβας αὐτός τε λωβηθεὶς καὶ τοὺς αὑτοῦ ἐπιδὼν παῖδάς τε καὶ γυναῖκα τὸ ἔσχατον ἀνασταυρωθῇ ἢ καταπιττωθῇ, οὗτος εὐδαιμονέστερος ἔσται ἢ ἐὰν διαφυγὼν τύραννος καταστῇ καὶ ἄρχων ἐν τῇ πόλει διαβιῷ ποιῶν ὅ τι ἂν βούληται, ζηλωτὸς ὢν καὶ εὐδαιμονιζόμενος ὑπὸ τῶν πολιτῶν καὶ τῶν | D ἄλλων ξένων; ταῦτα λέγεις ἀδύνατον εἶναι ἐξελέγχειν;

ΣΩ. Μορμολύττει αὖ, ὦ γενναῖε Πῶλε, καὶ οὐκ ἐλέγχεις· ἄρτι δὲ ἐμαρτύρου. ὅμως δὲ ὑπόμνησόν με σμικρόν· ἐὰν ἀδίκως ἐπιβουλεύων τυραννίδι, εἶπες;

ΠΩΛ. Ἔγωγε.

ΣΩ. Εὐδαιμονέστερος μὲν τοίνυν οὐδέποτε ἔσται οὐδέτερος αὐτῶν, οὔτε ὁ κατειργασμένος τὴν τυραννίδα ἀδίκως οὔτε ὁ δίκην διδούς· δυοῖν γὰρ ἀθλίοιν εὐδαιμονέστερος μὲν οὐκ ἂν εἴη· ἀθλιώτερος μέντοι ὁ διαφεύγων | E καὶ τυραννεύσας.—τί τοῦτο, ὦ Πῶλε; γελᾷς; ἄλλο αὖ

473 τοῦτο εἶδος ἐλέγχου ἐστίν, ἐπειδάν τίς τι εἴπῃ, καταγελᾶν, ἐλέγχειν δὲ μή;

ΠΩΛ. Οὐκ οἴει ἐξεληλέγχθαι, ὦ Σώκρατες, ὅταν τοιαῦτα λέγῃς, ἃ οὐδεὶς ἂν φήσειεν ἀνθρώπων; ἐπεὶ ἐροῦ τινα τουτωνί.

by appeal to the general judgment.

ΣΩ. Ὦ Πῶλε, οὐκ εἰμὶ τῶν πολιτικῶν· καὶ πέρυσι βουλεύειν λαχών, ἐπειδὴ ἡ φυλὴ ἐπρυτάνευε καὶ ἔδει με ἐπιψηφίζειν, γέλωτα
474 παρεῖχον | καὶ οὐκ ἠπιστάμην ἐπιψηφίζειν. μὴ οὖν μηδὲ νῦν με κέλευε ἐπιψηφίζειν τοὺς παρόντας, ἀλλ' εἰ μὴ ἔχεις τούτων βελτίω ἔλεγχον, ὅπερ νῦν δὴ ἐγὼ ἔλεγον, ἐμοὶ ἐν τῷ μέρει παράδος, καὶ πείρασαι τοῦ ἐλέγχου, οἷον ἐγὼ οἶμαι δεῖν εἶναι. ἐγὼ γὰρ ὧν ἂν λέγω ἕνα μὲν παρασχέσθαι μάρτυρα ἐπίσταμαι, αὐτὸν πρὸς ὃν ἄν μοι ὁ λόγος ᾖ, τοὺς δὲ πολλοὺς ἐῶ χαίρειν, καὶ ἕνα ἐπιψηφίζειν ἐπίσταμαι, τοῖς δὲ πολλοῖς οὐδὲ διαλέγομαι.
B ὅρα οὖν, εἰ ἐθελήσεις | ἐν τῷ μέρει διδόναι ἔλεγχον ἀποκρινόμενος τὰ ἐρωτώμενα. ἐγὼ γὰρ δὴ οἶμαι καὶ ἐμὲ καὶ σὲ καὶ τοὺς ἄλλους ἀνθρώπους τὸ ἀδικεῖν τοῦ ἀδικεῖσθαι κάκιον ἡγεῖσθαι καὶ τὸ μὴ διδόναι δίκην τοῦ διδόναι.

But Socrates proves, first, that to do wrong is worse than to suffer wrong;

ΠΩΛ. Ἐγὼ δέ γε οὔτ' ἐμὲ οὔτ' ἄλλον ἀνθρώπων οὐδένα. ἐπεὶ σὺ δέξαι' ἂν μᾶλλον ἀδικεῖσθαι ἢ ἀδικεῖν;

ΣΩ. Καὶ σύ γ' ἂν καὶ οἱ ἄλλοι πάντες.

ΠΩΛ. Πολλοῦ γε δεῖ, ἀλλ' οὔτ' ἐγὼ οὔτε σὺ οὔτ' ἄλλος οὐδείς.

ΣΩ. Οὔκουν | ἀποκρινεῖ; 474

ΠΩΛ. Πάνυ μὲν οὖν· καὶ γὰρ ἐπιθυμῶ C
εἰδέναι ὅ τι ποτ' ἐρεῖς.

ΣΩ. Λέγε δή μοι, ἵν' εἰδῇς, ὥσπερ ἂν εἰ ἐξ ἀρχῆς σε ἠρώτων· πότερον δοκεῖ σοι, ὦ Πῶλε, κάκιον εἶναι τὸ ἀδικεῖν ἢ τὸ ἀδικεῖσθαι;

ΠΩΛ. Τὸ ἀδικεῖσθαι ἔμοιγε.

ΣΩ. Τί δὲ δή; αἴσχιον πότερον τὸ ἀδικεῖν ἢ τὸ ἀδικεῖσθαι; ἀποκρίνου.

ΠΩΛ. Τὸ ἀδικεῖν.

ΣΩ. Οὐκοῦν καὶ κάκιον, εἴπερ αἴσχιον.

ΠΩΛ. Ἥκιστά γε.

ΣΩ. Μανθάνω· οὐ ταὐτὸν ἡγεῖ σύ, ὡς ἔοικας, καλόν τε καὶ | ἀγαθόν, καὶ κακὸν καὶ D
αἰσχρόν.

ΠΩΛ. Οὐ δῆτα.

ΣΩ. Τί δὲ τόδε; τὰ καλὰ πάντα, οἷον καὶ σώματα καὶ χρώματα καὶ σχήματα καὶ φωνὰς καὶ ἐπιτηδεύματα, εἰς οὐδὲν ἀποβλέπων καλεῖς ἑκάστοτε καλά; οἷον πρῶτον τὰ σώματα τὰ καλὰ οὐχὶ ἤτοι κατὰ τὴν χρείαν λέγεις καλὰ εἶναι, πρὸς ὃ ἂν ἕκαστον χρήσιμον ᾖ, πρὸς τοῦτο, ἢ κατὰ ἡδονήν τινα, ἐὰν ἐν τῷ θεωρεῖσθαι χαίρειν ποιῇ τοὺς θεωροῦντας; ἔχεις τι ἐκτὸς τούτων λέγειν περὶ σώματος
| κάλλους; E

ΠΩΛ. Οὐκ ἔχω.

ΣΩ. Οὐκοῦν καὶ τἆλλα πάντα οὕτω καὶ σχήματα καὶ χρώματα ἢ διὰ ἡδονήν τινα ἢ διὰ ὠφέλειαν ἢ δι' ἀμφότερα καλὰ προσαγορεύεις;

474 ΠΩΛ. Ἔγωγε.

ΣΩ. Οὐ καὶ τὰς φωνὰς καὶ τὰ κατὰ τὴν μουσικὴν πάντα ὡσαύτως;

ΠΩΛ. Ναί.

ΣΩ. Καὶ μὴν τά γε κατὰ τοὺς νόμους καὶ τὰ ἐπιτηδεύματα οὐ δήπου ἐκτὸς τούτων ἐστίν, τὰ καλά, τοῦ ἢ ὠφέλιμα εἶναι ἢ ἡδέα ἢ ἀμφότερα.

ΠΩΛ. Οὐκ ἔμοιγε δοκεῖ.

475 ΣΩ. Οὐκοῦν καὶ | τὸ τῶν μαθημάτων κάλλος ὡσαύτως;

ΠΩΛ. Πάνυ γε· καὶ καλῶς γε νῦν ὁρίζει, ὦ Σώκρατες, ἡδονῇ τε καὶ ἀγαθῷ ὁριζόμενος τὸ καλόν.

ΣΩ. Οὐκοῦν τὸ αἰσχρὸν τῷ ἐναντίῳ, λύπῃ τε καὶ κακῷ;

ΠΩΛ. Ἀνάγκη.

ΣΩ. Ὅταν ἄρα δυοῖν καλοῖν θάτερον κάλλιον ᾖ, ἢ τῷ ἑτέρῳ τούτοιν ἢ ἀμφοτέροις ὑπερβάλλον κάλλιόν ἐστιν, ἤτοι ἡδονῇ ἢ ὠφελείᾳ ἢ ἀμφοτέροις.

ΠΩΛ. Πάνυ γε.

ΣΩ. Καὶ ὅταν δὲ δὴ δυοῖν αἰσχροῖν τὸ
B ἕτερον αἴσχιον | ᾖ, ἤτοι λύπῃ ἢ κακῷ ὑπερβάλλον αἴσχιον ἔσται· ἢ οὐκ ἀνάγκη;

ΠΩΛ. Ναί.

ΣΩ. Φέρε δή, πῶς ἐλέγετο νῦν δὴ περὶ τοῦ ἀδικεῖν καὶ ἀδικεῖσθαι; οὐκ ἔλεγες τὸ μὲν ἀδικεῖσθαι κάκιον εἶναι, τὸ δὲ ἀδικεῖν αἴσχιον;

ΠΩΛ. Ἔλεγον.

ΣΩ. Οὐκοῦν εἴπερ αἴσχιον τὸ ἀδικεῖν τοῦ

ἀδικεῖσθαι, ἤτοι λυπηρότερόν ἐστιν καὶ λύπῃ 475 ὑπερβάλλον αἴσχιον ἂν .εἴη ἢ κακῷ ἢ ἀμφοτέροις; οὐ καὶ τοῦτο ἀνάγκη;

ΠΩΛ. Πῶς γὰρ οὔ;

ΣΩ. Πρῶτον μὲν δὴ σκεψώμεθα, ἆρα λύπῃ | ὑπερβάλλει τὸ ἀδικεῖν τοῦ ἀδικεῖσθαι, καὶ C ἀλγοῦσι μᾶλλον οἱ ἀδικοῦντες ἢ οἱ ἀδικούμενοι;

ΠΩΛ. Οὐδαμῶς, ὦ Σώκρατες, τοῦτό γε.

ΣΩ. Οὐκ ἄρα λύπῃ γε ὑπερέχει.

ΠΩΛ. Οὐ δῆτα.

ΣΩ. Οὐκοῦν εἰ μὴ λύπῃ, ἀμφοτέροις μὲν οὐκ ἂν ἔτι ὑπερβάλλοι.

ΠΩΛ. Οὐ φαίνεται.

ΣΩ. Οὐκοῦν τῷ ἑτέρῳ λείπεται.

ΠΩΛ. Ναί.

ΣΩ. Τῷ κακῷ.

ΠΩΛ. Ἔοικεν.

ΣΩ. Οὐκοῦν κακῷ ὑπερβάλλον τὸ ἀδικεῖν κάκιον ἂν εἴη τοῦ ἀδικεῖσθαι.

ΠΩΛ. Δῆλον δὴ | ὅτι. D

ΣΩ. Ἄλλο τι οὖν ὑπὸ μὲν τῶν πολλῶν ἀνθρώπων καὶ ὑπὸ σοῦ ὡμολογεῖτο ἡμῖν ἐν τῷ ἔμπροσθεν χρόνῳ αἴσχιον εἶναι τὸ ἀδικεῖν τοῦ ἀδικεῖσθαι;

ΠΩΛ. Ναί.

ΣΩ. Νῦν δέ γε κάκιον ἐφάνη.

ΠΩΛ. Ἔοικε.

ΣΩ. Δέξαιο ἂν οὖν σὺ μᾶλλον τὸ κάκιον καὶ τὸ αἴσχιον ἀντὶ τοῦ ἧττον; μὴ ὄκνει ἀποκρίνασθαι, ὦ Πῶλε· οὐδὲν γὰρ βλαβήσει·

475 ἀλλὰ γενναίως τῷ λόγῳ ὥσπερ ἰατρῷ παρέχων
E ἀποκρίνου, καὶ | ἢ φάθι ἢ μὴ ἃ ἐρωτῶ.

ΠΩΛ. Ἀλλ᾽ οὐκ ἂν δεξαίμην, ὦ Σώκρατες.

ΣΩ. Ἄλλος δέ τις ἀνθρώπων;

ΠΩΛ. Οὔ μοι δοκεῖ κατά γε τοῦτον τὸν λόγον.

ΣΩ. Ἀληθῆ ἄρα ἐγὼ ἔλεγον, ὅτι οὔτ᾽ ἂν ἐγὼ οὔτ᾽ ἂν σὺ οὔτ᾽ ἄλλος οὐδεὶς ἀνθρώπων δέξαιτ᾽ ἂν μᾶλλον ἀδικεῖν ἢ ἀδικεῖσθαι· κάκιον γὰρ τυγχάνει ὄν.

ΠΩΛ. Φαίνεται.

ΣΩ. Ὁρᾷς οὖν, ὦ Πῶλε, ὁ ἔλεγχος παρὰ τὸν ἔλεγχον παραβαλλόμενος ὅτι οὐδὲν ἔοικεν, ἀλλὰ σοὶ μὲν οἱ ἄλλοι πάντες ὁμολογοῦσιν
πλὴν ἐμοῦ, ἐμοὶ δὲ σὺ ἐξαρκεῖς εἷς ὢν μόνος
476 καὶ ὁμολογῶν καὶ μαρτυρῶν, | καὶ ἐγὼ σὲ
μόνον ἐπιψηφίζων τοὺς ἄλλους ἐῶ χαίρειν. καὶ τοῦτο μὲν ἡμῖν οὕτως ἐχέτω· μετὰ τοῦτο δὲ περὶ οὗ τὸ δεύτερον ἠμφεσβητήσαμεν σκεψώμεθα, τὸ ἀδικοῦντα διδόναι δίκην ἆρα μέγιστον τῶν κακῶν ἐστιν, ὡς σὺ ᾤου, ἢ μεῖζον τὸ μὴ διδόναι, ὡς αὖ ἐγὼ ᾤμην. σκοπώμεθα δὲ τῇδε· τὸ διδόναι δίκην καὶ τὸ κολάζεσθαι δικαίως ἀδικοῦντα ἆρα τὸ αὐτὸ καλεῖς;

and then the paradox: the wrong-doer is better off if punished,

ΠΩΛ. Ἔγωγε.

B ΣΩ. Ἔχεις | οὖν λέγειν, ὡς οὐχὶ τά γε
δίκαια πάντα καλά ἐστιν, καθ᾽ ὅσον δίκαια; καὶ διασκεψάμενος εἰπέ.

ΠΩΛ. Ἀλλά μοι δοκεῖ, ὦ Σώκρατες.

ΣΩ. Σκόπει δὴ καὶ τόδε· ἆρα εἴ τίς τι

ποιεῖ, ἀνάγκη τι εἶναι καὶ πάσχον ὑπὸ τούτου 476 τοῦ ποιοῦντος;

ΠΩΛ. Ἔμοιγε δοκεῖ.

ΣΩ. Ἆρα τοῦτο πάσχον, ὃ τὸ ποιοῦν ποιεῖ, καὶ τοιοῦτον, οἷον ποιεῖ τὸ ποιοῦν; λέγω δὲ τὸ τοιόνδε· εἴ τις τύπτει, ἀνάγκη τι τύπτεσθαι;

ΠΩΛ. Ἀνάγκη.

ΣΩ. Καὶ εἰ σφόδρα τύπτει ἢ ταχὺ ὁ τύπτων, οὕτω καὶ τὸ | τυπτόμενον τύπτεσθαι; C

ΠΩΛ. Ναί.

ΣΩ. Τοιοῦτον ἄρα πάθος τῷ τυπτομένῳ ἐστίν, οἷον ἂν τὸ τύπτον ποιῇ;

ΠΩΛ. Πάνυ γε.

ΣΩ. Οὐκοῦν καὶ εἰ κάει τις, ἀνάγκη τι κάεσθαι;

ΠΩΛ. Πῶς γὰρ οὔ;

ΣΩ. Καὶ εἰ σφόδρα γε κάει ἢ ἀλγεινῶς, οὕτω κάεσθαι τὸ καόμενον ὡς ἂν τὸ κᾶον κάῃ;

ΠΩΛ. Πάνυ γε.

ΣΩ. Οὐκοῦν καὶ εἰ τέμνει τις, ὁ αὐτὸς λόγος; τέμνεται γάρ τι.

ΠΩΛ. Ναί.

ΣΩ. Καὶ εἰ μέγα γε ἢ βαθὺ τὸ τμῆμα ἢ ἀλγεινόν, τοιοῦτον τμῆμα | τέμνεται τὸ τεμνό- D μενον, οἷον τὸ τέμνον τέμνει;

ΠΩΛ. Φαίνεται.

ΣΩ. Συλλήβδην δὴ ὅρα εἰ ὁμολογεῖς, ὃ ἄρτι ἔλεγον, περὶ πάντων, οἷον ἂν ποιῇ τὸ ποιοῦν, τοιοῦτον τὸ πάσχον πάσχειν.

ΠΩΛ. Ἀλλ' ὁμολογῶ.

476 ΣΩ. Τούτων δὴ ὁμολογουμένων, τὸ δίκην διδόναι πότερον πάσχειν τί ἐστιν ἢ ποιεῖν;

ΠΩΛ. Ἀνάγκη, ὦ Σώκρατες, πάσχειν.

ΣΩ. Οὐκοῦν ὑπό τινος ποιοῦντος;

ΠΩΛ. Πῶς γὰρ οὔ; ὑπό γε τοῦ κολάζοντος.

E ΣΩ. Ὁ δὲ ὀρθῶς κολάζων δικαίως | κολάζει;

ΠΩΛ. Ναί.

ΣΩ. Δίκαια ποιῶν ἢ οὔ;

ΠΩΛ. Δίκαια.

ΣΩ. Οὐκοῦν ὁ κολαζόμενος δίκην διδοὺς δίκαια πάσχει;

ΠΩΛ. Φαίνεται.

ΣΩ. Τὰ δὲ δίκαιά που καλὰ ὡμολόγηται;

ΠΩΛ. Πάνυ γε.

ΣΩ. Τούτων ἄρα ὁ μὲν ποιεῖ καλά, ὁ δὲ πάσχει, ὁ κολαζόμενος.

ΠΩΛ. Ναί.

477 ΣΩ. Οὐκοῦν εἴπερ καλά, ἀγαθά; | ἢ γὰρ ἡδέα ἢ ὠφέλιμα.

ΠΩΛ. Ἀνάγκη.

ΣΩ. Ἀγαθὰ ἄρα πάσχει ὁ δίκην διδούς;

ΠΩΛ. Ἔοικεν.

ΣΩ. Ὠφελεῖται ἄρα;

ΠΩΛ. Ναί.

ΣΩ. Ἆρα ἥνπερ ἐγὼ ὑπολαμβάνω τὴν ὠφέλειαν; βελτίων τὴν ψυχὴν γίγνεται, εἴπερ δικαίως κολάζεται;

ΠΩΛ. Εἰκός γε.

ΣΩ. Κακίας ἄρα ψυχῆς ἀπαλλάττεται ὁ δίκην διδούς;

ΠΩΛ. Ναί. 477

ΣΩ. Ἆρα οὖν τοῦ μεγίστου ἀπαλλάττεται
κακοῦ; ὧδε δὲ σκόπει· ἐν χρημάτων | κατα- B
σκευῇ ἀνθρώπου κακίαν ἄλλην τινὰ ἐνορᾷς ἢ πενίαν;

ΠΩΛ. Οὔκ, ἀλλὰ πενίαν.

ΣΩ. Τί δ' ἐν σώματος κατασκευῇ; κακίαν ἂν φήσαις ἀσθένειαν εἶναι καὶ νόσον καὶ αἶσχος καὶ τὰ τοιαῦτα;

ΠΩΛ. Ἔγωγε.

ΣΩ. Οὐκοῦν καὶ ἐν ψυχῇ πονηρίαν ἡγεῖ τινὰ εἶναι;

ΠΩΛ. Πῶς γὰρ οὔ;

ΣΩ. Ταύτην οὖν οὐκ ἀδικίαν καλεῖς καὶ ἀμαθίαν καὶ δειλίαν καὶ τὰ τοιαῦτα;

ΠΩΛ. Πάνυ μὲν οὖν.

ΣΩ. Οὐκοῦν χρημάτων καὶ σώματος καὶ
ψυχῆς, τριῶν ὄντων, τριττὰς εἴρηκας | πονηρίας, C
πενίαν, νόσον, ἀδικίαν;

ΠΩΛ. Ναί.

ΣΩ. Τίς οὖν τούτων τῶν πονηριῶν αἰσχίστη; οὐχ ἡ ἀδικία καὶ συλλήβδην ἡ τῆς ψυχῆς πονηρία;

ΠΩΛ. Πολύ γε.

ΣΩ. Εἰ δὴ αἰσχίστη, καὶ κακίστη;

ΠΩΛ. Πῶς, ὦ Σώκρατες, λέγεις;

ΣΩ. Ὡδί· ἀεὶ τὸ αἴσχιστον ἤτοι λύπην μεγίστην παρέχον ἢ βλάβην ἢ ἀμφότερα αἴσχιστόν ἐστιν ἐκ τῶν ὡμολογημένων ἐν τῷ ἔμπροσθεν.

ΠΩΛ. Μάλιστα.

477 ΣΩ. Αἴσχιστον δὲ ἀδικία καὶ σύμπασα
D ψυχῆς πονηρία | νῦν δὴ ὡμολόγηται ἡμῖν ;

ΠΩΛ. Ὡμολόγηται γάρ.

ΣΩ. Οὐκοῦν ἢ ἀνιαρότατόν ἐστι καὶ ἀνίᾳ ὑπερβάλλον αἴσχιστον τούτων ἐστὶν ἢ βλάβῃ ἢ ἀμφότερα ;

ΠΩΛ. Ἀνάγκη.

ΣΩ. Ἆρ' οὖν ἀλγεινότερόν ἐστιν τοῦ πένεσθαι καὶ κάμνειν τὸ ἄδικον εἶναι καὶ ἀκόλαστον καὶ δειλὸν καὶ ἀμαθῆ ;

ΠΩΛ. Οὐκ ἔμοιγε δοκεῖ, ὦ Σώκρατες, ἀπὸ τούτων γε.

ΣΩ. Ὑπερφυεῖ τινι ἄρα ὡς μεγάλῃ βλάβῃ
καὶ κακῷ θαυμασίῳ ὑπερβάλλουσα τἆλλα
E ἡ τῆς ψυχῆς πονηρία αἴσχιστόν | ἐστι
πάντων, ἐπειδὴ οὐκ ἀλγηδόνι γε, ὡς ὁ σὸς
λόγος.

ΠΩΛ. Φαίνεται.

ΣΩ. Ἀλλὰ μήν που τό γε μεγίστῃ βλάβῃ ὑπερβάλλον μέγιστον ἂν κακὸν εἴη τῶν ὄντων.

ΠΩΛ. Ναί.

ΣΩ. Ἡ ἀδικία ἄρα καὶ ἡ ἀκολασία καὶ ἡ ἄλλη ψυχῆς πονηρία μέγιστον τῶν ὄντων κακόν ἐστιν ;

ΠΩΛ. Φαίνεται.

ΣΩ. Τίς οὖν τέχνη πενίας ἀπαλλαττει ; οὐ χρηματιστική ;

ΠΩΛ. Ναί.

ΣΩ. Τίς δὲ νόσου ; οὐκ ἰατρική ;

ΠΩΛ. Ἀνάγκη.

478 ΣΩ. Τίς δὲ πονηρίας καὶ | ἀδικίας ; εἰ μὴ

οὕτως εὐπορεῖς, ὧδε σκόπει· ποῖ ἄγομεν καὶ 478
παρὰ τίνας τοὺς κάμνοντας τὰ σώματα;

ΠΩΛ. Παρὰ τοὺς ἰατρούς, ὦ Σώκρατες.

ΣΩ. Ποῖ δὲ τοὺς ἀδικοῦντας καὶ τοὺς ἀκολασταίνοντας;

ΠΩΛ. Παρὰ τοὺς δικαστὰς λέγεις;

ΣΩ. Οὐκοῦν δίκην δώσοντας;

ΠΩΛ. Φημί.

ΣΩ. Ἆρ' οὖν οὐ δικαιοσύνῃ τινὶ χρώμενοι κολάζουσιν οἱ ὀρθῶς κολάζοντες;

ΠΩΛ. Δῆλον δή.

ΣΩ. Χρηματιστικὴ μὲν ἄρα πενίας ἀπαλλάττει, ἰατρικὴ | δὲ νόσου, δίκη δὲ ἀκολασίας B
καὶ ἀδικίας.

ΠΩΛ. Φαίνεται.

ΣΩ. Τί οὖν τούτων κάλλιστόν ἐστιν ὧν λέγω;

ΠΩΛ. Τίνων λέγεις;

ΣΩ. Χρηματιστικῆς, ἰατρικῆς, δίκης.

ΠΩΛ. Πολὺ διαφέρει, ὦ Σώκρατες, ἡ δίκη.

ΣΩ. Οὐκοῦν αὖ ἤτοι ἡδονὴν πλείστην ποιεῖ ἢ ὠφέλειαν ἢ ἀμφότερα, εἴπερ κάλλιστόν ἐστιν;

ΠΩΛ. Ναί.

ΣΩ. Ἆρ' οὖν τὸ ἰατρεύεσθαι ἡδύ ἐστιν, καὶ χαίρουσιν οἱ ἰατρευόμενοι;

ΠΩΛ. Οὐκ ἔμοιγε δοκεῖ.

ΣΩ. Ἀλλ' ὠφέλιμόν γε. ἦ γάρ;

ΠΩΛ. | Ναί. C

ΣΩ. Μεγάλου γὰρ κακοῦ ἀπαλλάττεται, ὥστε λυσιτελεῖ ὑπομεῖναι τὴν ἀλγηδόνα καὶ ὑγιῆ εἶναι.

478 ΠΩΛ. Πῶς γὰρ οὔ;

ΣΩ. Ἆρ' οὖν οὕτως ἂν περὶ σῶμα εὐδαιμονέστατος ἄνθρωπος εἴη, ἰατρευόμενος, ἢ μηδὲ κάμνων ἀρχήν;

ΠΩΛ. Δῆλον ὅτι μηδὲ κάμνων.

ΣΩ. Οὐ γὰρ τοῦτ' ἦν εὐδαιμονία, ὡς ἔοικε, κακοῦ ἀπαλλαγή, ἀλλὰ τὴν ἀρχὴν μηδὲ κτῆσις.

ΠΩΛ. Ἔστι ταῦτα.

ΣΩ. Τί δέ; ἀθλιώτερος πότερος δυοῖν D ἐχόντοιν | κακὸν εἴτ' ἐν σώματι εἴτ' ἐν ψυχῇ, ὁ ἰατρευόμενος καὶ ἀπαλλαττόμενος τοῦ κακοῦ, ἢ ὁ μὴ ἰατρευόμενος, ἔχων δέ;

ΠΩΛ. Φαίνεταί μοι ὁ μὴ ἰατρευόμενος.

ΣΩ. Οὐκοῦν τὸ δίκην διδόναι μεγίστου κακοῦ ἀπαλλαγὴ ἦν, πονηρίας;

as Polus at last reluctantly admits.

ΠΩΛ. Ἦν γάρ.

ΣΩ. Σωφρονίζει γάρ που καὶ δικαιοτέρους ποιεῖ καὶ ἰατρικὴ γίγνεται πονηρίας ἡ δίκη.

ΠΩΛ. Ναί.

E ΣΩ. Εὐδαιμονέστατος μὲν ἄρα ὁ μὴ ἔχων | κακίαν ἐν ψυχῇ, ἐπειδὴ τοῦτο μέγιστον τῶν κακῶν ἐφάνη.

ΠΩΛ. Δῆλον δή.

ΣΩ. Δεύτερος δὲ δήπου ὁ ἀπαλλαττόμενος.

ΠΩΛ. Ἔοικεν.

ΣΩ. Οὗτος δ' ἦν ὁ νουθετούμενός τε καὶ ἐπιπληττόμενος καὶ δίκην διδούς.

ΠΩΛ. Ναί.

ΣΩ. Κάκιστα ἄρα ζῇ ὁ ἔχων ἀδικίαν καὶ μὴ ἀπαλλαττόμενος.

ΠΩΛ. Φαίνεται. 478

ΣΩ. Οὐκοῦν οὗτος τυγχάνει ὢν ὃς ἂν τὰ μέγιστα ἀδικῶν καὶ χρώμενος μεγίστῃ ἀδικίᾳ διαπράξηται ὥστε μήτε νουθετεῖσθαι | μήτε 479 κολάζεσθαι μήτε δίκην διδόναι, ὥσπερ σὺ φῂς Ἀρχέλαον παρεσκευάσθαι καὶ τοὺς ἄλλους τυράννους καὶ ῥήτορας καὶ δυνάστας;

ΠΩΛ. Ἔοικε.

ΣΩ. Σχεδὸν γάρ που οὗτοι, ὦ ἄριστε, τὸ αὐτὸ διαπεπραγμένοι εἰσίν, ὥσπερ ἂν εἴ τις τοῖς μεγίστοις νοσήμασιν συνισχόμενος διαπράξαιτο μὴ διδόναι δίκην τῶν περὶ τὸ σῶμα ἁμαρτημάτων τοῖς ἰατροῖς μηδὲ ἰατρεύεσθαι, φοβούμενος, ὡσπερανεὶ παῖς, τὸ κάεσθαι καὶ τὸ τέμνεσθαι, ὅτι | ἀλγεινόν. ἢ οὐ δοκεῖ καὶ σοὶ οὕτω; B

ΠΩΛ. Ἔμοιγε.

ΣΩ. Ἀγνοῶν γε, ὡς ἔοικεν, οἷόν ἐστιν ἡ ὑγίεια καὶ ἀρετὴ σώματος. κινδυνεύουσι γὰρ ἐκ τῶν νῦν ἡμῖν ὡμολογημένων τοιοῦτόν τι ποιεῖν καὶ οἱ τὴν δίκην φεύγοντες, ὦ Πῶλε, τὸ ἀλγεινὸν αὐτοῦ καθορᾶν, πρὸς δὲ τὸ ὠφέλιμον τυφλῶς ἔχειν καὶ ἀγνοεῖν, ὅσῳ ἀθλιώτερόν ἐστι μὴ ὑγιοῦς σώματος μὴ ὑγιεῖ ψυχῇ συνοικεῖν, ἀλλὰ σαθρᾷ καὶ ἀδίκῳ καὶ ἀνοσίῳ. ὅθεν καὶ πᾶν | ποιοῦσιν ὥστε δίκην μὴ διδόναι C μηδ' ἀπαλλάττεσθαι τοῦ μεγίστου κακοῦ, καὶ χρήματα παρασκευαζόμενοι καὶ φίλους καὶ ὅπως ἂν ὦσιν ὡς πιθανώτατοι λέγειν. εἰ δὲ ἡμεῖς ἀληθῆ ὡμολογήκαμεν, ὦ Πῶλε, ἆρ' αἰσθάνει τὰ συμβαίνοντα ἐκ τοῦ λόγου; ἢ βούλει συλλογισώμεθα αὐτά; Summary.

479 ΠΩΛ. Εἴ σοί γε καλῶς δοκεῖ.

ΣΩ. Ἆρ᾽ οὖν συμβαίνει μέγιστον κακὸν ἡ ἀδικία καὶ τὸ ἀδικεῖν;

ΠΩΛ. Φαίνεταί γε.

D ΣΩ. Καὶ | μὴν ἀπαλλαγή γε ἐφάνη τούτου τοῦ κακοῦ τὸ δίκην διδόναι;

ΠΩΛ. Κινδυνεύει.

ΣΩ. Τὸ δέ γε μὴ διδόναι ἐμμονὴ τοῦ κακοῦ;

ΠΩΛ. Ναί.

ΣΩ. Δεύτερον ἄρα ἐστὶν τῶν κακῶν μεγέθει τὸ ἀδικεῖν· τὸ δὲ ἀδικοῦντα μὴ διδόναι δίκην πάντων μέγιστόν τε καὶ πρῶτον κακῶν πέφυκεν.

ΠΩΛ. Ἔοικεν.

ΣΩ. Ἆρ οὖν περὶ τούτου, ὦ φίλε, ἠμφεσβητήσαμεν, σὺ μὲν τὸν Ἀρχέλαον εὐδαιμονίζων τὸν τὰ μέγιστα ἀδικοῦντα δίκην οὐδεμίαν
E διδόντα, ἐγὼ δὲ τοὐναντίον | οἰόμενος, εἴτε Ἀρχέλαος εἴτ᾽ ἄλλος ἀνθρώπων ὁστισοῦν μὴ δίδωσι δίκην ἀδικῶν, τούτῳ προσήκειν ἀθλίῳ εἶναι διαφερόντως τῶν ἄλλων ἀνθρώπων, καὶ ἀεὶ τὸν ἀδικοῦντα τοῦ ἀδικουμένου ἀθλιώτερον εἶναι καὶ τὸν μὴ διδόντα δίκην τοῦ διδόντος; οὐ ταῦτ᾽ ἦν τὰ ὑπ᾽ ἐμοῦ λεγόμενα;

ΠΩΛ. Ναί.

ΣΩ. Οὐκοῦν ἀποδέδεικται ὅτι ἀληθῆ ἐλέγετο;

ΠΩΛ. Φαίνεται.

480 ΣΩ. | Εἶεν· εἰ οὖν δὴ ταῦτα ἀληθῆ, ὦ Πῶλε, τίς ἡ μεγάλη χρεία ἐστὶν τῆς ῥητορικῆς; δεῖ μὲν γὰρ δὴ ἐκ τῶν νῦν ὡμολογημένων αὐτὸν ἑαυτὸν μάλιστα

What then is the use of Rhetoric?

φυλάττειν ὅπως μὴ ἀδικήσῃ, ὡς ἱκανὸν κακὸν 480 ἕξοντα. οὐ γάρ;

ΠΩΛ. Πάνυ γε.

ΣΩ. Ἐὰν δέ γε ἀδικήσῃ ἢ αὐτὸς ἢ ἄλλος τις ὧν ἂν κήδηται, αὐτὸν ἑκόντα ἰέναι ἐκεῖσε, ὅπου ὡς τάχιστα δώσει δίκην, παρὰ τὸν δικαστήν, ὥσπερ παρὰ τὸν ἰατρόν, σπεύδοντα ὅπως μὴ ἐγχρονισθὲν τὸ | νόσημα τῆς ἀδικίας ὕπουλον B τὴν ψυχὴν ποιήσῃ καὶ ἀνίατον· ἢ πῶς λέγωμεν, ὦ Πῶλε, εἴπερ τὰ πρότερον μένει ἡμῖν ὁμολογήματα; οὐκ ἀνάγκη ταῦτα ἐκείνοις οὕτω μὲν συμφωνεῖν, ἄλλως δὲ μή;

ΠΩΛ. Τί γὰρ δὴ φῶμεν, ὦ Σώκρατες;

ΣΩ. Ἐπὶ μὲν ἄρα τὸ ἀπολογεῖσθαι ὑπὲρ τῆς ἀδικίας τῆς αὑτοῦ ἢ γονέων ἢ ἑταίρων ἢ παίδων ἢ πατρίδος ἀδικούσης οὐ χρήσιμος οὐδὲν ἡ ῥητορικὴ ἡμῖν, ὦ Πῶλε, εἰ μὴ εἴ τις ὑπολάβοι ἐπὶ τοὐναντίον, — | κατηγορεῖν δεῖν C μάλιστα μὲν ἑαυτοῦ, ἔπειτα δὲ καὶ τῶν οἰκείων καὶ τῶν ἄλλων, ὃς ἂν ἀεὶ τῶν φίλων τυγχάνῃ ἀδικῶν, καὶ μὴ ἀποκρύπτεσθαι, ἀλλ' εἰς τὸ φανερὸν ἄγειν τὸ ἀδίκημα, ἵνα δῷ δίκην καὶ ὑγιὴς γένηται, ἀναγκάζειν δὲ καὶ αὑτὸν καὶ τοὺς ἄλλους μὴ ἀποδειλιᾶν, ἀλλὰ παρέχειν μύσαντα καὶ ἀνδρείως, ὥσπερ τέμνειν καὶ κάειν ἰατρῷ, τὸ ἀγαθὸν καὶ καλὸν διώκοντα, μὴ ὑπολογιζόμενον τὸ ἀλγεινόν, ἐὰν μέν γε πληγῶν ἄξια ἠδικηκὼς | ᾖ, τύπτειν παρέχοντα, ἐὰν δὲ D δεσμοῦ, δεῖν, ἐὰν δὲ ζημίας, ἀποτίνοντα, ἐὰν δὲ φυγῆς, φεύγοντα, ἐὰν δὲ θανάτου, ἀποθνῄ-

Not for the criminal to defend himself with, but to use in pleading for his own punishment,

480 σκοντα, αὐτὸν πρῶτον ὄντα κατήγορον καὶ αὑτοῦ καὶ τῶν ἄλλων οἰκείων καὶ ἐπὶ τοῦτο χρώμενον τῇ ῥητορικῇ, ὅπως ἂν καταδήλων τῶν ἀδικημάτων γιγνομένων ἀπαλλάττωνται τοῦ μεγίστου κακοῦ, ἀδικίας. φῶμεν οὕτως ἢ μὴ φῶμεν, ὦ Πῶλε;

E ΠΩΛ. Ἄτοπα μέν, ὦ Σώκρατες, | ἔμοιγε δοκεῖ, τοῖς μέντοι ἔμπροσθεν ἴσως σοι ὁμολογεῖται.

ΣΩ. Οὐκοῦν ἢ κἀκεῖνα λυτέον ἢ τάδε ἀνάγκη συμβαίνειν;

ΠΩΛ. Ναί, τοῦτό γε οὕτως ἔχει.

ΣΩ. Τοὐναντίον δέ γε αὖ μεταβαλόντα, εἰ ἄρα δεῖ τινα κακῶς ποιεῖν, εἴτ' ἐχθρὸν εἴτε ὁντινοῦν, ἐὰν μόνον μὴ αὐτὸς ἀδικῆται ὑπὸ τοῦ ἐχθροῦ (τοῦτο μὲν γὰρ εὐλαβητέον),—ἐὰν δὲ ἄλλον ἀδικῇ ὁ ἐχθρός, παντὶ τρόπῳ παρασκευαστέον καὶ πράτ-
481 τοντα καὶ λέγοντα, | ὅπως μὴ δῷ δίκην μηδὲ ἔλθῃ παρὰ τὸν δικαστήν· ἐὰν δὲ ἔλθῃ, μηχανητέον, ὅπως ἂν διαφύγῃ καὶ μὴ δῷ δίκην ὁ ἐχθρός, ἀλλ' ἐάντε χρυσίον ἡρπακὼς ᾖ πολύ, μὴ ἀποδιδῷ τοῦτο, ἀλλ' ἔχων ἀναλίσκῃ καὶ εἰς ἑαυτὸν καὶ εἰς τοὺς ἑαυτοῦ ἀδίκως καὶ ἀθέως, ἐάντε θανάτου ἄξια ἠδικηκὼς ᾖ, ὅπως μὴ ἀποθανεῖται, μάλιστα μὲν μηδέποτε, ἀλλ' ἀθάνα-
B τος ἔσται πονηρὸς ὤν, εἰ δὲ μή, | ὅπως ὡς πλεῖστον χρόνον βιώσεται τοιοῦτος ὤν. ἐπὶ τὰ τοιαῦτα ἔμοιγε δοκεῖ, ὦ Πῶλε, ἡ ῥητορικὴ χρήσιμος εἶναι, ἐπεὶ τῷ γε μὴ μέλλοντι ἀδικεῖν οὐ μεγάλη τίς μοι δοκεῖ ἡ χρεία αὐτῆς εἶναι,

and for the acquittal of his enemies.

εἰ δὴ καὶ ἔστιν τις χρεία, ὡς ἔν γε τοῖς 481
πρόσθεν οὐδαμῇ ἐφάνη οὖσα.

ΚΑΛ. Εἰπέ μοι, ὦ Χαιρεφῶν, σπουδάζει ταῦτα Σωκράτης ἢ παίζει;

Is Socrates joking in this?

ΧΑΙ. Ἐμοὶ μὲν δοκεῖ, ὦ Καλλίκλεις, ὑπερφυῶς σπουδάζειν· οὐδὲν μέντοι οἷον τὸ αὐτὸν ἐρωτᾶν.

ΚΑΛ. | Νὴ τοὺς θεοὺς ἀλλ' ἐπιθυμῶ. εἰπέ μοι, C
ὦ Σώκρατες, πότερόν σε θῶμεν νυνὶ σπουδάζοντα ἢ παίζοντα; εἰ μὲν γὰρ σπουδάζεις τε καὶ τυγχάνει ταῦτα ἀληθῆ ὄντα ἃ λέγεις, ἄλλο τι ἢ ἡμῶν ὁ βίος ἀνατετραμμένος ἂν εἴη τῶν ἀνθρώπων καὶ πάντα τὰ ἐναντία πράττομεν, ὡς ἔοικεν, ἢ ἃ δεῖ;

Callicles holds that Might is Right. His Attack on a Life of Philosophy.

Καὶ ἔγωγε κατ' αὐτὸ τοῦτο οὐκ ἄγαμαι 482
Πῶλον, ὅτι σοι συνεχώρησεν τὸ ἀδικεῖν αἴσχιον
εἶναι τοῦ ἀδικεῖσθαι· ἐκ ταύτης γὰρ | αὖ τῆς E
ὁμολογίας αὐτὸς ὑπὸ σοῦ συμποδισθεὶς ἐν τοῖς λόγοις ἐπεστομίσθη, αἰσχυνθεὶς ἃ ἐνόει εἰπεῖν. σὺ γὰρ τῷ ὄντι, ὦ Σώκρατες, εἰς τοιαῦτα ἄγεις φορτικὰ καὶ δημηγορικά, φάσκων τὴν ἀλήθειαν διώκειν, ἃ φύσει μὲν οὐκ ἔστιν καλά, νόμῳ δέ. ὡς τὰ πολλὰ δὲ ταῦτα ἐναντί' ἀλλήλοις ἐστίν, ἥ τε φύσις καὶ ὁ νόμος·

Nature *vs.* convention, or law.

ἐὰν οὖν τις αἰσχύνηται καὶ μὴ τολμᾷ
| λέγειν ἅπερ νοεῖ, ἀναγκάζεται ἐναντία 483
λέγειν. ὃ δὴ καὶ σὺ τοῦτο τὸ σοφὸν κατανενοηκὼς κακουργεῖς ἐν τοῖς λόγοις, ἐὰν μέν

483 τις κατὰ νόμον λέγῃ, κατὰ φύσιν ὑπερωτῶν, ἐὰν δὲ τὰ τῆς φύσεως, τὰ τοῦ νόμου. ὥσπερ αὐτίκα ἐν τούτοις, τῷ ἀδικεῖν τε καὶ τῷ ἀδικεῖσθαι, Πώλου τὸ κατὰ νόμον αἴσχιον λέγοντος, σὺ τὸν νόμον ἐδιώκαθες κατὰ φύσιν. φύσει μὲν γὰρ πάναισχρόν ἐστιν (ὅπερ καὶ κάκιον) τὸ ἀδικεῖσθαι, νόμῳ δὲ τὸ ἀδικεῖν.

B οὐδὲ γὰρ ἀνδρὸς τοῦτό | γ' ἐστὶν τὸ πάθημα, τὸ ἀδικεῖσθαι, ἀλλ' ἀνδραπόδου τινός, ᾧ κρεῖττόν ἐστιν τεθνάναι ἢ ζῆν, ὅστις ἀδικούμενος καὶ προπηλακιζόμενος μὴ οἷόστε ἐστὶν αὐτὸς αὑτῷ βοηθεῖν μηδὲ ἄλλῳ οὗ ἂν κήδηται. ἀλλ', οἶμαι, οἱ τιθέμενοι τοὺς νόμους οἱ ἀσθενεῖς ἄνθρωποί εἰσιν καὶ οἱ πολλοί.

Laws and ethical distinctions are devised by the weaker.

πρὸς αὑτοὺς οὖν καὶ τὸ αὑτοῖς συμφέρον τούς τε νόμους τίθενται καὶ τοὺς ἐπαίνους ἐπαινοῦσιν καὶ τοὺς

C ψόγους | ψέγουσιν· ἐκφοβοῦντες τοὺς ἐρρωμενεστέρους τῶν ἀνθρώπων καὶ δυνατοὺς ὄντας πλέον ἔχειν, ἵνα μὴ αὐτῶν πλέον ἔχωσιν, λέγουσιν ὡς αἰσχρὸν καὶ ἄδικον τὸ πλεονεκτεῖν, καὶ τοῦτό ἐστιν τὸ ἀδικεῖν, τὸ πλέον τῶν ἄλλων ζητεῖν ἔχειν· ἀγαπῶσι γάρ, οἶμαι, αὐτοί, ἂν τὸ ἴσον ἔχωσι φαυλότεροι ὄντες. διὰ ταῦτα δὴ νόμῳ μὲν τοῦτο ἄδικον καὶ αἰσχρὸν λέγεται, τὸ πλέον ζητεῖν ἔχειν τῶν πολλῶν, καὶ ἀδικεῖν αὐτὸ καλοῦσιν· ἡ δέ γε,

D οἶμαι, φύσις | αὐτὴ ἀποφαίνει αὐτό, ὅτι δίκαιόν

Nature favours the stronger.

ἐστιν τὸν ἀμείνω τοῦ χείρονος πλέον ἔχειν καὶ τὸν δυνατώτερον τοῦ ἀδυνατωτέρου. δηλοῖ δὲ ταῦτα πολλαχοῦ ὅτι οὕτως

ἔχει, καὶ ἐν τοῖς ἄλλοις ζῴοις καὶ τῶν 483
ἀνθρώπων ἐν ὅλαις ταῖς πόλεσι καὶ τοῖς
γένεσιν, ὅτι οὕτω τὸ δίκαιον κέκριται, τὸν
κρείττω τοῦ ἥττονος ἄρχειν καὶ πλέον ἔχειν.
ἐπεὶ ποίῳ δικαίῳ χρώμενος Ξέρξης ἐπὶ τὴν
Ἑλλάδα ἐστράτευσεν ἢ ὁ πατὴρ | αὐτοῦ ἐπὶ E
Σκύθας ἢ — ἄλλα μυρία ἄν τις ἔχοι τοιαῦτα
λέγειν; ἀλλ', οἶμαι, οὗτοι κατὰ φύσιν [τὴν
τοῦ δικαίου] ταῦτα πράττουσιν, καὶ ναὶ μὰ
Δία κατὰ νόμον γε τὸν τῆς φύσεως, οὐ μέντοι
ἴσως κατὰ τοῦτον, ὃν ἡμεῖς τιθέμεθα· πλάτ-
τοντες τοὺς βελτίστους καὶ ἐρρωμενεστάτους
ἡμῶν αὐτῶν, ἐκ νέων λαμβάνοντες, ὥσπερ
λέοντας, κατεπᾴδοντές τε καὶ γοητεύοντες κατα-
δουλούμεθα, | λέγοντες ὡς τὸ ἴσον χρὴ ἔχειν καὶ 484
τοῦτό ἐστιν τὸ καλὸν καὶ τὸ δίκαιον. ἐὰν δέ γε,
οἶμαι, φύσιν ἱκανὴν γένηται ἔχων ἀνήρ, πάντα
ταῦτα ἀποσεισάμενος καὶ διαρρήξας καὶ δια-
φυγών, καταπατήσας τὰ ἡμέτερα γράμματα καὶ
μαγγανεύματα καὶ ἐπῳδὰς καὶ νόμους τοὺς παρὰ
φύσιν ἅπαντας, ἐπαναστὰς ἀνεφάνη δεσπότης
ἡμέτερος ὁ δοῦλος, καὶ ἐνταῦθα ἐξέλαμψεν τὸ
τῆς φύσεως | δίκαιον. δοκεῖ δέ μοι καὶ B
Πίνδαρος ἅπερ ἐγὼ λέγω ἐνδείκνυσθαι ἐν τῷ
ᾄσματι ἐν ᾧ λέγει ὅτι

> νόμος ὁ πάντων βασιλεὺς
> θνατῶν τε καὶ ἀθανάτων·

οὗτος δὲ δή, φησίν,

> ἄγει δικαιῶν τὸ βιαιότατον
> ὑπερτάτᾳ χειρί· τεκμαίρομαι
> ἔργοισιν Ἡρακλέος, ἐπεὶ ἀπριάτας—

484 λέγει οὕτω πως (τὸ γὰρ ᾆσμα οὐκ ἐπίσταμαι)· λέγει δ' ὅτι οὔτε πριάμενος οὔτε δόντος τοῦ Γηρυόνου ἠλάσατο τὰς βοῦς, ὡς τούτου ὄντος C τοῦ δικαίου φύσει, καὶ | βοῦς καὶ τἆλλα κτήματα εἶναι πάντα τοῦ βελτίονός τε καὶ κρείττονος τὰ τῶν χειρόνων τε καὶ ἡττόνων.

Digression. The evil effects of philosophy if continued too long.

Τὸ μὲν οὖν ἀληθὲς οὕτως ἔχει, γνώσει δέ, ἂν ἐπὶ τὰ μείζω ἔλθῃς ἐάσας ἤδη φιλοσοφίαν. φιλοσοφία γάρ τοί ἐστιν, ὦ Σώκρατες, χαρίεν, ἄν τις αὐτοῦ μετρίως ἅψηται ἐν τῇ ἡλικίᾳ· ἐὰν δὲ περαιτέρω τοῦ δέοντος ἐνδιατρίψῃ, διαφθορὰ τῶν ἀνθρώπων. ἐὰν γὰρ καὶ πάνυ εὐφυὴς ᾖ καὶ πόρρω τῆς ἡλικίας φιλοσοφῇ, D ἀνάγκη πάντων ἄπειρον | γεγονέναι ἐστίν, ὧν χρὴ ἔμπειρον εἶναι τὸν μέλλοντα καλὸν κἀγαθὸν καὶ εὐδόκιμον ἔσεσθαι ἄνδρα. καὶ γὰρ τῶν νόμων ἄπειροι γίγνονται τῶν κατὰ τὴν πόλιν, καὶ τῶν λόγων, οἷς δεῖ χρώμενον ὁμιλεῖν ἐν τοῖς συμβολαίοις τοῖς ἀνθρώποις καὶ ἰδίᾳ καὶ δημοσίᾳ, καὶ τῶν ἡδονῶν τε καὶ ἐπιθυμιῶν τῶν ἀνθρωπείων, καὶ συλλήβδην τῶν ἠθῶν παντάπασιν ἄπειροι γίγνονται. ἐπειδὰν οὖν ἔλθωσιν εἴς τινα ἰδίαν ἢ πολιτικὴν πρᾶξιν, E καταγέλαστοι γίγνονται, | ὥσπερ γε, οἶμαι, οἱ πολιτικοί, ἐπειδὰν αὖ εἰς τὰς ὑμετέρας διατριβὰς ἔλθωσιν καὶ τοὺς λόγους, καταγέλαστοί εἰσιν. συμβαίνει γὰρ τὸ τοῦ Εὐριπίδου· λαμπρός τ' ἐστὶν ἕκαστος ἐν τούτῳ, καὶ ἐπὶ τοῦτ' ἐπείγεται,

νέμων τὸ πλεῖστον ἡμέρας τούτῳ μέρος,
ἵν' αὐτὸς αὑτοῦ τυγχάνει βέλτιστος ὤν·

485 | ὅπου δ' ἂν φαῦλος ᾖ, ἐντεῦθεν φεύγει καὶ λοιδορεῖ τοῦτο, τὸ δ' ἕτερον ἐπαινεῖ, εὐνοίᾳ τῇ ἑαυτοῦ, ἡγούμενος οὕτως αὐτὸς ἑαυτὸν ἐπαινεῖν. ἀλλ', οἶμαι, τὸ ὀρθότατόν ἐστιν ἀμφοτέρων μετασχεῖν· φιλοσοφίας μὲν ὅσον παιδείας χάριν καλὸν μετεχειν, καὶ οὐκ αἰσχρὸν μειρακίῳ ὄντι φιλοσοφεῖν· ἐπειδὰν δὲ ἤδη πρεσβύτερος ὢν ἄνθρωπος ἔτι φιλοσοφῇ, καταγέλαστον, ὦ Σώκρατες, τὸ χρῆμα γίγνεται, καὶ ἔγωγε ὁμοιότατον πάσχω B | πρὸς τοὺς φιλοσοφοῦντας ὥσπερ πρὸς τοὺς ψελλιζομένους καὶ παίζοντας. ὅταν μὲν γὰρ παιδίον ἴδω (ᾧ ἔτι προσήκει διαλέγεσθαι οὕτω) ψελλιζόμενον καὶ παῖζον, χαίρω τε καὶ χαρίεν μοι φαίνεται καὶ ἐλευθέριον καὶ πρέπον τῇ τοῦ παιδίου ἡλικίᾳ, ὅταν δὲ σαφῶς διαλεγομένου παιδαρίου ἀκούσω, πικρόν τί μοι δοκεῖ χρῆμα εἶναι καὶ ἀνιᾷ μου τὰ ὦτα καί μοι δοκεῖ δουλοπρεπές τι εἶναι· ὅταν δὲ ἀνδρὸς ἀκούσῃ τις ψελλιζομένου C | ἢ παίζοντα ὁρᾷ, καταγέλαστον φαίνεται καὶ ἄνανδρον καὶ πληγῶν ἄξιον. ταὐτὸν οὖν ἔγωγε τοῦτο πάσχω καὶ πρὸς τοὺς φιλοσοφοῦντας. παρὰ νέῳ μὲν γὰρ μειρακίῳ ὁρῶν φιλοσοφίαν ἄγαμαι, καὶ πρέπειν μοι δοκεῖ, καὶ ἡγοῦμαι ἐλεύθερόν τινα εἶναι τοῦτον τὸν ἄνθρωπον, τὸν δὲ μὴ φιλοσοφοῦντα ἀνελεύθερον καὶ οὐδέποτε οὐδενὸς ἀξιώσοντα ἑαυτὸν οὔτε καλοῦ οὔτε γενναίου πράγματος· ὅταν δὲ δὴ πρεσβύτερον D | ἴδω ἔτι φιλοσοφοῦντα καὶ μὴ ἀπαλλαττόμενον, πληγῶν μοι δοκεῖ ἤδη δεῖσθαι, ὦ Σώκρατες, οὗτος ὁ ἀνήρ. ὃ γὰρ νῦν δὴ

No disgrace in youth, but ridiculous in a man,

485 ἔλεγον, ὑπάρχει τούτῳ τῷ ἀνθρώπῳ, κἂν πάνυ
and unmanly— εὐφυὴς ᾖ, ἀνάνδρῳ γενέσθαι φεύγοντι
τὰ μέσα τῆς πόλεως καὶ τὰς ἀγοράς,
ἐν αἷς ἔφη ὁ ποιητὴς τοὺς ἄνδρας ἀριπρεπεῖς
γίγνεσθαι, καταδεδυκότι δὲ τὸν λοιπὸν βίον
βιῶναι μετὰ μειρακίων ἐν γωνίᾳ τριῶν ἢ τετ-
E τάρων ψιθυρίζοντα, ἐλεύθερον | δὲ καὶ μέγα
καὶ ἱκανὸν μηδέποτε φθέγξασθαι.

Ἐγὼ δέ, ὦ Σώκρατες, πρὸς σὲ ἐπιεικῶς
ἔχω φιλικῶς· κινδυνεύω οὖν πεπονθέναι νῦν
ὅπερ ὁ Ζῆθος πρὸς τὸν Ἀμφίονα ὁ Εὐριπίδου,
οὗπερ ἐμνήσθην. καὶ γὰρ ἐμοὶ τοιαῦτ᾽ ἄττα
ἐπέρχεται πρὸς σὲ λέγειν, οἷάπερ ἐκεῖνος πρὸς
τὸν ἀδελφόν, ὅτι Ἀμελεῖς, ὦ Σώκρατες, ὧν
δεῖ σε ἐπιμελεῖσθαι, καὶ φύσιν ψυχῆς ὧδε
γενναίαν μειρακιώδει τινὶ διαπρέπεις μορφώ-
486 ματι, | καὶ οὔτ᾽ ἂν δίκης βουλαῖσι προσθεῖ᾽ ἂν
ὀρθῶς λόγον, οὔτ᾽ εἰκὸς ἂν καὶ πιθανὸν λάκοις,
οὔθ᾽ ὑπὲρ ἄλλου νεανικὸν βούλευμα βου-
λεύσαιο. καίτοι, ὦ φίλε Σώκρατες (καί μοι
μηδὲν ἀχθεσθῇς· εὐνοίᾳ γὰρ ἐρῶ τῇ σῇ), οὐκ
αἰσχρὸν δοκεῖ σοι εἶναι οὕτως ἔχειν, ὡς ἐγὼ
σὲ οἶμαι ἔχειν καὶ τοὺς ἄλλους τοὺς πόρρω
ἀεὶ φιλοσοφίας ἐλαύνοντας; νῦν γὰρ εἴ τις
leaving him helpless against the attacks of enemies. σοῦ λαβόμενος ἢ ἄλλου ὁτουοῦν τῶν
τοιούτων εἰς τὸ δεσμωτήριον ἀπάγοι,
φάσκων ἀδικεῖν μηδὲν ἀδικοῦντα, οἶσθ᾽
B ὅτι οὐκ ἂν ἔχοις | ὅ τι χρήσαιο
σαυτῷ, ἀλλ᾽ εἰλιγγιῴης ἂν καὶ χασμῷο οὐκ
ἔχων ὅ τι εἴποις, καὶ εἰς τὸ δικαστήριον ἀναβάς,
κατηγόρου τυχὼν πάνυ φαύλου καὶ μοχθηροῦ,

ἀποθάνοις ἄν, εἰ βούλοιτο θανάτου σοι τιμᾶ- 486
σθαι. καίτοι πῶς σοφὸν τοῦτό ἐστιν, ὦ
Σώκρατες, εἴ τις εὐφυᾶ λαβοῦσα τέχνη
φῶτα ἔθηκε χείρονα, μήτε αὐτὸν αὑτῷ
δυνάμενον βοηθεῖν μηδ' ἐκσῶσαι ἐκ τῶν μεγί-
στων κινδύνων μήτε ἑαυτὸν μήτε ἄλλον μηδένα,
ὑπὸ δὲ τῶν ἐχθρῶν περισυλᾶσθαι πᾶσαν | τὴν C
οὐσίαν, ἀτεχνῶς δὲ ἄτιμον ζῆν ἐν τῇ πόλει;
τὸν δὲ τοιοῦτον, εἴ τι καὶ ἀγροικότερον εἰρῆσθαι,
ἔξεστιν ἐπὶ κόρρης τύπτοντα μὴ διδόναι δίκην.
ἀλλ' ὠγαθέ, ἐμοὶ πείθου, παῦσαι δ' ἐλέγχων,
πραγμάτων δ' εὐμουσίαν ἄσκει, καὶ ἄσκει
ὁπόθεν δόξεις φρονεῖν, ἄλλοις τὰ κομψὰ
ταῦτ' ἀφείς, εἴτε ληρήματα χρὴ φάναι εἶναι
εἴτε φλυαρίας, ἐξ ὧν κενοῖσιν ἐγκατοικήσεις
δόμοις· ζηλῶν οὐκ ἐλέγχοντας ἄνδρας τὰ
μικρὰ | ταῦτα, ἀλλ' οἷς ἔστιν καὶ βίος καὶ D
δόξα καὶ ἄλλα πολλὰ ἀγαθά. * * *

Nature's Right demands the satisfaction of our desires, not their repression, as does Conventional Right.

Ἐπεὶ πῶς ἂν εὐδαίμων γένοιτο ἄνθρωπος 491
δουλεύων ὁτῳοῦν; ἀλλὰ τοῦτ' ἔστιν E
τὸ κατὰ φύσιν καλὸν καὶ δίκαιον, ὃ
ἐγώ σοι νῦν παρρησιαζόμενος λέγω,
ὅτι δεῖ τὸν ὀρθῶς βιωσόμενον τὰς
μὲν ἐπιθυμίας τὰς ἑαυτοῦ ἐᾶν ὡς
μεγίστας εἶναι καὶ μὴ κολάζειν,
ταύταις δὲ ὡς μεγίσταις οὔσαις
ἱκανὸν | εἶναι ὑπηρετεῖν δι' ἀνδρείαν καὶ φρόνη- 492
σιν, καὶ ἀποπιμπλάναι ὧν ἂν ἀεὶ ἡ ἐπιθυμία
γίγνηται. ἀλλὰ τοῦτ', οἶμαι, τοῖς πολλοῖς οὐ
δυνατόν· ὅθεν ψέγουσιν τοὺς τοιούτους δι' αἰ-
σχύνην, ἀποκρυπτόμενοι τὴν αὑτῶν ἀδυναμίαν,

492 καὶ αἰσχρὸν δή φασιν εἶναι τὴν ἀκολασίαν,
ὅπερ ἐν τοῖς πρόσθεν ἐγὼ ἔλεγον, δουλούμενοι
τοὺς βελτίους τὴν φύσιν ἀνθρώπους, καὶ αὐτοὶ
οὐ δυνάμενοι ἐκπορίζεσθαι ταῖς ἡδοναῖς πλή-
B ρωσιν ἐπαινοῦσιν τὴν σωφροσύνην | καὶ τὴν
δικαιοσύνην διὰ τὴν αὐτῶν ἀνανδρίαν. ἐπεὶ
οἷς γε ἐξ ἀρχῆς ὑπῆρξεν ἢ βασιλέων ὑέσιν
εἶναι ἢ αὐτοὺς τῇ φύσει ἱκανοὺς ἐκπορίσασθαι
ἀρχήν τινα ἢ τυραννίδα ἢ δυναστείαν, τί τῇ
ἀληθείᾳ αἴσχιον καὶ κάκιον <ἂν> εἴη σωφροσύ-
νης τούτοις τοῖς ἀνθρώποις· οἷς ἐξὸν ἀπολαύειν
τῶν ἀγαθῶν καὶ μηδενὸς ἐμποδὼν ὄντος, αὐτοὶ
ἑαυτοῖς δεσπότην ἐπαγάγοιντο τὸν τῶν πολλῶν
ἀνθρώπων νόμον τε καὶ λόγον καὶ ψόγον; ἢ
πῶς οὐκ ἂν ἄθλιοι γεγονότες εἴησαν ὑπὸ τοῦ |
C καλοῦ τοῦ τῆς δικαιοσύνης καὶ τῆς σωφροσύνης,
μηδὲν πλέον νέμοντες τοῖς φίλοις τοῖς αὑτῶν
ἢ τοῖς ἐχθροῖς, καὶ ταῦτα ἄρχοντες ἐν τῇ
ἑαυτῶν πόλει; ἀλλὰ τῇ ἀληθείᾳ, ὦ Σώκρατες,
ἣν φῂς σὺ διώκειν, ὧδ' ἔχει· τρυφὴ καὶ ἀκολα-
σία καὶ ἐλευθερία, ἐὰν ἐπικουρίαν ἔχῃ, τοῦτ'
ἔστιν ἀρετή τε καὶ εὐδαιμονία· τὰ δὲ ἄλλα
ταῦτ' ἐστὶν τὰ καλλωπίσματα, τὰ παρὰ φύσιν
συνθήματα ἀνθρώπων, φλυαρία καὶ οὐδενὸς ἄξια.

The True "Politics." The Judgment of the Dead.

521

A ΣΩ. Ἐπὶ ποτέραν οὖν με παρακαλεῖς τὴν
θεραπείαν τῆς πόλεως, διόρισόν μοι·
τὴν τοῦ διαμάχεσθαι Ἀθηναίοις,

True and false service to the state.

ὅπως ὡς βέλτιστοι ἔσονται, ὡς ἰατρόν, ἢ 521 ὡς διακονήσοντα καὶ πρὸς χάριν ὁμιλήσοντα; τἀληθῆ μοι εἰπέ, Καλλίκλεις· δίκαιος γὰρ εἶ, ὥσπερ ἤρξω παρρησιάζεσθαι πρὸς ἐμέ, διατελεῖν ἃ νοεῖς λέγων· καὶ νῦν εὖ καὶ γενναίως εἰπέ.

ΚΑΛ. Λέγω τοίνυν ὅτι ὡς διακονήσοντα.

ΣΩ. | Κολακεύσοντα ἄρα με, ὦ γενναιότατε, B παρακαλεῖς.

ΚΑΛ. Εἴ σοι Μυσόν γε ἥδιον καλεῖν, ὦ Σώκρατες· ὡς εἰ μὴ ταῦτά γε ποιήσεις—

Dangers of the former.

ΣΩ. Μὴ εἴπῃς ὃ πολλάκις εἴρηκας, ὅτι ἀποκτενεῖ με ὁ βουλόμενος, ἵνα μὴ αὖ καὶ ἐγὼ εἴπω ὅτι Πονηρός γε ὢν ἀγαθὸν ὄντα· μηδ' ὅτι ἀφαιρήσεται ἐάν τι ἔχω, ἵνα μὴ αὖ ἐγὼ εἴπω ὅτι Ἀλλ' ἀφελόμενος οὐχ ἕξει ὅ τι χρήσηται αὐτοῖς, ἀλλ' ὥσπερ με | ἀδίκως ἀφείλετο, οὕτως καὶ λαβὼν ἀδίκως C χρήσεται, εἰ δὲ ἀδίκως, αἰσχρῶς, εἰ δὲ αἰσχρῶς, κακῶς.

ΚΑΛ. Ὥς μοι δοκεῖς, Σώκρατες, πιστεύειν μηδ' ἂν ἓν τούτων παθεῖν, ὡς οἰκῶν ἐκποδὼν καὶ οὐκ ἂν εἰσαχθεὶς εἰς δικαστήριον ὑπὸ πάνυ ἴσως μοχθηροῦ ἀνθρώπου καὶ φαύλου.

ΣΩ. Ἀνόητος ἄρα εἰμί, ὦ Καλλίκλεις, ὡς ἀληθῶς, εἰ μὴ οἴομαι ἐν τῇδε τῇ πόλει ὁντινοῦν ἄν, ὅ τι τύχοι, τοῦτο παθεῖν. τόδε μέντοι εὖ οἶδ' ὅτι, ἐάνπερ εἰσίω εἰς δικαστήριον | περὶ D τούτων τινὸς κινδυνεύων ὃ σὺ λέγεις, πονηρός τίς μ' ἔσται ὁ εἰσάγων· οὐδεὶς γὰρ ἂν χρηστὸς μὴ ἀδικοῦντ' ἄνθρωπον εἰσαγάγοι· καὶ οὐδέν

521 γε ἄτοπον εἰ ἀποθάνοιμι. βούλει σοι εἴπω
δι' ὅ τι ταῦτα προσδοκῶ;

ΚΑΛ. Πάνυ γε.

ΣΩ. Οἶμαι μετ' ὀλίγων Ἀθηναίων, ἵνα μὴ
εἴπω μόνος, ἐπιχειρεῖν τῇ ὡς ἀληθῶς
πολιτικῇ τέχνῃ καὶ πράττειν τὰ
πολιτικὰ μόνος τῶν νῦν. ἅτε οὖν
οὐ πρὸς χάριν λέγων τοὺς λόγους οὓς λέγω
E ἑκάστοτε, ἀλλὰ πρὸς τὸ βέλτιστον, οὐ | πρὸς
τὸ ἥδιστον, καὶ οὐκ ἐθέλων ποιεῖν ἃ σὺ παραινεῖς,
τὰ κομψὰ ταῦτα, οὐχ ἕξω ὅ τι λέγω ἐν
τῷ δικαστηρίῳ. ὁ αὐτὸς δέ μοι ἥκει λόγος,
ὅνπερ πρὸς Πῶλον ἔλεγον· κρινοῦμαι γὰρ ὡς
ἐν παιδίοις ἰατρὸς ἂν κρίνοιτο κατηγοροῦντος
ὀψοποιοῦ. σκόπει γάρ, τί ἂν ἀπολογοῖτο ὁ
τοιοῦτος ἄνθρωπος ἐν τούτοις ληφθείς, εἰ αὐτοῦ
κατηγοροῖ τις λέγων ὅτι Ὦ παῖδες, πολλὰ
ὑμᾶς καὶ κακὰ ὅδε εἴργασται ἀνὴρ καὶ αὐτούς,
καὶ τοὺς νεωτάτους ὑμῶν διαφθείρει τέμνων
522 τε καὶ κάων, καὶ ἰσχναίνων | καὶ πνίγων
ἀπορεῖν ποιεῖ, πικρότατα πώματα διδοὺς
καὶ πεινῆν καὶ διψῆν ἀναγκάζων, οὐχ ὥσπερ
ἐγὼ πολλὰ καὶ ἡδέα καὶ παντοδαπὰ εὐώχουν
ὑμᾶς· τί ἂν οἴει ἐν τούτῳ τῷ κακῷ ἀπολη-
φθέντα ἰατρὸν ἔχειν εἰπεῖν; ἢ <εἰ> εἴποι
τὴν ἀλήθειαν, ὅτι Ταῦτα πάντα ἐγὼ ἐποίουν, ὦ
παῖδες, ὑγιεινῶς, ὁπόσον οἴει ἂν ἀναβοῆσαι τοὺς
τοιούτους δικαστάς; οὐ μέγα; οἴεσθαί γε χρή.

ΚΑΛ. Ἴσως.

ΣΩ. Οὐκοῦν οἴει ἐν πάσῃ ἀπορίᾳ ἂν αὐτὸν
B ἔχεσθαι, ὅ τι | χρὴ εἰπεῖν;

Socrates the only true politician of his time.

ΚΑΛ. Πάνυ γε. 522

ΣΩ. Τοιοῦτον μέντοι καὶ ἐγὼ οἶδ' ὅτι πάθος πάθοιμι ἂν εἰσελθὼν εἰς δικαστήριον. οὔτε γὰρ ἡδονὰς ἃς ἐκπεπόρικα ἕξω αὐτοῖς λέγειν, ἃς οὗτοι εὐεργεσίας καὶ ὠφελίας νομίζουσιν, ἐγὼ δὲ οὔτε τοὺς πορίζοντας ζηλῶ οὔτε οἷς πορίζεται· ἐάν τέ τίς με ἢ νεωτέρους φῇ διαφθείρειν ἀπορεῖν ποιοῦντα, ἢ τοὺς πρεσβυτέρους κακηγορεῖν λέγοντα πικροὺς λόγους ἢ ἰδίᾳ ἢ δημοσίᾳ, οὔτε τὸ ἀληθὲς ἕξω εἰπεῖν, ὅτι Δικαίως πάντα ταῦτα ἐγὼ | λέγω, καὶ πράττω C τὸ ὑμέτερον δὴ τοῦτο, ὦ ἄνδρες δικασταί, οὔτε ἄλλο οὐδέν· ὥστε ἴσως, ὅ τι ἂν τύχω, τοῦτο πείσομαι.

ΚΑΛ. Δοκεῖ οὖν σοι, ὦ Σώκρατες, καλῶς ἔχειν ἄνθρωπος ἐν πόλει οὕτως διακείμενος καὶ ἀδύνατος ὢν ἑαυτῷ βοηθεῖν;

ΣΩ. Εἰ ἐκεῖνό γε ἓν αὐτῷ ὑπάρχοι, ὦ Καλλίκλεις, ὃ σὺ πολλάκις ὡμολόγησας· εἰ βεβοηθηκὼς εἴη αὑτῷ, μήτε περὶ ἀνθρώπους μήτε περὶ | θεοὺς ἄδικον μηδὲν μήτε εἰρηκὼς D μήτε εἰργασμένος. αὕτη γάρ τις βοήθεια ἑαυτῷ πολλάκις ἡμῖν ὡμολόγηται κρατίστη εἶναι. εἰ μὲν οὖν ἐμέ τις ἐξελέγχοι ταύτην τὴν βοήθειαν ἀδύνατον ὄντα ἐμαυτῷ καὶ ἄλλῳ βοηθεῖν, αἰσχυνοίμην ἂν καὶ ἐν πολλοῖς καὶ ἐν ὀλίγοις ἐξελεγχόμενος καὶ μόνος ὑπὸ μόνου, καὶ εἰ διὰ ταύτην τὴν ἀδυναμίαν ἀποθνῄσκοιμι, ἀγανακτοίην ἄν· εἰ δὲ κολακικῆς ῥητορικῆς ἐνδείᾳ τελευτῴην ἔγωγε,

Righteousness, not Rhetoric, a man's best help before the court,—certainly before the Last Court.

522 εὖ | οἶδα ὅτι ῥᾳδίως ἴδοις ἄν με φέροντα τὸν
E θάνατον. αὐτὸ μὲν γὰρ τὸ ἀποθνῄσκειν οὐδεὶς φοβεῖται, ὅστις μὴ παντάπασιν ἀλόγιστός τε καὶ ἄνανδρός ἐστιν, τὸ δὲ ἀδικεῖν φοβεῖται· πολλῶν γὰρ ἀδικημάτων γέμοντα τὴν ψυχὴν εἰς Ἅιδου ἀφικέσθαι πάντων ἔσχατον κακῶν ἐστιν. εἰ δὲ βούλει, σοὶ ἐγώ, ὡς τοῦτο οὕτως ἔχει, ἐθέλω λόγον λέξαι.

ΚΑΛ. Ἀλλ' ἐπείπερ γε καὶ τἆλλα ἐπέρανας, καὶ τοῦτο πέρανον.

The Judgment of the Dead, as ordered by Zeus.

523 ΣΩ. | Ἄκουε δή, φασί, μάλα καλοῦ λόγου, ὃν σὺ μὲν ἡγήσει μῦθον, ὡς ἐγὼ οἶμαι, ἐγὼ δὲ λόγον· ὡς ἀληθῆ γὰρ ὄντα σοι λέξω ἃ μέλλω λέγειν. ὥσπερ γὰρ Ὅμηρος λέγει, διενείμαντο τὴν ἀρχὴν ὁ Ζεὺς καὶ ὁ Ποσειδῶν καὶ ὁ Πλούτων, ἐπειδὴ παρὰ τοῦ πατρὸς παρέλαβον. ἦν οὖν νόμος ὅδε περὶ ἀνθρώπων ἐπὶ Κρόνου, καὶ ἀεὶ καὶ νῦν ἔτι ἔστιν ἐν θεοῖς, τῶν ἀνθρώπων τὸν μὲν δικαίως τὸν βίον διελθόντα καὶ
B ὁσίως, ἐπειδὰν τελευτήσῃ, | εἰς μακάρων νήσους ἀπιόντα οἰκεῖν ἐν πάσῃ εὐδαιμονίᾳ ἐκτὸς κακῶν, τὸν δὲ ἀδίκως καὶ ἀθέως εἰς τὸ τῆς τίσεώς τε καὶ δίκης δεσμωτήριον, ὃ δὴ Τάρταρον καλοῦσιν, ἰέναι. τούτων δὲ δικασταὶ ἐπὶ Κρόνου καὶ ἔτι νεωστὶ τοῦ Διὸς τὴν ἀρχὴν ἔχοντος ζῶντες ἦσαν ζώντων, ἐκείνῃ τῇ ἡμέρᾳ δικάζοντες ᾗ μέλλοιεν τελευτᾶν. κακῶς οὖν αἱ δίκαι ἐκρίνοντο· ὅ τε οὖν Πλούτων καὶ οἱ ἐπιμεληταὶ οἱ ἐκ μακάρων νήσων ἰόντες ἔλεγον πρὸς τὸν Δία
C ὅτι φοιτῷέν | σφιν ἄνθρωποι ἑκατέρωσε ἀνάξιοι.

εἶπεν οὖν ὁ Ζεύς· Ἀλλ᾽ ἐγώ, ἔφη, παύσω τοῦτο 523
γιγνόμενον. νῦν μὲν γὰρ κακῶς αἱ δίκαι
δικάζονται. ἀμπεχόμενοι γάρ, ἔφη, οἱ κρινόμενοι
κρίνονται· ζῶντες γὰρ κρίνονται. πολλοὶ οὖν,
ἦ δ᾽ ὅς, ψυχὰς πονηρὰς ἔχοντες ἠμφιεσμένοι
εἰσὶ σώματά τε καλὰ καὶ γένη καὶ πλούτους,
καί, ἐπειδὰν ἡ κρίσις ᾖ, ἔρχονται αὐτοῖς
πολλοὶ μάρτυρες, μαρτυρήσοντες ὡς δικαίως
βεβιώκασιν· οἱ οὖν δικασταὶ ὑπό τε τούτων |
ἐκπλήττονται, καὶ ἅμα καὶ αὐτοὶ ἀμπεχόμενοι D
δικάζουσι, πρὸ τῆς ψυχῆς τῆς αὑτῶν ὀφθαλ-
μοὺς καὶ ὦτα καὶ ὅλον τὸ σῶμα προκεκαλυμμένοι.
ταῦτα δὴ αὐτοῖς πάντα ἐπίπροσθεν γίγνεται,
καὶ τὰ αὑτῶν ἀμφιέσματα καὶ τὰ τῶν κρινομέ-
νων. πρῶτον μὲν οὖν, ἔφη, παυστέον ἐστὶν
προειδότας αὐτοὺς τὸν θάνατον· νῦν γὰρ
προΐσασι. τοῦτο μὲν οὖν καὶ δὴ εἴρηται τῷ
Προμηθεῖ ὅπως ἂν παύσῃ αὐτῶν. |
ἔπειτα γυμνοὺς κριτέον ἁπάντων E
τούτων· τεθνεῶτας γὰρ δεῖ κρίνεσθαι.

Each soul to be stripped and alone,—

καὶ τὸν κριτὴν δεῖ γυμνὸν εἶναι, τεθνεῶτα,
αὐτῇ τῇ ψυχῇ αὐτὴν τὴν ψυχὴν θεωροῦντα
ἐξαίφνης ἀποθανόντος ἑκάστου, ἔρημον πάντων
τῶν συγγενῶν καὶ καταλιπόντα ἐπὶ τῆς γῆς
πάντα ἐκεῖνον τὸν κόσμον, ἵνα δικαία ἡ κρίσις
ᾖ. ἐγὼ μὲν οὖν ταῦτα ἐγνωκὼς πρότερος ἢ
ὑμεῖς ἐποιησάμην δικαστὰς υἱεῖς ἐμαυτοῦ, δύο
μὲν ἐκ τῆς Ἀσίας, Μίνω τε καὶ
Ῥαδάμανθυν, | ἕνα δὲ ἐκ τῆς Εὐρώπης, 524
Αἰακόν· οὗτοι οὖν ἐπειδὰν τελευ-
τήσωσι, δικάσουσιν ἐν τῷ λειμῶνι, ἐν τῇ

the judges—Minos, Rhadamanthus, and Aeacus.

524 τριόδῳ, ἐξ ἧς φέρετον τὼ ὁδώ, ἡ μὲν εἰς μακάρων νήσους, ἡ δ' εἰς Τάρταρον. καὶ τοὺς μὲν ἐκ τῆς Ἀσίας Ῥαδάμανθυς κρινεῖ, τοὺς δὲ ἐκ τῆς Εὐρώπης Αἰακός· Μίνῳ δὲ πρεσβεῖα δώσω ἐπιδιακρίνειν, ἐὰν ἀπορῆτόν τι τὼ ἑτέρω, ἵνα ὡς δικαιοτάτη ἡ κρίσις ᾖ περὶ τῆς πορείας τοῖς ἀνθρώποις.

Ταῦτ' ἐστίν, ὦ Καλλίκλεις, ἃ ἐγὼ ἀκηκοὼς **B** πιστεύω ἀληθῆ | εἶναι· καὶ ἐκ τούτων τῶν λόγων τοιόνδε τι λογίζομαι συμβαίνειν. ὁ θάνατος τυγχάνει ὤν, ὡς ἐμοὶ δοκεῖ, οὐδὲν ἄλλο ἢ δυοῖν πραγμάτοιν διάλυσις, τῆς ψυχῆς καὶ τοῦ σώματος, ἀπ' ἀλλήλοιν· ἐπειδὰν δὲ διαλυθῆτον ἄρα ἀπ' ἀλλήλοιν, οὐ πολὺ ἧττον ἑκάτερον αὐτοῖν ἔχει τὴν ἕξιν τὴν αὑτοῦ, ἥνπερ καὶ ὅτε ἔζη ὁ ἄνθρωπος, τό τε σῶμα τὴν φύσιν τὴν αὑτοῦ καὶ τὰ θεραπεύματα καὶ τὰ παθήματα ἔνδηλα πάντα. οἷον εἴ τινος **C** μέγα ἦν τὸ | σῶμα φύσει ἢ τροφῇ ἢ ἀμφότερα ζῶντος, τούτου καὶ ἐπειδὰν ἀποθάνῃ ὁ νεκρὸς μέγας, καὶ εἰ παχύς, παχὺς καὶ ἀποθανόντος, καὶ τἆλλα οὕτως· καὶ εἰ αὖ ἐπετήδευε κομᾶν, κομήτης τούτου καὶ ὁ νεκρός. μαστιγίας αὖ εἴ τις ἦν καὶ ἴχνη εἶχε τῶν πληγῶν οὐλὰς ἐν τῷ σώματι ἢ ὑπὸ μαστίγων ἢ ἄλλων τραυμάτων ζῶν, καὶ τεθνεῶτος τὸ σῶμα ἔστιν ἰδεῖν ταῦτα ἔχον· κατεαγότ' αὖ εἴ του ἦν μέλη ἢ διεστραμμένα ζῶντος, καὶ τεθνεῶτος ταῦτα **D** ἔνδηλα. | ἑνὶ δὲ λόγῳ, οἷος εἶναι παρεσκεύαστο τὸ σῶμα ζῶν, ἔνδηλα ταῦτα καὶ τελευτήσαντος

The living state continued, after death, both of the body,

ἢ πάντα ἢ τὰ πολλὰ ἐπί τινα χρόνον. ταὐτὸν 524
δή μοι δοκεῖ τοῦτ' ἄρα καὶ περὶ τὴν ψυχὴν
εἶναι, ὦ Καλλίκλεις· ἔνδηλα πάντα
ἐστὶν ἐν τῇ ψυχῇ, ἐπειδὰν γυμνωθῇ
τοῦ σώματος, τά τε τῆς φύσεως καὶ τὰ παθή-
ματα, ἃ διὰ τὴν ἐπιτήδευσιν ἑκάστου πράγ-
ματος ἔσχεν ἐν τῇ ψυχῇ ὁ ἄνθρωπος. ἐπειδὰν
οὖν ἀφίκωνται παρὰ τὸν δικαστήν, οἱ μὲν ἐκ
τῆς Ἀσίας παρὰ | τὸν Ῥαδάμανθυν, ὁ Ῥαδά- E
μανθυς ἐκείνους ἐπιστήσας θεᾶται ἑκάστου τὴν
ψυχήν, οὐκ εἰδὼς ὅτου ἐστίν, ἀλλὰ πολλάκις
τοῦ μεγάλου βασιλέως ἐπιλαβόμενος ἢ ἄλλου
ὁτουοῦν βασιλέως ἢ δυνάστου κατεῖδεν οὐδὲν
ὑγιὲς ὂν τῆς ψυχῆς, ἀλλὰ διαμεμαστιγωμένην
καὶ οὐλῶν μεστὴν ὑπὸ ἐπιορκιῶν καὶ ἀδικίας,
ἃ | ἑκάστη ἡ πρᾶξις αὐτοῦ ἐξωμόρξατο εἰς τὴν 525
ψυχήν, καὶ πάντα σκολιὰ ὑπὸ ψεύδους καὶ
ἀλαζονείας καὶ οὐδὲν εὐθὺ διὰ τὸ ἄνευ ἀληθείας
τεθράφθαι· καὶ ὑπὸ ἐξουσίας καὶ τρυφῆς καὶ
ὕβρεως καὶ ἀκρατίας τῶν πράξεων ἀσυμμετρίας
τε καὶ αἰσχρότητος γέμουσαν τὴν ψυχὴν εἶδεν·
ἰδὼν δὲ ἀτίμως ταύτην ἀπέπεμψεν εὐθὺ τῆς
φρουρᾶς, οἷ μέλλει ἐλθοῦσα ἀνατλῆναι τὰ
προσήκοντα πάθη.

and of the soul.

Προσήκει δὲ παντὶ τῷ ἐν τιμωρίᾳ ὄντι,
| ὑπ' ἄλλου ὀρθῶς τιμωρουμένῳ, ἢ B
βελτίονι γίγνεσθαι καὶ ὀνίνασθαι ἢ
παραδείγματι τοῖς ἄλλοις γίγνεσθαι,
ἵνα ἄλλοι ὁρῶντες πάσχοντα ἃ ἂν πάσχῃ
φοβούμενοι βελτίους γίγνωνται. εἰσὶν δὲ οἱ
μὲν ὠφελούμενοί τε καὶ δίκην διδόντες ὑπὸ

Punishment is for betterment or for warning;

525 θεῶν τε καὶ ἀνθρώπων οὗτοι, οἳ ἂν ἰάσιμα ἁμαρτήματα ἁμάρτωσιν· ὅμως δὲ δι' ἀλγηδόνων καὶ ὀδυνῶν γίγνεται αὐτοῖς ἡ ὠφελία καὶ ἐνθάδε καὶ ἐν Ἅιδου· οὐ γὰρ οἷόντε ἄλλως
C ἀδικίας ἀπαλλάττεσθαι. οἳ | δ' ἂν τὰ ἔσχατα ἀδικήσωσι καὶ διὰ τοιαῦτα ἀδικήματα ἀνίατοι γένωνται, ἐκ τούτων τὰ παραδείγματα γίγνεται, καὶ οὗτοι αὐτοὶ μὲν οὐκέτι ὀνίνανται οὐδέν, ἅτε ἀνίατοι ὄντες, ἄλλοι δὲ ὀνίνανται οἱ τούτους ὁρῶντες διὰ τὰς ἁμαρτίας τὰ μέγιστα καὶ ὀδυνηρότατα καὶ φοβερώτατα πάθη πάσχοντας τὸν ἀεὶ χρόνον, ἀτεχνῶς παραδείγματα ἀνηρτημένους ἐκεῖ ἐν Ἅιδου ἐν τῷ δεσμωτηρίῳ, τοῖς ἀεὶ τῶν ἀδίκων ἀφικνουμένοις θεάματα καὶ
D νουθετήματα. | ὧν ἐγώ φημι ἕνα καὶ Ἀρχέλαον ἔσεσθαι, εἰ ἀληθῆ λέγει Πῶλος, καὶ ἄλλον ὅστις ἂν τοιοῦτος τύραννος ᾖ· οἶμαι δὲ καὶ τοὺς πολλοὺς εἶναι τούτων τῶν παραδειγμάτων ἐκ τυράννων καὶ βασιλέων καὶ δυναστῶν καὶ τὰ τῶν πόλεων πραξάντων γεγονότας· οὗτοι γὰρ διὰ τὴν ἐξουσίαν μέγιστα καὶ ἀνοσιώτατα ἁμαρτήματα ἁμαρτάνουσι. μαρτυρεῖ δὲ τούτοις καὶ Ὅμηρος· βασιλέας γὰρ καὶ δυνάστας ἐκεῖνος πεποίηκεν
E τοὺς ἐν Ἅιδου τὸν | ἀεὶ χρόνον τιμωρουμένους, Τάνταλον καὶ Σίσυφον καὶ Τιτυόν· Θερσίτην δέ, καὶ εἴ τις ἄλλος πονηρὸς ἦν ἰδιώτης, οὐδεὶς πεποίηκεν μεγάλαις τιμωρίαις συνεχόμενον ὡς ἀνίατον· οὐ γάρ, οἶμαι, ἐξῆν αὐτῷ· διὸ καὶ εὐδαιμονέστερος ἦν ἢ οἷς ἐξῆν. ἀλλὰ γάρ, ὦ

[Margin: that of the greatest and incurable criminals, for the latter—]

[Margin: the most of them being from among the powerful;]

Καλλίκλεις, ἐκ τῶν δυναμένων εἰσὶ καὶ οἱ
σφόδρα πονηροὶ | γιγνόμενοι ἄνθρωποι· οὐδὲν 526
μὴν κωλύει καὶ ἐν τούτοις ἀγαθοὺς ἄνδρας
ἐγγίγνεσθαι, καὶ σφόδρα γε ἄξιον ἄγασθαι τῶν
γιγνομένων· χαλεπὸν γάρ, ὦ Καλλίκλεις, καὶ
πολλοῦ ἐπαίνου ἄξιον ἐν μεγάλῃ ἐξουσίᾳ τοῦ
ἀδικεῖν γενόμενον δικαίως διαβιῶναι. ὀλίγοι
δὲ γίγνονται οἱ τοιοῦτοι· ἐπεὶ καὶ
ἐνθάδε καὶ ἄλλοθι γεγόνασιν, οἶμαι
δὲ καὶ ἔσονται καλοὶ κἀγαθοὶ ταύτην
τὴν ἀρετὴν τοῦ δικαίως | διαχειρίζειν ἃ ἄν τις B
ἐπιτρέπῃ· εἷς δὲ καὶ πάνυ ἐλλόγιμος γέγονεν
καὶ εἰς τοὺς ἄλλους Ἕλληνας, Ἀριστείδης ὁ
Λυσιμάχου· οἱ δὲ πολλοί, ὦ ἄριστε, κακοὶ
γίγνονται τῶν δυναστῶν.

for few of these are good.

Ὅπερ οὖν ἔλεγον, ἐπειδὰν ὁ Ῥαδάμανθυς
ἐκεῖνος τοιοῦτόν τινα λάβῃ, ἄλλο μὲν
περὶ αὐτοῦ οὐκ οἶδεν οὐδέν, οὔθ’
ὅστις οὔθ’ ὧντινων, ὅτι δὲ πονηρός
τις· καὶ τοῦτο κατιδὼν ἀπέπεμψεν εἰς Τάρταρον,
ἐπισημηνάμενος, ἐάντε ἰάσιμος ἐάντε ἀνίατος
δοκῇ εἶναι· ὁ δὲ ἐκεῖσε | ἀφικόμενος τὰ προσ- C
ήκοντα πάσχει. ἐνίοτε δ’ ἄλλην εἰσιδὼν ὁσίως
βεβιωκυῖαν καὶ μετ’ ἀληθείας, ἀνδρὸς ἰδιώτου
ἢ ἄλλου τινός, μάλιστα μέν, ἔγωγέ φημι, ὦ
Καλλίκλεις, φιλοσόφου τὰ αὑτοῦ πράξαντος
καὶ οὐ πολυπραγμονήσαντος ἐν τῷ βίῳ,
ἠγάσθη τε καὶ ἐς μακάρων νήσους ἀπέπεμψε.
ταὐτὰ δὲ ταῦτα καὶ ὁ Αἰακός· ἑκάτερος
τούτων ῥάβδον ἔχων δικάζει· ὁ δὲ Μίνως
ἐπισκοπῶν κάθηται, μόνος ἔχων χρυσοῦν σκῆπ-

Tartarus, and the isles of the blest.

526 τρον, ὥς φησιν | Ὀδυσσεὺς ὁ Ὁμήρου ἰδεῖν
D αὐτὸν

χρύσεον σκῆπτρον ἔχοντα, θεμιστεύοντα νέκυσσιν.

In preparation for this trial I, Socrates, spend my life, and summon others to the same.

Ἐγὼ μὲν οὖν, ὦ Καλλίκλεις, ὑπὸ τούτων τῶν λόγων πέπεισμαι, καὶ σκοπῶ ὅπως ἀποφανοῦμαι τῷ κριτῇ ὡς ὑγιεστάτην τὴν ψυχήν· χαίρειν οὖν ἐάσας τὰς τιμὰς τὰς τῶν πολλῶν ἀνθρώπων, τὴν ἀλήθειαν σκοπῶν πειράσομαι τῷ ὄντι ὡς ἂν δύνωμαι βέλτιστος ὢν καὶ ζῆν καὶ ἐπειδὰν ἀποθνῄσκω ἀποθνῄσκειν.
E παρακαλῶ | δὲ καὶ τοὺς ἄλλους πάντας ἀνθρώπους, καθ' ὅσον δύναμαι, καὶ δὴ καὶ σὲ ἀντιπαρακαλῶ ἐπὶ τοῦτον τὸν βίον καὶ τὸν ἀγῶνα τοῦτον, ὃν ἐγώ φημι ἀντὶ πάντων τῶν ἐνθάδε ἀγώνων εἶναι, καὶ ὀνειδίζω σοι, ὅτι οὐχ οἷόστ' ἔσει σαυτῷ βοηθῆσαι, ὅταν ἡ δίκη σοι ᾖ καὶ ἡ κρίσις ἣν νῦν δὴ ἐγὼ ἔλεγον, ἀλλὰ ἐλθὼν παρὰ τὸν δικαστὴν τὸν τῆς Αἰγίνης ὑόν,
527 ἐπειδάν σου ἐπιλαβόμενος | ἄγῃ, χασμήσει καὶ εἰλιγγιάσεις οὐδὲν ἧττον ἢ ἐγὼ ἐνθάδε σὺ ἐκεῖ, καί σε ἴσως τυπτήσει τις καὶ ἐπὶ κόρρης ἀτίμως, καὶ πάντως προπηλακιεῖ.

You three wisest men of Greece can show nothing wiser.

Τάχα δ' οὖν ταῦτα μῦθός σοι δοκεῖ λέγεσθαι ὥσπερ γραός, καὶ καταφρονεῖς αὐτῶν. καὶ οὐδέν γ' ἂν ἦν θαυμαστὸν καταφρονεῖν τούτων, εἴ πῃ ζητοῦντες εἴχομεν αὐτῶν βελτίω καὶ ἀληθέστερα εὑρεῖν· νῦν δὲ ὁρᾷς, ὅτι τρεῖς ὄντες ὑμεῖς, οἵπερ σοφώτατοί ἐστε τῶν νῦν Ἑλλήνων, σύ

τε καὶ Πῶλος καὶ Γοργίας, | οὐκ ἔχετε ἀπο- 527
δεῖξαι, ὡς δεῖ ἄλλον τινὰ βίον ζῆν ἢ τοῦτον, B
ὅσπερ καὶ ἐκεῖσε φαίνεται συμφέρων. ἀλλ' ἐν
τοσούτοις λόγοις τῶν ἄλλων ἐλεγχο-
μένων μόνος οὗτος ἠρεμεῖ ὁ λόγος,
ὡς εὐλαβητέον ἐστὶν τὸ ἀδικεῖν μᾶλλον ἢ τὸ
ἀδικεῖσθαι, καὶ παντὸς μᾶλλον ἀνδρὶ μελετητέον
οὐ τὸ δοκεῖν εἶναι ἀγαθὸν ἀλλὰ τὸ εἶναι, καὶ
ἰδίᾳ καὶ δημοσίᾳ· ἐὰν δέ τις κατά τι κακὸς
γίγνηται, κολαστέος ἐστί, καὶ τοῦτο δεύτερον
ἀγαθὸν μετὰ τὸ εἶναι δίκαιον, | τὸ γίγνεσθαι C
καὶ κολαζόμενον διδόναι δίκην· καὶ πᾶσαν
κολακείαν καὶ τὴν περὶ ἑαυτὸν καὶ τὴν περὶ
τοὺς ἄλλους, καὶ περὶ ὀλίγους καὶ περὶ πολ-
λούς, φευκτέον· καὶ τῇ ῥητορικῇ οὕτω χρηστέον,
ἐπὶ τὸ δίκαιον ἀεί, καὶ τῇ ἄλλῃ πάσῃ πράξει.
ἐμοὶ οὖν πειθόμενος ἀκολούθησον
ἐνταῦθα, οἷ ἀφικόμενος εὐδαιμονήσεις
καὶ ζῶν καὶ τελευτήσας, ὡς ὁ σὸς λόγος
σημαίνει. καὶ ἔασόν τινά σου καταφρονῆσαι
ὡς ἀνοήτου καὶ προπηλακίσαι, ἐὰν βούληται,
καὶ ναὶ μὰ Δία, | σύ γε θαρρῶν, πατάξαι τὴν D
ἄτιμον ταύτην πληγήν· οὐδὲν γὰρ δεινὸν πείσει,
ἐὰν τῷ ὄντι ᾖς καλὸς κἀγαθός, ἀσκῶν ἀρετήν.
κἄπειτα οὕτω κοινῇ ἀσκήσαντες, τότε ἤδη, ἐὰν
δοκῇ χρῆναι, ἐπιθησόμεθα τοῖς πολιτικοῖς, ἢ
ὁποῖον ἄν τι ἡμῖν δοκῇ, τότε βουλευσόμεθα,
βελτίους ὄντες βουλεύεσθαι ἢ νῦν. αἰσχρὸν
γὰρ ἔχοντάς γε ὡς νῦν φαινόμεθα ἔχειν, ἔπειτα
νεανιεύεσθαι ὥς τι ὄντας, οἷς οὐδέποτε ταὐτὰ
δοκεῖ περὶ τῶν αὐτῶν, καὶ ταῦτα περὶ τῶν

Summary.

Final exhortation.

527 μεγίστων· | εἰς τοσοῦτον ἥκομεν ἀπαιδευσίας·
E ὥσπερ οὖν ἡγεμόνι τῷ λόγῳ χρησώμεθα τῷ νῦν παραφανέντι, ὃς ἡμῖν σημαίνει ὅτι οὗτος ὁ τρόπος ἄριστος τοῦ βίου, καὶ τὴν δικαιοσύνην καὶ τὴν ἄλλην ἀρετὴν ἀσκοῦντας καὶ ζῆν καὶ τεθνάναι. τούτῳ οὖν ἑπώμεθα, καὶ τοὺς ἄλλους παρακαλῶμεν, μὴ ἐκείνῳ, ᾧ σὺ πιστεύων ἐμὲ παρακαλεῖς· ἔστι γὰρ οὐδενὸς ἄξιος, ὦ Καλλίκλεις.

EUTHYDEMUS

The Sophisms of the Sophists.

SOCRATES. CRITO.

The two sophists and their pretensions.

271 Τίς ἦν, ὦ Σώκρατες, ᾧ χθὲς ἐν Λυκείῳ διελέγου; ἦ πολὺς ὑμᾶς ὄχλος περιειστήκει, ὥστ' ἔγωγε βουλόμενος ἀκούειν προσελθὼν οὐδὲν οἷός τ' ἦν ἀκοῦσαι σαφές· ὑπερκύψας μέντοι κατεῖδον, καί μοι ἔδοξεν εἶναι ξένος τις, ᾧ διελέγου. τίς ἦν;

ΣΩ. Ὁπότερον καὶ ἐρωτᾷς, ὦ Κρίτων; οὐ γὰρ εἷς, ἀλλὰ δύ' ἤστην.

ΚΡ. Ὃν μὲν ἐγὼ λέγω, ἐκ δεξιᾶς τρίτος
B ἀπὸ σοῦ καθῆστο· ἐν | μέσῳ δ' ὑμῶν τὸ Ἀξιόχου μειράκιον ἦν. καὶ μάλα πολύ, ὦ Σώκρατες, ἐπιδεδωκέναι μοι ἔδοξεν, καὶ τοῦ ἡμετέρου οὐ πολύ τι τὴν ἡλικίαν διαφέρειν Κριτοβούλου. ἀλλ' ἐκεῖνος μὲν σκληφρός, οὗτος δὲ προφερὴς καὶ καλὸς κἀγαθὸς τὴν ὄψιν.

ΣΩ. Εὐθύδημος οὗτός ἐστιν, ὦ Κρίτων, ὃν

ἐρωτᾷς· ὁ δὲ παρ' ἐμὲ καθήμενος ἐξ ἀριστερᾶς 271
ἀδελφὸς τούτου, Διονυσόδωρος· μετεῖχε δὲ καὶ
οὗτος τῶν λόγων.

ΚΡ. Οὐδέτερον γιγνώσκω, ὦ Σώκρατες.
καινοί τινες αὖ | οὗτοι, ὡς ἔοικε, σοφισταί· C
ποδαποί; καὶ τίς ἡ σοφία;

ΣΩ. Οὗτοι τὸ μὲν γένος, ὡς ἐγᾦμαι, ἐντεῦ-
θέν ποθέν εἰσιν ἐκ Χίου, ἀπῴκησαν δὲ ἐς
Θουρίους· φεύγοντες δὲ ἐκεῖθεν πόλλ' ἤδη ἔτη
περὶ τούσδε τοὺς τόπους διατρίβουσιν. ὃ δὲ
σὺ ἐρωτᾷς τὴν σοφίαν αὐτοῖν, θαυμασία, ὦ
Κρίτων· πάσσοφοι ἀτεχνῶς. ὡς ἔγωγε οὐδ'
ᾔδη πρὸ τοῦ, ὅ τι εἶεν οἱ παγκρατιασταί·
τούτω γάρ ἐστον κομιδῇ παμμάχω, οὐ κατὰ
τὼ 'Ακαρνᾶνε τὼ παγκρατιαστὰ ἀδελφώ· ἐκείνω
μὲν γὰρ | τῷ σώματι μόνον οἵωτε μάχεσθαι· D
τούτω δὲ πρῶτον μὲν τῷ σώματι δεινοτάτω
ἐστὸν καὶ μάχῃ πάντων κρατεῖν (ἐν ὅπλοις
γὰρ αὐτώ τε σοφὼ πάνυ μάχεσθαι καὶ ἄλλον,
ὃς ἂν | διδῷ μισθόν, οἵωτε ποιῆσαι)· ἔπειτα 272
τὴν ἐν τοῖς δικαστηρίοις μάχην κρατίστω καὶ
ἀγωνίσασθαι καὶ ἄλλον διδάξαι λέγειν τε καὶ
συγγράφεσθαι λόγους οἵους εἰς τὰ δικαστήρια.
πρὸ τοῦ μὲν οὖν ταῦτα δεινὼ ἤστην μόνον, νῦν
δὲ τέλος ἐπιτεθήκατον παγκρατιαστικῇ τέχνῃ.
ἣ γὰρ ἦν λοιπὴ αὐτοῖν μάχη ἀργός, ταύτην
νῦν ἐξείργασθον, ὥστε μηδ' ἂν ἕνα αὐτοῖς
οἷόντ' εἶναι μηδ' ἀντᾶραι· οὕτω δεινὼ γεγόνατον
ἐν τοῖς λόγοις μάχεσθαί τε καὶ ἐξελέγχειν τὸ
ἀεὶ λεγόμενον, ὁμοίως ἐάντε ψεῦδος | ἐάντε B
ἀληθὲς ᾖ. ἐγὼ μὲν οὖν, ὦ Κρίτων, ἐν νῷ

272 ἔχω τοῖν ἀνδροῖν παραδοῦναι ἐμαυτόν· καὶ γάρ φατον ἐν ὀλίγῳ χρόνῳ ποιῆσαι ἂν καὶ ἄλλον ὁντινοῦν τὰ αὐτὰ ταῦτα δεινόν. * * *

They are asked and are willing to give an exhibition.

275 Ὑμεῖς ἄρα, ἦν δ' ἐγώ, ὦ Διονυσόδωρε, τῶν νῦν ἀνθρώπων κάλλιστ' ἂν προτρέψαιτε εἰς φιλοσοφίαν καὶ ἀρετῆς ἐπιμέλειαν; Οἰόμεθά γε δή, ὦ Σώκρατες. Τῶν μὲν τοίνυν ἄλλων τὴν ἐπίδειξιν ἡμῖν, ἔφην, εἰς αὖθις ἀπόθεσθον, τοῦτο δ' αὐτὸ ἐπιδείξασθον· τουτονὶ τὸν νεανίσκον πείσατον, ὡς χρὴ φιλοσοφεῖν καὶ ἀρετῆς ἐπιμελεῖσθαι, καὶ χαριεῖσθον ἐμοί τε καὶ τουτοισὶ πᾶσιν. συμβέβηκεν γάρ τι τοιοῦτον τῷ μειρακίῳ τούτῳ· ἐγώ τε καὶ οἵδε πάντες τυγχάνομεν ἐπιθυμοῦντες ὡς βέλτιστον αὐτὸν γενέσθαι. ἔστι δὲ οὗτος Ἀξιόχου μὲν ὑὸς τοῦ
B Ἀλκιβιάδου τοῦ παλαιοῦ, | αὐτανεψιὸς δὲ τοῦ νῦν ὄντος Ἀλκιβιάδου· ὄνομα δ' αὐτῷ Κλεινίας· ἔστι δὲ νέος· φοβούμεθα δὴ περὶ αὐτῷ (οἷον εἰκὸς περὶ νέῳ) μή τις φθῇ ἡμᾶς ἐπ' ἄλλο τι ἐπιτήδευμα τρέψας τὴν διάνοιαν καὶ διαφθείρῃ. σφὼ οὖν ἥκετον εἰς κάλλιστον. ἀλλ' εἰ μή τι διαφέρει ὑμῖν, λάβετον πεῖραν τοῦ μειρακίου καὶ διαλέχθητον ἐναντίον ἡμῶν. εἰπόντος οὖν ἐμοῦ σχεδόν τι αὐτὰ ταῦτα ὁ Εὐθύδημος ἅμα ἀνδρείως τε καὶ θαρραλέως,
C Ἀλλ' οὐδὲν διαφέρει, | ὦ Σώκρατες, ἔφη, ἐὰν μόνον ἐθέλῃ ἀποκρίνεσθαι ὁ νεανίσκος. Ἀλλὰ μὲν δή, ἔφην ἐγώ, τοῦτο γε καὶ εἴθισται· θαμὰ γὰρ αὐτῷ οἵδε προσιόντες πολλὰ ἐρωτῶσίν τε καὶ διαλέγονται, ὥστε ἐπιεικῶς θαρρεῖ τὸ ἀποκρίνασθαι.

Τὰ δὴ μετὰ ταῦτα, ὦ Κρίτων, πῶς ἂν 275
καλῶς σοι διηγησαίμην; οὐ γὰρ σμικρὸν τὸ
ἔργον, δύνασθαι ἀναλαβεῖν διεξιόντα σοφίαν
ἀμήχανον ὅσην· ὥστ᾽ ἔγωγε, καθάπερ οἱ
ποιηταί, | δέομαι ἀρχόμενος τῆς διηγήσεως D
Μούσας τε καὶ Μνήμην ἐπικαλεῖσθαι.
ἤρξατο δ᾽ οὖν ἐνθένδε ποθὲν ὁ Εὐθύδημος, ὡς
ἐγᾦμαι· Ὦ Κλεινία, πότεροί εἰσι τῶν ἀνθρώ-
πων οἱ μανθάνοντες, οἱ σοφοὶ ἢ οἱ
ἀμαθεῖς; καὶ τὸ μειράκιον, ἅτε
μεγάλου ὄντος τοῦ ἐρωτήματος, ἠρυ-
θρίασέν τε καὶ ἀπορήσας ἔβλεπεν εἰς ἐμέ.

First fallacy, by Euthydemus;

καὶ ἐγὼ γνοὺς αὐτὸν τεθορυβημένον, Θάρρει,
ἦν δ᾽ ἐγώ, ὦ Κλεινία, καὶ ἀπόκριναι | ἀνδρείως, E
ὁπότερά σοι φαίνεται· ἴσως γάρ τοι ὠφελεῖ
τὴν μεγίστην ὠφελίαν. καὶ ἐν τούτῳ ὁ Διονυ-
σόδωρος προσκύψας μοι μικρὸν πρὸς τὸ οὖς,
πάνυ μειδιάσας τῷ προσώπῳ, Καὶ μήν, ἔφη,
σοί, ὦ Σώκρατες, προλέγω, ὅτι ὁπότερ᾽ ἂν
ἀποκρίνηται τὸ μειράκιον, ἐξελεγχθήσεται. καὶ
αὐτοῦ μεταξὺ ταῦτα λέγοντος ὁ Κλεινίας ἔτυχεν
ἀποκρινάμενος, ὥστε οὐδὲ παρακελεύσασθαί
μοι ἐξεγένετο εὐλαβηθῆναι τῷ μειρακίῳ, |
ἀλλ᾽ ἀπεκρίνατο ὅτι οἱ σοφοὶ εἶεν οἱ μανθά- 276
νοντες. καὶ ὁ Εὐθύδημος, Καλεῖς δέ τινας,
ἔφη, διδασκάλους, ἢ οὔ; Ὡμολόγει. Οὐκοῦν
τῶν μανθανόντων οἱ διδάσκαλοι διδάσκαλοί
εἰσιν ὥσπερ ὁ κιθαριστὴς καὶ ὁ γραμματιστὴς
διδάσκαλοι δήπου ἦσαν σοῦ καὶ τῶν ἄλλων
παίδων, ὑμεῖς δὲ μαθηταί; Συνέφη. Ἄλλο
τι οὖν, ἡνίκα ἐμανθάνετε, οὔπω ἠπίστασθε

276 ταῦτα, ἃ ἐμανθάνετε; Οὐκ ἔφη. Ἆρ' οὖν
B σοφοὶ ἦτε, ὅτε | ταῦτα οὐκ ἠπίστασθε; Οὐ δῆτα, ἦ δ' ὅς. Οὐκοῦν εἰ μὴ σοφοί, ἀμαθεῖς; Πάνυ γε. Ὑμεῖς ἄρα μανθάνοντες ἃ οὐκ ἠπίστασθε, ἀμαθεῖς ὄντες ἐμανθάνετε. Ἐπένευσε τὸ μειράκιον. Οἱ ἀμαθεῖς ἄρα σοφοὶ μανθάνουσιν, ὦ Κλεινία, ἀλλ' οὐχ οἱ σοφοί, ὡς σὺ οἴει. ταῦτ' οὖν εἰπόντος αὐτοῦ, ὥσπερ ὑπὸ διδασκάλου χορὸς ἀποσημήναντος, ἅμα ἀνεθορύβησάν τε καὶ ἐγέλασαν οἱ ἑπόμενοι ἐκεῖνοι μετὰ τοῦ Διονυσοδώρου τε καὶ Εὐθυδήμου. |
C καὶ πρὶν ἀναπνεῦσαι καλῶς τε καὶ εὖ τὸ μειράκιον, ἐκδεξάμενος ὁ Διονυσόδωρος, Τί δέ, ὦ Κλεινία, ἔφη, ὁπότε ἀποστοματίζοι ὑμῖν ὁ γραμματιστής, πότεροι ἐμάνθανον τῶν παίδων τὰ ἀποστοματιζόμενα, οἱ σοφοὶ ἢ οἱ ἀμαθεῖς; Οἱ σοφοί, ἔφη ὁ Κλεινίας. Οἱ σοφοὶ ἄρα μανθάνουσιν, ἀλλ' οὐχ οἱ ἀμαθεῖς, καὶ οὐκ εὖ ἄρτι Εὐθυδήμῳ ἀπεκρίνω.

is "caught up" by Dionysodorus.

D Ἐνταῦθα δὴ καὶ πάνυ ἐγέλασάν | τε καὶ ἐθορύβησαν οἱ ἐρασταὶ τοῖν ἀνδροῖν, ἀγασθέντες τῆς σοφίας αὐτοῖν· οἱ δ' ἄλλοι ἡμεῖς ἐκπεπληγμένοι ἐσιωπῶμεν. γνοὺς δὲ ἡμᾶς ὁ Εὐθύδημος ἐκπεπληγμένους, ἵν' ἔτι μᾶλλον θαυμάζοιμεν αὐτόν, οὐκ ἀνίει τὸ μειράκιον, ἀλλ' ἠρώτα· ὥσπερ οἱ ἀγαθοὶ ὀρχησταί, διπλᾶ ἔστρεφε τὰ ἐρωτήματα περὶ τοῦ αὐτοῦ, καὶ ἔφη· Πότερον γὰρ οἱ μανθάνοντες μανθάνουσιν ἃ ἐπίστανται ἢ ἃ μὴ ἐπίστανται; καὶ ὁ Διονυσόδωρος πάλιν μικρὸν πρός με

Second fallacy, by Euthydemus;

ψιθυρίσας, | Καὶ τοῦτ᾽, ἔφη, ὦ Σώκρατες, ἕτερον 276 E τοιοῦτον, οἷον τὸ πρότερον. Ὦ Ζεῦ, ἔφην ἐγώ, ἦ μὴν καὶ τὸ πρότερόν γε καλὸν ἡμῖν ἐφάνη τὸ ἐρώτημα. Πάντ᾽, ἔφη, ὦ Σώκρατες, τοιαῦτα ἡμεῖς ἐρωτῶμεν ἄφυκτα. Τοιγάρτοι, ἦν δ᾽ ἐγώ, δοκεῖτέ μοι εὐδοκιμεῖν παρὰ τοῖς μαθηταῖς. ἐν δὲ τούτῳ ὁ μὲν Κλεινίας τῷ Εὐθυδήμῳ ἀπεκρίνατο ὅτι μανθάνοιεν οἱ μανθάνοντες ἃ οὐκ ἐπίσταιντο· ὁ δὲ ἤρετο αὐτὸν διὰ τῶν αὐτῶν ὧνπερ τὸ πρότερον· | Τί δέ; 277 ἦ δ᾽ ὅς, οὐκ ἐπίστασαι σὺ γράμματα; Ναί, ἔφη. Οὐκοῦν ἅπαντα; Ὡμολόγει. Ὅταν οὖν τις ἀποστοματίζῃ ὁτιοῦν, οὐ γράμματα ἀποστοματίζει; Ὡμολόγει. Οὐκοῦν ὧν τι σὺ ἐπίστασαι, ἔφη, ἀποστοματίζει, εἴπερ πάντα ἐπίστασαι; Καὶ τοῦτο ὡμολόγει. Τί οὖν; ἦ δ᾽ ὅς, ἆρα οὐ μανθάνεις ἅττ᾽ ἂν ἀποστοματίζῃ τις, ὁ δὲ μὴ ἐπιστάμενος γράμματα μανθάνει; Οὔκ, ἀλλ᾽, ἦ δ᾽ ὅς, μανθάνω. Οὐκοῦν ἃ ἐπίστασαι, ἔφη, μανθάνεις, εἴπερ γε ἅπαντα τὰ | γράμματα B ἐπίστασαι. Ὡμολόγησεν. Οὐκ ἄρ᾽ ὀρθῶς ἀπεκρίνω, ἔφη. καί οὔπω σφόδρα τι ταῦτα εἴρητο τῷ Εὐθυδήμῳ, καὶ ὁ Διονυσόδωρος ὥσπερ σφαῖραν ἐκδεξάμενος τὸν λόγον πάλιν ἐστοχάζετο τοῦ μειρακίου, καὶ εἶπεν· Ἐξαπατᾷ σε Εὐθύδημος, ὦ Κλεινία. εἰπὲ γάρ μοι, τὸ μανθάνειν οὐκ ἐπιστήμην ἐστὶ λαμβάνειν τούτου, οὗ ἄν τις μανθάνῃ; Ὡμολόγει ὁ Κλεινίας. Τὸ δ᾽ ἐπίστασθαι, ἦ δ᾽ ὅς, ἄλλο τι ἢ ἔχειν ἐπιστήμην ἤδη ἐστίν; Συνέφη. Τὸ ἄρα μὴ ἐπίστασθαι | μήπω C

again caught by the brother.

277 ἔχειν ἐπιστήμην ἐστίν; Ὡμολόγει αὐτῷ. Πότερον οὖν εἰσιν οἱ λαμβάνοντες ὁτιοῦν οἱ ἔχοντες ἤδη ἢ οἳ ἂν μή; Οἳ ἂν μὴ ἔχωσιν. Οὐκοῦν ὡμολόγηκας εἶναι τούτων καὶ τοὺς μὴ ἐπισταμένους, τῶν μὴ ἐχόντων; Κατένευσε. Τῶν λαμβανόντων ἄρ' εἰσὶν οἱ μανθάνοντες, ἀλλ' οὐ τῶν ἐχόντων; Συνέφη. Οἱ μὴ ἐπιστάμενοι ἄρα, ἔφη, μανθάνουσιν, ὦ Κλεινία, ἀλλ' οὐχ οἱ ἐπιστάμενοι. * * *

Dionysodorus takes the lead.

283 Ἐγὼ μὲν οὖν ταῦτα εἶπον, ὦ Κρίτων· τῷ δὲ μετὰ τοῦτο ἐσομένῳ πάνυ σφόδρα προσεῖχον τὸν νοῦν, καὶ ἐπεσκόπουν, τίνα ποτὲ τρόπον ἅψοιντο τοῦ λόγου καὶ ὁπόθεν ἄρξοιντο παρακελευόμενοι τῷ νεανίσκῳ σοφίαν τε καὶ ἀρετὴν ἀσκεῖν. ὁ οὖν πρεσβύτερος αὐτῶν, ὁ Διονυσόδωρος, πρότερος ἤρχετο τοῦ λόγου, καὶ ἡμεῖς πάντες ἐβλέπομεν πρὸς αὐτὸν ὡς αὐτίκα μάλα ἀκουσόμενοι θαυμασίους τινὰς λόγους. ὅπερ οὖν καὶ συνέβη ἡμῖν· θαυμαστὸν
B γάρ τινα, | ὦ Κρίτων, ἀνὴρ κατῆρχεν λόγον, οὗ σοι ἄξιον ἀκοῦσαι, ὡς παρακελευστικὸς ὁ λόγος ἦν ἐπ' ἀρετήν.

Third fallacy.

Εἰπέ μοι, ἔφη, ὦ Σώκρατές τε καὶ ὑμεῖς οἱ ἄλλοι, ὅσοι φατὲ ἐπιθυμεῖν τόνδε τὸν νεανίσκον σοφὸν γενέσθαι, πότερον παίζετε ταῦτα λέγοντες ἢ ὡς ἀληθῶς ἐπιθυμεῖτε καὶ σπουδάζετε; κἀγὼ διενοήθην ὅτι ᾠηθήτην ἄρα ἡμᾶς τὸ πρότερον παίζειν, ἡνίκα ἐκελεύομεν διαλεχθῆναι τῷ νεανίσκῳ αὐτώ, καὶ διὰ ταῦτα προσεπαισάτην τε καὶ
C οὐκ | ἐσπουδασάτην· ταῦτα οὖν διανοηθεὶς ἔτι

μᾶλλον εἶπον ὅτι θαυμαστῶς σπουδάζοιμεν. 283
καὶ ὁ Διονυσόδωρος, Σκόπει μήν, ἔφη, ὦ Σώκρατες, ὅπως μὴ ἔξαρνος ἔσει ἃ νῦν λέγεις. Ἔσκεμμαι, ἦν δ' ἐγώ· οὐ γὰρ μή ποτ' ἔξαρνος γένωμαι. Τί οὖν; ἔφη· φατὲ βούλεσθαι αὐτὸν σοφὸν γενέσθαι; Πάνυ μὲν οὖν. Νῦν δέ, ἦ δ' ὅς, Κλεινίας πότερον σοφός ἐστιν ἢ οὔ; Οὔκουν φησί γέ πω· ἔστιν δὲ οὐκ ἀλαζών. Ὑμεῖς δέ, ἔφη, βούλεσθε γενέσθαι αὐτὸν | σοφόν, D
ἀμαθῆ δὲ μὴ εἶναι; Ὡμολογοῦμεν. Οὐκοῦν ὃς μὲν οὐκ ἔστιν, βούλεσθε αὐτὸν γενέσθαι, ὃς δ' ἔστι νῦν, μηκέτι εἶναι. καὶ ἐγὼ ἀκούσας ἐθορυβήθην· ὁ δ' ἐμοῦ θορυβουμένου ὑπολαβών, Ἄλλο τι οὖν, ἔφη, ἐπεὶ βούλεσθε αὐτόν, ὃς νῦν ἐστιν, μηκέτι εἶναι, βούλεσθε αὐτόν, ὡς ἔοικεν, ἀπολωλέναι; καίτοι πολλοῦ ἂν ἄξιοι οἱ τοιοῦτοι εἶεν φίλοι τε καὶ ἐρασταί, οἵτινες τὰ παιδικὰ περὶ παντὸς ἂν ποιήσαιντο ἐξολωλέναι.

Καὶ ὁ Κτήσιππος ἀκούσας ἠγανάκτησέν | τε ὑπὲρ τῶν παιδικῶν καὶ εἶπεν· E

Ktesippus angered.

Ὦ ξένε Θούριε, εἰ μὴ ἀγροικότερον, ἔφη, ἦν εἰπεῖν, εἶπον ἄν, Σοὶ εἰς κεφαλήν, ὅ τι μαθὼν ἐμοῦ καὶ τῶν ἄλλων καταψεύδει τοιοῦτον πρᾶγμα, ὃ ἐγὼ οἶμαι οὐδ' ὅσιον εἶναι λέγειν, ὡς ἐγὼ τόνδε βουλοίμην ἂν ἐξολωλέναι. Τί δέ, ἔφη, ὦ Κτήσιππε, ὁ Εὐθύδημος, ἦ δοκεῖ σοι οἷόν τ' εἶναι ψεύδεσθαι;

Fourth fallacy.

Νὴ Δία, ἔφη, εἰ μὴ μαίνομαί γε. Πότερον λέγοντα τὸ πρᾶγμα, περὶ οὗ ἂν ὁ λόγος ᾖ, ἢ μὴ λέγοντα; Λέγοντα, | ἔφη. 284

284 Οὐκοῦν εἴπερ λέγει αὐτό, οὐκ ἄλλο λέγει [τῶν ὄντων] ἢ ἐκεῖνο ὅπερ λέγει; Πῶς γὰρ ἄν; ἔφη ὁ Κτήσιππος. Ἓν μὴν κἀκεῖνό γ' ἐστὶν τῶν ὄντων, ὃ λέγει, χωρὶς τῶν ἄλλων. Πάνυ γε. Οὐκοῦν ὁ ἐκεῖνο λέγων τὸ ὄν, ἔφη, λέγει; Ναί. Ἀλλὰ μὴν ὅ γε τὸ ὂν λέγων καὶ τὰ ὄντα τἀληθῆ λέγει· ὥστε ὁ Διονυσόδωρος, εἴπερ λέγει τὰ ὄντα, λέγει τἀληθῆ καὶ οὐδὲν κατὰ σοῦ ψεύδεται. Ναί, ἔφη· ἀλλ'
B ὁ ταῦτα λέγων, ἔφη ὁ Κτήσιππος, | ὦ Εὐθύδημε, οὐ τὰ ὄντα λέγει. καὶ ὁ Εὐθύδημος, Τὰ δὲ μὴ ὄντα, ἔφη, ἄλλο τι ἢ οὐκ ἔστιν;

* * * * *

Ninth fallacy, by Euthydemus.

293 Πότερον δή σε, ἔφη, ὦ Σώκρατες, | ταύτην
B τὴν ἐπιστήμην, περὶ ἣν πάλαι ἀπορεῖτε, διδάξω, ἢ ἐπιδείξω ἔχοντα; Ὦ μακάριε, ἦν δ' ἐγώ, ἔστι δὲ ἐπὶ σοὶ τοῦτο; Πάνυ μὲν οὖν, ἔφη. Ἐπίδειξον τοίνυν νὴ Δί', ἔφην ἐγώ, ἔχοντα· πολὺ γὰρ ῥᾷον ἢ μανθάνειν τηλικόνδε ἄνδρα. Φέρε δή μοι ἀπόκριναι, ἔφη· ἔστιν ὅ τι ἐπίστασαι; Πάνυ γε, ἦν δ' ἐγώ, καὶ πολλά, σμικρά γε. Ἀρκεῖ, ἔφη. ἆρ' οὖν δοκεῖς οἷόν τέ τι τῶν ὄντων τοῦτο, ὃ τυγχάνει ὄν, αὐτὸ τοῦτο μὴ εἶναι; Ἀλλὰ μὰ Δί' οὐκ |
C ἔγωγε. Οὐκοῦν σύ, ἔφη, ἐπίστασαί τι; Ἔγωγε. Οὐκοῦν ἐπιστήμων εἶ, εἴπερ ἐπίστασαι; Πάνυ γε, τούτου γε αὐτοῦ. Οὐδὲν διαφέρει. ἀλλ' οὐκ ἀνάγκη σε ἔχει πάντα ἐπίστασθαι ἐπιστήμονά γε ὄντα; Μὰ Δί', ἔφην ἐγώ· ἐπεὶ πολλὰ ἄλλ' οὐκ ἐπίσταμαι. Οὐκοῦν εἴ τι μὴ ἐπίστασαι, οὐκ ἐπιστήμων εἶ. Ἐκείνου γε, ὦ φίλε,

ἦν δ' ἐγώ. Ἧττον οὖν τι, ἔφη, οὐκ ἐπιστήμων 293
εἶ; ἄρτι δὲ ἐπιστήμων ἔφησθα εἶναι· καὶ
οὕτως τυγχάνεις ὢν αὐτὸς οὗτος, ὃς εἶ, | καὶ D
αὖ πάλιν οὐκ εἶ, κατὰ ταὐτὰ ἅμα. Εἶεν, ἦν
δ' ἐγώ, Εὐθύδημε· τὸ γὰρ λεγόμενον, καλὰ δὴ
παταγεῖς. πῶς οὖν ἐπίσταμαι ἐκείνην τὴν ἐπι-
στήμην, ἣν ἐζητοῦμεν; ὡς δὴ τοῦτο ἀδύνατόν
ἐστιν, τὸ αὐτὸ εἶναί τε καὶ μή, εἴπερ ἓν
ἐπίσταμαι, ἅπαντα ἐπίσταμαι· οὐ γὰρ ἂν εἴην
ἐπιστήμων τε καὶ ἀνεπιστήμων ἅμα· ἐπεὶ δὲ
πάντα ἐπίσταμαι, κἀκείνην δὴ τὴν ἐπιστήμην
ἔχω· ἆρα οὕτως λέγεις, καὶ τοῦτό ἐστιν | τὸ E
σοφόν; Αὐτὸς σαυτόν γε δὴ ἐξελέγχεις, ἔφη,
ὦ Σώκρατες. Τί δέ, ἦν δ' ἐγώ, ὦ Εὐθύδημε,
σὺ οὐ πέπονθας τοῦτο τὸ αὐτὸ πάθος; ἐγὼ
γάρ τοι μετὰ σοῦ ὁτιοῦν ἂν πάσχων καὶ μετὰ
Διονυσοδώρου τοῦδε, φίλης κεφαλῆς, οὐκ ἂν
πάνυ ἀγανακτοίην. εἰπέ μοι, σφὼ οὐχὶ τὰ
μὲν ἐπίστασθον τῶν ὄντων, τὰ δὲ οὐκ ἐπί-
στασθον; Ἥκιστά γε, ἔφη, ὦ Σώκρατες, ὁ
Διονυσόδωρος. Πῶς λέγετον; ἔφην ἐγώ· ἀλλ'
οὐδὲν ἄρα ἐπίστασθον; Καὶ μάλα, ἦ δ' ὅς.
Πάντ' ἄρα, | ἔφην ἐγώ, ἐπίστασθον, ἐπειδήπερ 294
καὶ ὁτιοῦν; Πάντ', ἔφη· καὶ σύ γε πρός,
εἴπερ καὶ ἓν ἐπίστασαι, πάντα ἐπίστασαι.
Ὦ Ζεῦ, ἔφην ἐγώ, ὡς θαυμαστὸν λέγεις καὶ
ἀγαθὸν μέγα πεφάνθαι. μῶν καὶ οἱ ἄλλοι
πάντες ἄνθρωποι πάντ' ἐπίστανται, ἢ οὐδέν;
Οὐ γὰρ δήπου, ἔφη, τὰ μὲν ἐπίστανται, τὰ δ'
οὐκ ἐπίστανται, καί εἰσιν ἅμα ἐπιστήμονές
τε καὶ ἀνεπιστήμονες. Ἀλλὰ τί; ἦν δ' ἐγώ.

294 Πάντες, ἦ δ᾽ ὅς, πάντα ἐπίστανται, εἴπερ καὶ ἕν.
B Ὦ πρὸς τῶν θεῶν, ἦν | δ᾽ ἐγώ, ὦ Διονυσόδωρε (δῆλοι γάρ μοί ἐστον ἤδη ὅτι σπουδάζετον, καὶ μόλις ὑμᾶς προὐκαλεσάμην σπουδάζειν), αὐτὼ τῷ ὄντι πάντα ἐπίστασθον—οἷον τεκτονικὴν καὶ σκυτικήν; Πάνυ γ᾽, ἔφη. Ἦ καὶ νευρορραφεῖν δυνατώ ἐστον; Καὶ ναὶ μὰ Δία καττύειν, ἔφη. Ἦ καὶ τὰ τοιαῦτα, τοὺς ἀστέρας, ὁπόσοι εἰσί, καὶ τὴν ἄμμον; Πάνυ γε, ἦ δ᾽ ὅς· εἶτ᾽ οὐκ ἂν οἴει ὁμολογῆσαι ἡμᾶς;

Καὶ ὁ Κτήσιππος ὑπολαβών· Πρὸς Διός, ἔφη, Διονυσόδωρε, τεκμήριόν τί | μοι
C τούτων ἐπιδείξατον τοιόνδε, ᾧ εἴσομαι ὅτι ἀληθῆ λέγεις. Τί ἐπιδείξω; ἔφη. Οἶσθα Εὐθύδημον, ὁπόσους ὀδόντας ἔχει, καὶ ὁ Εὐθύδημος, ὁπόσους σύ; Οὐκ ἐξαρκεῖ σοι, ἔφη, ἀκοῦσαι ὅτι πάντα ἐπιστάμεθα; Μηδαμῶς, ἦ δ᾽ ὅς, ἀλλὰ τοῦτο ἔτι ἡμῖν μόνον εἴπατον καὶ ἐπιδείξατον ὅτι ἀληθῆ λέγετον. καὶ ἐὰν εἴπητον, ὁπόσους ἑκάτερος ἔχει ὑμῶν, καὶ φαίνησθε γνόντες ἡμῶν ἀριθμησάντων, ἤδη πεισόμεθα ὑμῖν καὶ τἆλλα. ἡγουμένω οὖν
D σκώπτεσθαι οὐκ | ἠθελέτην, ἀλλ᾽ ὡμολογησάτην πάντα χρήματα ἐπίστασθαι, καθ᾽ ἓν ἕκαστον ἐρωτώμενοι ὑπὸ Κτησίππου. ὁ γὰρ Κτήσιππος πάνυ ἀπαρακαλύπτως οὐδὲν ὅ τι οὐκ ἠρώτα τελευτῶν, καὶ τὰ αἴσχιστα, εἰ ἐπισταίσθην· τὼ δὲ ἀνδρειότατα ὁμόσε ᾔτην τοῖς ἐρωτήμασιν, ὁμολογοῦντες εἰδέναι, ὥσπερ οἱ κάπροι οἱ πρὸς τὴν πληγὴν ὁμόσε ὠθούμενοι, ὥστ᾽ ἔγωγε καὶ αὐτός, ὦ Κρίτων, ὑπ᾽ ἀπιστίας ἠναγκάσθην

Ktesippus proposes a test, which is refused.

τελευτῶν ἐρέσθαι τὸν Εὐθύδημον, εἰ καὶ ὀρχεῖ- 294
σθαι | ἐπίσταιτο ὁ Διονυσόδωρος. ὁ δέ, Πάνυ E
γ', ἔφη. Οὐ δήπου, ἦν δ' ἐγώ, καὶ ἐς μαχαίρας
γε κυβιστᾶν καὶ ἐπὶ τροχοῦ δινεῖσθαι τηλικοῦ-
τος ὤν; οὕτω πόρρω σοφίας. ἥκει; Οὐδέν,
ἔφη, ὅ τι οὔ. Πότερον δέ, ἦν δ' ἐγώ, πάντα
νῦν μόνον ἐπίστασθον ἢ καὶ ἀεί; Καὶ ἀεί,
ἔφη. Καὶ ὅτε παιδία ἤστην καὶ
εὐθὺς γενόμενοι ἠπίστασθε πάντα;

Tenth contention.

ἐφάτην ἅμα ἀμφοτέρω. καὶ ἡμῖν μὲν | ἄπιστον 295
ἐδόκει τὸ πρᾶγμα εἶναι· ὁ δ' Εὐθύδημος, Ἀπι-
στεῖς, ἔφη, ὦ Σώκρατες; Πλήν γ' ὅτι, ἦν δ'
ἐγώ, εἰκὸς ὑμᾶς ἐστι σοφοὺς εἶναι. Ἀλλ' ἤν,
ἔφη, ἐθελήσῃς μοι ἀποκρίνεσθαι, ἐγὼ ἐπιδείξω
καὶ σὲ ταῦτα τὰ θαυμαστὰ ὁμολογοῦντα.
Ἀλλὰ μήν, ἦν δ' ἐγώ, ἥδιστα ταῦτα ἐξελέγχο-
μαι. εἰ γάρ τοι λέληθα ἐμαυτὸν σοφὸς ὤν,
σὺ δὲ τοῦτο ἐπιδείξεις, ὡς πάντα ἐπίσταμαι
καὶ ἀεί, τί μεῖζον ἕρμαιον αὐτοῦ ἂν εὕροιμι ἐν
παντὶ τῷ βίῳ; * * * *

Φεύγεις, ἔφη, ὦ Σώκρατες, ὁ Διονυσόδωρος, 297
καὶ οὐκ ἐθέλεις ἀποκρίνεσθαι. Εἰκότως γ',
εἶπον ἐγώ· ἥττων γάρ εἰμι καὶ τοῦ ἑτέρου
ὑμῶν, ὥστε | πολλοῦ δέω μὴ οὐ δύο γε φεύγειν. C
πολὺ γάρ πού εἰμι φαυλότερος τοῦ Ἡρακλέους,
ὃς οὐχ οἷόστε ἦν τῇ τε ὕδρᾳ διαμά-
χεσθαι—σοφιστρίᾳ οὔσῃ καὶ διὰ τὴν

Hydra-headed sophistry.

σοφίαν ἀνιείσῃ (εἰ μίαν κεφαλὴν ἀποτμηθείη
τοῦ λόγου) πολλὰς ἀντὶ τῆς μιᾶς—καὶ καρκίνῳ
τινὶ ἑτέρῳ σοφιστῇ, ἐκ θαλάττης ἀφιγμένῳ,
νεωστί μοι δοκεῖν καταπεπλευκότι· ὃς ἐπειδὴ

297 αὐτὸν ἐλύπει οὕτως ἐκ τοῦ ἐπ᾽ ἀριστερὰ λέγων
καὶ δάκνων, τὸν Ἰόλεων τὸν ἀδελφιδοῦν βοηθὸν
D ἐπεκαλέσατο, ὁ δὲ αὐτῷ ἱκανῶς | ἐβοήθησεν. ὁ
δ᾽ ἐμὸς Ἰόλεως εἰ ἔλθοι, πλέον ἂν θάτερον
ποιήσειεν.

Eleventh fallacy.

Ἀπόκριναι δή, ἔφη ὁ Διονυσόδωρος (ὁπότε
σοι ταῦτα ὕμνηται), πότερον ὁ Ἰόλεως
τοῦ Ἡρακλέους μᾶλλον ἦν ἀδελφιδοῦς
ἢ σός; Κράτιστον τοίνυν μοι, ὦ Διονυσόδωρε,
ἦν δ᾽ ἐγώ, ἀποκρίνασθαί σοι. οὐ γὰρ μὴ
ἀνῇς ἐρωτῶν (σχεδόν τι ἐγὼ τοῦτ᾽ εὖ οἶδα),
φθονῶν καὶ διακωλύων, ἵνα μὴ διδάξῃ με
Εὐθύδημος ἐκεῖνο τὸ σοφόν. Ἀποκρίνου δή,
ἔφη. Ἀποκρίνομαι δή, εἶπον, ὅτι τοῦ Ἡρα-
κλέους ἦν ὁ Ἰόλεως ἀδελφιδοῦς, ἐμὸς δ᾽, ὡς
E ἐμοὶ δοκεῖ, οὐδ᾽ ὁπωστιοῦν. | οὐ γὰρ Πατροκλῆς
ἦν αὐτῷ πατήρ, ὁ ἐμὸς ἀδελφός, ἀλλὰ παρα-
πλήσιος μὲν τοὔνομα Ἰφικλῆς, ὁ Ἡρακλέους
ἀδελφός. Πατροκλῆς δέ, ἦ δ᾽ ὅς, σός; Πάνυ
γ᾽, ἔφην ἐγώ, ὁμομήτριός γε, οὐ μέντοι ὁμοπά-
τριος. Ἀδελφὸς ἄρα ἐστί σοι καὶ οὐκ ἀδελφός.
Οὐχ ὁμοπάτριός γε, ὦ βέλτιστε, ἔφην· ἐκείνου
μὲν γὰρ Χαιρέδημος ἦν πατήρ, ἐμὸς δὲ Σω-
φρονίσκος. Πατὴρ δὲ ἦν, ἔφη, Σωφρονίσκος
καὶ Χαιρέδημος; Πάνυ γ᾽, ἔφην· ὁ μέν γε
298 ἐμός, ὁ δὲ ἐκείνου. Οὐκοῦν, | ἦ δ᾽ ὅς, ἕτερος
ἦν Χαιρέδημος τοῦ πατρός; Τοὐμοῦ γ᾽, ἔφην
ἐγώ. Ἆρ᾽ οὖν πατὴρ ἦν ἕτερος ὢν πατρός;
ἢ σὺ εἶ ὁ αὐτὸς τῷ λίθῳ; Δέδοικα μὲν ἔγωγ᾽,
ἔφην, μὴ φανῶ ὑπὸ σοῦ ὁ αὐτός· οὐ μέντοι
μοι δοκῶ. Οὐκοῦν ἕτερος εἶ, ἔφη, τοῦ λίθου;

Ἕτερος μέντοι. Ἄλλο τι οὖν ἕτερος, ἦ δ᾽ ὅς, 298
ὢν λίθου οὐ λίθος εἶ; καὶ ἕτερος ὢν χρυσοῦ
οὐ χρυσὸς εἶ; Ἔστι ταῦτα. Οὐκοῦν καὶ ὁ
Χαιρέδημος, ἔφη, ἕτερος ὢν πατρὸς οὐκ ἂν
πατὴρ εἴη. Ἔοικεν, ἦν δ᾽ ἐγώ, οὐ πατὴρ |
εἶναι. Εἰ γὰρ δήπου, ἔφη, πατήρ ἐστιν ὁ B
Χαιρέδημος, ὑπολαβὼν ὁ Εὐθύδημος, πάλιν αὖ
ὁ Σωφρονίσκος ἕτερος ὢν πατρὸς οὐ πατήρ
ἐστιν, ὥστε σύ, ὦ Σώκρατες, ἀπάτωρ εἶ. καὶ
ὁ Κτήσιππος ἐκδεξάμενος, Ὁ δὲ ὑμέτερος, ἔφη,
αὖ πατὴρ οὐ ταὐτὰ ταῦτα πέπονθεν; ἕτερός
ἐστιν τοὐμοῦ πατρός; Πολλοῦ γ᾽, ἔφη, δεῖ, ὁ
Εὐθύδημος. Ἀλλά, ἦ δ᾽ ὅς, ὁ αὐτός; Ὁ
αὐτὸς μέντοι. Οὐκ ἂν συμβουλοίμην. ἀλλὰ
πότερον, ὦ Εὐθύδημε, ἐμὸς μόνον | Twelfth
ἐστὶ πατὴρ ἢ καὶ τῶν ἄλλων ἀνθρώ- fallacy. C
πων; Καὶ τῶν ἄλλων, ἔφη· ἢ οἴει τὸν αὐτὸν
πατέρα ὄντα οὐ πατέρα εἶναι; Ὤιμην δῆτα,
ἔφη ὁ Κτήσιππος. Τί δέ; ἦ δ᾽ ὅς· χρυσὸν
ὄντα μὴ χρυσὸν εἶναι; ἢ ἄνθρωπον ὄντα μὴ
ἄνθρωπον; Μὴ γάρ, ἔφη ὁ Κτήσιππος, ὦ
Εὐθύδημε· τὸ λεγόμενον, οὐ λίνον λίνῳ συν-
άπτεις· δεινὸν γὰρ λέγεις πρᾶγμα, εἰ ὁ σὸς
πατὴρ πάντων ἐστὶν πατήρ. Ἀλλ᾽ Thirteenth
ἔστιν, ἔφη. Πότερον ἀνθρώπων; ἦ fallacy.
δ᾽ ὃς ὁ Κτήσιππος, ἢ καὶ ἵππων; ἢ καὶ τῶν
ἄλλων | πάντων ζῴων; Πάντων, ἔφη. Ἦ καὶ D
μήτηρ ἡ μήτηρ; Καὶ ἡ μήτηρ γε. Καὶ τῶν ἐχίνων
ἄρα, ἔφη, ἡ σὴ μήτηρ μήτηρ ἐστὶν τῶν θαλατ-
τίων. Καὶ ἡ σή γ᾽, ἔφη. Καὶ σὺ ἄρα ἀδελφὸς εἶ
τῶν βοιδίων καὶ κυναρίων καὶ χοιριδίων. Καὶ

298 γὰρ σύ, ἔφη. Καὶ πρὸς ἄρα σοι πατήρ ἐστι
καὶ κύων. Καὶ γὰρ σοί, ἔφη. Αὐτίκα δέ γε,
ἦ δ' ὃς ὁ Διονυσόδωρος, ἄν μοι ἀποκρίνῃ, ὦ
Κτήσιππε, ὁμολογήσεις ταῦτα. εἰπὲ γάρ μοι,
ἔστι σοι κύων; Καὶ μάλα πονηρός, ἔφη ὁ
E Κτήσιππος. Ἔστιν οὖν | αὐτῷ κυνίδια; Καὶ
μάλ', ἔφη, ἕτερα τοιαῦτα. Οὐκοῦν πατήρ ἐστιν
αὐτῶν ὁ κύων; Ναί. Τί οὖν; οὐ σός ἐστιν
ὁ κύων; Πάνυ γ', ἔφη. Οὐκοῦν πατὴρ ὢν
σός ἐστιν, ὥστε σὸς πατὴρ γίγνεται ὁ κύων
καὶ σὺ κυναρίων ἀδελφός; καὶ αὖθις ταχὺ
ὑπολαβὼν ὁ Διονυσόδωρος, ἵνα μὴ πρότερόν τι
εἴποι ὁ Κτήσιππος, Καὶ ἔτι γέ μοι μικρόν,
ἔφη, ἀπόκριναι· τύπτεις τὸν κύνα τοῦτον; καὶ
ὁ Κτήσιππος γελάσας, Νὴ τοὺς θεούς, ἔφη·
οὐ γὰρ δύναμαι σέ. Οὐκοῦν τὸν σαυτοῦ
299 πατέρα, ἔφη, τύπτεις; | Πολὺ μέντοι, ἔφη,
δικαιότερον <ἂν> τὸν ὑμέτερον πατέρα τύπτοιμι,
ὅ τι μαθὼν σοφοὺς ὑεῖς οὕτως ἔφυσεν.

THEAETETUS

Philosopher vs. Rhetorician.

THEODORUS. SOCRATES.

172 ΘΕΟ. Οὐκοῦν σχολὴν ἄγομεν, ὦ Σώκρατες;
C ΣΩ. Φαινόμεθα. καὶ πολλάκις μέν γε δή, ὦ δαιμόνιε, καὶ ἄλλοτε κατενόησα, ἀτὰρ καὶ νῦν, ὡς εἰκότως οἱ ἐν ταῖς φιλοσοφίαις πολὺν χρόνον διατρίψαντες εἰς τὰ δικαστήρια ἰόντες γελοῖοι φαίνονται ῥήτορες.

Slave *vs* freeman; haste and "business" *vs.* leisure.

ΘΕΟ. Πῶς δὴ οὖν λέγεις; 172

ΣΩ. Κινδυνεύουσιν οἱ ἐν δικαστηρίοις καὶ
τοῖς τοιούτοις ἐκ νέων κυλινδούμενοι πρὸς τοὺς
ἐν φιλοσοφίᾳ καὶ τῇ τοιᾷδε διατριβῇ | τεθραμ- D
μένους ὡς οἰκέται πρὸς ἐλευθέρους τεθράφθαι.

ΘΕΟ. Πῇ δή;

ΣΩ. Ἧι τοῖς μὲν τοῦτο, ὃ σὺ εἶπες, ἀεὶ πάρεστι, σχολή, καὶ τοὺς λόγους ἐν εἰρήνῃ ἐπὶ σχολῆς ποιοῦνται· ὥσπερ ἡμεῖς νυνὶ τρίτον ἤδη λόγον ἐκ λόγου μεταλαμβάνομεν, οὕτω κἀκεῖνοι, ἐὰν αὐτοὺς ὁ ἐπελθὼν τοῦ προκειμένου μᾶλλον καθάπερ ἡμᾶς ἀρέσῃ· καὶ διὰ μακρῶν ἢ βραχέων μέλει οὐδὲν λέγειν, ἂν μόνον τύχωσι τοῦ ὄντος· οἱ δὲ ἐν ἀσχολίᾳ τε ἀεὶ λέγουσι (κατεπείγει γὰρ ὕδωρ ῥέον) καὶ
οὐκ | ἐγχωρεῖ περὶ οὗ ἂν ἐπιθυμήσωσιν τοὺς E
λόγους ποιεῖσθαι, ἀλλ' ἀνάγκην ἔχων ὁ ἀντίδικος ἐφέστηκεν καὶ ὑπογραφὴν παραναγιγνωσκομένην, ὧν ἐκτὸς οὐ ῥητέον, ἣν ἀντωμοσίαν καλοῦσιν· οἱ δὲ λόγοι ἀεὶ περὶ ὁμοδούλου πρὸς δεσπότην καθήμενον, ἐν χειρί τινα δίκην ἔχοντα, καὶ οἱ ἀγῶνες οὐδέποτε τὴν ἄλλως ἀλλ' ἀεὶ τὴν περὶ αὐτοῦ· πολλάκις δὲ καὶ περὶ ψυχῆς ὁ δρόμος·
ὥστ' ἐξ | ἁπάντων τούτων ἔντονοι 173
καὶ δριμεῖς γίγνονται, ἐπιστάμενοι τὸν δεσπότην λόγῳ τε θωπεῦσαι καὶ ἔργῳ χαρίσασθαι, σμικροὶ δὲ καὶ οὐκ ὀρθοὶ τὰς ψυχάς. τὴν γὰρ αὔξην καὶ τὸ εὐθύ τε καὶ τὸ ἐλεύθερον ἡ ἐκ νέων δουλεία ἀφῄρηται, ἀναγκάζουσα πράττειν σκολιά, μεγάλους κινδύνους καὶ φόβους ἔτι ἁπαλαῖς ψυχαῖς ἐπιβάλλουσα, οὓς

The clever pettifogger and his little soul.

173 οὐ δυνάμενοι μετὰ τοῦ δικαίου καὶ ἀληθοῦς ὑποφέρειν, εὐθὺς ἐπὶ τὸ ψεῦδός τε καὶ τὸ ἀλλήλους ἀνταδικεῖν τρεπόμενοι πολλὰ κάμπτονται B καὶ | συγκλῶνται, ὥσθ' ὑγιὲς οὐδὲν ἔχοντες τῆς διανοίας εἰς ἄνδρας ἐκ μειρακίων τελευτῶσι, δεινοί τε καὶ σοφοὶ γεγονότες, ὡς οἴονται. καὶ οὗτοι μὲν δὴ τοιοῦτοι, ὦ Θεόδωρε· τοὺς δὲ τοῦ ἡμετέρου χοροῦ πότερον βούλει διελθόντες ἢ ἐάσαντες πάλιν ἐπὶ τὸν λόγον τρεπώμεθα, ἵνα μὴ καί, ὃ νῦν δὴ ἐλέγομεν, λίαν πολὺ τῇ ἐλευθερίᾳ καὶ μεταλήψει τῶν λόγων καταχρώμεθα ;

ΘΕΟ. Μηδαμῶς, ὦ Σώκρατες, ἀλλὰ διελ- C θόντες. πάνυ γὰρ εὖ τοῦτο εἴρηκας, ὅτι | οὐχ ἡμεῖς οἱ ἐν τῷ τοιῷδε χορεύοντες τῶν λόγων ὑπηρέται, ἀλλ' οἱ λόγοι ἡμέτεροι ὥσπερ οἰκέται, καὶ ἕκαστος αὐτῶν περιμένει ἀποτελεσθῆναι ὅταν ἡμῖν δοκῇ· οὔτε γὰρ δικαστὴς οὔτε θεατὴς ὥσπερ ποιηταῖς ἐπιτιμήσων τε καὶ ἄρξων ἐπιστατεῖ παρ' ἡμῖν.

ΣΩ. Λέγωμεν δή, ὡς ἔοικεν, ἐπεὶ σοί γε δοκεῖ, περὶ τῶν κορυφαίων· (τί γὰρ ἄν τις τούς γε φαύλως διατρίβοντας ἐν φιλοσοφίᾳ λέγοι ;) οὗτοι δέ που ἐκ νέων πρῶτον μὲν εἰς ἀγορὰν οὐκ ἴσασι τὴν ὁδόν, οὐδὲ | D ὅπου δικαστήριον ἢ βουλευτήριον ἤ τι κοινὸν ἄλλο τῆς πόλεως συνέδριον· νόμους δὲ καὶ ψηφίσματα λεγόμενα ἢ γεγραμμένα οὔτε ὁρῶσιν οὔτε ἀκούουσι· σπουδαὶ δὲ ἑταιρειῶν ἐπ' ἀρχὰς καὶ σύνοδοι καὶ δεῖπνα καὶ σὺν αὐλητρίσι κῶμοι,—οὐδὲ ὄναρ πράττειν

The aloofness of the philosopher.

προσίσταται αὐτοῖς. εἰ δὲ εὖ ἢ κακῶς τις 173
γέγονεν ἐν πόλει, ἤ τί τῳ κακόν ἐστιν ἐκ
προγόνων γεγονὸς ἢ πρὸς ἀνδρῶν ἢ γυναικῶν,
μᾶλλον αὐτὸν λέληθεν ἢ οἱ τῆς θαλάττης
λεγόμενοι χόες. καὶ ταῦτα πάντ' | οὐδ' ὅτι E
οὐκ οἶδεν οἶδεν· οὐδὲ γὰρ αὐτῶν ἀπέχεται τοῦ
εὐδοκιμεῖν χάριν, ἀλλὰ τῷ ὄντι τὸ σῶμα μόνον
ἐν τῇ πόλει κεῖται αὐτοῦ καὶ ἐπιδημεῖ, ἡ δὲ
διάνοια, ταῦτα πάντα ἡγησαμένη σμικρὰ καὶ
οὐδέν, ἀτιμάσασα πανταχῇ φέρεται κατὰ Πίν-
δαρον, τά τε γᾶς ὑπένερθε καὶ τὰ ἐπίπεδα
γεωμετροῦσα, οὐρανοῦ τε ὕπερ ἀστρονομοῦσα,
καὶ πᾶσαν πάντῃ φύσιν | ἐρευνωμένη τῶν ὄντων 174
ἑκάστου ὅλου, εἰς τῶν ἐγγὺς οὐδὲν αὑτὴν
συγκαθιεῖσα.

ΘΕΟ. Πῶς τοῦτο λέγεις, ὦ Σώκρατες;

ΣΩ. Ὥσπερ καὶ Θαλῆν ἀστρονομοῦντα, ὦ
Θεόδωρε, καὶ ἄνω βλέποντα, πεσόντα
εἰς φρέαρ, Θρᾷττά τις ἐμμελὴς καὶ
χαρίεσσα θεραπαινὶς ἀποσκῶψαι λέγεται, ὡς
τὰ μὲν ἐν οὐρανῷ προθυμοῖτο εἰδέναι, τὰ δ'
ἔμπροσθεν αὐτοῦ καὶ παρὰ πόδας λανθάνοι
αὐτόν. ταὐτὸν δὲ ἀρκεῖ σκῶμμα ἐπὶ πάντας
ὅσοι ἐν φιλοσοφίᾳ | διάγουσι. τῷ γὰρ ὄντι B
τὸν τοιοῦτον ὁ μὲν πλησίον καὶ ὁ γείτων
λέληθεν, οὐ μόνον ὅ τι πράττει, ἀλλ' ὀλίγου
καὶ εἰ ἄνθρωπός ἐστιν ἤ τι ἄλλο θρέμμα· τί
δέ ποτ' ἐστὶν ἄνθρωπος καὶ τί τῇ τοιαύτῃ
φύσει προσήκει διάφορον τῶν ἄλλων ποιεῖν ἢ
πάσχειν, ζητεῖ τε καὶ πράγματ' ἔχει διερευνώ-
μενος. μανθάνεις γάρ που, ὦ Θεόδωρε,—ἢ οὔ;

The abstracted Thales.

174 ΘΕΟ. Ἔγωγε· καὶ ἀληθῆ λέγεις.

ΣΩ. Τοιγάρτοι, ὦ φίλε, ἰδίᾳ τε συγγιγνόμενος ὁ τοιοῦτος ἑκάστῳ καὶ δη-
The philosopher an idiot in court,
C μοσίᾳ, ὅπερ ἀρχόμενος | ἔλεγον, ὅταν ἐν δικαστηρίῳ ἤ που ἄλλοθι ἀναγκασθῇ περὶ τῶν παρὰ πόδας καὶ τῶν ἐν ὀφθαλμοῖς διαλέγεσθαι, γέλωτα παρέχει οὐ μόνον Θρᾴτταις ἀλλὰ καὶ τῷ ἄλλῳ ὄχλῳ, εἰς φρέατά τε καὶ πᾶσαν ἀπορίαν ἐμπίπτων ὑπὸ ἀπειρίας, καὶ ἡ ἀσχημοσύνη δεινή, δόξαν ἀβελτερίας παρεχομένη. ἔν τε γὰρ ταῖς λοιδορίαις ἴδιον ἔχει οὐδὲν οὐδένα λοιδορεῖν, ἅτ' οὐκ εἰδὼς κακὸν οὐδὲν οὐδενὸς ἐκ τοῦ μὴ μεμελετηκέναι (ἀπορῶν οὖν
D γελοῖος φαίνεται), ἔν | τε τοῖς ἐπαίνοις καὶ ταῖς τῶν ἄλλων μεγαλαυχίαις, οὐ προσποιήτως, ἀλλὰ τῷ ὄντι γελῶν ἔνδηλος γιγνόμενος ληρώδης δοκεῖ εἶναι. τύραννόν τε γὰρ ἢ βασιλέα ἐγκωμιαζόμενον ἕνα τῶν νομέων (οἷον συβώτην ἢ ποιμένα ἤ τινα βουκόλον) ἡγεῖται ἀκούειν εὐδαιμονιζόμενον πολὺ βδάλλοντα· δυσκολώτερον δὲ ἐκείνων ζῷον καὶ ἐπιβουλότερον ποιμαίνειν τε καὶ βδάλλειν νομίζει αὐτούς, ἄγροικον δὲ καὶ ἀπαίδευτον ὑπὸ ἀσχολίας οὐδὲν ἧττον τῶν
E νομέων τὸν | τοιοῦτον ἀναγκαῖον γίγνεσθαι, σηκὸν ἐν ὄρει τὸ τεῖχος περιβεβλημένον. γῆς δὲ ὅταν μύρια πλέθρα ἢ ἔτι πλείω ἀκούσῃ ὥς τις ἄρα κεκτημένος θαυμαστὰ πλήθει κέκτηται, πάνσμικρα δοκεῖ ἀκούειν εἰς ἅπασαν εἰωθὼς τὴν γῆν βλέπειν. τὰ δὲ δὴ γένη ὑμνούντων, ὡς γενναῖός τις ἑπτὰ πάππους πλουσίους ἔχων ἀποφῆναι, παντάπασιν ἀμβλὺ καὶ ἐπὶ σμικρὸν

ὁρώντων ἡγεῖται τὸν ἔπαινον, ὑπὸ | ἀπαιδευσίας 175 οὐ δυναμένων εἰς τὸ πᾶν ἀεὶ βλέπειν οὐδὲ λογίζεσθαι ὅτι πάππων καὶ προγόνων μυριάδες ἑκάστῳ γεγόνασιν ἀναρίθμητοι, ἐν αἷς πλούσιοι καὶ πτωχοὶ καὶ βασιλῆς καὶ δοῦλοι βάρβαροί τε καὶ Ἕλληνες πολλάκις μύριοι γεγόνασιν ὁτῳοῦν· ἀλλ' ἐπὶ πέντε καὶ εἴκοσι καταλόγῳ προγόνων σεμνυνομένων καὶ ἀναφερόντων εἰς Ἡρακλέα τὸν Ἀμφιτρύωνος ἄτοπα αὐτῷ καταφαίνεται τῆς σμικρολογίας, ὅτι δὲ ὁ ἀπ' Ἀμφιτρύωνος εἰς τὸ | ἄνω πεντεκαιεικοστὸς B τοιοῦτος ἦν, οἵα συνέβαινεν αὐτῷ τύχη, καὶ ὁ πεντηκοστὸς ἀπ' αὐτοῦ, γελᾷ οὐ δυναμένων λογίζεσθαί τε καὶ χαυνότητα ἀνοήτου ψυχῆς ἀπαλλάττειν. ἐν ἅπασι δὴ τούτοις ὁ τοιοῦτος ὑπὸ τῶν πολλῶν καταγελᾶται, τὰ μὲν ὑπερηφάνως ἔχων, ὡς δοκεῖ, τὰ δ' ἐν ποσὶν ἀγνοῶν τε καὶ ἐν ἑκάστοις ἀπορῶν.

ΘΕΟ. Παντάπασι τὰ γιγνόμενα λέγεις, ὦ Σώκρατες.

The pettifogger an idiot in philosophy.

ΣΩ. Ὅταν δέ γέ τινα αὐτός, ὦ φίλε, ἑλκύσῃ ἄνω, καὶ ἐθελήσῃ τις αὐτῷ | ἐκβῆναι ἐκ τοῦ Τί ἐγὼ σὲ ἀδικῶ ἢ C σὺ ἐμέ; εἰς σκέψιν αὐτῆς δικαιοσύνης τε καὶ ἀδικίας, τί τε ἑκάτερον αὐτοῖν καὶ τί τῶν πάντων ἢ ἀλλήλων διαφέρετον, ἢ ἐκ τοῦ Εἰ βασιλεὺς εὐδαίμων κεκτημένος τ' αὖ πολὺ χρυσίον, βασιλείας πέρι καὶ ἀνθρωπίνης ὅλως εὐδαιμονίας καὶ ἀθλιότητος ἐπὶ σκέψιν, ποίω τέ τινε ἐστὸν καὶ τίνα τρόπον ἀνθρώπου φύσει προσήκει τὸ μὲν κτήσασθαι αὐτοῖν, τὸ

175 δὲ ἀποφυγεῖν — περὶ τούτων ἁπάντων ὅταν
D αὖ δέῃ λόγον διδόναι τὸν | σμικρὸν ἐκεῖνον τὴν
ψυχὴν καὶ δριμὺν καὶ δικανικόν, πάλιν αὖ τὰ
ἀντίστροφα ἀποδίδωσιν· εἰλιγγιῶν τε ἀπὸ
ὑψηλοῦ κρεμασθεὶς καὶ βλέπων μετέωρος ἄνωθεν
ὑπὸ ἀηθείας, ἀδημονῶν τε καὶ ἀπορῶν καὶ
βαρβαρίζων, γέλωτα Θρᾴτταις μὲν οὐ παρέχει
οὐδ' ἄλλῳ ἀπαιδεύτῳ οὐδενί (οὐ γὰρ αἰσθά-
νονται), τοῖς δ' ἐναντίως ἢ ὡς ἀνδραπόδοις
τραφεῖσιν ἅπασιν. οὗτος δὴ ἑκατέρου τρόπος,
ὦ Θεόδωρε, ὁ μὲν τῷ ὄντι ἐν ἐλευθερίᾳ τε καὶ
E σχολῇ τεθραμμένου, | ὃν δὴ φιλόσοφον καλεῖς,
ᾧ ἀνεμέσητον εὐήθει δοκεῖν καὶ οὐδενὶ εἶναι,
ὅταν εἰς δουλικὰ ἐμπέσῃ διακονήματα, οἷον
στρωματόδεσμον μὴ ἐπισταμένου συσκευάσασθαι
μηδὲ ὄψον ἡδῦναι ἢ θῶπας λόγους· ὁ δ' αὖ
τὰ μὲν τοιαῦτα πάντα δυναμένου τορῶς τε καὶ
ὀξέως διακονεῖν, ἀναβάλλεσθαι δὲ οὐκ ἐπιστα-
μένου ἐπιδέξια ἐλευθέρως οὐδέ γ' ἁρμονίαν
176 λόγων λαβόντος | ὀρθῶς ὑμνῆσαι θεῶν τε καὶ
ἀνδρῶν εὐδαιμόνων βίον ἀληθῆ.

ΘΕΟ. Εἰ πάντας, ὦ Σώκρατες, πείθοις ἃ
λέγεις ὥσπερ ἐμέ, πλείων ἂν εἰρήνη καὶ κακὰ
ἐλάττω κατ' ἀνθρώπους εἴη.

ΣΩ. Ἀλλ' οὔτ' ἀπολέσθαι τὰ κακὰ δυνατόν,
ὦ Θεόδωρε (ὑπεναντίον γάρ τι τῷ ἀγαθῷ ἀεὶ
εἶναι ἀνάγκη), οὔτ' ἐν θεοῖς αὐτὰ ἱδρῦσθαι, τὴν
δὲ θνητὴν φύσιν καὶ τόνδε τὸν τόπον περιπολεῖ
ἐξ ἀνάγκης. διὸ καὶ πειρᾶσθαι χρὴ ἐνθένδε
B ἐκεῖσε φεύγειν ὅτι τάχιστα. φυγὴ | δὲ ὁμοίω-
σις θεῷ κατὰ τὸ δυνατόν· ὁμοίωσις δὲ δίκαιον

Likeness to God the escape from human nothingness;

καὶ ὅσιον μετὰ φρονήσεως γενέσθαι. 176
ἀλλὰ γάρ, ὦ ἄριστε, οὐ πάνυ ῥᾴδιον
πεῖσαι ὡς ἄρα οὐχ ὧν ἕνεκα οἱ
πολλοί φασι δεῖν πονηρίαν μὲν φεύγειν, ἀρετὴν
δὲ διώκειν, τούτων χάριν τὸ μὲν ἐπιτηδευτέον,
τὸ δ' οὔ, ἵνα μὴ κακὸς καὶ ἵνα ἀγαθὸς δοκῇ
εἶναι—ταῦτα γάρ ἐστιν ὁ λεγόμενος γραῶν
ὕθλος, ὡς ἐμοὶ φαίνεται· τὸ δὲ ἀληθὲς ὧδε
λέγωμεν. | θεὸς οὐδαμῇ οὐδαμῶς ἄδικος, ἀλλ' C
ὡς οἷόντε δικαιότατος, καὶ οὐκ ἔστιν αὐτῷ
ὁμοιότερον οὐδὲν ἢ ὃς ἂν ἡμῶν αὖ γένηται ὅτι
δικαιότατος. περὶ τούτου καὶ ἡ ὡς ἀληθῶς
δεινότης ἀνδρὸς καὶ οὐδενία τε καὶ ἀνανδρία.
ἡ μὲν γὰρ τούτου γνῶσις σοφία καὶ ἀρετὴ
ἀληθινή, ἡ δὲ ἄγνοια ἀμαθία καὶ κακία ἐναργής·
αἱ δ' ἄλλαι δεινότητές τε δοκοῦσαι καὶ σοφίαι
ἐν μὲν πολιτικαῖς δυναστείαις γιγνόμεναι φορ-
τικαί, ἐν δὲ τέχναις βάναυσοι. τῷ οὖν ἀδικοῦντι
καὶ ἀνόσια λέγοντι ἢ | πράττοντι μακρῷ ἄριστ' D
ἔχει τὸ μὴ συγχωρεῖν δεινῷ ὑπὸ πανουργίας
εἶναι· ἀγάλλονται γὰρ τῷ ὀνείδει καὶ οἴονται
ἀκούειν ὅτι οὐ λῆροί εἰσι, γῆς ἄλλως ἄχθη,
ἀλλ' ἄνδρες οἵους δεῖ ἐν πόλει τοὺς σωθη-
σομένους. λεκτέον οὖν τἀληθές, ὅτι τοσούτῳ
μᾶλλόν εἰσιν οἷοι οὐκ οἴονται, ὅτι οὐχὶ οἴονται·
ἀγνοοῦσι γὰρ ζημίαν ἀδικίας, ὃ δεῖ ἥκιστα
ἀγνοεῖν. οὐ γάρ ἐστιν ἣν δοκοῦσι, πληγαί τε
καὶ θάνατοι, ὧν ἐνίοτε πάσχουσιν οὐδὲν ἀδικοῦν-
τες, ἀλλὰ ἣν ἀδύνατον | ἐκφυγεῖν. E

ΘΕΟ. Τίνα δὴ λέγεις;

ΣΩ. Παραδειγμάτων, ὦ φίλε, ἐν τῷ ὄντι

Likeness to evil the punishment of evil.

176 ἑστώτων, τοῦ μὲν θείου εὐδαιμονε-
στάτου, τοῦ δὲ ἀθέου ἀθλιωτάτου,
οὐχ ὁρῶντες ὅτι οὕτως ἔχει, ὑπὸ
ἠλιθιότητός τε καὶ τῆς ἐσχάτης ἀνοίας λανθά-
177 νουσι τῷ μὲν ὁμοιούμενοι διὰ τὰς | ἀδίκους
πράξεις, τῷ δὲ ἀνομοιούμενοι. οὗ δὴ τίνουσι
δίκην ζῶντες τὸν εἰκότα βίον ᾧ ὁμοιοῦνται·
ἐὰν δ' εἴπωμεν ὅτι, ἂν μὴ ἀπαλλαγῶσι τῆς
δεινότητος, καὶ τελευτήσαντας αὐτοὺς ἐκεῖνος
μὲν ὁ τῶν κακῶν καθαρὸς τόπος οὐ δέξεται,
ἐνθάδε δὲ τὴν αὑτοῖς ὁμοιότητα τῆς διαγωγῆς
ἀεὶ ἕξουσι, κακοὶ κακοῖς συνόντες, ταῦτα δὴ
καὶ παντάπασιν ὡς δεινοὶ καὶ πανοῦργοι ἀνοήτων
τινῶν ἀκούσονται.

ΘΕΟ. Καὶ μάλα δή, ὦ Σώκρατες.

B ΣΩ. Οἶδά τοι, | ὦ ἑταῖρε· ἓν μέντοι τι
αὐτοῖς συμβέβηκεν, ὅτι, ἂν ἰδίᾳ λόγον δέῃ
δοῦναί τε καὶ δέξασθαι περὶ ὧν ψέγουσι, καὶ
ἐθελήσωσιν ἀνδρικῶς πολὺν χρόνον ὑπομεῖναι
καὶ μὴ ἀνάνδρως φεύγειν, τότε ἀτόπως, ὦ
δαιμόνιε, τελευτῶντες οὐκ ἀρέσκουσιν αὐτοὶ
αὑτοῖς περὶ ὧν λέγουσι, καὶ ἡ ῥητορικὴ ἐκείνη
πως ἀπομαραίνεται, ὥστε παίδων μηδὲν δοκεῖν
διαφέρειν. περὶ μὲν οὖν τούτων, ἐπειδὴ καὶ
πάρεργα τυγχάνει λεγόμενα, ἀποστῶμεν· εἰ δὲ
C μή, πλείω ἀεὶ | ἐπιρρέοντα καταχώσει ἡμῶν
τὸν ἐξ ἀρχῆς λόγον· ἐπὶ δὲ τὰ ἔμπροσθεν
ἴωμεν, εἰ καὶ σοὶ δοκεῖ.

ΘΕΟ. Ἐμοὶ μὲν τὰ τοιαῦτα, ὦ Σώκρατες, οὐκ ἀηδέστερα ἀκούειν· ῥᾴω γὰρ τηλικῷδε ὄντι ἐπακολουθεῖν· εἰ μέντοι δοκεῖ, πάλιν ἐπανίωμεν.

MENON

Learning is Reminiscence. A Lesson in Geometry.

SOCRATES. MENON. BOY.

ΣΩ. Ἀπόκριναι τοίνυν πάλιν ἐξ ἀρχῆς· τί 79
φῇς ἀρετὴν εἶναι καὶ σὺ καὶ ὁ ἑταῖρός σου; E

MEN. Ὦ Σώκρατες, ἤκουον μὲν ἔγωγε, πρὶν καὶ συγγενέσθαι σοι, ὅτι σὺ
οὐδὲν ἄλλο ἢ αὐτός | τε ἀπορεῖς καὶ 80
τοὺς ἄλλους ποιεῖς ἀπορεῖν· καὶ νῦν, ὥς γέ μοι δοκεῖς, γοητεύεις με καὶ φαρμάττεις καὶ ἀτεχνῶς κατεπᾴδεις, ὥστε μεστὸν ἀπορίας γεγονέναι. καὶ δοκεῖς μοι παντελῶς, εἰ δεῖ τι καὶ σκῶψαι, ὁμοιότατος εἶναι τό τε εἶδος καὶ τἆλλα ταύτῃ τῇ πλατείᾳ νάρκῃ τῇ θαλαττίᾳ. καὶ γὰρ αὕτη τὸν ἀεὶ πλησιάζοντα καὶ ἁπτόμενον ναρκᾶν ποιεῖ· καὶ σὺ δοκεῖς μοι νῦν ἐμὲ τοιοῦτόν τι πεποιηκέναι,—ναρκᾶν. ἀληθῶς γὰρ ἔγωγε καὶ τὴν ψυχὴν καὶ τὸ | στόμα B
ναρκῶ, καὶ οὐκ ἔχω ὅ τι ἀποκρίνωμαί σοι. καίτοι μυριάκις γε περὶ ἀρετῆς παμπόλλους λόγους εἴρηκα καὶ πρὸς πολλούς, καὶ πάνυ εὖ, ὥς γε ἐμαυτῷ ἐδόκουν· νῦν δὲ οὐδ᾽ ὅ τι ἐστὶν τὸ παράπαν ἔχω εἰπεῖν. καί μοι δοκεῖς εὖ βουλεύεσθαι οὐκ ἐκπλέων ἐνθένδε οὐδ᾽ ἀποδημῶν· εἰ γὰρ ξένος ἐν ἄλλῃ πόλει τοιαῦτα ποιοῖς, τάχ᾽ ἂν ὡς γόης ἀπαχθείης.

Socrates numbs his adversary like the torpedo,—

80 ΣΩ. Πανοῦργος εἶ, ὦ Μένων, καὶ ὀλίγου ἐξηπάτησάς με.

ΜΕΝ. Τί μάλιστα, ὦ Σώκρατες;

C ΣΩ. Γιγνώσκω | οὗ ἕνεκά με ᾔκασας.

ΜΕΝ. Τίνος δὴ οἴει;

ΣΩ. Ἵνα σε ἀντεικάσω. ἐγὼ δὲ τοῦτο οἶδα περὶ πάντων τῶν καλῶν, ὅτι χαίρουσιν εἰκαζόμενοι. λυσιτελεῖ γὰρ αὐτοῖς· καλαὶ γάρ, οἶμαι, τῶν καλῶν καὶ αἱ εἰκόνες. ἀλλ' οὐκ ἀντεικάσομαί σε. ἐγὼ δέ, εἰ μὲν ἡ νάρκη αὐτὴ ναρκῶσα οὕτω καὶ τοὺς ἄλλους ποιεῖ ναρκᾶν, ἔοικα αὐτῇ· εἰ δὲ μή, οὔ. οὐ γὰρ εὐπορῶν αὐτὸς τοὺς ἄλλους ποιῶ ἀπορεῖν, ἀλλὰ παντὸς μᾶλλον αὐτὸς ἀπορῶν οὕτως καὶ τοὺς ἄλλους ποιῶ ἀπορεῖν.

but not, he says, from his greater knowledge.

D καὶ | νῦν περὶ ἀρετῆς, ὅ ἐστιν, ἐγὼ μὲν οὐκ οἶδα, σὺ μέντοι ἴσως πρότερον μὲν ᾔδησθα πρὶν ἐμοῦ ἅψασθαι, νῦν μέντοι ὅμοιος εἶ οὐκ εἰδότι. ὅμως δὲ ἐθέλω μετὰ σοῦ σκέψασθαι καὶ συζητῆσαι ὅ τι ποτέ ἐστιν.

ΜΕΝ. Καὶ τίνα τρόπον ζητήσεις, ὦ Σώκρατες, τοῦτο, ὃ μὴ οἶσθα τὸ παράπαν ὅ τι ἐστίν; ποῖον γὰρ ὧν οὐκ οἶσθα προθέμενος ζητήσεις; ἢ εἰ καὶ ὅτι μάλιστα ἐντύχοις αὐτῷ, πῶς εἴσει ὅτι τοῦτό ἐστιν, ὃ σὺ οὐκ ᾔδησθα;

ΣΩ. Μανθάνω οἷον βούλει λέγειν, ὦ Μένων.

E | ὁρᾷς, τοῦτον ὡς ἐριστικὸν λόγον κατάγεις, ὡς οὐκ ἄρα ἔστιν ζητεῖν ἀνθρώπῳ οὔτε ὃ οἶδεν οὔτε ὃ μὴ οἶδεν; οὔτε γὰρ ἄν γε ὃ οἶδε ζητοῖ (οἶδε γάρ, καὶ οὐδὲν δεῖ τῷ γε τοιούτῳ ζητή-

Yet he does not believe that knowledge is unattainable.

σεως), οὔτε ὃ μὴ οἶδεν· οὐδὲ γὰρ οἶδεν ὅ τι ζητήσει.

MEN. | Οὐκοῦν καλῶς σοι δοκεῖ λέγεσθαι 81
ὁ λόγος οὗτος, ὦ Σώκρατες;

ΣΩ. Οὐκ ἔμοιγε.

MEN. Ἔχεις λέγειν ὅπῃ;

ΣΩ. Ἔγωγε· ἀκήκοα γὰρ ἀνδρῶν τε καὶ γυναικῶν σοφῶν περὶ τὰ θεῖα πράγματα—

MEN. Τίνα λόγον λεγόντων;

ΣΩ. Ἀληθῆ, ἔμοιγε δοκεῖν, καὶ καλόν.

MEN. Τίνα τοῦτον, καὶ τίνες οἱ λέγοντες;

ΣΩ. Οἱ μὲν λέγοντές εἰσι τῶν ἱερέων τε καὶ τῶν ἱερειῶν ὅσοις μεμέληκε, περὶ ὧν μεταχειρίζονται, λόγον οἵοισ τ' εἶναι διδόναι· λέγει δὲ καὶ Πίνδαρος | καὶ ἄλλοι πολλοὶ τῶν B
ποιητῶν, ὅσοι θεῖοί εἰσιν. ἃ δὲ λέγουσι, ταυτί ἐστιν· ἀλλὰ σκόπει εἴ σοι δοκοῦσιν ἀληθῆ λέγειν. φασὶ γὰρ τὴν ψυχὴν τοῦ ἀνθρώπου εἶναι ἀθάνατον, καὶ τοτὲ μὲν τελευτᾶν (ὃ δὴ ἀποθνῄσκειν καλοῦσι), τοτὲ δὲ πάλιν γίγνεσθαι, ἀπόλλυσθαι δ' οὐδέποτε· δεῖν δὴ διὰ ταῦτα ὡς ὁσιώτατα διαβιῶναι τὸν βίον·

For man's soul is immortal,

οἷσι γὰρ ἂν Φερσεφόνα ποινὰν παλαιοῦ πένθεος
δέξεται, εἰς τὸν ὕπερθεν ἅλιον κείνων ἐνάτῳ ἔτει
ἀνδιδοῖ ψυχὰν πάλιν,
ἐκ τᾶν βασιλῆες | ἀγαυοὶ καὶ σθένει κραιπνοὶ σοφίᾳ C
τε μέγιστοι
ἄνδρες αὔξοντ'· ἐς δὲ τὸν λοιπὸν χρόνον ἥρωες ἁγνοὶ
πρὸς ἀνθρώπων καλεῦνται.

Ἅτε οὖν ἡ ψυχὴ ἀθάνατός τε οὖσα καὶ

81 has learned all things,

πολλάκις γεγονυῖα, καὶ ἑωρακυῖα καὶ
τὰ ἐνθάδε καὶ τὰ ἐν Ἅιδου καὶ
πάντα χρήματα, οὐκ ἔστιν ὅ τι οὐ μεμάθηκεν·
ὥστε οὐδὲν θαυμαστὸν καὶ περὶ ἀρετῆς καὶ
περὶ ἄλλων οἷόντε εἶναι αὐτὴν ἀναμνησθῆναι,
ἅ γε καὶ πρότερον ἠπίστατο. ἅτε γὰρ τῆς
D φύσεως ἁπάσης συγγενοῦς | οὔσης, καὶ μεμαθη-
κυίας τῆς ψυχῆς ἅπαντα, οὐδὲν κωλύει ἓν
μόνον ἀναμνησθέντα (ὃ δὴ μάθησιν καλοῦσιν

and can recall them.

ἄνθρωποι) τἆλλα πάντα αὐτὸν ἀν-
ευρεῖν, ἐάν τις ἀνδρεῖος ᾖ καὶ μὴ
ἀποκάμνῃ ζητῶν· τὸ γὰρ ζητεῖν ἄρα καὶ τὸ
μανθάνειν ἀνάμνησις ὅλον ἐστίν. οὔκουν δεῖ
πείθεσθαι τούτῳ τῷ ἐριστικῷ λόγῳ· οὗτος μὲν
γὰρ ἂν ἡμᾶς ἀργοὺς ποιήσειεν καὶ ἔστιν τοῖς
μαλακοῖς τῶν ἀνθρώπων ἡδὺς ἀκοῦσαι, ὅδε δὲ
E ἐργαστικούς | τε καὶ ζητητικοὺς ποιεῖ. ᾧ ἐγὼ
πιστεύων ἀληθεῖ εἶναι ἐθέλω μετὰ σοῦ ζητεῖν
ἀρετὴ ὅ τι ἐστίν.

ΜΕΝ. Ναί, ὦ Σώκρατες· ἀλλὰ πῶς λέγεις τοῦτο, ὅτι οὐ μανθάνομεν, ἀλλὰ ἣν καλοῦμεν μάθησιν ἀνάμνησίς ἐστιν; ἔχεις με τοῦτο διδάξαι ὡς οὕτως ἔχει;

ΣΩ. Καὶ ἄρτι εἶπον, ὦ Μένων, ὅτι πανοῦρ-
γος εἶ· καὶ νῦν ἐρωτᾷς εἰ ἔχω σε διδάξαι, ὃς οὔ
82 φημι διδαχὴν | εἶναι ἀλλ' ἀνάμνησιν, ἵνα δὴ
εὐθὺς φαίνωμαι αὐτὸς ἐμαυτῷ τἀναντία λέγων.

ΜΕΝ. Οὐ μὰ τὸν Δία, ὦ Σώκρατες, οὐ πρὸς τοῦτο βλέψας εἶπον, ἀλλ' ὑπὸ τοῦ ἔθους· ἀλλ' εἴ πώς μοι ἔχεις ἐνδείξασθαι ὅτι ἔχει ὥσπερ λέγεις, ἔνδειξαι.

ΣΩ. Ἀλλ' ἔστι μὲν οὐ ῥᾴδιον, ὅμως δὲ 82
ἐθέλω προθυμηθῆναι σοῦ ἕνεκα. ἀλλά μοι
προσκάλεσον τῶν πολλῶν ἀκολούθων τουτωνὶ
τῶν σαυτοῦ ἕνα, ὅντινα βούλει, | ἵνα ἐν τούτῳ B
σοι ἐπιδείξωμαι.

Illustration given in the case of a slave,—subject, geometry.

MEN. Πάνυ γε. δεῦρο πρόσελθε.

ΣΩ. Ἕλλην μέν ἐστι καὶ ἑλληνίζει;

MEN. Πάνυ γε σφόδρα, οἰκογενής.

ΣΩ. Πρόσεχε δὴ τὸν νοῦν, ὁπότερ' ἄν σοι φαίνηται, ἢ ἀναμιμνῃσκόμενος ἢ μανθάνων παρ' ἐμοῦ.

MEN. Ἀλλὰ προσέξω.

ΣΩ. Εἰπὲ δή μοι, ὦ παῖ, γιγνώσκεις τετράγωνον χωρίον ὅτι τοιοῦτόν ἐστιν;

ΠΑΙ. Ἔγωγε.

ΣΩ. Ἔστιν οὖν τετράγωνον χωρίον ἴσας |
ἔχον τὰς γραμμὰς ταύτας πάσας, τέτταρας C
οὔσας;

ΠΑΙ. Πάνυ γε.

ΣΩ. Οὐ καὶ ταυτασὶ τὰς διὰ μέσου ἐστὶν ἴσας ἔχον;

ΠΑΙ. Ναί.

ΣΩ. Οὐκοῦν εἴη ἂν τοιοῦτον χωρίον καὶ μεῖζον καὶ ἔλαττον;

ΠΑΙ. Πάνυ γε.

ΣΩ. Εἰ οὖν εἴη αὕτη ἡ πλευρὰ δυοῖν ποδοῖν καὶ αὕτη δυοῖν, πόσων ἂν εἴη ποδῶν τὸ ὅλον; ὧδε δὲ σκόπει· εἰ ἦν ταύτῃ δυοῖν ποδοῖν, ταύτῃ δὲ ἑνὸς ποδὸς μόνον, ἄλλο τι ἅπαξ ἂν ἦν δυοῖν ποδοῖν τὸ χωρίον;

82 ΠΑΙ. Ναί.

D ΣΩ. Ἐπειδὴ | δὲ δυοῖν ποδοῖν καὶ ταύτῃ, ἄλλο τι ἢ δὶς δυοῖν γίγνεται;

ΠΑΙ. Γίγνεται.

ΣΩ. Δυοῖν ἄρα δὶς γίγνεται ποδῶν;

ΠΑΙ. Ναί.

ΣΩ. Πόσοι οὖν εἰσιν οἱ δύο δὶς πόδες; λογισάμενος εἰπέ.

ΠΑΙ. Τέτταρες, ὦ Σώκρατες.

ΣΩ. Οὐκοῦν γένοιτ᾽ ἂν τούτου τοῦ χωρίου ἕτερον διπλάσιον, τοιοῦτον δέ, ἴσας ἔχον πάσας τὰς γραμμὰς ὥσπερ τοῦτο;

ΠΑΙ. Ναί.

ΣΩ. Πόσων οὖν ἔσται ποδῶν;

ΠΑΙ. Ὀκτώ.

ΣΩ. Φέρε δή, πειρῶ μοι εἰπεῖν πηλίκη τις

E ἔσται ἐκείνου | ἡ γραμμὴ ἑκάστη; ἡ μὲν γὰρ τοῦδε δυοῖν ποδοῖν· τί δὲ ἡ ἐκείνου τοῦ διπλασίου;

ΠΑΙ. Δῆλον δή, ὦ Σώκρατες, ὅτι διπλασία.

ΣΩ. Ὁρᾷς, ὦ Μένων, ὡς ἐγὼ τοῦτον οὐδὲν διδάσκω, ἀλλ᾽ ἐρωτῶ πάντα; καὶ νῦν οὗτος οἴεται εἰδέναι, ὁποία ἐστὶν ἀφ᾽ ἧς τὸ ὀκτώπουν χωρίον γενήσεται· ἢ οὐ δοκεῖ σοι;

He is questioned merely, not instructed.

ΜΕΝ. Ἔμοιγε.

ΣΩ. Οἶδεν οὖν;

ΜΕΝ. Οὐ δῆτα.

ΣΩ. Οἴεται δέ γε ἀπὸ τῆς διπλασίας;

ΜΕΝ. Ναί.

ΣΩ. Θεῶ δὴ αὐτὸν ἀναμιμνῃσκόμενον ἐφεξῆς, ὡς δεῖ ἀναμιμνῄσκεσθαι. σὺ δέ μοι λέγε· ἀπὸ τῆς διπλασίας γραμμῆς φῂς τὸ διπλάσιον | χωρίον γίγνεσθαι; τοιόνδε λέγω, μὴ ταύτῃ 83 μὲν μακρόν, τῇ δὲ βραχύ, ἀλλὰ ἴσον πανταχῇ ἔστω ὥσπερ τουτί, διπλάσιον δὲ τούτου, ὀκτώπουν· ἀλλ' ὅρα, εἰ ἔτι σοι ἀπὸ τῆς διπλασίας δοκεῖ ἔσεσθαι.

ΠΑΙ. Ἔμοιγε.

ΣΩ. Οὐκοῦν διπλασία αὕτη ταύτης γίγνεται, ἂν ἑτέραν τοσαύτην προσθῶμεν ἐνθένδε;

ΠΑΙ. Πάνυ γε.

ΣΩ. Ἀπὸ ταύτης δή, φῄς, ἔσται τὸ ὀκτώπουν χωρίον, ἂν τέτταρες τοσαῦται γένωνται;

ΠΑΙ. Ναί.

ΣΩ. Ἀναγραψώμεθα | δὴ ἀπ' αὐτῆς ἴσας B τέτταρας. ἄλλο τι ἢ τουτὶ ἂν εἴη ὃ φῂς τὸ ὀκτώπουν εἶναι;

ΠΑΙ. Πάνυ γε.

ΣΩ. Οὐκοῦν ἐν αὐτῷ ἐστιν ταυτὶ τέτταρα, ὧν ἕκαστον ἴσον τούτῳ ἐστὶν τῷ τετράποδι;

ΠΑΙ. Ναί.

ΣΩ. Πόσον οὖν γίγνεται; οὐ τετράκις τοσοῦτον;

ΠΑΙ. Πῶς δ' οὔ;

ΣΩ. Διπλάσιον οὖν ἐστιν τὸ τετράκις τοσοῦτον;

ΠΑΙ. Οὐ μὰ Δία.

ΣΩ. Ἀλλὰ ποσαπλάσιον;

ΠΑΙ. Τετραπλάσιον.

ΣΩ. Ἀπὸ τῆς διπλασίας ἄρα, ὦ παῖ, | οὐ C διπλάσιον ἀλλὰ τετραπλάσιον γίγνεται χωρίον.

ΠΑΙ. Ἀληθῆ λέγεις.

83 ΣΩ. Τεττάρων γὰρ τετράκις ἐστὶν ἑκκαίδεκα. οὐχί;

ΠΑΙ. Ναί.

ΣΩ. Ὀκτώπουν δ' ἀπὸ ποίας γραμμῆς; οὐχὶ ἀπὸ μὲν ταύτης τετραπλάσιον;

ΠΑΙ. Φημί.

ΣΩ. Τετράπουν δὲ ἀπὸ τῆς ἡμισέας—ταυτησὶ τουτί;

ΠΑΙ. Ναί.

ΣΩ. Εἶεν· τὸ δὲ ὀκτώπουν οὐ τοῦδε μὲν διπλάσιόν ἐστιν, τούτου δὲ ἥμισυ;

ΠΑΙ. Πάνυ γε.

D ΣΩ. Οὐκ ἀπὸ μὲν μείζονος ἔσται | ἢ τοσαύτης γραμμῆς, ἀπὸ ἐλάττονος δὲ ἢ τοσησδί; ἢ οὔ;

ΠΑΙ. Ἔμοιγε δοκεῖ οὕτω.

ΣΩ. Καλῶς· τὸ γάρ σοι δοκοῦν τοῦτο ἀποκρίνου. καί μοι λέγε· οὐχ ἥδε μὲν δυοῖν ποδοῖν ἦν, ἡ δὲ τεττάρων;

ΠΑΙ. Ναί.

ΣΩ. Δεῖ ἄρα τὴν τοῦ ὀκτώποδος χωρίου γραμμὴν μείζω μὲν εἶναι τῆσδε τῆς δίποδος, ἐλάττω δὲ τῆς τετράποδος.

ΠΑΙ. Δεῖ.

E ΣΩ. Πειρῶ δὴ | λέγειν πηλίκην τινὰ φῂς αὐτὴν εἶναι.

ΠΑΙ. Τρίποδα.

ΣΩ. Οὐκοῦν ἄνπερ τρίπους ᾖ, τὸ ἥμισυ ταύτης προσληψόμεθα καὶ ἔσται τρίπους; δύο μὲν γὰρ οἵδε, ὁ δὲ εἷς· καὶ ἐνθένδε ὡσαύτως —δύο μὲν οἵδε, ὁ δὲ εἷς· καὶ γίγνεται τοῦτο τὸ χωρίον ὃ φῄς.

ΠΑΙ. Ναί. 83

ΣΩ. Οὐκοῦν ἂν ᾖ τῇδε τριῶν καὶ τῇδε τριῶν, τὸ ὅλον χωρίον τριῶν τρὶς ποδῶν γίγνεται;

ΠΑΙ. Φαίνεται.

ΣΩ. Τρεῖς δὲ τρὶς πόσοι εἰσὶ πόδες;

ΠΑΙ. Ἐννέα.

ΣΩ. Ἔδει δὲ τὸ διπλάσιον πόσων εἶναι ποδῶν;

ΠΑΙ. Ὀκτώ.

ΣΩ. Οὐδ᾽ ἄρα ἀπὸ τῆς τρίποδός πω τὸ ὀκτώπουν χωρίον γίγνεται.

ΠΑΙ. Οὐ δῆτα.

ΣΩ. Ἀλλ᾽ ἀπὸ ποίας; πειρῶ ἡμῖν εἰπεῖν
ἀκριβῶς· | καὶ εἰ μὴ βούλει ἀριθμεῖν, ἀλλὰ 84
δεῖξον ἀπὸ ποίας.

ΠΑΙ. Ἀλλὰ μὰ τὸν Δία, ὦ Σώκρατες, ἔγωγε οὐκ οἶδα.

ΣΩ. Ἐννοεῖς αὖ, ὦ Μένων, οὗ ἐστιν ἤδη βαδίζων ὅδε τοῦ ἀναμιμνῄσκεσθαι; ὅτι τὸ μὲν πρῶτον ᾔδει μὲν οὔ, ἥτις ἐστὶν ἡ τοῦ ὀκτώποδος χωρίου γραμμή, ὥσπερ οὐδὲ νῦν πω οἶδεν, ἀλλ᾽ οὖν ᾤετό γ᾽ αὐτὴν τότε εἰδέναι, καὶ θαρραλέως ἀπεκρίνετο ὡς εἰδώς, καὶ οὐχ ἡγεῖτο ἀπορεῖν· νῦν δὲ ἡγεῖται ἀπορεῖν ἤδη, καὶ ὥσπερ οὐκ
οἶδεν, οὐδ᾽ οἴεται | εἰδέναι. B

He is at first perplexed and numbed (though that is good for him),

ΜΕΝ. Ἀληθῆ λέγεις.

ΣΩ. Οὐκοῦν νῦν βέλτιον ἔχει περὶ τὸ πρᾶγμα ὃ οὐκ ᾔδει;

ΜΕΝ. Καὶ τοῦτό μοι δοκεῖ.

84 ΣΩ. Ἀπορεῖν οὖν αὐτὸν ποιήσαντες καὶ ναρκᾶν ὥσπερ ἡ νάρκη, μῶν τι ἐβλάψαμεν;

ΜΕΝ. Οὐκ ἔμοιγε δοκεῖ.

ΣΩ. Προὔργου γοῦν τι πεποιήκαμεν, ὡς ἔοικε, πρὸς τὸ ἐξευρεῖν ὅπῃ ἔχει· νῦν μὲν γὰρ καὶ ζητήσειεν ἂν ἡδέως οὐκ εἰδώς, τότε δὲ ῥᾳδίως ἂν καὶ πρὸς πολλοὺς καὶ πολλάκις ᾤετ' ἂν εὖ λέγειν περὶ τοῦ διπλασίου |
C χωρίου, ὡς δεῖ διπλασίαν τὴν γραμμὴν ἔχειν μήκει.

ΜΕΝ. Ἔοικεν.

ΣΩ. Οἴει οὖν ἂν αὐτὸν πρότερον ἐπιχειρῆσαι ζητεῖν ἢ μανθάνειν τοῦτο, ὃ ᾤετο εἰδέναι οὐκ εἰδώς, πρὶν εἰς ἀπορίαν κατέπεσεν ἡγησάμενος μὴ εἰδέναι, καὶ ἐπόθησεν τὸ εἰδέναι;

ΜΕΝ. Οὔ μοι δοκεῖ, ὦ Σώκρατες.

ΣΩ. Ὤνητο ἄρα ναρκήσας;

ΜΕΝ. Δοκεῖ μοι.

ΣΩ. Σκέψαι δὴ ἐκ ταύτης τῆς ἀπορίας ὅ τι καὶ ἀνευρήσει ζητῶν μετ' ἐμοῦ, οὐδὲν ἀλλ'
D ἢ ἐρωτῶντος ἐμοῦ καὶ | οὐ διδάσκοντος· φύλαττε δὲ ἄν που εὕρῃς με διδάσκοντα καὶ διεξιόντα αὐτῷ, ἀλλὰ μὴ τὰς τούτου δόξας ἀνερωτῶντα. Λέγε γάρ μοι σύ· οὐ τὸ μὲν τετράπουν τοῦτο ἡμῖν ἐστι χωρίον; μανθάνεις;

ΠΑΙ. Ἔγωγε.

ΣΩ. Ἕτερον δὲ αὐτῷ προσθεῖμεν ἂν τουτὶ ἴσον;

ΠΑΙ. Ναί.

ΣΩ. Καὶ τρίτον τόδε ἴσον ἑκατέρῳ τούτων;

ΠΑΙ. Ναί.

ΣΩ. Οὐκοῦν προσαναπληρωσαίμεθ' ἂν τὸ ἐν 84
τῇ γωνίᾳ τόδε;

ΠΑΙ. Πάνυ γε.

ΣΩ. Ἄλλο τι οὖν γένοιτ' ἂν τέτταρα ἴσα χωρία τάδε;

ΠΑΙ. | Ναί. E

ΣΩ. Τί οὖν; τὸ ὅλον τόδε ποσαπλάσιον τοῦδε γίγνεται;

ΠΑΙ. Τετραπλάσιον.

ΣΩ. Ἔδει δὲ διπλάσιον ἡμῖν γενέσθαι· ἢ οὐ μέμνησαι;

ΠΑΙ. Πάνυ γε.

ΣΩ. Οὐκοῦν ἔστιν αὕτη γραμμὴ ἐκ γωνίας εἰς γωνίαν τείνουσα, τέμνουσα δίχα ἕκαστον
τούτων τῶν χωρίων; 85

ΠΑΙ. Ναί.

ΣΩ. Οὐκοῦν τέτταρες αὗται γίγνονται γραμμαὶ ἴσαι, περιέχουσαι τουτὶ τὸ χωρίον;

ΠΑΙ. Γίγνονται.

ΣΩ. Σκόπει δή· πηλίκον τί ἐστιν τοῦτο τὸ χωρίον;

ΠΑΙ. Οὐ μανθάνω.

ΣΩ. Οὐχὶ τεττάρων ὄντων τούτων ἥμισυ ἑκάστου ἑκάστη ἡ γραμμὴ ἀποτέτμηκεν ἐντός; ἢ οὔ;

ΠΑΙ. Ναί.

ΣΩ. Πόσα οὖν τηλικαῦτα ἐν τούτῳ ἔνεστιν;

ΠΑΙ. Τέτταρα.

ΣΩ. Πόσα δὲ ἐν τῷδε;

ΠΑΙ. Δύο.

ΣΩ. Τὰ δὲ τέτταρα τοῖν δυοῖν τί ἐστιν;

85 ΠΑΙ. Διπλάσια.

B ΣΩ. Τόδε οὖν | ποσάπουν γίγνεται;

ΠΑΙ. Ὀκτώπουν.

ΣΩ. Ἀπὸ ποίας γραμμῆς;

ΠΑΙ. Ἀπὸ ταύτης.

ΣΩ. Ἀπὸ τῆς ἐκ γωνίας εἰς γωνίαν τεινούσης τοῦ τετράποδος;

ΠΑΙ. Ναί.

ΣΩ. Καλοῦσιν δέ γε ταύτην διάμετρον οἱ σοφισταί· ὥστ' εἰ ταύτῃ διάμετρος ὄνομα, ἀπὸ τῆς διαμέτρου ἄν, ὡς σὺ φῄς, ὦ παῖ Μένωνος, γίγνοιτ' ἂν τὸ διπλάσιον χωρίον.

ΠΑΙ. Πάνυ μὲν οὖν, ὦ Σώκρατες.

ΣΩ. Τί σοι δοκεῖ, ὦ Μένων; ἔστιν ἥντινα δόξαν οὐχ αὑτοῦ οὗτος ἀπεκρίνατο;

but at last has *true opinions* wakened in him (i.e. knowledge),

C ΜΕΝ. | Οὔκ, ἀλλ' ἑαυτοῦ.

ΣΩ. Καὶ μὴν οὐκ ᾔδει γε, ὡς ἔφαμεν ὀλίγον πρότερον.

ΜΕΝ. Ἀληθῆ λέγεις.

ΣΩ. Ἐνῆσαν δέ γε αὐτῷ αὗται αἱ δόξαι· ἢ οὔ;

ΜΕΝ. Ναί.

ΣΩ. Τῷ οὐκ εἰδότι ἄρα περὶ ὧν ἂν μὴ εἰδῇ ἔνεισιν ἀληθεῖς δόξαι περὶ τούτων ὧν οὐκ οἶδεν;

ΜΕΝ. Φαίνεται.

ΣΩ. Καὶ νῦν μέν γε αὐτῷ ὥσπερ ὄναρ ἄρτι ἀνακεκίνηνται αἱ δόξαι αὗται· εἰ δὲ αὐτόν τις ἀνερήσεται πολλάκις τὰ αὐτὰ ταῦτα καὶ πολλαχῇ, οἶσθ' ὅτι τελευτῶν οὐδενὸς ἧττον ἀκριβῶς

D ἐπιστήσεται | περὶ τούτων.

ΜΕΝ. Ἔοικεν. 85

ΣΩ. Οὐκοῦν οὐδενὸς διδάξαντος ἀλλ' ἐρωτήσαντος ἐπιστήσεται, ἀναλαβὼν αὐτὸς ἐξ αὑτοῦ τὴν ἐπιστήμην;

ΜΕΝ. Ναί.

ΣΩ. Τὸ δὲ ἀναλαμβάνειν αὐτὸν ἐν αὑτῷ ἐπιστήμην οὐκ ἀναμιμνῄσκεσθαί ἐστιν;

ΜΕΝ. Πάνυ γε.

ΣΩ. Ἆρ' οὖν οὐ τὴν ἐπιστήμην, ἣν νῦν οὗτος ἔχει, ἤτοι ἔλαβέν ποτε ἢ ἀεὶ εἶχεν;

ΜΕΝ. Ναί.

though never taught geometry in his life.

ΣΩ. Οὐκοῦν εἰ μὲν ἀεὶ εἶχεν, ἀεὶ καὶ ἦν ἐπιστήμων· εἰ δὲ ἔλαβέν ποτε, οὐκ ἂν ἔν γε τῷ νῦν βίῳ εἰληφὼς εἴη.
ἢ δεδίδαχέν τις τοῦτον | γεωμετρεῖν; E
οὗτος γὰρ ποιήσει περὶ πάσης γεωμετρίας ταὐτὰ ταῦτα, καὶ τῶν ἄλλων μαθημάτων ἁπάντων. ἔστιν οὖν ὅστις τοῦτον πάντα δεδίδαχεν; δίκαιος γάρ που εἶ εἰδέναι, ἄλλως τε ἐπειδὴ ἐν τῇ σῇ οἰκίᾳ γέγονε καὶ τέθραπται.

ΜΕΝ. Ἀλλ' οἶδα ἔγωγε ὅτι οὐδεὶς πώποτε ἐδίδαξεν.

ΣΩ. Ἔχει δὲ ταύτας τὰς δόξας, ἢ οὐχί;

ΜΕΝ. Ἀνάγκη, ὦ Σώκρατες, φαίνεται.

ΣΩ. Εἰ δὲ μὴ ἐν τῷ νῦν βίῳ λαβών, οὐκ
ἤδη τοῦτο | δῆλον, ὅτι ἐν ἄλλῳ τινὶ χρόνῳ 86
εἶχε καὶ ἐμεμαθήκει;

ΜΕΝ. Φαίνεται.

ΣΩ. Οὐκοῦν οὗτός γέ ἐστιν ὁ χρόνος, ὅτ' οὐκ ἦν ἄνθρωπος;

ΜΕΝ. Ναί.

86 ΣΩ. Εἰ οὖν ὅν τ' ἂν ᾖ χρόνον καὶ ὃν ἂν μὴ ᾖ ἄνθρωπος, ἐνέσονται αὐτῷ ἀληθεῖς δόξαι, αἳ ἐρωτήσει ἐπεγερθεῖσαι ἐπιστῆμαι γίγνονται, ἆρ' οὖν τὸν ἀεὶ χρόνον μεμαθηκυῖα ἔσται ἡ ψυχὴ αὐτοῦ; δῆλον γὰρ ὅτι τὸν πάντα χρόνον ἔστιν ἢ οὐκ ἔστιν ἄνθρωπος.

ΜΕΝ. Φαίνεται.

B ΣΩ. Οὐκοῦν εἰ | ἀεὶ ἡ ἀλήθεια ἡμῖν τῶν ὄντων ἐστὶν ἐν τῇ ψυχῇ, ἀθάνατος ἂν ἡ ψυχὴ εἴη, ὥστε θαρροῦντα χρή, ὃ μὴ τυγχάνεις ἐπιστάμενος νῦν—τοῦτο δ' ἐστὶν ὃ μὴ μεμνημένος—ἐπιχειρεῖν ζητεῖν καὶ ἀναμιμνῄσκεσθαι;

Hence knowledge is reminiscence by the immortal soul.

ΜΕΝ. Εὖ μοι δοκεῖς λέγειν, ὦ Σώκρατες, οὐκ οἶδ' ὅπως.

ΣΩ. Καὶ γὰρ ἐγὼ ἐμοί, ὦ Μένων. καὶ τὰ μέν γε ἄλλα οὐκ ἂν πάνυ ὑπὲρ τοῦ λόγου διισχυρισαίμην· ὅτι δ' οἰόμενοι δεῖν ζητεῖν, ἃ μή τις οἶδεν, βελτίους ἂν εἶμεν καὶ ἀνδρικώτεροι καὶ ἧττον ἀργοὶ ἢ εἰ οἰοίμεθα, ἃ μὴ
C ἐπιστάμεθα, | μηδὲ δυνατὸν εἶναι εὑρεῖν μηδὲ δεῖν ζητεῖν—περὶ τούτου πάνυ ἂν διαμαχοίμην, εἰ οἷόστε εἴην, καὶ λόγῳ καὶ ἔργῳ.

ΜΕΝ. Καὶ τοῦτο μέν γε δοκεῖς μοι εὖ λέγειν, ὦ Σώκρατες.

REPUBLIC I

Cephalus "De Senectute"

A chance meeting in Peiraeus.

Κατέβην χθὲς εἰς Πειραιᾶ μετὰ Γλαύκωνος 327 τοῦ Ἀρίστωνος, προσευξόμενός τε τῇ θεῷ καὶ ἅμα τὴν ἑορτὴν βουλόμενος θεάσασθαι, τίνα τρόπον ποιήσουσιν, ἅτε νῦν πρῶτον ἄγοντες. καλὴ μὲν οὖν μοι καὶ ἡ τῶν ἐπιχωρίων πομπὴ ἔδοξεν εἶναι, οὐ μέντοι ἧττον ἐφαίνετο πρέπειν ἣν οἱ Θρᾷκες ἔπεμπον. προσευξάμενοι δὲ καὶ θεωρήσαντες | ἀπῇμεν πρὸς τὸ ἄστυ. κατιδὼν B οὖν πόρρωθεν ἡμᾶς οἴκαδε ὡρμημένους Πολέμαρχος ὁ Κεφάλου ἐκέλευσε δραμόντα τὸν παῖδα περιμεῖναί ἑ κελεῦσαι. καί μου ὄπισθεν ὁ παῖς λαβόμενος τοῦ ἱματίου, Κελεύει ὑμᾶς, ἔφη, Πολέμαρχος περιμεῖναι. καὶ ἐγὼ μετεστράφην τε καὶ ἠρόμην ὅπου αὐτὸς εἴη. Οὗτος, ἔφη, ὄπισθεν προσέρχεται· ἀλλὰ περιμένετε. Ἀλλὰ περιμενοῦμεν, ἦ δ' ὃς ὁ Γλαύκων. καὶ ὀλίγῳ ὕστερον ὅ τε Πολέμαρχος | ἧκε καὶ C Ἀδείμαντος ὁ τοῦ Γλαύκωνος ἀδελφὸς καὶ Νικήρατος ὁ Νικίου καὶ ἄλλοι τινές, ὡς ἀπὸ τῆς πομπῆς. ὁ οὖν Πολέμαρχος ἔφη Ὦ Σώκρατες, δοκεῖτέ μοι πρὸς ἄστυ ὡρμῆσθαι ὡς ἀπιόντες. Οὐ γὰρ κακῶς δοξάζεις, ἦν δ' ἐγώ. Ὁρᾷς οὖν ἡμᾶς, ἔφη, ὅσοι ἐσμέν; Πῶς γὰρ οὔ; Ἢ τοίνυν τούτων, ἔφη, κρείττους γένεσθε ἢ μένετ' αὐτοῦ. Οὐκοῦν, ἦν δ' ἐγώ,

327 ἔτι ἓν | λείπεται τὸ ἢν πείσωμεν ὑμᾶς ὡς
D χρὴ ἡμᾶς ἀφεῖναι; Ἦ καὶ δύναισθ' ἄν, ἦ δ'
ὅς, πεῖσαι μὴ ἀκούοντας; Οὐδαμῶς, ἔφη ὁ
Γλαύκων. Ὡς τοίνυν μὴ ἀκουσομένων, οὕτω
328 διανοεῖσθε. καὶ ὁ Ἀδείμαντος, Ἆρά γε, | ἦ
δ' ὅς, οὐδ' ἴστε ὅτι λαμπὰς ἔσται πρὸς ἑσπέραν ἀφ' ἵππων τῇ θεῷ; Ἀφ' ἵππων; ἦν δ' ἐγώ· καινόν γε τοῦτο. λαμπάδια ἔχοντες διαδώσουσιν ἀλλήλοις ἁμιλλώμενοι τοῖς ἵπποις; ἢ πῶς λέγεις; Οὕτως, ἔφη ὁ Πολέμαρχος· καὶ πρός γε παννυχίδα ποιήσουσιν, ἣν ἄξιον θεάσασθαι. ἐξαναστησόμεθα γὰρ μετὰ τὸ δεῖπνον καὶ τὴν παννυχίδα θεασόμεθα καὶ ξυνεσόμεθά τε πολλοῖς τῶν νέων αὐτόθι καὶ διαλεξόμεθα.
B ἀλλὰ μένετε καὶ μὴ ἄλλως | ποιεῖτε. καὶ
ὁ Γλαύκων, Ἔοικεν, ἔφη, μενετέον εἶναι. Ἀλλ' εἰ δοκεῖ, ἦν δ' ἐγώ, οὕτω χρὴ ποιεῖν.

The visit to Cephalus, now an old man.

Ἤιμεν οὖν οἴκαδε εἰς τοῦ Πολεμάρχου, καὶ Λυσίαν τε αὐτόθι κατελάβομεν καὶ Εὐθύδημον, τοὺς τοῦ Πολεμάρχου ἀδελφούς, καὶ δὴ καὶ Θρασύμαχον τὸν Καλχηδόνιον καὶ Χαρμαντίδην τὸν Παιανιέα καὶ Κλειτοφῶντα τὸν Ἀριστωνύμου· ἦν δ' ἔνδον καὶ ὁ πατὴρ ὁ τοῦ Πολεμάρχου Κέφαλος. καὶ μάλα πρεσβύτης μοι ἔδοξεν εἶναι· διὰ
C χρόνου | γὰρ καὶ ἑωράκη αὐτόν. καθῆστο δὲ
ἐστεφανωμένος ἐπί τινος προσκεφαλαίου τε καὶ δίφρου· τεθυκὼς γὰρ ἐτύγχανεν ἐν τῇ αὐλῇ. ἐκαθεζόμεθα οὖν παρ' αὐτόν· ἔκειντο γὰρ δίφροι τινὲς αὐτόθι κύκλῳ. εὐθὺς οὖν με ἰδὼν ὁ Κέφαλος ἠσπάζετό τε καὶ εἶπεν Ὦ Σώκρατες,

οὐ δὲ θαμίζεις ἡμῖν καταβαίνων εἰς τὸν Πει- 328
ραιᾶ· χρῆν μέντοι. εἰ μὲν γὰρ ἐγὼ ἔτι ἐν
δυνάμει ἦν τοῦ ῥᾳδίως πορεύεσθαι πρὸς τὸ
ἄστυ, οὐδὲν ἄν σε ἔδει δεῦρο ἰέναι, | ἀλλ' ἡμεῖς D
ἂν παρὰ σὲ ᾖμεν· νῦν δέ σε χρὴ πυκνότερον
δεῦρο ἰέναι· ὡς εὖ ἴσθι ὅτι ἔμοιγε, ὅσον αἱ
ἄλλαι αἱ κατὰ τὸ σῶμα ἡδοναὶ ἀπομαραίνονται,
τοσοῦτον αὔξονται αἱ περὶ τοὺς λόγους ἐπι-
θυμίαι τε καὶ ἡδοναί. μὴ οὖν ἄλλως ποίει,
ἀλλὰ τοῖσδέ τε τοῖς νεανίαις ξύνισθι καὶ δεῦρο
παρ' ἡμᾶς φοίτα ὡς παρὰ φίλους τε καὶ πάνυ
οἰκείους. Καὶ μήν, ἦν δ' ἐγώ, ὦ Κέφαλε,
χαίρω διαλεγόμενος τοῖς σφόδρα πρεσβύταις.
δοκεῖ γάρ | μοι χρῆναι παρ' αὐτῶν πυνθάνεσθαι, E
ὥσπερ τινὰ ὁδὸν προεληλυθότων, ἣν καὶ ἡμᾶς
ἴσως δεήσει πορεύεσθαι, ποία τίς ἐστιν,—τραχεῖα
καὶ χαλεπή, ἢ ῥᾳδία καὶ εὔπορος. καὶ δὴ
καὶ σοῦ ἡδέως ἂν πυθοίμην, ὅ τι σοι φαίνεται
τοῦτο, ἐπειδὴ ἐνταῦθα ἤδη εἶ τῆς ἡλικίας, ὃ
δὴ ἐπὶ γήραος οὐδῷ φασιν εἶναι οἱ ποιηταί,
πότερον χαλεπὸν τοῦ βίου ἢ πῶς σὺ αὐτὸ
ἐξαγγέλλεις.

Old age brings him privations, but also calm. For this reason it is endurable,

Ἐγώ σοι, ἔφη, νὴ τὸν Δία ἐρῶ, ὦ Σώκρατες,
οἷόν γέ μοι | φαίνεται. πολλάκις γὰρ 329
συνερχόμεθά τινες εἰς ταὐτὸν παρα-
πλησίαν ἡλικίαν ἔχοντες, διασῴζοντες
τὴν παλαιὰν παροιμίαν. οἱ οὖν
πλεῖστοι ἡμῶν ὀλοφύρονται ξυνιόντες, τὰς ἐν
τῇ νεότητι ἡδονὰς ποθοῦντες καὶ ἀναμιμνῃσκό-
μενοι περί τε τἀφροδίσια καὶ περὶ πότους καὶ
εὐωχίας καὶ ἄλλ' ἄττα ἃ τῶν τοιούτων ἔχεται,

329 καὶ ἀγανακτοῦσιν ὡς μεγάλων τινῶν ἀπεστερη-
μένοι καὶ τότε μὲν εὖ ζῶντες, νῦν δὲ οὐδὲ
B ζῶντες· ἔνιοι δὲ καὶ τὰς τῶν | οἰκείων προπη-
λακίσεις τοῦ γήρως ὀδύρονται, καὶ ἐπὶ τούτῳ
δὴ τὸ γῆρας ὑμνοῦσιν ὅσων κακῶν σφίσιν
αἴτιον. ἐμοὶ δὲ δοκοῦσιν, ὦ Σώκρατες, οὗτοι
οὐ τὸ αἴτιον αἰτιᾶσθαι. εἰ γὰρ ἦν τοῦτ' αἴτιον,
κἂν ἐγὼ τὰ αὐτὰ ταῦτα ἐπεπόνθη ἕνεκά γε
γήρως καὶ οἱ ἄλλοι πάντες ὅσοι ἐνταῦθα ἦλθον
ἡλικίας. νῦν δ' ἔγωγε ἤδη ἐντετύχηκα οὐχ
οὕτως ἔχουσιν καὶ ἄλλοις—καὶ δὴ καὶ Σοφοκλεῖ
ποτε τῷ ποιητῇ παρεγενόμην ἐρωτωμένῳ ὑπό
C τινος Πῶς, ἔφη, ὦ | Σοφόκλεις, ἔχεις πρὸς
τἀφροδίσια; καὶ ὅς, Εὐφήμει, ἔφη, ὦ ἄνθρωπε·
ἁσμενέστατα μέντοι αὐτὸ ἀπέφυγον, ὥσπερ
λυττῶντά τινα καὶ ἄγριον δεσπότην ἀποφυγών.
εὖ οὖν μοι καὶ τότε ἔδοξεν ἐκεῖνος εἰπεῖν καὶ
νῦν οὐχ ἧττον. παντάπασι γὰρ τῶν γε τοιού-
των ἐν τῷ γήρᾳ πολλὴ εἰρήνη γίγνεται καὶ
ἐλευθερία—ἐπειδὰν αἱ ἐπιθυμίαι παύσωνται
κατατείνουσαι καὶ χαλάσωσι—παντάπασιν τὸ
D τοῦ Σοφοκλέους γίγνεται— | δεσποτῶν πάνυ
πολλῶν [ἔστι] καὶ μαινομένων ἀπηλλάχθαι.
ἀλλὰ καὶ τούτων πέρι καὶ τῶν γε πρὸς τοὺς
οἰκείους μία τις αἰτία ἐστίν, οὐ τὸ γῆρας, ὦ
Σώκρατες, ἀλλ' ὁ τρόπος τῶν ἀνθρώπων. ἂν
μὲν γὰρ κόσμιοι καὶ εὔκολοι ὦσιν, καὶ τὸ γῆρας
μετρίως ἐστὶν ἐπίπονον· εἰ δὲ μή, καὶ γῆρας,
ὦ Σώκρατες, καὶ νεότης χαλεπὴ τῷ τοιούτῳ
ξυμβαίνει.

Καὶ ἐγὼ ἀγασθεὶς αὐτοῦ εἰπόντος ταῦτα,

not because he has wealth,

βουλόμενος ἔτι λέγειν αὐτὸν ἐκίνουν 329
καὶ εἶπον Ὦ Κέφαλε, | οἶμαί σου E
τοὺς πολλούς, ὅταν ταῦτα λέγῃς, οὐκ ἀποδέ-
χεσθαι, ἀλλ' ἡγεῖσθαί σε ῥᾳδίως τὸ γῆρας
φέρειν οὐ διὰ τὸν τρόπον, ἀλλὰ διὰ τὸ πολλὴν
οὐσίαν κεκτῆσθαι· τοῖς γὰρ πλουσίοις πολλὰ
παραμύθιά φασιν εἶναι. Ἀληθῆ, ἔφη, λέγεις·
οὐ γὰρ ἀποδέχονται. καὶ λέγουσι μέν τι, οὐ
μέντοι γε ὅσον οἴονται, ἀλλὰ τὸ τοῦ Θεμιστο-
κλέους εὖ ἔχει, ὃς τῷ Σεριφίῳ λοιδορουμένῳ
καὶ λέγοντι ὅτι οὐ δι' αὐτὸν | ἀλλὰ διὰ τὴν 330
πόλιν εὐδοκιμοῖ, ἀπεκρίνατο ὅτι οὔτ' ἂν αὐτὸς
Σερίφιος ὢν ὀνομαστὸς ἐγένετο οὔτ' ἐκεῖνος
Ἀθηναῖος. καὶ τοῖς δὴ μὴ πλουσίοις χαλεπῶς
δὲ τὸ γῆρας φέρουσιν εὖ ἔχει ὁ αὐτὸς λόγος,
ὅτι οὔτ' ἂν ὁ ἐπιεικὴς πάνυ τι ῥᾳδίως γῆρας
μετὰ πενίας ἐνέγκοι, οὔθ' ὁ μὴ ἐπιεικὴς πλουτή-
σας εὔκολός ποτ' ἂν ἑαυτῷ γένοιτο. Πότερον
δέ, ἦν δ' ἐγώ, ὦ Κέφαλε, ὧν κέκτησαι τὰ
πλείω παρέλαβες ἢ ἐπεκτήσω; Ποῖ' ἐπεκτη-
σάμην, | ἔφη, ὦ Σώκρατες; μέσος τις γέγονα B
χρηματιστὴς τοῦ τε πάππου καὶ τοῦ πατρός.
ὁ μὲν γὰρ πάππος τε καὶ ὁμώνυμος ἐμοὶ
σχεδόν τι ὅσην ἐγὼ νῦν οὐσίαν κέκτημαι παρα-
λαβὼν πολλάκις τοσαύτην ἐποίησεν, Λυσανίας
δὲ ὁ πατὴρ ἔτι ἐλάττω αὐτὴν ἐποίησε τῆς νῦν
οὔσης· ἐγὼ δὲ ἀγαπῶ, ἐὰν μὴ ἐλάττω καταλίπω
τούτοισιν, ἀλλὰ βραχεῖ γέ τινι πλείω ἢ
παρέλαβον. Οὗ τοι ἕνεκα ἠρόμην, ἦν δ' ἐγώ,
ὅτι μοι ἔδοξας οὐ σφόδρα ἀγαπᾶν τὰ | χρήματα. C
τοῦτο δὲ ποιοῦσιν, ὡς τὸ πολύ, οἳ ἂν μὴ αὐτοὶ

330 κτήσωνται· οἱ δὲ κτησάμενοι διπλῇ ἢ οἱ ἄλλοι ἀσπάζονται αὐτά. ὥσπερ γὰρ οἱ ποιηταὶ τὰ αὑτῶν ποιήματα καὶ οἱ πατέρες τοὺς παῖδας ἀγαπῶσιν, ταύτῃ τε δὴ καὶ οἱ χρηματισάμενοι περὶ τὰ χρήματα σπουδάζουσιν ὡς ἔργον ἑαυτῶν, καὶ κατὰ τὴν χρείαν, ᾗπερ οἱ ἄλλοι. χαλεποὶ οὖν καὶ ξυγγενέσθαι εἰσίν, οὐδὲν ἐθέλοντες ἐπαινεῖν ἀλλ' ἢ τὸν πλοῦτον. Ἀληθῆ, ἔφη, λέγεις.

D Πάνυ μὲν οὖν, | ἦν δ' ἐγώ. ἀλλά μοι ἔτι τοσόνδε εἰπέ· τί μέγιστον οἴει ἀγαθὸν ἀπολελαυκέναι τοῦ πολλὴν οὐσίαν κεκτῆσθαι; Ὅ, ἦ δ' ὅς, ἴσως οὐκ ἂν πολλοὺς πείσαιμι λέγων. εὖ γὰρ ἴσθι, ἔφη, ὦ Σώκρατες, ὅτι, ἐπειδάν τις ἐγγὺς ᾖ τοῦ οἴεσθαι τελευτήσειν, εἰσέρχεται αὐτῷ δέος καὶ φροντὶς περὶ ὧν ἔμπροσθεν οὐκ εἰσῄει. οἵ τε γὰρ λεγόμενοι μῦθοι περὶ τῶν ἐν Ἅιδου, ὡς τὸν ἐνθάδε ἀδικήσαντα δεῖ ἐκεῖ διδόναι δίκην, καταγελώμενοι τέως, τότε δὴ

though it too contributes not a little to happiness in helping us to a life of justice.

E στρέφουσιν | αὐτοῦ τὴν ψυχὴν μὴ ἀληθεῖς ὦσιν· καὶ αὐτὸς ἤτοι ὑπὸ τῆς τοῦ γήρως ἀσθενείας ἢ καὶ ὥσπερ ἤδη ἐγγυτέρω ὢν τῶν ἐκεῖ μᾶλλόν τι καθορᾷ αὐτά. ὑποψίας δ' οὖν καὶ δείματος μεστὸς γίγνεται καὶ ἀναλογίζεται ἤδη καὶ σκοπεῖ, εἴ τινά τι ἠδίκηκεν. ὁ μὲν οὖν εὑρίσκων ἑαυτοῦ ἐν τῷ βίῳ πολλὰ ἀδικήματα καὶ ἐκ τῶν ὕπνων, ὥσπερ οἱ παῖδες, θαμὰ ἐγειρόμενος δειμαίνει καὶ ζῇ μετὰ κακῆς
331 ἐλπίδος· τῷ | δὲ μηδὲν ἑαυτῷ ἄδικον ξυνειδότι ἡδεῖα ἐλπὶς ἀεὶ πάρεστι καὶ ἀγαθὴ γηροτρόφος,

331 ὡς καὶ Πίνδαρος λέγει. χαριέντως γάρ τοι, ὦ Σώκρατες, τοῦτ' ἐκεῖνος εἶπεν, ὅτι ὃς ἂν δικαίως καὶ ὁσίως τὸν βίον διαγάγῃ,

γλυκεῖά οἱ καρδίαν ἀτάλλοισα γηροτρόφος συναορεῖ
ἐλπίς, ἃ μάλιστα θνατῶν πολύστροφον γνώμαν κυβερνᾷ.

εὖ οὖν λέγει θαυμαστῶς ὡς σφόδρα. πρὸς δὴ τοῦτ' ἔγωγε τίθημι τὴν τῶν χρημάτων κτῆσιν πλείστου ἀξίαν εἶναι, οὔ τι | B παντὶ ἀνδρί, ἀλλὰ τῷ ἐπιεικεῖ. τὸ γὰρ μηδὲ ἄκοντά τινα ἐξαπατῆσαι ἢ ψεύσασθαι, μηδ' αὖ, ὀφείλοντα ἢ θεῷ θυσίας τινὰς ἢ ἀνθρώπῳ χρήματα, ἔπειτα ἐκεῖσε ἀπιέναι δεδιότα,—μέγα μέρος εἰς τοῦτο ἡ τῶν χρημάτων κτῆσις συμβάλλεται. ἔχει δὲ καὶ ἄλλας χρείας πολλάς· ἀλλὰ ἕν γε ἀνθ' ἑνὸς οὐκ ἐλάχιστον ἔγωγε θείην ἂν εἰς τοῦτο ἀνδρὶ νοῦν ἔχοντι, ὦ Σώκρατες, πλοῦτον χρησιμώτατον εἶναι.

Socrates: But what is justice?

Παγκάλως, ἦν δ' ἐγώ, λέγεις, ὦ Κέφαλε. | C τοῦτο δ' αὐτό, τὴν δικαιοσύνην, πότερα τὴν ἀλήθειαν αὐτὸ φήσομεν εἶναι ἁπλῶς οὕτως καὶ τὸ ἀποδιδόναι, ἄν τίς τι παρά του λάβῃ, ἢ καὶ αὐτὰ ταῦτα ἔστιν ἐνίοτε μὲν δικαίως, ἐνίοτε δὲ ἀδίκως ποιεῖν; οἷον τοιόνδε λέγω· πᾶς ἄν που εἴποι, εἴ τις λάβοι παρὰ φίλου ἀνδρὸς σωφρονοῦντος ὅπλα, εἰ μανεὶς ἀπαιτοῖ, ὅτι οὔτε χρὴ τὰ τοιαῦτα ἀποδιδόναι, οὔτε δίκαιος ἂν εἴη ὁ ἀποδιδούς, οὐδ' αὖ πρὸς τὸν οὕτως ἔχοντα πάντα ἐθέλων τἀληθῆ λέγειν. | D Ὀρθῶς, ἔφη, λέγεις. Οὐκ ἄρα οὗτος ὅρος ἐστὶν δικαιοσύνης,

331 ἀληθῆ τε λέγειν καὶ ἃ ἂν λάβῃ τις ἀποδιδόναι. Πάνυ μὲν οὖν, ἔφη, ὦ Σώκρατες, ὑπολαβὼν ὁ Πολέμαρχος, εἴπερ γέ τι χρὴ Σιμωνίδῃ πείθεσθαι. Καὶ μέντοι, ἔφη ὁ Κέφαλος, καὶ παραδίδωμι ὑμῖν τὸν λόγον· δεῖ γάρ με ἤδη τῶν ἱερῶν ἐπιμεληθῆναι. Οὐκοῦν, ἔφην ἐγώ, ὁ Πολέμαρχος τῶν γε σῶν κληρονόμος; Πάνυ γε, ἦ δ᾽ ὃς γελάσας· καὶ ἅμα ᾔει πρὸς τὰ ἱερά.

A Sophist's Notion of Justice.

THRASYMACHUS.

Justice is another's good.

343 C Καὶ οὕτω πόρρω εἶ | περί τε τοῦ δικαίου καὶ δικαιοσύνης καὶ ἀδίκου τε καὶ ἀδικίας, ὥστε ἀγνοεῖς ὅτι ἡ μὲν δικαιοσύνη καὶ τὸ δίκαιον ἀλλότριον ἀγαθὸν τῷ ὄντι, τοῦ κρείττονός τε καὶ ἄρχοντος ξυμφέρον, οἰκεία δὲ τοῦ πειθομένου τε καὶ ὑπηρετοῦντος βλάβη, ἡ δὲ ἀδικία τοὐναντίον, καὶ ἄρχει τῶν ὡς ἀληθῶς εὐηθικῶν τε καὶ δικαίων, οἱ δ᾽ ἀρχόμενοι ποιοῦσιν τὸ ἐκείνου ξυμφέρον κρείττονος ὄντος, καὶ εὐδαίμονα ἐκεῖνον
D ποιοῦσιν ὑπηρετοῦντες αὐτῷ, ἑαυτοὺς δὲ | οὐδ᾽ ὁπωστιοῦν. Σκοπεῖσθαι δέ, ὦ εὐηθέστατε Σώκρατες, οὑτωσὶ χρή, ὅτι δίκαιος ἀνὴρ ἀδίκου πανταχοῦ ἔλαττον ἔχει.

The just man has the worst of it everywhere.

πρῶτον μὲν ἐν τοῖς πρὸς ἀλλήλους ξυμβολαίοις, ὅπου ἂν ὁ τοιοῦτος τῷ τοιούτῳ κοινωνήσῃ, οὐδαμοῦ ἂν εὕροις ἐν τῇ διαλύσει τῆς κοινωνίας πλέον ἔχοντα τὸν δίκαιον τοῦ ἀδίκου ἀλλ᾽ ἔλαττον· ἔπειτα ἐν τοῖς πρὸς τὴν πόλιν,

ὅταν τέ τινες εἰσφοραὶ ὦσιν, ὁ μὲν δίκαιος ἀπὸ 343
τῶν ἴσων πλέον εἰσφέρει, ὁ δ' ἔλαττον, ὅταν
τε λήψεις, | ὁ μὲν οὐδέν, ὁ δὲ πολλά, κερδαίνει. E
καὶ γὰρ ὅταν ἀρχήν τινα ἄρχῃ ἑκάτερος, τῷ
μὲν δικαίῳ ὑπάρχει, καὶ εἰ μηδεμία ἄλλη
ζημία, τά γε οἰκεῖα δι' ἀμέλειαν μοχθηροτέρως
ἔχειν, ἐκ δὲ τοῦ δημοσίου μηδὲν ὠφελεῖσθαι
διὰ τὸ δίκαιον εἶναι, πρὸς δὲ τούτοις ἀπεχθέσθαι
τοῖς τε οἰκείοις καὶ τοῖς γνωρίμοις, ὅταν μηδὲν
ἐθέλῃ αὐτοῖς ὑπηρετεῖν παρὰ τὸ δίκαιον· τῷ
δὲ ἀδίκῳ πάντα τούτων τἀναντία ὑπάρχει.
λέγω γὰρ ὅνπερ νῦν δὴ ἔλεγον, τὸν μεγάλα |
δυνάμενον πλεονεκτεῖν. τοῦτον οὖν σκόπει, 344
εἴπερ βούλει κρίνειν ὅσῳ μᾶλλον ξυμφέρει ἰδίᾳ
αὐτῷ ἄδικον εἶναι ἢ τὸ δίκαιον. πάντων δὲ
ῥᾷστα μαθήσει, ἐὰν ἐπὶ τὴν τελεωτάτην ἀδικίαν
ἔλθῃς, ἣ τὸν μὲν ἀδικήσαντα εὐδαι-
μονέστατον ποιεῖ, τοὺς δὲ ἀδικηθέντας
καὶ ἀδικῆσαι οὐκ ἂν ἐθέλοντας ἀθλιω-
τάτους. ἔστι δὲ τοῦτο τυραννίς, ἣ

The more colossal your injustice, the happier you are.

οὐ κατὰ σμικρὸν τἀλλότρια καὶ λάθρᾳ καὶ
βίᾳ ἀφαιρεῖται, καὶ ἱερὰ καὶ ὅσια καὶ ἴδια και
δημόσια, ἀλλὰ ξυλλήβδην· | ὧν ἐφ' ἑκάστῳ B
μέρει ὅταν τις ἀδικήσας μὴ λάθῃ, ζημιοῦταί τε
καὶ ὀνείδη ἔχει τὰ μέγιστα· καὶ γὰρ ἱερόσυλοι
καὶ ἀνδραποδισταὶ καὶ τοιχωρύχοι καὶ ἀπο-
στερηταὶ καὶ κλέπται οἱ κατὰ μέρη ἀδικοῦντες
τῶν τοιούτων κακουργημάτων καλοῦνται· ἐπειδὰν
δέ τις πρὸς τοῖς τῶν πολιτῶν χρήμασιν καὶ
αὐτοὺς ἀνδραποδισάμενος δουλώσηται, ἀντὶ
τούτων τῶν αἰσχρῶν ὀνομάτων εὐδαίμονες καὶ

344 μακάριοι κέκληνται, οὐ μόνον ὑπὸ τῶν πολιτῶν
C | ἀλλὰ καὶ ὑπὸ τῶν ἄλλων, ὅσοι ἂν πύθωνται
αὐτὸν τὴν ὅλην ἀδικίαν ἠδικηκότα· οὐ γὰρ τὸ
ποιεῖν τὰ ἄδικα ἀλλὰ τὸ πάσχειν φοβούμενοι
ὀνειδίζουσιν οἱ ὀνειδίζοντες τὴν ἀδικίαν. οὕτως,
ὦ Σώκρατες, καὶ ἰσχυρότερον καὶ ἐλευθεριώτερον
καὶ δεσποτικώτερον ἀδικία δικαιοσύνης
ἐστὶν ἱκανῶς γιγνομένη, καὶ ὅπερ ἐξ ἀρχῆς
ἔλεγον, τὸ μὲν τοῦ κρείττονος ξυμφέρον τὸ
δίκαιον τυγχάνει ὄν, τὸ δ' ἄδικον ἑαυτῷ λυσιτελοῦν
τε καὶ ξυμφέρον.

II

The Myths of the Poets about the Gods are not to be told to Children.

SOCRATES. ADEIMANTUS.

"Music" and gymnastic make up education.

376 Τίς οὖν ἡ παιδεία; ἢ χαλεπὸν εὑρεῖν βελτίω
E τῆς ὑπὸ τοῦ πολλοῦ χρόνου ηὑρημένης;
ἔστι δέ που ἡ μὲν ἐπὶ σώμασι γυμναστική,
ἡ δ' ἐπὶ ψυχῇ μουσική.
Ἔστιν γάρ. Ἆρ' οὖν οὐ μουσικῇ πρότερον
ἀρξόμεθα παιδεύοντες ἢ γυμναστικῇ; Πῶς δ'
οὔ; Μουσικῆς δ', εἶπον, τίθης λόγους, ἢ οὔ;
Ἔγωγε. Λόγων δὲ διττὸν εἶδος, τὸ μὲν ἀληθές,
377 ψεῦδος δ' ἕτερον; Ναί. Παιδευτέον δ' | ἐν
ἀμφοτέροις, πρότερον δ' ἐν τοῖς ψευδέσιν; Οὐ
μανθάνω, ἔφη, πῶς λέγεις. Οὐ μανθάνεις, ἦν
δ' ἐγώ, ὅτι πρῶτον τοῖς παιδίοις μύθους λέγομεν;

τοῦτο δέ που ὡς τὸ ὅλον εἰπεῖν ψεῦδος, ἔνι δὲ 377
καὶ ἀληθῆ. πρότερον δὲ μύθοις πρὸς τὰ παιδία ἢ γυμνασίοις χρώμεθα. Ἔστι ταῦτα. Τοῦτο δὴ ἔλεγον, ὅτι μουσικῆς πρότερον ἁπτέον ἢ γυμναστικῆς. Ὀρθῶς, ἔφη. Οὐκοῦν οἶσθ' ὅτι ἀρχὴ παντὸς ἔργου μέγιστον, ἄλλως τε καὶ νέῳ καὶ ἁπαλῷ | ὁτῳοῦν; μάλιστα B
γὰρ δὴ τότε πλάττεται καὶ ἐνδύεται τύπος, ὃν ἄν τις βούληται ἐνσημήνασθαι ἑκάστῳ. Κομιδῇ μὲν οὖν. Ἆρ' οὖν ῥᾳδίως οὕτω παρήσομεν τοὺς ἐπιτυχόντας ὑπὸ τῶν ἐπιτυχόντων μύθους πλασθέντας ἀκούειν τοὺς παῖδας καὶ λαμβάνειν ἐν ταῖς ψυχαῖς, ὡς ἐπὶ τὸ πολύ, ἐναντίας δόξας ἐκείναις, ἅς, ἐπειδὰν τελεωθῶσιν, ἔχειν οἰησόμεθα δεῖν αὐτούς; Οὐδ' ὁπωστιοῦν παρήσομεν. Πρῶτον δὴ ἡμῖν, ὡς ἔοικεν, ἐπιστατητέον τοῖς μυθοποιοῖς, καὶ ὃν μὲν ἂν | καλὸν ποιήσωσιν, ἐγκριτέον, ὃν δ' ἂν C
μή, ἀποκριτέον. τοὺς δ' ἐγκριθέντας πείσομεν τὰς τροφούς τε καὶ μητέρας λέγειν τοῖς παισὶ καὶ πλάττειν τὰς ψυχὰς αὐτῶν τοῖς μύθοις πολὺ μᾶλλον ἢ τὰ σώματα ταῖς χερσίν, ὧν δὲ νῦν λέγουσι τοὺς πολλοὺς ἐκβλητέον. Ποίους δή; ἔφη. Ἐν τοῖς μείζοσιν, ἦν δ' ἐγώ, μύθοις ὀψόμεθα καὶ τοὺς ἐλάττους. δεῖ γὰρ δὴ τὸν αὐτὸν τύπον εἶναι καὶ ταὐτὸν δύνασθαι τούς τε μείζους καὶ |
τοὺς ἐλάττους. ἢ οὐκ οἴει; Ἔγωγ', D
ἔφη· ἀλλ' οὐκ ἐννοῶ οὐδὲ τοὺς μείζους, τίνας λέγεις. Οὓς Ἡσίοδός τε, εἶπον, καὶ Ὅμηρος ἡμῖν ἐλεγέτην

The importance of the first steps.

The tales told must be selected.

Those of Homer and Hesiod are false, making the gods do wicked deeds.

377 καὶ οἱ ἄλλοι ποιηταί. οὗτοι γάρ που μύθους
τοῖς ἀνθρώποις ψευδεῖς συντιθέντες ἔλεγόν τε
καὶ λέγουσι. Ποίους δή, ἦ δ᾽ ὅς, καὶ τί
αὐτῶν μεμφόμενος λέγεις; Ὅπερ, ἦν δ᾽ ἐγώ,
χρὴ καὶ πρῶτον καὶ μάλιστα μέμφεσθαι, ἄλλως
E τε καὶ ἐάν τις μὴ καλῶς ψεύδηται. | Τί τοῦτο;
Ὅταν εἰκάζῃ τις κακῶς τῷ λόγῳ περὶ θεῶν τε
καὶ ἡρώων, οἷοί εἰσιν, ὥσπερ γραφεὺς μηδὲν
ἐοικότα γράφων οἷς ἂν ὅμοια βουληθῇ γράψαι.
Καὶ γάρ, ἔφη, ὀρθῶς ἔχει τά γε τοιαῦτα μέμ-
φεσθαι. ἀλλὰ πῶς δὴ λέγομεν καὶ ποῖα;
Πρῶτον μέν, ἦν δ᾽ ἐγώ, τὸ μέγιστον καὶ περὶ
τῶν μεγίστων ψεῦδος ὁ εἰπὼν οὐ καλῶς ἐψεύ-
σατο, ὡς Οὐρανός τε ἠργάσατο ἅ φησι δρᾶσαι
αὐτὸν Ἡσίοδος, ὅ τε αὖ Κρόνος ὡς ἐτιμωρή-
378 σατο αὐτόν· τὰ δὲ δὴ | τοῦ Κρόνου ἔργα καὶ
πάθη ὑπὸ τοῦ ὑέος, οὐδ᾽ ἂν εἰ ἦν ἀληθῆ
ᾤμην δεῖν ῥᾳδίως οὕτω λέγεσθαι πρὸς ἄφρονάς
τε καὶ νέους, ἀλλὰ μάλιστα μὲν σιγᾶσθαι, εἰ
δὲ ἀνάγκη τις ἦν λέγειν, δι᾽ ἀπορρήτων ἀκούειν
ὡς ὀλιγίστους, θυσαμένους οὐ χοῖρον, ἀλλά τι
μέγα καὶ ἄπορον θῦμα, ὅπως ὅτι ἐλαχίστοις
συνέβη ἀκοῦσαι. Καὶ γάρ, ἦ δ᾽ ὅς, οὗτοί γε
οἱ λόγοι χαλεποί. Καὶ οὐ λεκτέοι γ᾽, ἔφην,
B ὦ Ἀδείμαντε, | ἐν τῇ ἡμετέρᾳ πόλει· οὐδὲ λεκ-
τέον νέῳ ἀκούοντι ὡς ἀδικῶν τὰ ἔσχατα οὐδὲν
ἂν θαυμαστὸν ποιοῖ, οὐδ᾽ αὖ ἀδικοῦντα πατέρα
κολάζων παντὶ τρόπῳ, ἀλλὰ δρῴη ἂν ὅπερ
θεῶν οἱ πρῶτοί τε καὶ μέγιστοι. Οὐ μὰ τὸν
Δία, ἦ δ᾽ ὅς, οὐδὲ αὐτῷ μοι δοκεῖ ἐπιτήδεια
εἶναι λέγειν. Οὐδέ γε, ἦν δ᾽ ἐγώ, τὸ παράπαν,

ὡς θεοὶ θεοῖς πολεμοῦσί τε καὶ ἐπιβουλεύουσι 378
καὶ μάχονται (οὐδὲ γὰρ ἀληθῆ), | εἴ γε δεῖ C
ἡμῖν τοὺς μέλλοντας τὴν πόλιν φυλάξειν αἴσχι-
στον νομίζειν τὸ ῥᾳδίως ἀλλήλοις ἀπεχθάνεσθαι,
πολλοῦ δεῖ γιγαντομαχίας τε μυθολογητέον
αὐτοῖς καὶ ποικιλτέον, καὶ ἄλλας ἔχθρας πολλὰς
καὶ παντοδαπὰς θεῶν τε καὶ ἡρώων πρὸς
συγγενεῖς τε καὶ οἰκείους αὐτῶν. ἀλλ' εἴ πως
μέλλομεν πείσειν ὡς οὐδεὶς πώποτε πολίτης
ἕτερος ἑτέρῳ ἀπήχθετο οὐδ' ἐστὶ τοῦτο ὅσιον,
τοιαῦτα λεκτέα μᾶλλον πρὸς τὰ παιδία εὐθὺς
καὶ γέρουσι | καὶ γραυσί, καὶ πρεσβυτέροις D
γιγνομένοις καὶ τοὺς ποιητὰς ἐγγὺς τούτων
ἀναγκαστέον λογοποιεῖν. Ἥρας δὲ δεσμοὺς
ὑπὸ ὑέος καὶ Ἡφαίστου ῥίψεις ὑπὸ πατρός
(μέλλοντος τῇ μητρὶ τυπτομένῃ ἀμύνειν), καὶ
θεομαχίας ὅσας Ὅμηρος πεποίηκεν οὐ παρα-
δεκτέον εἰς τὴν πόλιν, οὔτ' ἐν ὑπονοίαις πεποιη-
μένας οὔτε ἄνευ ὑπονοιῶν. ὁ γὰρ νέος οὐχ
οἷόστε κρίνειν ὅ τι τε ὑπόνοια καὶ ὃ
μή, ἀλλ' ἃ ἂν τηλικοῦτος ὢν λάβῃ
ἐν ταῖς δόξαις, δυσέκνιπτά | τε καὶ E
ἀμετάστατα φιλεῖ γίγνεσθαι. ὧν δὴ ἴσως
ἕνεκα περὶ παντὸς ποιητέον, ἃ πρῶτα ἀκούου-
σιν ὅτι κάλλιστα μεμυθολογημένα πρὸς ἀρετὴν
ἀκούειν.

A child does not see the hidden meaning.

Ἔχει γάρ, ἔφη, λόγον. ἀλλ' εἴ τις αὖ καὶ
ταῦτα ἐρωτῴη ἡμᾶς αὐτά, ἅττα ἐστὶ καὶ τίνες
οἱ μῦθοι, τίνας ἂν φαῖμεν; καὶ ἐγὼ εἶπον Ὦ
Ἀδείμαντε, οὐκ ἐσμὲν ποιηταὶ ἐγώ τε καὶ σὺ ἐν
τῷ παρόντι, | ἀλλ' οἰκισταὶ πόλεως. οἰκισταῖς 379

379 δὲ τοὺς μὲν τύπους προσήκει εἰδέναι, ἐν οἷς
δεῖ μυθολογεῖν τοὺς ποιητάς, παρ᾽ οὓς ἐὰν
ποιῶσιν οὐκ ἐπιτρεπτέον, οὐ μὴν αὐτοῖς γε
ποιητέον μύθους. Ὀρθῶς, ἔφη· ἀλλ᾽ αὐτὸ δὴ
τοῦτο, οἱ τύποι περὶ θεολογίας τίνες ἂν εἶεν;
Τοιοίδε πού τινες, ἦν δ᾽ ἐγώ· οἷος τυγχάνει ὁ
θεὸς ὤν, ἀεὶ δήπου ἀποδοτέον, ἐάντε
τις αὐτὸν ἐν ἔπεσιν ποιῇ, ἐάντε ἐν
μέλεσιν, ἐάντε ἐν τραγῳδίᾳ. Δεῖ

God must be made good, as he is.

B γάρ. Οὐκοῦν ἀγαθὸς ὅ γε θεὸς τῷ ὄντι | τε
καὶ λεκτέον οὕτω; Τί μήν; Ἀλλὰ μὴν οὐδέν
γε τῶν ἀγαθῶν βλαβερόν· ἦ γάρ; Οὔ μοι
δοκεῖ. Ἆρ᾽ οὖν, ὃ μὴ βλαβερόν, βλάπτει;
Οὐδαμῶς. Ὃ δὲ μὴ βλάπτει, κακόν τι ποιεῖ;
Οὐδὲ τοῦτο. Ὃ δέ γε μηδὲν κακὸν ποιεῖ, οὐδ᾽
ἄν τινος εἴη κακοῦ αἴτιον; Πῶς γάρ; Τί δέ;
ὠφέλιμον τὸ ἀγαθόν; Ναί. Αἴτιον ἄρα εὐ-
πραγίας; Ναί. Οὐκ ἄρα πάντων γε αἴτιον τὸ
ἀγαθόν, ἀλλὰ τῶν μὲν εὖ ἐχόντων αἴτιον, τῶν
C δὲ κακῶν ἀναίτιον. Παντελῶς | γ᾽, ἔφη. Οὐδ᾽
ἄρα, ἦν δ᾽ ἐγώ, ὁ θεός, ἐπειδὴ ἀγαθός, πάντων
ἂν εἴη αἴτιος, ὡς οἱ πολλοὶ λέγουσιν, ἀλλ᾽
ὀλίγων μὲν τοῖς ἀνθρώποις αἴτιος, πολλῶν δὲ
ἀναίτιος (πολὺ γὰρ ἐλάττω τἀγαθὰ τῶν κακῶν
ἡμῖν)· καὶ τῶν μὲν ἀγαθῶν οὐδένα ἄλλον
αἰτιατέον, τῶν δὲ κακῶν ἄλλ᾽ ἄττα δεῖ ζητεῖν
τὰ αἴτια, ἀλλ᾽ οὐ τὸν θεόν. Ἀληθέστατα, ἔφη,
δοκεῖς μοι λέγειν. Οὐκ ἄρα, ἦν δ᾽ ἐγώ,
ἀποδεκτέον οὔτε Ὁμήρου οὔτ᾽ ἄλλου ποιητοῦ
D ταύτην | τὴν ἁμαρτίαν περὶ τοὺς θεοὺς ἀνοήτως
ἁμαρτάνοντος καὶ λέγοντος ὡς δοιοὶ πίθοι

κατακείαται ἐν Διὸς οὔδει 379
κηρῶν ἔμπλειοι, ὁ μὲν ἐσθλῶν, αὐτὰρ ὃ δειλῶν·

καὶ ᾧ μὲν ἂν μίξας ὁ Ζεὺς δῷ ἀμφοτέρων,

ἄλλοτε μέν τε κακῷ ὅ γε κύρεται, ἄλλοτε δ' ἐσθλῷ,

ᾧ δ' ἂν μή, ἀλλ' ἄκρατα τὰ ἕτερα, τὸν δὲ

κακὴ βούβρωστις ἐπὶ χθόνα δῖαν ἐλαύνει·

| οὐδ' ὡς ταμίας ἡμῖν Ζεὺς E

ἀγαθῶν τε κακῶν τε τέτυκται.

Τὴν δὲ τῶν ὅρκων καὶ σπονδῶν σύγχυσιν, ἣν ὁ Πάνδαρος συνέχεεν, ἐάν τις φῇ δι' Ἀθηνᾶς τε καὶ Διὸς γεγονέναι, οὐκ ἐπαινεσόμεθα· οὐδὲ θεῶν ἔριν τε καὶ κρίσιν | διὰ Θέμιτός τε 380
καὶ Διός· οὐδ' αὖ, ὡς Αἰσχύλος λέγει, ἐατέον ἀκούειν τοὺς νέους ὅτι

θεὸς μὲν αἰτίαν φύει βροτοῖς,
ὅταν κακῶσαι δῶμα παμπήδην θέλῃ.

ἀλλ' ἐάν τις ποιῇ, ἐν οἷς ταῦτα τὰ ἰαμβεῖα ἔνεστι, τὰ τῆς Νιόβης πάθη ἢ τὰ Πελοπιδῶν ἢ τὰ Τρωϊκὰ ἤ τι ἄλλο τῶν τοιούτων, ἢ οὐ θεοῦ ἔργα ἐατέον αὐτὰ λέγειν, ἢ εἰ θεοῦ, ἐξευρετέον αὐτοῖς σχεδὸν ὃν νῦν ἡμεῖς λόγον ζητοῦμεν, καὶ λεκτέον ὡς ὁ μὲν θεὸς δίκαιά τε καὶ ἀγαθὰ | ηργάζετο, οἱ δὲ ὠνίναντο B
κολαζόμενοι. ὡς δὲ ἄθλιοι μὲν οἱ δίκην διδόντες, ἦν δὲ δὴ ὁ δρῶν ταῦτα θεός, οὐκ ἐατέον λέγειν τὸν ποιητήν· ἀλλ' εἰ μὲν ὅτι ἐδεήθησαν κολάσεως λέγοιεν, ὡς ἄθλιοι

Good he is, even when he punishes.

380 οἱ κακοί, διδόντες δὲ δίκην ὠφελοῦντο ὑπὸ τοῦ θεοῦ, ἐατέον· κακῶν δὲ αἴτιον φάναι θεόν τινι γίγνεσθαι ἀγαθὸν ὄντα, — διαμαχετέον παντὶ τρόπῳ μήτε τινὰ λέγειν ταῦτα ἐν τῇ αὑτοῦ πόλει, εἰ μέλλει εὐνομήσεσθαι, μήτε τινὰ ἀκούειν,
C μήτε νεώτερον | μήτε πρεσβύτερον, μήτε ἐν μέτρῳ μήτε ἄνευ μέτρου μυθολογοῦντα, ὡς οὔτε ὅσια ἂν λεγόμενα, εἰ λέγοιτο, οὔτε ξύμφορα ἡμῖν οὔτε σύμφωνα αὐτὰ αὑτοῖς. Σύμψηφός σοί εἰμι, ἔφη, τούτου τοῦ νόμου, καί μοι ἀρέσκει. Οὗτος μὲν τοίνυν, ἦν δ' ἐγώ, εἷς ἂν εἴη τῶν περὶ θεοὺς νόμων τε καὶ τύπων, ἐν ᾧ δεήσει τοὺς λέγοντας λέγειν καὶ τοὺς ποιοῦντας ποιεῖν, μὴ πάντων αἴτιον τὸν θεὸν ἀλλὰ τῶν ἀγαθῶν. Καὶ μάλ', ἔφη, ἀπόχρη.

III

Youth's Surroundings should be Fair.

401 Ἆρ' οὖν τοῖς ποιηταῖς ἡμῖν μόνον | ἐπι-
B στατητέον καὶ προσαναγκαστέον τὴν τοῦ ἀγαθοῦ εἰκόνα ἤθους ἐμποιεῖν τοῖς ποιήμασιν (ἢ μὴ παρ' ἡμῖν ποιεῖν), ἢ καὶ τοῖς ἄλλοις δημιουργοῖς ἐπιστατητέον καὶ διακωλυτέον τὸ κακόηθες τοῦτο καὶ ἀκόλαστον καὶ ἀνελεύθερον καὶ ἄσχημον μήτε ἐν εἰκόσι ζῴων μήτε ἐν οἰκοδομήμασι μήτε ἐν ἄλλῳ μηδενὶ δημιουργουμένῳ ἐμποιεῖν, ἢ ὁ μὴ οἷόστε ὢν οὐκ ἐατέος παρ' ἡμῖν δημιουργεῖν, ἵνα μὴ ἐν κακίας εἰκόσι τρεφό-

Fair works of art should feed his soul.

μενοι ἡμῖν οἱ φύλακες ὥσπερ ἐν κακῇ βοτάνῃ, 401
| πολλὰ ἑκάστης ἡμέρας κατὰ σμικρὸν ἀπὸ C
πολλῶν δρεπόμενοί τε καὶ νεμόμενοι, ἕν τι
ξυνιστάντες λανθάνωσι κακὸν μέγα ἐν τῇ αὑτῶν
ψυχῇ· ἀλλ' ἐκείνους ζητητέον τοὺς δημιουργοὺς
τοὺς εὐφυῶς δυναμένους ἰχνεύειν τὴν τοῦ καλοῦ
τε καὶ εὐσχήμονος φύσιν, ἵνα ὥσπερ ἐν ὑγιεινῷ
τόπῳ οἰκοῦντες οἱ νέοι ἀπὸ παντὸς ὠφελῶνται,
ὁπόθεν ἂν αὐτοῖς ἀπὸ τῶν καλῶν ἔργων ἢ πρὸς
ὄψιν ἢ πρὸς ἀκοήν τι προσβάλῃ, ὥσπερ αὔρα
φέρουσα ἀπὸ χρηστῶν τόπων ὑγίειαν, καὶ εὐθὺς
| ἐκ παίδων λανθάνῃ εἰς ὁμοιότητά τε καὶ φιλίαν D
καὶ ξυμφωνίαν τῷ καλῷ λόγῳ ἄγουσα; Πολὺ
γὰρ ἄν, ἔφη, κάλλιστα οὕτω τραφεῖεν. Ἆρ'
οὖν, ἦν δ' ἐγώ, ὦ Γλαύκων, τούτων ἕνεκα
κυριωτάτη ἐν μουσικῇ τροφή, ὅτι μάλιστα καταδύεται
εἰς τὸ ἐντὸς τῆς ψυχῆς ὅ τε ῥυθμὸς καὶ
ἁρμονία, καὶ ἐρρωμενέστατα ἅπτεται αὐτῆς,
φέροντα τὴν εὐσχημοσύνην, καὶ ποιεῖ εὐσχήμονα,
ἐάν τις ὀρθῶς τραφῇ, εἰ δὲ μή, τοὐναντίον;
| καὶ ὅτι αὖ τῶν παραλειπομένων καὶ E
μὴ καλῶς δημιουργηθέντων ἢ μὴ καλῶς φύντων
ὀξύτατ' ἂν αἰσθάνοιτο ὁ ἐκεῖ τραφεὶς ὡς ἔδει, καὶ
ὀρθῶς δὴ χαίρων καὶ δυσχεραίνων τὰ μὲν καλὰ
ἐπαινοῖ καὶ καταδεχόμενος εἰς τὴν ψυχὴν τρέφοιτ'
ἂν ἀπ' αὐτῶν καὶ γίγνοιτο καλός τε κἀγαθός, | τὰ 402
δ' αἰσχρὰ ψέγοι τ' ἂν ὀρθῶς καὶ μισοῖ ἔτι νέος
ὤν, πρὶν λόγον δυνατὸς εἶναι λαβεῖν, ἐλθόντος δὲ
τοῦ λόγου ἀσπάζοιτ' ἂν αὐτὸν γνωρίζων δι' οἰκειότητα
μάλιστα ὁ οὕτω τραφείς; Ἐμοὶ γοῦν δοκεῖ,
ἔφη, τῶν τοιούτων ἕνεκα ἐν μουσικῇ εἶναι ἡ τροφή.

There is too much Doctoring.

With modern physic sickliness lives to old age—if rich.

405 C Τὸ δὲ ἰατρικῆς, ἦν δ᾽ ἐγώ, δεῖσθαι, ὅτι μὴ τραυμάτων ἕνεκα ἤ τινων ἐπετείων
D νοσημάτων ἐπιπεσόντων, ἀλλὰ | δι᾽ ἀργίαν τε καὶ δίαιταν οἵαν διήλθομεν, ῥευμάτων τε καὶ πνευμάτων ὥσπερ λίμνας ἐμπιμπλαμένους φύσας τε καὶ κατάρρους νοσήμασιν ὀνόματα τίθεσθαι ἀναγκάζειν τοὺς κομψοὺς Ἀσκληπιάδας, οὐκ αἰσχρὸν δοκεῖ; Καὶ μάλ᾽, ἔφη, ὡς ἀληθῶς καινὰ ταῦτα καὶ ἄτοπα νοσημάτων ὀνόματα. Οἷα, ἦν δ᾽ ἐγώ, ὡς οἶμαι, οὐκ ἦν ἐπ᾽ Ἀσκληπιοῦ· τεκμαίρομαι
E δέ, ὅτι αὐτοῦ οἱ ὑεῖς ἐν Τροίᾳ | Εὐρυπύλῳ τετρωμένῳ ἐπ᾽ οἶνον Πράμνειον ἄλφιτα πολλὰ
406 ἐπιπασθέντα καὶ τυρὸν ἐπιξυσθέντα, | ἃ δὴ δοκεῖ φλεγματώδη εἶναι, οὐκ ἐμέμψαντο τῇ δούσῃ πιεῖν, οὐδὲ Πατρόκλῳ τῷ ἰωμένῳ ἐπετίμησαν. Καὶ μὲν δή, ἔφη, ἄτοπόν γε τὸ πῶμα οὕτως ἔχοντι. Οὔκ, εἰ γ᾽ ἐννοεῖς, εἶπον, ὅτι τῇ παιδαγωγικῇ τῶν νοσημάτων ταύτῃ τῇ νῦν ἰατρικῇ πρὸ τοῦ Ἀσκληπιάδαι οὐκ ἐχρῶντο, ὥς φασι, πρὶν Ἡρόδικον γενέσθαι· Ἡρόδικος δὲ παιδοτρίβης ὢν καὶ νοσώδης γενόμενος, μείξας γυμναστικὴν ἰατρικῇ, ἀπέκναισε πρῶτον
B μὲν | καὶ μάλιστα ἑαυτόν, ἔπειτ᾽ ἄλλους ὕστερον πολλούς. Πῇ δή; ἔφη. Μακρόν, ἦν δ᾽ ἐγώ, τὸν θάνατον αὑτῷ ποιήσας. παρακολουθῶν γὰρ τῷ νοσήματι θανασίμῳ ὄντι οὔτε ἰάσασθαι, οἶμαι, οἷός τ᾽ ἦν ἑαυτόν, ἐν ἀσχολίᾳ τε πάντων ἰατρευόμενος διὰ βίου ἔζη ἀποκναιόμενος, εἴ τι

τῆς εἰωθυίας διαίτης ἐκβαίη, δυσθανατῶν δὲ 406
ὑπὸ σοφίας εἰς γῆρας ἀφίκετο. Καλὸν ἄρα
τὸ γέρας, ἔφη, τῆς τέχνης ἠνέγκατο. Οἷον
εἰκός, ἦν δ' ἐγώ, τὸν | μὴ εἰδότα ὅτι Ἀσκλη- C
πιὸς οὐκ ἀγνοίᾳ οὐδὲ ἀπειρίᾳ τούτου τοῦ εἴδους
τῆς ἰατρικῆς τοῖς ἐκγόνοις οὐ κατέδειξεν αὐτό,
ἀλλ' εἰδὼς ὅτι πᾶσι τοῖς εὐνομουμένοις ἔργον
τι ἑκάστῳ ἐν τῇ πόλει προστέτακται, ὃ ἀναγ-
καῖον ἐργάζεσθαι, καὶ οὐδενὶ σχολὴ διὰ βίου
κάμνειν ἰατρευομένῳ. ὃ ἡμεῖς γελοίως ἐπὶ μὲν
τῶν δημιουργῶν αἰσθανόμεθα, ἐπὶ δὲ τῶν
πλουσίων τε καὶ εὐδαιμόνων δοκούντων εἶναι
οὐκ αἰσθανόμεθα. Πῶς; ἔφη.

Τέκτων μέν, ἦν δ' | ἐγώ, κάμνων ἀξιοῖ παρὰ D
τοῦ ἰατροῦ φάρμακον πιὼν ἐξεμέσαι
τὸ νόσημα ἢ κάτω καθαρθεὶς ἢ
καύσει ἢ τομῇ χρησάμενος ἀπηλ-
λάχθαι· ἐὰν δέ τις αὐτῷ μακρὰν δίαιταν προσ-
τάττῃ, πιλίδιά τε περὶ τὴν κεφαλὴν περιτιθεὶς
καὶ τὰ τούτοις ἑπόμενα, ταχὺ εἶπεν ὅτι οὐ
σχολὴ κάμνειν οὐδὲ λυσιτελεῖ οὕτω ζῆν, νοσή-
ματι τὸν νοῦν προσέχοντα, τῆς δὲ προκειμένης
ἐργασίας ἀμελοῦντα. καὶ μετὰ ταῦτα χαίρειν
εἰπὼν τῷ τοιούτῳ ἰατρῷ, | εἰς τὴν εἰωθυῖαν E
δίαιταν ἐμβάς, ὑγιὴς γενόμενος ζῇ τὰ ἑαυτοῦ
πράττων· ἐὰν δὲ μὴ ἱκανὸν ᾖ τὸ σῶμα ὑπενεγ-
κεῖν, τελευτήσας πραγμάτων ἀπηλλάγη. Καὶ
τῷ τοιούτῳ μέν γ', ἔφη, δοκεῖ πρέπειν οὕτω
ἰατρικῇ χρῆσθαι. Ἆρ', ἦν δ' ἐγώ, ὅτι ἦν τι
αὐτῷ ἔργον, | ὃ εἰ μὴ πράττοι, οὐκ ἐλυσιτέλει 407
ζῆν; Δῆλον, ἔφη. Ὁ δὲ δὴ πλούσιος, ὥς

But the artisan has no time for physic.

407 φαμεν, οὐδὲν ἔχει τοιοῦτον ἔργον προκείμενον,
οὗ ἀναγκαζομένῳ ἀπέχεσθαι ἀβίωτον. Οὔκουν
δὴ λέγεταί γε. Φωκυλίδου γάρ, ἦν δ' ἐγώ, οὐκ
ἀκούεις, πῶς φησι δεῖν, ὅταν τῳ ἤδη βίος ᾖ,
ἀρετὴν ἀσκεῖν. Οἶμαι δέ γε, ἔφη, καὶ πρό-
τερον. Μηδέν, εἶπον, περὶ τούτου αὐτῷ μαχώ-
μεθα, ἀλλ' ἡμᾶς αὐτοὺς διδάξωμεν, πότερον
μελετητέον τοῦτο τῷ πλουσίῳ καὶ ἀβίωτον τῷ
B μὴ | μελετῶντι, ἢ νοσοτροφία τεκτονικῇ μὲν καὶ
ταῖς ἄλλαις τέχναις ἐμπόδιον τῇ προσέξει τοῦ
νοῦ, τὸ δὲ Φωκυλίδου παρακέλευμα
οὐδὲν ἐμποδίζει. Ναὶ μὰ τὸν Δία, ἦ
δ' ὅς, σχεδόν γέ τι πάντων μάλιστα ἥ
γε περαιτέρω γυμναστικῆς ἡ περιττὴ
αὕτη ἐπιμέλεια τοῦ σώματος. Καὶ γὰρ πρὸς
οἰκονομίας καὶ πρὸς στρατείας καὶ πρὸς ἑδραίους
ἐν πόλει ἀρχὰς δύσκολος. τὸ δὲ δὴ μέγιστον,
ὅτι καὶ πρὸς μαθήσεις ἁστινασοῦν καὶ ἐννοήσεις
C τε καὶ μελέτας | πρὸς ἑαυτὸν χαλεπή, κεφαλῆς
τινὰς ἀεὶ διατάσεις καὶ ἰλίγγους ὑποπτεύουσα
καὶ αἰτιωμένη ἐκ φιλοσοφίας ἐγγίγνεσθαι, ὥστε,
ὅπῃ ταύτῃ ἀρετὴ ἀσκεῖται καὶ δοκιμάζεται,
πάντῃ ἐμπόδιος· κάμνειν γὰρ οἴεσθαι ποιεῖ ἀεὶ
καὶ ὠδίνοντα μήποτε λήγειν περὶ τοῦ σώματος.
Εἰκός γ', ἔφη. Οὐκοῦν ταῦτα γιγνώσκοντα
φῶμεν καὶ Ἀσκληπιὸν τοὺς μὲν φύσει τε καὶ
διαίτῃ ὑγιεινῶς ἔχοντας τὰ σώματα
D νόσημα δέ τι ἀποκεκριμένον | ἴσχον-
τας ἐν αὑτοῖς, τούτοις μὲν καὶ ταύτῃ
τῇ ἕξει καταδεῖξαι ἰατρικήν, φαρμάκοις τε καὶ
τομαῖς τὰ νοσήματα ἐκβάλλοντα αὐτῶν τὴν

Nursing one's ailments hinders any vocation, active or mental.

Asclepius would not save the sickly.

εἰωθυῖαν προστάττειν δίαιταν, ἵνα μὴ τὰ πολι- 407
τικὰ βλάπτοι, τὰ δ᾽ εἴσω διὰ παντὸς νενοσηκότα
σώματα οὐκ ἐπιχειρεῖν διαίταις κατὰ σμικρὸν
ἀπαντλοῦντα καὶ ἐπιχέοντα μακρὸν καὶ κακὸν
βίον ἀνθρώπῳ ποιεῖν, καὶ ἔκγονα αὐτῶν, ὡς τὸ
εἰκός, ἕτερα τοιαῦτα φυτεύειν, ἀλλὰ τὸν μὴ
δυνάμενον | ἐν τῇ καθεστηκυίᾳ περιόδῳ ζῆν μὴ E
οἴεσθαι δεῖν θεραπεύειν, ὡς οὔτε αὑτῷ οὔτε πόλει
λυσιτελῆ; Πολιτικόν, ἔφη, λέγεις Ἀσκληπιόν.
Δῆλον, ἦν δ᾽ ἐγώ, ὅτι τοιοῦτος ἦν· καὶ οἱ
παῖδες αὐτοῦ, οὐχ ὁρᾷς ὡς καὶ ἐν Τροίᾳ
ἀγαθοὶ πρὸς τὸν πόλεμον | ἐφάνησαν, καὶ τῇ 408
ἰατρικῇ, ὡς ἐγὼ λέγω, ἐχρῶντο; ἢ οὐ μέμνησαι
ὅτι καὶ τῷ Μενέλεῳ ἐκ τοῦ τραύματος οὗ ὁ
Πάνδαρος ἔβαλεν

αἷμ᾽ ἐκμύζησάν τ᾽ ἐπί τ᾽ ἤπια φάρμακ᾽ ἔπασσον,

ὅ τι δ᾽ ἐχρῆν μετὰ τοῦτο ἢ πιεῖν ἢ φαγεῖν
οὐδὲν μᾶλλον ἢ τῷ Εὐρυπύλῳ προσέταττον,
ὡς ἱκανῶν ὄντων τῶν φαρμάκων ἰάσασθαι
ἄνδρας πρὸ τῶν τραυμάτων ὑγιεινούς τε καὶ
κοσμίους ἐν διαίτῃ, | κἂν εἰ τύχοιεν ἐν τῷ B
παραχρῆμα κυκεῶνα πιόντες, νοσώδη δὲ φύσει
τε καὶ ἀκόλαστον οὔτε αὐτοῖς οὔτε τοῖς ἄλλοις
ᾤοντο λυσιτελεῖν ζῆν, οὐδ᾽ ἐπὶ τούτοις τὴν
τέχνην δεῖν εἶναι, οὐδὲ θεραπευτέον αὐτούς, οὐδ᾽
εἰ Μίδου πλουσιώτεροι εἶεν. Πάνυ κομψούς,
ἔφη, λέγεις Ἀσκληπιοῦ παῖδας.

The Story of the Metals in Men,—in the Rulers, Gold.

414 Τίς ἂν οὖν ἡμῖν, ἦν δ' ἐγώ, μηχανὴ γένοιτο
B τῶν ψευδῶν τῶν ἐν δέοντι γιγνομένων, ὧν νῦν
C δὴ ἐλέγομεν, γενναῖόν τι ἓν ψευδομένους | πεῖσαι μάλιστα μὲν καὶ αὐτοὺς τοὺς ἄρχοντας, εἰ δὲ μή, τὴν ἄλλην πόλιν; Ποῖόν τι; ἔφη. Μηδὲν καινόν, ἦν δ' ἐγώ, ἀλλὰ Φοινικικόν τι, πρότερον μὲν ἤδη πολλαχοῦ γεγονός, ὥς φασιν οἱ ποιηταὶ καὶ πεπείκασιν, ἐφ' ἡμῶν δὲ οὐ γεγονὸς οὐδ' οἶδα εἰ γενόμενον ἄν, πεῖσαι δὲ συχνῆς πειθοῦς. Ὡς ἔοικας, ἔφη, ὀκνοῦντι λέγειν. Δόξω δέ σοι, ἦν δ' ἐγώ, καὶ μάλ' εἰκότως ὀκνεῖν, ἐπειδὰν εἴπω.

A noble fiction.

D Λέγ', ἔφη, καὶ μὴ φοβοῦ. Λέγω δή· | καίτοι οὐκ οἶδα ὁποίᾳ τόλμῃ ἢ ποίοις λόγοις χρώμενος ἐρῶ· καὶ ἐπιχειρήσω πρῶτον μὲν αὐτοὺς τοὺς ἄρχοντας πείθειν καὶ τοὺς στρατιώτας, ἔπειτα δὲ καὶ τὴν ἄλλην πόλιν, ὡς ἄρ' ἃ ἡμεῖς αὐτοὺς ἐτρέφομέν τε καὶ ἐπαιδεύομεν, ὥσπερ ὀνείρατα ἐδόκουν ταῦτα πάντα πάσχειν τε καὶ γίγνεσθαι περὶ αὐτούς, ἦσαν δὲ τότε τῇ ἀληθείᾳ ὑπὸ γῆς ἐντὸς πλαττόμενοι καὶ τρεφόμενοι καὶ αὐτοὶ καὶ τὰ ὅπλα αὐτῶν

You men are sons of Earth,

E καὶ ἡ ἄλλη σκευὴ δημιουργουμένη ἔτι. | ἤδη δὲ παντελῶς ἐξειργασμένοι ἦσαν, καὶ ἡ γῆ αὐτοὺς μήτηρ οὖσα ἀνῆκεν, καὶ νῦν δεῖ ὡς περὶ μητρὸς καὶ τροφοῦ τῆς χώρας ἐν ᾗ εἰσὶ βουλεύεσθαί τε καὶ ἀμύνειν αὐτούς, ἐάν τις ἐπ' αὐτὴν ἴῃ, καὶ ὑπὲρ τῶν ἄλλων πολιτῶν ὡς ἀδελφῶν

ὄντων καὶ γηγενῶν διανοεῖσθαι. Οὐκ ἐτός, ἔφη, 414
πάλαι ᾐσχύνου τὸ ψεῦδος λέγειν. Πάνυ, ἦν
δ' ἐγώ, | εἰκότως· ἀλλ' ὅμως ἄκουε καὶ τὸ 415
λοιπὸν τοῦ μύθου. ἐστὲ μὲν γὰρ δὴ πάντες
οἱ ἐν τῇ πόλει ἀδελφοί, ὡς φήσομεν πρὸς αὐτοὺς
μυθολογοῦντες, ἀλλ' ὁ θεὸς πλάττων, ὅσοι μὲν
ὑμῶν ἱκανοὶ ἄρχειν, χρυσὸν ἐν τῇ γενέσει
ξυνέμειξεν αὐτοῖς, διὸ τιμιώτατοί
εἰσιν· ὅσοι δ' ἐπίκουροι, ἄργυρον·
σίδηρον δὲ καὶ χαλκὸν τοῖς τε γεωρ-
γοῖς καὶ τοῖς ἄλλοις δημιουργοῖς. ἅτε οὖν
ξυγγενεῖς ὄντες πάντες τὸ μὲν πολὺ ὁμοίους ἂν
ὑμῖν αὐτοῖς γεννῷτε, ἔστι δ' ὅτε ἐκ | χρυσοῦ B
γεννηθείη ἂν ἀργυροῦν καὶ ἐξ ἀργυροῦ χρυσοῦν
ἔκγονον καὶ τἆλλα πάντα οὕτως ἐξ ἀλλήλων.
τοῖς οὖν ἄρχουσι καὶ πρῶτον καὶ μάλιστα
παραγγέλλει ὁ θεός, ὅπως μηδενὸς οὕτω φύλακες
ἀγαθοὶ ἔσονται μηδ' οὕτω σφόδρα φυλάξουσι
μηδὲν ὡς τοὺς ἐκγόνους, ὅ τι αὐτοῖς τούτων ἐν
ταῖς ψυχαῖς παραμέμικται, καὶ ἐάντε σφέτερος
ἔκγονος ὑπόχαλκος ἢ ὑποσίδηρος γένηται,
μηδενὶ | τρόπῳ κατελεήσουσιν, ἀλλὰ τὴν τῇ C
φύσει προσήκουσαν τιμὴν ἀποδόντες ὤσουσιν
εἰς δημιουργοὺς ἢ εἰς γεωργούς, καὶ ἂν αὖ ἐκ
τούτων τις ὑπόχρυσος ἢ ὑπάργυρος φυῇ, τιμή-
σαντες ἀνάξουσι τοὺς μὲν εἰς φυλακήν, τοὺς
δὲ εἰς ἐπικουρίαν, ὡς χρησμοῦ ὄντος τότε τὴν
πόλιν διαφθαρῆναι, ὅταν αὐτὴν ὁ σίδηρος ἢ ὁ
χαλκὸς φυλάξῃ. τοῦτον οὖν τὸν μῦθον ὅπως
ἂν πεισθεῖεν, ἔχεις τινὰ μηχανήν; Οὐδαμῶς,
ἔφη, ὅπως γ' ἂν αὐτοὶ οὗτοι· | ὅπως μεντἂν οἱ D

with metal in your composition, by which ye are ranked.

415 τούτων ὑεῖς καὶ οἱ ἔπειτα οἵ τ' ἄλλοι ἄνθρωποι οἱ ὕστερον. Ἀλλὰ καὶ τοῦτο, ἦν δ' ἐγώ, εὖ ἂν ἔχοι πρὸς τὸ μᾶλλον αὐτοὺς τῆς πόλεώς τε καὶ ἀλλήλων κήδεσθαι· σχεδὸν γάρ τι μανθάνω ὃ λέγεις.

The "Guardians" in camp.

Καὶ τοῦτο μὲν δὴ ἕξει ὅπῃ ἂν αὐτὸ ἡ φήμη ἀγάγῃ· ἡμεῖς δὲ τούτους τοὺς γηγενεῖς ὁπλίσαντες προάγωμεν ἡγουμένων τῶν ἀρχόντων. ἐλθόντες δὲ θεασάσθων τῆς πόλεως ὅπου κάλλιστον στρατο-
E πεδεύσασθαι, ὅθεν τούς τε ἔνδον | μάλιστ' ἂν κατέχοιεν, εἴ τις μὴ ἐθέλοι τοῖς νόμοις πείθεσθαι, τούς τε ἔξωθεν ἀπαμύνοιεν, εἰ πολέμιος ὥσπερ λύκος ἐπὶ ποίμνην τις ἴοι· στρατοπεδευσάμενοι δέ, θύσαντες οἷς χρή, εὐνὰς ποιησάσθων· ἢ πῶς; Οὕτως, ἔφη. Οὐκοῦν τοιαύτας, οἵας χειμῶνός τε στέγειν καὶ θέρους ἱκανὰς εἶναι; Πῶς γὰρ οὐχί; οἰκήσεις γάρ, ἔφη, δοκεῖς μοι λέγειν. Ναί, ἦν δ' ἐγώ, στρατιω-
416 τικάς γε, ἀλλ' οὐ χρηματιστικάς. | Πῶς, ἔφη, αὖ τοῦτο λέγεις διαφέρειν ἐκείνου; Ἐγώ σοι, ἦν δ' ἐγώ, πειράσομαι εἰπεῖν. δεινότατον γάρ που πάντων καὶ αἴσχιστον ποιμέσι τοιούτους γε καὶ οὕτω τρέφειν κύνας ἐπικούρους ποιμνίων, ὥστε ὑπὸ ἀκολασίας ἢ λιμοῦ ἤ τινος ἄλλου κακοῦ ἔθους αὐτοὺς τοὺς κύνας ἐπιχειρῆσαι τοῖς προβάτοις κακουργεῖν καὶ ἀντὶ κυνῶν λύκοις ὁμοιωθῆναι. Δεινόν, ἦ δ' ὅς· πῶς δ'
B οὔ; Οὐκοῦν φυλακτέον | παντὶ τρόπῳ, μὴ τοιοῦτον ἡμῖν οἱ ἐπίκουροι ποιήσωσι πρὸς τοὺς πολίτας, ἐπειδὴ αὐτῶν κρείττους εἰσίν, ἀντὶ

ξυμμάχων εὐμενῶν δεσπόταις ἀγρίοις ἀφομοιω- 416
θῶσιν; Φυλακτέον, ἔφη. Οὐκοῦν τὴν μεγίστην
τῆς εὐλαβείας παρεσκευασμένοι ἂν εἶεν, εἰ τῷ
ὄντι καλῶς πεπαιδευμένοι εἰσίν; Ἀλλὰ μὴν
εἰσίν γ', ἔφη. καὶ ἐγὼ εἶπον, Τοῦτο μὲν οὐκ
ἄξιον διισχυρίζεσθαι, ὦ φίλε Γλαύκων· ὃ
μέντοι ἄρτι ἐλέγομεν, ἄξιον, ὅτι δεῖ αὐτοὺς τῆς
ὀρθῆς | τυχεῖν παιδείας, ἥτις ποτέ ἐστιν, εἰ C
μέλλουσι τὸ μέγιστον ἔχειν πρὸς τὸ ἥμεροι
εἶναι αὑτοῖς τε καὶ τοῖς φυλαττομένοις ὑπ'
αὐτῶν. Καὶ ὀρθῶς γε, ἦ δ' ὅς. Πρὸς τοίνυν
τῇ παιδείᾳ ταύτῃ φαίη ἄν τις νοῦν ἔχων δεῖν
καὶ τὰς οἰκήσεις καὶ τὴν ἄλλην οὐσίαν τοι-
αύτην αὐτοῖς παρεσκευάσθαι, ἥτις μήτε τοὺς
φύλακας ὡς ἀρίστους εἶναι παύσοι αὐτούς,
κακουργεῖν τε μὴ ἐπαροῖ περὶ τοὺς ἄλλους
| πολίτας. Καὶ ἀληθῶς γε φήσει. Ὅρα δή, D
εἶπον ἐγώ, εἰ τοιόνδε τινὰ τρόπον δεῖ αὐτοὺς ζῆν
τε καὶ οἰκεῖν, εἰ μέλλουσι τοιοῦτοι ἔσεσθαι·
πρῶτον μὲν οὐσίαν κεκτημένον μηδεμίαν μηδένα
ἰδίαν, ἂν μὴ πᾶσα ἀνάγκη· ἔπειτα
οἴκησιν καὶ ταμιεῖον μηδενὶ εἶναι
μηδὲν τοιοῦτον, εἰς ὃ οὐ πᾶς ὁ βου-
λόμενος εἴσεισι· τὰ δ' ἐπιτήδεια, ὅσων δέονται
ἄνδρες ἀθληταὶ πολέμου σώφρονές τε καὶ
ἀνδρεῖοι, ταξαμένους | παρὰ τῶν ἄλλων πολι- E
τῶν δέχεσθαι μισθὸν τῆς φυλακῆς τοσοῦτον,
ὅσον μήτε περιεῖναι αὐτοῖς εἰς τὸν ἐνιαυτὸν
μήτε ἐνδεῖν· φοιτῶντας δὲ εἰς ξυσσίτια ὥσπερ
ἐστρατοπεδευμένους κοινῇ ζῆν· χρυσίον δὲ καὶ
ἀργύριον εἰπεῖν αὐτοῖς ὅτι θεῖον παρὰ θεῶν

They are to possess no property—

416 Gold and silver are within them. ἀεὶ ἐν τῇ ψυχῇ ἔχουσι καὶ οὐδὲν προσδέονται τοῦ ἀνθρωπείου, οὐδὲ ὅσια τὴν ἐκείνου κτῆσιν τῇ τοῦ θνητοῦ χρυσοῦ κτήσει ξυμμιγνύντας μιαίνειν, διότι πολλὰ καὶ ἀνόσια
417 περὶ τὸ τῶν | πολλῶν νόμισμα γέγονεν, τὸ παρ᾽ ἐκείνοις δὲ ἀκήρατον· ἀλλὰ μόνοις αὐτοῖς τῶν ἐν τῇ πόλει μεταχειρίζεσθαι καὶ ἅπτεσθαι χρυσοῦ καὶ ἀργύρου οὐ θέμις, οὐδ᾽ ὑπὸ τὸν αὐτὸν ὄροφον ἰέναι οὐδὲ περιάψασθαι οὐδὲ πίνειν ἐξ ἀργύρου ἢ χρυσοῦ. καὶ οὕτω μὲν σῴζοιντό τ᾽ ἂν καὶ σῴζοιεν τὴν πόλιν· ὁπότε δ᾽ αὐτοὶ γῆν τε ἰδίαν καὶ οἰκίας καὶ νομίσματα κτήσονται, οἰκονόμοι μὲν καὶ γεωργοὶ ἀντὶ φυλάκων ἔσονται, δεσπόται δ᾽ ἐχθροὶ ἀντὶ
B ξυμμάχων | τῶν ἄλλων πολιτῶν γενήσονται, μισοῦντες δὲ δὴ καὶ μισούμενοι καὶ ἐπιβουλεύοντες καὶ ἐπιβουλευόμενοι διάξουσι πάντα τὸν βίον, πολὺ πλείω καὶ μᾶλλον δεδιότες τοὺς ἔνδον ἢ τοὺς ἔξωθεν πολεμίους, θέοντες ἤδη τότε ἐγγύτατα ὀλέθρου αὐτοί τε καὶ ἡ ἄλλη πόλις. τούτων οὖν πάντων ἕνεκα, ἦν δ᾽ ἐγώ, φῶμεν οὕτω δεῖν κατεσκευάσθαι τοὺς φύλακας οἰκήσεώς τε πέρι καὶ τῶν ἄλλων, καὶ ταῦτα νομοθετήσωμεν, ἢ μή; Πάνυ γε, ἦ δ᾽ ὃς ὁ Γλαύκων.

V

Philosophers must be our Kings.

472 B Οὐκοῦν, ἦν δ᾽ ἐγώ, πρῶτον μὲν τόδε χρὴ ἀναμνησθῆναι, ὅτι ἡμεῖς ζητοῦντες δικαιοσύνην

Ideal Justice our theme, not whether it can be realized.

472 οἷόν ἐστι καὶ ἀδικίαν δεῦρο ἥκομεν. Χρή· ἀλλὰ τί τοῦτο; ἔφη. Οὐδέν· ἀλλ' ἐὰν εὕρωμεν οἷόν ἐστι δικαιοσύνη, ἆρα καὶ ἄνδρα τὸν δίκαιον ἀξιώσομεν μηδὲν δεῖν αὐτῆς ἐκείνης διαφέρειν, ἀλλὰ πανταχῇ τοιοῦτον εἶναι, οἷον δικαιοσύνη | C ἐστίν, ἢ ἀγαπήσομεν, ἐὰν ὅτι ἐγγύτατα αὐτῆς ᾖ καὶ πλεῖστα τῶν ἄλλων ἐκείνης μετέχῃ; Οὕτως, ἔφη· ἀγαπήσομεν. Παραδείγματος ἄρα ἕνεκα, ἦν δ' ἐγώ, ἐζητοῦμεν αὐτό τε δικαιοσύνην οἷόν ἐστι, καὶ ἄνδρα τὸν τελέως δίκαιον (εἰ γένοιτο), καὶ οἷος ἂν εἴη γενόμενος, καὶ ἀδικίαν αὖ καὶ τὸν ἀδικώτατον, ἵνα εἰς ἐκείνους ἀποβλέποντες, οἷοι ἂν ἡμῖν φαίνωνται εὐδαιμονίας τε πέρι καὶ τοῦ ἐναντίου, ἀναγκαζώμεθα καὶ περὶ ἡμῶν αὐτῶν ὁμολογεῖν, ὃς ἂν | D ἐκείνοις ὅτι ὁμοιότατος ᾖ, τὴν ἐκείνοις μοῖραν ὁμοιοτάτην ἕξειν, ἀλλ' οὐ τούτου ἕνεκα, ἵν' ἀποδείξωμεν ὡς δυνατὰ ταῦτα γίγνεσθαι. Τοῦτο μέν, ἔφη, ἀληθὲς λέγεις. Οἴει ἂν οὖν ἧττόν τι ἀγαθὸν ζῳγράφον εἶναι, ὃς ἂν γράψας παράδειγμα, οἷον ἂν εἴη ὁ κάλλιστος ἄνθρωπος, καὶ πάντα εἰς τὸ γράμμα ἱκανῶς ἀποδοὺς μὴ ἔχῃ ἀποδεῖξαι ὡς καὶ δυνατὸν γενέσθαι τοιοῦτον ἄνδρα; Μὰ Δί' οὐκ ἔγωγ', ἔφη. Τί οὖν; οὐ καὶ ἡμεῖς, φαμέν, παράδειγμα | E ἐποιοῦμεν λόγῳ ἀγαθῆς πόλεως; Πάνυ γε. Ἧττόν τι οὖν οἴει ἡμᾶς εὖ λέγειν τούτου ἕνεκα, ἐὰν μὴ ἔχωμεν ἀποδεῖξαι ὡς δυνατὸν οὕτω πόλιν οἰκῆσαι ὡς ἐλέγετο; Οὐ δῆτα, ἔφη. Τὸ μὲν τοίνυν ἀληθές, ἦν δ' ἐγώ, οὕτω· εἰ δὲ δὴ καὶ τοῦτο προθυμηθῆναι δεῖ

472 σὴν χάριν, ἀποδεῖξαι, πῇ μάλιστα καὶ κατὰ τί δυνατώτατ᾽ ἂν εἴη, πάλιν μοι πρὸς τὴν τοιαύτην ἀπόδειξιν τὰ αὐτὰ διομολόγησαι. Τὰ
473 ποῖα; Ἆρ᾽ οἷόν τέ τι | πραχθῆναι ὡς λέγεται, ἢ φύσιν ἔχει πρᾶξιν λέξεως ἧττον ἀληθείας ἐφάπτεσθαι, κἂν εἰ μή τῳ δοκεῖ; ἀλλὰ σὺ πότερον ὁμολογεῖς οὕτως ἢ οὔ; Ὁμολογῶ, ἔφη. Τοῦτο μὲν δὴ μὴ ἀνάγκαζέ με, οἷα τῷ λόγῳ διήλθομεν, τοιαῦτα παντάπασι καὶ τῷ ἔργῳ δεῖν γιγνόμενα ἀποφαίνειν· ἀλλ᾽, ἐὰν οἷοί τε γενώμεθα εὑρεῖν ὡς ἂν ἐγγύτατα τῶν εἰρημένων πόλις οἰκήσειεν, φάναι ἡμᾶς ἐξηυρηκέναι ὡς δυνατὰ ταῦτα γίγνεσθαι,
B ἃ σὺ ἐπιτάττεις. | ἢ οὐκ ἀγαπήσεις τούτων τυγχάνων; ἐγὼ μὲν γὰρ ἂν ἀγαπῴην. Καὶ γὰρ ἐγώ, ἔφη.

Approximation all that is to be hoped for.

Τὸ δὲ δὴ μετὰ τοῦτο, ὡς ἔοικε, πειρώμεθα ζητεῖν τε καὶ ἀποδεικνύναι, τί ποτε νῦν κακῶς ἐν ταῖς πόλεσι πράττεται, δι᾽ ὃ οὐχ οὕτως οἰκοῦνται, καὶ τίνος ἂν σμικροτάτου μεταβαλόντος ἔλθοι εἰς τοῦτον τὸν τρόπον τῆς πολιτείας πόλις, μάλιστα μὲν ἑνός, εἰ δὲ μή, δυοῖν, εἰ δὲ μή, ὅτι ὀλιγίστων τὸν ἀριθμὸν καὶ σμικροτάτων τὴν δύναμιν. Παντά-
C πασι | μὲν οὖν, ἔφη. Ἑνὸς μὲν τοίνυν, ἦν δ᾽ ἐγώ, μεταβαλόντος δοκοῦμέν μοι ἔχειν δεῖξαι ὅτι μεταπέσοι ἄν, οὐ μέντοι σμικροῦ γε οὐδὲ ῥᾳδίου, δυνατοῦ δέ. Τίνος; ἔφη. Ἐπ᾽ αὐτὸ δή, ἦν δ᾽ ἐγώ, εἶμι, ὃ τῷ μεγίστῳ προῃκάζομεν κύματι· εἰρήσεται δ᾽ οὖν, εἰ καὶ μέλλει γέλωτί τε ἀτεχνῶς ὥσπερ κῦμα ἐκγελῶν καὶ ἀδοξίᾳ

How best attained?

κατακλύσειν. σκόπει δὲ ὃ μέλλω λέγειν. Λέγε, 473
ἔφη. Ἐὰν μή, ἦν δ' ἐγώ, ἢ οἱ φιλόσοφοι
βασιλεύσωσιν ἐν ταῖς | πόλεσιν D
ἢ οἱ βασιλῆς τε νῦν λεγόμενοι
καὶ δυνάσται φιλοσοφήσωσι γνη-
σίως τε καὶ ἱκανῶς, καὶ τοῦτο εἰς ταὐτὸν
ξυμπέσῃ, δύναμίς τε πολιτικὴ καὶ φιλο-
σοφία, τῶν δὲ νῦν πορευομένων χωρὶς ἐφ'
ἑκάτερον αἱ πολλαὶ φύσεις ἐξ ἀνάγκης
ἀποκλεισθῶσιν, οὐκ ἔστι κακῶν παῦλα, ὦ
φίλε Γλαύκων, ταῖς πόλεσι, δοκῶ δ' οὐδὲ
τῷ ἀνθρωπίνῳ γένει, οὐδὲ αὕτη ἡ πολι-
τεία μή ποτε πρότερον φυῇ | τε εἰς τὸ E
δυνατὸν καὶ φῶς ἡλίου ἴδῃ, ἣν νῦν λόγῳ
διεληλύθαμεν. ἀλλὰ τοῦτό ἐστιν, ὃ ἐμοὶ
πάλαι ὄκνον ἐντίθησι λέγειν, ὁρῶντι ὡς πολὺ
παρὰ δόξαν ῥηθήσεται· χαλεπὸν γὰρ ἰδεῖν ὅτι
οὐκ ἂν ἄλλῃ τις εὐδαιμονήσειεν οὔτε ἰδίᾳ οὔτε
δημοσίᾳ. καὶ ὅς, Ὦ Σώκρατες, ἔφη, τοιοῦτον
ἐκβέβληκας ῥῆμά τε καὶ λόγον, ὃν εἰπὼν ἡγοῦ
ἐπὶ σὲ πάνυ πολλούς τε καὶ οὐ φαύλους νῦν
οὕτως, οἷον ῥίψαντας τὰ ἱμάτια, | γυμνούς, λα- 474
βόντας ὅ τι ἑκάστῳ παρέτυχεν ὅπλον,
θεῖν διατεταμένους ὡς θαυμάσια
ἐργασομένους· οὓς εἰ μὴ ἀμυνεῖ τῷ
λόγῳ καὶ ἐκφεύξει, τῷ ὄντι τωθαζόμενος δώσεις
δίκην. Οὐκοῦν σύ μοι, ἦν δ' ἐγώ, τούτων
αἴτιος; Καλῶς γ', ἔφη, ἐγὼ ποιῶν· ἀλλά τοί
σε οὐ προδώσω, ἀλλ' ἀμυνῶ οἷς δύναμαι· δύνα-
μαι δὲ εὐνοίᾳ τε καὶ τῷ παρακελεύεσθαι, καὶ
ἴσως ἂν ἄλλου του ἐμμελέστερόν σοι | ἀπο- B

If philosophers be kings,—

a saying Socrates will be stoned for.

474 κρινοίμην. ἀλλ᾽ ὡς ἔχων τοιοῦτον βοηθὸν
πειρῶ τοῖς ἀπιστοῦσιν ἐνδείξασθαι ὅτι ἔχει ᾗ
σὺ λέγεις. Πειρατέον, ἦν δ᾽ ἐγώ, ἐπειδὴ καὶ
σὺ οὕτω μεγάλην ξυμμαχίαν παρέχει.

VI

How Democracy is the Arch-Sophist in Corruption.

492 Ἣν τοίνυν ἔθεμεν | τοῦ φιλοσόφου φύσιν,
ἂν μέν, οἶμαι, μαθήσεως προσηκούσης τύχῃ,
εἰς πᾶσαν ἀρετὴν ἀνάγκη αὐξανομένην ἀφι-
κνεῖσθαι, ἐὰν δὲ μὴ ἐν προσηκούσῃ σπαρεῖσά τε
καὶ φυτευθεῖσα τρέφηται, εἰς πάντα τἀναντία
αὖ,—ἐὰν μή τις αὐτῇ βοηθήσας θεῶν τύχῃ.
ἢ καὶ σὺ ἡγεῖ, ὥσπερ οἱ πολλοί, διαφθειρομέ-
νους τινὰς εἶναι ὑπὸ σοφιστῶν νέους, διαφθεί-
ροντας δέ τινας σοφιστὰς ἰδιωτικούς, ὅ τι καὶ
ἄξιον λόγου, ἀλλ᾽ οὐκ αὐτοὺς τοὺς ταῦτα λέγον-
B τας μεγίστους μὲν | εἶναι σοφιστάς, παιδεύειν
δὲ τελεώτατα καὶ ἀπεργάζεσθαι οἵους βούλον-
ται εἶναι καὶ νέους καὶ πρεσβυτέρους καὶ ἄνδρας
καὶ γυναῖκας; Πότε δή; ἦ δ᾽ ὅς. Ὅταν,
εἶπον, ξυγκαθεζόμενοι ἁθρόοι | <οἱ> πολλοὶ
εἰς ἐκκλησίας ἢ εἰς δικαστήρια ἢ θέατρα ἢ
στρατόπεδα ἤ τινα ἄλλον κοινὸν πλήθους ξύλ-
λογον ξὺν πολλῷ θορύβῳ τὰ μὲν ψέγωσι τῶν
λεγομένων ἢ πραττομένων, τὰ δὲ ἐπαινῶσιν,
ὑπερβαλλόντως ἑκάτερα, καὶ ἐκβοῶντες καὶ
C κροτοῦντες, | πρὸς δ᾽ αὐτοῖς αἵ τε πέτραι καὶ

ὁ τόπος ἐν ᾧ ἂν ὦσιν ἐπηχοῦντες διπλάσιον 492
θόρυβον παρέχωσι τοῦ ψόγου καὶ ἐπαίνου. ἐν
δὴ τῷ τοιούτῳ τὸν νέον, τὸ λεγόμενον, τίνα
οἴει καρδίαν ἴσχειν; ἢ ποίαν ἂν αὐτῷ παι-
δείαν ἰδιωτικὴν ἀνθέξειν, ἣν οὐ κατακλυσθεῖσαν
ὑπὸ τοῦ τοιούτου ψόγου ἢ ἐπαίνου οἰχήσε-
σθαι φερομένην κατὰ ῥοῦν, ᾗ ἂν οὗτος φέρῃ, καὶ
φήσειν τε τὰ αὐτὰ τούτοις καλὰ καὶ αἰσχρὰ
εἶναι, καὶ ἐπιτηδεύσειν | ἅπερ ἂν οὗτοι, καὶ ἔσε- D
σθαι τοιοῦτον; Πολλή, ἦ δ' ὅς, ὦ Σώκρατες,
ἀνάγκη.

Καὶ μήν, ἦν δ' ἐγώ, οὔπω τὴν μεγίστην
ἀνάγκην εἰρήκαμεν. Ποίαν; ἔφη. Ἣν ἔργῳ
προστιθέασι, λόγῳ μὴ πείθοντες, οὗτοι οἱ
παιδευταί τε καὶ σοφισταί. ἢ οὐκ οἶσθα,
ὅτι τὸν μὴ πειθόμενον ἀτιμίαις τε καὶ χρή-
μασι καὶ θανάτοις κολάζουσι; Καὶ μάλα, ἔφη,
σφόδρα. Τίνα οὖν ἄλλον σοφιστὴν οἴει ἢ
ποίους ἰδιωτικοὺς λόγους ἐναντία τούτοις |
τείνοντας κρατήσειν; Οἶμαι μὲν οὐδένα, ἦ δ' E
ὅς. Οὐ γάρ, ἦν δ' ἐγώ, ἀλλὰ καὶ τὸ ἐπι-
χειρεῖν πολλὴ ἄνοια. οὔτε γὰρ γίγνεται οὔτε
γέγονεν οὐδὲ οὖν μὴ γένηται ἀλλοῖον ἦθος πρὸς
ἀρετὴν παρὰ τὴν τούτων παιδείαν πεπαιδευμένον,
ἀνθρώπειον, ὦ ἑταῖρε· θεῖον μέντοι κατὰ τὴν
παροιμίαν ἐξαιρῶμεν λόγου. εὖ γὰρ χρὴ εἰδέναι,
ὅ τι περ ἂν σωθῇ τε καὶ γένηται οἷον δεῖ ἐν
τοιαύτῃ καταστάσει πολιτειῶν, | θεοῦ μοῖραν 493
αὐτὸ σῶσαι λέγων οὐ κακῶς ἐρεῖς. Οὐδ' ἐμοὶ
ἄλλως, ἔφη, δοκεῖ. Ἔτι τοίνυν σοι, ἦν δ' ἐγώ,
πρὸς τούτοις καὶ τόδε δοξάτω. Τὸ ποῖον;

Professional sophists do but humour the great beast.

493 Ἕκαστος τῶν μισθαρνούντων ἰδιωτῶν, οὓς δὴ οὗτοι σοφιστὰς καλοῦσι καὶ ἀντιτέχνους ἡγοῦνται, μὴ ἄλλα παιδεύειν ἢ ταῦτα τὰ τῶν πολλῶν δόγματα, ἃ δοξάζουσιν ὅταν ἀθροισθῶσιν, καὶ σοφίαν ταύτην καλεῖν· οἷόνπερ ἂν εἰ θρέμματος μεγάλου καὶ ἰσχυροῦ τρεφομένου τὰς ὀργάς τις

B καὶ ἐπιθυμίας κατεμάνθανεν, | ὅπῃ τε προσελθεῖν χρὴ καὶ ὅπῃ ἅψασθαι αὐτοῦ, καὶ ὁπότε χαλεπώτατον ἢ πραότατον καὶ ἐκ τίνων γίγνεται, καὶ φωνὰς δὴ ἐφ᾽ οἷς ἑκάστας εἴωθεν φθέγγεσθαι, καὶ οἵας αὖ ἄλλου φθεγγομένου ἡμεροῦταί τε καὶ ἀγριαίνει, καταμαθὼν δὲ ταῦτα πάντα ξυνουσίᾳ τε καὶ χρόνου τριβῇ σοφίαν τε καλέσειεν καὶ ὡς τέχνην συστησάμενος ἐπὶ διδασκαλίαν τρέποιτο, μηδὲν εἰδὼς τῇ ἀληθείᾳ τούτων τῶν δογμάτων τε καὶ ἐπιθυμιῶν, ὅ τι καλὸν ἢ αἰσχρὸν ἢ ἀγαθὸν ἢ κακὸν ἢ δίκαιον ἢ ἄδικον, |

C ὀνομάζοι δὲ πάντα ταῦτα ἐπὶ ταῖς τοῦ μεγάλου ζῴου δόξαις, οἷς μὲν χαίροι ἐκεῖνο ἀγαθὰ καλῶν, οἷς δὲ ἄχθοιτο κακά, ἄλλον δὲ μηδένα ἔχοι λόγον περὶ αὐτῶν, ἀλλὰ τἀναγκαῖα δίκαια καλοῖ καὶ καλά, τὴν δὲ τοῦ ἀναγκαίου καὶ ἀγαθοῦ φύσιν, ὅσον διαφέρει τῷ ὄντι, μήτε ἑωρακὼς εἴη μήτε ἄλλῳ δυνατὸς δεῖξαι. τοιοῦτος δὴ ὢν πρὸς Διὸς οὐκ ἄτοπος ἄν σοι δοκεῖ εἶναι παιδευτής; Ἔμοιγ᾽, ἔφη. Ἦ οὖν τι τούτου δοκεῖ διαφέρειν ὁ τὴν τῶν πολλῶν καὶ παν-

D τοδαπῶν | ξυνιόντων ὀργὴν καὶ ἡδονὰς κατανενοηκέναι σοφίαν ἡγούμενος, εἴτ᾽ ἐν γραφικῇ εἴτ᾽ ἐν μουσικῇ εἴτε δὴ ἐν πολιτικῇ; ὅ τι μὲν

γὰρ ἄν τις τούτοις ὁμιλῇ ἐπιδεικνύμενος, ἢ 493
ποίησιν ἤ τινα ἄλλην δημιουργίαν ἢ πόλει διακονίαν, κυρίους αὑτοῦ ποιῶν τοὺς πολλοὺς πέρα τῶν ἀναγκαίων, ἡ Διομηδεία λεγομένη ἀνάγκη ποιεῖν αὐτῷ ταῦτα ἃ ἂν οὗτοι ἐπαινῶσιν· ὡς δὲ καὶ ἀγαθὰ καὶ καλὰ ταῦτα τῇ ἀληθείᾳ, ἤδη πώποτέ του ἤκουσας αὐτῶν λόγον διδόντος οὐ καταγέλαστον; Οἶμαι δέ γε, ἦ δ'
ὅς, | οὐδ' ἀκούσομαι. E

Again the Philosopher-King.

Ἐλέγομεν, ὑπὸ τἀληθοῦς ἠναγκασμένοι, ὅτι 499
οὔτε πόλις οὔτε πολιτεία οὐδέ γ' ἀνὴρ ὁμοίως B
μήποτε γένηται τέλεος, πρὶν ἂν τοῖς φιλοσόφοις τούτοις τοῖς ὀλίγοις καὶ οὐ πονηροῖς, ἀχρήστοις δὲ νῦν κεκλημένοις, ἀνάγκη τις ἐκ τύχης περιβάλῃ, εἴτε βούλονται εἴτε μή, πόλεως ἐπιμεληθῆναι καὶ τῇ πόλει κατηκόῳ γενέσθαι, ἢ τῶν νῦν ἐν δυναστείαις ἢ βασιλείαις ὄντων υἱέσιν ἢ αὐτοῖς ἔκ τινος θείας ἐπιπνοίας |
ἀληθινῆς φιλοσοφίας ἀληθινὸς ἔρως ἐμπέσῃ. C

How the Philosopher would paint the State.

Οὐδὲ γάρ που, ὦ Ἀδείμαντε, σχολὴ τῷ γε 500
ὡς ἀληθῶς πρὸς τοῖς οὖσι τὴν διάνοιαν ἔχοντι κάτω βλέπειν εἰς
ἀνθρώπων | πραγματείας, καὶ μαχόμενον αὐτοῖς C
φθόνου τε καὶ δυσμενείας ἐμπίμπλασθαι, ἀλλ' εἰς τεταγμένα ἄττα καὶ κατὰ ταὐτὰ ἀεὶ ἔχοντα

His previous training.

500 ὁρῶντας καὶ θεωμένους οὔτ' ἀδικοῦντα οὔτ'
ἀδικούμενα ὑπ' ἀλλήλων, κόσμῳ δὲ πάντα καὶ
κατὰ λόγον ἔχοντα, ταῦτα μιμεῖσθαί τε καὶ ὅτι
μάλιστα ἀφομοιοῦσθαι. ἢ οἴει τινὰ μηχανὴν
εἶναι, ὅτῳ τις ὁμιλεῖ ἀγάμενος, μὴ μιμεῖσθαι
ἐκεῖνο; Ἀδύνατον, ἔφη. Θείῳ δὴ καὶ κοσμίῳ
D ὅ γε φιλόσοφος ὁμιλῶν κόσμιός | τε καὶ θεῖος
εἰς τὸ δυνατὸν ἀνθρώπῳ γίγνεται· διαβολὴ δ'
ἐν πᾶσι πολλή. Παντάπασι μὲν οὖν. Ἂν
οὖν τις, εἶπον, αὐτῷ ἀνάγκη γένηται, ἃ ἐκεῖ
ὁρᾷ, μελετῆσαι εἰς ἀνθρώπων ἤθη καὶ ἰδίᾳ καὶ
δημοσίᾳ τιθέναι καὶ μὴ μόνον ἑαυτὸν πλάττειν,
ἆρα κακὸν δημιουργὸν αὐτὸν οἴει γενήσεσθαι
σωφροσύνης τε καὶ δικαιοσύνης καὶ ξυμπάσης
τῆς δημοτικῆς ἀρετῆς; Ἥκιστά γε, ἦ δ' ὅς.
Ἀλλ' ἐὰν δὴ αἴσθωνται οἱ πολλοὶ ὅτι ἀληθῆ
περὶ αὐτοῦ λέγομεν, | χαλεπανοῦσι δὴ τοῖς
E φιλοσόφοις καὶ ἀπιστήσουσιν ἡμῖν λέγουσιν
ὡς οὐκ ἄν ποτε ἄλλως εὐδαιμονήσειε πόλις, εἰ
μὴ αὐτὴν διαγράψειαν οἱ τῷ θείῳ παραδείγματι
χρώμενοι ζωγράφοι; Οὐ χαλεπανοῦσιν, ἦ δ'
501 ὅς, ἐάνπερ αἴσθωνται. ἀλλὰ δὴ τίνα | λέγεις
τρόπον τῆς διαγραφῆς; Λαβόντες, ἦν δ' ἐγώ,
ὥσπερ πίνακα πόλιν τε καὶ ἤθη ἀνθρώπων,
His clean canvas. πρῶτον μὲν καθαρὰν ποιήσειαν ἄν· ὃ
οὐ πάνυ ῥᾴδιον· ἀλλ' οὖν οἶσθ' ὅτι
τούτῳ ἂν εὐθὺς τῶν ἄλλων διενέγκοιεν, τῷ
μήτε ἰδιώτου μήτε πόλεως ἐθελῆσαι ἂν ἅψα-
σθαι μηδὲ γράφειν νόμους, πρὶν ἢ παραλαβεῖν
καθαρὰν ἢ αὐτοὶ ποιῆσαι. Καὶ ὀρθῶς γ', ἔφη.
Οὐκοῦν μετὰ ταῦτα οἴει ὑπογράψασθαι ἂν τὸ

σχῆμα τῆς πολιτείας; Τί μήν; Ἔπειτα, οἶμαι, 501
ἀπεργαζόμενοι πυκνὰ ἂν ἑκατέρωσε ἀποβλέποιεν, B
πρός τε τὸ φύσει δίκαιον καὶ καλὸν
καὶ σῶφρον καὶ πάντα τὰ τοιαῦτα
καὶ πρὸς ἐκεῖνο αὖ ὃ ἐν τοῖς ἀνθρώ-
ποις ἐμποιοῖεν, ξυμμιγνύντες τε καὶ κεραννύντες
ἐκ τῶν ἐπιτηδευμάτων τὸ ἀνδρείκελον, ἀπ᾽ ἐκεί-
νου τεκμαιρόμενοι, ὃ δὴ καὶ Ὅμηρος ἐκάλεσεν
ἐν τοῖς ἀνθρώποις ἐγγιγνόμενον θεοειδές τε καὶ
θεοείκελον. Ὀρθῶς, ἔφη. Καὶ τὸ μὲν ἄν,
οἶμαι, ἐξαλείφοιεν, τὸ δὲ πάλιν ἐγγράφοιεν,
ἕως ὅτι μάλιστα ἀνθρώπεια ἤδη (εἰς ὅσον C
ἐνδέχεται) θεοφιλῆ ποιήσειαν. Καλλίστη γοῦν
ἄν, ἔφη, ἡ γραφὴ γένοιτο. Ἆρ᾽ οὖν, ἦν δ᾽
ἐγώ, πείθομέν πῃ ἐκείνους, οὓς δια-
τεταμένους ἐφ᾽ ἡμᾶς ἔφησθα ἰέναι,
ὡς τοιοῦτός ἐστι πολιτειῶν ζωγράφος, ὃν τότ᾽
ἐπῃνοῦμεν πρὸς αὐτούς, δι᾽ ὃν ἐκεῖνοι ἐχαλέ-
παινον, ὅτι τὰς πόλεις αὐτῷ παρεδίδομεν, καί
τι μᾶλλον αὐτὸ νῦν ἀκούοντες πραΰνονται;
Καὶ πολύ γε, ἦ δ᾽ ὅς, εἰ σωφρονοῦσιν. Πῇ
γὰρ δὴ ἕξουσιν ἀμφισβητῆσαι; πότερον μὴ D
τοῦ ὄντος τε καὶ ἀληθείας ἐραστὰς εἶναι τοὺς
φιλοσόφους; Ἄτοπον μεντἄν, ἔφη, εἴη. Ἀλλὰ
μὴ τὴν φύσιν αὐτῶν οἰκείαν εἶναι τοῦ ἀρίστου,
ἣν ἡμεῖς διήλθομεν; Οὐδὲ τοῦτο. Τί δέ; τὴν
τοιαύτην τυχοῦσαν τῶν προσηκόντων ἐπιτηδευ-
μάτων οὐκ ἀγαθὴν τελέως ἔσεσθαι καὶ φιλό-
σοφον εἴπερ τινὰ ἄλλην; ἢ ἐκείνους φήσειν
μᾶλλον, οὓς ἡμεῖς ἀφωρίσαμεν; Οὐ δήπου. E
Ἔτι οὖν ἀγριανοῦσι λεγόντων ἡμῶν ὅτι, πρὶν ἂν

His constant reference to the ideal.

The result.

The philosopher must be the painter.

501 πόλεως τὸ φιλόσοφον γένος ἐγκρατὲς γένηται, οὔτε πόλει οὔτε πολίταις κακῶν παῦλα ἔσται, οὐδὲ ἡ πολιτεία, ἣν μυθολογοῦμεν λόγῳ, ἔργῳ τέλος λήψεται; Ἴσως, ἔφη, ἧττον. Βούλει οὖν, ἦν δ' ἐγώ, μὴ ἧττον φῶμεν αὐτούς, ἀλλὰ παντάπασι πρᾴους
502 γεγονέναι καὶ πεπεῖσθαι, ἵνα, | εἰ μή τι ἄλλο, αἰσχυνθέντες ὁμολογήσωσιν; Πάνυ μὲν οὖν, ἔφη.

VII

The Parable of the Cave.

Man is born as in an underground chamber.

514 Μετὰ ταῦτα δή, εἶπον, ἀπείκασον τοιούτῳ πάθει τὴν ἡμετέραν φύσιν παιδείας τε πέρι καὶ ἀπαιδευσίας. ἰδὲ γὰρ ἀνθρώπους οἷον ἐν καταγείῳ οἰκήσει σπηλαιώδει, ἀναπεπταμένην πρὸς τὸ φῶς τὴν εἴσοδον ἐχούσῃ μακρὰν παρ' ἅπαν τὸ σπήλαιον, ἐν ταύτῃ ἐκ παίδων ὄντας ἐν δεσμοῖς καὶ τὰ σκέλη καὶ τοὺς αὐχένας, ὥστε μένειν τε αὐτοὺς
B εἴς τε | τὸ πρόσθεν μόνον ὁρᾶν, κύκλῳ δὲ τὰς κεφαλὰς ὑπὸ τοῦ δεσμοῦ ἀδυνάτους περιάγειν, φῶς δὲ αὐτοῖς πυρὸς ἄνωθεν καὶ πόρρωθεν καόμενον ὄπισθεν αὐτῶν, μεταξὺ δὲ τοῦ πυρὸς καὶ τῶν δεσμωτῶν ἐπάνω ὁδόν, παρ' ἣν ἰδὲ τειχίον παρῳκοδομημένον, ὥσπερ τοῖς θαυματοποιοῖς πρὸ τῶν ἀνθρώπων πρόκειται τὰ παραφράγματα, ὑπὲρ ὧν τὰ θαύματα δεικνύασιν. Ὁρῶ, ἔφη. Ὅρα τοίνυν παρὰ τοῦτο τὸ τειχίον φέροντας ἀνθρώπους σκεύη τε παντοδαπὰ ὑπερέ-

χοντα τοῦ τειχίου καὶ ἀνδριάντας | καὶ ἄλλα ζῷα 515
λίθινά τε καὶ ξύλινα καὶ παντοῖα εἰργασμένα,
οἷον εἰκός, τοὺς μὲν φθεγγομένους, τοὺς δὲ
σιγῶντας τῶν παραφερόντων. Ἄτοπον, ἔφη,
λέγεις εἰκόνα καὶ δεσμώτας ἀτόπους. Ὁμοίους
ἡμῖν, ἦν δ' ἐγώ· τοὺς γὰρ τοιούτους πρῶτον
μὲν ἑαυτῶν τε καὶ ἀλλήλων οἴει ἄν τι ἑωρα-
κέναι ἄλλο πλὴν τὰς σκιὰς τὰς ὑπὸ
τοῦ πυρὸς εἰς τὸ καταντικρὺ αὐτῶν

He sees but shadow,

τοῦ σπηλαίου προσπιπτούσας; Πῶς γάρ, ἔφη,
εἰ ἀκινήτους γε τὰς κεφαλὰς ἔχειν ἠναγκασμένοι
| εἶεν διὰ βίου; Τί δὲ τῶν παραφερομένων; οὐ B
ταὐτὸν τοῦτο; Τί μήν; Εἰ οὖν διαλέγεσθαι
οἷοί τ' εἶεν πρὸς ἀλλήλους, οὐ ταῦτα ἡγεῖ ἂν τὰ
παριόντα αὐτοὺς νομίζειν ὀνομάζειν, ἅπερ ὁρῷεν;
Ἀνάγκη. Τί δ'; εἰ καὶ ἠχὼ τὸ δεσμωτήριον
ἐκ τοῦ καταντικρὺ ἔχοι, ὁπότε τις
τῶν παριόντων φθέγξαιτο, οἴει ἂν

hears but echo,

ἄλλο τι αὐτοὺς ἡγεῖσθαι τὸ φθεγγόμενον ἢ
τὴν παριοῦσαν σκιάν; Μὰ Δί' οὐκ ἔγωγ', ἔφη.
Παντάπασι δή, ἦν δ' ἐγώ, οἱ | τοιοῦτοι οὐκ C
ἂν ἄλλο τι νομίζοιεν τὸ ἀληθὲς ἢ τὰς τῶν
σκευαστῶν σκιάς. Πολλὴ ἀνάγκη, ἔφη. Σκόπει
δή, ἦν δ' ἐγώ, αὐτῶν λύσιν τε καὶ ἴασιν τῶν
δεσμῶν καὶ τῆς ἀφροσύνης, οἵα τις
ἂν εἴη, εἰ φύσει τοιάδε ξυμβαίνοι
αὐτοῖς· ὁπότε τις λυθείη καὶ ἀναγκά-

which he takes for reality even after release,

ζοιτο ἐξαίφνης ἀνίστασθαί τε καὶ περιάγειν τὸν
αὐχένα καὶ βαδίζειν καὶ πρὸς τὸ φῶς ἀναβλέ-
πειν, πάντα δὲ ταῦτα ποιῶν ἀλγοῖ τε καὶ διὰ
τὰς μαρμαρυγὰς ἀδυνατοῖ καθορᾶν ἐκεῖνα, ὧν |

515 τότε τὰς σκιὰς ἑώρα, τί ἂν οἴει αὐτὸν εἰπεῖν,
D εἴ τις αὐτῷ λέγοι ὅτι τότε μὲν ἑώρα φλυαρίας,
νῦν δὲ μᾶλλόν τι ἐγγυτέρω <ὢν> τοῦ ὄντος
καὶ πρὸς μᾶλλον ὄντα τετραμμένος ὀρθότερον
βλέποι, καὶ δὴ καὶ ἕκαστον τῶν παριόντων
δεικνὺς αὐτῷ ἀναγκάζοι ἐρωτῶν ἀποκρίνεσθαι
ὅ τι ἐστίν; οὐκ οἴει αὐτὸν ἀπορεῖν τε ἂν καὶ
ἡγεῖσθαι τὰ τότε ὁρώμενα ἀληθέστερα ἢ τὰ
νῦν δεικνύμενα; Πολύ γ', ἔφη. Οὐκοῦν κἂν εἰ
E πρὸς αὐτὸ τὸ φῶς ἀναγκάζοι αὐτὸν | βλέπειν,
ἀλγεῖν τε ἂν τὰ ὄμματα καὶ φεύγειν ἀπο-
στρεφόμενον πρὸς ἐκεῖνα, ἃ δύναται καθορᾶν,
καὶ νομίζειν ταῦτα τῷ ὄντι σαφέστερα τῶν
δεικνυμένων; Οὕτως, ἔφη. Εἰ δέ, ἦν δ' ἐγώ,
ἐντεῦθεν ἕλκοι τις αὐτὸν βίᾳ διὰ τραχείας
τῆς ἀναβάσεως καὶ ἀνάντους, καὶ μὴ ἀνείη
πρὶν ἐξελκύσειεν εἰς τὸ τοῦ ἡλίου φῶς, ἆρα
οὐχὶ ὀδυνᾶσθαί τε ἂν καὶ ἀγανακτεῖν ἑλκόμενον,
516 καὶ ἐπειδὴ πρὸς τὸ φῶς | ἔλθοι, αὐγῆς ἂν
ἔχοντα τὰ ὄμματα μεστὰ ὁρᾶν οὐδ' ἂν ἓν
δύνασθαι τῶν νῦν λεγομένων ἀληθῶν; Οὐ γὰρ
ἄν, ἔφη, ἐξαίφνης γε. Συνηθείας δή, οἶμαι,
δέοιτ' ἄν, εἰ μέλλοι τὰ ἄνω ὄψεσθαι· καὶ
πρῶτον μὲν τὰς σκιὰς ἂν ῥᾷστα
καθορῷ, καὶ μετὰ τοῦτο ἐν τοῖς
ὕδασι τά τε τῶν ἀνθρώπων καὶ τὰ
τῶν ἄλλων εἴδωλα, ὕστερον δὲ αὐτά·
ἐκ δὲ τούτων τὰ ἐν τῷ οὐρανῷ καὶ αὐτὸν τὸν
οὐρανὸν νύκτωρ ἂν ῥᾷον θεάσαιτο (προσβλέπων
B τὸ τῶν ἄστρων τε καὶ | σελήνης φῶς) ἢ μεθ'
ἡμέραν τὸν ἥλιόν τε καὶ τὸ τοῦ ἡλίου. Πῶς

until in time, and painfully, seeing the light, he learns the truth,

δ᾽ οὔ; Τελευταῖον δή, οἶμαι, τὸν ἥλιον, οὐκ ἐν 516
ὕδασιν οὐδ᾽ ἐν ἀλλοτρίᾳ ἕδρᾳ φαντάσματα
αὐτοῦ, ἀλλ᾽ αὐτὸν καθ᾽ αὑτὸν ἐν τῇ αὑτοῦ
χώρᾳ δύναιτ᾽ ἂν κατιδεῖν καὶ θεάσασθαι οἷός
ἐστιν. Ἀναγκαῖον, ἔφη. Καὶ μετὰ ταῦτ᾽ ἂν
ἤδη συλλογίζοιτο περὶ αὐτοῦ ὅτι αὐτὸς ὁ τάς
τε ὥρας παρέχων καὶ ἐνιαυτοὺς καὶ πάντα
ἐπιτροπεύων τὰ ἐν τῷ ὁρωμένῳ τόπῳ, καὶ
ἐκείνων, ὧν | σφεῖς ἑώρων, τρόπον τινὰ πάν- C
των αἴτιος. Δῆλον, ἔφη, ὅτι ἐπὶ ταῦτα ἂν
μετ᾽ ἐκεῖνα ἔλθοι. Τί οὖν; ἀναμιμνῃσκόμενον
αὐτὸν τῆς πρώτης οἰκήσεως καὶ τῆς
ἐκεῖ σοφίας καὶ τῶν τότε ξυνδεσμω-
τῶν οὐκ ἂν οἴει αὑτὸν μὲν εὐδαιμονίζειν τῆς
μεταβολῆς, τοὺς δὲ ἐλεεῖν; Καὶ μάλα. Τιμαὶ
δὲ καὶ ἔπαινοι εἴ τινες αὐτοῖς ἦσαν τότε παρ᾽
ἀλλήλων καὶ γέρα τῷ ὀξύτατα καθορῶντι τὰ
παριόντα καὶ μνημονεύοντι μάλιστα, ὅσα τε
πρότερα αὐτῶν καὶ | ὕστερα εἰώθει καὶ ἅμα D
πορεύεσθαι, καὶ ἐκ τούτων δὴ δυνατώτατα
ἀπομαντευομένῳ τὸ μέλλον ἥξειν, δοκεῖς ἂν
αὐτὸν ἐπιθυμητικῶς αὐτῶν ἔχειν καὶ ζηλοῦν
τοὺς παρ᾽ ἐκείνοις τιμωμένους τε καὶ ἐνδυνα-
στεύοντας, ἢ τὸ τοῦ Ὁμήρου ἂν πεπονθέναι καὶ
σφόδρα βούλεσθαι ἐπάρουρον ἐόντα θητευέ-
μεν ἄλλῳ ἀνδρὶ παρ᾽ ἀκλήρῳ, καὶ ὁτιοῦν
ἂν πεπονθέναι μᾶλλον ἢ ᾽κεῖνά τε δοξάζειν καὶ
ἐκείνως ζῆν; Οὕτως, | ἔφη, ἔγωγε οἶμαι, πᾶν E
μᾶλλον πεπονθέναι ἂν δέξασθαι ἢ ζῆν ἐκείνως.
Καὶ τόδε δὴ ἐννόησον, ἦν δ᾽ ἐγώ. εἰ πάλιν ὁ
τοιοῦτος καταβὰς εἰς τὸν αὐτὸν θᾶκον καθίζοιτο,

and repents his delusions.

Returning to the cave, he would be thought to have lost his eyesight.

516 ἆρ' οὐ σκότους ἂν πλέως σχοίη τοὺς ὀφθαλμούς, ἐξαίφνης ἥκων ἐκ τοῦ ἡλίου; Καὶ μάλα γ', ἔφη. Τὰς δὲ δὴ σκιὰς ἐκείνας πάλιν εἰ δέοι αὐτὸν γνωματεύοντα διαμιλλᾶσθαι τοῖς ἀεὶ δεσμώταις
517 ἐκείνοις, ἐν ᾧ ἀμβλυώττει, | πρὶν καταστῆναι τὰ ὄμματα, οὗτος δ' ὁ χρόνος μὴ πάνυ ὀλίγος εἴη τῆς συνηθείας, ἆρ' οὐ γέλωτ' ἂν παράσχοι, καὶ λέγοιτο ἂν περὶ αὐτοῦ, ὡς ἀναβὰς ἄνω διεφθαρμένος ἥκει τὰ ὄμματα, καὶ ὅτι οὐκ ἄξιον οὐδὲ πειρᾶσθαι ἄνω ἰέναι; καὶ τὸν ἐπιχειροῦντα λύειν τε καὶ ἀνάγειν, εἴ πως ἐν ταῖς χερσὶ δύναιντο λαβεῖν καὶ ἀποκτιννύναι, ἀποκτείνειαν ἄν; Σφόδρα γ', ἔφη.

The application.

Ταύτην τοίνυν, ἦν δ' ἐγώ, τὴν εἰκόνα, ὦ φίλε Γλαύκων, προσαπτέον ἅπασαν
B τοῖς ἔμπροσθεν | λεγομένοις, τὴν μὲν δι' ὄψεως φαινομένην ἕδραν τῇ τοῦ δεσμωτηρίου οἰκήσει ἀφομοιοῦντα, τὸ δὲ τοῦ πυρὸς ἐν αὐτῇ φῶς τῇ τοῦ ἡλίου δυνάμει· τὴν δὲ ἄνω ἀνάβασιν καὶ θέαν τῶν ἄνω τὴν εἰς τὸν νοητὸν τόπον τῆς ψυχῆς ἄνοδον τιθεὶς οὐχ ἁμαρτήσει τῆς γ' ἐμῆς ἐλπίδος, ἐπειδὴ ταύτης ἐπιθυμεῖς ἀκούειν· θεὸς δέ που οἶδεν, εἰ ἀληθὴς οὖσα τυγχάνει. τὰ δ' οὖν ἐμοὶ φαινόμενα οὕτω φαίνεται· ἐν τῷ γνωστῷ τελευταία ἡ τοῦ ἀγαθοῦ ἰδέα καὶ μόγις ὁρᾶσθαι, ὀφθεῖσα δὲ |
C συλλογιστέα εἶναι ὡς ἄρα πᾶσι πάντων αὕτη ὀρθῶν τε καὶ καλῶν αἰτία, ἔν τε ὁρατῷ φῶς καὶ τὸν τούτου κύριον τεκοῦσα, ἔν τε νοητῷ αὐτὴ κυρία ἀλήθειαν καὶ νοῦν παρασχομένη,

καὶ ὅτι δεῖ ταύτην ἰδεῖν τὸν μέλλοντα ἐμφρό- 517
νως πράξειν ἢ ἰδίᾳ ἢ δημοσίᾳ. Ξυνοίομαι, ἔφη,
καὶ ἐγώ, ὅν γε δὴ τρόπον δύναμαι. Ἴθι τοί-
νυν, ἦν δ' ἐγώ, καὶ τόδε ξυνοιήθητι καὶ μὴ
θαυμάσῃς ὅτι οἱ ἐνταῦθα ἐλθόντες οὐκ ἐθέλουσιν
τὰ τῶν ἀνθρώπων πράττειν, ἀλλ' ἄνω ἀεὶ
ἐπείγονται | αὐτῶν αἱ ψυχαὶ διατρίβειν· εἰκὸς D
γάρ που οὕτως, εἴπερ αὖ κατὰ τὴν προειρημέ-
νην εἰκόνα τοῦτ' ἔχει. Εἰκὸς μέντοι, ἔφη. Τί
δέ; τόδε οἴει τι θαυμαστόν, εἰ ἀπὸ θείων, ἦν
δ' ἐγώ, θεωριῶν ἐπὶ τὰ ἀνθρώπειά
τις ἐλθὼν κακὰ ἀσχημονεῖ τε καὶ
φαίνεται σφόδρα γελοῖος, ἔτι ἀμ-
βλυώττων καί, πρὶν ἱκανῶς συνήθης
γενέσθαι τῷ παρόντι σκότῳ, ἀναγκα-
ζόμενος ἐν δικαστηρίοις ἢ ἄλλοθί που ἀγωνίζε-
σθαι περὶ τῶν τοῦ δικαίου σκιῶν ἢ ἀγαλμάτων
ὧν αἱ σκιαί, καὶ διαμιλλᾶσθαι περὶ τούτου,
ὅπῃ ποτὲ | ὑπολαμβάνεται ταῦτα ὑπὸ τῶν E
αὐτὴν δικαιοσύνην μὴ πώποτε ἰδόντων; Οὐδ'
ὁπωστιοῦν θαυμαστόν, ἔφη. Ἀλλ' εἰ νοῦν γε
ἔχοι τις, | ἦν δ' ἐγώ, μεμνῇτ' ἂν ὅτι διτταὶ καὶ 518
ἀπὸ διττῶν γίγνονται ἐπιταράξεις ὄμμασιν, ἔκ τε
φωτὸς εἰς σκότος μεθισταμένων καὶ ἐκ σκότους
εἰς φῶς· ταὐτὰ δὲ ταῦτα νομίσας γίγνεσθαι καὶ
περὶ ψυχήν, ὁπότε ἴδοι θορυβουμένην τινὰ καὶ
ἀδυνατοῦσάν τι καθορᾶν, οὐκ ἂν ἀλογίστως
γελῷ, ἀλλ' ἐπισκοποῖ ἄν, πότερον ἐκ φανοτέρου
βίου ἥκουσα ὑπὸ ἀηθείας ἐσκότωται ἢ ἐξ
ἀμαθίας πλείονος εἰς φανότερον | ἰοῦσα ὑπὸ B
λαμπροτέρου μαρμαρυγῆς ἐμπέπλησται, καὶ

Those who have had the Vision of the Good are ridiculous among men of the world.

518 οὕτω δὴ τὴν μὲν εὐδαιμονίσειεν ἂν τοῦ πάθους τε καὶ βίου, τὴν δὲ ἐλεήσειεν, καὶ εἰ γελᾶν ἐπ' αὐτῇ βούλοιτο, ἧττον ἂν καταγέλαστος ὁ γέλως αὐτῷ εἴη ἢ ὁ ἐπὶ τῇ ἄνωθεν ἐκ φωτὸς ἡκούσῃ. Καὶ μάλα,, ἔφη, μετρίως λέγεις.

* * * * *

Shall these or those oversee the State?

519 Τί δέ; τόδε οὐκ εἰκός, ἦν δ' ἐγώ, καὶ ἀνάγ-
B κη ἐκ τῶν προειρημένων, μήτε τοὺς ἀπαιδεύτους καὶ ἀληθείας ἀπείρους ἱκανῶς ἄν ποτε πόλιν ἐπιτροπεῦσαι, |
C μήτε τοὺς ἐν παιδείᾳ ἐωμένους διατρίβειν διὰ τέλους, τοὺς μέν, ὅτι σκοπὸν ἐν τῷ βίῳ οὐκ ἔχουσιν ἕνα, οὗ στοχαζομένους δεῖ ἅπαντα πράττειν ἃ ἂν πράττωσιν ἰδίᾳ τε καὶ δημοσίᾳ, τοὺς δέ, ὅτι ἑκόντες εἶναι οὐ πράξουσιν, ἡγούμενοι ἐν μακάρων νήσοις ζῶντες ἔτι ἀπῳκίσθαι;

The former, even if compelled.

Ἀληθῆ, ἔφη. Ἡμέτερον δὴ ἔργον, ἦν δ' ἐγώ, τῶν οἰκιστῶν τάς τε βελτίστας φύσεις ἀναγκάσαι ἀφικέσθαι πρὸς τὸ μάθημα, ὃ ἐν τῷ πρόσθεν ἔφα-
D μεν εἶναι μέγιστον, ἰδεῖν τε τὸ ἀγαθὸν | καὶ ἀναβῆναι ἐκείνην τὴν ἀνάβασιν, καὶ ἐπειδὰν ἀναβάντες ἱκανῶς ἴδωσι, μὴ ἐπιτρέπειν αὐτοῖς ὃ νῦν ἐπιτρέπεται. Τὸ ποῖον δή; Τὸ αὐτοῦ, ἦν δ' ἐγώ, καταμένειν καὶ μὴ ἐθέλειν πάλιν καταβαίνειν παρ' ἐκείνους τοὺς δεσμώτας μηδὲ μετέχειν τῶν παρ' ἐκείνοις πόνων τε καὶ τιμῶν, εἴτε φαυλότεραι εἴτε σπουδαιότεραι. Ἔπειτ', ἔφη, ἀδικήσομεν αὐτούς, καὶ ποιήσομεν χεῖρον ζῆν, δυνατὸν αὐτοῖς ὂν ἄμεινον; Ἐπελάθου, |
E ἦν δ' ἐγώ, πάλιν, ὦ φίλε, ὅτι νόμῳ οὐ τοῦτο

μέλει, ὅπως ἕν τι γένος ἐν πόλει διαφερόντως 519
εὖ πράξει, ἀλλ᾽ ἐν ὅλῃ τῇ πόλει τοῦτο μηχα-
νᾶται ἐγγενέσθαι, ξυναρμόττων τοὺς πολίτας
πειθοῖ τε καὶ ἀνάγκῃ, ποιῶν μεταδιδόναι ἀλλή-
λοις τῆς ὠφελείας, ἣν ἂν ἕκαστοι τὸ κοινὸν |
δυνατοὶ ὦσιν ὠφελεῖν, καὶ αὐτὸς ἐμποιῶν τοιού- 520
τους ἄνδρας ἐν τῇ πόλει, οὐχ ἵνα ἀφίῃ τρέ-
πεσθαι ὅπῃ ἕκαστος βούλεται, ἀλλ᾽ ἵνα κατα-
χρῆται αὐτὸς αὐτοῖς ἐπὶ τὸν ξύνδεσμον τῆς πόλεως.
Ἀληθῆ, ἔφη· ἐπελαθόμην γάρ. Σκέψαι τοίνυν,
εἶπον, ὦ Γλαύκων, ὅτι οὐδ᾽ ἀδικήσομεν τοὺς
παρ᾽ ἡμῖν φιλοσόφους γιγνομένους, ἀλλὰ δίκαια
πρὸς αὐτοὺς ἐροῦμεν, προσαναγκάζοντες τῶν
ἄλλων ἐπιμελεῖσθαί τε καὶ φυλάττειν. ἐροῦμεν
γὰρ ὅτι οἱ μὲν | ἐν ταῖς ἄλλαις πόλεσι τοιοῦ- B
τοι γιγνόμενοι εἰκότως οὐ μετέχουσι τῶν ἐν
αὐταῖς πόνων· αὐτόματοι γὰρ ἐμφύονται ἀκού-
σης τῆς ἐν ἑκάστῃ πολιτείας, δίκην δ᾽ ἔχει τό
γε αὐτοφυές, μηδενὶ τροφὴν ὀφεῖλον, μηδ᾽ ἐκτί-
νειν τῳ προθυμεῖσθαι τὰ τροφεῖα· ὑμᾶς δ᾽
ἡμεῖς ὑμῖν τε αὐτοῖς τῇ τε ἄλλῃ πόλει ὥσπερ
ἐν σμήνεσιν ἡγεμόνας τε καὶ βασιλέας ἐγεννή-
σαμεν, ἄμεινόν τε καὶ τελεώτερον ἐκείνων πεπαι-
δευμένους | καὶ μᾶλλον δυνατοὺς ἀμφοτέρων C
μετέχειν. καταβατέον οὖν ἐν μέρει ἑκάστῳ εἰς
τὴν τῶν ἄλλων ξυνοίκησιν καὶ ξυνεθιστέον τὰ
σκοτεινὰ θεάσασθαι· ξυνεθιζόμενοι γὰρ μυρίῳ
βέλτιον ὄψεσθε τῶν ἐκεῖ, καὶ γνώσεσθε ἕκαστα
τὰ εἴδωλα ἅττα ἐστὶ καὶ ὧν, διὰ τὸ τἀληθῆ
ἑωρακέναι καλῶν τε καὶ δικαίων καὶ ἀγαθῶν
πέρι. καὶ οὕτω ὕπαρ ἡμῖν καὶ ὑμῖν ἡ πόλις

520 οἰκήσεται, ἀλλ' οὐκ ὄναρ, ὡς νῦν αἱ πολλαὶ
ὑπὸ σκιαμαχούντων τε πρὸς ἀλλήλους καὶ
D στασιαζόντων | περὶ τοῦ ἄρχειν οἰκοῦνται, ὡς
μεγάλου τινὸς ἀγαθοῦ ὄντος. τὸ δέ που ἀληθὲς
ὧδ' ἔχει· ἐν πόλει ᾗ ἥκιστα πρόθυμοι
ἄρχειν οἱ μέλλοντες ἄρξειν, ταύτην ἄριστα
καὶ ἀστασιαστότατα ἀνάγκη οἰκεῖσθαι,
τὴν δ' ἐναντίους ἄρχοντας σχοῦσαν ἐναν-
τίως. Πάνυ μὲν οὖν, ἔφη. Ἀπειθήσουσιν
οὖν ἡμῖν, οἴει, οἱ τρόφιμοι ταῦτ' ἀκούοντες, καὶ
οὐκ ἐθελήσουσιν ξυμπονεῖν ἐν τῇ πόλει ἕκαστοι
ἐν μέρει, τὸν δὲ πολὺν χρόνον μετ' ἀλλήλων
οἰκεῖν ἐν τῷ καθαρῷ; Ἀδύνατον, ἔφη· δίκαια |
E γὰρ δὴ δικαίοις ἐπιτάξομεν· παντὸς μὴν μᾶλ-
λον ὡς ἐπ' ἀναγκαῖον αὐτῶν ἕκαστος εἶσι τὸ
ἄρχειν, τοὐναντίον τῶν νῦν ἐν ἑκάστῃ πόλει
ἀρχόντων.

Young Logicians.

539 Ἆρ' οὖν οὐ μία μὲν εὐλάβεια αὕτη συχνή,
B τὸ | μὴ νέους ὄντας αὐτῶν γεύεσθαι;
οἶμαι γάρ σε οὐ λεληθέναι ὅτι οἱ
μειρακίσκοι, ὅταν τὸ πρῶτον λόγων

Are like puppies for destruction.

γεύωνται, ὡς παιδιᾷ αὐτοῖς καταχρῶνται, ἀεὶ
εἰς ἀντιλογίαν χρώμενοι, καὶ μιμούμενοι τοὺς
ἐξελέγχοντας αὐτοὶ ἄλλους ἐλέγχουσι, χαίροντες
ὥσπερ σκυλάκια τῷ ἕλκειν τε καὶ σπαράττειν
τῷ λόγῳ τοὺς πλησίον ἀεί. Ὑπερφυῶς μὲν
οὖν, ἔφη. Οὐκοῦν ὅταν δὴ πολλοὺς μὲν αὐτοὶ
ἐλέγξωσιν, ὑπὸ πολλῶν δὲ ἐλεγχθῶσι, σφόδρα
C καὶ | ταχὺ ἐμπίπτουσιν εἰς τὸ μηδὲν ἡγεῖσθαι

ὧνπερ πρότερον· καὶ ἐκ τούτων δὴ αὐτοί τε 539
καὶ τὸ ὅλον φιλοσοφίας πέρι εἰς τοὺς ἄλλους
διαβέβληνται. Ἀληθέστατα, ἔφη. Ὁ δὲ δὴ
πρεσβύτερος, ἦν δ' ἐγώ, τῆς μὲν τοιαύτης
μανίας οὐκ ἂν ἐθέλοι μετέχειν, τὸν δὲ διαλέ-
γεσθαι ἐθέλοντα καὶ σκοπεῖν τἀληθὲς μᾶλλον
μιμήσεται ἢ τὸν παιδιᾶς χάριν παίζοντα καὶ
ἀντιλέγοντα, καὶ αὐτός τε μετριώτερος | ἔσται D
καὶ τὸ ἐπιτήδευμα τιμιώτερον ἀντὶ ἀτιμοτέρου
ποιήσει. Ὀρθῶς, ἔφη. Οὐκοῦν καὶ τὰ προ-
ειρημένα τούτου ἐπ' εὐλαβείᾳ πάντα προείρηται,
τὸ τὰς φύσεις κοσμίους εἶναι καὶ στασίμους,
οἷς τις μεταδώσει τῶν λόγων, καὶ μὴ ὡς νῦν
ὁ τυχὼν καὶ οὐδὲν προσήκων ἔρχεται ἐπ' αὐτό;
Πάνυ μὲν οὖν, ἔφη.

VIII

Democracy.—Its Rise, Estate, and End.

Origin.

Δημοκρατία δή, οἶμαι, γίγνεται, ὅταν οἱ 557
πένητες νικήσαντες τοὺς μὲν ἀπο-
κτείνωσι τῶν ἑτέρων, τοὺς δὲ ἐκβά-
λωσι, τοῖς δὲ λοιποῖς ἐξ ἴσου μεταδῶσι πολι-
τείας τε καὶ ἀρχῶν, καὶ ὡς τὸ πολὺ ἀπὸ
κλήρων αἱ ἀρχαὶ ἐν αὐτῇ γίγνωνται. Ἔστι
γάρ, ἔφη, αὕτη ἡ κατάστασις δημοκρατίας,
ἐάντε καὶ δι' ὅπλων γένηται ἐάντε καὶ διὰ
φόβον ὑπεξελθόντων τῶν ἑτέρων. Τίνα δὴ οὖν,
ἦν δ' ἐγώ, οὗτοι τρόπον οἰκοῦσι; καὶ ποία τις
ἡ τοιαύτη | αὖ πολιτεία; δῆλον γὰρ ὅτι ὁ B

557 τοιοῦτος ἀνὴρ δημοκρατικός τις ἀναφανήσεται.

Its motley character: each does as he likes—

Δῆλον, ἔφη. Οὐκοῦν πρῶτον μὲν δὴ ἐλεύθεροι, καὶ ἐλευθερίας ἡ πόλις μεστὴ καὶ παρρησίας γίγνεται, καὶ ἐξουσία ἐν αὐτῇ ποιεῖν ὅ τι τις βούλεται; Λέγεταί γε δή, ἔφη. Ὅπου δέ γε ἐξουσία, δῆλον ὅτι ἰδίαν ἕκαστος ἂν κατασκευὴν τοῦ αὑτοῦ βίου κατασκευάζοιτο ἐν αὐτῇ, ἥτις ἕκαστον ἀρέσκοι. Δῆλον. Παντοδαποὶ δὴ ἄν, οἶμαι, ἐν
C ταύτῃ | τῇ πολιτείᾳ μάλιστ᾽ ἐγγίγνοιντο ἄνθρωποι. Πῶς γὰρ οὔ; Κινδυνεύει, ἦν δ᾽ ἐγώ, καλλίστη αὕτη τῶν πολιτειῶν εἶναι· ὥσπερ ἱμάτιον ποικίλον πᾶσιν ἄνθεσι πεποικιλμένον, οὕτω καὶ αὕτη πᾶσιν ἤθεσι πεποικιλμένη καλλίστη ἂν φαίνοιτο. καὶ ἴσως μέν, ἦν δ᾽ ἐγώ, καὶ ταύτην, ὥσπερ οἱ παῖδές τε καὶ αἱ γυναῖκες τὰ ποικίλα θεώμενοι, καλλίστην ἂν πολλοὶ κρίνειαν. Καὶ μάλ᾽, ἔφη. Καὶ ἔστιν γε, ὦ μακάριε, ἦν δ᾽ |
D ἐγώ, ἐπιτήδειον ζητεῖν ἐν αὐτῇ πολιτείαν. Τί δή; Ὅτι πάντα γένη πολιτειῶν ἔχει διὰ τὴν ἐξουσίαν, καὶ κινδυνεύει τῷ βουλομένῳ πόλιν κατασκευάζειν, ὃ νῦν δὴ ἡμεῖς ἐποιοῦμεν, ἀναγκαῖον εἶναι εἰς δημοκρατουμένην ἐλθόντι πόλιν, ὃς ἂν αὐτὸν ἀρέσκῃ τρόπος, τοῦτον ἐκλέξασθαι, ὥσπερ εἰς παντοπώλιον ἀφικομένῳ πολιτειῶν, καὶ ἐκλεξαμένῳ οὕτω κατοικίζειν. Ἴσως γοῦν,
E ἔφη, οὐκ ἂν ἀποροῖ | παραδειγμάτων.

no compulsion on any one—

Τὸ δὲ μηδεμίαν ἀνάγκην, εἶπον, εἶναι ἄρχειν ἐν ταύτῃ τῇ πόλει, μηδ᾽ ἂν ᾖς ἱκανὸς ἄρχειν, μηδὲ αὖ ἄρχεσθαι, ἐὰν μὴ βούλῃ, μηδὲ πολεμεῖν πολεμούντων, μηδὲ εἰρήνην ἄγειν τῶν

ἄλλων ἀγόντων, ἐὰν μὴ ἐπιθυμῇς εἰρήνης, μηδ᾽ 557
αὖ, ἐάν τις ἄρχειν νόμος σε διακωλύῃ ἢ δικάζειν,
μηδὲν ἧττον καὶ ἄρχειν καὶ δικάζειν, ἐὰν αὐτῷ
σοι ἐπίῃ, | ἆρ᾽ οὐ θεσπεσία καὶ ἡδεῖα ἡ τοιαύτη 558
διαγωγὴ ἐν τῷ παραυτίκα; Ἴσως, ἔφη, ἔν γε
τούτῳ. Τί δέ; ἡ πραότης ἐνίων τῶν δικα-
σθέντων οὐ κομψή; ἢ οὔπω εἶδες ἐν τοιαύτῃ
πολιτείᾳ, ἀνθρώπων καταψηφισθέντων θανάτου
ἢ φυγῆς, οὐδὲν ἧττον αὐτῶν μενόντων τε καὶ
ἀναστρεφομένων ἐν μέσῳ, καὶ ὡς οὔτε φροντί-
ζοντος οὔτε ὁρῶντος οὐδενὸς περινοστεῖ ὥσπερ
ἥρως; Καὶ πολλούς γ᾽, ἔφη. Ἡ δὲ συγγνώμη
καὶ | οὐδ᾽ ὁπωστιοῦν σμικρολογία αὐτῆς, ἀλλὰ B
καταφρόνησις ὧν ἡμεῖς ἐλέγομεν σεμνύνοντες,
ὅτε τὴν πόλιν ᾠκίζομεν, ὡς εἰ μή τις ὑπερ-
βεβλημένην φύσιν ἔχοι, οὔποτ᾽ ἂν γένοιτο
ἀνὴρ ἀγαθός, εἰ μὴ παῖς ὢν εὐθὺς παίζοι ἐν
καλοῖς καὶ ἐπιτηδεύοι τὰ τοιαῦτα πάντα,—ὡς
μεγαλοπρεπῶς καταπατήσασ᾽ ἅπαντα ταῦτα
οὐδὲν φροντίζει, ἐξ ὁποίων ἄν τις
ἐπιτηδευμάτων ἐπὶ τὰ πολιτικὰ ἰὼν
πράττῃ, ἀλλὰ τιμᾷ, ἐὰν φῇ μόνον
εὔνους εἶναι τῷ | πλήθει. Πάνυ γ᾽, ἔφη, C
γενναία. Ταῦτά τε δή, ἔφην, ἔχοι ἂν καὶ
τούτων ἄλλα ἀδελφὰ δημοκρατία, καὶ εἴη, ὡς
ἔοικεν, ἡδεῖα πολιτεία καὶ ἄναρχος καὶ ποικίλη,
ἰσότητά τινα ὁμοίως ἴσοις τε καὶ ἀνίσοις διανέ-
μουσα. Καὶ μάλ᾽, ἔφη, γνώριμα λέγεις.

all equally fit for offices of state.

* * * * *

Ὃ προὔθεντο, ἦν δ᾽ ἐγώ, ἀγαθόν, καὶ 562
δι᾽ οὗ ἡ ὀλιγαρχία καθίστατο — τοῦτο δ᾽ B

562 But its passion for Freedom destroys it.

ἦν ὑπὲρ πλούτου· ἦ γάρ; Ναί. Ἡ πλούτου τοίνυν ἀπληστία καὶ ἡ τῶν ἄλλων ἀμέλεια διὰ χρηματισμὸν αὐτὴν ἀπώλλυ. Ἀληθῆ, ἔφη. Ἆρ' οὖν καὶ ὃ δημοκρατία ὁρίζεται ἀγαθόν, ἡ τούτου ἀπληστία καὶ ταύτην καταλύει; Λέγεις δ' αὐτὴν τί ὁρίζεσθαι; Τὴν ἐλευθερίαν, εἶπον. τοῦτο γάρ που ἐν δημοκρατουμένῃ πόλει C ἀκούσαις | ἂν ὡς ἔχει τε κάλλιστον καὶ διὰ ταῦτα ἐν μόνῃ ταύτῃ ἄξιον οἰκεῖν ὅστις φύσει ἐλεύθερος. Λέγεται γὰρ δή, ἔφη, καὶ πολὺ τοῦτο τὸ ῥῆμα. Ἆρ' οὖν, ἦν δ' ἐγώ, ὅπερ ᾖα νῦν δὴ ἐρῶν, ἡ τοῦ τοιούτου ἀπληστία καὶ ἡ τῶν ἄλλων ἀμέλεια καὶ ταύτην τὴν πολιτείαν μεθίστησί τε καὶ παρασκευάζει τυραννίδος δεηθῆναι; Πῶς; ἔφη. Ὅταν, οἶμαι, δημοκρατουμένη πόλις ἐλευθερίας διψήσασα κακῶν D οἰνοχόων προστατούντων τύχῃ, | καὶ πορρωτέρω

Drunken with Freedom,

τοῦ δέοντος ἀκράτου αὐτῆς μεθυσθῇ, τοὺς ἄρχοντας δή, ἂν μὴ πάνυ πρᾷοι ὦσι καὶ πολλὴν παρέχωσι τὴν ἐλευθερίαν, κολάζει αἰτιωμένη ὡς μιαρούς τε καὶ ὀλιγαρχικούς. Δρῶσιν γάρ, ἔφη, τοῦτο. Τοὺς δέ γε, εἶπον, τῶν ἀρχόντων κατηκόους προπηλακίζει ὡς ἐθελοδούλους τε καὶ οὐδὲν ὄντας, τοὺς δὲ ἄρχοντας μὲν ἀρχομένοις, ἀρχομένους δὲ ἄρχουσιν ὁμοίους ἰδίᾳ τε καὶ δημοσίᾳ ἐπαινεῖ τε καὶ E τιμᾷ. ἆρ' οὐκ ἀνάγκη ἐν τοιαύτῃ | πόλει ἐπὶ πᾶν τὸ τῆς ἐλευθερίας ἰέναι; Πῶς γὰρ οὔ;

anarchy permeates all its members—

Καὶ καταδύεσθαί γε, ἦν δ' ἐγώ, ὦ φίλε, εἴς τε τὰς ἰδίας οἰκίας καὶ τελευτᾶν μέχρι τῶν θηρίων τὴν ἀναρ-

χίαν ἐμφυομένην. Πῶς, ἦ δ᾽ ὅς, τὸ τοιοῦτον 562
λέγομεν; Οἷον, ἔφην, πατέρα μὲν ἐθίζεσθαι
παιδὶ ὅμοιον γίγνεσθαι καὶ φοβεῖσθαι τοὺς ὑεῖς,
ὑὸν δὲ πατρί, καὶ μήτε αἰσχύνεσθαι μήτε δεδιέναι
τοὺς γονέας, ἵνα δὴ ἐλεύθερος ᾖ· μέτοικον | δὲ 563
ἀστῷ καὶ ἀστὸν μετοίκῳ ἐξισοῦσθαι, καὶ ξένον
ὡσαύτως. Γίγνεται γὰρ οὕτως, ἔφη. Ταῦτά
τε, ἦν δ᾽ ἐγώ, καὶ σμικρὰ τοιάδε ἄλλα γίγνεται·
διδάσκαλός τε ἐν τῷ τοιούτῳ φοιτητὰς φοβεῖται
καὶ θωπεύει, φοιτηταί τε διδασκάλων ὀλιγωροῦσιν, οὕτω δὲ καὶ παιδαγωγῶν· καὶ ὅλως
οἱ μὲν νέοι πρεσβυτέροις ἀπεικάζονται καὶ
διαμιλλῶνται καὶ ἐν λόγοις καὶ ἐν ἔργοις, οἱ
δὲ γέροντες ξυγκαθιέντες τοῖς νέοις εὐτραπελίας
τε καὶ χαριεντισμοῦ | ἐμπίμπλανται, μιμούμενοι B
τοὺς νέους, ἵνα δὴ μὴ δοκῶσιν ἀηδεῖς εἶναι μηδὲ
δεσποτικοί. Πάνυ μὲν οὖν, ἔφη. Τὸ δέ γε,
ἦν δ᾽ ἐγώ, ἔσχατον, ὦ φίλε, τῆς ἐλευθερίας
τοῦ πλήθους, ὅσον γίγνεται ἐν τῇ τοιαύτῃ
πόλει, ὅταν δὴ οἱ ἐωνημένοι καὶ αἱ
ἐωνημέναι μηδὲν ἧττον ἐλεύθεροι ὦσι
τῶν πριαμένων. ἐν γυναιξὶ δὲ πρὸς ἄνδρας
καὶ ἀνδράσι πρὸς γυναῖκας ὅση ἡ ἰσονομία καὶ
ἐλευθερία γίγνεται, ὀλίγου ἐπελαθόμεθ᾽ εἰπεῖν.
Οὐκοῦν κατ᾽ Αἰσχύλον, | ἔφη, ἐροῦμεν ὅ τι νῦν C
ἦλθ᾽ ἐπὶ στόμα; Πάνυ γε, εἶπον. καὶ ἔγωγε
οὕτω λέγω· τὸ μὲν γὰρ τῶν θηρίων τῶν ὑπὸ
τοῖς ἀνθρώποις ὅσῳ ἐλευθερώτερά ἐστιν ἐνταῦθα
ἢ ἐν ἄλλῃ, οὐκ ἄν τις πείθοιτο ἄπειρος. ἀτεχνῶς
γὰρ αἵ τε κύνες κατὰ τὴν παροιμίαν οἷαίπερ αἱ
δέσποιναι, γίγνονταί τε δὴ καὶ ἵπποι καὶ ὄνοι,

its very slaves,

563 dogs, and donkeys.

πάνυ ἐλευθέρως καὶ σεμνῶς εἰθισμένοι
πορεύεσθαι, κατὰ τὰς ὁδοὺς ἐμβάλ-
λοντες τῷ ἀεὶ ἀπαντῶντι, ἐὰν μὴ ἐξίστηται·
D καὶ τἆλλα πάντα οὕτως | μεστὰ ἐλευθερίας
γίγνεται. Τὸ ἐμόν γ', ἔφη, ἐμοὶ λέγεις ὄναρ·
αὐτὸς γὰρ εἰς ἀγρὸν πορευόμενος θαμὰ αὐτὸ
πάσχω. Τὸ δὲ δὴ κεφάλαιον, ἦν δ' ἐγώ,
πάντων τούτων ξυνηθροισμένων ἐννοεῖς, ὡς
ἁπαλὴν τὴν ψυχὴν τῶν πολιτῶν ποιεῖ, ὥστε,
κἂν ὁτιοῦν δουλείας τισὶ προσφέρηται, ἀγανα-
κτεῖν καὶ μὴ ἀνέχεσθαι; τελευτῶντες γάρ που
οἶσθ' ὅτι οὐδὲ τῶν νόμων φροντίζουσι γεγραμ-
μένων ἢ ἀγράφων, ἵνα δὴ μηδαμῇ μηδεὶς αὐτοῖς
E | ᾖ δεσπότης. Καὶ μάλ', ἔφη, οἶδα.

Αὕτη μὲν τοίνυν, ἦν δ' ἐγώ, ὦ φίλε, ἡ ἀρχὴ
οὑτωσὶ καλὴ καὶ νεανική, ὅθεν τυραννὶς φύεται,
ὡς ἐμοὶ δοκεῖ. Νεανικὴ δῆτα, ἔφη·

Hence springs Tyranny.

ἀλλὰ τί τὸ μετὰ τοῦτο; Ταὐτόν, ἦν
δ' ἐγώ, ὅπερ ἐν τῇ ὀλιγαρχίᾳ νόσημα ἐγγενόμενον
ἀπώλεσεν αὐτήν, τοῦτο καὶ ἐν ταύτῃ πλέον τε
καὶ ἰσχυρότερον ἐκ τῆς ἐξουσίας ἐγγενόμενον
καταδουλοῦται δημοκρατίαν· καὶ τῷ ὄντι τὸ
ἄγαν τι ποιεῖν μεγάλην φιλεῖ εἰς τοὐναντίον
μεταβολὴν ἀνταποδιδόναι, ἐν ὥραις τε καὶ ἐν |
564 φυτοῖς καὶ ἐν σώμασι, καὶ δὴ καὶ ἐν πολιτείαις
οὐχ ἥκιστα. Εἰκός, ἔφη. Ἡ γὰρ ἄγαν
ἐλευθερία ἔοικεν οὐκ εἰς ἄλλο τι ἢ εἰς
ἄγαν δουλείαν μεταβάλλειν καὶ ἰδιώτῃ
καὶ πόλει. Εἰκὸς γάρ. Εἰκότως τοίνυν,
εἶπον, οὐκ ἐξ ἄλλης πολιτείας τυραννὶς καθί-
σταται ἢ ἐκ δημοκρατίας, ἐξ οἶμαι τῆς ἀκρο-

τάτης ἐλευθερίας δουλεία πλείστη τε καὶ ἀγριωτάτη. Ἔχει γάρ, ἔφη, λόγον.

IX

The Soul three Creatures in one.

Εἶεν δή, εἶπον· ἐπειδὴ ἐνταῦθα λόγου | 588
γεγόναμεν, ἀναλάβωμεν τὰ πρῶτα λεχθέντα, B
δι' ἃ δεῦρ' ἥκομεν· ἦν δέ που λεγόμενον,
λυσιτελεῖν ἀδικεῖν τῷ τελέως μὲν ἀδίκῳ
δοξαζομένῳ δὲ δικαίῳ. ἢ οὐχ οὕτως ἐλέχθη;
Οὕτω μὲν οὖν. Νῦν δή, ἔφην, αὐτῷ διαλεγώμεθα, ἐπειδὴ διωμολογησάμεθα τό τε ἀδικεῖν
καὶ τὸ δίκαια πράττειν ἣν ἑκάτερον ἔχει
δύναμιν. Πῶς; ἔφη. Εἰκόνα πλάσαντες τῆς
ψυχῆς λόγῳ, ἵνα εἰδῇ ὁ ἐκεῖνα λέγων οἷα
ἔλεγεν. Ποίαν τινά; ἦ δ' | ὅς. Τῶν τοιούτων C
τινά, ἦν δ' ἐγώ, οἷαι μυθολογοῦνται παλαιαὶ
γενέσθαι φύσεις, ἥ τε Χιμαίρας καὶ ἡ Σκύλλης καὶ Κερβέρου, καὶ ἄλλαι τινὲς συχναὶ
λέγονται ξυμπεφυκυῖαι ἰδέαι πολλαὶ εἰς ἓν
γενέσθαι. Λέγονται γάρ, ἔφη. Πλάττε τοίνυν
μίαν μὲν ἰδέαν θηρίου ποικίλου καὶ
πολυκεφάλου, ἡμέρων δὲ θηρίων

A monster many-headed,

ἔχοντος κεφαλὰς κύκλῳ καὶ ἀγρίων, καὶ δυνατοῦ
μεταβάλλειν καὶ φύειν ἐξ αὑτοῦ πάντα ταῦτα.
Δεινοῦ πλάστου, ἔφη, τὸ ἔργον· | ὅμως δέ, D
ἐπειδὴ εὐπλαστότερον κηροῦ καὶ τῶν τοιούτων
λόγος, πεπλάσθω. Μίαν δὴ τοίνυν
ἄλλην ἰδέαν λέοντος, μίαν δὲ ἀνθρώ-

a lion, and a man.

588 που· πολὺ δὲ μέγιστον ἔστω τὸ πρῶτον καὶ
δεύτερον τὸ δεύτερον. Ταῦτα, ἔφη, ῥᾴω· καὶ
πέπλασται. Σύναπτε τοίνυν αὐτὰ εἰς ἓν τρία
ὄντα, ὥστε πῃ ξυμπεφυκέναι ἀλλήλοις. Συν-
ῆπται, ἔφη. Περίπλασον δὴ αὐτοῖς ἔξωθεν
ἑνὸς εἰκόνα, τὴν τοῦ ἀνθρώπου, ὥστε τῷ μὴ
E δυναμένῳ τὰ ἐντὸς ὁρᾶν ἀλλὰ | τὸ ἔξω μόνον
ἔλυτρον ὁρῶντι, ἓν ζῷον φαίνεσθαι, ἄνθρωπον.
Περιπέπλασται, ἔφη. Λέγωμεν δὴ τῷ λέγοντι
ὡς λυσιτελεῖ τούτῳ ἀδικεῖν τῷ ἀνθρώπῳ,
δίκαια δὲ πράττειν οὐ ξυμφέρει, ὅτι
οὐδὲν ἄλλο φησὶν ἢ λυσιτελεῖν αὐτῷ
τὸ παντοδαπὸν θηρίον εὐωχοῦντι

Wrong-doing fattens the first two,

ποιεῖν ἰσχυρὸν καὶ τὸν λέοντα καὶ τὰ περὶ
589 τὸν λέοντα, τὸν δὲ ἄνθρωπον λιμοκτονεῖν | καὶ
ποιεῖν ἀσθενῆ, ὥστε ἕλκεσθαι ὅπῃ ἂν ἐκείνων
ὁπότερον ἄγῃ, καὶ μηδὲν ἕτερον ἑτέρῳ ξυνεθίζειν
μηδὲ φίλον ποιεῖν, ἀλλ' ἐᾶν αὐτὰ ἐν αὑτοῖς
δάκνεσθαί τε καὶ μαχόμενα ἐσθίειν ἄλληλα.
Παντάπασι γάρ, ἔφη, ταῦτ' ἂν λέγοι ὁ τὸ
ἀδικεῖν ἐπαινῶν. Οὐκοῦν αὖ ὁ τὰ δίκαια
λέγων λυσιτελεῖν φαίη ἂν δεῖν ταῦτα
πράττειν καὶ ταῦτα λέγειν, ὅθεν τοῦ
ἀνθρώπου ὁ ἐντὸς ἄνθρωπος ἔσται

Right tames the lion and helps the man.

B ἐγκρατέστατος, | καὶ τοῦ πολυκεφάλου θρέμ-
ματος ἐπιμελήσεται (ὥσπερ γεωργός, τὰ μὲν
ἥμερα τρέφων καὶ τιθασεύων, τὰ δὲ ἄγρια
ἀποκωλύων φύεσθαι), ξύμμαχον ποιησάμενος
τὴν τοῦ λέοντος φύσιν, καὶ κοινῇ πάντων
κηδόμενος, φίλα ποιησάμενος ἀλλήλοις τε καὶ
αὑτῷ, οὕτω θρέψει; Κομιδῇ γὰρ αὖ λέγει

ταῦτα ὁ τὸ δίκαιον ἐπαινῶν. Κατὰ πάντα 589
τρόπον δὴ ὁ μὲν τὰ δίκαια ἐγκωμιάζων ἀληθῆ
ἂν λέγοι, | ὁ δὲ τὰ ἄδικα ψεύδοιτο. πρός C
τε γὰρ ἡδονὴν καὶ πρὸς εὐδοξίαν καὶ ὠφελίαν
σκοπουμένῳ ὁ μὲν ἐπαινέτης τοῦ δικαίου
ἀληθεύει, ὁ δὲ ψέκτης οὐδὲν ὑγιὲς οὐδ' εἰδὼς
ψέγει ὅ τι ψέγει. Οὔ μοι δοκεῖ, ἦ δ' ὅς,
οὐδαμῇ γε. Πείθωμεν τοίνυν αὐτὸν πράως
(οὐ γὰρ ἑκὼν ἁμαρτάνει), ἐρωτῶντες· Ὦ
μακάριε, οὐ καὶ τὰ καλὰ καὶ αἰσχρὰ νόμιμα
διὰ τὰ τοιαῦτ' ἂν φαῖμεν γεγονέναι—τὰ μὲν |
καλὰ τὰ ὑπὸ τῷ ἀνθρώπῳ (μᾶλλον δὲ ἴσως τὰ D
ὑπὸ τῷ θείῳ) τὰ θηριώδη ποιοῦντα τῆς φύσεως,
αἰσχρὰ δὲ τὰ ὑπὸ τῷ ἀγρίῳ τὸ ἥμερον δουλού-
μενα; ξυμφήσει ἢ πῶς; Ἐὰν ἐμοί, ἔφη,
πείθηται. Ἔστιν οὖν, εἶπον, ὅτῳ λυσιτελεῖ ἐκ
τούτου τοῦ λόγου χρυσίον λαμβά-
νειν ἀδίκως, εἴπερ τοιόνδε τι γίγνεται,
λαμβάνων τὸ χρυσίον ἅμα καταδουλοῦται τὸ
βέλτιστον ἑαυτοῦ τῷ μοχθηροτάτῳ; ἢ εἰ μὲν
| λαβὼν χρυσίον ὑὸν ἢ θυγατέρα ἐδουλοῦτο, E
καὶ ταῦτ' εἰς ἀγρίων τε καὶ κακῶν ἀνδρῶν,
οὐκ ἂν αὐτῷ ἐλυσιτέλει οὐδ' ἂν πάμπολυ ἐπὶ
τούτῳ λαμβάνειν, εἰ δὲ τὸ ἑαυτοῦ θειότατον
ὑπὸ τῷ ἀθεωτάτῳ τε καὶ μιαρωτάτῳ δουλοῦται
καὶ μηδὲν ἐλεεῖ, οὐκ ἄρα ἄθλιός ἐστι καὶ | πολὺ 590
ἐπὶ δεινοτέρῳ ὀλέθρῳ χρυσὸν δωροδοκεῖ ἢ Ἐρι-
φύλη ἐπὶ τῇ τοῦ ἀνδρὸς ψυχῇ τὸν ὅρμον δεξα-
μένη; Πολὺ μέντοι, ἦ δ' ὃς ὁ Γλαύκων· ἐγὼ
γάρ σοι ὑπὲρ ἐκείνου ἀποκρινοῦμαι.
Οὐκοῦν καὶ τὸ ἀκολασταίνειν οἴει διὰ

What theft does, and intemperance, self-will, and like qualities.

590 τοιαῦτα πάλαι ψέγεσθαι, ὅτι ἀνίεται ἐν τῷ
τοιούτῳ τὸ δεινὸν τὸ μέγα ἐκεῖνο καὶ πολυειδὲς
θρέμμα πέρα τοῦ δέοντος; Δῆλον, ἔφη. Ἡ δ'
αὐθαδία καὶ δυσκολία ψέγεται οὐχ ὅταν τὸ λεον-
B τῶδές | τε καὶ ὀφεῶδες αὔξηται καὶ συντείνηται
ἀναρμόστως; Πάνυ μὲν οὖν. Τρυφὴ δὲ καὶ
μαλθακία οὐκ ἐπὶ τῇ αὐτοῦ τούτου χαλάσει
τε καὶ ἀνέσει ψέγεται, ὅταν ἐν αὐτῷ δειλίαν
ἐμποιῇ; Τί μήν; Κολακεία δὲ καὶ ἀνελευθερία
οὐχ ὅταν τις τὸ αὐτὸν τοῦτο, τὸ θυμοειδές,
ὑπὸ τῷ ὀχλώδει θηρίῳ ποιῇ, καὶ ἕνεκα
χρημάτων καὶ τῆς ἐκείνου ἀπληστίας προ-
πηλακιζόμενον ἐθίζῃ ἐκ νέου ἀντὶ λέοντος
C πίθηκον γίγνεσθαι; | Καὶ μάλα, ἔφη. Βαναυσία
δὲ καὶ χειροτεχνία διὰ τί, οἴει, ὄνειδος φέρει;
ἢ δι' ἄλλο τι φήσομεν ἢ ὅταν τις ἀσθενὲς
φύσει ἔχῃ τὸ τοῦ βελτίστου εἶδος, ὥστε μὴ
ἂν δύνασθαι ἄρχειν τῶν ἐν αὐτῷ θρεμμάτων,
ἀλλὰ θεραπεύειν ἐκεῖνα, καὶ τὰ θωπεύματα
αὐτῶν μόνον δύνηται μανθάνειν; Ἔοικεν, ἔφη.

He should be ruled who cannot rule himself.

Οὐκοῦν ἵνα καὶ ὁ τοιοῦτος ὑπὸ
ὁμοίου ἄρχηται οἵουπερ ὁ βέλτιστος,
δοῦλον αὐτόν φαμεν δεῖν εἶναι ἐκείνου
D τοῦ | βελτίστου, ἔχοντος ἐν αὐτῷ τὸ θεῖον
ἄρχον, οὐκ ἐπὶ βλάβῃ τῇ τοῦ δούλου οἰόμενοι
δεῖν ἄρχεσθαι αὐτόν, ὥσπερ Θρασύμαχος ᾤετο
τοὺς ἀρχομένους, ἀλλ' ὡς ἄμεινον ὂν παντὶ
ὑπὸ θείου καὶ φρονίμου ἄρχεσθαι, μάλιστα μὲν
οἰκείως ἔχοντος ἐν αὐτῷ, εἰ δὲ μή, ἔξωθεν
ἐφεστῶτος, ἵνα εἰς δύναμιν πάντες ὅμοιοι ὦμεν
καὶ φίλοι τῷ αὐτῷ κυβερνώμενοι; Καὶ ὀρθῶς

γ', ἔφη. Δηλοῖ δέ γε, ἦν δ' ἐγώ, καὶ ὁ 590
νόμος | ὅτι τοιοῦτον βούλεται, πᾶσι τοῖς ἐν τῇ E
πόλει ξύμμαχος ὤν· καὶ ἡ τῶν παίδων ἀρχή,
τὸ μὴ ἐᾶν ἐλευθέρους εἶναι, ἕως ἂν ἐν αὐτοῖς
ὥσπερ ἐν πόλει πολιτείαν καταστήσωμεν, καὶ
τὸ βέλτιστον θεραπεύσαντες | τῷ παρ' ἡμῖν 591
τοιούτῳ ἀντικαταστήσωμεν φύλακα ὅμοιον καὶ
ἄρχοντα ἐν αὐτῷ, καὶ τότε δὴ ἐλεύθερον
ἀφίεμεν. Δηλοῖ γάρ, ἦ δ' ὅς. Πῇ δὴ οὖν
φήσομεν, ὦ Γλαύκων, καὶ κατὰ τίνα λόγον λυσι-
τελεῖν ἀδικεῖν ἢ ἀκολασταίνειν ἤ τι αἰσχρὸν
ποιεῖν, ἐξ ὧν πονηρότερος μὲν ἔσται, πλείω δὲ
χρήματα ἢ ἄλλην τινὰ δύναμιν κεκτήσεται;
Οὐδαμῇ, ἦ δ' ὅς. Πῇ δ' ἀδικοῦντα λανθάνειν
καὶ μὴ διδόναι δίκην λυσιτελεῖν; ἢ οὐχὶ ὁ μὲν
λανθάνων | ἔτι πονηρότερος γίγνεται, τοῦ δὲ μὴ B
λανθάνοντος καὶ κολαζομένου τὸ μὲν
θηριῶδες κοιμίζεται καὶ ἡμεροῦται,
τὸ δὲ ἥμερον ἐλευθεροῦται, καὶ ὅλη
ἡ ψυχὴ εἰς τὴν βελτίστην φύσιν καθισταμένη
τιμιωτέραν ἕξιν λαμβάνει, σωφροσύνην τε καὶ
δικαιοσύνην μετὰ φρονήσεως κτωμένη, ἢ σῶμα
ἰσχύν τε καὶ κάλλος μετὰ ὑγιείας λαμβάνον, το-
σούτῳ ὅσῳπερ ψυχὴ σώματος τιμιωτέρα; Παν-
τάπασι μὲν οὖν, ἔφη. Οὐκοῦν ὅ γε νοῦν ἔχων
πάντα | τὰ αὑτοῦ εἰς τοῦτο ξυντείνας βιώσεται, C
πρῶτον μὲν τὰ μαθήματα τιμῶν, ἃ τοιαύτην αὐτοῦ
τὴν ψυχὴν ἀπεργάσεται, τὰ δὲ ἄλλα
ἀτιμάζων; Δῆλον, ἔφη. Ἔπειτά γ',
εἶπον, τὴν τοῦ σώματος ἕξιν καὶ τροφὴν οὐχ ὅπως
τῇ θηριώδει καὶ ἀλόγῳ ἡδονῇ ἐπιτρέψας ἐνταῦθα

The wrong-doer is better punished.

One's duty to himself.

591 τετραμμένος ζήσει, ἀλλ᾽ οὐδὲ πρὸς ὑγίειαν
βλέπων, οὐδὲ τοῦτο πρεσβεύων, ὅπως ἰσχυρὸς
ἢ ὑγιὴς ἢ καλὸς ἔσται, ἐὰν μὴ καὶ σωφρονήσειν
D μέλλῃ ἀπ᾽ αὐτῶν, | ἀλλ᾽ ἀεὶ τὴν ἐν τῷ σώματι
ἁρμονίαν τῆς ἐν τῇ ψυχῇ ἕνεκα ξυμφωνίας
ἁρμοττόμενος [φαίνηται]. Παντάπασι μὲν οὖν,
ἔφη, ἐάνπερ μέλλῃ τῇ ἀληθείᾳ μουσικὸς εἶναι.
Οὐκοῦν, εἶπον, καὶ τὴν ἐν τῇ τῶν χρημάτων
κτήσει ξύνταξίν τε καὶ ξυμφωνίαν; καὶ τὸν
ὄγκον τοῦ πλήθους οὐκ ἐκπληττόμενος ὑπὸ
τοῦ τῶν πολλῶν μακαρισμοῦ ἄπειρον αὐξήσει,
ἀπέραντα κακὰ ἔχων; Οὐκ οἴομαι, ἔφη.
E Ἀλλ᾽ ἀποβλέπων γε, εἶπον, | πρὸς τὴν ἐν
αὑτῷ πολιτείαν καὶ φυλάττων, μή τι παρακινῇ
αὑτοῦ τῶν ἐκεῖ διὰ πλῆθος οὐσίας ἢ δι᾽
ὀλιγότητα, οὕτως κυβερνῶν προσθήσει καὶ
ἀναλώσει τῆς οὐσίας καθ᾽ ὅσον ἂν οἷός τ᾽ ᾖ.
Κομιδῇ μὲν οὖν, ἔφη. Ἀλλὰ μὴν καὶ τιμάς
592 γε, εἰς ταὐτὸν ἀποβλέπων, | τῶν μὲν μεθέξει
καὶ γεύσεται ἑκών, ἃς ἂν ἡγῆται ἀμείνω αὑτὸν
ποιήσειν, ἃς δ᾽ ἂν λύσειν τὴν ὑπάρχουσαν
ἕξιν, φεύξεται ἰδίᾳ καὶ δημοσίᾳ. Οὐκ ἄρα,
ἔφη, τά γε πολιτικὰ ἐθελήσει πράττειν, ἐάνπερ
τούτου κήδηται. Νὴ τὸν κύνα, ἦν δ᾽ ἐγώ, ἔν
γε τῇ ἑαυτοῦ πόλει καὶ μάλα, οὐ
μέντοι ἴσως ἔν γε τῇ πατρίδι, ἐὰν
μὴ θεία τις ξυμβῇ τύχη. Μανθάνω,
ἔφη· ἐν ᾗ νῦν διήλθομεν οἰκίζοντες

The ideal Republic is possible in each one's soul.

πόλει λέγεις, τῇ ἐν λόγοις κειμένῃ ἐπεὶ γῆς
B γε | οὐδαμοῦ οἶμαι αὐτὴν εἶναι. Ἀλλ᾽, ἦν δ᾽
ἐγώ, ἐν οὐρανῷ ἴσως παράδειγμα ἀνάκειται τῷ

βουλομένῳ ὁρᾶν καὶ ὁρῶντι εἰς αὑτὸν κατοικίζειν. 592
διαφέρει δὲ οὐδέν, εἴτε που ἔστιν εἴτε ἔσται·
τὰ γὰρ ταύτης μόνης ἂν πράξειεν, ἄλλης δὲ
οὐδεμιᾶς. Εἰκός γ', ἔφη.

X

The Apocalypse of Er.

Ἃ μὲν τοίνυν, ἦν δ' ἐγώ, ζῶντι τῷ δικαίῳ
παρὰ θεῶν τε καὶ ἀνθρώπων | ἆθλά τε καὶ 614
μισθοὶ καὶ δῶρα γίγνεται πρὸς ἐκείνοις τοῖς ἀγαθοῖς οἷς αὐτὴ παρείχετο ἡ δικαιοσύνη, τοιαῦτ' ἂν εἴη. Καὶ μάλ', ἔφη, καλά τε καὶ βέβαια. Ταῦτα τοίνυν, ἦν δ' ἐγώ, οὐδέν ἐστι πλήθει οὐδὲ μεγέθει πρὸς ἐκεῖνα, ἃ τελευτήσαντα ἑκάτερον περιμένει. χρὴ δ' αὐτὰ ἀκοῦσαι, ἵνα τελέως ἑκάτερος αὐτῶν ἀπειλήφῃ τὰ ὑπὸ τοῦ λόγου ὀφειλόμενα ἀκοῦσαι. Λέγοις ἄν, ἔφη,
ὡς οὐ πολλὰ ἄλλ' ἥδιον | ἀκούοντι. Ἀλλ' οὐ B
μέντοι σοι, ἦν δ' ἐγώ, Ἀλκίνου γε ἀπόλογον ἐρῶ, ἀλλ' ἀλκίμου μὲν ἀνδρός, Ἠρὸς τοῦ Ἀρμενίου, τὸ γένος Παμφύλου· ὅς ποτε ἐν πολέμῳ τελευτήσας, ἀναιρεθέντων δεκαταίων τῶν νεκρῶν ἤδη διεφθαρμένων, ὑγιὴς μὲν ἀνῃρέθη, κομισθεὶς δ' οἴκαδε μέλλων θάπτεσθαι δωδεκαταῖος ἐπὶ τῇ πυρᾷ κείμενος ἀνεβίω, ἀναβιοὺς δ' ἔλεγεν ἃ ἐκεῖ ἴδοι. ἔφη δέ, ἐπειδὴ οὗ ἐκβῆναι τὴν ψυχήν, πορεύ-
εσθαι μετὰ πολλῶν, καὶ ἀφικνεῖσθαι | σφᾶς εἰς C
τόπον τινὰ δαιμόνιον, ἐν ᾧ τῆς τε γῆς δύ'

The apocalypse of Er. His tale.

The meeting-place for judgment.

614 εἶναι χάσματα ἐχομένω ἀλλήλοιν καὶ
τοῦ οὐρανοῦ αὖ ἐν τῷ ἄνω ἄλλα
καταντικρύ· δικαστὰς δὲ μεταξὺ τού-
των καθῆσθαι, οὕς, ἐπειδὴ διαδικάσειαν, τοὺς
μὲν δικαίους κελεύειν πορεύεσθαι τὴν εἰς δεξιάν
τε καὶ ἄνω διὰ τοῦ οὐρανοῦ, σημεῖα περιά-
ψαντας τῶν δεδικασμένων ἐν τῷ πρόσθεν, τοὺς
δὲ ἀδίκους τὴν εἰς ἀριστεράν τε καὶ κάτω,
ἔχοντας καὶ τούτους ἐν τῷ ὄπισθεν σημεῖα |
D πάντων ὧν ἔπραξαν. ἑαυτοῦ δὲ προσελθόντος
εἰπεῖν ὅτι δέοι αὐτὸν ἄγγελον ἀνθρώποις γενέ-
σθαι τῶν ἐκεῖ καὶ διακελεύοιντό οἱ ἀκούειν τε
καὶ θεᾶσθαι πάντα τὰ ἐν τῷ τόπῳ. ὁρᾶν δὴ
ταύτῃ μὲν καθ' ἑκάτερον τὸ χάσμα τοῦ οὐρανοῦ
τε καὶ τῆς γῆς ἀπιούσας τὰς ψυχάς, ἐπειδὴ
αὐταῖς δικασθείη, κατὰ δὲ τὼ ἑτέρω ἐκ μὲν τοῦ
ἀνιέναι ἐκ τῆς γῆς μεστὰς αὐχμοῦ τε καὶ
κόνεως, ἐκ δὲ τοῦ ἑτέρου καταβαίνειν ἑτέρας
E ἐκ τοῦ οὐρανοῦ καθαράς· καὶ | τὰς ἀεὶ ἀφι-
κνουμένας ὥσπερ ἐκ πολλῆς πορείας φαίνεσθαι
ἥκειν, καὶ ἁσμένας εἰς τὸν λειμῶνα ἀπιούσας
οἷον ἐν πανηγύρει κατασκηνᾶσθαι, καὶ ἀσπά-
ζεσθαί τε ἀλλήλας ὅσαι γνώριμαι, καὶ πυνθά-
νεσθαι τάς τε ἐκ τῆς γῆς ἡκούσας παρὰ τῶν
ἑτέρων τὰ ἐκεῖ καὶ τὰς ἐκ τοῦ οὐρανοῦ τὰ
παρ' ἐκείναις, διηγεῖσθαι δὲ ἀλλήλαις τὰς μὲν
ὀδυρομένας τε καὶ κλαιούσας, ἀναμιμνῃσκομένας |
615 ὅσα τε καὶ οἷα πάθοιεν καὶ ἴδοιεν ἐν τῇ ὑπὸ
γῆς πορείᾳ (εἶναι δὲ τὴν πορείαν χιλιέτη) τὰς
δ' αὖ ἐκ τοῦ οὐρανοῦ εὐπαθίας διηγεῖσθαι καὶ
θέας ἀμηχάνους τὸ κάλλος. τὰ μὲν οὖν πολλά,

Tenfold penalty, tenfold reward.

ὦ Γλαύκων, πολλοῦ χρόνου διηγήσασθαι· τὸ 615
δ᾽ οὖν κεφάλαιον ἔφη τόδε εἶναι· ὅσα πώποτέ
τινα ἠδίκησαν καὶ ὅσους ἕκαστοι,
ὑπὲρ ἁπάντων δίκην δεδωκέναι ἐν
μέρει, ὑπὲρ ἑκάστου δεκάκις (τοῦτο δ᾽ εἶναι
κατὰ ἑκατονταετηρίδα ἑκάστην, ὡς | βίου ὄντος B
τοσούτου τοῦ ἀνθρωπίνου), ἵνα δεκαπλάσιον τὸ
ἔκτισμα τοῦ ἀδικήματος ἐκτίνοιεν· καὶ οἷον εἴ
τινες πολλῶν θανάτων ἦσαν αἴτιοι, ἢ πόλεις
προδόντες ἢ στρατόπεδα καὶ εἰς δουλείας ἐμβε-
βληκότες, ἤ τινος ἄλλης κακουχίας μεταίτιοι,
πάντων τούτων δεκαπλασίας ἀλγηδόνας ὑπὲρ
ἑκάστου κομίσαιντο, καὶ αὖ εἴ τινας εὐεργεσίας
εὐεργετηκότες καὶ δίκαιοι καὶ ὅσιοι
γεγονότες εἶεν, κατὰ ταὐτὰ τὴν ἀξίαν
κομίζοιντο. τῶν | δὲ εὐθὺς γενομένων καὶ C
ὀλίγον χρόνον βιούντων πέρι ἄλλα ἔλεγεν οὐκ
ἄξια μνήμης· εἰς δὲ θεοὺς ἀσεβείας τε καὶ εὐ-
σεβείας (καὶ γονέας), καὶ αὐτόχειρος φόνου, μείζους
ἔτι τοὺς μισθοὺς διηγεῖτο.

The fate of Ardiaeus.

Ἔφη γὰρ δὴ παραγενέσθαι ἐρωτωμένῳ ἑτέρῳ
ὑπὸ ἑτέρου, ὅπου εἴη Ἀρδιαῖος ὁ
μέγας. ὁ δὲ Ἀρδιαῖος οὗτος τῆς
Παμφυλίας ἔν τινι πόλει τύραννος ἐγεγόνει,
ἤδη χιλιοστὸν ἔτος εἰς ἐκεῖνον τὸν χρόνον,
γέροντά τε πατέρα ἀποκτείνας καὶ | πρεσβύ- D
τερον ἀδελφόν, καὶ ἄλλα δὴ πολλά τε καὶ
ἀνόσια εἰργασμένος, ὡς ἐλέγετο. ἔφη οὖν τὸν
ἐρωτώμενον εἰπεῖν, Οὐχ ἥκει, φάναι, οὐδ᾽ ἂν
ἥξει δεῦρο. ἐθεασάμεθα γὰρ οὖν δὴ καὶ τοῦτο
τῶν δεινῶν θεαμάτων· ἐπειδὴ ἐγγὺς τοῦ στομίου

615 ἦμεν μέλλοντες ἀνιέναι καὶ τἆλλα πάντα πεπονθότες, ἐκεῖνόν τε κατείδομεν ἐξαίφνης καὶ ἄλλους, σχεδόν τι αὐτῶν τοὺς πλείστους τυράννους— ἦσαν δὲ καὶ ἰδιῶταί τινες τῶν μεγάλα ἡμαρ-
E τηκότων· οὓς οἰομένους | ἤδη ἀναβήσεσθαι οὐκ ἐδέχετο τὸ στόμιον, ἀλλ᾽ ἐμυκᾶτο, ὁπότε τις τῶν οὕτως ἀνιάτως ἐχόντων εἰς πονηρίαν ἢ μὴ ἱκανῶς δεδωκὼς δίκην ἐπιχειροῖ ἀνιέναι. ἐνταῦθα δὴ ἄνδρες, ἔφη, ἄγριοι, διάπυροι ἰδεῖν, παρεστῶτες καὶ καταμανθάνοντες τὸ φθέγμα τοὺς μὲν διαλαβόντες ἦγον, τὸν δὲ Ἀρδιαῖον καὶ ἄλλους συμποδίσαντες χεῖράς τε καὶ πόδας |
616 καὶ κεφαλήν, καταβαλόντες καὶ ἐκδείραντες, εἷλκον παρὰ τὴν ὁδὸν ἐκτὸς ἐπ᾽ ἀσπαλάθων κνάπτοντες καὶ τοῖς ἀεὶ παριοῦσι σημαίνοντες, ὧν ἕνεκά τε καὶ εἰς ὅ τι [τὸν τάρταρον] ἐμπεσούμενοι ἄγοιντο. ἔνθα δὴ φόβων, ἔφη, πολλῶν καὶ παντοδαπῶν σφίσι γεγονότων, τοῦτον ὑπερβάλλειν, μὴ γένοιτο ἑκάστῳ τὸ φθέγμα, ὅτε ἀναβαίνοι, καὶ ἁσμενέστατα ἕκαστον σιγήσαντος ἀναβῆναι.

Καὶ τὰς μὲν δὴ δίκας τε καὶ τιμωρίας
B τοιαύτας | τινὰς εἶναι, καὶ αὖ τὰς εὐεργεσίας ταύταις ἀντιστρόφους· ἐπειδὴ δὲ τοῖς ἐν τῷ λειμῶνι ἑκάστοις ἑπτὰ ἡμέραι γένοιντο, ἀναστάντας ἐντεῦθεν δεῖν τῇ ὀγδόῃ πορεύεσθαι, καὶ ἀφικνεῖσθαι τεταρταίους ὅθεν καθορᾶν ἄνωθεν διὰ παντὸς τοῦ οὐρανοῦ καὶ γῆς τεταμένον φῶς εὐθύ, οἷον κίονα, μάλιστα τῇ ἴριδι προσφερῆ, λαμπρότερον δὲ καὶ καθαρώτερον. εἰς ὃ ἀφικέσθαι προελθόντας

Forward to the pillar of light and spindle of Necessity.

ἡμερησίαν ὁδόν, καὶ ἰδεῖν αὐτόθι κατὰ μέσον | 616
τὸ φῶς ἐκ τοῦ οὐρανοῦ τὰ ἄκρα αὐτοῦ τῶν C
δεσμῶν τεταμένα· εἶναι γὰρ τοῦτο τὸ φῶς ξύνδεσμον τοῦ οὐρανοῦ, οἷον τὰ ὑποζώματα τῶν τριήρων, οὕτω πᾶσαν ξυνέχον τὴν περιφοράν· ἐκ δὲ τῶν ἄκρων τεταμένον Ἀνάγκης ἄτρακτον, δι' οὗ πάσας ἐπιστρέφεσθαι τὰς περιφοράς· οὗ τὴν μὲν ἠλακάτην τε καὶ τὸ ἄγκιστρον εἶναι ἐξ ἀδάμαντος, τὸν δὲ σφόνδυλον μεικτὸν ἔκ τε τούτου καὶ ἄλλων γενῶν.

* * * * *

Στρέφεσθαι δὲ αὐτὸν ἐν τοῖς τῆς Ἀνάγκης 617
γόνασιν. ἐπὶ δὲ τῶν κύκλων αὐτοῦ ἄνωθεν B
ἐφ' ἑκάστου βεβηκέναι Σειρῆνα συμπεριφερομένην, φωνὴν μίαν ἱεῖσαν—ἕνα τόνον· ἐκ πασῶν δὲ ὀκτὼ οὐσῶν μίαν ἁρμονίαν ξυμφωνεῖν. ἄλλας δὲ καθημένας πέριξ δι' ἴσου τρεῖς, ἐν
θρόνῳ | ἑκάστην, θυγατέρας τῆς Ἀνάγκης, Μοί- C
ρας, λευχειμονούσας, στέμματα ἐπὶ τῶν κεφαλῶν ἐχούσας, Λάχεσίν τε καὶ Κλωθὼ καὶ Ἄτροπον, ὑμνεῖν πρὸς τὴν τῶν Σειρήνων ἁρμονίαν, Λάχεσιν μὲν τὰ γεγονότα, Κλωθὼ δὲ τὰ ὄντα, Ἄτροπον δὲ τὰ μέλλοντα.

The three Fates.

καὶ τὴν μὲν Κλωθὼ τῇ δεξιᾷ χειρὶ ἐφαπτομένην συνεπιστρέφειν τοῦ ἀτράκτου τὴν ἔξω περιφοράν, διαλείπουσαν χρόνον, τὴν δὲ Ἄτροπον τῇ ἀριστερᾷ τὰς ἐντὸς αὖ ὡσαύτως· τὴν δὲ Λάχε-
σιν | ἐν μέρει ἑκατέρας ἑκατέρᾳ τῇ χειρὶ ἐφά- D
πτεσθαι. σφᾶς οὖν, ἐπειδὴ ἀφικέσθαι, εὐθὺς δεῖν ἰέναι πρὸς τὴν Λάχεσιν. προφήτην οὖν τινα σφᾶς πρῶτον μὲν ἐν τάξει διαστῆσαι,

617 Lachesis gives to choose.

ἔπειτα λαβόντα ἐκ τῶν τῆς Λαχέσεως γονάτων κλήρους τε καὶ βίων παραδείγματα, ἀναβάντα ἐπί τι βῆμα ὑψηλὸν εἰπεῖν· Ἀνάγκης θυγατρὸς κόρης Λαχέσεως λόγος. ψυχαὶ ἐφήμεροι, ἀρχὴ ἄλλης περιόδου
E θνητοῦ γένους θανατηφόρου. οὐχ ὑμᾶς | δαίμων λήξεται, ἀλλ᾽ ὑμεῖς δαίμονα αἱρήσεσθε. πρῶτος δ᾽ ὁ λαχὼν πρῶτος αἱρείσθω βίον, ᾧ συνέσται ἐξ ἀνάγκης. ἀρετὴ δὲ ἀδέσποτον, ἣν τιμῶν καὶ ἀτιμάζων πλέον καὶ ἔλαττον αὐτῆς ἕκαστος ἕξει. αἰτία ἑλομένου· θεὸς ἀναίτιος. ταῦτα εἰπόντα ῥῖψαι ἐπὶ πάντας τοὺς κλήρους, τὸν δὲ παρ᾽ αὑτὸν πεσόντα ἕκαστον ἀναιρεῖσθαι, πλὴν οὗ· ἓ δὲ οὐκ ἐᾶν· τῷ δὲ ἀνελομένῳ δῆλον εἶναι, ὁπόστος εἰλήχειν· |

618 Lives of all varieties before the souls.

μετὰ δὲ τοῦτο αὖθις τὰ τῶν βίων παραδείγματα εἰς τὸ πρόσθεν σφῶν θεῖναι ἐπὶ τὴν γῆν, πολὺ πλείω τῶν παρόντων, εἶναι δὲ παντοδαπά· ζῴων τε γὰρ πάντων βίους καὶ δὴ καὶ τοὺς ἀνθρωπίνους ἅπαντας· τυραννίδας τε γὰρ ἐν αὐτοῖς εἶναι, τὰς μὲν διατελεῖς, τὰς δὲ καὶ μεταξὺ διαφθειρομένας καὶ εἰς πενίας τε καὶ φυγὰς καὶ εἰς πτωχείας τελευτώσας· εἶναι δὲ καὶ δοκίμων ἀνδρῶν βίους, τοὺς μὲν ἐπὶ εἴδεσιν καὶ κατὰ
B κάλλη καὶ τὴν ἄλλην ἰσχύν τε | καὶ ἀγωνίαν, τοὺς δ᾽ ἐπὶ γένεσιν καὶ προγόνων ἀρεταῖς, καὶ ἀδοκίμων κατὰ ταὐτά, ὡσαύτως δὲ καὶ γυναικῶν· ψυχῆς δὲ τάξιν οὐκ ἐνεῖναι διὰ τὸ ἀναγκαίως ἔχειν ἄλλον ἑλομένην βίον ἀλλοίαν γίγνεσθαι· τὰ δ᾽ ἄλλα ἀλλήλοις τε καὶ πλούτοις καὶ

πενίαις, τὰ δὲ νόσοις, τὰ δὲ ὑγιείαις μεμῖχθαι, 618
τὰ δὲ καὶ μεσοῦν τούτων.—Ἔνθα δή, ὡς
ἔοικεν, ὦ φίλε Γλαύκων, ὁ πᾶς κίνδυνος ἀν-
θρώπῳ, καὶ διὰ ταῦτα μάλιστα ἐπιμελητέον,
ὅπως ἕκαστος ἡμῶν | τῶν ἄλλων μαθημάτων C
ἀμελήσας τούτου τοῦ μαθήματος καὶ
ζητητὴς καὶ μαθητὴς ἔσται, ἐάν
ποθεν οἷόστ' ᾖ μαθεῖν καὶ ἐξευρεῖν, τίς αὐτὸν
ποιήσει δυνατὸν καὶ ἐπιστήμονα, βίον καὶ
χρηστὸν καὶ πονηρὸν διαγιγνώσκοντα, τὸν
βελτίω ἐκ τῶν δυνατῶν ἀεὶ πανταχοῦ αἱρεῖσθαι·
ἀναλογιζόμενον πάντα τὰ νῦν δὴ ῥηθέντα,
ξυντιθέμενα ἀλλήλοις καὶ διαιρούμενα, πρὸς
ἀρετὴν βίου πῶς ἔχει, εἰδέναι, τί κάλλος πενίᾳ
ἢ πλούτῳ κραθὲν | καὶ μετὰ ποίας τινὸς ψυχῆς D
ἕξεως κακὸν ἢ ἀγαθὸν ἐργάζεται, καὶ τί εὐγέ-
νειαι καὶ δυσγένειαι καὶ ἰδιωτεῖαι καὶ ἀρχαὶ
καὶ ἰσχύες καὶ ἀσθένειαι καὶ εὐμαθίαι καὶ
δυσμαθίαι καὶ πάντα τὰ τοιαῦτα τῶν φύσει
περὶ ψυχὴν ὄντων καὶ τῶν ἐπικτήτων τί ξυγ-
κεραννύμενα πρὸς ἄλληλα ἐργάζεται, ὥστε ἐξ
ἁπάντων αὐτῶν δυνατὸν εἶναι συλλογισάμενον
αἱρεῖσθαι, πρὸς τὴν τῆς ψυχῆς φύσιν ἀποβλέ-
ποντα, τόν τε χείρω καὶ τὸν ἀμείνω βίον,
χείρω | μὲν καλοῦντα ὃς αὐτὴν ἐκεῖσε ἄξει, εἰς E
τὸ ἀδικωτέραν γίγνεσθαι, ἀμείνω δὲ ὅστις εἰς
τὸ δικαιοτέραν, τὰ δὲ ἄλλα πάντα χαίρειν
ἐάσει· ἑωράκαμεν γὰρ ὅτι ζῶντί τε καὶ τελευ-
τήσαντι αὕτη κρατίστη αἵρεσις. ἀδαμαντίνως |
δὴ δεῖ ταύτην τὴν δόξαν ἔχοντα εἰς Ἅιδου 619
ἰέναι, ὅπως ἂν ᾖ καὶ ἐκεῖ ἀνέκπληκτος ὑπὸ

The dangers of the choice.

619 πλούτων τε καὶ τῶν τοιούτων κακῶν, καὶ μὴ
ἐμπεσὼν εἰς τυραννίδας καὶ ἄλλας τοιαύτας
πράξεις πολλὰ μὲν ἐργάσηται καὶ ἀνήκεστα
κακά, ἔτι δὲ αὐτὸς μείζω πάθῃ ἀλλὰ γνῷ τὸν
μέσον ἀεὶ τῶν τοιούτων βίον αἱρεῖσθαι
καὶ φεύγειν τὰ ὑπερβάλλοντα ἑκατέρωσε καὶ
ἐν τῷδε τῷ βίῳ κατὰ τὸ δυνατὸν καὶ ἐν παντὶ
B τῷ ἔπειτα· οὕτω γὰρ εὐδαιμονέστατος | γίγνεται
ἄνθρωπος.

Καὶ δὴ οὖν καὶ τότε ὁ ἐκεῖθεν ἄγγελος
ἤγγελλε τὸν μὲν προφήτην οὕτως
εἰπεῖν· Καὶ τελευταίῳ ἐπιόντι, ξὺν

How they chose,

νῷ ἑλομένῳ, συντόνως ζῶντι κεῖται βίος ἀγα-
πητός, οὐ κακός· μήτε ὁ ἄρχων αἱρέσεως
ἀμελείτω μήτε ὁ τελευτῶν ἀθυμείτω. εἰπόντος
δὲ ταῦτα τὸν πρῶτον λαχόντα ἔφη εὐθὺς
ἐπιόντα τὴν μεγίστην τυραννίδα ἑλέσθαι, καὶ
ὑπὸ ἀφροσύνης τε καὶ λαιμαργίας οὐ πάντα
C ἱκανῶς ἀνασκεψάμενον ἑλέσθαι, | ἀλλ' αὐτὸν
λαθεῖν ἐνοῦσαν εἱμαρμένην, παίδων αὑτοῦ βρώ-
σεις καὶ ἄλλα κακά· ἐπειδὴ δὲ κατὰ σχολὴν
σκέψασθαι, κόπτεσθαί τε καὶ ὀδύρεσθαι τὴν
αἵρεσιν, οὐκ ἐμμένοντα τοῖς προρρηθεῖσιν ὑπὸ
τοῦ προφήτου· οὐ γὰρ ἑαυτὸν αἰτιᾶσθαι τῶν
κακῶν, ἀλλὰ τύχην τε καὶ δαίμονας καὶ πάντα
μᾶλλον ἀνθ' ἑαυτοῦ. εἶναι δὲ αὐτὸν τῶν ἐκ
τοῦ οὐρανοῦ ἡκόντων, ἐν τεταγμένῃ πολιτείᾳ
ἐν τῷ προτέρῳ βίῳ βεβιωκότα, ἔθει ἄνευ
D φιλοσοφίας ἀρετῆς | μετειληφότα. ὡς δὲ καὶ
εἰπεῖν, οὐκ ἐλάττους εἶναι ἐν τοῖς τοιούτοις
ἁλισκομένους τοὺς ἐκ τοῦ οὐρανοῦ ἥκοντας, ἅτε

πόνων ἀγυμνάστους· τῶν δ' ἐκ τῆς γῆς τοὺς 619
πολλούς, ἅτε αὐτούς τε πεπονηκότας ἄλλους
τε ἑωρακότας, οὐκ ἐξ ἐπιδρομῆς τὰς αἱρέσεις
ποιεῖσθαι. διὸ δὴ καὶ μεταβολὴν τῶν κακῶν
καὶ τῶν ἀγαθῶν ταῖς πολλαῖς τῶν ψυχῶν
γίγνεσθαι, καὶ διὰ τὴν τοῦ κλήρου τύχην.
ἐπεὶ εἴ τις ἀεί, ὁπότε εἰς τὸν ἐνθάδε βίον
ἀφικνοῖτο, ὑγιῶς φιλοσοφοῖ | καὶ ὁ κλῆρος E
αὐτῷ τῆς αἱρέσεως μὴ ἐν τελευταίοις πίπτοι,
κινδυνεύει ἐκ τῶν ἐκεῖθεν ἀπαγγελλομένων οὐ
μόνον ἐνθάδε εὐδαιμονεῖν ἄν, ἀλλὰ καὶ τὴν
ἐνθένδε ἐκεῖσε καὶ δεῦρο πάλιν πορείαν οὐκ ἂν
χθονίαν καὶ τραχεῖαν πορεύεσθαι, ἀλλὰ λείαν
τε καὶ οὐρανίαν. ταύτην γὰρ δὴ ἔφη τὴν
θέαν ἀξίαν εἶναι ἰδεῖν, ὡς ἕκασται αἱ ψυχαὶ
ᾑροῦντο τοὺς βίους· | ἐλεεινήν τε γὰρ ἰδεῖν 620
εἶναι καὶ γελοίαν καὶ θαυμασίαν. κατὰ συνή-
θειαν γὰρ τοῦ προτέρου βίου τὰ πολλὰ αἱρεῖ-
σθαι. ἰδεῖν μὲν γὰρ ψυχὴν ἔφη τήν ποτε
Ὀρφέως γενομένην κύκνου βίον αἱ-
ρουμένην, μίσει τοῦ γυναικείου γένους
διὰ τὸν ὑπ' ἐκείνων θάνατον οὐκ
ἐθέλουσαν ἐν γυναικὶ γεννηθεῖσαν γενέσθαι·
ἰδεῖν δὲ τὴν Θαμύρου ἀηδόνος ἑλομένην· ἰδεῖν
δὲ καὶ κύκνον μεταβάλλοντα εἰς ἀνθρωπίνου
βίου αἵρεσιν, καὶ ἄλλα ζῷα μουσικὰ ὡσαύτως.
| εἰκοστὴν δὲ λαχοῦσαν ψυχὴν ἑλέσθαι λέοντος B
βίον· εἶναι δὲ τὴν Αἴαντος τοῦ Τελαμωνίου,
φεύγουσαν ἄνθρωπον γενέσθαι, μεμνημένην τῆς
τῶν ὅπλων κρίσεως· τὴν δ' ἐπὶ τούτῳ Ἀγαμέμ-
νονος· ἔχθρᾳ δὲ καὶ ταύτην τοῦ ἀνθρωπίνου

For example, Orpheus, Ajax, Odysseus.

620 γένους διὰ τὰ πάθη ἀετοῦ διαλλάξαι βίον. ἐν μέσοις δὲ λαχοῦσαν τὴν Ἀταλάντης ψυχήν, κατιδοῦσαν μεγάλας τιμὰς ἀθλητοῦ ἀνδρός, οὐ C δύνασθαι παρελθεῖν, ἀλλὰ λαβεῖν. μετὰ | δὲ ταύτην ἰδεῖν τὴν Ἐπειοῦ τοῦ Πανοπέως εἰς τεχνικῆς γυναικὸς ἰοῦσαν φύσιν· πόρρω δ' ἐν ὑστάτοις ἰδεῖν τὴν τοῦ γελωτοποιοῦ Θερσίτου πίθηκον ἐνδυομένην· κατὰ τύχην δὲ τὴν Ὀδυσσέως, λαχοῦσαν πασῶν ὑστάτην, αἱρησομένην ἰέναι· μνήμῃ δὲ τῶν προτέρων πόνων φιλοτιμίας λελωφηκυῖαν ζητεῖν περιιοῦσαν χρόνον πολὺν βίον ἀνδρὸς ἰδιώτου ἀπράγμονος, καὶ μόγις εὑρεῖν κείμενόν που καὶ παρημελημένον D ὑπὸ τῶν ἄλλων, καὶ εἰπεῖν | ἰδοῦσαν ὅτι τὰ αὐτὰ ἂν ἔπραξεν καὶ πρώτη λαχοῦσα, καὶ ἁσμένην ἑλέσθαι. καὶ ἐκ τῶν ἄλλων δὴ θηρίων ὡσαύτως εἰς ἀνθρώπους ἰέναι καὶ εἰς ἄλληλα, τὰ μὲν ἄδικα εἰς τὰ ἄγρια, τὰ δὲ δίκαια εἰς τὰ ἥμερα μεταβάλλοντα, καὶ πάσας μίξεις μίγνυσθαι. ἐπειδὴ δ' οὖν πάσας τὰς ψυχὰς

Assignment to each of his genius.

τοὺς βίους ᾑρῆσθαι, ὥσπερ ἔλαχον, ἐν τάξει προσιέναι πρὸς τὴν Λάχεσιν· ἐκείνην δ' ἑκάστῳ, ὃν εἵλετο δαίμονα, E τοῦτον φύλακα ξυμπέμπειν | τοῦ βίου καὶ ἀποπληρωτὴν τῶν αἱρεθέντων. ὃν πρῶτον μὲν

Clotho and Atropus do their work.

ἄγειν αὐτὴν πρὸς τὴν Κλωθὼ ὑπὸ τὴν ἐκείνης χεῖρά τε καὶ ἐπιστροφὴν τῆς τοῦ ἀτράκτου δίνης, κυροῦντα ἣν λαχὼν εἵλετο μοῖραν· ταύτης δ' ἐφαψάμενον αὖθις ἐπὶ τὴν τῆς Ἀτρόπου ἄγειν νῆσιν, ἀμετάστροφα τὰ ἐπικλωσθέντα ποιοῦντα· ἐντεῦ-

θεν δὲ δὴ ἀμεταστρεπτὶ ὑπὸ τὸν τῆς | Ἀνάγκης 621
ἰέναι θρόνον, καὶ δι' ἐκείνου διεξελθόντα, ἐπειδὴ
καὶ οἱ ἄλλοι διῆλθον, πορεύεσθαι ἅπαντας εἰς
τὸ τῆς Λήθης πεδίον διὰ καύματός τε καὶ
πνίγους δεινοῦ· καὶ γὰρ εἶναι αὐτὸ κενὸν δένδρων
τε καὶ ὅσα γῆ φύει. σκηνᾶσθαι οὖν σφᾶς
ἤδη ἑσπέρας γιγνομένης παρὰ τὸν
Ἀμέλητα ποταμόν, οὗ τὸ ὕδωρ ἀγγεῖον
οὐδὲν στέγειν. μέτρον μὲν οὖν τι τοῦ ὕδατος
πᾶσιν ἀναγκαῖον εἶναι πιεῖν, τοὺς δὲ φρονήσει
μὴ σῳζομένους πλέον πίνειν τοῦ μέτρου· τὸν
δὲ ἀεὶ πιόντα | πάντων ἐπιλανθάνεσθαι. ἐπειδὴ B
δὲ κοιμηθῆναι καὶ μέσας νύκτας γενέσθαι,
βροντήν τε καὶ σεισμὸν γενέσθαι, καὶ ἐντεῦθεν
ἐξαπίνης ἄλλον ἄλλῃ φέρεσθαι ἄνω εἰς τὴν
γένεσιν, ᾄττοντας ὥσπερ ἀστέρας. αὐτὸς δὲ
τοῦ μὲν ὕδατος κωλυθῆναι πιεῖν· ὅπῃ μέντοι
καὶ ὅπως εἰς τὸ σῶμα ἀφίκοιτο, οὐκ εἰδέναι,
ἀλλ' ἐξαίφνης ἀναβλέψας ἰδεῖν ἕωθεν αὑτὸν
κείμενον ἐπὶ τῇ πυρᾷ.

The river of Forgetfulness.

Καὶ οὕτως, ὦ Γλαύκων, μῦθος ἐσώθη καὶ
οὐκ ἀπώλετο, καὶ ἡμᾶς | ἂν σώσειεν, C
ἂν πειθώμεθα αὐτῷ, καὶ τὸν τῆς
Λήθης ποταμὸν εὖ διαβησόμεθα καὶ τὴν ψυχὴν
οὐ μιανθησόμεθα. ἀλλ' ἂν ἐμοὶ πειθώμεθα,
νομίζοντες ἀθάνατον ψυχὴν καὶ δυνατὴν πάντα
μὲν κακὰ ἀνέχεσθαι, πάντα δὲ ἀγαθά, τῆς ἄνω
ὁδοῦ ἀεὶ ἑξόμεθα καὶ δικαιοσύνην μετὰ φρονή-
σεως παντὶ τρόπῳ ἐπιτηδεύσομεν, ἵνα καὶ ἡμῖν
αὐτοῖς φίλοι ὦμεν καὶ τοῖς θεοῖς, αὐτοῦ τε
μένοντες ἐνθάδε, καὶ ἐπειδὰν τὰ ἆθλα | αὐτῆς D

The final word.

621 κομιζώμεθα, ὥσπερ οἱ νικηφόροι περιαγειρόμενοι, καὶ ἐνθάδε καὶ ἐν τῇ χιλιέτει πορείᾳ, ἣν διεληλύθαμεν, εὖ πράττωμεν.

PHAEDRUS

Socrates in the Country.

Socrates. Phaedrus.

'Αλλα ποῦ δὴ βούλει καθιζόμενοι ἀναγνῶμεν ; |

229 ΣΩ. Δεῦρ' ἐκτραπόμενοι κατὰ τὸν 'Ιλισσὸν ἴωμεν, εἶτα, ὅπου ἂν δόξῃ, ἐν ἡσυχίᾳ καθιζησόμεθα.

The walk by the Ilissus.

ΦΑΙ. Εἰς καιρόν, ὡς ἔοικεν, ἀνυπόδητος ὢν ἔτυχον· σὺ μὲν γὰρ δὴ ἀεί. ῥᾷστον οὖν ἡμῖν κατὰ τὸ ὑδάτιον βρέχουσι τοὺς πόδας ἰέναι, καὶ οὐκ ἀηδές, ἄλλως τε καὶ τήνδε τὴν ὥραν τοῦ ἔτους τε καὶ τῆς ἡμέρας.

ΣΩ. Πρόαγε δή, καὶ σκόπει ἅμα ὅπου καθιζησόμεθα.

ΦΑΙ. 'Ορᾷς οὖν ἐκείνην τὴν ὑψηλοτάτην πλάτανον ;

ΣΩ. Τί μήν ;

B ΦΑΙ. 'Εκεῖ | σκιά τ' ἐστὶν καὶ πνεῦμα μέτριον, καὶ πόα καθίζεσθαι ἤ, ἂν βουλώμεθα, κατακλινῆναι.

ΣΩ. Προάγοις ἄν.

ΦΑΙ. Εἰπέ μοι, ὦ Σώκρατες, οὐκ ἐνθένδε μέντοι ποθὲν ἀπὸ τοῦ 'Ιλισσοῦ λέγεται ὁ Βορέας τὴν 'Ωρείθυιαν ἁρπάσαι ;

ΣΩ. Λέγεται γάρ. **229**

ΦΑΙ. Ἆρ' οὖν ἐνθένδε; χαρίεντα γοῦν καὶ καθαρὰ καὶ διαφανῆ τὰ ὑδάτια φαίνεται, καὶ ἐπιτήδεια κόραις παίζειν παρ' αὐτά.

ΣΩ. Οὔκ, ἀλλὰ κάτωθεν ὅσον δύ' ἢ τρία στάδια, | ᾗ πρὸς τὸ τῆς Ἄγρας διαβαίνομεν· **C**
καί πού τίς ἐστι βωμὸς αὐτόθι Βορέου.

ΦΑΙ. Οὐ πάνυ νενόηκα· ἀλλ' εἰπὲ πρὸς Διός, ὦ Σώκρατες· σὺ τοῦτο τὸ μυθολόγημα πείθει ἀληθὲς εἶναι;

ΣΩ. Ἀλλ' εἰ ἀπιστοίην, ὥσπερ οἱ σοφοί, οὐκ ἂν ἄτοπος εἴην, εἶτα σοφιζόμενος φαίην αὐτὴν πνεῦμα Βορέου κατὰ τῶν πλησίον πετρῶν σὺν Φαρμακείᾳ παίζουσαν ὦσαι, καὶ οὕτω δὴ τελευτήσασαν λεχθῆναι ὑπὸ τοῦ Βορέου ἀνάρπαστον | γεγονέ- **D**
ναι. (ἢ ἐξ Ἀρείου πάγου· λέγεται γὰρ αὖ καὶ οὗτος ὁ λόγος, ὡς ἐκεῖθεν ἀλλ' οὐκ ἐνθένδε ἡρπάσθη.) ἐγὼ δέ, ὦ Φαῖδρε, ἄλλως μὲν τὰ τοιαῦτα χαρίεντα ἡγοῦμαι, λίαν δὲ δεινοῦ καὶ ἐπιπόνου καὶ οὐ πάνυ εὐτυχοῦς ἀνδρός, κατ' ἄλλο μὲν οὐδέν, ὅτι δ' αὐτῷ ἀνάγκη μετὰ τοῦτο τὸ τῶν Ἱπποκενταύρων εἶδος ἐπανορθοῦσθαι, καὶ αὖθις τὸ τῆς Χιμαίρας· καὶ ἐπιρρεῖ δὲ ὄχλος τοιούτων Γοργόνων καὶ Πηγάσων καὶ ἄλλων ἀμηχάνων πλήθει τε καὶ
| ἀτοπίᾳ τερατολόγων τινῶν φύσεων· αἷς εἴ **E**
τις ἀπιστῶν προσβιβᾷ κατὰ τὸ εἰκὸς ἕκαστον, ἅτε ἀγροίκῳ τινὶ σοφίᾳ χρώμενος, πολλῆς αὐτῷ σχολῆς δεήσει. ἐμοὶ δὲ πρὸς αὐτὰ οὐδαμῶς ἐστι σχολή. τὸ δὲ αἴτιον, ὦ φίλε, τούτου

The rationalists.

τόδε· οὐ δύναμαί πω κατὰ τὸ Δελφικὸν γραμμα γνῶναι ἐμαυτόν· γελοῖον δέ μοι φαίνεται, |
230 τοῦτο ἔτι ἀγνοοῦντα, τὰ ἀλλότρια σκοπεῖν. ὅθεν δὴ χαίρειν ἐάσας ταῦτα, πειθόμενος δὲ τῷ νομιζομένῳ περὶ αὐτῶν, ὃ νῦν δὴ ἔλεγον, σκοπῶ οὐ ταῦτα ἀλλ' ἐμαυτόν, εἴτε τι θηρίον τυγχάνω Τυφῶνος πολυπλοκώτερον καὶ μᾶλλον ἐπιτεθυμμένον, εἴτε ἡμερώτερόν τε καὶ ἁπλούστερον ζῷον, θείας τινὸς καὶ ἀτύφου μοίρας φύσει μετέχον. ἀτάρ, ὦ ἑταῖρε, μεταξὺ τῶν λόγων, ἆρ' οὐ τόδε ἦν τὸ δένδρον, ἐφ' ὅπερ ἦγες ἡμᾶς;

B ΦΑΙ. Τοῦτο | μὲν οὖν αὐτό.

ΣΩ. Νὴ τὴν Ἥραν, καλή γε ἡ καταγωγή. ἥ τε γὰρ πλάτανος αὕτη μάλ' ἀμφιλαφής τε καὶ ὑψηλή, τοῦ τε ἄγνου τὸ ὕψος καὶ τὸ σύσκιον πάγκαλον, καὶ ὡς ἀκμὴν ἔχει τῆς ἄνθης, ὡς ἂν εὐωδέστατον παρέχοι τὸν τόπον· ἥ τε αὖ πηγὴ χαριεστάτη ὑπὸ τῆς πλατάνου ῥεῖ μάλα ψυχροῦ ὕδατος, ὥς γε τῷ ποδὶ τεκμήρασθαι· Νυμφῶν τέ τινων καὶ Ἀχελῴου ἱερὸν ἀπὸ τῶν κορῶν τε καὶ
C ἀγαλμάτων ἔοικεν εἶναι. εἰ δ' αὖ | βούλει, τὸ εὔπνουν τοῦ τόπου ὡς ἀγαπητὸν καὶ σφόδρα ἡδύ· θερινόν τε καὶ λιγυρὸν ὑπηχεῖ τῷ τῶν τεττίγων χορῷ. πάντων δὲ κομψότατον τὸ τῆς πόας, ὅτι ἐν ἠρέμα προσάντει ἱκανὴ πέφυκε κατακλινέντι τὴν κεφαλὴν παγκάλως ἔχειν. ὥστε ἄριστά σοι ἐξενάγηται, ὦ φίλε Φαῖδρε.

The scenery fair,

ΦΑΙ. Σὺ δέ γε, ὦ θαυμάσιε, ἀτοπώτατός τις φαίνει. ἀτεχνῶς γάρ, ὃ λέγεις, ξεναγουμένῳ

τινὶ καὶ οὐκ ἐπιχωρίῳ ἔοικας· οὕτως ἐκ τοῦ 230
ἄστεως οὔτ' εἰς | τὴν ὑπερορίαν ἀποδημεῖς, οὔτ' D
ἔξω τείχους ἔμοιγε δοκεῖς τὸ παράπαν ἐξιέναι.

ΣΩ. Συγγίγνωσκέ μοι, ὦ ἄριστε. φιλομαθὴς
γάρ εἰμι. τὰ μὲν οὖν χωρία καὶ τὰ
δένδρα οὐδέν μ' ἐθέλει διδάσκειν, οἱ
δ' ἐν τῷ ἄστει ἄνθρωποι. σὺ μέντοι
δοκεῖς μοι τῆς ἐξόδου τὸ φάρμακον ηὑρηκέναι.
ὥσπερ γὰρ οἱ τὰ πεινῶντα θρέμματα θαλλὸν
ἤ τινα καρπὸν προσείοντες ἄγουσιν, σὺ ἐμοὶ
λόγους οὕτω προτείνων ἐν βιβλίοις τήν τε
᾿Αττικὴν φαίνει | περιάξειν ἅπασαν καὶ ὅποι E
ἂν ἄλλοσε βούλῃ. νῦν οὖν ἐν τῷ παρόντι
δεῦρ' ἀφικόμενος ἐγὼ μέν μοι δοκῶ κατακεῖ-
σθαι, σὺ δ' ἐν ὁποίῳ σχήματι οἴει ῥᾷστα
ἀναγνώσεσθαι, τοῦτο ἑλόμενος ἀναγίγνωσκε.

but trees will not teach as men.

ΦΑΙ. Ἄκουε δή.

MENEXENUS

The Call of our Forefathers to Virtue.

Ὦ παῖδες, ὅτι μέν ἐστε πατέρων ἀγαθῶν, | 246
αὐτὸ μηνύει τὸ νῦν παρόν· ἡμῖν δὲ ἐξὸν ζῆν D
μὴ καλῶς, καλῶς αἱρούμεθα μᾶλλον τελευτᾶν,
πρὶν ὑμᾶς τε καὶ τοὺς ἔπειτα εἰς ὀνείδη κατα-
στῆσαι καὶ πρὶν τοὺς ἡμετέρους πατέρας καὶ
πᾶν τὸ πρόσθεν γένος αἰσχῦναι, ἡγούμενοι τῷ
τοὺς αὑτοῦ αἰσχύνοντι ἀβίωτον εἶναι, καὶ τῷ
τοιούτῳ οὔτε τινὰ ἀνθρώπων οὔτε θεῶν φίλον
εἶναι οὔτ' ἐπὶ γῆς οὔθ' ὑπὸ γῆς τελευτήσαντι.

246 χρὴ οὖν μεμνημένους τῶν ἡμετέρων λόγων, ἐάν
E τι καὶ ἄλλο | ἀσκῆτε, ἀσκεῖν μετ᾽ ἀρετῆς, εἰδό-
τας ὅτι τούτου λειπόμενα πάντα, καὶ κτήματα
καὶ ἐπιτηδεύματα, αἰσχρὰ καὶ κακά. οὔτε γὰρ
πλοῦτος κάλλος φέρει τῷ κεκτημένῳ μετ᾽
ἀνανδρίας (ἄλλῳ γὰρ ὁ τοιοῦτος πλουτεῖ καὶ
οὐχ ἑαυτῷ), οὔτε σώματος κάλλος καὶ ἰσχὺς
δειλῷ καὶ κακῷ ξυνοικοῦντα πρέποντα φαίνεται
ἀλλ᾽ ἀπρεπῆ, καὶ ἐπιφανέστερον ποιεῖ τὸν
ἔχοντα καὶ ἐκφαίνει τὴν δειλίαν· πᾶσά τε
247 ἐπιστήμη χωριζομένη δικαιοσύνης | καὶ τῆς
ἄλλης ἀρετῆς πανουργία, οὐ σοφία, φαίνεται.
ὧν ἕνεκα καὶ πρῶτον καὶ ὕστατον καὶ διὰ
παντὸς πᾶσαν πάντως προθυμίαν πειρᾶσθε
ἔχειν, ὅπως μάλιστα μὲν ὑπερβαλεῖσθε καὶ
ἡμᾶς καὶ τοὺς πρόσθεν εὐκλείᾳ· εἰ δὲ μή, * * *
ἴστε ὡς ἡμῖν, ἂν μὲν νικῶμεν ὑμᾶς ἀρετῇ, ἡ
νίκη αἰσχύνην φέρει, ἡ δὲ ἧττα, ἐὰν ἡττώμεθα,
εὐδαιμονίαν. μάλιστα δ᾽ ἂν ἡττῴμεθα καὶ
ὑμεῖς νικῴητε, εἰ παρασκευάσαισθε τῇ τῶν
B προγόνων δόξῃ μὴ καταχρησόμενοι | μηδ᾽ ἀναλώ-
σοντες αὐτήν, γνόντες ὅτι ἀνδρὶ οἰομένῳ τι
εἶναι οὐκ ἔστιν αἴσχιον οὐδὲν ἢ παρέχειν
ἑαυτὸν τιμώμενον μὴ δι᾽ ἑαυτὸν ἀλλὰ διὰ
δόξαν προγόνων. εἶναι μὲν γὰρ τιμὰς γονέων
ἐκγόνοις καλὸς θησαυρὸς καὶ μεγαλοπρεπής·
χρῆσθαι δὲ καὶ χρημάτων καὶ τιμῶν θησαυρῷ,
καὶ μὴ τοῖς ἐκγόνοις παραδιδόναι, αἰσχρὸν καὶ
ἄνανδρον, ἀπορίᾳ ἰδίων αὑτοῦ κτημάτων τε καὶ
εὐδοξιῶν. καὶ ἐὰν μὲν ταῦτα ἐπιτηδεύσητε,
C φίλοι παρὰ | φίλους ἡμᾶς ἀφίξεσθε, ὅταν ὑμᾶς

ᾗ προσήκουσα μοῖρα κομίσῃ· ἀμελήσαντας δὲ 247
ὑμᾶς καὶ κακισθέντας οὐδεὶς εὐμενῶς ὑποδέξεται.
τοῖς μὲν οὖν παισὶ ταῦτ' εἰρήσθω.

ALCIBIADES I

Not Walls, but Virtue, the Need of the State.

ΣΩ. Οὐκ ἄρα τειχῶν οὐδὲ τριήρων οὐδὲ 134
νεωρίων δέονται αἱ πόλεις, ὦ Ἀλκιβιάδη, εἰ B
μέλλουσιν εὐδαιμονήσειν, οὐδὲ πλήθους οὐδὲ
μεγέθους ἄνευ ἀρετῆς.

ΑΛ. Οὐ μέντοι.

ΣΩ. Εἰ δὴ μέλλεις τὰ τῆς πόλεως πράξειν
ὀρθῶς καὶ καλῶς, ἀρετῆς σοι μεταδοτέον | τοῖς C
πολίταις.

ΑΛ. Πῶς γὰρ οὔ;

ΣΩ. Δύναιτο δ' ἄν τις μεταδιδόναι ὃ μὴ ἔχει;

ΑΛ. Καὶ πῶς;.

ΣΩ. Αὐτῷ ἄρα σοὶ πρῶτον κτητέον ἀρετήν, καὶ ἄλλῳ ὃς μέλλει μὴ ἰδίᾳ μόνον αὑτοῦ τε καὶ τῶν αὑτοῦ ἄρξειν καὶ ἐπιμελήσεσθαι, ἀλλὰ πόλεως καὶ τῶν τῆς πόλεως.

ΑΛ. Ἀληθῆ λέγεις.

Without Virtue, we had better have a Master.

Πρὶν δέ γε ἀρετὴν ἔχειν, τὸ ἄρχεσθαι ἄμει- 135
νον ὑπὸ τοῦ βελτίονος ἢ τὸ ἄρχειν ἀνδρί, οὐ B
μόνον παιδί.

PROTAGORAS

The Care paid to Virtue in Greek Schooling.

Virtue inculcated in the home,

325 Ἐκ παίδων σμικρῶν ἀρξάμενοι, μέχρι οὗπερ ἂν ζῶσι, καὶ διδάσκουσι καὶ νουθετοῦσιν. ἐπειδὰν θᾶττον συνιῇ τις τὰ λεγόμενα, καὶ τροφὸς καὶ μήτηρ καὶ παιδαγωγὸς καὶ αὐτὸς ὁ πατὴρ περὶ τούτου
D διαμάχονται, ὅπως | <ὡς> βέλτιστος ἔσται ὁ παῖς, παρ' ἕκαστον καὶ ἔργον καὶ λόγον διδάσκοντες καὶ ἐνδεικνύμενοι ὅτι τὸ μὲν δίκαιον, τὸ δὲ ἄδικον, καὶ τόδε μὲν καλόν, τόδε δὲ αἰσχρόν, καὶ τόδε μὲν ὅσιον, τόδε δὲ ἀνόσιον, καὶ τὰ μὲν ποίει, τὰ δὲ μὴ ποίει. καὶ ἐὰν μὲν ἑκὼν πείθηται,—εἰ δὲ μή, ὥσπερ ξύλον διαστρεφόμενον καὶ καμπτόμενον εὐθύνουσιν ἀπειλαῖς καὶ πληγαῖς. μετὰ δὲ ταῦτα εἰς διδασκάλων πέμποντες πολὺ μᾶλλον ἐντέλλονται ἐπιμελεῖσθαι εὐκοσμίας τῶν

in the schools,

E παίδων ἢ | γραμμάτων τε καὶ κιθαρίσεως· οἱ δὲ διδάσκαλοι τούτων τε ἐπιμελοῦνται, καὶ ἐπειδὰν αὖ γράμματα μάθωσιν καὶ μέλλωσιν συνήσειν τὰ γεγραμμένα, ὥσπερ τότε τὴν φωνήν, παρατιθέασιν αὐτοῖς ἐπὶ τῶν βάθρων ἀναγιγνώσκειν ποιητῶν ἀγαθῶν ποιήματα καὶ ἐκμανθάνειν ἀναγκάζουσιν, ἐν οἷς πολλαὶ
326 μὲν νουθετήσεις | ἔνεισιν, πολλαὶ δὲ διέξοδοι καὶ ἔπαινοι καὶ ἐγκώμια παλαιῶν ἀνδρῶν ἀγαθῶν, ἵνα ὁ παῖς ζηλῶν μιμῆται καὶ ὀρέγηται τοιοῦτος γενέσθαι. οἵ τ' αὖ κιθαρισταὶ ἕτερα

τοιαῦτα σωφροσύνης τε ἐπιμελοῦνται καὶ ὅπως 326
ἂν οἱ νέοι μηδὲν κακουργῶσιν· πρὸς δὲ τούτοις,
ἐπειδὰν κιθαρίζειν μάθωσιν, ἄλλων αὖ ποιητῶν
ἀγαθῶν ποιήματα διδάσκουσι | μελοποιῶν, εἰς B
τὰ κιθαρίσματα ἐντείνοντες, καὶ τοὺς ῥυθμούς
τε καὶ τὰς ἁρμονίας ἀναγκάζουσιν οἰκειοῦσθαι
ταῖς ψυχαῖς τῶν παίδων, ἵνα ἡμερώτεροί τε
ὦσιν, καὶ εὐρυθμότεροι καὶ εὐαρμοστότεροι
γιγνόμενοι χρήσιμοι ὦσιν εἰς τὸ λέγειν τε καὶ
πράττειν· πᾶς γὰρ ὁ βίος τοῦ ἀνθρώπου εὐρυθ-
μίας τε καὶ εὐαρμοστίας δεῖται. ἔτι τοίνυν
πρὸς τούτοις εἰς παιδοτρίβου πέμ- in the gymnasium,
πουσιν, ἵνα τὰ σώματα βελτίω
ἔχοντες ὑπηρετῶσι τῇ διανοίᾳ χρηστῇ | οὔσῃ, C
καὶ μὴ ἀναγκάζωνται ἀποδειλιᾶν διὰ τὴν
πονηρίαν τῶν σωμάτων καὶ ἐν τοῖς πολέμοις
καὶ ἐν ταῖς ἄλλαις πράξεσιν· καὶ ταῦτα
ποιοῦσιν οἱ μάλιστα δυνάμενοι <μάλιστα>·
μάλιστα δὲ δύνανται οἱ πλουσιώτατοι· καὶ οἱ
τούτων ὑεῖς, πρῳαίτατα εἰς διδασκάλων τῆς
ἡλικίας ἀρξάμενοι φοιτᾶν, ὀψιαίτατα ἀπαλ-
λάττονται. ἐπειδὰν δὲ ἐκ διδασκάλων ἀπαλ-
λαγῶσιν, ἡ πόλις αὖ τούς τε νόμους and in the State.
ἀναγκάζει μανθάνειν καὶ κατὰ τού-
τους | ζῆν [κατὰ παράδειγμα], ἵνα μὴ αὐτοὶ D
ἐφ' αὑτῶν εἰκῇ πράττωσιν, ἀλλ' ἀτεχνῶς ὥσπερ
οἱ γραμματισταὶ τοῖς μήπω δεινοῖς γράφειν
τῶν παίδων ὑπογράψαντες γραμμὰς τῇ γραφίδι
οὕτω τὸ γραμματεῖον διδόασιν καὶ ἀναγκάζουσι
γράφειν κατὰ τὴν ὑφήγησιν τῶν γραμμῶν, ὣς
δὲ καὶ ἡ πόλις νόμους ὑπογράψασα, ἀγαθῶν

326 καὶ παλαιῶν νομοθετῶν εὑρήματα, κατὰ τού-
τους ἀναγκάζει καὶ ἄρχειν καὶ ἄρχεσθαι· ὃς
δ' ἂν ἐκτὸς βαίνῃ τούτων, κολάζει, καὶ ὄνομα
τῇ κολάσει ταύτῃ καὶ παρ' ὑμῖν καὶ ἄλλοθι
E πολλαχοῦ, ὡς εὐθυνούσης | τῆς δίκης, εὐθῦναι.
τοσαύτης οὖν τῆς ἐπιμελείας οὔσης περὶ ἀρετῆς
ἰδίᾳ καὶ δημοσίᾳ, θαυμάζεις, ὦ Σώκρατες, καὶ
ἀπορεῖς, εἰ διδακτόν ἐστιν ἀρετή; ἀλλ' οὐ
χρὴ θαυμάζειν, ἀλλὰ πολὺ μᾶλλον, εἰ μὴ
διδακτόν.

BRIEFER EXTRACTS

Orphaned Philosophy married by the bald-headed little Tinker.

(*Republic VI.*)

495 Οὗτοι μὲν δὴ οὕτως ἐκπίπτοντες, οἷς μά-
C λιστα | προσήκει, ἔρημον καὶ ἀτελῆ φιλοσοφίαν
λείποντες αὐτοί τε βίον οὐ προσήκοντα οὐδ'
ἀληθῆ ζῶσιν, τὴν δέ, ὥσπερ ὀρφανὴν ξυγγενῶν,
ἄλλοι ἐπεισελθόντες ἀνάξιοι ᾔσχυνάν τε καὶ
ὀνείδη περιῆψαν, οἷα καὶ σὺ φῂς ὀνειδίζειν
τοὺς ὀνειδίζοντας, ὡς οἱ ξυνόντες αὐτῇ οἱ μὲν
οὐδενός, οἱ δὲ πολλοὶ πολλῶν κακῶν ἄξιοί
εἰσιν. Καὶ γὰρ οὖν, ἔφη, τά γε λεγόμενα
ταῦτα. Εἰκότως γε, ἦν δ' ἐγώ, λεγόμενα.
καθορῶντες γὰρ ἄλλοι ἀνθρωπίσκοι κενὴν τὴν
χώραν ταύτην γιγνομένην, καλῶν δὲ ὀνομάτων
D καὶ προσχημάτων | μεστήν, ὥσπερ οἱ ἐκ τῶν
εἱργμῶν εἰς τὰ ἱερὰ ἀποδιδράσκοντες ἄσμενοι
καὶ οὗτοι ἐκ τῶν τεχνῶν ἐκπηδῶσιν εἰς τὴν

φιλοσοφίαν, οἳ ἂν κομψότατοι ὄντες τυγχάνωσι 495
περὶ τὸ αὑτῶν τεχνίον. ὅμως γὰρ δὴ πρός γε τὰς ἄλλας τέχνας καίπερ οὕτω πραττούσης φιλοσοφίας τὸ ἀξίωμα μεγαλοπρεπέστερον λείπεται· οὗ δὴ ἐφιέμενοι πολλοὶ ἀτελεῖς μὲν τὰς φύσεις, ὑπὸ δὲ τῶν τεχνῶν τε καὶ δημιουργιῶν ὥσπερ τὰ σώματα λελώβηνται, οὕτω
καὶ τὰς | ψυχὰς ξυγκεκλασμένοι τε καὶ ἀποτε- E
θρυμμένοι διὰ τὰς βαναυσίας τυγχάνουσιν—ἢ οὐκ ἀνάγκη; Καὶ μάλα, ἔφη. Δοκεῖς οὖν τι, ἦν δ' ἐγώ, διαφέρειν αὐτοὺς ἰδεῖν ἀργύριον κτησαμένου χαλκέως φαλακροῦ καὶ σμικροῦ, νεωστὶ μὲν ἐκ δεσμῶν λελυμένου, ἐν βαλανείῳ δὲ λελουμένου, νεουργὸν ἱμάτιον ἔχοντος, ὡς νυμφίου παρεσκευασμένου, διὰ πενίαν καὶ ἐρημίαν τοῦ δεσπότου τὴν θυγατέρα μέλλοντος
γαμεῖν; Οὐ | πάνυ, ἔφη, διαφέρει. Ποῖ' ἄττα 496
οὖν εἰκὸς γεννᾶν τοὺς τοιούτους; οὐ νόθα καὶ φαῦλα; Πολλὴ ἀνάγκη. Τί δέ; τοὺς ἀναξίους παιδεύσεως, ὅταν αὐτῇ πλησιάζοντες ὁμιλῶσι μὴ κατ' ἀξίαν, ποῖ' ἄττα φῶμεν γεννᾶν διανοήματά τε καὶ δόξας; ἆρ' οὐχ ὡς ἀληθῶς προσήκοντα ἀκοῦσαι σοφίσματα, καὶ οὐδὲν γνήσιον οὐδὲ φρονήσεως [ἄξιον] ἀληθινῆς ἐχόμενον; Παντελῶς μὲν οὖν, ἔφη.

The Philosopher under the Wall.

(*Republic VI.*)

Καὶ τούτων δὴ τῶν ὀλίγων οἱ γενόμενοι 496
καὶ γευσάμενοι ὡς ἡδὺ καὶ μακάριον τὸ κτῆμα, C
καὶ τῶν πολλῶν αὖ ἱκανῶς ἰδόντες τὴν μανίαν,

496 καὶ ὅτι οὐδεὶς οὐδὲν ὑγιὲς ὡς ἔπος εἰπεῖν περι
τὰ τῶν πόλεων πράττει, οὐδ᾽ ἔστι ξύμμαχος,
D μεθ᾽ ὅτου τις ἰὼν ἐπὶ | τὴν τῷ δικαίῳ βοή-
θειαν σῴζοιτ᾽ ἄν, ἀλλ᾽ ὥσπερ εἰς θηρία
ἄνθρωπος ἐμπεσών, οὔτε ξυναδικεῖν ἐθέλων
οὔτε ἱκανὸς ὢν εἷς πᾶσιν ἀγρίοις ἀντέχειν,
πρίν τι τὴν πόλιν ἢ φίλους ὀνῆσαι προαπολό-
μενος ἀνωφελὴς αὑτῷ τε καὶ τοῖς ἄλλοις ἂν
γένοιτο, ταῦτα πάντα λογισμῷ λαβὼν ἡσυχίαν
ἔχων καὶ τὰ αὑτοῦ πράττων, οἷον ἐν χειμῶνι
κονιορτοῦ καὶ ζάλης ὑπὸ πνεύματος φερομένου
ὑπὸ τειχίον ἀποστάς, ὁρῶν τοὺς ἄλλους κατα-
πιμπλαμένους ἀνομίας ἀγαπᾷ, εἴ πῃ αὐτὸς
E καθαρὸς ἀδικίας τε | καὶ ἀνοσίων ἔργων τόν τε
ἐνθάδε βίον βιώσεται καὶ τὴν ἀπαλλαγὴν
αὐτοῦ μετὰ καλῆς ἐλπίδος ἵλεώς τε καὶ εὐ-
μενὴς ἀπαλλάξεται. Ἀλλά τοι, ἦ δ᾽ ὅς, οὐ
497 τὰ ἐλάχιστα ἂν | διαπραξάμενος ἀπαλλάττοιτο.
Οὐδέ γε, εἶπον, τὰ μέγιστα, μὴ τυχὼν πολι-
τείας προσηκούσης· ἐν γὰρ προσηκούσῃ αὐτός
τε μᾶλλον αὐξήσεται καὶ μετὰ τῶν ἰδίων τὰ
κοινὰ σώσει.

The kicking, butting Herd.

(*Republic IX.*)

586 Οἱ ἄρα φρονήσεως καὶ ἀρετῆς ἄπειροι,
A εὐωχίαις | δὲ καὶ τοῖς τοιούτοις ἀεὶ ξυνόντες,
κάτω, ὡς ἔοικεν, καὶ μέχρι πάλιν πρὸς τὸ
μεταξὺ φέρονταί τε καὶ ταύτῃ πλανῶνται διὰ
βίου, ὑπερβάντες δὲ τοῦτο πρὸς τὸ ἀληθῶς
ἄνω οὔτε ἀνέβλεψαν πώποτε οὔτε ἠνέχθησαν,

οὐδὲ τοῦ ὄντος τῷ ὄντι ἐπληρώθησαν, οὐδὲ 586
βεβαίου τε καὶ καθαρᾶς ἡδονῆς ἐγεύσαντο,
ἀλλὰ βοσκημάτων δίκην κάτω ἀεὶ βλέποντες
καὶ κεκυφότες εἰς γῆν καὶ εἰς τραπέζας βό-
σκονται χορταζόμενοι . . ., καὶ ἕνεκα | τῆς τούτων B
πλεονεξίας λακτίζοντες καὶ κυρίττοντες ἀλλή-
λους σιδηροῖς κέρασί τε καὶ ὁπλαῖς ἀπο-
κτιννύασι δι' ἀπληστίαν, ἅτε οὐχὶ τοῖς οὖσιν
οὐδὲ τὸ ὂν οὐδὲ τὸ στέγον ἑαυτῶν πιμπλάντες.
Παντελῶς, ἔφη ὁ Γλαύκων, τὸν τῶν πολλῶν,
ὦ Σώκρατες, χρησμῳδεῖς βίον.

The purging Effect of Dialectic.

(*Sophistes.*)

ΞΕΝΟΣ. Διερωτῶσιν ὧν ἂν οἴηταί τίς τι 230
πέρι λέγειν λέγων μηδέν· εἶθ' ἅτε πλανωμένων B
τὰς δόξας ῥᾳδίως ἐξετάζουσι, καὶ συνάγοντες δὴ
τοῖς λόγοις εἰς ταὐτὸν τιθέασι παρ' ἀλλήλας,
τιθέντες δὲ ἐπιδεικνύουσιν αὐτὰς αὑταῖς ἅμα
περὶ τῶν αὐτῶν πρὸς τὰ αὐτὰ κατὰ ταὐτὰ
ἐναντίας· οἱ δ' ὁρῶντες ἑαυτοῖς μὲν χαλεπαί-
νουσι, πρὸς δὲ τοὺς ἄλλους ἡμεροῦνται, καὶ
τούτῳ δὴ τῷ τρόπῳ τῶν περὶ αὑτοὺς μεγάλων
καὶ | σκληρῶν δοξῶν ἀπαλλάττονται πασῶν C
ἀπαλλαγῶν ἀκούειν τε ἡδίστην καὶ τῷ πάσχοντι
βεβαιότατα γιγνομένην. νομίζοντες γάρ, ὦ
παῖ φίλε, οἱ καθαίροντες αὐτούς, ὥσπερ οἱ
περὶ τὰ σώματα ἰατροὶ νενομίκασι μὴ πρότερον
ἂν τῆς προσφερομένης τροφῆς ἀπολαύειν
δύνασθαι σῶμα, πρὶν ἂν τὰ ἐμποδίζοντα ἐν
αὐτῷ τις ἐκβάλῃ, ταὐτὸν καὶ περὶ ψυχῆς

230 διενοήθησαν ἐκεῖνοι, μὴ πρότερον αὐτὴν ἕξειν
τῶν προσφερομένων μαθημάτων ὄνησιν, πρὶν |
D ἂν ἐλέγχων τις τὸν ἐλεγχόμενον εἰς αἰσχύνην
καταστήσας, τὰς τοῖς μαθήμασιν ἐμποδίους
δόξας ἐξελών, καθαρὸν ἀποφήνῃ καὶ ταῦτα
ἡγούμενον, ἅπερ οἶδεν, εἰδέναι μόνα, πλείω δὲ μή.

ΘΕΑΙΤΗΤΟΣ. Βελτίστη γοῦν καὶ σωφρονεστάτη τῶν ἕξεων αὕτη.

ΞΕ. Διὰ ταῦτα δὴ πάντα ἡμῖν, ὦ Θεαίτητε,
καὶ τὸν ἔλεγχον λεκτέον ὡς ἄρα μεγίστη καὶ
κυριωτάτη τῶν καθάρσεών ἐστι, καὶ τὸν
ἀνέλεγκτον αὖ νομιστέον, ἂν καὶ τυγχάνῃ
βασιλεὺς ὁ μέγας ὤν, τὰ μέγιστα ἀκάθαρτον |
E ὄντα, ἀπαίδευτόν τε καὶ αἰσχρὸν γεγονέναι
ταῦτα, ἃ καθαρώτατον καὶ κάλλιστον ἔπρεπε
τὸν ὄντως ἐσόμενον εὐδαίμονα εἶναι.

ΘΕΑΙ. Παντάπασι μὲν οὖν.

Misanthropy and Misology.

(*Phaedo.*)

89 Ἀλλὰ πρῶτον εὐλαβηθῶμέν τι πάθος μὴ
πάθωμεν. Τὸ ποῖον; ἦν δ' ἐγώ. Μὴ γενώ-
D μεθα, ἦ δ' ὅς, μισόλογοι, | ὥσπερ οἱ μισάν-
θρωποι γιγνόμενοι· ὡς οὐκ ἔστιν, ἔφη, ὅ τι ἄν
τις μεῖζον τούτου κακὸν πάθοι—ἢ λόγους
μισήσας. γίγνεται δὲ ἐκ τοῦ αὐτοῦ τρόπου
μισολογία τε καὶ μισανθρωπία. ἥ τε γὰρ
μισανθρωπία ἐνδύεται ἐκ τοῦ σφόδρα τινὶ
πιστεῦσαι ἄνευ τέχνης, καὶ ἡγήσασθαι παντάπασί τε ἀληθῆ εἶναι καὶ ὑγιῆ καὶ πιστὸν τὸν
ἄνθρωπον, ἔπειτα ὀλίγον ὕστερον εὑρεῖν τοῦτον

πονηρόν τε καὶ ἄπιστον καὶ αὖθις ἕτερον· καὶ 89
ὅταν τοῦτο πολλάκις πάθῃ τις καὶ ὑπὸ τούτων
μάλιστα, οὓς ἂν ἡγήσαιτο οἰκειοτάτους τε καὶ
ἑταιροτάτους, τελευτῶν | δὴ θαμὰ προσκρούων E
μισεῖ τε πάντας καὶ ἡγεῖται οὐδενὸς οὐδὲν
ὑγιὲς εἶναι τὸ παράπαν. ἢ οὐκ ᾔσθησαι σὺ
τοῦτο γιγνόμενον; Πάνυ γε, ἦν δ' ἐγώ.

The ultimate Value of Physical Science.

(*Timaeus.*)

Διὸ δὴ χρὴ δύ' αἰτίας εἴδη διορίζεσθαι, τὸ 68
μὲν ἀναγκαῖον, τὸ δὲ θεῖον, καὶ τὸ μὲν θεῖον ἐν E
ἅπασι ζητεῖν κτήσεως ἕνεκα εὐδαίμονος βίου,
καθ' ὅσον ἡμῶν ἡ φύσις | ἐνδέχεται, τὸ δὲ 69
ἀναγκαῖον ἐκείνων χάριν, λογιζομένους, ὡς ἄνευ
τούτων οὐ δυνατὰ αὐτὰ ἐκεῖνα, ἐφ' οἷς
σπουδάζομεν, μόνα κατανοεῖν οὐδ' αὖ λαβεῖν
οὐδ' ἄλλως πως μετασχεῖν.

Learning must be Play.

(*Republic VII.*)

Οὐδὲν μάθημα | μετὰ δουλείας τὸν ἐλεύθερον 536
χρὴ μανθάνειν. οἱ μὲν γὰρ τοῦ σώματος E
πόνοι βίᾳ πονούμενοι χεῖρον οὐδὲν τὸ σῶμα
ἀπεργάζονται, ψυχῇ δὲ βίαιον οὐδὲν ἔμμονον
μάθημα. Ἀληθῆ, ἔφη. Μὴ τοίνυν βίᾳ, εἶπον,
ὦ ἄριστε, τοὺς παῖδας ἐν τοῖς μαθήμασιν
ἀλλὰ παίζοντας | τρέφε, ἵνα καὶ μᾶλλον οἷός τ' 537
ᾖς καθορᾶν ἐφ' ὃ ἕκαστος πέφυκεν. Ἔχει ὃ
λέγεις, ἔφη, λόγον.

Wonder the Beginning of Wisdom.

(*Theaetetus.*)

155 D | ΣΩ. Θεόδωρος γάρ, ὦ φίλε, φαίνεται οὐ κακῶς τοπάζειν περὶ τῆς φύσεώς σου. μάλα γὰρ φιλοσόφου τοῦτο τὸ πάθος, τὸ θαυμάζειν· οὐ γὰρ ἄλλη ἀρχὴ φιλοσοφίας ἢ αὕτη, καὶ ἔοικεν ὁ τὴν Ἶριν Θαύμαντος ἔκγονον φήσας οὐ κακῶς γενεαλογεῖν.

Your solid Materialist believes only what he touches.

(*Theaetetus.*)

155 E ΣΩ. Ἄθρει δὴ περισκοπῶν, μή τις τῶν ἀμυήτων ἐπακούῃ. εἰσὶν δὲ οὗτοι οἱ οὐδὲν ἄλλο οἰόμενοι εἶναι ἢ οὗ ἂν δύνωνται ἀπρὶξ τοῖν χεροῖν λαβέσθαι, πράξεις δὲ καὶ γενέσεις καὶ πᾶν τὸ ἀόρατον οὐκ ἀποδεχόμενοι ὡς ἐν οὐσίας μέρει.

ΘΕΑΙ. Καὶ μὲν δή, ὦ Σώκρατες, σκληρούς
156 γε λέγεις καὶ | ἀντιτύπους ἀνθρώπους.

ΣΩ. Εἰσὶν γάρ, ὦ παῖ, μάλ' εὖ ἄμουσοι.

Need of Exercise for Mind, as for Body.

(*Theaetetus.*)

153 B ΣΩ. Τί δέ; ἡ τῶν σωμάτων ἕξις οὐχ ὑπὸ ἡσυχίας μὲν καὶ ἀργίας διόλλυται, ὑπὸ γυμνασίων δὲ καὶ κινήσεων ἐπὶ τὸ πολὺ σῴζεται;

ΘΕΑΙ. Ναί.

ΣΩ. Ἡ δ' ἐν τῇ ψυχῇ ἕξις οὐχ ὑπὸ μαθή-

σεως μὲν καὶ μελέτης, κινήσεων ὄντων, κτᾶταί 153
τε μαθήματα καὶ σῴζεται καὶ γίγνεται βελτίων,
ὑπὸ δ' ἡσυχίας, ἀμελετησίας τε καὶ ἀμαθίας
οὔσης, οὔτε τι μανθάνει ἅ τε ἂν μάθῃ ἐπιλανθάνεται;

ΘΕΑΙ. | Καὶ *μάλα.* C

Don't be a Pedant.

(*Theaetetus.*)

ΣΩ. Τὸ *δὲ εὐχερὲς τῶν* | *ὀνομάτων τε καὶ* 184
ῥημάτων καὶ μὴ δι' ἀκριβείας ἐξεταζόμενον τὰ C
μὲν πολλὰ οὐκ ἀγεννές, ἀλλὰ μᾶλλον τὸ τούτου ἐναντίον ἀνελεύθερον, ἔστι δὲ ὅτε ἀναγκαῖον, οἷον καὶ νῦν ἀνάγκη ἐπιλαβέσθαι τῆς ἀποκρίσεως ἣν ἀποκρίνει, ᾗ οὐκ ὀρθή.

Nor over-anxious about mere Words.

(*Politicus.*)

Ἂν *διαφυλάξῃς τὸ μὴ σπουδάζειν ἐπὶ τοῖς* 261
ὀνόμασι, πλουσιώτερος εἰς τὸ γῆρας ἀναφανήσει E
φρονήσεως.

The would-be Poet.

(*Phaedrus.*)

Ὃς *δ' ἂν ἄνευ μανίας* Μουσῶν *ἐπὶ ποιη-* 245
τικὰς θύρας ἀφίκηται, πεισθεὶς ὡς ἄρα ἐκ A
τέχνης ἱκανὸς ποιητὴς ἐσόμενος, ἀτελὴς αὐτός τε καὶ ἡ ποίησις ὑπὸ τῆς τῶν μαινομένων ἡ τοῦ σωφρονοῦντος ἠφανίσθη.

True Object of Punishment.

(*Protagoras.*)

324 Οὐδεὶς γὰρ κολάζει τοὺς ἀδικοῦντας πρὸς
B τούτῳ τὸν νοῦν ἔχων καὶ | τούτου ἕνεκα, ὅτι ἠδίκησεν, ὅστις μὴ ὥσπερ θηρίον ἀλογίστως τιμωρεῖται· ὁ δὲ μετὰ λόγου ἐπιχειρῶν κολάζειν οὐ τοῦ παρεληλυθότος ἕνεκα ἀδικήματος τιμωρεῖται (οὐ γὰρ ἂν τό γε πραχθὲν ἀγένητον θείη), ἀλλὰ τοῦ μέλλοντος χάριν, ἵνα μὴ αὖθις ἀδικήσῃ μήτε αὐτὸς οὗτος μήτε ἄλλος ὁ τοῦτον ἰδὼν κολασθέντα.

The Great W's: Well, Wealthy, and Wise.

(*Laws.*)

743 Χρημάτων ἐπιμέλειαν οὐχ ἅπαξ εἰρήκαμεν
E ὡς χρὴ τελευταῖον τιμᾶν· ὄντων γὰρ τριῶν τῶν ἁπάντων, περὶ ἃ πᾶς ἄνθρωπος σπουδάζει, τελευταῖον καὶ τρίτον ἐστὶν ἡ τῶν χρημάτων ὀρθῶς σπουδαζομένη σπουδή, σώματος δὲ πέρι μέση, πρώτη δὲ ἡ τῆς ψυχῆς.

Truth the Beginning of all Good.

(*Laws.*)

730 Ἀλήθεια δὴ πάντων μὲν ἀγαθῶν θεοῖς
B ἡγεῖται, πάντων δὲ ἀνθρώποις· ἧς ὁ γενήσεσθαι μέλλων μακάριός τε καὶ εὐδαίμων ἐξ ἀρχῆς εὐθὺς μέτοχος εἴη, ἵνα ὡς πλεῖστον χρόνον ἀληθὴς ὢν διαβιῷ.

Self-love a False Shame.

(*Laws.*)

Πάντα ἄνθρωπον χρὴ φεύγειν τὸ σφόδρα 732
φιλεῖν αὑτόν, τὸν δ' ἑαυτοῦ βελτίω διώκειν B
ἀεί, μηδεμίαν αἰσχύνην ἐπὶ τῷ τοιούτῳ πρόσθεν
ποιούμενον.

The Useful is the Noble.

(*Republic.*)

Κάλλιστα γὰρ δὴ τοῦτο καὶ λέγεται καὶ 457
λελέξεται, ὅτι τὸ μὲν ὠφέλιμον καλόν, τὸ δὲ B
βλαβερὸν αἰσχρόν.

Faint Heart never won Fair Lady.

(*Critias.*)

Ἀλλὰ γὰρ ἀθυμοῦντες ἄνδρες οὔπω τρό- 108
παιον ἔστησαν, ὦ Κριτία. C

Quality, not Quantity.

(*Theaetetus.*)

Κρεῖττον γάρ που σμικρὸν εὖ ἢ πολὺ μὴ 187
ἱκανῶς περᾶναι. E

A Man's Soul.

(*Laws.*)

Πάντων γὰρ τῶν αὑτοῦ κτημάτων μετὰ 726
θεοὺς ψυχὴ θειότατον, οἰκειότατον ὄν. A

Fair Play in the Race for Excellence.

(*Laws*).

Φιλονικείτω δὲ ἡμῖν πᾶς πρὸς ἀρετὴν ἀφθό- 731
νως. A

NOTES

G. = Goodwin's *Greek Grammar* (revised edition, 1893).
H. = Hadley's *Greek Grammar* (revised by Allen, 1884).
(These are cited by the section-numbers.)
L. & S. = Liddell and Scott's *Greek-English Lexicon*, seventh edition.
G. M. T. = Goodwin's *Greek Moods and Tenses*, enlarged edition.

References such as 36,17 are to page and line of the present volume.

The figures down the outer margin of the notes refer to the paging of the text; those before each note give the line of the page. The heavy-faced figures and letters at the head of each paragraph (and on the outer margin of the Greek text) give the paging and its five divisions of the edition of Plato in three volumes published by Henri Estienne (Latin, *Stephanus*) in Paris, 1578.

APOLOGY

THE *Apology* reads as the defence spoken by Socrates when on trial at the age of seventy before an Athenian court on the charge of impiety. Is it that defence? The unanimous answer of scholars, and for sufficient reasons, is—no. How nearly does it reproduce that real defence? Here, opinions differ widely. Written "when the words of Socrates were still fresh in his memory," says one; "in *substance* the real defence," says another; "*not* the real speech of Socrates, but a *free creation* of Plato's," still a third. All agree that it "sounds like Socrates." But the reason for this is as well explained from the third as from the first point of view. Hamlet's soliloquy sounds strikingly like Hamlet. And the reason is obvious.

Further, if we recall the ideals of literary creation in Plato's time and race, and recall that Plato was the idealist of idealists (literalism, stenography, footnote references, and all such belonging to a later unhappy age), we must incline to the notion not only that Plato is not here a verbatim reporter, but that he of all men was incapable of being such, or approximately such. Giotto drew his circle with a free hand ; if he had undertaken it with a string-radius, he probably would have bungled. To Rubinstein playing Beethoven's music, the *notes* could have been but a hindrance. To picture Plato seated as court-reporter, or as a writer of memoirs is utterly distasteful and belittling. Nor is such a view necessary to preserve the greatness or the truth of the Socratic picture. Plato, if any man (recall his theory of Ideas), knew that the characteristic alone is true, while the actual is often aberration and untruth. A man is sometimes not himself—quite conceivably not himself on a trial involving life or death. Therefore it is that the words here put into the mouth of Socrates may be more truly the words of Socrates than those he actually uttered. "We have the whole of Socrates summed up ; the search after knowledge, the interrogation of all persons pretending to have knowledge, the negative result, the irony, the indifference to popular opinion, the offence taken by those whose ignorance is exposed or their opinion despised, the dauntless courage, the almost defiance of those who administer the law as compared with the law itself" (Purves).

It has been almost certainly proved that the piece is one of Plato's earlier writings, composed not many years after the death of his master. The latest and most exhaustive discussion of its composition and of its relation to the writings of Xenophon and others for and against Socrates is to be found in Schanz's edition of 1893.

1 **17 A** 1. **ὅ τι μὲν ὑμεῖς . . πεπόνθατε** 'how *you* have been affected'; 'you' emphatic, because *ὑμεῖς* is expressed. **πεπόνθατε ὑπὸ . . κατηγόρων**: for *ὑπό* c. gen. of the agent after intrans. verbs (as *πάσχω, ἀποθνῄσκω, ἀπόλλυμαι, γίγνομαι, φεύγω*), see H. 820, G. 1241. It is used also with quasi-passive expressions such as *αἰτίαν ἔχειν* 'to be blamed' (36,17), *δίκην ὀφλεῖν* 'to be cast in a suit' (37,28). Often it may be rendered by 'at the hands of,' 'by reason of.' 3. **δ' οὖν** '(but) certainly,' 'at all events,' regularly vouches for the truth of what follows, be the preceding true or not. (Or, secondly, it marks resumption of some previous matter, after a longer or shorter digression.) As the collocation is a fixed one, it might well be written as one word, *δοῦν*. Cf. *γοῦν* (from *γε οὖν*), *μῶν* (*μὴ οὖν*), *γάρ* (*γε ἄρα*). **καὶ αὐτός** 'likewise' (lit. 'even myself'; see n. on 3,1). **ὑπ' αὐτῶν**: *ὑπό*, as above, with agent of the intrans. verb *ἐπ-ελαθόμην* ('was made to forget myself'). 4. **ὀλίγου** was perhaps originally a gen. of the time *within which* (H. 759, G. 1136) ; 'within a little

(=almost) I had forgotten myself.' (For the usu. explanation—an ellipsis of the infin. absolute *δεῖν*, 'lacking little,' see H. 743 b, G. 1116 b.) 5. **καίτοι** 'and mark you' (*τοι*=*σοί*, an ethical dat.) continues the matter in hand (*καί*), yet introduces a noteworthy (*τοι*) consideration usually *at variance* with what has preceded. Transl. 'and yet,' 'although.' 6. **ὡς ἔπος εἰπεῖν** (an infin. absolute, i.e. *absolved* from construction in the sent.) qualifies here the too sweeping negat. *οὐδέν*; 'almost,' 'about.' H. 956, G. 1534. Cf. *ὀλίγου* (li. 4.). 7. **αὐτῶν ἓν ἐθαύμασα**: *αὐτῶν* is best taken, not with *ἕν*, but directly with the verb; '*in* them'—a sort of gen. of the whole, *within the sphere of which* the verb acts. So G. 1102; *contra* H. 733. 8. **ὧν**: the regular "attract." or "assimilation" of case from acc.; H. 994, G. 1031. **τοῦτο** 'viz., that,' in appos. to *ἕν*. **ἐν ᾧ** 'where.' 9. **μὴ . . ἐξαπατηθῆτε** 'lest you —.' H. 885 b, G. 1374–75 10. **ὡς δεινοῦ ὄντος λέγειν** 'because a clever speaker.' *ὡς* c. ptc. is a form of indir. discourse ('alleging that—,' 'in the belief that—,' 'supposing that—.' 'because,' etc.) marking the thought as that of some one other than the speaker or writer; H. 978, G. 1574. For the infin. *λέγειν* depending on the adj. *δεινός* ('clever *as* to speaking'), see H. 952, G. 1526.

17 B 11. **αὐτίκα**: in answer to *πην-ίκα* (H. 283, G. 436) 'at just what point of time?', *αὐτ-ίκα* replies 'on the very (*αὐτό*) instant,' 'at once.' 12. **ἔργῳ**: his poor speech is to be, itself, the 'deed' or 'fact' that will refute them. **μηδ' ὁπωσ-τι-οῦν** 'not in any way whatsoever.' On *-τι-οῦν*, see H. 285, G. 432, 1. 13. **τοῦτο** sums in one word all that precedes, resuming specifically *τὸ μὴ αἰσχυνθῆναι*. **αὐτῶν** again is '*in* them' (li. 7). 14. **εἰ μὴ ἄρα** 'unless forsooth,' ironical. **δεινὸν . . λέγειν**: when a syntactic unit (as here, 'clever speaker') is broken by intervening words, the part to be emphasized usu. precedes (as here, 'clever'). Attention to this point often offers the key to the sense. 15. **εἰ μὲν γάρ** 'for if *indeed*,' 'for *verily* if,' with no *δέ* following. *μέν* not rarely betrays its origin (*μήν*) and asseverating sense; as in the phrase of assent *πάνυ μὲν οὖν*. ('yes indeed,' 'aye truly'), in mén-toi ('surely'), in *ἀλλά . . μέν* ('*at . . certe*'), in *μέν δή*, and other collocations. 16. **οὐ κατὰ τούτους . . ῥήτωρ**: again the syntactic group is, for emphasis, broken (li. 14); 'I might admit to being a not-in-*their*-line (of *their* measure, after *their* fashion) orator.' *κατά* means 'down along, and *within*, the line of,' 'in accord with,' 'by the measure of'; while *παρά* is also 'along, but *outside* of.' Cf. *κατά τοὺς νόμους, παρὰ τοὺς νόμους*; and recall *κατά τὸν ποταμόν* ('down the river-*bed*'), *παρὰ τὸν ποταμόν* ('along the river*bank*'). 17. **ὥσπερ ἐγὼ λέγω** 'as I *said*.' The present in such phrases (*ὅπερ λέγω, ὡς ἐγώ φημι*) is frequent; e.g. 3, 30.

1 7,23. 28,19. 18. **ἤ τι ἤ οὐδέν** 'little or nothing.' 19. **ὑμεῖς δ' ἐμοῦ** are both emphatic—*ἐμοῦ* by form, *ὑμεῖς* by position and because expressed at all. The truth is for *you* and *me*; *these* men (*οὗτοι*) have no truth to them. 20. **οὐ μέντοι**: *μέντοι*, from *μήν τοι* ('verily, look you'), at times has only its simple earlier function—that of strong asseveration ('indeed," 'in truth,' 'surely'), in which usage it is often accompanied by *νὴ* **Δ***ία*, *μὰ*, **Δ***ία*, etc.; at other times again, it strongly asseverates a *contrast* to the preceding, and so becomes an **adversative conjunction** ('however'). See L. & S. s.v. *μέν*, B II 4, a & b. Cf. n. on *καίτοι*, supra li. 5. **κεκαλλιεπημένους**: *καλλι-επέομαι* 'to make fine phrases' is here pass. (deponents are not rarely so in the perf.); 'beautified.'
2 1. **ῥήμασί τε καὶ ὀνόμασιν** 'phrases and words,' with *κεκαλλιεπημένους*.

17 C 3. **εἰκῇ λεγόμενα τοῖς ἐπιτυχοῦσιν ὀνόμασι**: note (1) the substantival use of the partic., though without art. (*λεγόμενα* 'a speech spoken'), (2) that *τοῖς . . ὀνόμασι* duplicates and explains *εἰκῇ*. Such clauses of explanation (*ἐπ-εξ-ήγησις*, epexegésis) are characteristic of easy conversation and constantly found in Plato. 5. **οὐδὲ γάρ** 'for not . . either.' Just as *καί* is now the conjunct. 'and,' now the adv. 'even' or also,' so is *οὐδέ* sometimes 'and not,' 'but not,' 'nor' (conj.), sometimes an adv., as here. Consult constantly the lexicon for the particles and conjunctions that "everybody knows." 6. **δήπου** (stronger than *πού*) is used when your statement is, you think, pretty sure to obtain assent; 'doubtless,' 'I presume,' 'you will admit.' *πού* is not so sure—is 'perhaps,' 'maybe,' 'I suppose.' **τῇδε τῇ ἡλικίᾳ**=*ἐμοὶ τηλικῷδε ὄντι* 'for me at my age'; hence *πλάττοντι* is masc. according to the sense (*κατὰ σύν-εσιν*), not femin. in agreement with *ἡλικίᾳ*, according to grammar 7. **ὥσπερ μειρακίῳ** 'sophomoric fashion.' **εἰς ὑμᾶς** 'into your presence.' 8. **καὶ μέντοι καὶ πάνυ**: *καί* conjoins, *μέντοι* asseverates, the second *καί* is an adv. with *πάνυ* (as often); 'and in-truth very strongly.' 9. **παρ-ίεμαι**: *παρ-ίημι* (active) is 'to let go,' 'to concede'; the mid. is 'to get (or try to get) something conceded,' 'to ask as a favour.' 10. **διὰ . . λόγων**: *διά* c. gen. ('through the use of') often differs little from the dat. of instrument; but, as a rule, it is to be sharply disting. from *διά* c. acc. 'on account of,' 'by reason of,' 'thanks to.' 11. **καὶ ἐν ἀγορᾷ . . καὶ ἄλλοθι**: the two *καί*'s are correlative (i.e. relate, refer, each to the other); 'both . . and.' For *ἐν ἀγορᾷ* without art., see H. 661, G. 958. We too say 'in market,' 'at market.' 12. **ἐπὶ τῶν τραπεζῶν** 'at the (money-changers') tables.' For the haunts of Socrates and his mode of life, see Introd., n. 17. **ἵνα** 'where.'

17 D 14. **ἔχει . . οὑτωσί** 'it stands thus ; *ἔχει* intrans. 2
For appended *-ί* in *οὑτωσί*, H. 274, G. 412. 15. **ἐπὶ δικαστήριον ἀναβέβηκα** 'have appeared at court' (orig. 'stepped up,' with reference to the *βήματα* 'platforms'). **γεγονώς** 'born'; Engl. 'old.' 16. **ἀτεχνῶς** (adv. of *ἀτεχνής*) 'simply,' 'literally,' 'veritably,' 'really.' **ξένως ἔχω**=*ξένος εἰμί* (an adv. with *ἔχω* intrans. differs little from the corresponding adj. with *εἰμί*), 'am a stranger to,' 'am unacquainted with,' followed by *λέξεως* a gen. of separation; H. 753 g, G. 1141. 17. **ὥσπερ οὖν ἄν** *κτλ.*: for the form of apodosis, see H. 895, G. 1397. Note the repetition of *ἄν*; H. 864, G. 1312. For **δήπου**, see n. on 2,6. **εἰ τῷ ὄντι** 'supposing really,' a preliminary basis of supposition, upon which rests the condition that follows—*εἰ . . ἔλεγον*. 19. **φωνῇ** 'dialect.'

18 A 19. **ἐτεθράμμην** 'had been reared' (*τρέφω*), still a part of the condition, and hence, by assimilation, in a past tense; H. 919 b, G. 1440. 20. **καὶ δὴ καὶ νῦν** ('and so too in the present case') for *οὕτω καὶ νῦν*, which should properly follow *ὥσπερ* of li. 17. Failure to follow out the original plan of a sentence is called anacoluthon (*ἀνα-κολουθία*, from *ἀκολουθέω* 'to follow'), i.e. is an *in-consequence*; H. 1063. **τοῦτο . . δίκαιον** 'this . . in simple justice.' 25. **αὕτη ἀρετή** subject and predicate, not 'this virtue.' Why not? H. 674, G. 974. *αὕτη*, resumptive of the clause *αὐτὸ . . μή*, would be neuter *τοῦτο*, but for the attraction of the feminine predic. *ἀρετή*; H. 632 a.—This closes the introduction (*exordium*, *προοίμιον*). Next follows a statement of the case (*propositio*, *πρόθεσις*) with a division into heads (*partitio*).—26. **πρῶτον μὲν οὖν . . ἔπειτα δέ**: never ignore the guide-post words. Here, e.g., the conjunct. *οὖν* points backward, the particle *μέν* forward, giving warning of a contrast, thus:

μὲν οὖν . . . . . . δέ.

δίκαιός εἰμι '*it* is right that I'; H. 944 a, G. 1527. 28. **πρῶτά μου ψευδῆ κατηγορημένα** 'the first falsehoods charged against me,' or 'the first charges falsely brought etc.' For the gen. with *κατηγορέω*, see H. 752, G. 1123.

18 B 1. **καὶ πάλαι**: cf. *καὶ πάνυ* 2,8; and once for all 3
note the *adverbial* use of *καί* 'even,' 'aye,' in the phrases *καὶ πάνυ*, *καὶ σφόδρα*, *καὶ μάλα* (*μάλιστα*),—*καὶ πάλαι*, *καὶ πρότερον*, *καὶ νῦν*, *καὶ τότε*, *καὶ πρῴην*, *καὶ ἔναγχος*,—*καὶ ὥς*, *καὶ οὕτως*, *καὶ αὐτός*, etc. **πολλὰ ἤδη ἔτη** ('now many years') merely repeats *καὶ πάλαι* (see n. on 2,3). This is pleonasm (*πλεονα-*

3 *σμός*, see L. & S.) or tautology (*ταὐτο-λογία*). 3. **τοὺς ἀμφὶ Ἄνυτον**, i.e. Anytus, Melētus, Lyco—the three accusers. Though it was really Meletus who had brought the indictment, he is here passed over in contempt. Anytus, it would seem, was the only influential one of the trio (see Index of Proper Names), hence is here made the central figure. **καὶ τούτους**: is *καί* adv. or conjunct.? 4. **δεινούς** 'to be feared' (*δέ-ος*, *δέ*-**δοι**-*κα*). 5. **ἐκ παίδων** 'from childhood.' **παραλαμβάνοντες**: this verb (used of teachers '*taking* boys in hand *from*' their parents) shows how sedulously the enemies of Socrates schooled the rising generation to mistrust this scientist. 6. **ἔπειθον**: observe the tense. **μᾶλλον οὐδὲν ἀληθές** is the compar. degree of the quasi-compound *οὐδὲν ἀληθές* (='falsehood,' 'untruth') used in li. 1. These old accusers were more to be feared (*δεινότεροι*) because they charged 'greater untruth.' 7. **τις Σωκράτης** 'a person named Socrates'—"uncomplimentary indefiniteness" (Dyer). **σοφὸς ἀνήρ**: used thus in warning admonition, the appellation must have had a bad sense with the people. Wisdom beyond the ordinary is apt to be eyed askance. 8. **τὰ μετέωρα** (*ἀείρω*) = not 'heavenly bodies' only, but all atmospheric phenomena. Aristotle's *Meteorologica* discusses Milky Way, comets, orbits, air, water, wind, rain, snow, lightning, earthquakes. 9. **τὸν ἥττω λόγον κρείττω ποιῶν**: this 'making the weaker cause the stronger,' 'making the worse cause win,' was an achievement of the rhetoric taught by the sophists of the time. Naturally, plain people feared and hated such glib gentlemen, as they do now the lawyers that prove black white.

18 C 11. **κατασκεδάσαντες** 'by scattering.' 12. **δεινοί** is empathic. Why? (1,14). 13. **οὐδὲ θεοὺς νομίζειν** 'do not believe in gods *either*' (*οὐδέ*). 16. **ἔτι δὲ καί** 'and further too' (*καί* adv.). 17. **ἂν . . ἐπιστεύσατε** 'may well have been most credulous'; G. 1337, H. silent. 18. **παῖδες ὄντες** 'children as ye were.' Primary rule of translation: Keep the Greek order of words if possible, even though it involve a change in the syntax. For the syntax is not so important as the *march of thought*. 19. **ἀτεχνῶς**: 2,16. **ἐρήμην** (sc. *δίκην*, H. 621 c). **κατηγοροῦντες** ('prosecuting a deserted suit') is explained by the foll. genit. absolute *ἀπολογουμένου οὐδενός*, a clause of *ἐπ-εξήγησις* (2,3). 20. **ὃ δὲ πάντων** (*ἐστὶν*) **ἀλογώτατον**, (*ἐστιν*) **ὅτι**: in translat., however, instead of supplying the second *ἐστί*, we may omit *ὅτι*. 21. **οἷόντε** (sc. *ἐστίν*) 'it is possible.' *οἷόστε* 'able' is quite distinct from *οἷος* '(of such nature) as'; hence, perhaps, may be written as one word. Cf. *ὥστε*, *ἐφ' ᾧτε*.

18 D 22. **πλὴν εἰ** ('except if' =) 'unless.' **κω-**

μῳδοποιός, for ex., an Aristophanes, Eupolis, or Ameipsias. 3
See Introd., § 6. **ὅσοι δέ**: in contrast (*δέ*) to the comedy-writers (who may have been moved by the pure spirit of fun) stood 'all those who out of envy or prejudice etc.' 24. **οἱ δέ** 'and others,' added as an after-thought; hence (1) no preceding *μέν*, (2) *πείθοντες*, loosely repeating *ἀνέπειθον*. 25. **ἀπορώτατοι** 'hardest to deal with.' **οὐδὲ γάρ**: 2,5. 26. **ἀναβιβάσασθαι . . ἐνταυθοῖ** 'to make to *ἀναβαίνειν* ('step up') here (sc. upon the *βῆμα*).' Note *ἐνταυθοῖ* 'hither' as the correlative of *ποῖ* 'whither.' 27. **οὐδ' ἐλέγξαι** 'nor refute'; *οὐδέ* has nothing to do with the preceding *οὐδὲ γάρ*. I.e., two *οὐδέ*'s are not correlative, as are *οὔτε . . οὔτε*. The first gives no hint that a second is to follow. **ἀτεχνῶς ὥσπερ** *κτλ.* 'simply (2,16) to fight shadows as it were (*ὥσπερ*) in my defence.' Following this metaphor closely (note *τὲ καί*) is a clause of interpretation (2,3): 'to cross-examine, with no one making answer':

{ *σκιαμαχεῖν ἀπολογούμενόν τε*
{ *καὶ ἐλέγχειν, μηδενὸς ἀποκρινομένου.*

29. **ἀξιώσατε** 'assume,' 'grant.' Cf. *ἀξίωμα* 'axiom,' 'assumption.'

18 E 2. **οἰήθητε** aor. imperat. from *οἴομαι* a pass. depon. 4
3. **καὶ γάρ**: the real sense is 'aye truly.' It may be translated 'indeed,' 'and indeed,' 'for truly,' etc.—almost anything rather than the stereotyped and abominable phrase 'and (this is right) for,' on the theory of an ellipsis. H. 1050,4 d. (But note that sometimes *καί* and *γάρ* are to be separated, *καί* going with the word after *γάρ* (in the sense of 'also,' 'even' as in 10,1), or correlated with a second *καί*.) 6. **εἶεν** 'so be it,' 'good,' 'well.' See L. & S. **ἀπολογητέον δή**: *δή* is here a particle of transition, a sentence-adverb, a quasi-conjunction; 'then.'

19 A 7. **ὑμῶν ἐξελέσθαι** 'take out of your *minds*.' 9. **ἔσχετε** 'conceived,' 'acquired.' *ἔχω* 'I have,' *ἔσχον* (aor.) 'I got.' **ταύτην**, summary and resumptive (1,13), gathers into one word the preceding eight, to contrast sharply '*all* that prejudice' with the little time allowed for removing it. 10. **βουλοίμην μὲν οὖν**: function of *μέν* and of *οὖν*? (2,26). 11. **εἴ τι ἄμεινον** *κτλ.*: the thought in his mind was: "'Tis not the whole of life to live." 12. **πλέον τί με ποιῆσαι** 'to effect (accomplish) something,' depends, as does *γενέσθαι*, on *βουλοίμην*. 13. **οὐ πάνυ με λανθάνει** 'I am not *wholly* unaware' = 'I am quite well aware.' Such understatement is called *λιτότης* 'simplicity,' *μείωσις* 'diminution,' or *εἰρωνεία* 'irony.' 14. **οἷόν ἐστι** 'the nature' of the difficulty. *ποῖος* asks for the quality, nature, or likeness of a

4 person. (In translation, the free interchange of the various parts of speech—noun for verb, adject. for noun, etc.—as well as of clauses with single words, is necessary, and affords good discipline.) **ὅπῃ τῷ θεῷ**: for all relat. adverbs (*ᾗ*, *ὅπῃ*, *οἷ*, *ὅποι*, *ὅθεν*, *ὁπόθεν*, etc.), of which there is large use in Plato, see H. 283, G. 436—paragraphs notoriously neglected by young students. **τῷ θεῷ**: as the generic art. in *ὁ ἄνθρωπος* 'man' marks off man from other *genera*, e.g. from brutes, so in *ὁ θεός* here it marks off 'divinity,' 'god,' from men. It does not point to any particular god.

After *προ-οίμιον* (17 A–18 A) and *πρό-θεσις* (18 A–19 A), there follows now the defence proper (*πίστις*, *confutatio*; 19 A–28 A); and first against his old accusers (19 A–24 B). 16. **ἀναλάβωμεν** 'take up.' 17. **ἡ ἐμὴ διαβολή** : *ἐμή* is objective: 'against me' (H. 694, G. 999). 18. **ᾗ δὴ καὶ πιστεύων** 'upon which in fact (*καί*) Meletus relied when—'; the first ex. in the *Apol.* of *δή* with a pronoun.

Its use is very frequent with pronouns of all classes—e.g. with relatives 14,1. 19,1,23. 25,20. 39,11. 24,13. 27,3. 37,6; with demonstratives at head of clause 10,27. 34,22. 35,18; with interrogatives 4,20. 7,4. 41,13. Its presence should be noted and *felt*, even when left untranslated. For various approximates in Engl., see H. 1037,4. L. & S. s.v. I 5.

19 B 18. **με ἐγράψατο τὴν γραφήν** : for the two accusatives (one a "cognate"), see H. 725, G. 1076. 19. **εἶεν· τί δή**: li. 6. 21. **ὥσπερ οὖν** *κτλ.* : the comparison is condensed; 'as if then of (formal) prosecutors must I read their affidavit,' calling their *διαβολή* 'slander' by the legal term *ἀντ-ωμοσία* (*ὄμ-νυμι*), for which see L. & S. 23. **καὶ περιεργάζεται** is, I think, solemnly (i.e. ironically) added to *ἀδικεῖ*, to show what after all his criminality amounted to. 'To be over-busy,' 'to waste one's labour' is hardly a crime.

19 C 26. **τοιαύτη τις** 'something like that.' 27. **καὶ αὐτοί**: *καί* is for us superfluous. See n. on 3,1. 28. **κωμῳδίᾳ**, viz. the *Clouds* (*Nubes*), where we find Socrates on his first appearance hung aloft, swinging around (*περιφερόμενον*) in a basket. In explanation of this singular situation he says: *ἀεροβατῶ καὶ περιφρονῶ τὸν ἥλιον* 'I tread the air and contemplate the sun.' See the Introd., § 6. 30. **ὧν . . πέρι** : the most notable instance in Attic prose of the postponement of the prepos. *περί*—six words distant from its case. For the anastrophe (*ἀνα-στροφή* 'turning back') of accent, see H. 109, G. 116. 31. **ὡς ἀτιμάζων** *κτλ.* '*with the idea of* discrediting' (1,10). **οὐ . . λέγω . ., μή πως . . φύγοιμι** : the sense is: "I am not disparaging physical science (by calling it *φλυαρία*) just to recommend myself to (or, in fear of) Meletus, lest somehow (*μή πως*)—in addition to the counts against me of introducing new gods and of corrupting the youth

(infra 27 B)—he might vamp this other old charge about physical speculation. Not at all. The fact is, I know nothing about it." *λέγω* pres. for past (1,17) hence the optat. *φύγοιμι* rather than subjunctive.—For the legal sense of *φεύγω* see L. & S.; on its construct. with *ὑπό* c. gen. see n. on 1,1. 4
3. **τοσαύτας δίκας**: cognate acc.; H. 715 b, G. 1051. 5
ἀλλὰ γάρ (from *γ' ἄρ'*) 'but indeed'; H. 1050,4 d. *γάρ* is the Irish 'sure.' "I'll not go; it's raining sure"=*οὐκ εἶμι· ὕει γάρ.* (Note too the inversion: "Sure it's raining; I'll not go"=*ὕει γάρ, οὐκ εἶμι*—a common order in Herodotus.) Those who insist on translating *γάρ* always by 'for' are driven to the assumption of an ellipsis in *ἀλλὰ γάρ*, as in *καὶ γάρ* above 4,3. But see App. 4. **μέτεστι**: c. gen. et dat. (*ἐμοὶ τούτων*); H. 734, G. 1161. **μάρτυρας δὲ αὐτοὺς ὑμῶν τοὺς πολλούς**: distinguish the object-accus. (c. art.) from the predic. acc.; 'as witnesses I offer the majority of you yourselves'; H. 726 a, G. 1080. We might have had *αὐτῶν*, in agreement with *ὑμῶν*; but the identity of the *majority* with the witnesses is better shown by *αὐτούς*.

19 D 6. **ἀξιῶ** 'I demand (deem it *ἄξιον*, reasonable).' 8. **πολλοὶ . . οἱ τοιοῦτοι**: predic. and subj. (c. art.) respectively. In Engl. too the predic. comes first: 'many of you are of that class,' i.e. have been my hearers. 9. **ἢ μικρὸν ἢ μέγα**: cf. 4,30. 11. **ἐκ τούτων** 'from *this*'; as in *μετὰ ταῦτα* 'after *that*,' Greek idiom prefers, though it does not demand, the plural. 13. **ἀλλὰ γάρ**: 5,3. **οὔτε . . οὐδέ γε** 'neither . . but no more.' *οὐδέ γε* is a strong contrasting substitute for the second *οὔτε* which should respond to the first. H. 1044 b. 16. **πράττομαι**: see L. & S. s.v. *πράσσω*, v 2.

19 E 16. **οὐδὲ τοῦτο ἀληθές** repeats the previous *οὐδέ*; 'nor is that true *either*.' Cf. 2,5. 17. **ἐπεὶ καὶ τοῦτο** *κτλ.*: Socrates has just stated a fact—that the report of his teaching for pay was untrue. The *ἐπεί*-clause assigns the reason, not for the fact but for his *statement* of the fact. '(I say this, make this disclaimer) *for*, while I think the ability to teach is a fine thing, yet I do not possess it (*ἀλλ' οὐ γὰρ ἐπίσταμαι* 6,18).' But before he reaches this final repudiation, a long anecdote must intervene. Cf. in Engl.: "It weighs ten pounds; for I weighed it myself." Here is no reason for its weighing ten pounds, but rather for my saying so. *γάρ* is used in like manner; cf. 36,2. 19. **Γοργίας** *κτλ.*: see the Index of Proper Names. 21. **οἷόσ τ' ἐστὶν . . τοὺς νέους . . τούτους πείθουσι**: we should expect the infin. *πείθειν* ('is able to persuade'); but after the relat. clause *οἷς ἔξεστι κτλ.* ('who are free to associate . . '), *τοὺς νέους* is taken up again by *τούτους* (1,13) and the original construction is then dropped (anacoluthon; 2,20); hence *πείθουσι indicat.* and *plural.*

5 **20 A** 26. **χάριν προσ-ειδέναι** 'to feel gratitude besides (*πρός*).' We should have expected a ptc., matching *διδόντας*. **ἐπεὶ καί**, as above (17), does not give the reason for the *fact stated* —that these eminent sophists have power to persuade—but the reason for *stating the fact*. '(I say this of the great sophists) *since indeed* this pitiful Parian can persuade.' The general statement is true, *for* it is true in the following instance.
27. **ἄλλος ἀνήρ ἐστι** *κτλ.* 'another man, a Parian, is here, a wise man.' Retain the original homely colloquial order of words when possible. The Greek is a language of low plane even at its highest. See the Index of Proper Names for *Πάριος*.
28. **ᾐσθόμην** 'heard,' 'learned.' **ἐπιδημοῦντα** 'residing here'; contrast *ἀπο-δημέω* 'to be (reside) abroad.' Cf. *epi-demic* 'among the people.' 29. **τετέλεκε** 'has paid,' 'spent'—the second and much-used meaning of *τελέω*.
30. **ξύμπαντες** 'all put together.' On Callias consult the Index. 31. **ἀν-ηρόμην** 'I questioned,' 'interrogated.' *ἠρόμην* as the aor. of *ἐρωτάω* is more common in Attic prose
6 than *ἠρώτησα*; but the latter is also good. 1. **ὑέε**: in Att. prose at Plato's time *υἱός* was probably spelled *ὑός*. For its double inflection (by 2nd and by 3rd declens.), see H. 216, G. 291. **ἦν δ' ἐγώ** 'said I'; H. 485, G. s.v. *ἠμί* in the Catalogue of Verbs. 2. **ἐγενέσθην** 'had been born.' **εἴχομεν ἂν . . λαβεῖν** 'we should be able to —,' i.e. *now*. The imperf. is regularly used to present a state of things contrary to the *present* reality, when the condition is contrary to reality; H. 895, G. 1397. 3. **μισθώσασθαι**: disting. the mid. from the active; H. 816, G. 1245. 4. **ἔμελλεν . . ποιήσειν** 'would make,' a mere *περί-φρασις* ('circumlocution') for the fut., *when the fut. must be thrown into the past*—as here, because depending on a past tense, *εἴχομεν*. See n. on 2,19. **καλώ τε κἀγαθώ** 'perfect.'

20 B 5. **προσ-ήκουσαν**: trace the sense 'to have come to,' 'to become,' 'beseem,' 'be proper.' **ἀρετήν** 'excellence' of any kind—of land, animals, things, people—not merely the morality 'virtue.' Here it is an acc. of specific. with *καλὼ καὶ ἀγαθώ*; H. 718, G. 1058. 6. **γεωργικῶν**: *γῆ*, *ἔργον*. What does "George" mean? **νῦν δέ** 'but as it is (as the case stands),' often introduces the fact, after an hypothesis contrary to fact. 8. **τοιαύτης** 'that kind of' refers to *ἀνθρώπω* in preceding line; but its sense is rendered more explicit by the added clause *τῆς ἀνθρωπίνης κτλ.*; cf. 5,8.
10. **ἐσκέφθαι**: perf. inf. from *σκέπτομαι*. 11. **πάνυ γε**, *πάνυ μὲν οὖν*, *καὶ πάνυ γε*, are answers of entire assent; 'quite so,' 'to be sure,' 'certainly.' **ἦ δ' ὅς**: for *ἦ* see li. 1; for *ὅς* ('he'), H. 655 a; G. 1023,2. Also in our own old-fashioned phrase "quoth he," *quoth* is all there is left of a verb

at one time fully inflected. 12. **πόσου**: gen. of price. So 6
μνῶν, li. 14. The following table should be learned :—

(1	*ὀβολός*	=circa 3 cents)
6	*ὀβολοί*	=1 *δραχμή* (c. 18 cents)
100	*δραχμαί*	=1 *μνᾶ* (c. $ 18.00)
60	*μναῖ*	=1 *τάλαντον* (c. $ 1080.00)

14. **ὡς ἀληθῶς** '(thus) truly,' '(so) truly.' 15. **ἔχοι . . διδάσκει**: both are in (implied) indir. discourse, after the secondary tense *ἐμακάρισα*. Hence both, or neither, or either, may be shifted to the optative.

20 C 15. **ἐμμελῶς**=*ἐν μέλει* (*τὸ μέλος*='*mel*-ody') 'in tune,' 'harmoniously,' 'fitly,' 'reasonably'—perhaps here used with irony. The fee of the great Protagoras was twenty times five minae; and Socrates may mean that the fee and the teaching of Evenus were on a par—both cheap. 16. **ἐγὼ γοῦν καὶ αὐτός** 'for my own part certainly.' On *καί* see n. on 3,1. In the following, carefully note the tenses and the presence of *ἄν*. *ἡβρυνόμην* from *ἁβρύνομαι*. 18. **ἀλλ' οὐ γάρ** 'but indeed (*γάρ*) I do not ——.' See n. on 5,3. 20. **τὸ σὸν . . πρᾶγμα**: the unit is broken by the inserted *τί ἐστι*; hence a heavy emphasis on *τὸ σόν*: '*your* profession—what is it?'—if teaching be that of the sophists. See on 1,14. 22. **δήπου**: 2,6. **σοῦ γε οὐδὲν . . πραγματευομένου**: a gen. absol. of fact, not of condition, as shown by *οὐδέν* rather than *μηδέν*. A more transparent form for presenting the inconsistency between this fact and the next would have been :—

οὐ γὰρ δήπου { *σὺ μὲν οὐδὲν . . πραγματεύει,*
τοσαύτη δὲ φήμη . . γέγονεν.

(Here *οὐ* denies neither the one nor the other statement, but their *combination*. 'For it is not true, I presume (*δήπου*), that (at the same time) you do nothing more than the rest of the world, and yet so great a talk has arisen about you.') But often, as here, one or the other member is thrown into participial or other subordinate form. 24. **ἔπειτα** 'then,' 'under those circumstances,' viz. those indicated by the participial clause preceding. 25. **εἰ μή τι** *κτλ.* represents the thought of the participial clause above, but this time not as a fact (*οὐ*), but as a condition (*μή*). The speaker weakens; it may be Socrates' business *was* different from most men's.

20 D 27. **ταυτί μοι δοκεῖ** *κτλ.* 'this I think he justly says who says it.' Greek order. 29. **τί ποτε**: lit. 'whatever?' But in Engl. we generalize in space, not in time, asking 'what *in the world*?' 31. **ἀκούετε δή** 'listen then,' 'listen now,' *δή* common c. imperat., e.g. 13,24. 15,17. 17,31. 26,9.

7 See n. on 4,18 for its use with pronouns. 1. **εὖ μέντοι ἴστε** 'be assured however' (for the form *ἴστε* see H. 491, G. 820). *μέντοι* is a strong substitute for *δέ*, in responsion to *μέν*. For its origin, see on 1,20. 2. **ἐρῶ**: a fut. of *φημί* (or *λέγω*). **οὐδὲν ἀλλ' ἤ** was once perhaps *οὐδὲν ἄλλο ἤ* 'nothing other than,' but hardly so in the classic period, since the variations of the phrase show that *ἀλλ'* had detached itself from *οὐδέν* and fused with *ἤ* = 'but,' 'except.' E.g. 29,29 *τίνα ἄλλον ἔχουσι λόγον . . ἀλλ' ἢ τὸν ὀρθόν;* H. 1046,2 c. 3. **ἔσχηκα** cf. *ἔσχετε* 4,9. 4. **ποίαν δὴ σοφίαν ταύτην;** supply *διά*. Not 'this wisdom'; see n. on 2,25. 5. **τῷ ὄντι**: H. 779 b, G. 1181; used above 2,17. **κινδυνεύω** c. infin. 'I run the risk of —,' 'I probably —,' 'it is likely that I —'; much used by Plato. 6. **ταύτην**: with *σοφός* (6,5). **τάχ' ἄν** 'perhaps' goes with *εἶεν*, li. 8. See L. & S. s.v. II.

20 E 7. **κατ' ἄνθρωπον**: an adj. phrase with *σοφίαν*, yet not quite equiv. to *ἀνθρωπίνην*. It is rather 'of human *measure*, according to the *standard* of man.' See n. on *κατά* 1,16. 8. **τί λέγω**: a deliberat. subjunct., indirect; 'I know not what I am to call it,' Ironical, of course. The wisdom of these professional wise ones was something beyond man's common sense, or—nonsense. 9. **γὰρ δή** 'for indeed (in truth, in fact, you know),' a freq. combination always to be noted and felt, not necessarily translated. Cf. 7,24. 8,1. 13,5,13. 28,24. 36,17,21. Do not ignore **ἔγωγε** following: 'for my part.' 10. **ἐπὶ διαβολῇ τῇ ἐμῇ** 'to my prejudice.' *ἐπί* c. dat. 'with a view to,' 'for the purpose of,' equiv. to a *ἵνα*-clause. On the objective *ἐμή*, see 4,17. 11. **καί μοι** 'and pray,' 'and please.' The "ethical" dat. (H. 770, G. 1171) makes it a personal matter between them, as 'please' in English. **μὴ θορυβήσητε** 'no noise, please (*μοι*),' prohibition; H. 874, G. 1346. In li. 23 the *present* imperat. is used (*μὴ θορυβεῖτε*) 'don't be making a noise,' i.e. 'stop making.' 12. **μηδὲ ἄν** (*ἄν* for *ἐάν*) repeats the negative. **μέγα λέγειν** 'to boast.' 13. **οὐκ ἐμὸν τὸν λόγον**: predicate posit. is given to an adject. when it is—not a mere attribute of the subject, defining and preparing it for predication—but itself is part of the predication or information conveyed by the sentence; 'not mine is the word that I —.' See H. 618, G. 972. 14. **ἀξιόχρεων**, masc. acc., is also in predic. position. **ἀν-οίσω** (*ἀνα-φέρω*): lit. 'refer' (sc. *τὸν λόγον*). **τῆς γὰρ ἐμῆς** sc. *σοφίας*. But Socrates modestly substitutes 'if indeed it is a modicum of wisdom.' 15. **καὶ οἵα** 'and as to its quality' (a sort of indir. question), 'as witness I will offer.' For *οἵα* 'quality' see n. on 4,14. 17. **Χαιρεφῶντα γάρ**: the ground, thus introduced by *γάρ*, 'for' offering Apollo

as a witness to his wisdom is not reached till li. 25, since 7
Socrates must first explain how the matter came about. Cf.
ἐπεί 5,17 for this long *carrying power* of a logical connective.
On **που** see n. on 2,6 (*δήπου*). **ἴστε** is here indic., not as in
li. 1, imperat.

21 A 17. **οὗτος** *κτλ.* : the scheme of the sent. is :

οὗτος { *ἐμός τε ἑταῖρος ἦν ἐκ νέου,*
{ *καὶ ὑμῶν τῷ πλήθει* { *ἑταῖρός τε (ἦν),*
{ *καὶ ξυνέφυγε—*

In the first clause, *ἑταῖρος* is 'friend,' 'comrade'; in the second, 'adherent'—its political sense. *τὸ πλῆθος* has also its political sense, 'democracy.' With *ἐκ νέου* cf. *ἐκ παίδων* 3,5.—Socrates refers to the revolution of 404–403 B.C. At the close of Athens' disastrous war with Sparta (431–404 B.C.), an oligarchy of thirty men (the infamous "Thirty"), backed by the Spartan victor Lysander, had got itself established in Athens and had proceeded to the wholesale confiscation of property, with condemnation of hundreds of citizens to death and exile. In a few months, however (eight months), under the brave marshalling of Thrasybūlus, the exiles were sufficiently strong to force their way back to Athens and re-establish the democracy. 19. **τὴν φυγὴν ταύτην,** because so recent. 20. **κατῆλθε** the regular compound for the return of exiles. **ἴστε δή** 'you know, of course.' 21. **ὡς σφοδρός** *κτλ.* 'how intense (vehement, impetuous) in whatever he went at.' For the opt. *ὁρμήσειε* (past repetition), see H. 914 B 2 ; G. 1431,2. And once for all note that Att. prose prefers the inflection *-σαιμι, -σειας, -σειε(ν)*, third plur. *-σειαν*, and *not -σαιμι, -σαις, -σαι*, H. 434, G. 732. **καὶ δή ποτε καί** 'and so once too' (2,20). *καὶ δὴ καί* is used either after a general statement as here, or after a mere reference to other instances (*ἄλλα τε . .*), to come to the important instance, the main point. 22. **τοῦτο μαντεύσασθαι** : *τοῦτο* is a cognate acc. ('thus to question the oracle')—the quest. itself being postponed a line by reason of the parenthesis (*παρ-έν-θεσις*). 23. **ὅπερ λέγω** *κτλ.* : see 1,17 for the tense of *λέγω* ; li. 11 above for that of *θορυβεῖτε*. 24. **γὰρ δή**: li. 9. 25. **ἀνεῖλε . . ἡ Πυθία** (sc. *ἱέρεια* 'priestess') : *ἀν-αιρέω* the usu. term for the response of an oracle ; Xen. *Anab.* III 1,6. 26. **τούτων πέρι**: 4,31. 27. **οὑτοσί** (on *-ί*, see 2,14). It is a deictic (i.e. pointing, *δείκ-νυμι*, demonstrative) pronoun ; hence freq. corresponds to our adv. 'here.' 28. **ὧν ἕνεκα** 'why.'

21 B 29. **ὅθεν . . γέγονε** 'the origin'; noun for verb
(4,14). 31. **λέγει** 'mean,' as often. 1. **αἰνίττεται** : from 8
this, the word *αἴνιγμα* 'enigma.' **γὰρ δή** : 7,9. 4. **δήπου** :
2,6. 6. **μόγις πάνυ** 'with great (inward) struggle'; *μόγις*
adv. from *μόγος* 'toil,' 'distress.' 8. **δοκούντων** 'reputed.'

8 **21 C** 9. **που**: local sense 'anywhere,' not as in 7,17. **μαντεῖον, χρησμῷ** 'oracle,' 'response.' 10. **ὅτι,** introducing direct discourse, is to be dropped in transl. 12. **ὀνόματι** 'by name'; H. 780, G. 1182. 14. **πρὸς ὅν** '*with* whom' (a freq. sense) goes with *ἔπαθον*. 15. **σκοπῶν** 'in my investigations.' 16. **διαλεγόμενος** resumes *διασκοπῶν*. **ἔδοξέ μοι,** after the nomin. ptc., is anacoluthic (2,20) for *ᾐσθόμην* or *ἔγνων*. 17. **δοκεῖν μέν**: with heavy emphasis on the verb, as below in *οἴοιτο μέν*. 18. **κἄπειτα** crasis of *καὶ ἔπειτα*.

21 D 20. **ἐντεῦθεν** 'from this (attempt).' 21. **ἀπηχθόμην** (aor. of *ἀπεχθάνομαι*) 'became odious,' 'incurred the hatred of.' **πρὸς ἐμαυτὸν . . ἐλογιζόμην**: not quite 'I *said* to myself' nor 'I *thought*,' but rather the Yankee 'I reckoned' 'calculated.' 22. **δ' οὖν**: 1,3. **τούτου μέν**: *μέν* = *μήν* 'surely' (1,15). 23. **κινδυνεύει**: 7,5. *μέν* following is answered by *ἀλλά*. The scheme is :—

{ *κινδυνεύει μὲν γὰρ . . οὐδέτερος . . ,*
{ *ἀλλ'* { *οὗτος μὲν οἴεται . . ,*
{ *ἐγὼ δὲ . . οὐδὲ οἴομαι.*

24. **καλὸν κἀγαθὸν εἰδέναι** 'to have *perfect* knowledge.' The phrase *καλὸς κἀγαθός* is usu. applied to persons—'perfect without and within.' But see 6,4 and L. & S. s.v. *καλοκἀγαθός*. 26. **ὥσπερ οὖν** 'as certainly.' *οὖν* refers to, and re-enforces, his previous statement (li. 2) that he was not conscious of any superior knowledge. 27. **οὐδέ** (adv.) 'no more' do I —. **γ' οὖν** 'at least, then.' **σμικρῷ τινι**: dat. of measure ('to some small degree'), **αὐτῷ τούτῳ**: dat. of respect; H. 780, G. 1182. 28. **ἃ μὴ οἶδα**: note the negat. (not *οὐ*); H. 914, G. 1430. 29. **ἐντεῦθεν**: temporal. **ᾖα**: imperf. of *εἶμι*.

9 **21 E** 31. **κἀκείνῳ**: crasis of *καὶ ἐκείνῳ*. 2. **ᾖα**: the syntax goes to pieces on the long digression *αἰσθανόμενος . . ποιεῖσθαι*. Not till after the resumptive *ἰτέον* is it stated *to whom* he went. **αἰσθανόμενος μὲν . . ὅτι** go together; what intervenes is subordinate ('with grief and apprehension'). After this, the finite verb *ὅμως δὲ . . ἐδόκει* is anacoluthic for *ἡγούμενος* or the like. 5. **τὸ τοῦ θεοῦ** 'the matter (word) of the god'; H. 730 b, G. 953. **περὶ πλείστου ποιεῖσθαι** (*mid.*) 'to regard of most importance.' So often *περὶ πολλοῦ* (*πλείονος, πλείστου,—ὀλίγου, ἐλάττονος, ἐλαχίστου,—παντός*) *ποιοῦμαι* (N.B. mid. voice). See L. & S. s.v. *περί* A IV. 6. **σκοποῦντι** *κτλ.* (sc. *μοι*) 'in my investigation of what the oracle meant.' For the dat. with verbals (*ἰτέον*), see H. 769, & b; G. 1188 and 1187. 7. **νὴ τὸν κύνα** (see L. & S.): one of the many curious Greek oaths (as—"by the plane-tree," "goose," "cabbage," "almond"), used perhaps

"to get the relief of swearing without incurring the sin" 9
(Adam). For the acc. see H. 723, G. 1066–67.

22 A 9. **ἦ μήν**: the usual initial phrase in an oath; 'verily, verily,' 'so help me Heaven.' 10. **ὀλίγου δεῖν**: see n. on *ὡς ἔπος εἰπεῖν* 1,6. 12. **ἐπιεικέστεροι . . πρός** 'more promising for (in the matter of),' lit. 'more likely' (*εἰκός*). Cf. the colloquial Engl. 'a *likely* youth.' 13. **φρονίμως ἔχειν**: the equiv. of adj. with *εἶναι* (2,16). 14. **δή**: quasi-conjunct. (4,6). **ὥσπερ** 'as it were' (3,28). 15. **πονοῦντος**: sc. *μου*, implied in *ἐμήν*. **ἵνα <μή> μοι καί** 'lest of a truth,' i.e. lest (as it seemed, so) *indeed* it might *prove* irrefutable (*ἀν-έλεγκτος*). *γένοιτο* is opt. because depend. upon *πονοῦντος* a virtual imperfect.

22 B 19. **ὡς** c. ptc.; 4,31. **ἐπ' αὐτοφώρῳ** 'palpably,' 'manifestly'; a common phrase. See L. & S. for its lit. meaning. 21. **ἀναλαμβάνων**: 4,16. 22. **πεπραγματεῦσθαι**: pass., though the verb is depon. So *κεκαλλιεπημένους* 1,20. For *αὐτοῖς* dat., see H. 769, but better G. 1186–87. 23. **δι-ηρώτων ἄν**: iterative *ἄν*, the *ἄν* of occasion; H. 835, G. 1296. *ἐρωτάω* is 'to ask a question'; *ἀν-ερωτάω* 'to ask one a *series* of questions,' 'to question him' (5,31); *δι-ερωτάω* 'to cross-question.' **τί λέγοιεν** 'what they *meant*,' as often. 26. **ῥη-τέον**: *ἐρ-ρή-θην*, *ῥῆ-μα*, *ῥῆ-σις*. **γάρ**: note postponement. **ὡς ἔπος . . εἰπεῖν ὀλίγου . . ἅπαντες** 'briefly, almost all.' On both phrases see p. 1. 27. **ἂν . . ἔλεγον**, i.e. if called on—a condit. contrary to fact, hence *ἄν*. 28. **ἐπεποιήκεσαν** 'made,' i.e. 'composed' poetry; hence *ποιητής* 'poet,' properly any 'maker of fiction.' 29. **ἐν ὀλίγῳ**: temporal.

22 C 30. **φύσει τινί** 'by some instinct,' 'naturally,' i.e. unconsciously. The true poet does not say to himself: "I will now to manufacture some poetry." He is rather the trumpet through which divinity speaks to man. See Plato's *Ion* 533 D.
1. **καὶ γάρ**: not here in combination, as in 4,3. *καί* goes 10
with *οὗτοι*, 'these too'; H. 1050,4 e. 3. **ἐφάνησαν** (2nd aor. pass.): c. ptc.; H. 986; G. 1592,1. 4. **ᾐσθόμην αὐτῶν**: note the genit. 5. **καὶ τἆλλα** 'also in other matters.' **ἀνθρώπων**: a predic. genit. *of the whole* (so-called "partitive"). Note the separation of *σοφωτάτων* from its substantive (1,14). **ἅ**, like *τἆλλα*, an acc. of specification. 6. **ἐντεῦθεν**: here of persons, 'from them.' **τῷ αὐτῷ**: dat. of respect (8,27). 7. **περιγεγονέναι** 'to *be* superior'—present state; c. gen. H. 749, G. 1120. **ᾧπερ καί**: in Engl. we may have an 'also' or 'too' in the main clause, but not in the relat. clause. The Greek often uses them in both (**e.g.** "I too believe what you also do") or in the relat.

10 alone ("I believe what you also do"). Recall the freq. *ὥς τις καὶ ἄλλος* 'as *also* any other.' See L. & S. s.v. *καί*, B 2. For the redundancy of expression, cf. the doubling of the negative. 8. **τελευτῶν**: in Engl. an adv. — 'finally'; H. 968 a, G. 1564. 9. **ξυν-ῄδη**: H. 491, G. 820 for the form.

22 D 9. **ὡς ἔπος εἰπεῖν** qualifies the too strong *οὐδέν* (1,6). 10. **τούτους δέ γε**: *γε* italicizes *τούτους*, though yielding posit. to the conjunction. 11. **πολλὰ καὶ καλά**: drop *καί* in translat. 12. **τούτου μέν**: answered, not by a *δέ*-clause, but by *ἀλλά* in li. 14. For the genit. after *ψεύδομαι*, see H. 748, G. 1117. 15. **ὅπερ καί**: n. on 7. Here *καί* stands also in the main clause—*καὶ οἱ ἀγαθοί*. 17. **ἐξ-εργάζεσθαι**: note *ἐξ-*. Cf. '*e*-labor-ate.' **ἠξίου** 'assumed' (3,29). **τὰ μέγιστα** (appos. to *τἆλλα*) 'the affairs of state.' 19. **πλημ-μέλεια** (*πλήν-μέλος*) 'out-of-tune-ness,' 'discordance,' 'inconsistency.' Cf. *ἐμ-μελῶς* 6,15. The *πλημμέλεια* of these artisans in assuming knowledge of the matters of state is a quite natural one (and rather encouraged) under any democratic form of government. **ἀπ-έκρυπτεν** 'dimmed.' 20. **ὥστε**: with acc. c. infin.; as the result actually occurs, we might have had the indic. (the mood of facts); H. 927, G. 1450. **ἀν-ερωτᾶν**: see n. on *δι-ηρώτων* 9,23.

22 E 20. **ὑπέρ** 'in behalf of.' 21. **πότερα** (= *πότερον*): the alternative is *ἢ ἀμφότερα*, li. 23. **οὕτως . . ἔχειν**: intrans. *ἔχω* c. adv. (2,16). **ὥσπερ ἔχω** is explained by the *μήτε*-clauses. 22. **μήτε τι** go together. See L. & S. s.v. *τις* (enclit.), A 12 c. 25. **λυσι-τελοῖ** (*λύω* 'to atone for,' 'to pay,' *τέλος* 'expense') = 'to profit,' 'to advantage.' 27. **δή**: quasi-conjunct. (4,6). See 4,18 on its affinity for pronouns. 28. **ἀπέχθεια**: cf. its verb *ἀπεχθάνομαι* 9,1.

23 A 29. **οἷαι** = *τοιαῦται οἷαί εἰσι*. 31. **ὄνομα δὲ τοῦτο λέγεσθαι**: *λέγομαι*, in correspond. with the finite verb of the *μέν*-clause above, might have been expected. But the clause has fallen under the influence of the nearer *ὥστε*. *ὄνομα* is perhaps an adv. accus. *τοῦτο* is a predic. nomin., introducing *σοφὸς εἶναι*. *σοφός* is nomin. *κατὰ σύνεσιν* (2,6), because Socrates is the real subject of thought, if *not* the grammatical subj. of the sentence. *εἶναι* is a rather freq. pleonasm after verbs
11 of *naming*. 2. **ἑκάστοτε** 'each time' is a sort of detailed *ἀεί*. **αὐτόν** is the intensive pronoun 'self,' going with *με*. But this is, of course, not the same thing as *ἐμαυτόν*, reflexive, 'myself.' No reflexive sense is possible here. 3. **ἅ**, like its antecedent, is an acc. of specif. **τὸ δέ** 'but on the other hand' (= 'whereas'); an adverbial acc. much used by Plato to introduce a statement *counter* (*δέ*) to the preceding—as if responding to some omitted *τὸ μέν*. Cf. the adverbial *τοῦτο μὲν . . τοῦτο δέ*. 4. **κινδυνεύει**: 7,5. For the order of words in

transl., see 3,18. **τῷ ὄντι**: 7,5. 6. **ὀλίγου τινὸς . . καὶ οὐδενός**: Engl. 'little *or* nothing'; Greek, 'little—aye, nothing,' offering, not an alternative with, but a climax in, littleness. 7. **φαίνεται**: here c. infin. Disting. from its use c. ptc. (10,3). **τοῦτον λέγειν τὸν Σωκράτη** *κτλ.* 'to mention by name *this* Socrates ('this' is emphat. by position) and to use-for-his-purpose (*προσ-*) *my* name ('my' is emphat. because *ἐμῷ* in attributive rather than *μου* in predic. position) because making *me* (*ἐμέ*, not *με*) his (middle voice) example.' 11

23 B 10. **ὥσπερ ἂν**: sc. *ποιοῖτο*; H. 863, G. 1313. 12. **τῇ ἀληθείᾳ**: H. 779 b, G. 1181. Note the synonyms already had: *τῷ ὄντι* (2,17), *ὡς ἀληθῶς* (6,14). 13. **πρὸς σοφίαν**: cf. *πρὸς τὸ φρονίμως ἔχειν* 9,13. **ταῦτ'** (adverbial accus., as if adv. *οὕτω*) 'so,' 'thus.' It is often said to be for *διὰ ταῦτα* 'therefore' (H. 719 c, G. 1060); but it is not to be supposed that there was an ellipsis of *διά*. See the App. for the true explanation. 15. **ἄν τινα,** followed by subjunct., is of course for *ἐάν*. 17. **ἐνδείκνυμαι** 'in-dicate,' 'show.' Cf. *δεικνύναι* 8,19. 18. **ὑπό**: c. gen. with intrans. verb (1,1). **τι τῶν τῆς πόλεως** 'any of the affairs of —' (9,5).

23 C 20. **πενίᾳ μυρίᾳ** 'untold poverty.' For the fact, see Introd., n. 2. 22. **πρὸς δὲ τούτοις**: i.e. 'in addition to' the results of his *ἐξέτασις* (10,27) as narrated in the previous paragraph. 23. **οἱ τῶν πλουσιωτάτων**, sc. *υἱοί*. 24. **αὐτόματοι χαίρουσιν ἀκούοντες**: Socrates had no *claqueurs* (paid applauders) in his suite. The pleasure his audience felt was spontaneous (*αὐτόματοι*). [*αὐτόματοι* is usu. taken with *ἐπακολουθοῦντες*—an improbable syntax, I think.] 27. **εἶτα** 'and then,' as often. 28. **ἀφθονίαν**: the adj. *ἄ-φθονος* is 'un-grudging,' 'without stint,' hence 'abounding in.' *ἀφθονία* the derivative is hence 'abundance,' 'plenty.' 29. **οἰομένων μέν**: *μέν* italicizes *οἰομένων*. 30. **ἐντεῦθεν** 'as a consequence.' Cf. its previous temporal and personal uses 8,29. 10,6. 31. **ἐμοί**: would *μοι* serve as well? (Note the contrast—*αὐτοῖς*.) **οὐχ αὑτοῖς,** as they should be, for laying themselves open to refutation, through assumption of knowledge they did not possess. 1. **λέγουσιν ὡς** 'tell 12
how,' not 'say *that*.'

23 D 1. **τίς**: does it go with *Σωκράτης* (cf. 3,7), or is it predic. with *μιαρώτατος* ('a most pestilent fellow')? Editors differ. 2. **διαφθείρει** 'corrupts.' 3. **ὅ τι ποιῶν,** sc. *διαφθείρει* (an indir. quest.), 'what he does to corrupt them.' 4. **ἔχουσι μέν**: is the answering clause *ἀλλ' ἀγνοοῦσιν* or *ἵνα δέ*? It would be well to make a scheme, as above 6,22; 7,17; 8,23. 5. **κατά**: c. gen. pers. 'against,' as in *κατήγορος*. Distinguish sharply from its use with accus. 1,16. **τὰ . . πρόχειρα** 'the stock (lit., 'at hand') charges.' After

12 *ὅτι* supply *διδάσκων* 'by teaching' viz. (1) *τὰ μετέωρα*, (2) *μὴ νομίζειν* ('disbelief'), (3) *ποιεῖν*. 10. **ὅτι κατάδηλοι** *κτλ.* explains *τἀληθῆ*: 'that they are getting shown up as *pretending* (*μέν*) etc.' 11. **ἅτε**: see L. & S. s.v.; or H. 977, G. 1575.

23 E 12. **σφοδροί**: 7,21. 13. **ξυν-τε-τα-μένως** 'with might and main,' 'strenuously'; adv. from mid. perf. partic. of *συν-τείνω*; mid. = 'to strain all one's powers.' Lat. *contendere*. 14. **καὶ πάλαι**: *καί* is probably not a conjunct. but an adv. with *πάλαι*; 3,1. 15. **ἐκ τούτων** 'hence' = *ἐντεῦθεν* above 11,30. The *καί* following is an adv., not the correlative 'both.' 16. **Μέλητος** *κτλ.*: for these three accusers see the Index. The three classes represented by them are the three that Socrates has examined and convicted of ignorance (21 B–22 E),—poets, craftsmen, and politicians (or, as the last are here called, public speakers). There is here special humiliation perhaps for Anytus the prominent politician, in being made to stand for the craftsmen merely—since he was a tanner. Failing to see this, some reader has probably added the bracketed words *καὶ τῶν πολιτικῶν*.

24 A 19. **ἀρχόμενος**: cf. *τελευτῶν* 10,8 and grammar refer. for the Engl. equiv. Socrates refers to what he said at 4,6–15. 23. **ταῦτ' ἔστιν ὑμῖν . . τἀληθῆ** 'there you have the truth' (Greek order of words). *ταῦτα* is 'there'; 7,27. 25. **ἀποκρυψάμενος** takes two accusatives. For *ὑποστειλάμενος*, study L. & S. 26. **καί-τοι** 'although' (1,5) goes closely with the preceding. A comma indeed would be sufficient punctuation. **οἶδα σχεδόν** 'I about know' is litotes (4,13) for 'I know quite well.' **τούτοις αὐτοῖς** 'by (with) just this (frankness).' 29. **ἐάντε . . ἐάντε** (lit. 'both if . . and if' =) 'whether . . or.' For the writing as one word, cf. *εἴτε, οὔτε, μήτε*.

24 B 31. **μὲν οὖν . . δέ**: 2,26. **περὶ . . ὧν** (for *περὶ τούτων ἅ*, H. 996, G. 1032) 'on the charges that—,' the
13 noun 'charges' lying in the verb *κατηγόρουν*. 3. **φιλόπολιν** 'patriotic.' 4. **μετὰ ταῦτα** 'next.' 5. **αὖθις** 'again,' refers to 4,16. **γὰρ δή**: 7,9. 6. **ὥσπερ ἑτέρων** *κτλ.* '*as if* these were another set of accusers.' Though these are indeed his accusers before the court, Socrates, with *ὥσπερ*, makes light of them. They are not his real accusers. Their strength lies not so much in their formal charge of atheism as in the old *φθόνος* and *διαβολή*. 7. **αὖ** repeats *αὖθις*; pleonasm (3,1). **τὴν τούτων ἀντωμοσίαν** '*their* affidavit.' Disting. sharply from *τὴν ἀντωμοσίαν αὐτῶν* 'their *affidavit*.' For *οὗτος* is the emphatic third personal pronoun, *αὐτοῦ* (-*ῷ*, -*όν*) the unemphatic. Note also the difference in their position, and see n. on *ἐμός* and *μου* 11,7. 8. **ἔχει δέ πως ὧδε** 'it runs somehow so (in some such fashion)';

again only approximate accuracy. Cf. *τοιαύτη τις* 4,26. 9. 13
ἀδικεῖν: scheme

ἀδικεῖν { *τούς τε νέους διαφθείροντα*
καὶ θεοὺς . . οὐ νομίζοντα.

11. **δαιμόνια**: the adj. *δαιμόνιος* 'supernatural,' 'of a *δαίμων*,' was often used in the neut. as a substantive, 'divine power,' 'divinity.' The plural was still more concrete — 'spirits,' 'divinities,' as the accusers meant it here, with special reference to the *δαιμόνιόν τι* that guided Socrates.

24 C 12. **δή**: conjunct. (4,6). See n. on 2,26 for the scheme. **τοιοῦτον**: in the best MSS. of Plato the neuter of *τοιοῦτος* and *τοσοῦτος* ends in *ν*. So too *ταὐτόν* is preferred to *ταὐτό*. 13. **ἓν ἕκαστον** 'each count.' **γὰρ δή**: 7,9. 14. **τοὺς νέους**: emphatically separated from *διαφθείροντα*. 'The youth forsooth,' as if with their welfare Meletus concerned himself! **ἐγὼ δέ γε**: *γε* with *ἐγώ*; 10,10. 16. **Μέλητον**: last in the clause, with emphasis. **σπουδῇ χαριεντίζεται** 'is playing a serious joke'—explained by the following participles. *σπουδῇ* a quasi-adv.; H. 776, G. 1181. **ῥᾳδίως** 'lightly,' 'recklessly.' **εἰς ἀγῶνα καθιστάς** 'bringing to trial,' 'involving in a suit.' 18. **ὧν . . τούτῳ . . ἐμέλησεν**: for the gen. and dat. c. *μέλει* see H. 742, G. 1161. In *ἐμέλησεν*, here and later (li. 26. 14,2. 15,5. 16,12), Socrates seems to be punning on his accuser's name *Μέλητος*, as if Mr. *Care-y*. 21. **καί μοι δεῦρο** *κτλ.* 'come, just tell me.' *δεῦρο* lit. 'hither,' *καί* is 'just'; it levels or evens up the *fact* with the *requirement* or *expectation*. 'As I require, do you *just*, or *also*, tell me.'—Socrates here avails himself of the right granted by Attic legal procedure, but foreign to our own courts of law, to question his adversary directly. **ἄλλο τι ἤ** and *ἄλλο τι* in questions = Lat. *nonne*; H. 1015 b, G. 1604. 22. **περὶ πολλοῦ ποιεῖ**: 9,5.

24 D 22. **ὅπως . . ἔσονται**: H. 885, G. 1372. — *ὡς* goes of course with *βέλτιστοι*. 24. **ἴθι δή**: again *δή* c. imperat. (6,31). 26. **μέλον γέ σοι**: acc. absol. 'being (since it is) your care'; H. 973 a, G. 1569. 27. **τουτοισί**, if correct, seems to be for *εἰς τουτουσί*. 28. **δὲ δή**: like *γὰρ δή*, a freq. collocation = 'but now,' 'but then,' 'well, but.' 14,12. 15,24. 16,13. 33,2. 38,3. With *δή* we arrive at a certain point, reach a conclusion, and are ready for a fresh start, a new direction, a complete change. 31. **καίτοι**: 1,5. 1. **οὗ** 14
δή: 4,18. 2. **ὠγαθέ**: crasis of *ὦ ἀγαθέ* 'Good Sir.'

24 E 4. **οὐ τοῦτο ἐρωτῶ** 'that is not my question,' 'it is not that, that I am asking.' Greek order (3,18). **ὦ βέλτιστε** 'my excellent man.' 5. **ὅστις πρῶτον** *κτλ.* 'some one that, to begin with, has just (*καί*) that very (*αὐτό*)

14 knowledge, viz. of the laws.' 6. **οἱ δικασταί**: an appositive explanation of *οὗτοι*. The flattery is so direct that Socrates bluntly exclaims: 'How do you mean, Meletus? *These* gentlemen etc.?' The Athenian jury-trial notoriously miscarried. 9. **μάλιστα** = *πάνυ γε, πάνυ μὲν οὖν*, and other phrases of entire assent; 'to be sure,' 'most certainly.' 10. **εὖ γε . . λέγεις** 'good news!' (*not* 'you speak well at least'). *λέγεις* has a second construction with *ἀφθονίαν*: 'and a great abundance do you report.' 12. **τί δὲ δή** lit. 'but what *now*?' *τί δέ* (without *δή*) marks but the merest transition, as in line 13.

25 A 13. **τί δὲ οἱ βουλευταί**: though a verb of *doing* or *faring* may be supplied, the Greeks perhaps felt no more need of one than we in: 'but what of the senators?'—The senate (*βουλή*) consisted of 500 *βουλευταί* chosen by lot, 50 from each of the 10 tribes (*φυλαί*). 14. **ἀλλ' ἄρα . . μή** *κτλ.* 'but surely it cannot be that the men of the assembly corrupt . . ?' For *ἄρα*, see n. on *γάρ* (=*γ' ἄρ'* 5,3). *μή* is used in questions, assent to which one does not wish (or pretends he does not wish) to obtain, but fears lest, or *maybe*, he may; 'surely not,' 'I hope not,' 'you cannot mean that —.' H. 1015, G. 1603. (*μή* deprecates.) 15. **οἱ ἐκκλησιασταί**: all freemen of Attica over twenty years of age, if not debarred by *ἀτιμία* (curtailment of civil privileges), had the right to vote in the *ἐκκλησία* ('assembly,' 'town-meeting'), i.e. were *ἐκκλησιασταί*. Note the regularity of formation and accent in the substantives *δικασ-τής* (*δικάζομαι*), *ἀκροα-τής* (*ἀκροάομαι*), *βουλευ-τής* (*βουλεύω*), *ἐκκλησιασ-τής* (*ἐκκλησιάζω*). 17. **ἄρα** is not here the original 'surely,' nor the ironical 'forsooth' (1,14), but an inferential 'then.' H. 1048,1. L. & S. s.v., B 1. 21. **μου κατέγνωκας**: for the gen. after *κατά* in composit., H. 752, 752 a; G. 1123. 'Certainly (*γε*) great is the unhappiness you have condemned me to'; or literally: 'great the misfortune you have discovered (noted) in me.' Ironical. **καί μοι ἀπόκριναι**: for *καί* 'just,' see 13,21. Disting. *ἀπόκριναι* imperat. from *ἀποκρῖναι* infin. act.; H. 390, G. 485 end. 22. **ἦ** interrog. particle; H. 1015, G. 1603. **οἱ μὲν . . ποιοῦντες αὐτούς**: subj. of a *δοκοῦσι* to be supplied.

25 B 24. **τοὐναντίον** (*τὸ ἐναντ.*) **τούτου πᾶν** 'quite the reverse of this,' is an apposit. to the sent.; i.e., if expanded, is a brief predication or affirmation about the sent. = and what I now say *is* 'quite the reverse of this.' H. 926 a & b, G. 915. 27. **ξυνῶσι**: from *σύν-ειμι*, not *συν-ίημι*. 30. **δήπου**: 2,6. **ἐάντε . . ἐάντε**: 12,29. 31. **ἂν . . εἴη** 'must be'—a freq.
15 transl. of the potent. optative. 1. **εἰ . . διαφθείρει**: the indic. rather than the optat. assumes the statement of Meletus

to be true ; 'if (as you say) —.' 2. **ἀλλὰ γάρ** : 5,3. 15
3. **ἐφρόντισας** : c. gen., like *μέλει, ἐπιμελοῦμαι*; H. 742, G. 1102.

25 C 5. **ὅτι οὐδέν** *κτλ.* : a clause expanding *ἀμέλειαν*. 7. **πρὸς Διός** : an oath of entreaty, not of asseveration ; 'before Zeus.' H. 805,1 ; G. 1216,1. Note separation of *ὦ* from its vocat. *Μέλητε*. 8. **οἰκεῖν** 'residence' ; noun for verb (4,14). 9. **ὦταν** (or *ὦ τάν*, or *ὦ 'τᾶν*) ; orthography and exact meaning are disputed. Perhaps 'my good sir.' See L. & S. s.v. *τᾶν*. **γάρ τοι** 'for mark you,' 'for observe,' 'for I assure you.' *τοι* makes the matter a personal one, belonging to feeling rather than to fact. Cf. *μοι* 'please.' Disting. from *γὰρ δήπου* 2,6. The words could well be written in Plato as one (*γάρτοι*), since he never interposes others ; e.g. 21,11. 69,26. 157,15. 163,16. 197,1. 11. **ἀεί** 'for the time being,' 'at any time'—a not uncommon sense.

25 D 14. **ἀποκρίνου** : note pres. tense ; '*be* about your answer.' Meletus was perhaps hesitating. In li. 9 it was aor., *ἀπόκριναι* a summary 'answer.' 17. **δῆτα** : H. 1037,6. L. & S. **φέρε δή** : L. & S. s.v. *φέρω*, IX ; and cf. *ἄγε*. 18. **ὡς** 'on the charge of' (1,10). 20. **τοσοῦτον** : adv. acc. ; might have been *τοσούτῳ* dat. of measure. 21. **τηλικούτου ὄντος τηλικόσδε ὤν** 'I at my age, you at yours' ; juxtaposit. for strong contrast. Cf. n. on *ταύτην* 4,9. 22. **ὥστε** *κτλ.* : scheme is

ὥστε { *σὺ μὲν ἔγνωκας ὅτι* { *οἱ μὲν κακοὶ . .* / *οἱ δὲ ἀγαθοὶ . .* } / *ἐγὼ δέ . .* }

25 E 24. **ἐγὼ δὲ δή** (13,28) 'while I of course,' ironical. 26. **τινά** : with *τῶν ξυνόντων*. 29. **ταῦτα ἐγώ** *κτλ.* '*there* I do not believe you' ; Greek order.—The argument has been : Bad men work ill to those about them. But no one desires ill-treatment. Hence no one would voluntarily make his associates bad,—to be ill-treated by them in return.

26 A 1. **κατ' ἀμφότερα** 'either way.' 2. **τῶν τοιού-** 16
των ἁμαρτημάτων : gen. of the *crime* with *εἰσάγειν* in its legal sense (H. 745, G. 1121) : 'for offences like that,' i.e. such as one commits *ἄκων* 'involuntarily.' The bracketed words *καὶ ἀκουσίων* were added probably by some one who did not find the reference of *τοιούτων* sufficiently clear. But cf. 6,8. 3. **δεῦρο** : emphatic, by separation from *εἰσάγειν*. **ἰδίᾳ** 'privately' ; H. 779, G. 1181. 6. **ξυγγενέσθαι** 'intercourse' ; noun for verb. 7. **οἷ** : relat. adv. ; see n. on *ὅπῃ* 4,14. 10. **ἀλλὰ γάρ** : 5,3. 11. **ἤδη** 'by this time.' **Μελήτῳ τούτων** : for the cases, see 13,18.

26 B 13. **δὲ δή** : 13, 28. 14. **ἤ** often does not introduce an alternative to the previous question (whether . . *or*),

16 but withdraws it altogether, substituting another that is either less general or that should properly anticipate the other. **ὅτι**: supply before it *με φῄς διαφθείρειν τοὺς νεωτέρους.* 16. **μὴ νομίζειν** 'disbelief'; noun for verb. 17. **ταῦτα** goes with *διδάσκων*, but is emphatic by separation. 18. **πάνυ μὲν οὖν σφόδρα** *κτλ.* is vehement assent. Cf. the more usual *πάνυ γε* 6,11. *μάλιστα* 14,9. *πάνυ σφόδρα* 14,20. For *μέν* (= *μήν*), see 1,15. 19. **πρός**: 15,7. **τοίνυν** 'then'—never temporal but either merely transitional as here (='now'), or inferential (='therefore').

26 C 23. **νομίζειν εἶναι** 'belief in the existence'; noun for verb, and Greek order retained. 24. **τινάς** 'some.' **ἄρα** 'consequently,' 'in that case' (14,17). 25. **τὸ παράπαν** 'wholly,' 'utterly.' 26. **ταύτῃ** 'that way'; adv. (4,14). **οὐ μέντοι** 'not however,' going back to '*some* gods.' 29. **παντάπασι** = *τὸ παράπαν*. **οὔτε . . τε** 'both utterly *dis*-believe, myself (*αὐτόν* 11,2), in gods, and —.' 31. **ὦ θαυμάσιε Μέλητε** 'my admirable Meletus'; ironical, like our 'my dear Sir,' though not always so. Often
17 it is used in expostulation with friends, as infra 52,5. 1. **ἵνα τί**, sc. *γένηται*; orig. 'to what end,' 'with what intent'; then merely 'why.' **οὐδὲ . . οὐδέ** ('not even . . nor') are not correlatives (3,27).

26 D 2. **ἄρα**: 14,17. 3. **οἱ ἄλλοι ἄνθρωποι** 'the rest of the world.' **μὰ Δία,** even without *οὐ*, is an oath of denial—though if *ναί* precedes, it is affirmative; H. 723, G. 1067. 5. **'Αναξαγόρου** *κτλ.* 'it is Anaxagoras you fancy etc.'; Greek order. 6. **οὕτω** goes with both *καταφρονεῖς* and *ἀπείρους*: 'you so scorn them and fancy them *so* ignorant of letters as to —.' 7. **τῶνδε**: gen. after *κατα-* in composit. Cf. supra li. 5, and 12,5. 10. **καὶ δὴ καί** *κτλ.* 'and then too the youth learn from *me* these [doctrines], on buying which sometimes (*ἐνίοτε*) in the orchestra for a drachma at the highest (lit., if very high), they may have the laugh on Socrates, if he pretends —?' 12. **πριαμένοις**: dat. in agreement with *αὐτοῖς* to be supplied for *ἔξεστι*, 'it is possible for them.'—An *ὀρχήστρα* is properly that great circular space of a Greek theatre round which rose the seats of the spectators and in which the chorus sang and danced (*ὀρχέομαι*). In the present passage it may be either (1) the orchestra of the great theatre of Dionysus at Athens—the sense being that from the dramas there enacted the youth could learn these no longer new doctrines about the sun and moon (a drachma would be the price of admission for the whole festival of three days), or (2) it may refer to a certain locality near the Agora which seems to have been called the *Orchestra*,—where perhaps books were sold. But no hint is elsewhere found that such was the case; nor does ἐνίοτε quite fall in with this explanation. 17

26 E 14. **ἄλλως τε καί** ('both in other ways and')= 'especially'; H. 1042 b. 15. **οὑτωσί,** i.e. in the Anaxagoras-fashion, explaining away the gods by physics. Meletus does not answer the quest., but reiterates the charge of flat atheism. 16. **μέντοι**: here asseverative 'indeed,' not adversative (1,20). **ὁπωστιοῦν**: 1.12. 17. **ἄπιστος** 'not to be believed.' **καὶ ταῦτα μέντοι** 'and that too indeed.' L. & S. s.v. οὗτος, C IX 2. 18. **σαυτῷ** 'in your own judgment (eyes)'; H. 771, G. 1172. **ἐμοί**: note form and position. 19. **πάνυ,** though an adv., goes with ὑβριστής, 'wholly wanton.' Note the emphasis by separation. 20. **ἀτεχνῶς**: 2,16.

27 A 22. **αἴνιγμα**: cf. αἰνίττομαι 8,1. **ἔοικε . . ξυντιθέντι** (sc. τινί) 'he is like one that composes as it were a riddle' ='he seems to be composing.' **διαπειρωμένῳ** 'trying to see.' 23. **ἆρα**: interrog. particle (H. 1015, G. 1603) to be disting. from ἄρα 'therefore,' though originating from it. **σοφὸς δή**: ironical δή, 'your wise man.' 24. **ἐμοῦ** κτλ.: gen. instead of accus. after γνώσεται. Cf. gen. with ᾐσθόμην 10,4. **ἐναντί' ἐμαυτῷ λέγοντος** 'contra-dicting myself.' 27. **αὐτὸς ἑαυτῷ**: an emphasis on the nomin. common in Greek but to be dropped in Engl. For the juxtaposit., see τηλικούτου τηλικόσδε 15,21. **ὥσπερ ἄν**: without verb; 11,10. 29. **καίτοι**: 1,5. **παίζοντος** sc. τινός, as τινί with ξυντιθέντι, li. 22. 31. **ξυν-επισκέψασθε**: συν-='with me'; 'let us examine.' **δή** c. imperat. 6,31. **ᾗ**: see n. on 4,14 or L. & S. 2. **κατ' ἀρχάς** 'at the outset,' viz. in 2,9 ff. 18

27 B 3. **μοι**: 7,11. **ἐν τῷ εἰωθότι τρόπῳ**: well might the judges be tempted to raise an outcry. Once more—his ruling passion strong in death — Socrates is about to exemplify his 'usual manner' (already so terribly well known to them) of catechizing a man into hopeless self-contradiction. 4. **τοὺς λόγους ποιῶμαι**: cf. *verba facio*. For this periphrasis (6,4) of a verb (here of λέγω) by means of its corresponding substantive with the *middle* voice of ποιέω, see L. & S. s.v. ποιέω, A II 5. 6. **ἀποκρινέσθω** and **μὴ . . θορυβείτω** 'be answering' . . 'not be raising disturbance.' Observe the tense. Meletus is evidently evasive. See n. on 15,14. 11. **σὺ . . ἐγώ**: emphatic. 13. **τὸ ἐπὶ τούτῳ γε** 'the *next* quest. at least'; for he now comes to the application of his parallels. ἐπί is 'after,' as in ἐπ-ῳδός 'after-song,' ἐπί-λογος 'after-speech.' **ἀπόκριναι**: the aor. hints at dispatch again, now that Meletus has been helped over the first question.

18 **27 C** 13. **δαιμόνια . . πράγματα**: Socrates is careful to call back the word *δαιμόνια* to its proper adjectival use. Cf. n. on 13,11. *δαίμονες* are 'supernatural beings,' spirits intermediate between the divine and human. So Plato *Symp.* 202 E *πᾶν τὸ δαιμόνιον μεταξύ ἐστι θεοῦ τε καὶ θνητοῦ.* 15. **ὤνησας**: from *ὀνίνημι.* **ὡς** is exclamatory. **μόγις**: 8,6. 16. **οὐκοῦν** 'therefore.' When so accented, the negative is not to be translated. But *οὔκουν* is '*not* therefore.' The scheme is:

οὐκοῦν { *δαιμόνια μὲν φῄς . .,* / *εἰ δὲ δαιμόνια . ., καὶ δαίμονας κτλ.*

In these last words lies the *result* (introduced by *οὐκοῦν*) of the admission made in li. 15—that no men can believe in *δαιμόνια πράγματα* without believing 'also in *δαίμονες.*' 18. **εἴτε . . εἴτε**: cf. *ἐάντε . . ἐάντε* 12,29. *οὖν*, an accentuating 'indeed,' is often found in one or the other clause, sometimes in both (infra 31,1), **ἀλλ' οὖν . . γε** 'whether new or old, *at any rate*' = *δ' οὖν* (1,3). 19. **καὶ δι-ωμόσω** and **καὶ δαίμονας** (21): *καί* is adverb. 21. **δήπου**: 2,6. **πολλὴ ἀνάγκη** 'every necessity.' 24. **ἤτοι . . ἤ**: *τοι* ('mark you') introduces the alternatives as the only ones the speaker will admit. Of the two, *either* this or that. *γε* is often added, as here, to the first number, emphasizing it as the more probable choice.

27 D 26. **εἴ-περ** '*if* indeed' '*if*, that is' ("much virtue in *εἴπερ*" Touchstone), like *εἰ τῷ ὄντι* (2,17), supplies a preliminary basis of supposition upon which, in the present passage, rest the alternate conditions *εἰ μέν, εἰ δ' αὖ.* 27. **τοῦτ' ἂν εἴη** *κτλ.* 'this would be what I say is your riddle and witticism.' The nouns are in the verbs (4,14). 29. **φάναι** interprets *τοῦτο*; 'this declaration,' viz. 'that I, while not believing etc.' **αὖ . . πάλιν**: pleonasm as *αὖθις . . αὖ* 13,7. 30. **ἐπειδήπερ** *κτλ.* restates the preliminary supposition, as above (6,25) *εἰ μή τι ἔπραττες* repeated in a different form the participial clause. **εἰ δ' αὖ** 'but if
19 again (on the other hand)'; H. 1047,1. 1. **ὧν δὴ καὶ λέγονται** 'from whom in fact (*καί*) they are said to be,' '*just* as they are said to be.' With *ὧν* supply *ἐξ* from its antecedent; H. 1007, G. 1025. Note *δή* c. relat. (4,18). 3. **ὥσπερ ἄν**, sc. *εἴη* (11,10).

27 E 4. **παῖδας** 'offspring.' **ἢ καὶ ὄνων** 'or asses as well,' 'or asses if you like' (Adam), 'or asses, as the case may be.' It is the same well-nigh superfluous *καί* that is found in relat. clauses (10,7). Socrates draws his illustrations from common life. [*τοὺς ἡμιόνους* was probably inserted by some reader who failed to observe the *ἤ* in *ἢ καί*, and who supposed that as *ἵπποι* stood for *δαίμονες* so *ὄνοι* must stand for *νύμφαι*,

and hence concluded that *something* had to correspond to *παῖδες* 19
νόθοι.] 6. **οὐκ ἔστιν ὅπως . . οὐχί** (*fieri non potest quin*) = 'it must be.' 7. **ταῦτα** 'herein' goes perhaps with *ἀποπειρώμενος*, which is best made the main verb in English ; 'it must be that herein you were making trial of us when you etc.' 8. **ὅ τι ἐγκαλοῖς**: indir. discourse for Meletus's orig. dubitative subjunct. *τί ἐγκαλῶ*. 9. **ὅπως . . πείθοις ἄν** depends on *οὐδεμία μηχανή ἐστιν* at the end. The second *τοῦ αὐτοῦ* repeats the first—unnecessarily, but Socrates is speaking *ἐν τῷ εἰωθότι τρόπῳ*, explicit to redundancy. The sense is: You will never by any possibility persuade a man of the least sense that one and the same person can believe in supernatural and divine things yet on the other hand believe in neither supernatural nor divine beings, nor heroes. [*μήτε ἥρωας*, if genuine, is added to recall how sweepingly Meletus had denied Socrates' faith in divinity (*οὐδ' ὁπωστιοῦν* 17,16). How could a man so completely atheistic as to be compelled to deny even the heroes —those best incarnate and historic proofs of the existence of gods, how could such a one talk of *θεῖα* and *δαιμόνια*? Impossible.]

The defence proper is now closed. There follows a *παρ-έκβασις* 'digression.'

28 A 17. **ἐν τοῖς ἔμπροσθεν** 'before,' viz. in 10,28. 19. **πρός** 'with' (8,14). 21. **αἱρήσει**: in its legal sense 'to convict,' said of the prosecutor (*ὁ διώκων*), who 'captures' the defendant (*ὁ φεύγων*). 22. **ἃ δή**: 4,18. 23. **πολλοὺς καὶ ἄλλους καὶ ἀγαθούς**: the first *καί* is 'also,' the second is the one regularly connecting *πολλοί* with another adj.—in transl. to be dropped (10,11); 'many other good men too.' 24. **οὐδὲν δὲ δεινόν, μὴ . . στῇ** 'there is no fear lest (no danger that) they will stay themselves (come to a halt) in my case.' Prejudice and spite will continue to convict men.

28 B 26. **ἴσως δ' ἂν οὖν** *κτλ.* 'be that as it may (*δ' οὖν*), somebody may perhaps say.' **εἶτα** 'then,' freq. in questions of emotion, espec. of indignation. 27. **ἐπιτηδεύσας** 'at having practised'; H. 986, G. 1581. Cf. *αἰσχύνομαι* c. *infin.* 9,24. 29. **καλῶς λέγεις**: this does *not* mean 'you speak beautifully'—the usu. undergraduate belief. 1. **ἄνδρα**, 20
ὅτου (= *οὗτινος*): in Engl. we transfer the indefin. *τις* from *ὅστις* to the antecedent; '*any* man, of whom.' **τι καὶ σμικρὸν ὄφελος** ('any even little use' =) 'any use at all.' 2. **ὅταν πράττῃ** 'whenever he acts.' 3. **πότερα**: variant of *πότερον* in double question ; H. 1017, G. 1606.

28 C 4. **φαῦλοι** 'of no account,' 'futile.' **τῷ γε σῷ λόγῳ** = *κατά γε τὸν σὸν λόγον*. Cf. 18,19. 6. **οἵ τε ἄλλοι καί** amounts to 'above all.' *τε* and *καί* are like two scale-pans,

20 balancing their two clauses. When emphasis or prominence is desired for a person, as here for Achilles, he is usu. put into the second pan, and the rest of the world weighed against him in the first. Thus all the *individuals* against him are insignificant. He is 'above all.' Cf. n. on *ἄλλως τε καί* 17,14. 8. **παρὰ τὸ . . ὑπομεῖναι** 'compared with —,' lit. 'by the side of.' Cf. para-ble (*παρα-βολή, βάλλω*). 10. **θεὸς οὖσα**, hence she would know the truth. Note *θεός* regularly used in Att. prose for the feminine *θεά*. 11. **εἰ τιμωρήσεις**: in threats and warnings, not subjunct. but fut. indic. is preferred in *εἰ*-clauses. See G. 1405 (H. 899 incorrect). 13. **αὐτίκα**: 1,11. **τοι** is an Epic *σοι*. 14. **ὁ δέ**: the result of his having 'so much scorned danger' was expected after *ὥστε*, li. 8. But, having been so long postponed, it is now introduced afresh by *ὁ δέ* (anacoluthon; 2,20). **τοῦ θανάτου** *κτλ.* '*the* death (namely) and danger prophesied by his mother.' 15. **ὠλιγώρησε** c. gen.; H. 742, G. 1102. To remember the word, see its etymology in L. & S. s.v. *ὀλίγωρος*.

28 D 16. **κακὸς ὤν** 'as a coward.' Note the nomin. (not acc.), though following an 'articular' infin. (*τὸ ζῆν*); H. 940, G. 927. 17. **τιμωρεῖν**: the *τό* before *ζῆν* belongs equally to *τιμωρεῖν*. **τεθναίην**: though the perf. tense should express not so much the act as the resulting state, yet exceptionally *τεθνάναι* is often 'to die' rather than 'to be dead,' as infra 23,16. 38,30. 44,5. 18. **ἐπιθείς** '*after* inflicting'; note the aorist. For this incident, see *Iliad* 18,94 ff. 20. **μή**: in question; 14,14. **φροντίσαι**: c. gen.; 15,3. So *ὀλιγωρέω*, li. 15. 21. **τῇ ἀληθείᾳ**: 11,12. 22. **οὗ**: adv., relat. of *ποῦ*. 23. **ἢ . . ταχθῇ**: stands as an alternate with *τάξῃ*—by anacoluthon; for, following *ἢ ἡγησάμενος*, we should expect *ἢ ταχθείς*. **ἄρχοντος** 'commander,' not 'ruler,' in military life. 25. **πρό** of preference; 'before,' 'rather than.' 27. **ἂν εἴην εἰργασμένος** 'should prove to have done.' The scheme is:

δεινά, εἰ { *ὅτε μὲν . . τότε μὲν ἔμενον,*
τοῦ δὲ θεοῦ τάττοντος . . ἐνταῦθα δὲ λίποιμι.

The 'dreadful thing' is, the *inconsistency* of obeying mortal rulers, yet disobeying God. For the places, see Index of Proper Names.

21 **28 E** 3. **ὑπέλαβον** 'understood,' not as in 6,19. 4. **με δεῖν ζῆν**: *δεῖν* repeats *τάττοντος*, and must be dropped in transl. Such pleonastic infinitives are not rare. See 47,24 App. for many examples. **καί** joins the two participles.

29 A 6. **ὁτιοῦν**: orig. with a verb to be supplied; 'whatever it be' = 'whatsoever.' See H. 1002 a, or L. & S. s.v.

ὅστις, IV 2 b. 7. **τἂν** (*τοι ἄν*) 'dreadful surely.' **ὡς** 21
ἀληθῶς: 6,14. 11. **γάρ τοι**: 15,9. 13. **ἐστίν**, sc. *τὸ θάνατον δεδιέναι* subject. 14. **θάνατον οὐδ' εἰ τυγχάνει**: prolepsis (*πρό-ληψις*) is taking (*λαβ-*) a substant. out of the subord. clause *beforehand* (*προ-*), to put it into the principal clause; H. 878. Translate (noting *οὐ***δέ**): 'no one *knows* (*μέν*) but what death *may* be (*τυγχάνει ὄν*) even the greatest of all blessings for man.' 17. **τοῦτο** might have been *αὕτη*, through attract. by the predicate *ἀμαθία*; cf. 2,25.

29 B 17. **αὕτη ἡ ἐπονείδιστος**: added to *ἀμαθία* to specify: 'that ıeprehensible kind,' viz. of thinking etc. 18. **τοῦ οἴεσθαι** a sort of appositive genit.; 'the ignorance *that consists in* thinking'; H. 729 g. 19. **τούτῳ**: dat. of respect, repeated two lines below. **καὶ ἐνταῦθα** 'here too.' 20. **εἰ δή** 'if indeed.' **τῳ** and **του** (enclit.) are *not* the art. 21. **τούτῳ ἄν**, sc. *φαίην σοφώτερος εἶναι.* **οὐκ εἰδὼς ἱκανῶς** 'with no adequate knowledge.' 22. **ἐν Ἅιδου**: L. & S. s.v. *ἐν*, I 2, H. 730 a. Cf. *εἰς Ἅιδου* 40,25 and frequently. 24. **καὶ θεῷ καὶ ἀνθρώπῳ**: distribut. apposit. to *τῷ βελτίονι*; 'whether . . or.' 25. **πρό**: 20,25. 26. **ὧν οἶδα** *κτλ.* 'which I know to be ills'; *ὧν* by attract. for *ἅ*; H. 994, G. 1031. **ἅ** for *ταῦτα ἅ*; *ταῦτα* obj. of *φοβήσομαι.*

29 C 30. **τὴν ἀρχήν**: adv. acc. usu. with negat.: 'at all'; H. 719 a, G. 1060. **δεῖν**: "imperf." infin., i.e. stands for *ἔδει* of the direct disc.; H. 853 a; G. 1285,1. 31. **οὐχ οἷόντ' εἶναι** *κτλ.* 'my acquittal was impossible'; noun for
verb (4,14). 1. **διαφευξοίμην**: fut. opt. in indir. disc. 22
for fut. indic. For the fut. indic. in conditions of *warning*, see 20,11. **ἄν . . διαφθαρήσονται** (fut. pass.): *ἄν* c. fut. indic. in Attic prose extremely rare; H. 845, G. 1303. 3. **εἰ . . εἴποιτε**: a restatement of the condition above, *εἰ ἀφίετε.* 5. **ἐπὶ τούτῳ** *κτλ.* 'upon this condition, however, that—.' For *ἐφ' ᾧτε* c. infin., H. 999 a, G. 1460. 8. **ἁλῷς**: 2nd aor. subj. of *ἁλίσκομαι*; H. 489,13; G. 799. **εἰ οὖν** for the third time states the condition, after which, at last, the apodosis *εἴποιμ' ἄν.*

29 D 10. **ὅτι** is omitted in translat. when direct disc. follows. So in 8,10. 12. **οὐ μὴ παύσωμαι** 'I shall never never cease.' Note this form of emphatic denial of the future —*both* negatives (objective and subjective) coupled with the *aorist* subjunctive; H. 1032, G. 1360. 14. **ἀεί**: 15,11. 15. **ὅτι** *κτλ.* depends on both *ἐνδεικνύμενος* and *λέγων*.
16. **'Αθηναῖος ὤν, πόλεως** 'citizen of Athens—a city.' The genit. is in apposit. to a genit. implied in the adject.; H. 633 b, G. 913. 17. **εἰς σοφίαν** 'for wisdom.' The prepos. aids a little in showing that the accus. is one of specification.

22 Cf. πρός 9,13. 11,13. 18. **αἰσχυνει**: c. ptc.; 19,27. For the prolepsis of χρημάτων, 21,14. 21. **ὅπως . . ἔσται**: on the construct., see 13,22.

29 E 21. **οὐκ ἐπιμελεῖ**: note the anacoluthon in the scheme:

χρημάτων μὲν } οὐκ αἰσχύνει { ἐπιμελούμενος,
φρονήσεως δὲ } { οὐκ ἐπιμελεῖ;

24. **ἐρήσομαι** and ἠρόμην are used as fut. and aor. of ἐρωτάω more freq. than the regular formations. 26. **ὀνειδιῶ**: for the form, see H. 425, G. 665,3. 27. **περὶ ἐλαχίστου ποιεῖται**: 9,5.

30 A 30. **ὅσῳ**: dat. of measure. The full expression would be τοσούτῳ μᾶλλον . . ὅσῳ ἐγγυτέρω (*tanto—quanto*); H. 781 a, G. 1184. ὅσῳ alone is often causal; 'inasmuch as.' 31.
23 **εὖ ἴστε**: 7,1. *Not* 'know well.' 6. **πρότερον**: we expect ἢ τῆς ψυχῆς; but the μηδέ-clause intervenes: 'sooner than, *or as much as*.' N.B. μηδέ is not correlat. with the two μήτε's, but introduces a sub-clause under the second μήτε.

30 B 10. **εἰ μὲν οὖν** κτλ.: note the indic. and see n. on 15,1. In Engl., for the μὲν . . δέ antithesis we should say rather: 'this then must be hurtful doctrine, if it be true that by teaching it I corrupt the youth; *for* I teach no other.' 12. **οὐδὲν λέγει,** and λέγει τι, its opposite, are still paralleled in our 'he talks much but says nothing' and '*now* you are talking' (sc. sense). 13. **πρὸς ταῦτα** 'in view of this.' πρός *faces* its object. 15. **ὡς** 'assured that —' (1,10). **ἂν ποιήσοντος** stands for ἄν c. fut. indic. in direct discourse. On this, see 22,1.

30 C 16. **τεθνάναι**: 20,17. 17. **μὴ θορυβεῖτε** 'don't *be* making uproar' (pres.). A round aorist follows—ἐμμείνατε 'stand by what —.' 19. **ἐφ' οἷς,** as in Engl., 'at what' (= ἐπὶ τούτοις ἅ 'at that which'). 20. **καὶ γάρ**: 4,3. 21. **ὀνήσεσθε**: the aor. ὤνησας in 18,15. **γὰρ οὖν** 'for certainly'—οὖν in its primitive use as a corroborating particle (cf. δ' οὖν 'but certainly,' γοῦν, καὶ γὰρ οὖν, τοιγαροῦν, πάνυ μὲν οὖν). Its conjunctional use (inferential and transitional) is of later (post-Homeric) origin. 22. **ἅττα** (= τινά pl.); H. 277 b; G. 416,2. 23. **εὖ ἴστε**: 7,1. 24. **ἐμέ**: note the emphatic form. 25. **μείζω,** and οὐδέν following, go with the acc. in the verb ("inner acc."); H. 716 b, G. 1054. 26. **ἐμὲ μέν**: ἐμέ is emphatic by form, position, and the presence of μέν. The antithesis, long postponed, is reached in 24,6 ἀλλ' ὑπὲρ ὑμῶν. Sense: 'you cannot harm *me*,—I do not plead for myself (24,4); it is for *you* I plead, lest —.'

30 D 29. **ἀποκτείνειε μεντἂν** κτλ. : μέντοι 'to be sure'; 23
1,20. The scheme :

ἀποκτείνειε μέντοι . .
ἀλλὰ ταῦτα { οὗτος μὲν ἴσως οἴεται . . / ἐγὼ δ' οὐκ οἴομαι . .

In translat., the clause οὗτος μέν must be subordinated: 'To be sure, a bad man may perhaps put a better man to death, but that, *though* this man maybe thinks it an evil, I for my part do not regard as such.' For ἀτιμώσειεν see L. & S. ἀτιμόω, II. 31. **ἄλλος τίς που** 'many another doubtless.' 3. 24
ἀποκτιννύναι: ἀποκτίννυμι (-ύω) or -κτείν(ν)υμι (-ύω), a not infreq. variant for ἀποκτείνω. 4. **πολλοῦ δέω** 'I am far from' (lit. 'lack much'); H. 743 b. 6. **τι**: its noun is in the verb. 7. **καταψηφισάμενοι** 'by condemning.' See App. for tense.

30 E 9. **ἀτεχνῶς** (2,16) goes with προσκείμενον. **εἰ καὶ γελοιότερον** 'even if it *is* (καί) rather ridiculous.' See App. 10. **προσκείμενον** 'put upon,' 'attached to.' κεῖμαι is regularly used as the perf. pass. of τίθημι; H. 820.—In the simile note the scheme :

ἵππῳ { μεγάλῳ μέν ('indeed')— / ὑπὸ μεγέθους δέ—

12. **νωθεστέρῳ** '*rather* sluggish.' 13. **μύωπος** 'gadfly.' **οἷον δή** 'just the way,' though of course grammatically οἷον is not adv. but masc. pron. Cf., for translat., *Od.* 4,611 αἵματός εἰς ἀγαθοῖο, φίλον τέκος, οἷ' ἀγορεύεις 'you are of good blood, my dear boy, *the way* you talk.'

31 A 17. **προσκαθίζων** 'settling upon.' 18. **ἐὰν ἐμοὶ πείθησθε** 'if you take *my* advice.' 19. **ἴσως τάχ' ἄν**: *we* commonly transl. both words by 'perhaps.' But that does not prove that the Greeks, when using them together, were guilty of tautology. Certainly in their lit. sense they are far enough apart ('equally,' 'quickly'). —Note ἄν thrice over, before the verb ἀποκτείναιτε is reached (2,17) 20. **ὥσπερ οἱ νυστάζοντες ἐγειρόμενοι** 'like nodding people when awakened.' 22. **εἶτα** 'and then'; 11,27. 24. **κηδόμενος**: c. gen., as φροντίζω (20,20), ἐπιμελοῦμαι (22,18), ὀλιγωρέω (20,15), ἀμελέω (infra, li. 28). 25. **οἷος . . δεδόσθαι**: H. 1000, G. 1526.

31 B 27. **τὸ ἐμέ** with the three foll. infinitives is subject of ἔοικε. The scheme :

τὸ ἐμὲ { τῶν μὲν ἐμαυτοῦ . . ἠμεληκέναι καὶ . . / τὸ δὲ ὑμέτερον πράττειν.

30. **ἰδίᾳ**: 16,3. 2. **καίτοι**: 1,5. 4. **εἶχον ἄν τινα** 25
λόγον 'I should have had some ground (could have given

25 some reason)' for my course of life. **νῦν δέ**: 6,6. 6. **ἀναισχύντως οὕτω** go together; 'though so shamelessly bringing all their other charges.' **τοῦτό γε** *κτλ.* 'this bit of shamelessness at least they did not prove equal to carrying out.' The *ἀπο-* in composit. is perhaps as in *ἀπ-εργάζεσθαι*.

31 C 8. **ἐπραξάμην**: 5,16. 9. **ἱκανὸν . . τὸν μάρτυρα**: see 7,13 for the significance of the predicative posit. Either '*an* adequate witness' in Engl., or 'adequate *is the* witness' I offer. 12. **ὅτι δή**: *δή* after *ὅτι* is not common. 13. **ταῦτα**: object of both *ξυμβουλεύω* and *πολυπραγμονῶ*—the latter recalling ironically *περιεργάζεται* (4,23) that his old slanderers made out to be criminal (*ἀδικεῖ*). 15. **ἀναβαίνων εἰς τὸ πλῆθος**: see 2,15. 2,7. 7,18 for the words respectively. 19. **θεῖόν τι καὶ δαιμόνιον** *κτλ.* 'something from God, and supernatural, comes to me.'

31 D 20. **ὃ δὴ καί** ('which you know (*δή*) in point of fact (*καί*),' 'which indeed is just what') is the obj. of *ἐπικωμῳδῶν* ('caricatured'), which should be made the principal verb in Engl. 21. **ἐγράψατο** 'when he —.' For *καί* in the relat. clause, cf. 4,18. **ἐκ παιδός**: cf. *ἐκ παίδων* (3,5), *ἐκ νέου* (7,18). 22. **φωνή τις γιγνομένη**: epexegetic apposit. to *τοῦτο*; H. 624 c. 23. **ἀπο-τρέπει** and **προ-τρέπει** 'dis-suade' and 'per-suade.' **τοῦτο**: obj. of *πράττειν*. With *μέλλω* supply *πράξειν* (or *πράττειν*). 29. **ἀπωλώλη . . ὠφελήκη**: note the ending of the pluperfect, contraction from *-εα*. Cf. *ξυν-ῄδη* 10,9. G. 683,1.

31 E 31. **ὅστις**: transfer *-τις* to main clause (20,1).
26 1. **πλήθει** 'democracy'; 7,18. 25,16. 2. **γνησίως** 'genuinely' (*γι-γεν-ομαι*, *gen*-uinus)=*τῷ ὄντι*, *ὡς ἀληθῶς*, *τῇ ἀληθείᾳ*.

32 A 4. **τὸν . . μαχούμενον**: note the tense. 5. **καὶ εἰ** 'even if,' 'aye, if.' 6. **ἀλλὰ μή**: in Engl. '*and* not,' as frequently, e.g. 11,31. 16,8. 7. **μεγάλα**: emphatic (1,14). 9. **δή**: 6,31. 11. **οὐδ' ἂν ἑνί**=*οὐδενὶ ἄν*, but more emphatic. H. 290 a, G. 378. **ὑπεικάθοιμι**: on the formation (from *εἴκω*), see H. 494, G. 779. **παρὰ τὸ δίκαιον**: n. on 1,16. 12. **μὴ ὑπείκων δέ**: conditional, as shown by *μή*; 'though (*δέ*) in the case of my not yielding.' 13. **φορτικὰ καὶ δικανικά** (*φορτικός*, from *φέρω*, 'burdensome') 'a tedious story and one of the law-court sort.' Socrates refers to the practice of rehearsing before the court one's services to the state, or the exemplary private life he has led. 15. **ἄλλην ἀρχήν**: *ἄλλην* had better be dropped in translation; for a seat in the *βουλή* (*ἐβούλευσα δέ* 16) was not properly called an *ἀρχή* ('office,' 'magistracy').

32 B 16. **ἐβούλευσα** 'was chosen senator'—though the

inceptive sense of the aor. (H. 841, G. 1260) need not be pressed 26
(H. 841 b). Cf. 120,8. 17. **ἡ φυλὴ . . πρυτανεύουσα**: the ten groups of fifty, chosen by lot into the *βουλή* from each tribe (*φυλή*), took turns in acting, for one-tenth of the year, as an executive committee of constant session in the round hall or Rotunda called *ἡ θόλος* (27,1). Its members were called *πρυτάνεις* (sing. *πρύτανις*), its period of office a *πρυτανεία*. Each day a chairman (*ἐπι-στάτης*) was chosen by lot, who presided also over the popular assembly (*ἐκκλησία*), if one was held.

(**Ἀντιοχίς**, the name of Socrates' tribe, was probably written on the margin of a copy of the *Apology* by some learned man of later times, and still later transferred by some copyist to the text.) 18. **ὅτε ὑμεῖς** *κτλ.*, referring to the crime committed by the Athenian people after their naval victory over the Lacedaemonians at the Arginūsae (three small islands near Lesbos) in 406 B.C.—seven years before the present trial. In their haste to follow up the victory the generals had not 'taken up' (*ἀν-αιρεῖσθαι*, the regular term) their dead and wounded—a neglect regarded by the Greeks as extreme impiety. Their plea was that two of their number had been detailed for this duty, but that a storm had prevented them from accomplishing it. Whether true or not (and it is not now easily decided), the Athenians certainly acted illegally (*παρανόμως*) in (1) refusing to the generals—as they did—an opportunity for a formal defence before the proper court, and (2) in passing judgment upon them in a body (*ἀθρόους κρίνειν*). A complete account of the battle and trial is found in Xenophon's *Greek History* (*Hellenica*) I 6,26—I 7,32. References to the trial he also makes in his *Memorabilia* I 1,18 ; IV 4,2.
τοὺς δέκα στρατηγούς is incorrect. It is true that ten was the number of generals annually elected—one for each tribe ; but in the battle off the Arginusae only eight took part. Indeed, of these, only six obeyed the summons to present themselves for trial. 19. **τοὺς ἐκ τῆς ναυμαχίας**: for *τοὺς ἐν τῇ ν.*, due to the verb of *motion from*, *ἀνελομένους*. Cf. Xen. *Anab.* I 2,3 *τοὺς ἐκ τῶν πόλεων* λαβών ; I 2,18 *οἱ ἐκ τῆς ἀγορᾶς ἔφυγον*, H. 788 a ; G. 1225,1. 22. **ἠναντιώθην μηδὲν ποιεῖν** 'opposed doing anything.' *μηδέν* is a doubling of the negat. idea already implied in the verb, but one that is not obligatory. Cf. 25,24 and *διακωλύων* above, li. 2. See H. 1029, G. 1615. 23. **καὶ ἐναντία ἐψηφισάμην**: if the text is sound (and some editors reject the words), it must describe a meeting of the greatest possible disorder. Apparently the *πρυτάνεις*, while actually presiding over the assembled people (*ἐκκλησία*), fell to disputing among themselves whether or not the *ἐπι-στάτης* should put the question (*ἐπι-ψηφίζειν*) to them. In Xen. *Mem.* I 1,18 and IV 4,2 it is stated that Socrates was himself the *ἐπι-στάτης* for the day ; and the same is implied in

26 Plat. *Gorg.* 473 E. **ἑτοίμων ὄντων**, as also the following gen. absol., is concessive. By *ὑμῶν* is meant, of course, the people at large, *τὸ πλῆθος*. 24. **ἐνδεικνύναι . . ἀπάγειν**: here in their technical, legal sense 'to denounce' and 'to summarily arrest.' See L. & S. The nouns are *ἔνδειξις* and *ἀπαγωγή*. **ῥητόρων** designates no recognized officials of state (cf. above 12,19), but merely those citizens who took most active part in *δημ-αγωγία*.

32 C 27. **δια-κινδυνεύειν**: the force of the prepos.? See L. & S., and cf. *δια-σκοπῶν* 8,12. **μεθ' ὑμῶν γενέσθαι** 'to side with you.' **μή**: c. partic.; condition. 28. **δεσμόν** (*δέω* 'I bind') 'imprisonment.' 31. **οἱ τριάκοντα**: see n. on 7,17.
27 1. **πέμπτον αὐτόν**: H. 681 b, G. 991. 2. **Σαλαμῖνος**: what and where was Salamis? Consult some map. 3. **ἀποθάνοι** 'be put to death,' regularly used as the pass. of *ἀποκτείνω*; H. 820, G. 1241. **οἷα δή** 'the sort of order' (the noun is in *προσέταττον*). Cf. 24,13. Note the following order of words (acc., dat., nom., dat., acc.), so impossible in English, so neat and clear in a language of inflections. Note too in li. 4 alliteration of *π*, and juxtaposit. of two forms of the same word, *πολλοῖς πολλά*. 5. **ἀναπλῆσαι**: from *ἀνα-πίμ-πλημι* (cf. *πλή-ρης*, *plē-nus*) 'to fill,' 'to infect,' 'to implicate in,' c. gen. *αἰτιῶν* 'crimes'; H. 743, G. 1113. Fellow-criminals, the Thirty thought, must "*hang* together." **μέντοι**: asseverat. (1,20); 'then *in very truth* I showed again (*αὖ*), not by word but by deed, that —.'

32 D 6. **ἐνεδειξάμην**: not here in the legal sense of the active voice as in 26,24, but as in 11,17. **ἐμοί** is not conciliatory, is not merely *μοι*. 7. **θανάτου μέν**: force of *μέν*? **εἰ μὴ ἀγροικότερον ἦν** 'were it not rather rude (blunt)' sc. than otherwise—the comparat. degree in both Engl. and Greek; cf. 24,12. The condition is stated as if *ἔλεγον ἄν* ('I should say') were to follow. Yet after all, he does say the 'blunt' thing, viz. *οὐδ' ὁτιοῦν* 'not a picayune.' Blunt indeed it was, before judges of life and death. With this strong negat. (see n. on 21,6) cf. *μηδ' ὁπωστιοῦν* 1,12; *οὐδ' ὁπωστιοῦν* 17,16. 9. **τούτου δέ**: *τούτου* resumptive, or summary (1,13; 5,16), *δέ* repetition of the preceding one. Cf. *τότε μέν* 20,31. **τὸ πᾶν** adverbial; cf. *τὸ παράπαν* (16,25,31), *παντάπασι* (16,29), *πάντως* (14,29). 10. **ἐμέ** is again defiant as *ἐμοί* in li. 6. **ἐκείνη ἡ ἀρχή**, i.e. *ἡ ὀλιγαρχία*; *ἐκείνη*, because *that* government succeeded with him no better than the democracy. **οὕτως . . οὖσα**: concessive; 'so strong as it was.' 14. **ᾠχόμην ἀπιών**: simply 'went off.' The partic. with *οἴχομαι* should usually be made the main verb in Engl. 15. **ἀπέθανον**: as in li. 3. **διὰ ταχέων**=

ταχέως. Such periphrases of adv. by means of *διά* c. gen. are 27
freq.; as *διὰ βραχέων* = *βραχέως*, *διὰ σπουδῆς* = *σπουδαίως*. L. & S. s.v. *διά*, A III c. Cf. the like periphrases by *κατά* c. acc., e.g. *κατὰ τάχος*; L. & S. s.v., B VIII.—For the brief domination of the Thirty, see n. on 7,17.

32 E 18. **ἄν**: *can* it go with *οἴεσθε*? H. 858 a, G. 1302. **δια-γενέσθαι**: cf. *δια-κινδυνεύειν* 26,27. *δια-σκοπῶν* 8,12. 19. **εἰ ἔπραττον**: in 2,17 and 6,17 the imperf. referred to a *present* state of things contrary to fact. Is it so here? H. 895 a, G. 1397. 20. **τοῖς δικαίοις**: prob. neuter. 21. **περὶ πλείστου**: 9,5. 22. **πολλοῦ γε δεῖ** 'far from it'; cf. 24,4. 23. **οὐδὲ γὰρ ἄν** *κτλ.*, sc. *τοσάδε ἔτη διεγένετο.* On *οὐδέ* see 2,5.

33 A 24. **εἴ πού τι** *κτλ.*: apologetic for his 'bit' of public work. On *που* see 2,6. 25. **τοιοῦτος** 'that kind of a man,' *ὁ αὐτὸς οὗτος* 'that same kind,' referring vaguely to the kind just described (cf. *τοιοῦτος* in 6,8; 16,2), but further explained by the following *οὐδενὶ ξυγχωρήσας.* 30. **μαθητάς**: Socrates himself preferred the term *οἱ συνόντες* 'companions.' **διδάσκαλος μέν**: the contrasted thought? 31. **λέγοντος καὶ τὰ ἐμαυτοῦ** (9,5) **πράττοντος**: the two activities were in
Socrates' case identical. 3. **ἐφθόνησα**: a sudden shift of 28
tense. From what precedes and follows, the present might be expected. **οὐδέ** negatives its clause as a whole, not its separate members:

οὐδὲ { *χρήματα μὲν λαμβάνων διαλέγομαι,*
 { *μὴ λαμβάνων δ' οὔ.*

Transl.: 'nor *is it true that* —.'

33 B 5. **ἐρωτᾶν** 'for questioning' = 'to be questioned'; infin. of purpose, and active rather than passive (H. 951, 952 a; G. 1532,1 & 2). 6. **ἀποκρινόμενος**, i.e. when questioned, in his turn, by Socrates. 7. **ὧν**: for *τούτων ἅ.* **τούτων**: a gen. of the whole with *τις* and also directly construed with *τὴν αἰτίαν ὑπέχοιμι* ('be responsible for,' 'have to answer for'). Alcibiades and Critias were the most famous of the 'pupils' who did 'not become useful citizens.' 9. **ὧν . . μηδενί** 'to no one of whom.' 11. **ὅ τι μή**: *μή*, not *οὐ* (as in li. 9 *μήτε*, not *οὔτε*). See on 8,28. 12. **καὶ οἱ ἄλλοι πάντες** 'all the rest.' For *καί*, see 10,7.

33 C 17. **ὅτι ἀκούοντες** *κτλ.* 'viz. that —,' explaining *τὴν ἀλήθειαν.* Others take *ὅτι* as 'because,' answering *διὰ τί* (li. 14). **χαίρουσι**: with supplementary ptc. *ἀκούοντες* (H. 983, G. 1580), and with also a dat. of cause *ἐξεταζομένοις τοῖς οἰομένοις* (H. 778); cf. 11,24. 22. **τινὶ . . καὶ ἄλλῳ**: see n. on 10,7. 23. **καὶ ὁτιοῦν**: 21,6; 27,8. 24. **εἰ γὰρ δή**: as in 2,17 (*εἰ τῷ ὄντι*) and 18,26 (*εἴπερ*), a preliminary

28 supposition is offered, on which, later, a condition is based (here, in li. 26).

33 D 26. **χρῆν**: the condition *εἴτε . . ἔγνωσαν* being contrary to fact, *ἄν* might be expected with *χρῆν*, the verb of the conclusion. But see H. 897, G. 1400,1. The infinitives depending on *χρῆν* are in line 30 and 29,3. **δήπου**: 2,6. **εἴτε**: note the substitute in li. 31 for the second *εἴτε*, and cf. *οὔτε . . οὐδέ* 5,13. 29. **αὐτούς** 'themselves,' the intensive use of the word. 30. **τιμωρεῖσθαι**: disting. the mid. from the active used in 20,11. H. 816,12; G. 1246.
29 Cf. n. on *μισθώσασθαι* 6,3. 1. **τῶν ἐκείνων**: not '*those* relatives,' but '*their* relatives.' Why? H. 673, G. 960.
2. **τοὺς προσήκοντας**: an appositive to *ἄλλους*, where in Engl. we should use a genit. **εἴπερ**: 'if indeed' (cf. 8,9. 14,27. 18,26. 19,21) calls to mind the original supposition *εἰ γὰρ δή* nine lines distant. 4. **πάντως δέ** 'and certainly (surely)'; 14,29. 5. **ἐνταυθοῖ** 'hither' for 'here' (*ἐνταῦθα*), as in Xen. *Anab.* I 2,2 *παρῆσαν εἰς Σάρδεις.* Pregnant construction; H. 788, G. 1225,1. 6. **οὑτοσί** goes with *Κρίτων*, though no article is present; H. 674, G. 945,2. For **-ί** see 2,14. **δημότης**: the *δῆμος*, or parish, was a subdivision of the *φυλή*, tribe. Socrates belonged to *Ἀλωπεκή* of the tribe *Ἀντιοχίς*.

33 E 7. **τοῦδε** 'here.' *ὅδε* is a "deictic" pronoun (7,27). Again the art. is absent. 8. **ὁ Σφήττιος** 'of the deme *Σφηττός*.' 9. **Κηφισιεύς** (9) 'of the deme *Κηφισιά*.' The Aeschines here spoken of is not the famous (and later) antagonist of Demosthenes, nor again this Antiphon the earlier orator Antiphon, who was from another deme (*ὁ Ῥαμνούσιος*). 10. **τοίνυν**: 16,19. **διατριβῇ** 'mode of life,' 'employment.' 11. **Θεοζοτίδου**: supply *υἱός*. 12. **ὁ μὲν Θεόδοτος**: *μέν solitarium* 1,15. 8,23. 13. **ἐκεῖνος**: an emphatic '*he*' (not 'that one'!!), i.e. the dead Theodotus. **καταδεηθείη**: *κατά* in composit. gives various shades of meaning. Perhaps here, as in *κατα-πολεμέω* ('to *down* one in war, to finish one off by it'), 'to *overcome* by entreaty.' The compound is nowhere else found. The negat. potent. optat. (*οὐκ ἂν καταδεηθείη*) may be translated 'he *cannot* —,' as often.

34 A 18. **ἐχρῆν**: apparently forgetting that *χρῆν* is *χρὴ ἦν*, the Greeks wrote also *ἐ-χρῆν*, augmenting the noun!
19. **μάλιστα μέν**: often = 'best of all.' **παρασχέσθαι**: for the significance of the tense, see G. 1400,2. 21. **παρασχέσθω**: the aor. pictures the act summarily and finished, while the pres. **λεγέτω** shows it in process, as do (inherently) our English words 'tell,' 'relate.' **παραχωρῶ** 'I give way,' 'yield place.' The speaker's limited time was measured by the *κλεψ-ύδρα* (*ὕδωρ*)—a kind of water-hourglass. The offer here made was a freq. one, often merely for show. 22.

τούτου πᾶν τοὐναντίον : 14,24. 24. **τῷ διαφθείροντι** 'the 29
corruptor' spoken with ironical emphasis.

34 B 26. **γάρ** : the reason *for* all being ready to aid him is not reached till li. 30 'because they know that Meletus is lying.' The intervening is subordinate ; 'for *whilst* (*μέν*) the corrupted themselves, etc.' **τάχ' ἂν** : 7,6. 27. **ἂν λόγον ἔχοιεν** 'would perhaps be excusable (have some reason)' ; 25,4. 29. **ἀλλ' ἤ** : 7,3. 30. **ξυνίσασι Μελήτῳ** 'they know *with* Meletus' = 'they know as well as he does.'

Here begins the *ἐπί-λογος* 'after-speech,' peroration.

1. **εἶεν** : 4,6,19. 3. **τάχα δ' ἂν** : 7,6. 30

34 C 5. **εἰ ὁ μέν** : for an *εἰ*-clause after *ἀγανακτέω*, see H. 926, G. 1423–24. *ὁ μέν* is a strong '*he*,' since the answering *ἐγὼ δέ* is five lines distant. Subordinate one or the other member with a 'while' or 'whereas.' For the scheme of sent., cf. 20,27 *δεινὰ ἂν εἴην*—. 8. **παιδία . . ἀναβιβασάμενος** : this was scandalously frequent. 11. **ἄρα** 'forsooth' (1,14). **καὶ ταῦτα** : 17,17 and H. 612 a, G. 1573. 13. **αὐθαδέστερον ἂν . . σχοίη** (2,16) 'may the more steel himself against me,' 'take a more stubborn attitude toward me.' 14. **αὐτοῖς τούτοις** : causal, H. 778. For the plur., see on 5,11. 16. **οὕτως ἔχει** 'feels that way.'

34 D 16. **οὐκ ἀξιῶ** *κτλ.* 'for while (*μέν*) I do not for my part think it right.' 17. **εἰ δ' οὖν** 'yet anyhow (i.e. right or not) if (he does feel so).' See 1,3 for *δ' οὖν*. **ἐπιεικῆ** 'fair,' 'reasonable.' Cf. 9,12. 18. **λέγων** 'when I say.' **ἐμοί** emphatic. **εἰσὶ μέν** : the sense of *μέν*, and its response? 10,12. 19. **καί** 'also.' **καὶ γάρ** : perhaps to be taken separately (10,1). **καὶ . . τοῦτο αὖ** *κτλ.* 'to quote again also this saying of Homer's.' He had been already quoted 20,13. For the case, cf. *τοὐναντίον πᾶν*, 14,24. 20. **οὐδ' ἐγώ** 'no more am I.' *Od.* 19,163 *οὐ γὰρ ἀπὸ δρυός ἐσσι παλαιφάτου οὐδ' ἀπὸ πέτρης*. 21. **πέφυκα** : one of the perfects active that are intrans. in meaning—an important list ; H. 501, G. silent. Cf. *ἀπόλωλα* 25,29. **καὶ . . καί** are not here correlative, but 'also' and 'even.' 23. **τρεῖς** : keep Greek order ; not 'three sons.' 24. **ἀναβιβασάμενος δεήσομαι** : in Engl. better two finite verbs in the fut. connected by 'and.' 25. **τί δὴ οὖν** (sometimes *τί οὖν δή*) 'why then?' 26. **αὐθαδιζόμενος** 'from stubbornness.' After *ἀλλά* the participial construction is dropped (anacoluthon).

34 E 27. **θαρραλέως . . ἔχω** : 2,16. 28. **λόγος** 'consideration,' 'question,' 'matter.' 29. **δ' οὖν** : 1,3.
31. **τηλικόνδε** : 15,21. **τοῦτο τοὔνομα** : *what* name?
(11,1). 1. **εἴτ' οὖν . . εἴτ' οὖν** : in 18,18 *οὖν* stands in the 31
first member only—'whether indeed.' For the second *οὖν* there

31 seems to be no rendering. **ψεῦδος**: note the subst., not *ψευδές*, as expected, after *ἀληθές*. 2. **ἀλλ' οὖν . . γε**: 18,18. 3. **τῶν πολλῶν ἀνθρώπων** 'most men.'

35 A 4. **δοκοῦντες**: 8,8. **διαφέρειν** 'to be superior.' 5. **ᾑ-τινι-οὖν** 'whatsoever.' **τοιοῦτοι** 'of that character,' referring (vaguely, as in 6,8. 16,2. 27,25) to the men above described, who would descend to prayers and tears to obtain acquittal. 6. **οἵουσπερ . . τινάς** 'the sort I have often seen specimens of.' 9. **πείσεσθαι**: *πάσχω*. 10. **ἐσομένων**: what case would be more regular? H. 972 d. **ἄν** at the head of its clause is always for *ἐάν*. 12. **ἄν . . ὑπολαβεῖν** stands for a potent. optat. 13. **εἰς**: 22,17.

35 B 13. **αὐτοὶ ἑαυτῶν**: 17,27. 15. **οὗτοι**: emphat. resumption of the subject (1,13). 17. **καὶ ὁπῃοῦν**: cf. 28,23. **τι εἶναι** 'to be *somebody*.' 19. **ἐνδείκνυσθαι**: 22,14. 27,6. 20. **κατα-ψηφιεῖσθε**: see 14,21 for *κατα-*; on the form, cf. *ὀνειδιῶ* 22,26. **ταῦτα**: in attributive position. Why permissible? H. 673 c, G. 975. 21. **εἰσάγοντος** 'introducing.' 23. **οὐδέ**: 2,5; the second *οὐδέ* is *not* its correlative; 3,27.

35 C 25. **ἀποφεύγειν**: in its legal sense, 'to be acquitted.' Note the prepos. 'to get *off*.' 26. **ἐπὶ τούτῳ** 'for this purpose, viz. —'; 7,10. H. 799,2 c; G. 1210,2 c. 27. **καταχαρίζεσθαι** *κτλ*. 'to make a favour of (give away as a present) justice.' 28. **ταῦτα**, viz. *τὰ δίκαια*. **ὀμώμοκεν**: *ὄμνυμι*. **οὐ** goes properly with *ὀμώμοκεν*. The dicast has *not* sworn *χαριεῖσθαι*, but *δικάσειν*. **χαριεῖσθαι**: tense and
32 formation? See li. 20. 29. **οὔκουν**: n. on 18,16. 1. **ἀξιοῦτε** 'expect'; cf. 3,29. 5,6. 10,17. 2. **πρὸς ὑμᾶς** 'have such transactions *with* you,' 'act in such a way *toward* you'; 8,14. 3. **ἄλλως τε** *κτλ*. (17,14) 'especially indeed (*μέντοι*) by Zeus when —.' (The phrase *ἄλλως τε καί* is strengthened sometimes by *μέντοι*, sometimes by *πάντως* (or other words), but hardly by both at once and *νὴ Δία* besides.)

35 D 4. **ἀσεβείας**: case? 16,2. 5. **τουτουΐ**: no art.; 29,6. 6. **βιαζοίμην ὀμωμοκότας** 'do violence to your oaths,' or 'to you, under oath as you are.' **θεοὺς . . εἶναι**: *θεούς* not so placed for nothing. For what? 8. **ἀπολογούμενος κατηγοροίην**: note the paradox and the juxtaposition of the words that form it, as also in li. 6 *δεῖσθαι βιαζοίμην*—cases of so-called *ὀξύ-μωρον*. See L. & S. For the juxtaposition, cf. 15,21; 17,27. 9. **πολλοῦ δεῖ**: cf. (24,4 and) 27,22.

In Attic procedure were recognized two sorts of trials—the *ἀγὼν ἀτίμητος*, in which the dicasts merely pronounced judgment (the penalty being fixed by law), and the *ἀγὼν τιμητός*, in

which they first pronounced judgment and then proceeded to 32
estimate the penalty (*τιμᾶν τὸ τίμημα*), choosing either the one proposed by the accuser (*ὁ διώκων τιμᾶται*—note the middle voice) or the counter-assessment proposed by the defendant (*ὁ φεύγων ἀντι-τιμᾶται*). The present trial is one of the latter sort. Socrates has been judged guilty. Meletus has proposed death as the penalty. Socrates now offers the counter-penalty.

35 E 14. **τὸ μὲν μὴ ἀγανακτεῖν** (sc. *ἐμέ*) 'the fact that I —' begins as if the subject of the sent., but proves to be the obj. of *ξυμβάλλεται* ('contributes') although properly this verb is followed by *εἰς* c. acc. Translate as a free accus.: '*as* to the fact that etc.' and supply a resumptive *εἰς αὐτό* ('to it') after the verb. Note *μέν solitarium*; 29,12. 15. **ἐπὶ τούτῳ τῷ γεγονότι** 'at this result (issue).' Is *ἐπί* necessary? See n. on *χαίρουσι* 28,17 and on *αὐτοῖς τούτοις* 30,14. For *ἐπί*, however, cf. 23,19 & 22. **ὅτι** 'viz. that —.'

36 A 17. **καὶ οὐκ**: answering *ἄλλα τε*, we should expect *καὶ* (*τοῦτο ὅτι*) *οὐκ* 'and this fact, that—.' But the second member often detaches itself by anacoluthon, becoming an independent clause, as in 30,27. **ἀνέλπιστον** 'unlooked for.' *ἐλπίζω* is 'to expect' (it may be good or bad), not merely 'to hope'—used only of desirables. 19. **γεγονότα** 'resulting.' 20. **οὕτω παρ' ὀλίγον**: observe the order of words. *παρ' ὀλίγον* goes as a unit, *οὕτω* modifies it. 'So by-a-little.' Cf. "quite a bad cold," "many good men," or the Shakespearian "good my lord" ('my lord'=*monsieur*, one word). 22. **μετέπεσον** 'fallen the other way.' *μετα-* in composit. often signifies *change*, e.g. in *μετα-βαίνω, -βάλλω, -γιγνώσκω, -γράφω, -μανθάνω, -νοέω*.—The number of dicasts that tried Socrates is not known, but is usu. assumed to be 500. Mention is found of dicasteries of 200, 500, 700 etc. to 6000. Any number from 400 up would satisfy the conditions of the *πέμπτον μέρος* of li. 28. 23. **ἀπ-επεφεύγη**: in legal sense (31,25), but in next line it is 'to escape,' 'get off from.' **Μέλητον μέν**: response in li. 1 of next page. 27. **κἂν ὦφλε** *κτλ.* 'he would have also incurred a fine of —',—evidently a law meant to discourage litigation.

36 B 27. **οὐ μεταλαβών** *κτλ.*: again a little contemptuous jest at the expense of the nominal accuser, as above in *τοὺς*
ἀμφὶ Ἄνυτον 3,3. 1. **τιμᾶται δ' οὖν**: the jest is dismissed 33
by the *δ' οὖν* 'be that as it may.' Note the self-interested *middle* voice, as in *ἀντι-τιμήσομαι*, li. 2. **θανάτου**: gen. of price, as in li. 4 *ἀξίας* (6,12. 17,11). **εἶεν**: 4,6. 30,1. 2. **ὑμῖν**: ethical dat. 'what would you have me etc.' (Adam). 3. **ἤ**: 16,14. 4. **ἀξίας** is a substantive. See L. & S. **ἄξιος** *κτλ.* 'deserve to suffer or pay' (*ἀπο-τίνω*)—a freq. formula of the courts. 5. **ὅ τι μαθών**: *τί μαθὼν* (*τί παθὼν*)

33 *τοῦτο ἐποίησας;* means 'what having learned (suffered) did you do that?' 'what possessed you (what was the matter with you) that you did that?' (H. 968 c, G. 1566.) The indir. quest. 'I asked you what possessed you etc.' is *ἠρόμην σε ὅ τι μαθὼν κτλ.* So here: What do I deserve to pay for whatever possessed me not to hold my peace? But the phrase is idiomatic and seems equiv. to a mere *ὅ τι* 'because,' or simply 'that.' 6. **ἀ-μελήσας ὧνπερ οἱ πολλοί** '*not* caring for what most men' [*do* care for, sc. *ἐπιμελοῦνται*]. 8. **καὶ τῶν ἄλλων**, 'and the rest, viz.,' 'and what not besides' (Stock), followed by the appositives *ἀρχῶν* etc. See L. & S. s.v. *ἄλλος*, II 8; or H. 705, G. 966,2. Xen. *Anab.* I 5,5 *οὐ γὰρ ἦν χόρτος οὐδὲ ἄλλο οὐδὲν δένδρον.* 10. **τῷ ὄντι**: 7,5. **ἐπιεικέστερον**: 9,12. 11. **ἢ ὥστε**: H. 954, G. 1458.

36 C 12. **ἐνταῦθα . . ᾖα** (and in li. 15): adv. of rest with verb of motion, the reverse of *ἐνταυθοῖ πάρεισι* (29,5) adv. of motion with verb of rest. **οἷ**: relat. to *ποῖ*; n. on 4,14. **μήτε**: not *οὔτε* (8,28). 13. **ἔμελλον . . εἶναι** (6,4): a periphrastic *past* fut., as in Engl. 'was going to be.' 14. **εὐεργετεῖν**: with two accusatives (outer and inner), as in 4,18. 15. **ἐνταῦθα** summarizes *ἐπὶ δὲ τό κτλ.* 16. **πρότερον . . πρίν**: a duplication that, like the doubled negat. or the *καί* in the relat. clause (10,7), is to be dropped in Engl. 17. **πρὶν . . ἐπιμεληθείη**: indir. disc. for *πρὶν ἂν* c. subjunct. So *ὅπως ἔσοιτο* following, for *ἔσται*, the construction of 13,22. 22,19. 23,7. 20. **οὕτω** and **κατὰ τὸν αὐτὸν τρόπον** are parallel expressions (2,3). 21. **τί οὖν** *κτλ.*, after a rambling sent., resumes the quest. of li. 4.

36 D 23. **τῇ ἀληθείᾳ**: 11,12. **τιμᾶσθαι**: mid., as in li. 1. **καὶ ταῦτα**: 17,17. 30,11. 24. **ὅ τι**=*οἷον* 'as.' 25. **εὐ-εργέτης** 'benefactor,' a word of special contents in Athens. Decrees were often passed bestowing it as a title of honour upon those who had done eminent service to the state, whether citizen or foreigner. 26. **ἐπί**: c. dat. of purpose (7,10. 31,26). 27. **μᾶλλον . . πρέπει οὕτως, ὡς** *κτλ.* 'more fitting to such degree as that such a man etc.' After *μᾶλλον*, we might expect *ἤ* 'than'; but *οὕτως* diverts the syntax. Cf. the somewhat different irregularity in 23,6; also *Childe Harold*, c. III 23 "His heart more truly knew that peal too well." 28. **ἐν πρυτανείῳ**: the prytanēum was the Townhall or Statehouse. Here were entertained guests of state, ambassadors, victors in the great games, and others. Sometimes permanent maintenance was granted, such as Socrates here, with splendid pride and defiance, suggests for himself. 30. **ἵππῳ ἢ ξυν-ωρίδι ἢ ζεύγει**: said to mean 'single race-horse,' 'pair,' and 'four abreast' respectively. **Ὀλυμπία-σιν**: a locat. like *Ἀθήνη-σιν*; H. 220, G. 296.

37 A 6. **ὥσπερ περὶ οἴκτου** *κτλ.*, viz. on p. 30. *οἶκτος* 34
'lamentation' recalls *δάκρυα* (30,8), *ἀντιβόλησις* (verb *ἀντιβολέω*) recalls *ἱκετεύω* (30,7). 7. **ἀπ-αυθαδιζόμενος**: cf. *αὐθαδέστερον* (30,13) and *αὐθαδιζόμενος* (30,26). **τὸ δέ**: *possibly* the demonstrat. subject 'but that is not so'; yet better as in 11,3 an adv. acc. 'whereas.' 8. **τοιόνδε μᾶλλον** 'as follows rather,' while *τοιοῦτον* refers to the preceding. 9. **ἑκὼν εἶναι**: for *εἶναι* see H. 956 a, G. 1535. **μηδένα ἀδικεῖν**: is *μηδένα* subject? See *ἑκών*, nom.—This belief of Socrates—that a man does not sin voluntarily, and that other, that virtue is knowledge, seem curious to us. We recall Paul's words (*Rom.* VII 15) *οὐ γὰρ ὃ θέλω, τοῦτο πράσσω· ἀλλ' ὃ μισῶ, τοῦτο ποιῶ.* But Socrates admitted no dissidence between right action and right knowledge. Wrong action indicated defective knowledge. The sinner merely *does not know well enough* what is good for him. Perhaps he was himself so thoroughly self-controlled, that he could not conceive the will as disobedient to reason. 11. **ἐγᾦμαι**: crasis of *ἐγὼ οἶμαι.* 12. **ὥσπερ καί**: what of *καί*? 10,7.—The reference is probably to the Spartans, whose state Socrates openly admired—an unpopular thing to do, surely, if we recall the long 27 years' war.

37 B 14. **νῦν δέ**: 6,6. 25,4. 15. **χρόνῳ ὀλίγῳ**: the same complaint as in 4,10 and 12,22. Criticism rather than entreaty! Socrates was surely not talking *πρὸς χάριν.* 16. **δή** 'then' (4,6), as below li. 22. **πολλοῦ δέω**: 24,4. 17. **ἀδικήσειν**: for the infrequency of the fut. inf. exc. in indir. disc. and after *μέλλω*, see G. 1277. 18. **αὐτός**: 17,27. **του**, not *τοῦ.* 19. **τί δείσας** 'in fear of what?' from which depends *μὴ πάθω* 'lest I —?' 22. **ἕλωμαι** (*αἱρέω*) 'am I to choose from what etc.?' Deliberative subjunct.; H. 866,3; G. 1358. **ὧν** is partit. genit. or (better named) gen. *of the whole.* **ὧν εὖ οἶδ' ὅτι κακῶν ὄντων**: after *οἶδα* should follow a *ὅτι*-clause (cf. 21,26) or the participial construction. Here both follow, complicated further by the attract. of the relat. from *ἃ εὖ οἶδα κακὰ ὄντα* into the genit. *ὧν.* As for *ὅτι*, it sometimes thus negligently appears also when the acc. c. infin. follows, e.g. Lysias 13,9 *λέγει ὅτι . . ποιήσειν*, and sometimes is tacked on to *οἶδα* at the end of a sent., e.g. Aristoph. *Aves* 1408 *οὐ παύσομαι, τοῦτ' ἴσθ' ὅτι.* 23. **τοῦ**=*τίνος.* **δεσμοῦ**: 26,28.

37 C 25. **ἀεὶ καθισταμένῃ** 'from time to time installed.' Cf. *ἀεί* in 15,11. 22,14. **τοῖς ἕνδεκα** (see L. & S.) is prob. a later learned marginal note. Why need Socrates have instructed the dicasts on a contemporary fact quite so well known? Even "colloquial repetition" can hardly excuse it. 26. **δεδέσθαι** (perf. tense=pres. state) 'imprisonment.'

34 27. *ἐκτίνω, -τείσω -έτεισα.* **νῦν δή** 'just now,' its regular sense, and by some printed as one word *νυνδή*. 28. **ὁπόθεν ἐκτείσω** ('to pay with') is here fut. indic.; H. 911, G. 1442. 29. **ἀλλὰ δή** 'well then.' 30. **τιμήσαιτε**: the act. used of the dicasts, the mid. of the parties interested. **πολλὴ μέντοι ἄν** *κτλ.* 'great indeed must be (14,31) my love of life.' 31. **ἔχοι**: lit. 'would possess.' **ἀ-λόγι-**
35 **στος** 'il-logical.' 3. **διατριβάς**: 29,10.

37 D 4. **βαρύτεραι** 'too burdensome.' 5. **αὐτῶν . . ἀπαλλαγῆναι** 'to get free from them'; H. 748, G. 1117. **ἄλλοι δέ** *κτλ.* is spiritedly anacoluthic. Logic would put it: if *you* did not prove able to endure me, still less will others. For this last, a quest. is substituted: will others forsooth (*ἄρα*)? (Note subordination of the *μέν*-clause by 'if.' Cf. n. on 23,29. 30,5,16.) 8. **ἐξελθόντι** 'after going into exile.' **τηλικῷδε**: 15,21. **ἄλλην ἐξ ἄλλης**: in Engl. reversed; 'from one to another.' 9. **ζῆν**: epexegetic of 'that life' (*ὁ βίος*), viz. 'to live wandering . . and ever driven forth' (pres.). 11. **κἄν**: *καὶ ἐάν.* 12. **ἐξ-ελῶσι** (*-ελαύνω*).

37 E 18. **ἡμῖν**: ethical dat. 'pray.' Cf. *μοι* 'please.' **ἐξελθὼν ζῆν** 'to go into exile *and* live' (n. on 30,24). **τουτὶ δή** 'now *that.*' 22. **ὡς**: c. ptc. (1,10).

38 A 23. **ἐάντ' αὖ** 'or again if,' i.e. 'on the other hand.' Cf. *εἰ δ' αὖ* 18,30. **ὅτι καί** 'that indeed.' 24. **ἑκά-στης ἡμέρας**: H. 759, G. 1136. 25. **τοὺς λόγους ποιεῖσθαι**: 18,4. 29. **ταῦτα δέ**: *δέ* in apodosis (G. 1422) breaks off as does our anacoluthic stop-gap 'why'; e.g. "If you see him in New York, why tell him etc." **τὰ δέ** is the *demonstrative* article, or rather not the art. at all. 30. **ἔχει μέν** '*stands* thus, but etc.' 31. **εἴθισμαι** '*am* in the habit'
36 (perf. tense gives pres. state). 1. **εἰ μὲν γάρ** *κτλ.*: *γάρ* gives here no reason for the previous fact (it makes no sense to say: 'I am not accustomed to regard myself as deserving of ill *because* I should have assessed a money-penalty etc.'), but gives the ground for the *statement* of the fact. 'Deserving of *ill*, I say, because, while I should have fixed a money-penalty if I had had any, yet I do not regard the loss of money as an evil.' Cf. the same use of *ἐπεί* in 5,17.

38 B 3. **ἔμελλον ἐκτείσειν**: 6,4. 4. **νῦν δέ**: 6,6. **οὐ γὰρ ἔστιν** 'indeed I have none.' On *γάρ*, see 5,3. **εἰ μὴ ἄρα** 'unless, to be sure.' Cf. 1,14. 6. **μνᾶν**: n. on 6,12. 10. **ἐγγυᾶσθαι**: supply *φασίν* from *κελεύουσι* in previous line. 12. **ἀξιόχρεῳ**: 7,14.

38 C 14. **ἕξετε . . αἰτίαν**: *ἔχω αἰτίαν* is the usu. pass. of *αἰτιάομαι* 'to blame.' **ὑπό** follows c. gen. agentis (1,2).

16. **ἀπεκτόνατε**: 2nd perf. 17. **εἰ καὶ μή εἰμι** 'suppos- 36
ing I am *not*.' The emphasis is due to *καί*, as in 24,9.
Translat. of *εἰ καί* by 'although' (H. 1053,1) blunts the
feeling for *καί*. 20. **ἀπὸ τοῦ αὐτομάτου** 'of itself,' 'in the
course of nature.' Cf. 11,24. 21. **ὁρᾶτε . . τὴν ἡλικίαν**:
prolepsis (21,14). **πόρρω . . τοῦ βίου**: *πόρρω* c. gen. is
either 'far on in,' or 'far from.' The context decides.

38 D 24. **τόδε** 'the following,' while *τοῦτο* in 22 refers to
the foregoing, Cf. *τοιόνδε, τοιοῦτον* 34,8. 26. **ἀ-πορίᾳ**;
as *ἀ-φθονία* ('without stint') is 'plenty,' so *ἀ-πορία* ('without
resource') is 'want,' 'lack.' **τοιούτων** 'of the kind.'
1. **μὲν . . μέντοι**: 7,1. 4. **θρηνοῦντός τέ μου** *κτλ.* is 37
epexegetic of *οἷα*, but depends upon *ἀκούω*.

38 E 5. **πολλὰ καί**: drop *καί*. 7. **εἴθισθε**: 35,31.
12. **ἐκείνως**, sc. *ἀπολογησάμενος*.

39 A 14. **πᾶν ποιῶν** 'by doing any- and everything.' So
παν-οῦργος (ἔργον) 'a man who will do *anything*,' i.e. a rascal.
Cf. 36,27 and infra li. 20. 15. **καὶ γάρ**: 10,1. 17.
ἐκφύγοι 'e-vade.' **ἀφ-είς**: *-ἵημι*. **ἱκετείαν** = *ἀντιβόλησιν*
34,7. 18. **τῶν διωκόντων** 'his pursuers.' 20. **δια-
φεύγειν** is properly 'to slip through.' Cf. *ἐκ-* in 17, *ἀπο-* in 14.
21. **μή** with an independ. subjunct. (as here *ᾖ*) originally
perhaps deprecated the matter (= 'I hope *not*,' 'God forbid'),
but came to be used (and by Plato frequently) to express the
suspicion that *maybe* the matter was as stated, undesirable or
otherwise. Translate 'maybe,' 'perhaps.' H. 867, G. 1350.
23. **θᾶττον . . θανάτου θεῖ**: mark alliteration; 'flies faster
than fate' (Dyer). **καὶ νῦν**: *καί* often adds a special
instance of some general statement = 'and so,' 'for example.'

39 B 24. **ἅτε**: 12,11. 27. **ὑπό** c. gen. and intrans.
verb; 1,2. 28. **δίκην ὀφλών** 'having incurred penalty.'
29. **ὠφληκότες**: note tense of present state (10,7); 'already
condemned to,' 'debtors to.' 31. **μέν που**: the answering
δέ is in 38,3. *που* (2,6) weakens the statement much as *ἴσως*
does. Cf. *ἴσως τάχ' ἂν* 24,19. 1. **οὕτως καὶ ἔδει σχεῖν** 'had 38
indeed (*καί*) to happen so.' For aor. of *ἔχω*, see 4,9. **μετρίως
ἔχειν** 'is fair' (2,16). 3. **τὸ δὲ δὴ μετὰ τοῦτο** 'and now (*δή*)
the next thing (is) —'; an apposit. to the sent. See 14,24 App.
τὸ μετὰ τοῦτο is an adverbial phrase, as in *τὸ πρὸ τούτου* 'here-
tofore,' *τὸ ἀπὸ τοῦδε* 'hereafter.'

39 C 7. **ὅταν** *κτλ.* 'viz. when—' in epexegesis. So pro-
phesied, before death, Patroclus; so Hector. 8. **ἀπεκτό-
νατε**: the perf. puts the will for the deed. We had better
transl. 'have *sentenced* to death.' 10. **ἢ οἵαν . . ἀπ-
εκτόνατε**, i.e. 'than the vengeance of death you have visited
on me'—a brachylogic cognate acc. for *οἵαν (τιμωρίαν) ἐμὲ*

38 *ἐτιμωρήσασθε ἀποκτείνοντες.* For the two accus. (inner and outer), cf. 4,18. 33,14. 12. **ἀπ-αλλάξεσθαι** : c. gen.; cf. 35,5. 13. **τὸ δέ** : again, probably, the adv. acc. of 11,3 and 34,7; 'whereas.' 16. **ὅσῳ** : 22,30.

39 D 18. **ἐπισχήσειν** 'to keep back,' 'hinder,' 'prevent' (=*κωλύω, ἀπείργω*). L. & S. s.v., IV c. For the dependent *τοῦ ὀνειδίζειν*, see H. 963, G. 1549. 20. **οὔτε πάνυ δυνατή** 'neither entirely efficient.' For the litotes, see 4,13. 24. **μέν** : its answer? 25. **ἀπαλλάττομαι** 'I have done.' L. & S. s.v., B II 7 b.

39 E 27. **ὑπέρ** : c. gen.; perhaps here 'for,' 'in behalf of' (for Socrates is "enamoured of death"), though freq. it is no more than *περί* 'concerning.' 28. **ἐν ᾧ** 'while'—very common. **οἱ ἄρχοντες** 'the officers,' *οἱ ἕνδεκα*, not of course the nine "archons," the mayors of Athens. **ἀσχολίαν ἄγουσι** 'are busy.' Note the negat. mode of expressing ideas that for us are positive: *ἀ-σχολία* 'business,' *ἀ-πορία* 'want,' *ἀ-φθονία* 'plenty.' 29. **οἷ ἐλθόντα** : cf. 33,12. 30. **τεθνάναι** : 20,17. **ἀλλά** c. imperat. is extremely common; 'nay.' Perhaps there was a movement for departure.
39 1. **δια-μυθολογῆσαι** : in Plato's time *μῦθοι* had come to its modern sense 'myths,' 'tales,' 'fancies.' The verb here then is 'to exchange (*δια-*) fancies'—not *διαλέγεσθαι*, for Socrates is not going into "dialectics," discussion, arguments, to prove anything.

40 A 3. **τὸ . . ξυμβεβηκός** : prolepsis (21,14). 4. **νοεῖ** 'means,' 'signifies,' 'the significance of —.' Cf. *quid sibi vult.* **ὦ ἄνδρες δικασταί** is the usu. address to the dicasts, but by Socrates used here for the first time. Was there ever a jury so defied and scorned as this that tried Socrates! 9. **πάνυ ἐπὶ σμικροῖς** 'on wholly trivial matters.' See n. on 32,20 for word-order. Prepositions compound with nouns as with verbs. Were *πάνυ* to intervene, it would be, for the Greeks, *tmesis.* **εἴ τι μέλλοιμι** : opt. of past general supposit. H. 894,2. G. 1393,2. 11. **ἅ γε δή** ('*which* to be sure') has a double function—acc. after *οἰηθείη*, nom. with *νομίζεται. οἴομαι* is 'to suppose, imagine, fancy' (see L. & S. and supra, e.g. 38,11,17. 32,20. 28,18, 8,19,27); *νομίζω* is 'to think,' 'have conviction,' 'believe in,' e.g. a creed, the gods, etc., as in 13,10 and freq. 13. **ἕωθεν** : designations of time and place oft. employ *whence* prepositions and adverbs rather than *where*; *ἐκ νυκτός, ἐκ δεξιᾶς*, etc.

40 B 15. **ἐν τῷ λόγῳ** 'during (in the course of) my speech.' 17. **ἐπέσχε** : 38,18. **λέγοντα μεταξύ** 'in the midst (act) of speaking'; H. 976, G. 1572. 18. **πρᾶξιν** 'affair

(matter, business).' 21. **κινδυνεύει**: 7,5. 11,4. 22. 39
οὐκ ἔσθ' ὅπως 'it is impossible that —.'

40 C 25. **οὐ γάρ** *κτλ.*: 19,6. 27. **ἀγαθὸν πράξειν**: intrans. 'to fare in some way (*τι*) well' (Adam). 29. **αὐτό**: we rarely see the unemphatic 'it' expressed; yet here it is necessary. 30. **θάτερον**: H. 77 d, G. 46. **ἢ γὰρ** (*τὸ τεθνάναι ἐστὶν τοιοῦτον*) **οἷον** *κτλ.*: lit. 'for either it is a sort of *being nothing* and having no perception of anything—the dead man (I mean).'
2. **μεταβολή τις** *κτλ.* 'may be some change.' *μετα-* in 40
compos. 32,22. 3. **μετοίκησις . . τοῦ τόπου** 'change (*μετα-*) of residence from, etc.' 4. **τοῦ ἐνθένδε** 'hence' for 'here' (*ἐνταῦθα*). Cf. 26,19. 29,5. 33,12. **καὶ εἴτε** takes up the first alternative. The second follows in li. 20 *εἰ δ' αὖ*. Cf. n. on 28,26.

40 D 5. **οἷον** 'a sort of,' 'as it were.' Cf. the vulgar: "a sleep *like*," "he fell over *like*." 6. **μηδέ** 'not even.' 7. **ἂν εἴη** 'must be'; 14,31. 34,30. 8. **ἂν οἶμαι**: *ἄν* is repeated in 14 and again in 16 before its infin. is reached. 11. **ἀντι-παρα-θέντα** 'after-placing over-against in-comparison.' 12. **δέοι**: repeated from 8; 'had, on consideration (*σκεψάμενον*), to say.' 14. **μὴ** (sc. *λέγω*) **ὅτι** 'not to speak of'; H. 1035 a, G. 1504. 15. **ἀλλά** 'nay.'

40 E 16. **αὐτόν** 'himself,' the great king. Despite exile, beheadings, and other drawbacks, kings popularly stand for the happiest of mortals.

> "The world is so full of a number of things,
> I am sure we should all be as happy as kings."
> R. L. Stevenson.

19. **φαίνεται . . εἶναι**: note inf., not ptc. (11,7). **οὕτω δή** 'under *these* circumstances.' 20. **εἰ δ' αὖ**: 18,30. **ἀποδημῆσαι** = *μετοίκησις*, li. 3. 22. **ὡς ἄρα** 'how namely,' 'how, that is'—a common formula of quotation. 25. **εἰς Ἅιδου**: see n. on *ἐν Ἅιδου* 21,22. **ἀπαλλαγείς**: 35,5. 38,12.

41 A 26. **φασκόντων** 'claiming,' 'alleging.' **τοὺς ἀληθῶς δικαστάς**: adv. for adject. Cf. *πάνυ ὑβριστής* 17,19. H. 641 a, G. 952,1. 27. **οἵπερ καί** 'who indeed' (19,1). 28. **Μίνως** *κτλ.* should stand in the accus. as appositives to *δικαστάς*, but are attracted by the intervening nom. *οἵπερ*. See
Index of Proper Names. 1. **ἐπὶ πόσῳ** 'on what condition?' 41
(22,5); yet oft. it is equiv. to a gen. of price. See L. & S. s.v. *ἐπί*, B III 4. 2. **ἄν** is doubled. **μέν** *solitarium* (29,12) is common with *ἐγώ* (about = *ἔγωγε*), leaving dissent or opposition (*δέ*) unexpressed. 3. **ἐθέλω** 'am willing.' **τεθνάναι**: 20,17. 4. **ἔμοιγε καὶ αὐτῷ** 'for myself personally.' 5. **διατριβή**: 29,10. 35,3.

41 **41 B** 6. **εἴ τις ἄλλος** 'whoever else.' *εἴ τις=ὅστις.* 7. **ἀντι-παρα-βάλλοντι** (c. *ἔμοιγε* in 4) = *ἀντι-παρα-θέντι* 40,11. 9. **οὐκ ἂν ἀηδὴς εἴη**: the sent. has lost its balance—the subordinate clause (*ὁπότε*) running nearly three times as long as the main clause (li. 4). To restore the equilibrium and *recall the main statement*, *οὐκ ἀηδής* (referring to *διατριβή* and merely repeating *θαυμαστή*) is attached by anacoluthon. Cf. notes on 6,25. 18,30. 29,2. 9. **καὶ δή** *κτλ.* 'and then best of all'; see 14,24 for case of *τὸ μέγιστον.* 12. **οἴεται** 'imagines' (39,11). 13. **δἄν**=*δὴ ἄν.* Cf. *ἐπειδάν*; also *μεντἄν* and *τἄν* (-*οι ἄν*).

41 C 18. **ἀμήχανον . . εὐδαιμονίας** 'inexpressible (amount) of happiness.' **πάντως οὐ δήπου**: so 14,29, and cf. 29,4. 19. **τούτου γε ἕνεκα,** sc. *τοῦ διαλέγεσθαι . . καὶ ἐξετάζειν.* 20. **τά τε γὰρ ἄλλα . . καί**: acc. of specif.; for this formula of dispatch, see 20,6. 22. **εἴπερ γε** 'if, that is' (29,2). 24. **πρὸς τὸν θάνατον** 'in view of —.' *πρός faces* its object (23,13). 25. **ἕν τι τοῦτο** *κτλ.* 'to regard one thing, viz. this, as true.' The verb is also in 38,20.

41 D 27. **τελευτήσαντι**: note tense. 28. **πράγματα** 'interests,' 'affairs,' 'fate.' 29. **ἀπὸ τοῦ αὐτομάτου**: 36,20. 30. **τεθνάναι**: used so much heretofore as the equiv. of *ἀποθνῄσκειν*, perhaps here too it is 'to die.' **ἤδη** 'now at length.' 31. **ἀπηλλάχθαι** 'to *be* quit of.' **βέλτιον ἦν** '*would be* better.' In phrases such as *βέλτιον* (*ἄξιον*, *κρεῖττον*, *εἰκός*) *ἦν*, the particle *ἄν* is regularly omitted. See H. 897,
42 G. 1400. 1. **ἀπέτρεψε**: 25,23. 3. **οὐ πάνυ**: 4,13 (litotes). 4. **διανοίᾳ** 'thought,' 'intention.' 5. **τοῦτο αὐτοῖς ἄξιον μέμφεσθαι** 'this it is fair to reproach them with'—inner accus. For the dat. *αὐτοῖς*, see H. 764,2 and G. 1160. Cf. the dat. c. *χαλεπαίνω* li. 3 and *ὀνειδίζετε* 13.

41 E 6. **τοσόνδε μέντοι** 'this much however,' viz. what follows. So *τοιόνδε* 34,8. *τόδε* 36,24.

42 A 19. **πρᾶγμα** 'lot,' 'fate,' 'state,' 'life.' 20. **πλὴν εἰ** in 3,22 was followed by a verb; here, and often, it stands without one, becoming a mere conjunctional 'except.' Cf. *ὁτιοῦν* without verb (21,6).

CRITO

"BUT he caused his associates to despise the established laws, arguing that it was folly to choose the rulers of the city 'by bean,' whereas etc." This, Xenophon says, was one of the charges brought against Socrates by his enemies. *ἀλλὰ . .*

ὑπεροράν ἐποίει τῶν καθεστώτων νόμων τοὺς συνόντας, λέγων ὡς 42
μῶρον εἴη τοὺς μὲν τῆς πόλεως ἄρχοντας ἀπὸ κυάμου καθιστάναι, κυβερνήτῃ δέ κτλ. Mem. I 2,9.

In answer to such charges Plato wrote the *Crito.* In the long delay between his condemnation and its execution, Socrates, with the aid of his many friends and their money, could easily have escaped. But he chose to remain and suffer the law. Why? In this little piece Plato tells why, pitching the reasons so high that there should be thereafter no doubt about the reverent patriotism of his master. Had he criticized the laws and customs of Athens? True. In speech (*λόγῳ*) he might be critical, but in deed (*ἔργῳ*) he was loyal. No man could be more so. He gave his life. The best patriotism is not of the screaming sort that upholds the government right or wrong in speech,—and in action vents itself in firecrackers and pension-drawing.

Crito is a faithful lifelong friend of Socrates, of the same age and deme (supra, 29,6)—a plain man, seeing things from the point of view of daily life and welfare—a man who builds, creates home and family, makes money, laws, and states. But he does not really understand Socrates. They talk together, but he hears not. To the last, Socrates remained, for him, *δαιμόνιος* (45,1). And naturally so. Socrates is of the mountain, Crito of the plain. Crito sees standing in his way merely the jailor, whom he would pass, by putting into his hand a few pieces of silver. But Socrates, like Moses on Sinai, is facing God, whom he cannot pass. And he stands, in that upper silence, isolated from all human friends, and misunderstood, like Antigone. But, like Antigone, he wins the victory—through death.

The piece is rhetorical, and full of assumptions allowed to go untested by dialectic. But we should like to believe that the words are truly those of Socrates. It would mean that even in the head of this lifelong questioner convictions claimed lodgment that had not entered by the door of ratiocination. For observe that nowhere in the *Crito* does he sift out why it is right *now* to obey the laws, when five years earlier he found it right to *disobey* the order of the lawfully established government of the Thirty (supra, 26,30).

43 A 21. **τηνικάδε** ‘at *this* hour.’ Cf. *αὐτίκα* (1,11), *τηνίκα, ἡνίκα,* H. 283, G. 436. **ἤ**: 16,14. 23. **πάνυ μὲν οὖν**: 6,11. *μέν = μήν* (1,15), and *οὖν* is corroborative (23,21). But in answers *μὲν οὖν* together have a special function, viz. *corrective* (= *immo vero*). Hence here it is not merely ‘early’—it is ‘nay, *quite* early.’
1. **πηνίκα μάλιστα**: 43
πηνίκα asks the preciso time, the hour, or minute; *πότε* is more indefinite. *μάλιστα* with numerals or as here = ‘about.’

43 2. **ὄρθρος βαθύς** (cf. *ὄρ-νυμι*, *or-ior*, Or-ient (the land of the *rising* sun)) is 'deep-dawn,' i.e. still dark. Cf. 106,2.
3. **ὅπως** 'how it was that—' (indir. quest.). 4. **ὑπακοῦσαι**: the usual verb for 'to hear and *answer*' a door-summons.
5. **ἤδη** 'by this time.' 6. **καί τι καί** 'and . . too.' *τι* (inner accus. retained with pass. voice. H. 725 c, G. 1239) was doubtless a "tip." 9. **ἐπιεικῶς** 'fairly (long ago)'; 9,12. 30,17. 33,10. 10. **εἶτα** : 19,26. **πῶς** 'how is it that—?' or briefly 'why?'

43 B 10. **ἐπ-ήγειρας**: *-εγείρω*. 12. Crito does not answer 'why' till li. 16. 'No, by Zeus, [I did not waken you] nor would I myself have willed to sit etc.,' i.e. he too would have slept, had it been possible. 14. **ἀλλὰ καί** 'but besides.' In addition to the fact that it was bad enough for *one* to watch, there was 'besides' another reason.
σοῦ πάλαι θαυμάζω : *σου* directly with the verb ; G. 1102 (and cf. 1,7). *πάλαι* with the pres. tense 'have been *this long time* wondering'; H. 826, G. 1258. **αἰσθανόμενος ὡς** 'seeing how' (*ὅπως*), 'seeing the way.' 16. **ἵνα . . διάγῃς**: subjunct, not opt., though after a past tense ; G. 1369, H. 881 (needs revision), *διάγω* we had in 41,11. **καὶ πολλάκις**: *καί* is prob. adverb, as in *καὶ πάνυ* and the rest (3,1). For the foll. *μὲν δὴ . . δέ*, cf. 13,11. 46,1. 168,21.
17. **καὶ πρότερον** : 3,1. 18. **τοῦ τρόπου** : a gen. of cause ; H. 744, G. 1126. 19. **παρ-εστώσῃ** : 2nd perf. ptc. (*ἑστώς*). **ὡς ῥᾳδίως** 'so easily.' (*ὡς* is usu. said to be for *ὅτι οὕτως*. See App. for a diff. explanation.) 21. **πλημ-μελές**: see on 10,19. 22. **ἀγανακτεῖν** 'to repine.' **τηλικοῦτον**: 15,21. **ἤδη** 'at length.'

43 C 24. **καί** is adv., not conjunct. 26. **ἐπιλύεται** 'frees,' 'absolves,' construed like verbs of *hindering*, with infin. with or without art. (38,18). 26. **μὴ οὐχί** : the infin. is doubly negatived when the verb of hindering is itself negatived : H. 1034 a, G. 1616. 27. **τῇ . . τύχῃ** : cause
44 (30,14). 2. **ἐν τοῖς βαρύτατα** '*about* the hardest'—a limited superlat. (not "strengthened," as H. 652 has it). See L. & S. s.v. *ὁ ἡ τό*, A VIII 7. (Originally *τοῖς* was a demonstrat. with definite reference 'them,' as *πρὸ τοῦ* meant 'before *that.*' Later both phrases became stereotyped ; *ἐν τοῖς* could even be used with a femin. context (e.g. *ἐν τοῖς πλεῖσται δὴ νῆες* 'about the most ships') and *πρὸ τοῦ* meant merely 'formerly.' Cf. the formal "it" in : You'll catch it, Plague take it, He lords it over us. 4. **τὸ πλοῖον** : *what* boat is told in *Phaedo* infra 65,11.

43 D 6. **οὔτοι δή** 'well (*δή*) no, faith (*τοι*), it has not—.' **ἀλλὰ . . μέν** ('*at . . certe*'; *μέν solitar.* = *μήν*) is a common formula after a negat. clause, as here. 9. **ἐκ . . τῶν**

ἀγγέλων, i.e. 'from what they *report*.' 10. **δή** 'of course.' 44
εἰς αὔριον: *εἰς* to us seems often useless, as in *εἰς ἑσπέραν* '*in* the evening,' *εἰς τρίτην* '*on* the third day,' *ἐς τέλος* '*at* last.' See L. & S. s.v., II 2 end. Cf., for the other point of view (viz. -*θεν*), *ἕωθεν* 39,13. 12. **τύχῃ ἀγαθῇ** 'good luck!'—a common wish-formula. **ταύτῃ** (adv.) 'if *so* the gods will, so let it be.' 13. **μέντοι**: 1,20.

44 A 16. **που**: n. on 2,6. **ὑστεραίᾳ** is comparat. in sense, hence a foll. genit. or, as here, *ἤ*. Dat. of time; H. 782, G. 1192. 18. **φασί γέ τοι δή** 'well (*δή*) certainly (*τοι*) they *say* (*γε*) so.' The *κύριοι* are the *ἕνδεκα*; cf. 34,25. 19. **τοίνυν**: 16,19. **τῆς ἐπ-ιούσης ἡμέρας** 'the (oncoming, i.e.) approaching'; it was already 'deep dawn.'. Gen. of time *within which* (cf. 35,24). 20. **τῆς ἑτέρας** 'the next day,' i.e. 'to-morrow.' 22. **ταύτης τῆς νυκτός** epexegetic to *ὀλίγον πρότερον* 'a little while ago.' **κινδυνεύεις**: 7,5. **ἐν καιρῷ τινι**: usu. without *τινί*='opportunely.' *With τινί*, it is a case of litotes (4,13)='not inopportunely.' 24. **δὲ δή** 'well but' (13,28).

44 B 26. **λευκὰ ἱμάτια**, hence, for a Greek, a messenger of joy. 27. **ἤματί κεν** *κτλ.*: from *Il.* 9,363 (but *ἱκοίμην* for *ἵκοιο*). Achilles, minded to desert the siege of Troy, says that with a fair wind on the third day he would reach fertile Phthia his home. Socrates, believer as he was in the significance of dreams (cf. 44,21. 70,11), would here interpret significantly for himself each item—time, destination, event. 29. **ἄτοπον** 'strange,' 'queer.' 30. **ἐναργές** 'clear,' 'plain.' **μὲν οὖν** corrective (42,23), 'nay rather.' 1. **ὦ** 45
δαιμόνιε: one whose words or deeds could not be accounted for by ordinary human motives was often addressed as *ὦ δαιμόνιε*; i.e. he was 'possessed by a *δαίμων*,' he was 'peculiar,' 'queer,' 'strange,' 'cracked.' The address was used in fun or earnest, anger or admiration, reproach, expostulation, or flattery. 2. **ἔτι καὶ νῦν** 'even yet.' 3. **ὡς**: causal; 'since.' 5. **χωρὶς μὲν . . ἔτι δέ** (7) instead of *χωρὶς δέ* as in *Phaedo* 76,26. It is not a single calamity, but two separate ones, first a deprivation of you, etc. **ἐστερῆσθαι** is used as a noun (sc. *ἐστί*); the perf. gives the pres. state (10, 7). 6. **οὐδένα μήποτε εὑρήσω** 'shall never never find'; H. 1032, G. 1360. See 22,12 for aor. subjunct. 7. **ἔτι δὲ καί**: 3,16. 8. **μή**, not *οὐ*: 8,28. **ὡς οἷόσ τ' ὤν** 'in the belief that (1,10) I was able' to save you, they will think that I neglected it. *ὡς* gives the ground for their judgment of neglect.

44 C 9. **καίτοι**: 1,5. 10. **ταύτης**, sc. *τῆς δόξης* 'reputation,' explained by *ἤ δοκεῖν* 'viz. than to —.' 11.

45 **περὶ πλείονος ποιεῖσθαι**: 9,5. 13. **οὐκ ἠθέλησας** 'refused.' 15. **τί** 'why.' **ὦ μακάριε**: see L. & S. Note the various forms of address *ὦ δαιμόνιε* (1), *ὠγαθέ* (14,2), *ὦ βέλτιστε* (14,4). 16. **δόξης** 'opinion.' **μέλει**: c. gen. et dat. (13,19). 17. **ἐπιεικέστατοι** 'fairest,' 'most reasonable'; cf. 9,12. 30,17. **ὧν**: c. *φροντίζειν*; 15,3. 20,20. 18. **αὐτά** 'it' 'the matter,' vaguely. **ὥσπερ ἂν πραχθῇ** 'just as it *may* be done.'

44 D 21. **αὐτά** 'just,' 'exactly.' 22. **δῆλα**: person. construct. (2,26). **ὅτι** *κτλ.* 'viz. that,' by anacoluthon; for he begins: 'it is plain that just the present situation is . . ' but dropping *τὰ παρόντα*, he substitutes *οἱ πολλοί*. 24. **σχεδόν**: 12,26. 30,2. **ἐν** 'among,' or (in its law-court use) 'before.' 26. **εἰ γὰρ ὤφελον**: H. 871 a, G. 1512–13. *γάρ* is *not* 'for.' 27. **ἵνα . . ἦσαν** 'that they might have been': why the indic. after *ἵνα*? H. 884, G. 1371. Cf. *ἐτεθράμμην* (2,19) and *ἔμελλεν* (6,4). 28. **καλῶς . . εἶχε**: 2,16. 29. **νῦν δέ**: 6,6.—Socrates regards the masses as children, in their irresponsibility and in their valuations. They, and Crito, look upon death as the greatest evil. (What death is, or may be, he has discussed in the *Apology*.) As for him, the greatest good is wisdom, the greatest evil ignorance. And if *that* be the domain of good and evil, the masses are ineffectual for either. They cannot make a man wise or foolish (li. 30). 31. **τύχωσι**, sc. *ποιοῦντες*: i.e. they treat him at haphazard, do with him as the moment suggests. For us, *τοῦτο* seems
46 needlessly precise, as was *οὕτω* before *ὥσπερ* in li. 18. 1. **ταῦτα . . τάδε**: 36,24. The scheme *μὲν δὴ . . δέ* is freq. in transitions. Cf. 99,21. 214,6.

44 E 2. **μή**: in quest. 14,14. 20,20. 3. **προμηθεῖ**: c. gen., as *φροντίζω* 45,17. 4. **μή** 'lest,' as aft. verbs of *fearing*. 6. **ὡς**: c. ptc. (1,10). 7. The scheme is probably:

$$\text{ἀναγκασθῶμεν}\begin{cases}\text{ἢ καὶ . . , ἢ . . ,}\\ \text{ἢ καὶ . . .}\end{cases}$$

For the symmetrical but superfluous *καί*'s, cf. those in relat. and main clause (10,7) as, e.g. Xen. *Anab.* II 1,22 *καὶ ἡμῖν ταὐτὰ δοκεῖ ἅπερ καὶ βασιλεῖ*. 7. **οὐσίαν** 'property' (*ὤν*, **οὖσα**, *ὄν*). **ἀποβαλεῖν** 'to lose.' 8. **πρός**: 11,22.

45 A 9. **ἔασον αὐτὸ χαίρειν** 'bid it goodbye,' 'dismiss it.' See L. & S. s.v. *χαίρω*, III, & V 2. 10. **που**: 44,16. **δίκαιοί ἐσμεν** '*it* is right etc.' (2,26). 11. **σώσαντες** '*in* saving'; for tense, see H. 856 b, G. 1290. 12. **ἀλλά**: c. imperat. (38,30). 13. **καὶ μὴ ἄλλως ποίει**: cf. our 'and don't be contrary.' 14. **ταῦτα προμηθοῦμαι**: an

inner acc. H. 716 b, G. 1054. Cf. the genit. in li. 3. 46
16. **μήτε**: where is its correlative? **τοίνυν**: 16,19. **καὶ γάρ**: 4,3. 19. **τούτους**: scornful. **ὡς εὐτελεῖς** 'how cheap (they are).' 21. **σοὶ δὲ ὑπάρχει μέν** 'you have, to *begin* with'—answered by *ἔπειτα* in next line.

45 B 22. **ἱκανά**: appositive. **ἔπειτα καί** 'then too.' 24. **καί** 'in fact,' 'actually.' Cf. 35,23. 38,1. 25. **ἐπ' αὐτὸ τοῦτο** 'for this very purpose.' 27. **μήτε** is a repetition from li. 16. **ὅπερ λέγω**: 1,17. 28. **ἀποκάμῃς** 'become weary' seems here misused. Socrates had made no efforts to escape. G. M. T. § 903,3 translates, but not without violence. **μήτε** is at last the correl. from li. 16. **ὃ ἔλεγες**, viz. in 35,7 ff. 30. **ἐξελθών**, i.e. from the country. Cf. 35,8. **ὅ τι χρῷο σαυτῷ**: H. 777, G. 1183. *ὅ τι* is an inner acc.; 'would not have anything to do,' 'would not know what to do with yourself.' 31. **καί**: adv., not conjunct. **ἄλλοσε** (by attract. of *ὅποι*, 'wherever else') for *ἄλλο-θι* with *πολλαχοῦ* 'many another place.'

45 C 5. **οὐδέ** 'not . . either.' Note emphasis of *δίκαιον*, 47
by separation from *πρᾶγμα*. 7. **ἐξόν**: acc. absol. (13,26). 11. **πρὸς δὲ τούτοις** (11,22) adds an item, as did *ἔτι δέ*, li. 5. 13. **ἐκ-θρέψαι καὶ ἐκ-παιδεῦσαι**: *ἐκ-* is 'to bring to an issue,' 'to complete' the action of the verb.

45 D 14. **τὸ σὸν μέρος**: adv. acc. (H. 719 a, G. 1060) 'for *your* part,' 'so far as *you* concern yourself.' **τύχωσι**, sc. *πράττοντες*; cf. 45,31. **πράξουσι**: intrans. 'to fare' (39,27). As in 45,31 the *τοῦτο* (inner acc.) is not needed in Engl.; 'they will fare as hap will.' 21. **φάσκοντα**: 40,26. 22. **δή** = sarcastic (17,24).

45 E 24. **μή** 'lest' (46,4). 25. **τῇ ἡμετέρᾳ** 'on our part,' keeping Greek order. 26. **καὶ ἡ εἴσοδος** *κτλ.*: 'the whole affair' (25) is here itemized by three *καί*'s, and in terms that would seem to allude as well to the dramatic stage as to the court, viz. *εἴσοδος* (the 'entrance' upon the stage, and the 'opening' of a suit—see L. & S.); *ἀγών* ('contest-debate,' a regular part of the old Attic comedy, and 'trial' of a case at law); and *κατάγελως* the laugh at the end of the farce (hardly a play on *καταστροφή* the 'catastrophe' in the plot, since this term seems to have been of later origin). 27. **ὡς εἰσῆλθεν** and 28 **ὡς ἐγένετο**: *ὡς* 'how,' 'as' (the relat. of *πῶς* which asks for the *manner*) recalls the *details.* At each point they might have fought the proceedings. 28. **καὶ τὸ τελευταῖον δὴ τουτί** *κτλ.* 'and now (*δή*) this *finale* here (-*ί*), a sort of *reductio ad absurdum*'—the last added bitterly; for by 'this *finale*' he means the imprisonment and death of his friend. *τουτί* is the last of the three items in apposit. to *πρᾶγμα* (25) which had

47 δόξῃ (24) for its verb. But δόξῃ is now left so far behind that it is resumed in δοκεῖν (31) though the *syntax* that is resumed is that of πεπρᾶχθαι which is dependent upon δόξῃ—anacoluthic, but entirely clear: 'lest this *finale* may seem to have given us the slip.' Note that ἀνανδρίᾳ (25) is also picked up again in 30. For δια-πεφευγέναι, see 37,20.

46 A 31. **οἵτινες**: why the *indefinite* relat. when the antecedent (here, ἡμᾶς) is definite? It often stands, as does ὅς γε, when the clause is causal ('seeing that we —,' *ut qui*, *quippe*
48 *qui*). Here the clause explains the charge of ἀνανδρία. 1. **οἷόντε ὄν**: accus. absol., 'feasible.' 2. **καὶ μικρόν**: 20,1. 3. **μή** 'lest'; H. 887 c, G. 1378. 5. **μᾶλλον δέ** 'or rather,' *vel potius*, the regular phrase to introduce some correction of statement. Note **οὐ-δέ** (2,5). 6. **βεβουλεῦσθαι** 'to *be* decided'; so πεπρᾶχθαι in 7, '*be* done.' 8. **περιμενοῦμεν**: significance of fut. indic. in condit. clause? (20,11).

46 B 13. **ὅσῳ . . τοσούτῳ**: 22,30. 16. **ὡς**: causal. 17. **οἷος**: c. infin.; 24,25. **τῶν ἐμῶν**: τὰ ἐμά is equiv. to 'me'; 'listen to nothing else in myself.' 18. **λόγῳ** 'argument.' 19. **ἐν τῷ ἔμπροσθεν** = πρὸ τοῦ, 'heretofore.' Cf. 19,17. 20. **ἐκβαλεῖν** 'throw over,' 'repudiate.' 21. **σχεδόν** oft. takes a τι with no perceptible diff. of meaning; 'pretty nearly.'

46 C 23. **οὕσπερ καί**: superflu. καί in relat. clause (10,7). **ὧν** 'than which.' 24. **εὖ ἴσθι**: 7,1. 25. **οὐ μή**: c. aor. subjunct.; 22,12. **ἄν** = ἐάν. **πλείω** (nt. plur.) goes with μορμολύττηται (27): 'bugaboo us more bugaboos.' Or, to keep Greek order, transl. as adv. '*more* than at present . . it bugaboo us.' 26. **ὥσπερ παῖδας ἡμᾶς**: the comparison coming first (as so freq. all relat. clauses do) is almost like an adj. to ἡμᾶς. The effect of the order is rather 'us children' than 'us, *like* children.' 27. **δεσμούς** 'imprisonments' (δεσμά neut. is 'chains'). To pluralize an abstract subst. is to render it concrete. We see it in the working; H. 636. 29. **πῶς οὖν ἄν** κτλ.: lines 11–28 form a προ-οίμιον ('preface'). Socrates *now* proceeds to formal argument. With **πρῶτον μέν** (30) he properly enough takes up and answers Crito's *first* argument (p. 45) on 'what people will think of us,' closing at 51,31. **αὐτά**: 45,18. 30. **ἀναλάβοιμεν**: 4,16.

49 46 D 4. **κατάδηλος** refers to λόγος (48,30). **ἄρα** 'forsooth' (1,14). **ἄλλως ἕνεκα λόγου** 'idly, for talk's sake'; pleonasm (3,1). See L. & S. for this idiomatic sense of ἄλλως, s.v. II 3. 5. **παιδιὰ καὶ φλυαρία**: the latter was used in 4,30; the verb for the former in 7,1. 17,29. 6. **ὡς ἀληθῶς**: 6,14. 7. **τι** 'at all,' 'somewhat'; adv. acc.

8. **ὧδε ἔχω** 'am in this present condition.' 9. **ἐάσομεν** 49
χαίρειν: 46,9. 10. **ἐγῷμαι**: 34,11. 11. **οἰομένων**:
39,11. **τι λέγειν**: n. on 23,12. **νῦν δή**: 34,27.

46 E 14. **πρὸς θεῶν**: tone of the oath? (15,7). 15. **ὅσα γε τἀνθρώπεια,** sc. *ἐστίν* 'in all human probability,' 'humanly speaking' (Dyer). Cf. the (also relat.) clause *ὡς τὸ εἰκός* 47,15. 16. **ἐκτός**: with *τοῦ μέλλειν*: lit. 'beyond the likelihood.'

47 A 18. **ἱκανῶς . . λέγεσθαι** 'adequately argued.' 19. **πάσας**: why emphatic? (1,14). 23. **οὐκοῦν . . τιμᾶν,** sc. *ὅτι χρή* (from 19) 'that we must therefore —.' On *οὐκοῦν*, see 18,16.

47 B 30. **τοῦτο πράττων** 'working at this,' viz. athletics,
'making this his business' (cf. *πρᾶγμα* in 6,20 and 62,3 or
ἐπιτήδευμα 19,27). 31. **παντὸς ἀνδρός** 'any- and every-
body': see n. on *πᾶν ποιῶν* 37,14. 2. **παιδοτρίβης** 50
'trainer' in gymnastic. 6. **ἀσπάζεσθαι** 'welcome (gratefully)'; cf. 22,10. 7. **ἀλλὰ μή** '*and* not'; 11,31. 16,8. 26,6. 9. **ἄρα**: inferential; 14,17. 16,24. **αὐτῷ**: so-called dat. of agent with verbals; n. on 9,6. 10. **καὶ . . γε** 'aye . . too,' 'aye even—.' **ἐδεστέον** and **ποτέον**: verbals of *ἐσθίω* (*ἔδομαι*) and *πίνω* (aor. pass. *ἐπόθην*). 11. **ἐπιστάτῃ** as if equiv. to *ἐπιστήμονι*. Cf. 110,13. **ἐπαΐοντι**: used in 4,31.

47 C 16. **καὶ μηδὲν ἐπαϊόντων**: added to *τῶν πολλῶν after the closure of the syntactic unit τοὺς τῶν πολλῶν λόγους*. Cf. *καὶ πράως* in 43,20. Such *post-scripts* (as we may call them) should be carefully indicated by the voice, in reading. See Index for examples, s. v. Word-order. 18. **πῶς γὰρ οὔ;** a *γάρ* that is *not* a *γάρ* (i.e. it is not 'for'). Lit. 'sure, how not?' See 5,3. 20. **τείνει**: L. & S. s v., B III 2. **τῶν τοῦ ἀπειθοῦντος**: cf. *τῶν ἐμῶν* 48,17. 23. **καὶ τἆλλα οὕτως,** sc. *ἔχει*. 24. **καὶ δὴ καί** 'and so too,' 'and then too,' 'and now too.' After the dispatching *τἆλλα* (see n. on 20,6), *καὶ δὴ καί* leads at once to the point. Cf. (though not the same) 2,20. 17,10.

47 D 31. **εἰ μὴ ἀκολουθήσομεν**: tone of the fut. indic.?
(20,11). 1. **ἐκεῖνο**: anteced. of *ὅ* in next line. **καὶ** 51
λωβησόμεθα: a "postscript" to *διαφθεροῦμεν*; 50,16. 43,20. 2. **τῷ δικαίῳ, τῷ ἀδίκῳ** 'right,' 'wrong'—more concrete names than the abstract *δικαιοσύνη, ἀδικία*. **ἐγίγνετο, ἀπώλλυτο**: past tense, referring to their old talks. 5. **τό** here fuses many words into one substantive phrase:

τὸ { *ὑπὸ τοῦ ὑγιεινοῦ μὲν βέλτιον γιγνόμενον*
{ *ὑπὸ τοῦ νοσώδους δὲ διαφθειρόμενον.*

51 By commoner usage *μέν* and *δέ* should stand after *ὑπό*. Again in *τοῦ ὑγιεινοῦ* and *τοῦ νοσώδους*, we have the more concrete for *ὑγιείας*, *νόσου*. 7. **διολέσωμεν**: tragic and Platonic is *δι-όλλυμι* for *ἀπ-όλλυμι*. **πειθόμενοι μή**: a negat. *after* its verb is in unusual and hence emphatic position; 'by heeding *not* the opinion of those who know' suggests an antithesis easily guessed.

47 E 9. **διεφθαρμένου αὐτοῦ** comes round again to the first clause *ἐάν κτλ*. Such returns we have had in 6,25. 18,30. 29,2. 41,9. 10. **που**: n. on 2,6. **τοῦτο** is subject, *τὸ σῶμα* predicate. 15. **ἐκείνου**: anteced. of *ᾧ*. What proves its emphasis? (1,14). 18. **τῶν ἡμετέρων** 'in us' (48,17).

48 A 19. **περὶ ὅ** *κτλ*. 'with which . . has to do.' 24. **ἄρα**: inferential. **ὦ βέλτιστε**: not here ironical, as in 14,4. **πάνυ . . οὕτω** did not, I think, belong together for the Greeks (not 'so wholly'), but rather 'altogether . . in this fashion,' sc. as Crito would wish. *οὐκ . . πάνυ* is litotes; 'not altogether mindful' means 'not mindful at all.' 25. **ἐροῦσι**: with two accus., 'will say *of* us.' 27. **πρῶτον μέν**: repeated from 48,30 and closing Socrates' argument on the first point. 28. **εἰσηγεῖ** (-*ηγέομαι*) ('to introduce') 'suggest,' 'propose.' 31. **ἀλλὰ μὲν δή**: *ἀλλὰ δή*, *ἀλλὰ γάρ*, *ἀλλὰ νὴ Δία* often introduce an objection anticipated from the opponent —here with a confirmatory *μέν* (=*μήν*) inserted; 'but surely
52 then,' 'well but surely.' Cf. *ἀλλὰ δή* 34,29. 1. **τις** is oft. not so innocently indefinite as it looks. *This τις* is Crito, who said what is here said in 45,20 ff. 2. **ἀποκτιννύναι**: 24,3 for form.

48 B 3. **δῆλα δὴ καὶ ταῦτα** 'plain enough that too'; i.e. this *objection* to disregarding the world's opinion was as plain as the argument of Socrates in *favour* of disregarding it—perhaps, to Crito, plainer. 5. **ἀληθῆ λέγεις** 'it is true (*τις* might say that).' **ὦ θαυμάσιε**: 17,1. 6. **οὗτός τε** *κτλ*. 'not merely this argument . . but again etc.' (*καὶ τόνδε αὖ*). **ἔμοιγε δοκεῖ** *κτλ*. 'in *my* judgment stands valid as before,' in spite of what a *τις* may say. For *καί*='as' aft. words denoting similarity and identity, as here *ὅμοιος*, see L. & S. s.v., A III. 8. **τόνδε**: 'the following' old discussion is not rehearsed at length, as was the previous one; Crito is merely asked if he still subscribes to its conclusions. 12. The contemporaries of Socrates did not all by any means identify *τὸ εὖ καὶ καλῶς ζῆν* with *τὸ δικαίως ζῆν*. 15. **οὐκοῦν** 'accordingly' (18,16). **τῶν ὁμολογουμένων**, i.e. the conclusions of the two old discussions to which Crito has given *fresh* assent (present tense). 17. **μὴ ἀφιέντων** 'if —' (*μή* conditional).

48 C 20. **ἃς δὲ σὺ λέγεις**: to this is added the apposit. *τὰς* 52
σκέψεις, by which *ἃς* (for *ἅ*) is antecedently attracted. The whole is thus fused into a single clause: 'as for the considerations you urge.' Socrates here dispatches in six lines Crito's second argument (p. 46) and his third *set* of arguments (beginning at *ἔτι* 47,5), that he may discuss in full (beginning at 26) what he has decided is the only question for him—*πότερον δίκαιον ἢ οὐ δίκαιον* (li. 16). 21. **ἀναλώσεως**: the noun of the verb *ἀναλίσκω*. 22. **μὴ . . ᾖ**: 37,21. 23. **σκέμματα** = *σκέψεις* in 20. 24. **καὶ . . γε**: 50,10. **ἂν** c. ptc. stands for *ἄν* c. imperf. indic., as shown by the protasis following, *εἰ οἷοίτ' ἦσαν* (H. 987 b, G. 1308,2); 'who would restore-to-life.' Note *ἀνα-* in compos. = Lat. prefix *re-* (*red-do*, *red-eo*). 25. **οὐδενὶ ξὺν νῷ**: for order, cf. 32,20. 39,9. 26. **ἡμῖν**: by posit. at head in sharp contrast to *τῶν πολλῶν* just preceding. **ὁ λόγος . . αἱρεῖ** 'prevails,' 'wins.' Plato constantly thus personifies, even deifies, *ὁ λόγος* 'reason' or 'the argument.' **μή**, as in 22, 'perhaps,' 'maybe.' 27. **νῦν δή**: 34,27. 28. **καὶ . . καί**: correlat. **τελοῦντες**: 5,29.

48 D 29. **ἐξάξουσι**: note tense. 30. **ἐξάγοντες**, i.e. Crito and the others who metaphorically *ἐξάγουσι*, by paying money to those who shall literally *ἐξάγειν* (29). **τῇ ἀληθείᾳ**:
11,12. 1. **φαινώμεθα**: c. ptc., not infin. (10,3). 2. 53
ὑπολογίζεσθαι: used in 19,31. 20,24. 4. **πρὸ τοῦ ἀδικεῖν**: cf. 20,25. 21,25. 6. Fine talk! but what to *do*? **δρῶμεν**: for mood, see 34,22.

48 E 9. **παῦσαι**: imperat. mid. 10. **μακάριε**: 45,15. 13. **ἄκοντος**, sc. *σου* 'without your approval.' **δὲ δή**: 13,28. 15. **πειρῶ**: imperat.

49 A 17. **ἀλλά** 'well.' 19. **τινὶ μέν**: why emphatic? (1,14). 22. **ἡμῖν**: dat. of "agent" (9,22). 24. **πᾶσαι**: emphasised (by posit.), because it is to be contrasted with *ὀλίγαις*. Cf. 4,9. **ἡμῖν**: the dat. properly consorts with the verb, as the genit. with nouns. Here, so far from the verb and so ensconced in the group *πᾶσαι . . ὁμολογίαι*, the dat. *ἡμῖν* is rather 'of ours.' 25. **ἐκ-κε-χυμέναι** (*χέω*) 'thrown away' (overboard). 26. **πάλαι**: with *ἐλάθομεν* in 28. **ἄρα** 'forsooth.' **γέροντες ἄνδρες**: *γέρων* and other names denoting age (e.g. *παρθένος*, *νεανίας*) are connected with *ἀνήρ* (*γυνή*) as adjectives. (This class of words should be added to those mentioned by H. 625 a.) 27. **σπουδῇ**: 13,16. **διαλεγόμενοι** 'when —.'

49 B 1. **εἴτε καί**: for the added *καί*, see n. on *ἢ . . ἢ καί* 54
19,1. 6. **οὐ δῆτα**: 15,17.

54 **49 C** 11. **τί δὲ δή**: 14,12. **κακουργεῖν** 'to do injury' and *ἀδικεῖν* 'to do wrong' seem about synonymous. But it is clear that the new term is introduced as in some way (perhaps by popular usage) more applicable to the act under consideration (*ἀποδιδράσκειν*), or, more generally, to the relation between individual and state. 13. **δήπου**: a reluctant 'I suppose.' 14. **τί δέ;** without *δή* here. The transition from *κακουργεῖν* to *ἀντικακουργεῖν* is too slight. 18. **γάρ που**: 44,16. 46,10. 21. **κακῶς ποιεῖν** merely replaces *κακουργεῖν*. From *ἀντ-αδικεῖν*, supply *ἀντι-*, as if *ἀντι-κακως-ποιεῖν*. 23. **καθομολογῶν** 'in giving entire (*κατα-*) assent.' See n. on *καταδέομαι* 29,13. 24. **ὅπως**: c. subjunct. aft. *ὅρα*, for the reg. fut. indic.; H. 885 b, G. 1374. **παρὰ δόξαν**: n. on 1,16 and cf. *paradox*.

49 D 25. **ὀλίγοις τισί** *κτλ.* For antiquity at large the *lex talionis* prevailed. Recall the prayer of Cyrus (X. *Anab.* I 9,11) *τοσοῦτον χρόνον ζῆν ἔστε* ('until') *νικῴη καὶ τοὺς εὖ καὶ τοὺς κακῶς ποιοῦντας ἀλεξόμενος.* 27. **οὐκ ἔστι κοινὴ βουλή**: the dissidence still exists. 30. **εὖ μάλα**: we reverse in Engl. 31. **ἀρχώμεθα**: note subjunct. (34,22). **ἐντεῦθεν**:
55 explained by the foll. gen. absol. 2. **πάσχοντα** 'when —.' 3. **ἀντιδρῶντα** 'by —.'

49 E 7. **τὸ μετὰ τοῦτο** 'the next point.' Cf. 18,13 *τὸ ἐπὶ τούτῳ γε ἀπόκριναι.* 9. **ἀλλὰ λέγε** 'do but go on' (pres. tense). 11. **μᾶλλον δέ**: 48,5. 12. **τῳ**=*τινί*. 15. **ἐκ** 'as a result of'; cf. 52,15. 16. **μή**: conditional.

50 A 17. **καὶ ταῦτα**: 17,17. 22. **οὐ γὰρ ἐννοῶ**: he did not *wish* to 'understand.' 23. **μέλλουσιν ἡμῖν**: dat. with *ἐλθόντες*. The scheme:

μέλλουσιν { *εἴτε ἀποδιδράσκειν*
εἴτε . .

24. **ὅπως δεῖ** *κτλ.* 'however we should name it.' 26. **τὸ κοινὸν τῆς πόλεως** 'the commonwealth.' **ἐπιστάντες**: the verb is freq. used of visions in dreams. See L. & S., B III. 28. **ἄλλο τι ἤ**: 13,21.

56 **50 B** 30. **τὸ σὸν μέρος**: 47,14. 1. **εἶναι** 'exist.' **ἀνατετράφθαι** (*-τρέπω*): note the tense (10,7). 2. **δίκαι** 'judgments,' not 'lawsuits' (the usu. Att. sense). 7. **ἀπολλυμένου** pres. tense (the action is incomplete) = 'in danger of annulment.' "It was a usage at Athens, whenever a law was about to be repealed, to appoint proper *συνήγοροι* (advocates) to defend it" (Wagner)—hence the reference to the *ῥήτωρ* in li. 6.

50 C 9. **γάρ** 'surely.' 13. **καὶ ταῦτα**, viz. the right to criticize the judgments. pronouncing them unjust.

ὡμολόγητο: as the perf. tense gives the present state, so the 56
pluperfect a past state; '*was* that too in the agreement?' **ἡμῖν**: 9,22. 15. **αὐτῶν θαυμάζοιμεν λεγόντων** 'wonder at their speaking' (lit. '*them* speaking'); for gen. c. *θαυμάζω* cf. 1,7. 43,14. 17. **μὴ θαύμαζε . . ἀποκρίνου**: Socrates is represented as loath to answer; hence the present tense: 'don't be expressing your surprise etc.' Cf. 18,6. 15,14. 18. **καί** 'in truth.' 19. **τί ἐγκαλῶν** *κτλ*. 'what is your charge against us that you—.' The ptc. in the Greek quest. is for us the main verb; cf. 12,3. H. 1012.

50 D 21. **δι' ἡμῶν**: *διά* c. gen.; 2,10. 22. **ἐλάμβανε** 'took to wife' (Adam). 23. **ἐφύτευσε** 'begot.' **φράσον**: the aor. imperat. aft. the pres. as in 18,13. 24. **τοῖς νόμοις . . μέμφει τι**: 42,6. 25. **ὡς** 'on the ground of' (1,10). 30. **μουσικῇ**: not in the narrow modern sense. It denoted the whole Greek schooling of the mind—reading, writing, arithmetic, poetry committed to memory, and lyre-playing. See infra p. 264.

50 E 2. **ἐξ-ετράφης**: 47,13. 3. **ἡμέτερος**: emphatic 57
by posit., equiv. in Engl. to a repetition: '*our* offspring and *our* slave.' 6. **ἐξ ἴσου** was to the Greek an adv. 'equally,' *ἴσως* the proper adv. having come to be used chiefly as 'perhaps.' Literally here: 'are equally to you and us.' Transl.: 'that you and we have equal rights.' 7. **ἅττα** = *ἅτινα*; H. 280 b, G. 426. 9. **πρός**: c. *τὸν πατέρα* 'in relation to' (8,14). **ἄρα** 'forsooth.' 10. **καὶ πρὸς τὸν δεσπότην**: a postscript to *πρὸς τὸν πατέρα* (50,16). 12. **πάσχοις**: 39,9 for mood. 13. **κακῶς ἀκούοντα**: H. 820, G. 1241. **ἀντιλέγειν** 'to talk *back*.'

51 A 15. **ἄρα**: repeated from 9. **ἐξέσται**: the scheme will show what this (in the affirm. clause) corresponds to in the negat. clause:

{ *πρὸς μὲν ἄρα τὸν πατέρα* | *οὐκ-ἐξ-ἴσου-ἦν-τὸ-δίκαιον*
{ *πρὸς δὲ ἄρα τὴν πατρίδα* | *ἐξέσται*— ·

'Can it be that in relation to your father you did *not* have the right, while in relation to your country it shall be permitted you —?' **ἐξέσται ὥστε**: impersonal verbs usu. take a subject-infin., but *ὥστε* sometimes intervenes (G. M. T. § 588). Here, therefore, we expect after *ὥστε* an infin. But the sent. is long—or so great an inconsistency is emerging between behaviour towards parent and behaviour towards state that the speaker is carried away by his feeling—but, whatever the reason, the sent. breaks (anacoluthon), and the *indic.* fut. is used instead (li. 19 *ἐπιχειρήσεις*). 16. **σέ**: emphatic. 17. **καὶ σὺ δέ** 'why, you too'; *δέ* in apodosis (35,29). 20. **ποιῶν . . πράττειν** 'do . . act.' **ὁ τῇ ἀληθείᾳ**

57 κτλ. with great scorn. 21. **σοφός**: a sneering reminder of the name he had acquired (11,1)—'*Professor* Socrates.'

51 B 25. **μοίρᾳ**: L. & S. s.v., IV 2. 26. **σέβεσθαι**, sc. *τινά*. 30. **ἐάντε τύπτεσθαι** κτλ.: apposit. explanation of *παθεῖν*. 31. **ἐάν τε**: *τε* is not much used "solitarium,"
58 to connect clauses as here and in 60,10. 1. **τρωθησόμενον**: *τι-τρώ-σκω*. 3. **ὑπεικτέον** κτλ. are all military terms.

51 C 6. **πείθειν**: supply *δεῖ* from *ποιη-τέον*. **ᾗ τὸ δίκαιον πέφυκε**: an object-clause of *πείθειν*; 'the path of real justice,' 'where natural justice lies.' See 30,20 for *intrans.* perf. act. *πέφυκα*. 8. **πολύ** goes with *ἧττον*; emphatic. 13. **ταῦτα ἀληθῆ**: object and predic.; 'if this that we say be true,' 'if herein we speak the truth.' So *δίκαια* in next line (5,4 n.). 16. **ἁπάντων ὧν οἱοίτ' ἦμεν καλῶν** for *ἁπάντων τῶν καλῶν ὧν* κτλ.—so-called "incorporation" or "attraction" of antecedent into its relat. clause, *with loss of article*; H. 995 & c, G. 1037.

51 D 18. **τῷ ἐξουσίαν πεποιηκέναι** 'by having granted permission.' 19. **τῷ βουλομένῳ** 'to whosoever will.' 20. **δοκιμασθῇ** 'has passed his examination,' i.e. in his 18th year, when he was enrolled in the register of his deme and entered on his two years' military duty previous to the attainment of his full rights as a citizen. 22. **ἐξεῖναι** depends on *προαγορεύομεν* in 18; 'we proclaim that he may.' But the true explanat. (anacoluthon) will be found in 47,24 App. **λαβόντα** κτλ. 'take his goods *and*—'; see n. on 30,24. 28. **μετοικεῖν ἄλλοσε ἐλθών** 'to go elsewhere *and* be a metic (i.e. a resident merely, but without citizenship). **ἰέναι** depends on *οὐδ' ἀπαγορεύει* 25. **ἐκεῖσε**: for us, otiose; cf. *τοῦτο* 45,31.

59 **51 E** 31. **τἆλλα**: adverbial. 1. **ἔργῳ**, viz. by remaining. 5. **ὁμολογήσας . . πείθεσθαι** 'after promising obedience,' *not* 'that he would obey'—which would call for a fut. infin. as in li. 2. 7. **προτιθέντων** 'though we merely propose.'

52 A 8. **ἐπιταττόντων** is harsher than *προσ-τάττω* heretofore used (e.g. 56,8,28. 57,30); it is 'to lord it over.' 9. **ἐφιέντων** 'leaving it to him,' 'granting.' **θάτερα**: 39,30. 10. **τούτων οὐδέτερα ποιεῖ**: another runaway sent., passing its proper end in li. 7 at the participles. It is brought to a halt by a brief restatement of *οὔτε πείθεται οὔτε πείθει*. See n. on 51,9. 11. **ταύταις**, thus remote from its noun, should be translated: '*these* then, Socrates, are the charges we say that *you*—.' **Σώκρατες** without *ὦ* is ominously stern. Note the warning fut. indic. *ποιήσεις* in the condition (20,11). 12. **εἴπερ**: 18,26. 14. **ἐν τοῖς μάλιστα**: 44,2.

19. **μεγάλα** : separated from its noun ; 'great are the proofs we 59
have etc.'

52 B. 22. **διαφερόντως** 'more.' **ἐν αὐτῇ**, i.e. Athens. **ἐπ-εδήμεις** : used in 5,28. 24. **θεωρίαν** : L. & S. s.v. II. **ἐπί** 'for the purpose of' (46,25). 25. **εἰ μή** 'except.' **στρατευσόμενος** : where, for instance? See 20,30–31. 26. **ἀποδημίαν ἐποιήσω** : periphrastic for *ἀπεδήμησας* (18,4). 27. **οὐδέ** : not correlated with the *οὔτε*'s. 29. **εἰδέναι** : added, as epexegesis, to *ἐπιθυμία* 'to know them, namely.'

52 C 1. **τά τε ἄλλα** : adv. acc. with *πολιτεύσεσθαι*. But the 60
responsion *καὶ παῖδας*, detaching itself, takes an independent verb *ἐποιήσω*. Cf. n. on 57,15. 2. **ἔτι τοίνυν** 'then further.' 3. **φυγῆς τιμήσασθαι** : for case and voice, see 33, 1. 6. **ἐκαλλωπίζου** : cf. *καλλύνομαι* 6,16. 7. **ὡς ἔφησθα**, viz. at 21,25. 8. **τοὺς λόγους αἰσχύνει** 'ashamed *before*—.' H. 712, G. 1049. 9. **ἡμῶν . . ἐντρέπει** : on the analogy of *ἐπιμελεῖσθαι*, *φροντίζειν*, and other verbs of *caring for*, *ἐντρέπομαι* 'to turn to,' 'give heed to,' takes the gen.

52 D 10. **τε** : 57,31. 12. **παρά** : 1,16. 13. **ξυνέθου** (*-τίθεμαι*) **πολιτεύεσθαι** 'agreed on citizenship,' *not* 'that you would live as a citizen.' See n. on 59,5. 17. **ἔργῳ** *κτλ.* : with *ὡμολογηκέναι*. **ἀλλ' οὐ** '*and* not' (26,6). 18. **φῶμεν** 'are we to— ' (34,22). 21. **ἄλλο τι οὖν** is part of the quotation ; *ἂν φαῖεν* is interjected but cannot be separated by punctuation, since *ἄν* does not stand first in its clause. 22. **πρός** 'with' (8,14). **ἡμᾶς αὐτούς** : not 'ourselves' reflexive (which makes no sense), but 'us ourselves' (i.e. 'us and no other,' 'us in person'), *αὐτούς* being the intensive pronoun (11,2). **παραβαίνεις**, i.e. in the *intended* flight. In heart, you already transgress (38,8).

52 E 25. **ἐν ἔτεσιν ἑβδομήκοντα** : cf. 2,15.

53 A 4. **δῆλον ὅτι** '[it is] evident that [it is so]' = 'evidently,' 61
added to a clause adverbially, as is *εὖ οἶδ' ὅτι* (see example in n. on 34,22), or the true adv. *εἰκότως*. 5. **οὐκ ἐμμένεις** : again the *intention* is present (as in *παραβαίνεις* 60,22), though the act is future. 9. **ταῦτα** is an inner accus. (sc. *τὰ ἁμαρτήματα*), not 'these laws.' **ἐξαμαρτάνων** '*being* a transgressor' ; pres. tense.

53 B 11. **ὅτι μὲν γάρ** *κτλ.* : a 'that'-clause, depending on *δῆλόν* (*ἐστι*) at the end. 12. **καὶ αὐτοί** 'they too,' as well as you. 14. **σχεδόν τι** : 48,21. 22. **τὴν δόξαν δοκεῖν** : cf. 45,10.

53 C 29. **ἀν-αισχυντήσεις** : for the word, cf. 25,6 & 7. 31. **ὡς** 'how,' correlat. of *πῶς*, hints at details (way, manner) more than the summary *ὅτι* that introduces the simple fact.

62 2. **ἂν φανεῖσθαι**: for *ἂν φανεῖται.* On *ἄν* c. fut. indic., see 22,1 and cf. 23,15.

53 D 3. **πρᾶγμα**: perhaps 'business,' 'profession'; n. on 49,30. 4. **ἀλλά** dismisses the suggestion (introduced by *πρῶτον μέν* 61,15) of residence in the nearer cities. **ἀπαρεῖς**: *-αίρω.* 5. **τοὺς ξένους**: see 47,1–2. 6. **πλείστη ἀταξία**: Thessaly was the seat of arrogant tyrannies, wild outbreaks, unbridled license. 8. **ὡς** 'how.' 9. **σκευήν τε**: response in *καὶ τὸ σχῆμα* 12. *σκευήν* is specified by the *ἢ* . . *ἢ*-clauses. 10. **ἄλλα οἷα** 'other such things as.' 13. **γέρων**: as adject.; 53,26. 14. **ὡς τὸ εἰκός**: cf. *ὅσα γε τἀνθρώπεια* 49,15.

53 E 14. **γλίσχρως** 'greedily.' 16. **εἰ δὲ μή**: a phrase used first as the alternative to an *affirmative* condition; then, becoming fixed, to *any* condition. 'Otherwise' serves the same purpose in English. 17. **ἀκούσει . . πολλὰ καί—**: cf. 57,13. Drop *καί* (19,23). 18. **ὑπερχόμενος δή**: emphatic (by position) and scornful; 'a *cringer* you will live —.' 19. **εὐωχούμενος**, sc. at the rich lords' tables.

54 A 23. **ἀλλὰ δή**: n. on 51,31 *ἀλλὰ μὲν δή.* 25. **τί δέ;** n. on 14,12 *τί δὲ δή;* **εἰς Θετταλίαν**: with disapproving emphasis. Thessaly was not like Ithaca—*ἀγαθὴ κουροτρόφος* (*Od.* 9,27). 27. **τοῦτο ἀπολαύσωσι**: ironical; for the Greeks were passionate home-lovers, though often so traitorous. *τοῦτο* is an inner acc. 28. **αὐτοῦ**: adv., sc. in Athens. 30. **σοι**: dat., the *οἵ* before it, relat. pron.
63 2. **εἴπερ γε**: 18,26.

54 B 10. **οὔτε . . ἐνθάδε**: the foll. negatives are added one by one without correlation (*οὐδέ*), until *οὔτε ἐκεῖσε* 13:

{ *οὔτε . . οὐδὲ . . οὐδὲ . . οὐδὲ*
{ *οὔτε—.*

54 C 19. **πρὸς ἡμᾶς**: *πρός* = 'with.' 24. **τὸ σὸν μέρος**: 47,14. 25. **ἀλλά** 'nay.' **μὴ πείσῃ**: prohibition; H. 866,2; G. 1346.

54 D 28. **οἱ κορυβαντιῶντες**: see L. & S. s.v. *Κορύβας.* Cf. 97,24. The worshippers of the *μεγάλη Μήτηρ* in Phrygia were wild, emotional religionists. The voice of the Laws to Socrates sounded as the voice of God. He stood upon the mount. Idle (*μάταιος*) were the words that came up to him from the valley
64 of human considerations and estimates. 2. **ὅσα γε** *κτλ.* 'as things seem to me now'; cf. *ὅσα γε τἀνθρώπεια* 49,15. 4. **πλέον ποιήσειν**: 4,12. 6. **ἔα**: imperat.

54 E 7. **ταύτῃ . . ταύτῃ**: 44,12. **ὑφηγεῖται** 'leads the way.'

PHAEDO

THE *Phaedo* reads as the last conversation of Socrates with his friends, held on the day of his death. Fittingly, it is concerned with the immortality of the soul. That such a dialogue took place is quite possible; that Plato, however, meant to give an accurate report of it, no one believes. One of the minor arguments for the soul's immortality involves a doctrine that belongs pretty certainly to Plato rather than to Socrates, viz. that Knowledge is a Reminiscence; while the whole ultimate weight of proof rests on the distinctly Platonic doctrine of Ideas. (See Archer-Hind's *Introduction*, p. xiii.) But, though the arguments may be Plato's, there is no reason to believe that the *incidents* narrated of the last day and hour are anything but historic. It is these, together with the introduction to the argument and one brief famous passage on the song of the dying swan, that are given in the present volume.

All the world, pagan and Christian, has read the *Phaedo*. and with various degrees of conviction. Some it has left still doubting, as Cicero, who believed while he read, but whose assent slipped away when the magical book was closed. (*Tuscul. Disput.* I 11 *nescio quo modo, dum lego, adsentior; cum posui librum et mecum ipse de immortalitate animorum coepi cogitare, adsensio omnis illa elabitur.*)—Others have been only too well persuaded not only of immortality but of the goodness of death that leads to it. We hear, for example, of a certain Cleombrotus of Ambracia, who finished its perusal, bade farewell to the Sun (*Ἥλιε, χαῖρε*), and threw himself down from a lofty wall into the sea. And again in Plutarch's *Lives* we read of Cato Uticensis, who on the last night of his life is said to have read the whole work twice through (*λέγεται δὶς ὅλον διεξελθεῖν*); and at cock-crow (*ἤδη δὲ ὄρνιθες ᾖδον*) he thrust his sword into his breast and shortly died.

57 A 13. **οὖν δή**: *δὴ οὖν* in 30,25. **ἅττα**: 57,7; 64
disting. from *ἄττα* 23,22. 15. **καὶ γάρ**: no ellipsis (4,3). 16. **Φλειασίων**: appositive. **πάνυ τι**: lit. 'much,' or, if by litotes (n. on 4,13), 'at all.' This depends on the relation—whether coolly friendly or hostile—in which Plato was thinking the two cities to be standing. As a matter of fact, they stood now in one, now the other relation. **ἐπιχωριάζει . . Ἀθήναζε** lit. 'stays *to* Athens'; pregnant construct. 29,5. 17. **τὰ νῦν** (H. 719 b, G. 1060) 'these days' =*ἐν τῷ παρόντι*.

64 57 B 18. **χρόνου συχνοῦ**: 44,19. **ἂν . . οἷόστ' ἦν** 'could have'—past potent. 20. **πλήν γε δή** '*except* of course.' 22. **οὐδέ** 'not even.' **τὰ περὶ τῆς δίκης** 'the details of the trial' by prolepsis (21,14); in Engl. to be made the subj. of ἐγένετο.

65 58 A 22. **ἄρα**: inferential. 1. **μέν**: *solitarium* (1,15). 2. **καὶ . . γε**: 50,10. 52,24. 3. **πολλῷ ὕστερον**: cf. Xen. *Mem.* IV 8,2 ἀνάγκη μὲν γὰρ ἐγένετο αὐτῷ μετὰ τὴν κρίσιν τριάκοντα ἡμέρας βιῶναι. 7. **τῆς δίκης** follows the comparat. τῇ προτεραίᾳ; H. 755, G. 1154. **ἐστεμμένη** (στέφω): note tense; 'to have been wreathed.' 10. **δὲ δή**: 13,28. 12. **τοὺς δὶς ἑπτά** 'the two sevens,' 'the seven pairs,' viz. of boys and maidens, whom Athens, according to the myth, had promised, by advice of Apollo, to send to king Minos of Crete every ninth year as an offering to the dread Minotaur of the Labyrinth, if he (Minos) should cease his desolating descents upon Attica. But when for the third time this human tribute came due, Theseus, the hero of Attica, of his own accord, accompanied the "twice seven," slew the Minotaur, escaped from the Labyrinth by aid of Ariadne's thread, and brought back safe the intended sacrifice. To commemorate this rescue, Athens henceforth sent an annual sacred embassy (θεωρία) to Delos, the small birth-island of Apollo and his sister Artemis. See Plutarch's *Life of Theseus*, chapters 15–20. 13. **ᾤχετο ἄγων** 'took off' (27,14).

58 B 14. **ηὔξαντο** 'vowed.' 15. **ἑκάστου ἔτους** (35, 24) = καθ' ἕκαστον ἔτος or κατ' ἐνιαυτόν as in li. 17. 16. **ἦν δή**: 4,18. 17. **κατά**: distributive; L. & S. s.v., B II 2. 18. **ἄρξωνται**: c. gen., H. 738, G. 1099. 19. **καθαρεύειν** 'to be καθαρός pure, unpolluted'; subj. is πόλιν. 20. **ἀπο-κτιννύναι**: 24,3 for form; subj. is πόλιν, or αὐτούς implied in it. 22. **δεῦρο**, i.e. Greece, the mainland. 23. **ἀπολαβόντες**: reg. term used of 'arresting' or 'detaining' winds. L. & S. s.v. IV. On the tense, see G. 1586. **αὐτούς**, i.e. those ἐν τῷ πλοίῳ.

58 C 26. **ὥσπερ λέγω**: 1,17. 27. **γεγονός**: c. ἔτυχεν: 'happened to *have* taken place.' 30. **δὲ δή**: 13,28.
66 2. **εἴων**: ἐάω. **οἱ ἄρχοντες**, i.e. οἱ ἕνδεκα 38,28. 68,20. 3. **ἔρημος**: c. φίλων. From this word comes ἐρημίτης, our *hermit.*

58 D 4. **καὶ πολλοί γε** 'aye, a good many' (65,2). 9. **ἀλλά** 'nay.' 10. **καὶ γάρ**: καί perhaps is adv. with τὸ μεμνῆσθαι, 'even,' as in 10,1. 11. **καὶ . . καί**: in Engl. 'whether . . or.' **αὐτόν** 'myself.' 13. **ἀλλὰ μήν** 'nay, indeed,' 'well, in truth,' differing little from καὶ μήν li. 16. **καί**: adv. 14. **τοιούτους**, i.e. like those who

find their memory of Socrates their greatest joy (*πάντων ἥδιστον*). **πειρῶ**: imperat. 16. **καὶ μήν** 'aye, truly.' The *καί* is perhaps adv. with *μήν*, as in the groups *καὶ μάλα*, *καὶ πάνυ*, etc. **θαυμάσια ἔπαθον** 'had a strange experience,' 'experienced strange feelings.' 66

58 E 17. **οὔτε**: where is its correlate? 18. **με . . εἰσῄει** 'entered my heart.' 19. **ἀνήρ**: note breathing. 20. **τοῦ τρόπου**: 43,18. **ὡς ἀ-δεῶς** 'so fearlessly.' Cf. 43,19. 21. **μοι . . παρ-ίστασθαι** 'occurred to me,' 'entered my head'; L. & S. s.v., B IV. The subject is the clause *ἐκεῖνον . . ἰέναι*. 22. **μηδ' . . ἰόντα** 'not even when going.' **εἰς "Αιδου**: H. 730 a, L. & S. s.v. *εἰς*, I 4 c. **θείας μοίρας**: 28,22. 23. **καί** 'even.' 24. **τις . . καὶ ἄλλος**: 10,7 for *καί*.

59 A 25. **οὐδὲν . . ἐλεεινόν** 'no feeling of pity.' Note also *μοι* with *εἰσῄει*, while in li. 18 *με*. 26. **εἰκός**: sc. *εἰσιέναι*. **παρόντι**: sc. *μοι*. **πένθει** '(scene of) mourning,' depends on *παρόντι*. **οὔτε αὖ**: correlat. (strengthened) to *οὔτε* in 17. 28. **τοιοῦτοι** 'of that character,' viz. philosophical. 29. **ἀτεχνῶς**: 2,16. **πάθος** 'feeling.' 30. **ἀ-ήθης**: for the root, cf. *ἦθος* 'custom' (which has become character); *εἴωθα* li. 28; *ξυνήθης* 43,5. **-κεκραμένη**: *κεράννυμι*, *κρᾶσις*. 2. **σχεδόν τι**: 48,21. **οὕτω**, i.e. 67
were of mixed emotions, as just described, but further explained by the foll. participles. **ὁτὲ μέν**: note accent (not *ὅτε*); see L. & S. s.v. *ὅτε*, C. 4. **διαφερόντως** 'especially'; cf. 59,22,23. 61,2. 5. **γάρ που**: cf. 7,17.

59 C 25. **οὐ δῆτα**: 15,16. 54,6. **ἐν Αἰγίνῃ**: emphatic by position, and perhaps with irony—as if these friends could not possibly come from so remote an island—only a dozen miles distant.

59 D 3. **φοιτᾶν** is 'to go repeatedly or regularly,' e.g. to 68
school; cf. 43,6. 70,11. 5. **ἕωθεν**: used in 39,13. 8. **ἕως ἀνοιχθείη** (*-οίγνυμι*): a past general supposition; H. 923, G. 1465. Cf. 39,9. **διατρίβοντες** 'whiling the time away,' 'loafing'—which for the Athenian always meant 'talking.' Cf. *διατριβή* 29,10. 35,3. 41,5. 11. **τὰ πολλά** 'generally'; H. 719 b, G. 1060. 12. **καὶ δὴ καί**: 2,20. 13. **[ἡμέρᾳ]**: cf. 65,6. 44,16; and, regularly, without *ἡμέρᾳ* (though, it is true, there seem to be exceptions).

59 E 17. **εἰς τὸ εἰωθός,** sc. 'place.' But the Greek felt no ellipse. *Their* word for 'place' is masc. (*τόπος*). **ἡμῖν** prob. goes with *εἶπεν*. 18. **ὑπακούειν**: 43,4. **εἶπεν**: c. dat. pers. et infin. $=$ *κελεύω*, L. & S. s.v. III. **περιμένειν . . ἕως** 'to wait until.' The clause *καὶ μὴ πρότερον παριέναι* is rather parenthetic. Were it felt as the main

68 clause, *πρίν* and not *ἕως* would follow. 21. **ὅπως ἄν** *κτλ.*: the clause states not only the purpose of *παραγγέλλουσιν* ('to the end that'), but is also virtually the order itself—an inner-object clause: 'are giving orders (how) that —.' Cf. *ut*-clauses after *impero, praecipio,* etc. See also G. 1373, for *ὅπως* c. *fut. indic.* used in this way, and cf. infra 147,18. 213,17. 22. **δ' οὖν**: 1,3. **ἐπισχών** 'delaying,' lit. 'holding on,' intrans.

60 A 28. **ἀν-ηυφήμησε**: lit. 'set *up* an *εὐφήμει*.' **ἅττα**: 23,22. 29. **ὕστατον δή** 'for the last time then'—
69 a pathetic use of *δή*. 2. **τῶν τοῦ Κρίτωνος**, sc. *ἀκολούθων* 'attendants.'

60 B 4. **ἀνα-καθιζόμενος** 'sitting *up*.' 5. **ἐξ-έτριψε**: the sense of *ἐξ-* is not obvious. Does it mean that Socrates rubbed the leg *out* or *down* to its extremity? or, as some suggest, till the pain was *out*? 6. **ὡς ἄτοπον** (44,29. 66,29): with *τι*; 'how queer a thing.' 8. **ὡς θαυμασίως** *κτλ.* 'how wonderfully is it by nature (*πέφυκε* 30,21) related to (*πρός*) —.' 10. **ἅμα μέν** 'at one and the same time'—to be contrasted with *sequence* in next line. **αὐτῷ**, i.e. 'pleasure' (*ἡδύ*) and 'pain' (*τὸ λυπηρόν*) its seeming opposite. 12. **ἀναγκάζεσθαι** is still under *τῷ* 'by the fact that'; its subject is to be got from *τις* in the condit. clause. 14. **συν-ημμένω**: *ἅπτω*.

60 C 15. **ἂν συν-θεῖναι** 'would have *composed*.' 16. **ὡς** 'how' (61,31). **διαλλάξαι** 'reconcile.' 17. **εἰς ταὐτόν** 'together,' practically, repeats *συν-* in the verb. No ellipse; 68,17. 18. **αὐτοῖς** 'for them.' 20. **ὥσπερ οὖν** *κτλ.* 'as indeed for myself too' (cf. 41,4); with *ἔοικεν* supply *ἐπακολουθεῖν*. 22. **ἥκειν δή** *κτλ.* 'there *now* comes, as it appears, accompanying it —'; Greek order. 25. **εὖ γ' ἐποίησας ἀναμνήσας**: a case where the action of the aor. partic. is *not* anterior to that of the main verb, since the acts are identical. Cf. 24,7. The aor. ptc. not infrequently shows thus its original timelessness, like any other unaugmented form of the aorist: H. 856 b, G. 1563,8 (G. M. T. § 150). 26. **γάρ τοι**: 15,9.

60 D 27. **ἐντείνας**: the reg. verb for setting prose into verse, or verse to music. Cf. our musical term "strain." (Different, apparently, is the sense of the word in 265,5.) 29. **καὶ . . ἀτὰρ καί** 'not merely . . but also.' 30. **ὅ τι ποτὲ διανοηθεὶς . . ἐποίησας**: the *partic.* asks the quest., not the fin. verb (56,19); 'what in the world you meant by —.' See 6,29 for *ποτέ*. 31. **ἐποίησας**: in the technical sense
70 'compose': hence *ποιη-τής* 'maker' = 'poet.' 7. **ᾔδη** (not *ἤδη*): *οἶδα*.

60 E 7. **οὐ ῥᾴδιον εἴη** is perh. ironical. Recall 6,14. 70
9. **ἀφοσιούμενος** 'in ex-piation'—exact corresponsion of the Greek and Latin. **πολλάκις**, espec. after *εἰ ἄρα* or *μή*, often is 'perchance,' as in li. 23. So *saepe*; e.g. Verg. *Aen.* I 148 *quum saepe coorta est seditio.* Cf. also the Germ. *vielleicht* = 'perhaps' (Geddes). 10. **ἦν** *κτλ.* 'they (the dreams) were something like this.' 11. **φοιτῶν**: 68,3. 12. **ἄλλοτ' ἐν ἄλλῃ ὄψει**: transl. briefly 'in *various* shapes.' 14. **ἐργάζου** 'practice,' 'cultivate.' 16. **ὑπελάμβανον**: as in 21,3. 39,20. **παρακελεύεσθαι . . ἐπικελεύειν . . διακελευόμενοι** are said to mean: 'exhort . . urge on . . separately (*δια-*) cheer on.'

61 A 18. **καὶ ἐμοὶ οὕτω**: *καί* is adv.; the sent. here begins to ramble and repeat; see n. on. 59,10. 51,9. *ἐπικελεύειν* in 19 still depends on *ὑπελάμβανον.* 20. **μεγίστης μουσικῆς**: Socrates took the term in even a larger than the large Greek sense. 23. **εἰ ἄρα** 'if sure enough,' 'if after all.' 24. **δημώδη** 'as popularly understood.'

61 B 31. **μύθους, ἀλλ' οὐ λόγους**, i.e. 'fictitious *λόγοι*,' and not narratives or stories (*λόγοι*) in general. 1. **ἦ** (indic. 71
imperf.): still under *ἐννοήσας ὅτι*, yet also semi-parenthetic and free, as shown by its tense (and mood), instead of *εἴην*. 2. **οὓς . . μύθους**: incorporation of anteced. in the relat. clause (58,16). **προχείρους**: used in 12,6. Observing Greek order: 'what I had at hand and remembered in the way of myths, that is, those of Aesop—*they* were the ones etc.' —homely English to be sure, but so is the Greek homely. 3. **ἐποίησα** here = *ἐντείνω* of 69,27. 6. **ἐρρῶσθαι**, sc. *φράζε*: 'bid him fare-well' (lit. 'be strong' *ῥώ-ννυμι*). Greek epistles closed with the imperat. perf. *ἔρ-ρωσο vale.*

61 C 9. **οἷον παρακελεύει** *κτλ.* 'what an exhortation is this —!' 11. **πολλά** 'many a time.' Cf. *τὰ πολλά* 68,11. **σχεδόν** approximates ('about,' 'nearly') and goes with *οὐδ' ὁπωστιοῦν* (1,12); 'probably (pretty surely) not at all.' 13. **ἑκὼν εἶναι** (34,9) with negat. = 'not if he can help it.' 15. **ἐθελήσει** 'will be willing.' Disting. *βούλομαι* the 'I wish' of a weak character from *ἐθέλω* the 'I will' or 'am willing' of a strong one. For *ἐθέλω* even when translated 'am willing' belongs to the stronger nature that concedes or permits to the weaker what it *could* have prevented or refused. So too in *οὐκ ἐθέλω* 'I refuse.' 16. **τοῦ πράγματος** 'pursuit,' 'study,' i.e. philosophy. 17. **μέντοι** 'however' (1,20). 18. **καθῆκε**: *ἵημι.*

61 D 20. **ἤδη** is often joined with other (sometimes duplicating) time-phrases, as here *τὰ λοιπά*: 'from that time forth.' 21. **λέγεις** 'mean.' 25. **συγγεγονότες** 'associates (i.e. pupils)

71 as you have been' of Philolāus. 26. **ἀλλὰ μήν**: 66,13. 27. **ἃ μέν**: *μέν solitarium* 1,15. 28. **φθόνος οὐδείς** 'I don't mind (lit. grudge) telling you.' 29. **καὶ μάλιστα**: cf. *καὶ πάνυ* (*μάλα*, etc.) 3,1.

61 E 30. **ἀποδημεῖν**: also in 40,20 death is a 'going abroad.' **διασκοπεῖν**: used in 8,12. For **μυθολογεῖν**, see 39,1. 31. **ἐκεῖ**: for *ἐκεῖσε* (i.e. *εἰς* "*Αιδου*); 33,12. **ποίαν τινά**: *τις* is indefinite and approximative; 'about
72 what kind—.' 1. **καὶ ποιοῖ**: for us, *καί* stresses the auxiliary verb (24,9); 'what else *could* one do?' 3. **κατὰ τί**=*διὰ τί*. 4. **αὐτόν** (intensive) we drop in Engl. 17,27. 31,13. 34,18. 5. **νῦν δή**: 34,27. 8. **περὶ αὐτῶν**, as in 71,27, refers to *τῶν τοιούτων* in 71,25. **οὐδενός**: gen. pers. c. *ἀκήκοα*.

62 A 10. **καὶ ἀκούσαις**: *καί* perhaps as in li. 1; '*may* or *will* hear.' **μέντοι** 'indeed.' 11. **τοῦτο**, i.e. this prohibition of suicide. **ἄλλων** we drop in Engl.; L. & S., II 8. 12. **ἁπλοῦν** *simplex*, i.e. 'unconditional,' 'without exception.' **καὶ οὐδέποτε** *κτλ.* 'and if it never proves for man as other rules do [to admit of exceptions, I mean], *some*times and for *some* people better to be dead than alive.' 13. **ἔστιν** belongs both to *ὅτε* and to *οἷς* = *ἐνίοτε* and *ἐνίοις*, but more emphatic. H. 998, G. 1029. On *καί* in the *ὥσπερ*-clause, see 10,7. 16. **ὅσιον**, sc. *ἐστίν*. 18. **ἐπι-γελάσας** 'with a laugh of *assent*.' Cf. *ἐπ-ευφημέω Il.* 1,22. **ἴττω**=*ἴστω*. 19. **φωνῇ** (2,19) 'dialect,' viz. Boeotian. "Gudeness kens" (Purves).

62 B 20. **οὕτω γε** 'so baldly stated.' **οὐ μέντοι** (*ἄλογόν ἐστιν*) **ἀλλά** 'it is not absurd however—nay perhaps' (*ἴσως γε*). So in li. 26. 21. **ἔχει τινὰ λόγον**: cf. 29,27. 25,4. **ἐν ἀπορρήτοις** 'in secret.' (The root *ῥε-* in *ῥῆμα*, *ἐρ-ρήθην*.) This 'doctrine spoken in secret' was perhaps one of those taught by Pythagoras. But instruction for an inner circle of pupils ("Seminar"-fashion) seems not infrequent in antiquity. See L. & S. s.v. *ἐσωτερικός*. 23. **φρουρᾷ**: said here to mean 'prison,' as in 149,23. 25. **μέγας . . τις** 'somewhat hard (deep).' 26. **τόδε**, viz. *τὸ θεοὺς εἶναι κτλ.* in 27. Cf. 73,9 and 12 and 13. 31. **οὐκοῦν**: 18,16.

73 **62 C** 1. **αὐτό**: an intensive that we drop, as in 72,4,16. But in li. 2 it is the 3rd pers. pron. 6. **πρὶν . . ἐπιπέμψῃ**: without *ἄν* (though here it may have dropped out before the *ἀν-* in *ἀνάγκη*); H. 921 a, G. 1473. 10. **ἂν ἐθέλειν** 'would be willing' (not 'wishing'); 71,15.

62 D 12. **εὐλόγως ἔχει**: 2,16. 14. **ἀγανακτεῖν** 'to repine' (43,22). 16. **ἄριστοι . . τῶν ὄντων** 'best in existence.' 17. **οὐκ ἔχει λόγον** 'is inconsistent (unreasonable).' 73

62 E 23. **ἀγαθοῦ**, sc. *δεσπότου*. 26. **οὕτως**=*ταύτῃ* li. 5='putting it *this* way,' 'on *this* view.' **τοὐναντίον . . ἤ** 'the opposite to —.' 30. **ἡσθῆναι** (*ἥδομαι*): c. dat. *τῇ πραγματείᾳ* ('earnestness'). Cf. the dat. c. *ὀργισθείς* 30,14; *χαλεπαίνοις* supra, li. 3. 31. **τοι** 'mark you,' *voilà*.

63 A 1. **ἀν-ερευνᾷ** 'tracks *back*' (?). 2. **ἐθέλει** 'is willing' (71,15). 3. **ἀλλὰ μήν**: 66,13. 4. **μοὶ . . καὶ αὐτῷ**: cf. 1,3. 69,20. 41,4. **τι . . λέγειν**: 49,11: n. on 23,12. **τί . . βουλόμενοι**: 56,19. 5. **ὡς ἀληθῶς**: with *σοφοί*, but emphat. by post-position (25,6). 8. **τείνειν τὸν λόγον** 'aiming his talk.' 74

63 B 11. **λέγειν** 'mean' (7,31). 14. **πειραθῶ** 'let me try.' 21. **νῦν δέ**: 6,6.

63 C 23. **δι-ισχυρισαίμην** 'strongly (*ἰσχυρός*) or dogmatically maintain.' 24. **μέντοι** (for *δέ*) after *μέν* (7,1. 37,1); it also replaces by anacoluthon *καὶ παρὰ θεούς*, which we should expect after *παρ' ἄνδρας τε*. 25. **ἥξειν**: after *ὅτι*, instead of indic.—prob. because felt as the mate of *ἀφίξεσθαι*, dependent upon *ἐλπίζω*. 27. **οὐχ ὁμοίως** 'not equally,' 'not so much,' as if without this hope. 28. **εἶναί τι** *κτλ*. 'a something there is for the dead.' 1. **ἐν νῷ**: with *ἔχεις*. 75
κἄν: *καί* with *ἡμῖν*.

63 D 6. **Κρίτωνα**: prolepsis (21,14). **τόνδε** needs no art. (29,7). 7. **τί . . ἄλλο γε ἤ** (*τοῦτο, ὅτι*). 8. **πάλαι** c. pres. t. (43,14). 10. **σοι φράζειν** 'to tell you.' 11. **θερμαίνεσθαι μᾶλλον** 'get rather heated.' The subj. is implied in *διαλεγομένους*. Cf. 17,22,29. 12. **δεῖν δὲ οὐδέν** *κτλ*. 'but that they ought not to bring any such influence to bear upon (=to counteract) the poison.' 13. **εἰ δὲ μή** 'otherwise' (62,16).

63 E 16. **ἔα . . χαίρειν**: 46,9. **τὸ ἑαυτοῦ**: cf. 24,28. 18. **μὲν . . ἀλλά**: 10,12. 30,18. 21. **ἤδη** ('now') marks a point of time as now attained (whether absolute or relative), and also *con*-notes other points of time in comparison—whether past or future. Hence its various translations: 'by now,' 'already,' 'now at length,' 'from now on.' Cf. *iam*. 22. **ἀπο-δοῦναι** *red-dere*. 23. **ἀνὴρ . . διατρίψας**=the generic *ὁ διατρίψας*. So 82,12. 87,13.

64 A 29. **κινδυνεύουσι**: c. inf.; 7,5. 30. **λεληθέναι** followed here, as infra 76,14, by a *ὅτι*-clause, not by a ptc. For exx., see L. & S., A 4. 31. **αὐτοί** 'personally' points the contrast with the masses (*τοὺς ἄλλους*). 1. 76
τεθνάναι 'death' the *state*, disting. from the present *ἀποθνή-*

76 *σκειν* 'dying,' the process towards that state. Yet see n. on 20,17. 3. **δήπου**: 2,6. 5. **ἀγανακτεῖν ὃ** *κτλ.* 'repine at what he had long been eager for.'

64 B 8. **γελασείοντα**: for the suffix *-σείω* in "desiderations," see H. 573, G. 868; 'though not by any means now desirous of laughing.' 10. **δοκεῖν**: with it, *ἄν* in 9; 'would think.' **εὖ πάνυ**: cf. *εὖ μάλα* 54,30 for order. 11. **τοὺς μὲν παρ' ἡμῖν ἀνθρώπους**, i.e. the Boeotians (Simmias being a Theban); a dull-witted folk, the Athenians thought. For *μέν solitarium*, 1,15. 12. **καὶ πάνυ**: cf. 71,29. 13. **θανατῶσι**: a desiderative in *-άω*; cf. li. 8. **σφᾶς**, i.e. *τοὺς πολλούς* of li. 9. 14. **λελήθασιν**, viz. the philosophers. 15. **καὶ . . γε**: 50,10. 18. **ὡς ἀληθῶς**: adv. as adj. (40,26); 6,14. 52,22.

64 C 21. **μή**: in quest. (14,14). **ἄλλο τι ἤ**: 13,21. 23. **ἀπαλλαγήν**: for the thought, cf. 148,10 ff. **τοῦτο** introduces the circumstantial definition by the two *χωρίς*-clauses which match throughout. 24. **χωρίς**: with *γεγονέναι.* 25. **αὐτὸ καθ' αὑτό** 'by itself.' The first *αὐτό* we drop as in 17,27. 27. **μὴ ἄλλο τι ᾖ θάνατος** *κτλ.*: *μή* c. subjunct. in cautious assertion we had in 37,21. 52,22,26. 53,1. Here we have perhaps the same, but in interrog. form; 'maybe death is something other than this?' G. M. T. § 268. 29. **ἐάν** *κτλ.*: the clause serves not only as the condition to, but as the object of, the imperat. *σκέψαι*; 'consider *whether* —.' **ἄρα** 'in very truth'; warning Simmias of the importance of his admission.

77 **64 D** 1. **ἀνδρός** (53,26): H. 625 a. 3. **οἷον** is practically an adverb (an absolved accus.): 'as,' 'for example.' L. & S., v 2 b. 8. **διαφερόντων** 'better' than other people's; cf. *διαφερόντως* 59,22,23. 61,2. 11. **μή** renders general.

64 E 14. **ἡ . . πραγματεία** 'concern.' Cf. 73,30. 16. **ἀφεστάναι αὐτοῦ** 'to stand aloof from it'; note the perf.

65 A 21. **καὶ . . γε**: 76,15. 22. **ᾧ**: 'for him to whom'; anteced. omitted. 23. **μηδὲ μετέχει**: in Engl. we should repeat the relat. in nomin. (*καὶ ὃς μὴ μετέχει*). But the Greek regularly omits; H. 1005, G. 1040. 24. **ἐγγύς** (modified by *τι*; cf. *σχεδόν τι*) goes with the genit. *τοῦ τεθνάναι.* **τείνειν** 'verges,' 'borders.' 25. **διά**: c. gen. instrum. or of channel; 2,10. 56,21. 27. **τί δὲ δή**: 14,12. **φρονήσεως**: perhaps 'wisdom' is the best translat. 30. **οἷον τοιόνδε λέγω**: lit. 'like this (following) I mean.'

78 **65 B** 31. **ἔχει**=*παρ-έχει.* 2. **ἢ τά γε τοιαῦτα** *κτλ.* 'or (is it) something like this [that] even the poets etc. viz.

that —?' 4. **αὗται τῶν . . αἰσθήσεων** '*these* (of the) 78
senses'; a partit. genit. after a demonstrat. pron. is rare. 6. **σχολῇ** (lit. 'at leisure,' 'slowly'; then) = 'scarcely,' 'hardly.'

65 C 12. **λογίζεσθαι** 'thinking.' 13. **τῶν ὄντων** 'realities.' 14. **δέ γε**: *γε* with *λογίζεται* (10,10). 16. **μηδέ** is not correlated with the *μήτε*'s, but contrasts *ἡδονή* with *ἀλγηδών*. Cf. *οὔτε . . οὐδέ* 5,13. 20. **ὀρέγηται** ('reach after') c. gen., like *τυγχάνω* infra 79,20; H. 739, G. 1099. **τοῦ ὄντος** 'reality,' 'the absolute.'

65 D 24. **τί δὲ δὴ** (*λέγεις*) **τὰ τοιάδε** 'of the following.' 25. **δίκαιον αὐτό** 'absolute justice.' 26. **μέντοι** asseverates. 27. **ἤδη** ('by now,' 'before to-day') with **πώποτε** = 'ever yet' (75,21). 30. **ἐφ-ήψω** (*ἐφ-άπτομαι*): 2nd sing. **λέγω** 'mean.' 31. **οἷον**: 77,3. **πέρι**: 4,31.

65 E 5. **αὐτὸ ἕκαστον** 'the essence of each thing.' **δια-** 79
νοηθῆναι 'to see *through*' intellectually, not merely *αἰσθέσθαι* 'to perceive with the senses.' 6. **ἐγγύτατα**: c. gen. (77,24). 9. **αὐτῇ** 'alone,' 'by itself,' 'just' the intellect. 11. **ἐφ-έλκων** 'dragging *after*.'

66 A 12. **λογισμοῦ** 'reasoning.' 16. **ὡς ἔπος εἰπεῖν**: 1,6. 21. **ὑπερφυῶς ὡς ἀληθῆ**: by inverse attraction for *ὑπερφυές* (*ἐστιν*) *ὡς*—'it is extraordinary how —'; H. 1003 b.

66 B 24. **παρίστασθαι**: 66,22. **τοιάνδε τινά** introduces the *ὅτι*-clause (li. 26), *not* the *ὥστε*-clause, which is semi-parenthetic. 25. **γνησίως**: 26,2. Cf. 76,18. 27. **κινδυνεύει** 'perhaps' (7,5). **τοι**: 73,31. **ὥσπερ** 'as it were' (3,28). The thing that is 'a sort of bye-path as it were,' which 'leads us to our goal' (*ἐκ-φέρειν*), seems from the whole context to be *death*. Perhaps the text is corrupt, and *θάνατος* rightly inserted after *ἀτραπός τις* by some editors, following Tournier. 29. **τοῦ λόγου** = *τοῦ λογισμοῦ* of li. 12. 31. **οὐ μή**: c. aor. subjunct.; 22,12.

66 C 5. **ἐρώτων**: *ἔρως*. 8. **τὸ λεγόμενον** 'as the saying 80
is'; perhaps an absolved (free, adverbial) acc., but see n. on 14,24. **ὡς ἀληθῶς τῷ ὄντι**: duplicate expressions; 2,3. **ὑπ' αὐτοῦ** 'by reason of the *body*,' namely. The next line gives what the saying is: 'we can't even *think* nothing *nohow*.' 9. **ἐγγίγνεται** '*becomes* possible,' as *ἔνεστι* = '*is* possible.' Cf. n. on 157,23 *ἐξεγένετο* as aor. of *ἔξεστι*.

66 D 18. **καὶ σχολὴ γένηται** '*does* get leisure'; 24,9. 72,1.

66 E 25. **τότε**, viz. *ἐπειδὰν κτλ.* li. 27. 26. **ἡμῖν ἔσται οὗ** *κτλ.* 'we shall have what we desire,' viz. wisdom. But when the subject of *ἔσται* is at last reached, it becomes *genit.*, *φρονήσεως*, by attraction of the intervening *οὗ*. 28. **ὁ**

λόγος 'the argument.' **ζῶσιν**: dat. c. ἡμῖν, li. 26. 30. (δυοῖν) **θάτερον**: an apposit. to the sent., as in li. 8.

81 **67 A** 2. **ἐν ᾧ**: 38,28. 3. **οὕτως**, viz. ἐὰν ὅτι κτλ. li.
4. 5. **ὅτι μή** 'except,' 'unless'; lit. 'what (ὅ τι) not'; H. 1049,1 rem. L. & S. s.v. ὅ τι, II. 6. **ἀναπιμπλώμεθα**: 27,5. 10. **τοιούτων**, i.e. καθαρῶν, prob. neut., referring to τὰ ὄντα of the discussion, i.e. the pure essences or realities.

67 B 13. **μὴ καθαρῷ**, sc. τινι or ἀνδρί, the μή generalizing. **μὴ οὐ**: 37,21. 19. **ἀφικομένῳ**, sc. μοι.

67 C 27. **ξυμβαίνει** (c. εἶναι) 'happen (prove) to be.' L. & S.
82 s.v., III b mid. 1. **κατὰ τὸ δυνατόν**: cf. 78,18 καθ' ὅσον δύναται.

67 D 7. **δέ γε**: 10,10. 78,14. 13. **παρασκευάζοντα**: here with a ptc. (ὄντα), not, as usually, with an infin. L. & S. cite Xen. *Cyrop.* I 6,18.

67 E 14. **οὕτω** ('so,' i.e. as just described in the participial clause) is frequently thus used in summary reinforcement of the ptc., but usu. best dropped in transl. H. 976 b, G. M. T. § 855. Cf. 71,19. 19. **εἰ . . διαβέβληνται** κτλ. is a preliminary basis, upon which rests the condit. εἰ φοβοῖντο (2,17. 18,26); 'if they have been set at variance with.' 24. **οὗ**: both verbs, τυχεῖν 'to obtain' and ἤρων (ἐράω), require the genit.

68 A 25. **τυχεῖν** and **ἀπηλλάχθαι** (26), joined by τε *solitarium* (57,31), depend on ἐλπίς ἐστιν. 26. **τούτου . . συνόντος**: the substantive *thought* lies in the ptc., not in τούτου. It is the '*association*' with this (body) that there is hope of riddance from. See 56,15 App. Note tense of ἀπηλλάχθαι—'*be* quit of.' 27. **ἀνθρωπίνων μέν**: the contrast comes in li. 31, the μέν-clause should be subordinated: if human wife-and-child love avail so much, what will that for wisdom? 29. **ἠθέλησαν** (71,15): Orpheus was such a one, in his love for Eurydice. 31. **ἄρα** 'forsooth,' used also in
83 49,4, in the same logical situation. 2. **ταύτην**: in attrib. posit. (31,20).

68 B 5. **οἴεσθαί γε χρή** (62,3. 63,4) 'we must *fancy* so at least,' i.e. that he will go more gladly than those others. 7. **ἄλλοθι . . ἀλλ' ἤ**: cf. 29,29. 7,3. 12. **τοῦτο**: what the 'this' is, is found in the relat. cl. (ὃν ἂν ἴδῃς) which belongs to ἀνδρός; 'if you see any man repining etc., "this" *repining* is etc.' Cf. n. on 76,29. 14. **οὐκ ἄρ' ἦν** 'he was not *then*' (as we thought him); an inference drawn from the fact of his repining. Or it may still be the original ἄρα 'i' Faith.'

68 C 16. **καί** is adv. 'also.' 17. **ἤτοι . . ἤ**: 18,24. 83
20. **ἡ ὀνομαζομένη ἀνδρεία** 'the quality called bravery' 'generally recognized as bravery.' **τοῖς οὕτω διακειμένοις** 'men of this (philosophic) temper' (Cope). 22. **ἣν καὶ οἱ πολλοί** *κτλ.* 'which again (as in the case of *ἀνδρεία*) the masses name temperance.' 23. **ἐπτοῆσθαι** (*πτοέω*) 'to *be* in a flutter' (perf. tense). 24. **ὀλιγώρως ἔχειν** 'maintain an attitude of indifference.'

68 D 27. **εἰ γὰρ ἐθέλεις** *κτλ.*: Socrates proceeds to show that though the masses had the names and knew the results of bravery and temperance, yet they had no conception of the true *source* of these virtues; hence *their* virtues were but spurious.
30. **ἄτοπος** 'inconsistent.' 1. **τῶν . . κακῶν**: predic. 84
genit. 3. **αὐτῶν**: genit. of the whole, with *οἱ ἀνδρεῖοι.* 4. **τῷ δεδιέναι . . καὶ δέει** 'through being afraid and from fear.' The verb pictures to us the man actually trembling, the substantive merely names the abstract quality without an image of it in play. "The verb is a noun in action, the noun is a verb at rest" (Gildersleeve, I believe). 6. **ἄλογον** = *ἀλογία* (82,23), *ἄτοπον* (76,2. 83,30).

68 E 7. **τί δέ** *κτλ.*: 14,13. 9. **καίτοι . . ἀλλ' ὅμως** 'although . . but still.' 11. **τούτῳ**, i.e. the 'case' (*πάθος*) of the pseudo-brave in li. 2. 14. **ἄλλων . . ἄλλων** 'some . . others.'

69 A 18. **ᾧ**: for *τούτῳ ὅ* (nom.); attraction from the nomin. is rare. G. 1033. 19. **τρόπον τινά** 'in a way.' 20. **ἔοικε γάρ**: *γάρ* in brief answers is still *γ' ἄρα.* See 5,3 App. 21. **μὴ . . οὐ** c. subj.; 81,13. **αὕτη** for *τοῦτο*; 2,25. 23. **καταλλάττεσθαι**: mid. (not pass.). 25. **ᾖ**: subjunct., going back to *μή* 'maybe' in 21. **ἐκεῖνο**: explained in 27, *φρόνησις.*

69 B 27. **τούτου**: gen. of price. 28. **μετά** 'along with.' **ὠνούμενα**: *ὠνέομαι* is usu. depon., but here pass. 31. **καὶ . . καί** 'whether . . or.' **προσ-, ἀπο-**, 'added
to,' 'subtracted from.' 4. **ἡ τοιαύτη ἀρετή** ('virtue like 85
that'): a compact appositive to the *χωριζόμενα* items of pleasure, fear, etc.

69 C 9. *καθαρ*-**μός** can hardly differ from *κάθαρ*-**σις**, li. 6. H. 551, G. 834. 10. **τελετάς**: see L. & S. for the connection between *τελέω* 'to end, perfect' and *τελετή* 'initiation' (*initium*). 11. **αἰνίττεσθαι**: used in 8,1. 18,28. 16. **πολλοὶ . . παῦροι**: a hexameter verse. For the sense, see L. & S. s.v. *ναρθηκοφόρος*, and cf. Matt. 22,14 *πολλοὶ γάρ εἰσι κλητοί, ὀλίγοι δὲ ἐκλεκτοί.*

69 D 19. **ὧν**: predic. c. *γενέσθαι.* 20. **ἀπέλιπον**: to connect this with *γενέσθαι*, we expect *πειρᾶσθαι*; 'never left off

85 *trying* to become.' But the sent. becomes affirmat. and we get ἀλλὰ . . προυθυμήθην. 22. **ἠνύσαμεν**: ἀνύτω.

In reviewing these opening pages of the *Phaedo*, the student should note Plato's skill in leading us by the most natural way in the world from the historic situation assumed to the subject now reached, usually regarded as the aim and end of the whole dialogue, viz. the immortality of the soul. We had first the release from chains and the attendant pleasure,—then the chance reference to Aesop, which puts Cebes in mind of the message from Evenus,—the return-message to that philosopher, leading on to the talk concerning suicide, the true philosopher, his aim in life (separation of soul from the confounding senses of the body, that it may attain to a vision of Truth, Reality (τὰ ὄντα), the Absolute (αὐτὸ καθ' αὐτό)),—the courage of the philosopher, and his hope, when facing death, as contrasted with the spurious courage of the body-lovers (φιλο-σώματοι).

* * * * *

All this is but introduction. Cebes next expresses the fear that on separation from the body, the soul may perish utterly and the philosopher's hope prove vain—thus leading directly to the various marshalled arguments for the soul's immortality. After a while, there comes a pause in the conversation, each silently busy with his own thoughts. Cebes and Simmias converse aside in a low voice. Socrates, rousing himself from reverie, observes them, and asks if they find the arguments anywhere at fault or are in doubt on any point. Then follows the next selection—the famous comparison of himself with the dying swan:

86 **84 D** 3. **καὶ μήν**: 66,16. 10. **ἦ που**: in this combination the doubt implied in που ('maybe,' 'I suppose') is merely assumed or ironical. For ἦ που is regularly used in *a fortiori* reasoning; 'hardly *indeed, methinks,* could I convince the rest of the world, when I am unable to persuade *even you.*'

84 E 12. **ὅτε γε** (*quandoquidem*): essentially causal, and yet conditional, as seen by the negat. μηδέ. 13. **φοβεῖσθε μὴ . . διάκειμαι**: H. 888, G. 1380 for the indic. **δυσκολώτερον**: adv. 16. **τὴν μαντικήν**: specific. with φαυλότερος ('inferior in'). Cf. 6,5.

85 A 19. **τὸν θεόν**, viz. Apollo. 21. **καί**: adv. 23. **ἐξᾴδειν**: for the usu. ἐκπνεῖν (τὸν βίον); i.e. 'to breathe forth, *in song,* their life.' 25. **αὐτή** 'herself,' 'even.' Why αὐτή is used, is seen on reaching the ἃ δή clause. 29. **ἅτε**: 12,11.

87 **85 B** 3. **διαφερόντως ἤ**: cf. 77,20 (genit. instead of ἤ). 5. **οὐ χεῖρον** 'no less.' 6. **μαντικὴν ἔχειν**: Socrates was now at last at the very hour referred to in 38,5–7. 9.

ἕως . . ἐῶσιν: the prose habit of the period would require here an ἄν with the subjunct. after ἕως. But we cannot be sure that ἄν was imperatively required, nor that Plato here meant to write plain prose—indeed there are many hints that he did not mean to. Certainly, however, the article would have been acceptable with ἄνδρες ἕνδεκα. 87

* * * * *

114 D 11. **ταῦτα.** After his various arguments for the soul's immortality, Socrates had next pictured the kind of place he imagined the underworld to be, with its rewards and punishments for human souls. To this description he now refers by ταῦτα (subj. of ἔχειν). **τὸ . . δι-ισχυρίσασθαι**: 74,23. 13. **μέντοι**: for δέ, after μέν; 7,1. 15. **ἀθάνατον**: nt. pred. 'an immortal *thing*'; H. 617, G. 925. 16. **πρέπειν**, i.e. to the νοῦν ἔχοντι man; supply also οἴεσθαι from the following οἰομένῳ; 'this, I think, is both proper for a sensible man to suppose and worth his taking the risk of imagining it to stand so.' Note that οἴομαι, not νομίζω (39,11), is used in contrast to διισχυρίσασθαι. 21. **περί** c. dat. is poetic, exc. after verbs of *fearing* and the contrary, and when used with articles of clothing *about* the body.

114 E 23. **τε . . καί** connect, and *show the equivalence* of, ὡς c. ptc. and a ptc. of *thinking*. 24. **θάτερον**: not rarely =τὸ κακόν. **ἡγησάμενος** 'because convinced.' **ἀπεργάζεσθαι**: subj. is τὰς περὶ τὸ σῶμα ἡδονάς. 25. **ἐσπούδασε** (subj. is still ὅστις, 21) is connected by τε καί to περιμένει.

115 A 1. **οὕτω** summarizes the κοσμήσας group of words; 88
82,14. 2. **εἱμαρμένη**; L. & S. s.v. μείρομαι must be consulted. The same root in μοῖρα, μέρος. 4. **εἰς αὖθις** 'hereafter.' Cf. εἰς αὔριον 44,10. 5. **ἀνήρ**: 53,26. Socrates jestingly (and characteristically) excuses his tragedian's phrase καλεῖ ἡ εἱμαρμένη. 8. **λουσάμενον πιεῖν**: in Engl. we reverse syntax; 'to bathe before drinking.'

115 B 15. **ἐν χάριτι μάλιστα** 'most acceptably.' 16. **καινότερον** 'new.' -τερος is 'rather' (sc. than old).

115 C 24. **πλέον ποιήσετε**: 4,12. 27. **ὅπως**, for the (in such connection) more freq. short form of relat. ὡς. Yet cf. οὕτως ὅπως 'in such way as' 89,23. 30. **ὡς ἐγώ εἰμι οὗτος** κτλ. 'that I here (οὗτος) am Socrates, I who am now conversing and marshalling one by one my arguments.'
3. **δή** perhaps is 'then.' 89

115 D 7. **ταῦτα** summarises the ὡς-clause and, by anacoluthon, ignores the ὅτι-clause with which the sent. began. **ἄλλως** 'in vain'; 49,4. 9. **ἐγγυήσασθε**: 36,10. 10. **ἐναντίαν . . ἤ**: cf. διαφερόντως ἤ 87,3. 11. **ἦ μήν** (9,9): quoted from the origin. oath implied in ἠγγυᾶτο (N.B. imperf.

89 tense of imperf. action; the offered bail was not received). 12. **μή**: in emphat. asseveration (oaths, etc.), regular. L. & S., B 5 c.

115 E 14. **μή**: c. *ἀγανακτῇ*, **ὁρῶν** 'when seeing.' 17. **προτίθεται** *κτλ.*: the regular terms for 'laying out' the dead, 'carrying forth' from the house, for 'burial.' 19. **εἰς αὐτὸ τοῦτο** 'in itself.' Socrates is true to his mission to the last. 'A wrong use of words' (*τὸ μὴ καλῶς λέγειν*) means confused thinking—a thinking you know what you do not know. 20. **πλημμελές**: 43,21. 21. **θαρρεῖν** *κτλ.*: the scheme is (I think):—

χρὴ { *θαρρεῖν τε καὶ φάναι . . ,*
καὶ θάπτειν.

116 A 23. **ὅπως** 'as' (88,27). 24. **νόμιμον** 'customary.' 25. **ἀνίστατο εἰς οἴκημα** 'got up [and went] into —.' See n. on 64,16. 28. **ἡμᾶς αὐτούς** = *ἀλλήλους*; H. 686 b, G. 996. 29. **ἀνα**-*σκοποῦντες* '*re*-considering.' **τοτὲ δ' αὖ**: as if *τοτὲ μέν* had preceded. 30. **ξυμφορᾶς, ὅση**:
90 prolepsis. 1. **ἔπειτα**: L. & S., I 2.

116 B 2. **τὰ παιδία**: 30,23. 4. **οἰκεῖαι** 'of his family.' 6. **ἅττα**: 64,13.

116 C 13. **καταγνώσομαι** 'shall pronounce the judgment on —' (14,21). 18. **καὶ ἄλλως . . καὶ δὴ καί**: 50,24. 2,20. 23. **ἃ ἦλθον ἀγγέλλων** 'what news I came with'; *not* a ptc. of purpose.

116 D 25. **δακρύσας**: inceptive aor. 'bursting into tears.' 28. **ἀστεῖος** 'courteous.' 29. **παρά** c. acc. temporal; we too say 'all *along*.' 31. **ἀπο**-*δακρύει* = '*de*-plorat.' L. & S. s.v. *ἀπό*, C 4 end.

91 **116 E** 5. **δεδυκέναι**: act. *intrans.* perf.; 30,21. 8. **εὖ μάλα**: 54,30 on order.

117 A 16. **παρ' ἐμαυτῷ** 'in my own eyes.' **φειδόμενος** *κτλ.* hints at an old proverb on the folly of economy when you have reached the bottom of the cup. 18. **μὴ ἄλλως ποίει**: 46,13. 25. **γάρ** we may transl. 'since,' though that is not its meaning.

117 B 28. **αὐτό** 'of itself,' i.e. *τὸ φάρμακον*. **ποιήσει** 'will act.' 29. **καὶ ὅς**: cf. *ἦ δ' ὅς* 6,11. 30. **καί**: adv. with *μάλα*; 'very graciously' (*ἵλεως*). 31. **διαφθείρας** 'changing.' The genitt. following are said to be "partitive." Perhaps they are like *αὐτῶν* 1,7; '*in* colour or countenance.'
92 1. **ταυρηδόν**: on adverbs in -*δόν*, see G. 860. Socrates seems to have had the habit of gazing with his protuberant eyes *set.*

3. **πρός** 'to,' 'as to.' 4. **τινί**, sc. *θεῷ*. 6. **μανθάνω** 92
'I understand,' 'good'—regular sense in conversation.

117 C 8. **τὴν μετοίκησιν . . γενέσθαι** is the obj. of *εὔχεσθαι*. 11. **ἐπισχόμενος** (mid.) 'putting (the cup) to (his lips).' **καί** before *μάλα* again perhaps an adv., though it *may* be correlated to the 2nd *καί*. 12. **τέως** is the demonstrat. correlat. to *ἕως*; 'up to that time.' **ἐπιεικῶς** 'fairly'; 43,9. 13. **κατέχειν** *κτλ*. 'to keep down our tears.' On *μή*, see H. 1029,963; G. 1615,1549. 15. **βίᾳ**: c. gen. 'in spite of,' L. & S. II. **καὶ αὐτοῦ**: with *ἐμοῦ*; 1,3. 15. **ἀστακτ-ί**: on *-ί*, see G. 860,3. 16. **ἀπ-έκλαιον**: cf. *ἀπο-δακρύει* 90,31. 18. **οἵου** *κτλ*. explains *τύχην*; 'that I was robbed of such a comrade.' For relat. *οἷος* as an ancient demonstrat., see App. on 43,19. For *ἀνήρ*, see 53,26. 77,1. The optat. *εἴην* is due to implied indir. discourse.

117 D 20. **ἐξ-αν-έστη** 'got up and went out.' So 107,22. 23. **οὐδένα ὅντινα οὐ** = *οὐδεὶς ἦν ὅντινα οὐ* = *πάντας*; H. 1003 a, G. 1035 end. 25. **οἷα** exclamatory 'how' (or, as ancient demonstr., 'the way' you do!). 26. **μέντοι** 'indeed.' **οὐχ-ἥκιστα** = *μάλιστα* 'particularly.'

117 E 31. **ἐπ-έσχομεν**: c. gen., L. & S., IV 2 b. 2. 93
κατ-εκλίνη: 2nd aor., so-called pass.; yet cf. *ἔστην*, *ἔβην*. 4. **δια-λιπών**: lit. 'leaving apart,' i.e. 'after an interval' of time. 6. **αἰσθάνοιτο**: 'felt it.'

118 A 9. **ψύχοιτο** *κτλ*.: *pres.* optat., 'was *growing* cold and stiffening.' 11. **γένηται**, sc. *τὸ φάρμακον*. 12. **τὰ περὶ τὸ ἦτρον** 'the abdominal parts.' **καί**: after an *ἤδη*-clause ('now,' 'already') our Engl. for *καί* is 'when.' So 99,26. 15. **τῷ Ἀσκληπιῷ**: to this god of healing those who had been cured often brought the thank-offering of a cock. The long malady of Socrates had been—life. Irony to the last! Hardy, defiant soul! 18. **εἴ τι ἄλλο λέγεις** 'if you have aught else to say.' 19. **ἔτι** 'further.' 20. **ἐκινήθη** 'he stirred (quivered).' 21. **καὶ ὅς**, i.e. Socrates. **ἔστησεν** 'fixed.' We should say: 'his eyes became fixed.' 22. **συνέλαβε** 'closed.' 24. **τῶν τότε** 'his contemporaries.' 25. **ὧν**: *πειράομαι* takes the genit.; 'to have experience (knowledge) of.' **ἀρίστου**: perhaps here (in view of his soldier's death) 'bravest'—the Homeric sense. **καὶ ἄλλως** 'and besides.'

SYMPOSIUM

PERHAPS only the mystic can hope to understand the *Symposium*, and perceive, in the mystic's fashion, how Plato has here led him up to stand "upon the back of heaven" (ἐπὶ τῷ τοῦ οὐρανοῦ νώτῳ *Phaedr.* 247 C); how from that highest scaffolding of the universe he has obtained a vision of the whole façade and grasped the pattern-thought and all its variations—even as it speaks from the eyes of his beloved; how the integer of the world and all its fractions is before him—the cosmic tidal wave, yet also the billion rippling duplications on its bosom. All this, to be sure, is ἀπόρρητα for the young, and even φλυαρία—and perhaps well so (ὑπὸ γῆς ἐντὸς πλαττόμενοι 212,20).

The following extracts are not concerned with the subject of the dialogue. They have been chosen because of the information we gain from them concerning Socrates. Plato represents Apollodōrus as repeating what he had heard from a certain Aristodēmus about a famous banquet, given years before (416 B.C.) by Agathon in celebration of his first prize as a tragic poet. Socrates had been invited, and had accepted the invitation. Arrayed in his best, "bathed and sandalled" (ἃ ἐκεῖνος ὀλιγάκις ἐποίει, adds the narrator), he set out to the rich man's house. On the way he meets Aristodemus, described as a little man, always barefoot and a devoted lover of Socrates (σμικρός, ἀνυπόδητος ἀεί, Σωκράτους ἐραστής 173 B). Without much urging Socrates persuades him, though uninvited by the host, to go along to the feast, agreeing to make due explanation and apology. As they proceed they talk.

94 **174 D** 1. **ἔφη**, sc. Aristodemus. **σφᾶς**: Aristod. and Socrates. 4. **οὗ**, sc. Aristod., as also οἷ 8, ἕ 25, etc. 6. **γενέσθαι**: inf. of indir. disc., though in a subordin. clause (after ἐπειδή). So after ὡς 11.

174 E 8. **οἷ**, c. ἀπαντήσαντα. 9. **οὗ** 'where.' 11. **φάναι** (sc. Ἀγάθωνα) depends on ἔφη 7. 12. **εἰς καλόν** 'at a good time.' Cf. 156,22 and ἐν καιρῷ 44,22. 13. **εἰς αὖθις** 'for another time' (lit. 'for again'). L. & S. εἰσαῦθις. Cf. 156,9. 14. **ἀναβαλοῦ** 'put it off.' L. & S., B II. Cf. 156,9 ἀπόθεσθον. **χθὲς ζητῶν σε**: a most considerate fabrication. 18. **καὶ αὐτός**: Aristod. is more puzzled than Agathon why Socrates is not there; 'I came with him *myself*.' 19. **καλῶς . . ποιῶν**, sc. ἥκεις: in Engl. the ptc. becomes the main verb; 'you are quite right in having come.' 20. **σύ** 'for your part,' in contrast to οὗτος '*he*.'

175 A 23. **ἔφη**, sc. Aristodemus. 24. **ἦ δ' ὅς**: 6,11.

Ἀριστόδημε, without ὦ; 59,11 App. **παρ' Ἐρυξίμαχον**: two 94
reclined on one couch (*κλίνη*) in dining. 25. **ἀπονίζειν**:
subj. is *παῖδα*. The mid. *ἀπονίζομαι* is used of hand-washing by
one's self. Here it was probably the feet of Aristodemus washed
by the boy, since he had come unexpectedly and *ἀνυπόδητος*.
27. **ἀγγέλλοντα** 'with the report'; not a ptc. of purpose.
1. **οὗτος** 'yonder'; 29,6. 4. **μὴ ἀφ-ήσεις**: for this usage 95
of *μή*, following the interrog. *οὐ καλεῖς* (fut.), see G. M. T. § 299.

175 B 4. **καὶ ὅς** (91,29), i.e. Aristod., the subj. also of *εἰπεῖν*. 10. **πάντως**: the proper sense ('everyhow') 'by all means' often passes to 'anyhow,' 'certainly (be the rest true or not).' Cf. *δ' οὖν*. But neither sense seems fitting here. L. & S. s.v., II 2, cite and translate by 'only.'

175 C 18. **κελεύειν** 'urged' sending after. 19. **ἕ**, sc. Aristod. 20. **ὡς εἰώθει**: an instance of longer abstraction is to be read on p. 99,24 ff. 21. **μάλιστα** 'about,' freq. in approximations; 43,1. 22. **Ἀγάθωνα**: subj. of *φάναι*. 24. **ἵνα καί** 'just to let me —.' *καί*, like 'just,' *evens up*, or matches, one act with another. See App.

175 D 25. **προσέστη** has the same sense as *παρίστασθαι* 66,22; *εἰσῄει* 66,25. 26. **γάρ** 'for (otherwise).' 28. **φάναι** repeats *εἰπεῖν*. 31. **ὥσπερ** *κτλ.*: it would be fine, Socrates thinks, if wisdom could flow from one person into another by simple contact, just as water flows by capillary attraction through a fillet of wool (*ἔριον*) from the fuller cup
(*κύλιξ*) into the emptier. 3. **πολλοῦ τιμῶμαι** 'value 96
highly.'

175 E 5. **φαύλη τις** *κτλ.* 'of a poor and questionable sort.' 7. **ἐπίδοσιν ἔχουσα** 'promises growth.' 9. **πρῴην** 'day before yesterday.' **ἐν μάρτυσι** *κτλ.*, i.e. during, perhaps, the greater of the two great annual festivals to the god Dionysus, when the city was full of strangers from all parts of the Greek world, and dramas given in the theatre from early morning. 10. **ὑβριστής**: usu. a 'bully' (97,1); translate as adj. 'insulting,' 'outrageous.' 12. **δια-***δικασόμεθα* 'we shall have it *out* (see it *through*).' 13. **δικαστῇ . . Διονύσῳ**: Agathon wittily turns off the irony by referring *σοφία* to their drinking-skill. He will leave it to Bacchus which is the *σοφώτερος*. (And he proved to be right. See n. on 102,12.) The drinking (*πότος*) regularly followed the *δεῖπνον*; hence *ὀλίγον ὕστερον* in li. 12.

After the *δεῖπνον* it was agreed by the company (1) that the drinking this time be moderate, (2) that they choose as their theme of conversation Eros, the god of Love, and that each in turn pronounce an encomium upon him. Among the orators are Phaedrus, Agathon the host, and Aristophanes the brilliant

96 comic poet. Socrates speaks last, with a deepening, widening, and lifting of the theme (as may be guessed) that leaves the others dwarfed. His is the Idealized Love—the much talked of, rarely comprehended, "Platonic" Love. Just as he closes, there is a loud knocking at the outer door, and presently they recognize the voice of Alcibiades in the court—Alcibiades the dearest idol then of Athens—"very drunk and shouting loud" for Agathon (*ἐν τῇ αὐλῇ σφόδρα μεθύοντος καὶ μέγα βοῶντος, ἐρωτῶντος ὅπου Ἀγάθων*). He is admitted and (ever graceful, even when maudlin) elects himself symposiarch, insisting that now there shall be some real drinking—himself leading off with a wine-cooler full. He is then informed that it is his turn to speak of Love. This he refuses to do; but he will glorify the ideal lover instead—Socrates his master. From this panegyric the following passages are taken.

215 A 17. **εἰκόνων** 'similes,' 'comparisons.' 18. **ἐπὶ τὰ γελοιότερα** 'for fun rather'; 24,9.

215 B 20. **τοῖς σιληνοῖς** *κτλ.* 'those Silēni that sit in the statuaries' shops' were probably some sort of cabinet, grotesquely carved to Silenus-shape, for holding the statuettes of gods and the like. 21. **οὕστινας** 'the sort that.' 23. **ἔνδοθεν** for *ἔνδον*. Cf. *ἐνθένδε* for *ἐνταῦθα* 40,4. 25. **Μαρσύᾳ**: for his musical contest with Apollo—flute against lyre—and its final outcome, see X. *Anab.* I 2,8. On the personal appearance
97 (*εἶδος*) of Socrates, see Introd., n. 3. 1. **ὑβριστής**: 96,10.

215 C 4. **ἐκήλει**: used in 114,15. 6. **Ὄλυμπος** *κτλ.*: Marsyas, it appears, had become in Plato's time a mere name—his music perished; but certain melodies were still ascribed to his (almost equally mythical) pupil Olympus. 8. **μόνα** *κτλ.* 'alone produce ecstasy' (lit. 'cause to be possessed, spell-bound'); L. & S. s.v. *κατέχω* II 10. 9. **τοὺς τῶν θεῶν . . δεομένους**: the divinity in us is here measured by our responsiveness to divine music. "The man that hath no music in himself, Nor is not moved with concord of sweet sounds, Is fit for treasons, stratagems, and spoils." 13. **γοῦν** introduces a confirmatory instance (1,3 App.); 'certainly *we*.'

215 D 20. **κομιδῇ** 'quite.' Cf. *πάνυ, παντάπασι, μάλα, σφόδρα.* 21. **ὀμόσας** 'on my oath.'

215 E 24. **κορυβαντιώντων**: cf. 63,28. 25. **ὑπὸ τῶν λόγων τούτου** *may* be a blundering repetition from li. 22 by some copyist (note the predicate position of *τούτου*); yet Alcibiades himself was just now in both a forgettive as well as "forgetive" condition. The position of *τούτου*, though rare, may be parallelled. 27. **Περικλέους**, whose oratory, if measured by persuasiveness, must not be ranked inferior even to that of Demosthenes. 28. **ἡγούμην**: Pericles had died

thirteen years before this (429 B.C.). 30. **ἐτεθορύβητο**: pluperf. gives a past state, as perf. gives a present; 56,13.
1. **διετέθην** 'affected.' 98

216 A 2. **ἔχοντι**: intrans., 'in the state.' 5. **ἐθέλοιμι** 'willing' (71,15). 9. **βίᾳ**: with *οἴχομαι φεύγων* 'I tear myself away and run' (Purves). **ἐπισχόμενος** 'covering.' 10. **αὐτοῦ**: adverb.

216 B 17. **ἡττημένῳ**: he is conscious of two things, (1) that he is not able etc., (2) that he 'has been worsted' (note tense) by his honour (i.e. desire for it) with the masses. The genit. c. *ἡττᾶσθαι* is regular. *τιμή* c. *ὑπό* and genit., as if *τιμᾶσθαι*.

216 C 22. **ὅ τι χρήσωμαι**: deliberat. subjunct.

219 E 24. **Ποτείδαιαν**: 20,30. 26. **πόνοις**: dat. of respect; H. 780, G. 1182. 27. **ἐμοῦ περιῆν** 'surpassed *me*' (100,30).
1. **ἀποληφθέντες** 'cut off.' L. & S. IV; 99
cf. 65,23. 2. **οἷα δή**, sc. *γίγνεται* 'as happens, you know.'

220 A 2. **ἐπὶ στρατείας** 'in time of warfare (service).' **οὐδέν**: as *we* say, 'nowhere.' 3. **πρός**: 9,13. 11,13. **τε** answers *μέν* 98,26. 5. **καὶ πίνειν**: properly with *τά τ' ἄλλα*, but by anacoluthon goes on to *πάντας ἐκράτει*. See 32,17 n. 60,1. and cf. *τά τ' ἄλλα* li. 11. 7. **Σωκράτη μεθύοντα**: see n. on 102,12. 10. **καρτερήσεις**: plur. perh. = 'powers of endurance,' or 'regular (usual) endurance.' See 48,27 n. and App.

220 B 12. **οἵου δεινοτάτου** for *τοιούτου οἷος δεινότατός ἐστι*. H. 1002, G. 1036. 14. **θαυμαστὰ . . ὅσα** for *θαυμαστόν ἐστιν ὅσα* (*ἠμφιεσμένοι ἦσαν*); 'an astonishing amount.' H. 1003 b. 15. **ἐν-ειλιγμένων**: *ἐν-ελίττω*. 16. **πίλους** *κτλ*. 'felts and sheepskins.' **οὗτος δέ** gives the runaway sent. a subject again. Cf. 35,29. 57,17 for *δέ*. 17. **ἱμάτιον** *κτλ*.: for his one cloak, winter and summer, see Introd. n. 5. 20. **ὑπ-***έβλεπον* 'glowered,' 'scowled'; 61,20. 92,2.

220 C 21. **μὲν δὴ . . δέ**: formula of transition. On *δή* see 14,12 n. 22. **οἷον δ' αὖ**: adapted from *Od.* 4,242; 'but what a deed was this he did and dared—the hardy hero.' 23. **ξυννοήσας τι**: note aor.; '*falling* into some meditation.' 25. **προὐχώρει**, sc. his subject of thought. **οὐκ ἀνίει**: force of imperf. c. negat. '*would* not—.' 26. **ἤδη . . καί**: 93,11.

220 D 4. **ἕως** 'dawn.' 6. **βούλεσθε**, sc. *ἀκοῦσαι οἷος ἦν*; 100
the apodosis 'listen' omitted. 7. **τοῦτο** 'this tribute.' 8. **γάρ** when beginning a narrative is dropped; 7,2 App. **ἐξ** 'in consequence'; 12,15.

220 E 16. **ἀξίωμα** 'rank.'

100 **221 A** 24. **οὗτός τε ἅμα καὶ Λάχης**: the subject of the verb is here taken up again (οὗτος) *and amplified*, resulting in an apparent non-agreement in number. But the thing is common. See App.

101 **221 B** 1. **τὸ σὸν δὴ τοῦτο** 'to quote that phrase of yours'; cf. 30,19. 41,10. 2. **βρενθυόμενος** κτλ. (Ar. *Nub.* 362) 'stalking (strutting) and walling his eyes'—perhaps without turning his body; for he was προκοίλιος. See Introd., notes 3 and 27. 4. **παρασκοπῶν** 'running his eye along.' 6. **εἴ τις ἅψεται**: 20,11 for fut. indic. in condit. 7. **διὸ καί**: καί after relat. 'indeed'; 4,18. 25,20.

221 C 10. **προ-τροπ-άδην**: cf. the adverbial formations in -δόν and in -τί 92,1,15. G. 860. 13. **ἐπιτηδευμάτων** ('ways,' 'practices'), a free genit. sometimes found at the head of its clause, as if περί c. gen.; H. 733 a. See n. on 1,7 and App. 17. **ἀπεικάσειεν**, sc. τοιούτῳ; 'to such' (as Achilles was).

221 D 21. **ταὔτ'**: τὰ αὐτά. 24. **εἰ μὴ . . εἰ** (lit. 'except, to be sure, if'=) 'unless to be sure.' 27. **καὶ γάρ**: to this an intensive (*not* inferential) οὖν is added; 'for in truth.' Cf. 23,21. *Lach.* 184 B. 29. **τοῖς διοιγομένοις**: note tense; 'those that open.'

102 **221 E** 1. **ὀνόματα καὶ ῥήματα**: 2,1. 3. **ὄνους . . λέγει**: Plato has him 'talk asses' in the *Apol.* 19,4. See Introd., n. 19. **χαλκέας τινάς** 'rag-tag smiths.'

222 A 11. **ἐπὶ πλεῖστον τείνοντας** 'of the widest application.' Cf. 74,8. 50,20. 12. **μᾶλλον δέ** 'or rather'; 48,5. 55,11.

The banquet goes on through the night. But Socrates maintains his reputation—Σωκράτη μεθύοντα οὐδεὶς ἑώρακε 99,7. Day-break found all overcome save three—Aristophanes and Agathon (comedian and tragedian, both drowsy and not well able to follow, οὐ σφόδρα ἑπομένους), to whom Socrates was arguing that a man who can write comedy can write tragedy, and *vice versa*. Being at last compelled to admit this, and when they too had fallen asleep, Socrates went off to the Lycēum, bathed, and spent the day as usual—in talk.

LACHES

FROM the *Laches*—a short dialogue on Bravery, in which the two generals Nicias and Laches are fittingly introduced as speakers—the following *testimonium* to the ruling passion of Socrates is drawn.

187 E 15. **ὥσπερ γένει** seems to have crept into the text 102
from the margin,—the note of some reader explaining the dat.
of respect λόγῳ by a similar dat. he recalled, viz. γένει, from
the *Apol.* 22,31. The next clause (πλησιάζῃ κτλ.) is epexe-
getic. 16. **αὐτῷ**: unemphat. resumption of ὃς ἄν; usually
οὗτος resumes. 19. **πρὶν ἐμπέσῃ**: so the best MSS., with-
out ἄν; 73,6.

188 B 5. **εἰς τὸν ἔπειτα βίον** 'thereafter.' 6. **προμηθέ-** 103
στερον: cf. the verb in 46,3,14. 7. **τὸ τοῦ Σόλωνος**:
Solon's verse (pentameter) is: γηράσκω δ' αἰεὶ πολλὰ διδασκό-
μενος. 9. **αὐτό** κτλ. 'fancying that old age *in itself* brings
sense to a man.' 10. **ἄηθες** (66,30) and **ἀηδές**: word-play
(παρονομασία 27,4 App.).

188 C 14. **τὸ μὲν ἐμόν** 'for myself'; adverbial.

THEAETETUS

Another simile for Socrates.

169 A 21. **ἀποδύεσθαι**: as did wrestlers. 22. **πρὸς τὸν Σκίρωνα . . τείνειν** 'come near to —,' 'are like —.' L. & S. s.v. τείνω, B III 3.

169 B 25. **τι . . μᾶλλον** 'somewhat rather' Antaeus-
fashion (who gave no choice). **τὸ δρᾶμα δρᾶν** 'do your
work.' 1. **πρὶν ἀναγκάσῃς**, without ἄν; 73,6. 6. 104
Ἡρακλέες: for Socrates, these were the mighty sophists of the
day—from the leaders Gorgias and Protagoras down to such as
Thrasymachus, Euthydēmus, Evēnus. 9. **οὕτω**: with
δεινός; 57,21. 61,2. 10. **μή . . μηδὲ σύ** don't you *either*
(120,11).

REPUBLIC

487 A 13. **ἐπιτήδευμα**: Socrates has been detailing the philosophic 'training' proper for future rulers of the state, as also the kind of mind fitted for that training. Adeimantus retorts on both Socratic method and doctrine.

487 B 1. **παρὰ . . παραγόμενοι** 'at each question led a 105
little astray.' L. & S. s.v. παρά, C II 2. 3. **τὸ σφάλμα**
. . ἀναφαίνεσθαι follows ἡγοῦνται by anacoluthon, since παρα-

105 γόμενοι leads us to expect a continuation of the same subject. 5. **οἱ μή**, sc. δεινοὶ πεττεύειν.

487 C 6. **οὐκ ἔχουσιν** κτλ. 'haven't a move.' For the mood of φέρωσι, see 98,22. 7. **σφεῖς** goes back to ἡγοῦνται. 10. **ἐπεί**: the clause does not tell why they 'have nothing to say,' but why they name dialectic a mere checker-game with words; "mere words," they think; "*for* the truth certainly (γε) lies not a whit more on that side (than on their own)." See App. 14. **ὅσοι . . ἐνδιατρίψωσι**: those here described fall into two classes—τοὺς μὲν πλείστους (17) and τοὺς δ' ἐπιεικεστάτους (19). 15. **μή**: with ἀπαλλάττωνται.

487 D 18. **ἀλλοκότους** 'strange,' 'eccentric.' 20. **τοῦτο,** viz. ἀχρήστους . . γιγνομένους. "*Wer zu viel bedenkt wird wenig leisten*" (Schiller).

PROTAGORAS

The introductory scene of the *Protagoras* (all that is here given) sets forth well the prominence and great popular influence of the sophists, as well as the attitude towards them of Socrates and Plato. The time feigned for the dialogue is perhaps about 432 B.C., or just before the beginning of the Peloponnesian War. For the Sophists, see Introd., § 26.

106 **310 A** 2. **ὄρθρου**: 43,2. 3. **δέ** is regular in adding a second relationship, as in 156,17.

310 B 6. **εἴσω . . ἐπειγόμενος** 'came hurrying in.' **τῃ φωνῇ μέγα** 'in a loud voice.' μικρόν is 'softly' (158,31). 7. **ἐγρήγορας**: active, but intrans. (30,21); 'are you awake?' 9. **οὗτος**, sc. ἐστί. **μή**: in quest., deprecates (14,14); 'no bad news, I hope?' On νεώτερον, H. 649. See also 24,9 App. 10. **ἦ δ' ὅς**: 6,11. **εἰ μή** 'except.' 11. **εὖ ἂν λέγοις** 'that will be fine.' 12. **τοῦ** = τίνος. **τηνικάδε**: 42,21. 13. **πρῴην** 'day before yesterday'; 96,9. 14. **ἑσπέρας**, i.e. '*yesterday* evening,' the Athenians reckoning their day from sunset to sunset.

310 C 17. **δῆτα** 'yes indeed.' 18. **Οἰνόης**: the deme Οἰνόη lay toward Boeotia, whither the slave (παῖς) was trying to escape. 20. **ὑπό**: 1,3 n. 21. **ἦλθον** = ἐπανῆλθον 'returned,' as frequently. 24. **λίαν**: 45,1. **πόρρω**: with νυκτῶν 'far into the night.' The plur. of νύξ (with reference to its *watches*, perhaps) is quite regular.

107 **310 D** 1. **οὕτω**: aft. ptc. 82,14. 88,1. 2. **ἀνδρείαν**

κτλ. 'eagerness and excitement' (Towle). Cf. *πτοέομαι* 83,23. 107
3. **μῶν** (*μὴ οὖν*), like *μή* (106,9), deprecates; 'I hope not,' 'surely not.' H. 1015, G. 1603. **τι**: indef. 4. **καὶ ὅς** 'and he' (91,29). 8. **εἰ γάρ** introduces wish; 45,26. 9. **ἐν τούτῳ εἴη** 'depended on that.' **ὡς**: causal.

310 E 10. **ἐπιλίποιμι** 'leave,' 'spare.' **τῶν φίλων** 'my friends,' for *τῶν τῶν φίλων* 'their property.' 11. **αὐτὰ ταῦτα . . ἥκω** 'that is just my errand'; an inner accus. such as *τί γελᾷς* (*quid rides?*) 'what is your joke or laugh?' To supply *διά* may help us to translation, but not to a knowledge of Greek. See 11,13 App. 16. **ἐπεδήμησε**: 5,28. **ἀλλὰ γάρ**: 5,3. 17. **σοφώτατον . . λέγειν**: 1,10 *δεινοῦ λέγειν*.

311 A 19. **καταλύει** 'is lodging.' L. & S. II 2. 22. **ἐξαναστῶμεν**: 92,20. 24. **καὶ γάρ**: 4,3. 25. **τὰ πολλά** 'for the most part'; 68,11. 28. **ἀναστάντες εἰς**: 89,25 and 29,5 n. 29. **ἀποπειρώμενος**: used in 70,8.

311 B 30. **ῥώμης**, sc. of purpose—or, perhaps, of his reasoning powers. **διεσκόπουν**, as in 8,12. 71,30. 2. 108
τελῶν: fut. ptc. 3. **ὡς** *κτλ.* 'with the notion that you will come to whom and become what?' The interrog. participial clause must be made the main clause in Engl.; 'to what (manner of) men do you suppose (*ὡς*) you are going, and what do you intend (*ὡς*) to become, in now resolving (*νῦν ἐπιχειρεῖς*) etc.?' 4. **ὥσπερ**: a good example of the Socratic method of teaching by analogy—'*just as* this is true, *so* isn't that?' The application in the present instance is not reached till li. 19. **ἄν** holds us in suspense till li. 10. **εἰ** 'supposing.' 6. **Ἱπποκράτη**: *this* Hippocrates, 'him of the Asclepiad guild' is the famous father of medicine. See Index of Proper Names. 8. **εἰ**: this condition rests on the previous one *εἰ ἐπενόεις*—a freq. occurrence; 2,17. 18,26.

311 C 10. **ἀπεκρίνω**: we should expect the imperf. 'what would you (now and here) answer?' But the aor. is sometimes used. H. 895 b, G. M. T. 414. So *εἶπον ἄν*. **ἄν**: repeated from 4. 19. **εἶεν**: 4,6.

311 D 19. **δὲ δή**: 14,12 and 13,28 notes. 22. **ἂν μὲν ἐξικνῆται** *κτλ.*: when a second contrary supposition is to follow (*εἰ δὲ μή*), the apodosis of the first is often omitted—perhaps being indicated by a shrug or gesture. *We* say 'good.' H. 904 a, G. 1416. 24. **προσ-***αναλίσκοντες* 'besides —'

311 E 1. **τί τοιοῦτον** ('what name like that') comes back to 109
the original quest., made now more definite by the *ὥσπερ*-clause. Such palin-dromic sentences are freq. (*παλίν-δρομος* 'running

109 back'); 41,9. 51,9. 59,10. 2. **δή τοι . . γε**: 44,18. 3. **εἶναι**: a freq. pleonasm aft. verbs of *naming*. Omit, or transl. *ὀνομάζω* 'pronounce.' **ὡς σοφιστῇ** goes with *τελοῦντες* (fut. ptc.), not with *ἐρχόμεθα*. The dat. aft. a verb of *motion* is very rare. See 55,23 App. 5. **προσ-***έροιτο* 'in addition —.'

312 A 8. **τι ἡμέρας** 'a bit of daylight.' 9. **εἰ μέν τι** *κτλ.* 'to be sure (*μέν*), if it's at all like —.' Though left unsaid, Hippocrates probably felt an objecting *δέ*-clause. 11. **πρὸς θεῶν**: 15,7. **αἰσχύνοιο** *κτλ.*: sophists taught for pay, while Hippocrates was a wealthy young aristocrat. 14. **ἀλλ' ἄρα . . μή** *κτλ.* (14,14) 'well then, maybe (*μή*) it is not of *that* kind that you suppose your instruction from Protagoras will be.'

312 B 18. **παιδοτρίβου**: 50,2. **τούτων** 'from them.' 19. **ἐπί**: c. dat. of purpose, '*for* a profession.' 21. **παιδείᾳ** 'general culture.' So 139,5. 22. **πάνυ μὲν οὖν**: 16,18. 26. **πέρι**: 4,31. **ὅτι μέλλεις** depends on *λανθάνει*.

312 C 28. **ποτε**: 6,29. 30. **οὐδὲ . . οἶσθα** 'no more
110 do you know.' 1. **πράγματι** 'thing,' applied to the sophist as an unknown quantity. 4. **τῶν σοφῶν ἐπι-στή-μονα**: i.e., he etymologizes the word as *σοφ-ιστή-ς*, connecting the latter part with *ἵστημι* and *ἐπίσταμαι*. In fact, of course, it is *σοφισ-τής*, from *σοφίζω* 'to make wise,' as *δικασ-τής* from *δικάζω*. **τῶν σοφῶν**: neut.; 'crafts,' 'branches of learning.'

312 D 8. **τῶν τί σοφῶν** 'crafts on what subject?' 9. **που**: 2,6 n. 10. **ἀπεργασίαν** 'turning out,' 'production.' 13. **ἐπιστάτης** replaces *ἐπιστήμων*. 14. **τί ἄν** 'how would it do?' verb omitted. 18. **ἡμῖν** = *ἡμῶν*; 'our' answer.

312 E 21. **ἐπιστήμονα**, sc. *ποιεῖ*. **ἦ γάρ** 'doesn't he?' (*n'est-ce pas? nicht wahr?*). Here too, as in *εἰ γάρ* of wishes, *γάρ* is not 'for'; 5,3 App. 26. **οὐκ-έτι** 'not likewise,' 'not as before.'

313 A 30. **ἤ**: 16,14. **εἰ μέν**: this condit. and its conclusion, though in Greek coordinated with the next (*δέ*, li. 5 of next page), is in Engl. to be subordinated by 'while,'
111 'whereas.' Cf. carefully with the sent. on 20,27. 1. **δια-***κινδυνεύοντα*: 26,27. 7. **πάντα . . τὰ σά** 'all your hopes (chances).' 8. **περὶ δὲ τούτου**: *δέ* is repeated from li. 5, *τούτου* resumptive; 'on this thing I say.'

313 B 11. **εἴτε . . εἴτε καί**: 54,1 n. 12. **τούτῳ**: in attribut. posit.; 31,20. 14. **οὐδένα λόγον οὐδὲ συμβουλὴν ποιεῖ** 'say not a word, ask no advice.' For the periphrasis with *ποιεῖσθαι* (note mid.), see 18,4. 18. **συν-εσ-τέον**:

σύν-ειμι. 19. **οὔτε διείλεξαι** 'nor *with whom* you have ever 111
conversed.' The Greek rarely repeats the relat. (as above, li. 6), though it often replaces it with a demonstrat. or *αὐτοῦ*, *-ῷ*, *-όν*.

313 C 20. **σοφιστήν**: prolepsis. 21. **φαίνει** c. ptc.; 'evidently' (10,3). 22. **ἔοικεν**, sc. *εἶναι*; 'it looks that way.' 24. **ἔμπορος** 'importer,' 'merchant'; *κάπηλος* 'retail-dealer.' 26. **φαίνεται γάρ**: Hippocrates is struck by the metaphor (Protagoras and the rest being indeed foreigners that "imported and peddled"), and so to the first part of Socrates' remark gives hearty assent (*γάρ* = 'certainly'). But the second part puzzles him; hence his question *τρέφεται . . ψυχὴ τίνι;* 29. **καὶ . . γε** 'aye . . and.' Socrates hastens to add an important warning. **ὅπως μή** introducing an independent clause, here c. aor. subjunct., usu. c. fut. indic.; G. M. T. § 283. Cf. 133,1,9.

313 D 1. **καὶ γάρ**: 4,3. 2. **ἀγωγίμων**: incorporated 112
into relat. clause; 58,16. 71,2. 4. **δέ** 'though.' 8. **ἀεί** 'each time'; 15,11. 11. **ὡς . . αὔτως** is perhaps the adv. of *ὁ αὐτός*; 'in the same way.' See L. & S. s.v. *αὔτως*, end, for accent and breathing. Cf. *ὡς ἀληθῶς* 6,14 App.

313 E 14. **τυγχάνεις**: *ὤν* is sometimes omitted. 17. **ὁτουοῦν**: H. 285, G. 432,1. 18. **περί** c. dat.; 87,21.

314 A 19. *καὶ γὰρ* ('for indeed') *δή* ('now'), *καί* ('even'). 26. **ἐπαΐοντα**: used 4,31. 50,11,17.

314 B 2. **ἡμεῖς . . ἔτι νέοι**: in 432 B.C., Socrates was c. 37 113
years of age. 3. **νέοι ὥστε** c. inf.; usu. it is a comparat. c. *ὥστε* (H. 954, G. 1531), unless it be such an adject. as *δεινός*, *ἱκανός*, etc. (H. 952, G. 1528).

314 C 9. **πολλοὶ καί**: drop *καί* (19,23). 10. **δόξαν.** aor. ptc., acc. absol. (13,26); here it is notable, *ταῦτα* failing to agree; G. M. T. § 854, H. 974 a, end. 11. **προθύρῳ**: probably the space for this part 'before the door' was obtained by a slightly projecting porch into the street (cf. 95,1,25), but also by an inset of the door. See the figure, p. 360. **ἐπιστάντες** 'halted and —' (30,24). 12. **διελεγόμεθα** 'went on talking' (imperf.). 14. **οὕτως** 'after going through with it, might *then*' (107,1). 17. **κατ**-*ήκουεν* '*over*-heard,' 'caught sound of.' **κινδυνεύει** 'perhaps'; 7,5 n.

314 D 19. **φοιτῶσιν**: 68,3. 43,6. 21. **ἔα** 'bah!' 22. **αὐτῷ**, i.e. his master, Callias; H. 681 c. 24. **ἐπ-ήραξεν**: *ἐπ-αράσσω.* 25. **ἐγ-κε-κλῃμένης**: note the tense; with the door 'shut.'

314 E 29. **γάρ τοι**: 15,9. 30. **μόγις**: 8,6. 2. 114

114 **προστῴῳ** 'cloister.' Upon these cloisters, running round the *αὐλή* or open inner court of a Greek house, opened the various chambers.

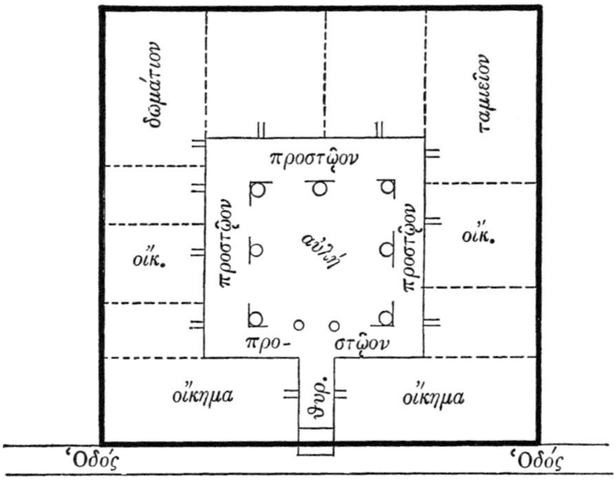

FIG. 1. SIMPLEST PLAN OF GREEK HOUSE.

3. **ἐκ μὲν τοῦ** *κτλ.* 'on the one side'; H. 788 c, G. 1225.

315 A 7. **τῶν,** sc. *ὑῶν.* 11. **οἵ:** this relat. clause is the subj. of *ἐφαίνοντο.* 12. **ἐπ-ακούοντες** 'listening, attending, to.' Disting. from *ὑπ-ακούω* (43,4. 68,18), and *κατ-ακούω* (113,17). 13. **τὸ μὲν πολύ** 'for the most part'; 107,25. 15. **κηλῶν:** used in 97,4. 16. **κατὰ τὴν φωνήν,** as *κατὰ τὴν ὁδόν*; lit., 'in the line of —.'

315 B 17. **ἐπιχωρίων:** in 67,13. 64,16. **χορῷ:** comparing them to the well-disciplined chorus of the drama, where exactness of position was required as rigorously as in a modern ballet. 19. **ἐν τῷ πρόσθεν,** sc. *Πρωταγόρου.* 22. **ἐπ-ήκοοι:** cf. *ἐπ-ακούοντες* li. 12. 25. **ἔφη:** in *Od.* 11,601, where Odysseus is telling what great heroes he saw in his visit to Hades. 25. **τόν** is the Homeric demonstrat. 'him,' viz. Hippias.

315 C 26. **κατ' ἀντικρύ** 'opposite.' 28. **ἐπὶ βάθρων** 'on benches,' contemptuously, as if Hippias kept school! See 264,21. 30. **πολῖται . . αὐτοῦ,** i.e. Elēans. 31. **φύσεως** (properly 'growing,' *φύσις, φύω*) = *natura*; 'the origin
115 of things.' 1. **μετεώρων:** 3,8 n. **ἄττα:** in 23,22. **δι-ερωτᾶν:** 9,23 n. 4. **καὶ μὲν δή** 'aye and then (*μέν* for

μήν), Tantalus too' (*Od.* 11,582); chosen here to typify the 115
wretched weakly Prodicus. 5. **γὰρ ἄρα** 'for sure enough.' Prodicus *was* in town, as Socrates had guessed 113,8.

315 D 11. **καί**: adv. c. *μάλα*. 14. **νέον τι** 'a bit young,' 'youngish.' 16. **φύσιν** 'growth,' 'stature.'

315 E 16. **δ' οὖν**: 1,3. **ἰδέαν** 'appearance.' 17. **ἔδοξα** 'I thought.' 19. **τοῦτ' ἦν** *κτλ.* 'there was this youth.'

GORGIAS

Debated under the heads Rhetoric *vs.* Philosophy, Politics *vs.* Ethics, the ultimate antithesis presented in the *Gorgias* is: The False *vs.* the True Aim of Life. Are we to live by the valuations of time or of eternity? of selfish petty might, or of everlasting right? The Rhetorician says: Learn my art of Persuasion; win your cause, whatever it be. The majority rules; become its leader. Thus will you best serve the state, and reach your personal highest goal as well. Socrates retorts: What profits the art of Persuasion, if thou knowest not the Truth—to which to persuade? Thou blind leader of the blind, first know thyself, and Truth. If thy cause be not righteous, better were it that it fail. Thy best duty to the State is, to contribute to it one good citizen—thyself. Reform *him*, and thou art the best of statesmen.

The place and date assumed for the dialogue are uncertain, and matter little. It reads as well for here and now (America, 1900), as for there and then. The moulds of Socrates, Polus, Callicles are not broken. A youth may pour his life into which he will. *θεὸς ἀναίτιος* (252,11).

471 E 9. **γάρ**: Polus had taken issue with the dictum of 116
Socrates that 'the wicked man is miserable,' and had confuted him, as he thought, by instancing Archelāus the king of Macedonia, at once one of the most powerful men of that time, and the wickedest, with whom not an Athenian but would gladly change places, beginning with Socrates himself. Socrates will not admit this kind of majority-refutation, '*for*' (*γάρ*) etc.

472 A 24. **ὧν**, c. *εἰσίν*. **οἱ ἑστῶτες** join to *ἐν τῷ* etc.
25. **τῷ Διονυσίῳ** 'the precinct sacred to Dionysus.' 2. 117
Πυθοῖ is itself locative ('at Delphi'), but sometimes a prepos. is added.

472 B 8. **τῆς οὐσίας**: a play on the word in its legal sense 'property,' 'realty,' 'inheritance,' and the philosophic sense 'reality,' 'essence.' That it is to be taken as a metaphor is

117 shown by the added explanation 'my heritage, the *truth*.' See 3,28 App.

472 C 18. **παραβαλόντες** 'putting side by side' = 'comparing.' Hence *παρα-βολή* 'parable.' L. & S. III 2.

472 D 25. **αὐτίκα** 'for example.' 28. **ἄλλο τι** : 13,21. 29. **ὡς . . νομίζοντος** ; where we should expect an object-
118 clause; G. 1593,2; G. M. T. 918. Cf. 192,4 App. 2. **ἆρα** '*really*'—the ultimate sense of the word, even when in its stereotyped place at the head of the question.

472 E 10. **πάντως** 'anyhow.'

119 **473 B** 29. **ἴσως** : ironical. 4. **χαλεπώτερον** : ironical. 9. **τυραννίδι ἐπι-** 'for (toward) a tyranny,' not 'against' it.

473 C 14. **ἐπ-ιδών** 'after looking upon,' sc. λωβηθέντας. **τὸ ἔσχατον** : adv. 15. **καταπιττωθῇ** : we 'tar and feather' in America, but rarely 'tar and set fire to.' 16. **ἤ** = 'than.'

473 D 19. **τῶν ἄλλων ξένων** 'strangers besides'; 33,8 n. 21. **αὖ** marks the shift from his previous attempt at refutation by plurality to this 'bugaboo' rhetoric. On *μορμολύττει*, see 48,27.

120 **473 E** 5. **ἐπεὶ ἐροῦ** 'for just ask' (aor.). *ἐπεί* gives no reason for the fact stated, but for the statement of the fact, as infra 27. See 5,17. 8. **πέρυσι βουλεύειν λαχών** : see 26,16 ff. This reference to 'last year' would fix the assumed date of the dialogue definitely at 405 B.C., did not other passages point with equal clearness to other dates. 9. **ἐπι-ψηφίζειν** 'to put to vote,' or, as in li. 18, 'to take one's vote'—regular term.

474 A 11. **μὴ . . μηδὲ νῦν** *κτλ.* 'don't ask me now *either*'; 104,10. 13. **ὅπερ** *κτλ.* prefaces what he is about to suggest, referring to what he had 'just now' (*νῦν δή*) said in 117,17. 14. **παράδος**, viz. *τὸν ἔλεγχον*. **πείρασαι** : imperat. mid.

121 **474 B** 29. **καὶ . . γε** 'aye—and.' 1. **οὔκουν** *κτλ.* 'then you won't answer?' 'Nay of course I will (*μὲν οὖν* corrective 42,23); for I *do* (*καί*) long —.' This 'no . . yes' *πάνυ μὲν οὖν* also 198,2.

474 C 4. **ὥσπερ ἄν** : 11, 10. 8. **αἴσχιον** 'fouler,' as disting. from *κάκιον* li. 6, stands with emphasis before *πότερον*. 9. **ἀποκρίνου** : 15,14 n.

474 D 17. **τί δὲ τόδε**, sc. (perhaps) λέγεις. Yet in 14,13; 84,7 a nomin. stands with *τί δέ*. **οἷον** : 77,3,8.

474 E 3. **ὡσαύτως**: 112,11. 5. **καὶ μὴν . . γε** 'aye 122
and certainly' holds fast to the points already won and presses on to add another. 7. **τὰ καλά** 'the fair' ones I mean, not all of them. **τοῦ . . εἶναι**: apposit. to *τούτων*.

475 A 20. **ὑπερβάλλον** 'by excelling. 23. **καὶ ὅταν δὲ δή** 'but then *also* whenever.'

475 B 1. **καὶ λύπῃ ὑπερβάλλον**: added with a fulness of 123
expression such as that in 84,5. 128,4.

475 C 6. **ὑπερ**-*βάλλει* and **ὑπερ**-*έχει* (10) c. genit. 13. **οὐκ-έτι** 'not *now*' ('no longer'); *ἔτι* corresponds to *ἤδη* in affirmat. sentences (Cope).

475 D 23. **ὡμολογεῖτο,** viz. in 121,10. 31. **βλαβήσει**:
fut. pass. 1. **παρέχων** 'submitting.' *σεαυτόν* need not be 124
expressed in Greek.

476 B 29. **διασκεψάμενος εἰπέ**: in Engl. 'don't speak till you have thoroughly considered,' or 'consider well before —.'
1. **τι εἶναι καὶ πάσχον** 'that there be a something that also 125
suffers.' 4. **τοῦτο** and **τοιοῦτον** (5): object of *πάσχον*.

477 A 26. **τὴν ὠφέλειαν**: for its posit. (in the relat. clause), 126
cf. 71,3. 112,2. 3. **ἐν χρημάτων** *κτλ.* 'in a man's 127
pecuniary condition' (Cope).

477 B 8. **αἶσχος** 'ugliness.'

477 D 3. **γάρ**: 84,20 n. 4. **ἀνιαρότατον** = *ἀλγεινότερον*. 128
5. **ὑπερβάλλον** 'because excelling,' 'by excelling.' 6. **ἀμφότερα**: adv. acc. 11. **ἀπὸ τούτων γε**: Polus catches sight of imminent refutation. 13. **ὑπερφυεῖ** *κτλ.*: for an original *ὑπερφυές τί ἐστιν ὡς* (see 79,21 n.); 'then because exceeding all else (*τἆλλα*) by some extraordinarily great harmfulness and amazing evil.'

477 E 19. **ἀλλὰ μήν** 'but surely'; 66,13.

478 A 31. **εἰ μὴ οὕτως εὐπορεῖς** 'if you're not just ready' with an answer.

478 B 27. **ἦ γάρ**: 110,21 n. 129

478 C 4. **ἀρχήν** 'at all'; 21,30. 130

478 E 28. **ἐπιπληττόμενος** 'rebuked' (Cope).

479 A 6. **παρεσκευάσθαι** 'has contrived to do' (Cope). 131
7. **ῥήτορας** begins to bring us back to the first question proposed in the dialogue—What is the value of Rhetoric? **δυνάστας** 'potentates.' 10. **ὥσπερ ἄν**: 11,10 n. 11. **συνισχόμενος** 'afflicted' (Cope). 14. **ὡσπερανεὶ παῖς** 'as (he would if he were) a child.'

479 B 19. **τοιοῦτόν τι,** viz. *καθορᾶν κτλ.* (21). 23. **μὴ**

131 **ὑγιοῦς σώματος** 'than with unsound body'—a rare use of the comparat. genit. for *ἤ* c. dat.; H. 643 b, G. 1155.

479 C 27. **ὅπως ἂν ὦσιν**: a third object of *παρασκευαζόμενοι*. 30. **συμβαίνοντα** 'issues,' 'results.' **βούλει**: c.
132 subjunct. of deliberat.; H. 866,3 b; G. 1358. 1. **καλῶς**: the MSS. read *ἄλλως*, with no sense. 5. **καὶ μὴν . . γε**: 122,5.

479 D 12. **πέφυκεν**: 30,21.

479 E 20. **διαφερόντως**: c. gen. 'more than' (59,22).

133 **480 A** 1. **ὅπως μὴ ἀδικήσῃ**: 111,30 App. So *ποιήσῃ* li. 9. **ἱκανόν**: litotes; 4,13 n.

480 B 18. **εἰ μὴ εἰ**: 101,24.

480 C 25. **παρέχειν**: 124,1 n.

134 **480 D** 1. **αὐτόν** 'himself.'

480 E 8. **σοι** 'perhaps, however, *in your eyes* it agrees with the previous'; 17,18. 13. **τοὐναντίον** *κτλ.*: a heaping up of adversative expression. **μεταβαλόντα** (acc. masc. intrans.) 'conversely' (lit. 'changing sides'). **εἰ ἄρα** 'if in truth'—as Greek ethics ran. 14. **τινα**: object of *κακῶς ποιεῖν*, aft. which a partit. apposit. 15. **ἐὰν μόνον μὴ αὐτός** *κτλ.*: ironical. It would be expecting *too* much of a man that he work for the acquittal of his enemy, when he himself had been the victim. 'But if it be some *other* man that his enemy is injuring —.'

481 A 26. **μάλιστα μέν** 'if possible'; 29,19.

135 **481 B** 31. **οὐ μεγάλη τις** 'no great one.' 1. **εἰ δὴ καί** *κτλ.* 'if, you know, it is *indeed* (*καί*).' 6. **οὐδὲν . . οἷον** *κτλ.* 'nothing like asking him.'

481 C 9. **θῶμεν**: 18,23. 13. **ἐναντία . . ἤ**: 89,10.

482 E 17. **συμποδισθείς**: Callicles here plays on the name of his frisky young friend Πῶλος (='filly,' Mr. 'Filli-kin'), who has been thoroughly broken—thrown down with his feet tied and a bit put in his mouth (*ἐπ-εστομίσθη*). 20. **φορτικὰ καὶ δημηγορικά** 'old-saw claptrap' (cf. 26,13). **φάσκων** 'with your pretence.' 21. **ἅ** refers to *τοιαῦτα*. 22. **ὡσ-τα-πολλά** is felt as one word (cf. 68,11); hence *δέ* only apparently stands in the fourth place.

483 A 26. **τοῦτο τὸ σοφόν**: an explanatory appos. to *ὅ*, inserted in the relat. clause much as in the so-called cases of
136 incorporation 71,3. 126,26. *σοφόν=σόφισμα* 'trick.' 1. **κατὰ νόμον** 'in a conventional sense,' 'on the conventional basis.' **ὑπ-***ερωτῶν*: either '*slyly* questioning,' or '*retorting*

with a question' (cf. ὑπο-λαβών, ὑπο-κρίνομαι). 3. **αὐτίκα**: 136
117,25. 5. **ἐδιώκαθες**: διώκω; H. 494, G. 779.

483 B 12. **αὐτὸς αὑτῷ**: 17,27. 13. **οἱ τιθέμενοι**: note voice (6,3). H. 816; L. & S., A v.

483 D 28. **αὐτό, ὅτι** 'just this, that.' 31. **δηλοῖ ταῦτα** κτλ.: a sort of prolepsis.

483 E 7. **ἄλλα μυρία** κτλ.: cf. 41,15. 137

484 A 19. **γράμματα** 'statute laws.' 21. **ἀνεφάνη** 'shows himself,' 'springs forth'—gnomic aor.; H. 840, G. 1292. So ἐξέλαμψε.

484 B 28. **οὗτος**, sc. νόμος. 29. **ἄγει** 'works,' 'effects.' **δικαιῶν** (ptc.) 'justifying.' In what follows, Pindar's attitude was probably religious. He was thinking of the might of Heracles' right. But the "statesman" of Plato's time would interpret rather as the right of his might. 31. **ἀ-πριάτας**
'unbought,' sc. βοῦς, as appears later. 1. **ἐπίσταμαι**: 71,2. 138

484 C 8. **ἐπὶ τὰ μείζω** 'to broader views (larger aims)'—ever the cry of superficialists, undisciplined, arrogant, empty. **ἤδη** 'at last.' 10. **χαρίεν** 'a pretty thing,' 'a nice thing.' 14. **πόρρω** c. gen.; 36,21.

484 D 16. **καλόν** κτλ. 'a gentleman and man of consideration.' 17. **καὶ γάρ**: καί is 'both,' with two correlat. καί's following. 19. **λόγων** 'principles.' 20. **συμβολαίοις** 'compacts,' 'covenants.' **τοῖς ἀνθρώποις**: c. ὁμιλεῖν. 22. **ἠθῶν** 'ways.'

484 E 28. **τὸ τοῦ Εὐριπίδου**: 30,19 n. 29. **τούτῳ** and **τοῦτο**: anteced. of ἵνα 'where,' li. 31. 31. **αὐτὸς αὑτοῦ . . βέλτιστος** 'at his best'; H. 644 a.

485 A 5. **ὅσον παιδείας χάριν** 'so far as necessary for the 139
sake of culture.' 9. **χρῆμα** 'business,' contemptuously. 10. **ὁμοιότατον πάσχω** 'have quite the same feeling.'

485 C 23. **παρά** 'in.' **νέῳ**: emphat. by posit.—before μέν, and separated from μειρακίῳ.

485 D 1. **ὑπάρχει** 'it is possible.' L. & S., B v 2. 140
4. **ὁ ποιητής** is Homer, when no name is given.

485 E 11. **ὁ Εὐριπίδου** 'the Zethus *in* Euripides,' i.e. in the (now lost) drama (Antiope) from which the verses were taken 138,30–31. 14. **ἀμελεῖς**: Callicles quotes, with a few changes, the words of Zethus, hunter and herdsman, to his brother Amphīon, musician. But he fails to add that in the building of the walls of Thebes the strength of Zethus' arm did not avail to raise the stones as much as Amphīon's lyre. 15. **φύσιν** κτλ. perhaps depends on some unquoted ἔχων; 'though

140 of so noble growth of soul, thou art conspicuous by thy boyish guise' (in the fragments of the drama, *γυναικομίμῳ* for *μειρακιώδει τινί*). Also what follows must be a free continuation of Euripides, to judge from the poetic form *βουλαῖσι* and the words *δίκης* (in the sense of 'justice') and *λάκοις* (*λάσκω* 'to speak').

486 A 19. **νεανικόν** 'gallant,' 'bold.' 21. **τῇ σῇ**: objective; '*toward* you' (4,17). 22. **ὡς**: adv. c. *ἔχειν*.

141 **486 B** 1. **τιμᾶσθαι**: 34,30 n. and the n. following 32,9. 4. **φῶτα**: poetic for *ἄνδρα*; **ἔθηκε** for *ἐποίησε*. 7. **περισυλᾶσθαι** depends prob. on *ἔθηκε*, and more fully explains *χείρονα*. 8. **οὐσίαν**: H. 724 a, G. 1239, for the acc. c. pass verb.

486 C 9. **εἴ τι καί** 'even if it *is* something'; cf. 24,9. 11. **ἐλέγχων**: prob. a ptc., since the original passage here shows one. 12. **εὐμουσίαν** 'accomplishment' (Cope). 16. **τὰ μικρά**: c. *ἐλέγχοντας*.

486 D 17. **βίος** = *βιότης* 'livelihood,' 'wealth,' opposed to *κενοῖσι δόμοις* above.

142 **492 A** 1. **δή** 'you know,' 'forsooth'; ironical.

492 B 7. **οἷς . . ὑπῆρξεν** 'whose fortune it was' (Lodge). 8. **αὐτούς** 'themselves.' 11. **οἷς ἐξόν** *κτλ.* 'if, when it was possible for them to —, should themselves bring in (*ἐπαγάγοιντο*)'; as if *οἵ, ἐξὸν αὐτοῖς*.

492 C 16. **καλοῦ τοῦ τῆς δικαιοσύνης**: an apposit. genit.; 21,18 and infra li. 27. 21. **ἐπικουρίαν** 'available succour,' 'power at disposal.' 22. **τὰ δὲ ἄλλα**, viz. *τὰ συνθήματα*. The predic. is *φλυαρία*. With *καλλωπίσματα* ('prettinesses,' 'airs,' 'fine talk'), cf. *καλλωπισμούς* 77,9. *ἐκαλλωπίζου* 60,6.

521 A 25. **ποτέραν**: predic. posit. (7,13); 'which, then, is the service to which you exhort me?' Callicles had exhorted in
143 141,11 ff. 1. **ἰατρόν**: reference to a previous sharply-drawn contrast between the physician, who is in constant warfare (*δια-μάχεσθαι*) with his patients for their own good, and the cook (*ὀψοποιός*, 'pastryman'), who tempts the palate with pleasant but unwholesome food. **ἢ ὡς διακονήσοντα** should be *ἢ τὴν τοῦ διακονεῖν*, but conforms to the intervening *ὡς ἰατρόν*; 'as one who would be their servant.' 2. **πρὸς χάριν** 'with the view to please.' See L. & S. s.v. *πρός*, C III 7. 3. **Καλλίκλεις**: no *ὦ*; nor in li. 21. See 59,11 App.

521 B 10. **Μυσόν**: Mysians were pusillanimous cringers. There was a proverb *Μυσῶν ἔσχατος* 'vilest of the vile' (Lodge). Callicles is angry at the way the argument has gone against him; and at this last comparison of the statesman with the *κόλαξ*, he answers hotly: 'Yes, if it's more agreeable to you to

call him a *toad-eater*'—putting Μυσόν for κόλακα. 11. **ὡς**: 143
causal. **ποιήσεις**: 20,11 n. for tense and mood. 14.
πονηρός γε κτλ.: cf. 23,27 for the thought. 15. **ἀφαιρή-
σεται**: mid., not pass.

521 C 21. **ὥς**: exclam.; 'how sure (*πιστεύων*) you seem to be.' 22. **μηδ' ἂν ἕν**: cf. *οὐδ' ἂν ἑνί* 26,11 n. **ἐκποδών** 'out of harm's way' (Cope). 23. **ἂν εἰσαχθείς** stands for a potent. optat. All this anticipation was written, of course, *post eventum.* 27. **ὅ τι τύχοι, τοῦτο παθεῖν**: cf. 47,14. 45,31. The optat. as in any condit. relat. clause; G. M. T. § 558.

521 D 29. **ὅ**: sing., by attract. of the nearer *τινός*, though
referring to *τούτων*. So *Gorg.* 486 D, *Theaet.* 209 A. 1. 144
βούλει: 131,30. 9. **οὐ πρὸς τὸ ἥδιστον** returns to *οὐ πρὸς
χάριν*; cf. 109,1 repeating 108,30.

521 E 11. **τὰ κομψὰ ταῦτα**: Callicles' phrase for philosophy (141,13) is retorted upon his own rhetoric. 13. **κρινοῦμαι**: mid. for pass. 18. **ὅδε . . ἀνήρ** 'here's a man that —.' **καὶ αὐτούς, καί** 'both yourselves and —.' But the second clause has its own verb; 32,17 n. 19. **διαφθείρει** 'cripples,' 'dis-ables'; but, writing *post eventum*, Plato uses the word to recall its use in the indictment against Socrates, the physician of souls (13,9).

522 A 21. **ἀπορεῖν ποιεῖ**: again one of the stock charges against Socrates—that of 'puzzling,' 'unsettling,' the minds of his associates. The phrase is perhaps hardly proper as a medical term, but in Platonic similes the expression is never more than the thinnest veil over the real subject, which often *breaks through* as here. See 145,7 where the application is made. Cf. infra 165,27 ff. 22. **οὐχ ὥσπερ ἐγώ** κτλ.: a common Greek mode of brief comparison that cannot be imitated in English. Transl. 'not (doing) as I (who).' 27. **ὑγιεινῶς** 'for your health.' **ὁπόσον οἴει** κτλ. is an indirect quest. (not *πόσον*), intended perhaps to depend upon an added "tell me that"—which, however, is omitted. Cf. infra 154,16. So in Engl. "But how to do it? [that's the question]," where the last is freq. unsaid. 28. **οἴεσθαί γε χρή**: 62,3. 30. **ἐν ἀπορίᾳ ἔχεσθαι** 'be held (caught) in —.' So freq. *ἐν ξυμφοραῖς, πένθεσι, ἀνάγκαις ἔχεσθαι.* L. & S. s.v. *ἔχω*, A I 8 end.

522 B 2. **οἶδ' ὅτι**: parenthetic and adverbial, as often. Cf. 145
δῆλον ὅτι. 3. **οὔτε**: *ἐάντε* (7) answers. 6. **ἐγὼ δέ** κτλ.:
parenthetic.

522 C 18. **εἰ . . γε** 'yes if —.' Cf. 143,10.

522 D 23. **αὕτη**: on gend. and function (predic.), see 2,25; 'this is the sort of (*τις*) self-help that —.'

146 **522 E** 3. **ἀλόγιστος**: for the thought, see 21,11. 8. **λόγον λέξαι** 'tell a tale.' On *λέξαι* (not *εἰπεῖν*), see 7,2 App. 9. **καὶ τἆλλα ἐπέρανας**: three or four times Callicles had wished to break off the conversation, at one point (506 c) actually leaving Socrates to 'finish' the argument by himself, answering his own questions.

523 A 11. **φασί**, viz. storytellers; for *ἄκουε δή* was the regular beginning. 12. **μῦθον** 'a mere story,' 'myth'—though Socrates will regard it as a *λόγος* 'true story,' 'true account.' There is *λόγος* 'reason' in it, though he cannot dogmatically maintain it (*δι-ισχυρίσασθαι* 87,11) any more than he can his teachings on the hereafter in the *Phaedo* or *Republic*, infra p. 247. 15. **λέγει**: in *Il.* 15,187 ff. 18. **νόμος ὅδε**: no art. (29,6). **ἐπὶ Κρόνου** 'in the time of Cronus' (99,2). 19. **καὶ . . καί** 'and . . even.'

523 B 25. **τούτων δικασταὶ . . ζῶντες ζώντων**: chiastic. 29. **οἱ ἐκ νήσων**: 26,19.

523 C 31. **σφιν**, i.e. to Pluto in Tartarus, and to the guardians in the Isles of the Blest.

147 **523 D** 13. **αὐτοῖς . . ἐπίπροσθεν γίγνεται** 'get in their way.' For the thought, cf. 78,9. 17. **τοῦτο**: proleptic subject of *εἴρηται*. Make it obj. of *παύσῃ*. **καὶ δή** '(even) already.' 18. **ὅπως ἂν παύσῃ**, instead of the infin.; 68,21 n. **αὐτῶν** 'in them'; 1,7,13.

523 E 20. **τούτων**: c. *γυμνούς*. 23. **ἐξαίφνης**, i.e. *οὐ προειδότας*. **ἔρημον**: masc. *κατὰ σύνεσιν* (2,6), though referring to *ψυχήν*.

148 **524 A** 5. **ἐπι-**_διακρίνειν_ 'to pass the *final* (or *after*-) judgment.'

524 B 10. **συμβαίνειν** 'result.' 12. **διάλυσις**: for the thought, cf. 76,21. 14. **ἄρα** 'sure enough' (at last). **οὐ πολὺ ἧττον** 'as much as ever.' 17. **τό τε σῶμα**: the *τε . . καί* scheme proves too small, as the *σῶμα*-half expands. Not till next page, li. 1, is the *ψυχή* taken up by *ταὐτὸν δή*. See 5,13 App. 18. **τὰ θεραπεύματα** *κτλ.* 'the results (-*μα* suffix) of training or accident' (Thompson). 19. **οἷον**: 77,3.

524 C 20. **ἀμφότερα**: adverbial; 128,6. 25. **ἴχνη** '*as* traces' (of the stripes). 28. **κατεαγότα**: -*ἄγνυμι*; intrans. perf. act.; 30,21.

149 **524 D** 1. **ἐπί** c. acc. of time, 'for.' 7. **ἔσχεν**: 4,9 n. 8. **οἱ μὲν . . παρὰ τὸν Ῥαδάμανθυν**: those who come before Aeacus are taken up 151,29.

524 E 10. **ἐπιστήσας**: cf. the *2nd* aor. (intrans.) 55,26. 149
113,11. 13. **δυνάστου**: 131,7. **κατεῖδεν**: gnomic, as in 21 and 22.

525 A 16. **ἐξωμόρξατο**: *-ομόργνυμι.* 22. **εὐθύ**, c. genit., 'straight to.'

525 B 31. **ὠφελούμενοι**: transl. *after δίκην διδόντες.* 1. 150
οὗτοι, οἳ ἄν is predic.; 'are those who.' 2. **ὅμως**: though their sins were not of the worst, 'still.' 4. **οὐ γὰρ οἷόντε ἄλλως** *κτλ.*: "this and similar passages in Plato doubtless laid the foundation of the theological idea of a purgatory, which seems to have been alien from the native Hebrew mind" (Thompson).

525 C 13. **ἀτεχνῶς**: c. *ἀνηρτημένους* (2,16); 'literally hung up as paradigms.'

525 E 27. **Τάνταλον** *κτλ.*: *Od.* 11,576–600. 28. **ἰδιώτης**: at end, for emphasis. 29. **συνεχόμενον**: 131,11. 30. **αὐτῷ**, i.e. *Θερσίτῃ*, and supply *τὰ μέγιστα ἁμαρτάνειν*, or the like. **διὸ καί**: 101,7. 31. **ἀλλὰ γάρ** *κτλ.* 'nay in truth, it is from the ranks of the powerful (and not from those in private station) that also (*καί*) those come who prove very wicked men (just as from their ranks came the paradigms).' Cf. 5,3; 104,24 for *ἀλλὰ γάρ.*

526 A 2. **οὐδὲν μὴν κωλύει** 'nothing, to be sure, *hinders*'— 151
answered by *ὀλίγοι δέ* in li. 7. 4. **σφόδρα**: best with *ἄγασθαι.* **τῶν γιγνομένων** (gen. c. *ἄγασθαι*) = the previous compound *ἐγ-γίγνεσθαι*, a preposit. being regularly dropped on repetition (45,27 App.); 'aye, and heartily should we admire those (good men) found among them.' 5. **χαλεπὸν γάρ** *κτλ.*: cf. *Luke* 18,25 *εὐκοπώτερον γάρ ἐστιν κάμηλον διὰ τρήματος βελόνης εἰσελθεῖν ἢ πλούσιον εἰς τὴν βασιλείαν τοῦ θεοῦ εἰσελθεῖν.* 9. **ἐνθάδε**: in Athens.

526 B 16. **ἔλεγον**: in 149,12. 17. **ἄλλο μέν**: 20,6 n.

526 C 25. **μάλιστα μέν** 'especially'; *μέν* = *μήν.* 28. **ἠγάσθη**: the line forms, doubtless by accident, a dactylic hexameter. See 257,15 n. 31. **ἐπι-***σκοπῶν*: cf. *ἐπι-διακρίνειν* 148,5.

526 D 3. **χρύσεον** *κτλ.*: *Od.* 11,569. 152

526 E 14. **ἀντι-***παρακαλῶ*: this invitation is 'in return' to that of Callicles 141,11. Cf. also 142,26. 15. **ἀντί** 'worth.' 16. **ἐνθάδε** 'on earth.' **οὐχ οἷόστ' ἔσει**: this terrible counter-invitation echoes the very words of the original. Cf. 140,24 ff. One is reminded of how Don Juan supped with the statue—in Hell.

527 A 22. **καὶ ἐπὶ κόρρης**: 141,10. *καί* is adv. 24. **δ' οὖν**, 'however,' dismisses the tale. See 1,3 App.

153 **527 B** 9. **κατά τι** 'in any respect.' 10. **τοῦτο**, viz. *τὸ γίγνεσθαι κτλ.* in next line.

527 C 15. **οὕτω**, viz. *ἐπὶ τὸ δίκαιον.* 18. **ἐνταῦθα, οἷ** for *ἐνταυθοῖ οἷ*: 33,12. 19. **ὁ σὸς λόγος**: it is rather the silence of Callicles than his argument (*λόγος*) that here 'indicates.' His last word had been a surly one (146,10). Yet Socrates may fairly claim him as the *εἷς μάρτυς* that he desired (117,14).

527 D 26. **τοῖς πολιτικοῖς**: neut., 'politics.' 28. **αἰσχρόν** (*ἐστιν*). 29. **ἔχοντας** intrans. **ἔπειτα**: 6,24.

154 **527 E** 2. **ὥσπερ ἡγεμόνι**: *λόγος* is personified; 52,26 n. 3. **οὗτος**, viz. *ζῆν κτλ.* in 5.

EUTHYDEMUS

"DRAMATIC vivacity and comic force, holding up various persons to ridicule or contempt, are attributes which Plato manifests often and abundantly. But the dialogue in which these qualities reach their maximum is the Euthydēmus" (Grote). Socrates narrates how two old sophists (ex-fencing masters) had been giving an exhibition of their skill in dialectic, involving their respondent in contradiction and confusion, winning for themselves great applause—and perhaps a pupil or so (with his fee). He had himself, he tells us, then endeavoured to show these professors how, by a proper use, dialectic conducted the pupil not to perplexity and humiliation, but to the truth that was latent within him.

Clearly, therefore, Plato wishes us to look first on this picture and then on that, comparing the self-display and emptiness of the frivolous sophists with the humility and sincerity of his master in his search for truth. That he has emphasized the contrast, there can be no doubt. Socrates is "depicted as a gentle, soothing, encouraging teacher with his claws drawn in" (Grote), while the sophist-brothers are made to talk such patent fallacy that we can regard them only as caricatures—just as Socrates himself had been caricatured by Aristophanes in the *Clouds*. The irony is the more sweeping in that it not only puts such triviality into the sophists' mouths, but also gives them rounds of applause for it from the bystanders. (So Aristophanes in the *Birds* gives his hero Peithetaerus a blazing (stage-)triumph at the end. So Molière in his *Précieuses Ridicules* throws Magdalen into a transport of praise over

Mascarille's verses: "J'aimerais mieux avoir fait ce *oh, oh!* qu'un poëme épique.") We are not, therefore, to suppose that this merry brace of quibblers ever existed, any more than the Aristophanic Socrates. We should not be so prone to the error, were not Plato so great a dramatist. Who knows but that, when the next dark age shall have rolled away Shakespeare may emerge as the best original (and perhaps contemporary) source for the history of Julius Caesar?

One should read the *Euthydemus* entire to enjoy it. It is true that, on the day he wrote it, Plato went forth for a mere skirmish with his life-long enemies (the Sophists) "lightly clad"—with but his arms of ridicule. Yet surely his success was never greater. He has veritably "arm-pitted" his adversaries. To this day the two toothless old brothers, vividly real, stalk the earth, allowed neither vengeance nor oblivion.

In the present extract, only a few of the fallacies are given, and the Socratic antithesis of method is omitted altogether, as well as the very important epilogue. The student should by all means consult Grote's *Plato*, ch. 19, and Zeller's *Pre-Socratic Philosophy* II p. 462 of the Engl. translation of 1881.

271 A 10. **ἐν Λυκείῳ**: Introd., n. 17. 11. **ἦ** 'truly' 154
—except in interrog. sentences, is not common outside of the groups *ἦ μήν, ἦ που.* 16. **ὁπότερον**: indirect; 'which one you are *asking* about (is the question).' See 144,27 n. *καί* stresses *ἐρωτᾷς* (24,9)? 18. **ἐκ δεξιᾶς** 'on your right' (114,3 n.).

271 B 19. **τὸ Ἀξιόχου μειράκιον**: Cleinias. 22. **ἡλικίαν**: here of *size*; L. & S. *sub verbo* v.

271 C 10. **ὅ**: inner acc.; 'as for your quest. concerning.' 155
The Greek, for us, would be simpler, if it read *ἡ δὲ σοφία, ἣν σὺ ἐρωτᾷς, θαυμασία ἐστί.* 12. **ὡς** 'since,' explaining why he employs superlatives. 15. **τὼ Ἀκαρνᾶνε**: ephemeral fame! Even their names are not now known.

271 D 18. **πάν**-*των* **κρατ**-*εῖν* plays on *παγ-κρατ-ιασταί.*

272 A 21. **καὶ . . καί**: anacoluthon; the 2nd member frees itself; 32,17 n. 23. **οἵους** for *οἷοί εἰσι*; 99,12 n. 26. **ἀργός**: passive. L. & S. II 2. 28. **ἀντ-ᾶραι**: *-αίρω.*

272 B 3. * * * Socrates in the part omitted tells how, 156
as he sat in the undressing room (*ἀπο-δυτήριον*) of the Lycēum, there had entered first the sophist-brothers with a crowd of pupils, and then the fair Cleinias with a band of friends, among them his devoted admirer Ktesippus. Since their last visit to Athens, the professors had added to their arts of arms and rhetoric that of dialectic. They now offered to teach *ἀρετή.* And Socrates proposes that they exhibit (*ἐπιδεῖξαι*).

156 **275 A** 7. **γε δή**: 64,20. 9. **εἰς αὖθις ἀπόθεσθον**: cf. 94,13. 12. **χαριεῖσθον**: fut. indic. 16. **τοῦ** goes back to Ἀξιόχου, 'the son of —.' 17. **τοῦ παλαιοῦ**, viz. grandfather of the great Alcibiades.

275 B 17. **δέ**: 106,3 n. 20. **φθῇ**: *φθάνω*. 22. **εἰς κάλλιστον**: 94,12 n.

275 C 28. **ἀλλὰ μὲν δή**: 51,31. 29. **καί**: not only willing is he, but 'even' *accustomed* to it. 31. **ἐπιεικῶς**
157 **θαρρεῖ** 'is fairly brave at —.' 1. **πῶς ἄν**: a freq. formula of wishing, espec. in tragedy; 'I wish I could —.' 4. **ἀμήχανον ὅσην**: inverse attract. (99,14).

275 D 5. **δέομαι** 'need.' 11. **ἠρυθρίασε**: 109,7. 12. **ἔβλεπε** 'sat looking,' imperf.

275 E 16. **ἐν τούτῳ** 'meanwhile' (159,7). 17. **προσκύψας**: cf. *ὑπερκύψας* 154,14. 18. **καὶ μήν** 'and (yet) in truth,' *καί*=*καίτοι*. 21. **μεταξύ** c. ptc.; 39,17. 23. **ἐξεγένετο** 'became possible,' aor. of *ἔξεστι*. Cf. 80,9 *ἐγ-γίγνεται*.

158 **276 B** 6. **σοφοί**: predic.; 'to *be* wise.' Evident as these fallacies are, it may be well for the student to think out and clearly state the source of each. 8. **ὑπό** *κτλ.* 'under a leader, at his signal'; 114,17 n. 9. **ἀν**-*εθορύβησαν*: cf. *ἀνα-βοάω* (144,27), *ἀν-ευφημέω* (68,28).

276 C 13. **ἐκ-δεξάμενος**: used of catching a ball.

276 D 22. **ἀγασθέντες** c. gen. (151,4). 27. **διπλᾶ ἔστρεφε**: a dance-figure not now known. 28. **πότερον γάρ**: for *γάρ* in quest., see H. 1050,4 b. 31. **μικρόν** 'softly'; cf. *μέγα* 106,6.

159 **276 E** 2. **τὸ πρότερον**: adv., 'the other time,' as infra lines 3 and 10, and 160,28. So too 273 E. 5. **τοιγάρτοι**: the first *τοι* is perhaps equiv. to, if not identical with, the demonstrat. Homeric *τῷ* (*τῶ*) at head of verse='by that,' 'therein,' 'therefore.' The appended *γάρτοι* is confirmatory; 'that's the reason surely' of your *εὐδοκιμεῖν*. 10. **ὧνπερ**: supply *διά*; 19,1.

277 A 14. **ὧν τι**=*τι τούτων ἅ*; the *τι* is object of *ἀποστοματίζει*. 15. **πάντα**, sc. *γράμματα*. 16. **τί οὖν**: 74,30. 110,28. 18. **γράμματα**: obj. of the ptc.

277 B 22. **οὔπω . . καί** 'not yet . . when.' So aft. *ἤδη* 93,11. 99,26. **σφόδρα τι**: *τι* as in *σχεδόν τι*.

160 **277 C** 4. **τούτων**, viz. *τῶν μὴ ἐχόντων* in next line. 5. **κατ**-*ένευσε*: cf. *ἐπ-ένευσε* 158,5.

283 A 10. **ἐγὼ . . ταῦτα εἶπον** refers to the exhibition (omitted) that Socrates had made of dialectic. 18. **μάλα**

reg. stands *after* rather than before *αὐτίκα* temporal. 19. 160
οὖν: not a conjunct. of course, when a relat. heads the sent. **καί** 'in fact,' or '*did*' happen.

283 B 21. **ὡς** 'how' (*οὗ* being proleptic). Others take it as causal. 28. **ἄρα** 'sure enough.'

283 C 4. **ἔσκεμμαι** 'I *have* considered.' Cf. 48,6. 161
οὐ μή c. aor. subjunct.; 22,12. 6. **νῦν**: strictly temporal here.

283 D 13. **ἐθορυβήθην**: note tense (that of entrance into a state) as compared with *θορυβουμένου*. 14. **ὅς**: a substitution for *οἷος*—hence the fallacy. 17. **φίλοι** '*as* friends,' predic.

283 E 22. **ἀγροικότερον**: 27,7. 23. **εἶπον ἄν**: 108,10 n. for tense. **σοὶ εἰς κεφαλήν**, sc. *τράποιτο τὸ ἐξολωλέναι*—a common brief imprecation for turning back any word of ill-luck upon the utterer. **ὅ τι μαθών**: 33,5. 24. **καταψεύδει** c. gen. pers. et acc. rei (cf. 14,21), 'lyingly charge one with —.' 25. **πρᾶγμα** is explained by *ὡς ἐγώ κτλ.*

284 A 2. **πῶς γὰρ ἄν**, sc. *ἄλλο λέγοι*. 6. **ἀλλὰ μήν** 162
'but surely'; 128,19.

293 B 14. **ταύτην**, viz. the knowledge Socrates had just been speaking of (omitted), *ἧς τυχόντες ἂν καλῶς τὸν ἐπίλοιπον βίον διέλθοιμεν*. 17 **ἔστι δέ**: a vocat. at the head of a sent. is not regarded as belonging to it. Hence *δέ* is only apparently in the fourth place. 'But, my angel, is this in your power (*ἐπί* c. dat.)?'

293 C 27. **τούτου γε**: supply *ἐπιστήμων*. Socrates, more cautious than Celinias in guarding his replies, will evidently give trouble to the sophists. 29. **μὰ Δία**: negat. oath.
1. **ἧττον οὖν** *κτλ.* (but because of this restriction) are you 163
then (*οὖν*) a whit the less unwise?—ironical, the implication being "no."

293 D 5. **Εὐθύδημε**: no *ὦ*; 59,11 App. **καλὰ δὴ παταγεῖς**: original use dubious. See L. & S. 7. **ὡς**: causal.

293 E 17. **φίλης κεφαλῆς**: strange are the habits of language. We may in Engl. call a man a sleepy-head, cabbage-head, dead-head, block-head; but here we must translate 'dear *heart*.' 22. **καὶ μάλα** 'yes indeed,' sc. we do know something.

294 A 24. **πρός**: adv., 'in addition,' 'to boot.' 27. **μῶν**: 107,3. 28. **ἢ οὐδέν** is not the alternative to *πάντα*, but withdraws the first quest. and substitutes another (16,14). 29. **οὐ γὰρ δήπου** 'it cannot be, I presume, that —.'

164 **294 B** 3. **καί** seems to be = *καίτοι* 'although' as in 21,16. *Gorg.* 519 c. Demos. 6,16. (Otherwise, should not *μόλις* be *μάτην* ?) 6. **ἦ** 'honour bright'—as boys say. 9. **εἶτα**: (simulated) surprise; 19,26. 43,10.

294 C 15. **ὁπόσους ὀδόντας**: splenetic hint at the toothlessness of the old imposters.

294 D 28. **τὼ δέ**: demonstrat. 29. **πρὸς τὴν πληγήν**: a syntactic substitute for the dat. of li. 28.

165 **294 E** 3. **μαχαίρας . . τροχοῦ**: see L. & S., *κυβιστάω* and *δινέω*. 9. **εὐθύς** 'straightway when born,' 'as soon as' born: properly c. *ἠπίστασθε*.

295 A 12. **πλήν γ' ὅτι**: ironical. His belief is clean gone, *except* as to *their* wisdom.

297 B 21. **φεύγεις** 'evade,' viz. the last point (omitted), though in truth it was the sophist-pair, not Socrates, that had been evading. 23. **τοῦ ἑτέρου** 'either one.'

297 C 24. **μὴ οὐ**: double negat. aft. the implied negat. in *πολλοῦ δέω* (= *ἀδύνατος*); H. 1034 b, G. 1617 (inadequate). Cf. 43,26. 26. **τε . . καί** (29). 27. **σοφιστρίᾳ** 'she-sophist.' So Aristoph. coined *συκοφάντρια* 'she-sycophant,' and *ἀλεκτρύαινα* 'she-cock.' 31. **νεωστί**: Socrates has rather *his* crab-sophist in mind ('lately' arrived in Athens) than that of Hercules. So *τοῦ λόγου* in 29, and *λέγων καὶ δάκνων* on next page. See n. on 144,21. **μοι δοκεῖν**: free infin. H. 956,
166 G. 1534. 1. **οὑτως**: deictic.

297 D 3. **ὁ ἐμὸς Ἰόλεως**: perhaps he means Ktesippus whose aid in the dialogue had already 'made bad worse.' *θάτερον* = *κακόν*: 87,24. 6. **ὁπότε** 'now that,' 'since.'

297 E 17. **ἀλλὰ . . μέν** (= *μήν*): 44,6.

298 A 26. **ἕτερος**, c. gen., 'other than.'

167 **298 C** 22. **λίνον λίνῳ**: L. & S.

298 D 31. 'Calf-ies, doggies, piggies.' **καὶ γὰρ σύ**: *καί* with *σύ*, as in next li. with *σοί*.

168 **299 A** 19. **ὅ τι μαθών**: 161,23. **ἔφυσεν** 'begot.'

THEAETETUS

"WHAT is Knowledge?" is the question of the *Theaetētus*. In the course of the long and abstruse debate occurs the welcome digression here given, which again contrasts, like the passage from the *Gorgias*, the philosopher and the Philistine, the man whose life is of the market-place and him whose life is concerned with Reality.

172 C 21. **καὶ πολλάκις**: *καί* may here be, not the conjunct., but the intensive adv., as in *καὶ μάλα*. Cf. 43,16. The *καί* in the next line, joining *πολλάκις* to *ἄλλοτε*, is of course to be dropped. 3. **κυλινδούμενοι** 'knocking about' (Campbell). 169
πρὸς τούς *κτλ.* '*stand* to those —,' **τεθράφθαι** 'in point of true culture.'

172 D 7. **ᾗ** 'by the fact that,' 'in so far as.' **τοῖς μέν**: antithesis is *οἱ δέ* 14. 9. **τρίτον . . λόγον** refers to two preceding arguments in the dialogue. 10. **ἐκ**, temporal, 'after'; 35,8. 12. **διὰ . . βραχέων**: 27,15. 15. **ὕδωρ**, viz. that in the *κλεψύδρα* (water-clock) which limited all pleadings.

172 E 16. **ἐγχωρεῖ** 'there is room.' 17. **ἀνάγκην**: what this is concretely, is explained first by *ὑπογραφήν* (itself here metaphorical, see 265,28 n., and hence) secondly by *ἀντωμοσίαν*. See 3,28 App. 18. **ἐφέστηκεν** 'stands over'; 95,11. **παρα-** 'alongside,' like the *parallel* lines of the *ὑπογραφή*; little chance therefore for speech *ἔξω τοῦ πράγματος*, as was this present digression. 19. **καλοῦσι** '*they* call,' not 'we.' An *ἐλεύθερος* is not expected to be up in lawyer's lingo. 20. **ὁμοδούλου**: all were 'fellow-slaves' who appeared before that 'seated despot' the people (*ὁ δῆμος*)—i.e. before the huge popular dicasteries of Athens—holding in its hand 'a *sort* of right,' viz. the *ψῆφος* or vote of the majority. By all means should be read those descriptions of *Δῆμος* by the cartoonist Aristophanes in his *Vespae* and *Equites*. 22. **τὴν ἄλλως**: L. & S. s.v. *τηνάλλως*. **τὴν περὶ αὑτοῦ**, i.e. small and narrow, never large and digressive.

173 B 7. **τοὺς δέ** *κτλ.* 'as for those —.' Transl. as a free 170
accus. 8. **χοροῦ**, viz. of philosophers. 10. **ἵνα μὴ καί** 'lest in very truth (*καί*).'

173 C 15. **τῷ τοιῷδε**, sc. *χορῷ*. 18. **θεατής**: the mention of *χορός* had brought to mind a new illustration of the compelling power of the many. 21. **ὡς ἔοικεν, ἐπεί—** 'as it seems (we must), since —.'

173 D 29. **σπουδαί** *κτλ.*: the 'race for offices' is not there-
fore an American novelty in 'machine' politics. 1. **προσ-** 171
ίσταται=**παρ-***ίστασθαι* 66,22. 3. **πρὸς ἀνδρῶν** *κτλ.* 'on the male or female side.' 4. **οἱ . . λεγόμενοι**: *we* should say 'the proverbial *sands* of the sea,' not 'quarts.'

173 E 5. **οὐδέ** 'not even,' with the second *οἶδεν*. 6. **οὐδέ**, 'not even,' leads to a stressed *εὐδοκιμεῖν*. 11. **τὰ**

171 **ἐπίπεδα γεωμετροῦσα**: Theodorus being a mathematician, Socrates illustrates to him with his own familiar (parallel-) 'epipeda' and the like—for these words can hardly be Pindar's. 12. **ὕπερ** belongs to the poetic quotation, as its anastrophe shows.

174 A 14. **ὅλου** 'in its universal aspect' (Campb.). 19. **ἐμμελής**: perhaps 'self-collected.' **χαρίεσσα** 'witty.'

174 B 27. **τί . . ἄνθρωπος** illustrates *ὅλου* above. The
172 philosopher is concerned with mankind, not manikins. 2. **τοιγάρτοι**: 159,5. **συγγιγνόμενος** in the *ἰδίᾳ*-clause is answered by *ὅταν κτλ.* aft. *δημοσίᾳ*.

174 C 10. **ἀσχημοσύνη** 'awkwardness,' lack of *savoir faire*. 11. **ἴδιον** 'personal.' 13. **οὐδενός** '*in* any one'; 1,7 n.

174 D 17. **τύραννόν τε γάρ** 'for as for a tyrant'; free acc. (170,7 n.)—a block left over as the construction of the sent. proceeded. So too *τε*, whose clause fills the whole sent., compelling *γῆς δέ* (25) to begin afresh. See 148,17 n. 18. **ἕνα**: obj. of *ἀκούειν*. 20. **πολὺ βδάλλοντα** 'as a good milker,' predicate. 21. **ἐκείνων**, viz. *νομέων*. **ζῷον**, viz. the people. 22. **ἄγροικον**: with *τὸν τοιοῦτον* below.

174 E 24. **ἀναγκαῖον**, sc. *εἶναι*, depends upon *ἡγεῖται* (19). 25. 'having surrounded himself with his castle as a mountain-pen,' i.e. as does the herdsman with a mountain-pen. **γῆς δέ** *κτλ.* 'and as for land,—when he hears how somebody, possessing 10,000 acres or more of it, possesses an enormous quantity—.' 26. **ὡς ἄρα**: freq. combination; 40,22. 30. **ὡς γενναῖος**, sc. *ἐστι* 'of how noble birth.' **ἔχων** 'because he has.'

173 **175 A** 8. **σεμνυνομένων**: better taken as gen. absol. 9. **ἄτοπα . . τῆς σμικρολογίας** 'the absurdity of their penny-reckoning pettiness becomes all too plain to him.' See 41,18 App. 11. **εἰς τὸ ἄνω** 'reckoning back.'

175 B 15. **ἅπασι** sums the items from p. 172, lines 11,14, 17,25,29. 21. **αὐτός** 'he in his turn.' 22. **αὐτῷ** whenever 'he can find' any one willing.

175 C 23. **τί ἐγὼ σέ**: the small question of personal rights and wrongs is the whole question of the dicastery—the habitat of the lawyer. 27. **εἰ βασιλεύς** *κτλ.* 'whether a king is happy, and one, again, who possessed great wealth'—referring, in order, to the king and the landowner of the previous page. 29. **ὅλως** 'in general'; cf. *ὅλου* 171,14. *τὸ πᾶν* 173,2. 30. **ἑστόν**, viz. happiness and wretchedness.

174 **175 D** 9. **ἐναντίως** *κτλ.* 'otherwise than as —.'

175 E 16. **ἡδῦναι . . θῶπας λόγους** recalls the suit of the

ὀψοποιός-orator of *Gorgias* 144,15 ff. **ὁ δ' αὖ**, sc. *τρόπος*. 174
18. **ἀναβάλλεσθαι . . ἐπιδέξια ἐλευθέρως** 'to wear his cloak like a gentleman' (Jowett). Yet see also L. & S., s.vv. 19. **ἁρμονίαν** *κτλ.* : the simile at last comes out clearly. Life is a picnic-banquet (*ἔρανος*), to which each contributes his share. Food must be prepared and traps packed. But the slave will see to those things. The philosopher is the world's guest—*his* contribution to the general happiness is, at the banquet itself, to seize the harmony of speech and reason (as a lyre) and hymn the true life of blessed gods and men.

176 B 1. **μετὰ φρονήσεως** : Plato scorned the "demotic" 175
justice and piety that lacked *φρόνησις*. Cp. 84,30. 245,22. 198,8 n. 3. **ὡς ἄρα** : 172,26.

176 C 16. **δεινότητες δοκοῦσαι** 'kinds of seeming cleverness.'

176 D 19. **ἄριστα** : adv. c. *ἔχει*. 20. **τὸ μὴ συγχωρεῖν** 'to refuse to admit.' 22. **ἀκούειν** : 57,13 n. **γῆς ἄλλως ἄχθη** : cf. 20,19 ; 'mere cumberers of the earth.' 26. **ὅ** : inner acc. c. *ἀγνοεῖν*. 28. **θάνατοι** ; 48,27 App. for the plur. **οὐδέν** c. *ὤν* ; cf. 85,20 App.

176 E 31. **ἐν τῷ ὄντι** 'in the world of reality' (not amid *φαινόμενα*). Cf. 246,31 *ἐν οὐρανῷ παράδειγμα ἀνάκειται*.

177 A 6. **οὗ** 'for which.' 7. **εἰκότα** (*τῷ παραδείγματι*) 176
ᾧ 'answering' (Jowett). 8. **ἐὰν δέ** : the apodosis begins at *ταῦτα δή* 12. 9. **καί** *κτλ.* 'also at their death.' 11. **τὴν αὐτοῖς** *κτλ.* = *αὐτοῖς ὁμοίαν τὴν διαγωγήν*, i.e. their life will be like themselves—bad. 12. **κακοῖς** : prob. neut. 15. **καὶ μάλα δή** : with this phrase and the response *οἶδά τοι*, cf. the words in 52,3–5, where the logical situation is the same.

177 B 22. **ἡ ῥητορικὴ . . ἀπομαραίνεται** : and Righteousness is his only aid. See 145,18 ff.

MENON

THE extract is made not merely for its matter, but as an example of Socratic pedagogy, his mid-wife art of helping others to bring forth their latent ideas. See, for Menon, the Index.

79 E 5. **οὐδὲν ἄλλο**, sc. *ποιεῖς*. So in Engl. you [do 177
nothing] but fall into perplexity yourself.'

177 **80 A** 7. **γοητεύεις** *κτλ.* : cf. 137,14 for words. 9. **δεῖ** 'may,' as oft. **εἰ . . καί** 'if indeed.' 10. **εἶδος** refers prob. to his flat snub-nosed face. See the cut:

178 

FIG. 2. Torpedo, or Cramp-fish (*Torpedo vulgaris*).

80 B 21. **οὐκ ἐκπλέων** : see 59,23 ff. 3. **τί μάλιστα** 'why, especially (particularly)?'

80 D 21. **τίνα τρόπον** *κτλ.*: the quibble did not originate with Menon, but was one of the stock fallacies of those "eristic" philosophs who did indeed 'numb' their pupils, like Euthydemus, merely to show their own cleverness. It appears in 158,28. 24. **καὶ ὅτι μάλιστα** is pleonastic. *εἰ καὶ ἐντύχοις* = 'if you *should* hit upon it,' and *εἰ ὅτι μάλιστα ἐντύχοις* = 'hit upon it as much as you like.'

80 E 27. **ἐριστικόν** : see L. & S. 28. **κατάγεις** 'are spinning.' L. & S. s.v. 4.

179 **81 A** 12. **ἱερέων**, viz. of the Eleusinian mysteries, teaching the Orphic doctrine. 13. **ὅσοις μεμέληκε** seems to be restrictive; 'as many as have cared.' Should we not expect *ὅσοις γε*?

81 B 16. **θεῖοι** 'inspired.' 24. **οἷσι** with *δέξεται* (H. 767 a, G. 1169) = *παρ' ὧν*. **πένθεος** : perhaps an apposit. gen.; 'a penalty *of long-drawn woe*' (*πάλαι* as c. pres. tense). Others take it as a poetic gracious name for 'crime.' 25. **δέξεται** : prob. the "short" subjunct. as so oft. in Hom., = *δέξηται*. **κείνων** = *ἐκείνων*. 26. **ἀνδιδοῖ** = *ἀναδίδωσι*. 27. **τᾶν** = *ὧν*.

180 **81 C** 30. **καλεῦνται** = *καλοῦνται*. 1. **πολλάκις γεγονυῖα**: Pythagoras's term was not *μετ-εμ-ψύχωσις*, but *παλιγ-γενεσία*. 6. **ἅ γε** : *γε* is freq. added if the relat. is causal.

81 D 12. **γὰρ . . ἄρα** 'for after all,' 'for sure enough.' 15. **ἂν ἡμᾶς ἀργοὺς ποιήσειεν** : i.e. it is an argument of despair.

81 E 18. **ζητεῖν ἀρετὴ ὅ τι ἐστίν** : a sort of half-evolved prolepsis for *ἀρετήν*. So *Lach.* 199 E, *Phaedr.* 271 D.

181 **82 B** 7. **μέν** = *μήν*. 10. **ὁπότερ' ἄν** is explained by *ἤ . . ἤ* 'whether—or.' For mood, see G. M. T. § 489. 15.

τοιοῦτον 'like this.' With his stick Socrates draws in the sand a square, supposably two feet each way—in the cut, ABCD. 181

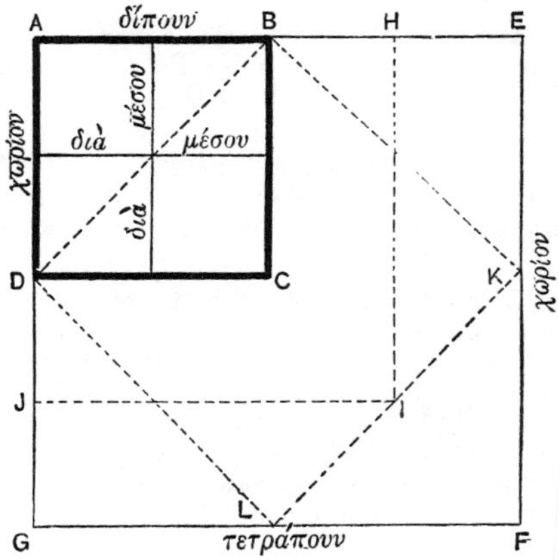

FIG. 3. Problem—to construct a square twice the size of ABCD.

82 C 21. **ἐστὶν . . ἔχον**: not merely periphrastic of *ἔχει*. *ἐστί* expresses existence as well. See 93,12 App. 29. **ταύτῃ . . ταύτῃ**: adv.; 'this way . . that way.' 31. **ἅπαξ . . δυοῖν** 'one time two.' So *δὶς δυοῖν*.

82 D 3. **γίγνεται** 'results,' 'turns out,' 'amounts to.' 182
11. **διπλάσιον**, c. gen., 'twice as large as,' H. 755 a, G. 1154. **τοιοῦτον δέ** 'but like it.' 12. **γραμμάς**, i.e. 'sides.' 16. **πηλίκη τις ἔσται**: properly *τις* is predic. ('will be something how long?'), but conventionally, we omit it or treat as an approximative 'about,' 'say.' 17. **ἐκείνου**, sc. *τοῦ χωρίου*. **γραμμή** 'base.'

82 E 30. **θεῶ**: imperat.

83 A 3. **τῇ** = *ταύτῃ*. 4. **διπλάσιον**: reg. c. gen. 183
9. **προσθῶμεν**: he here 'adds,' or as we say "produces" AB to E. **ἐνθένδε** 'on this side,' viz. the AB side. 14. **ἀναγραψώμεθα**: he completes the square AEFG.

83 B 18. **ταυτὶ τέτταρα**: pointing in turn to the four 2-foot squares, ABCD, BEKC, CKFL, DCLG.

83 C 1. **τεττάρων**, sc. *ποδῶν χωρίον*; four times a 4-ft. 184
square is a 16-ft. square. 4. **ὀκτώπουν**, sc. *χωρίον*. 5. **ταύτης**: pointing to the *γραμμή* AE. 7. **ταυτησί**, viz.

184 AB. **τουτί**: the *χωρίον* ABCD. So also *τοῦδε* in li. 10 11. **τούτου,** viz. the *χωρίον* AEFG.

83 D 13. **τοσαύτης**: AB. 14. **τοσησδί**: AE.

83 E 24. **τινα**: 182,16 n. 23. **ταύτης**: AB. 29. **οἵδε**: the two feet in AB. **ὁ δέ**: BH. **ἐνθένδε ὡσαύ-**
185 **τως** 'on this side likewise,' viz. AD+DJ. 11. **πω** c. negat., 'not yet.'

84 A 19. **οὗ** (adv.) c. the foll. genit. 21. **ὅτι** 'that' depends on *ἐννοεῖς*. 23. **ἀλλ' οὖν . . γε,** following *μέν*, is the strongest of substitutes for *δέ*. 26. **ὥσπερ οὐκ οἶδε** *κτλ.*: 8,26.

186 **84 B** 29. **βέλτιον** (adv.) **ἔχει** 'is better off.' 4. **προὔργου** (*πρὸ ἔργου*) 'of use,' 'serviceable.' (It is singular that no adj. *προὔργιος, -ον* arose, espec. as comparat. and superlat. forms are found *προὐργιαίτερος, -αίτατος.*) 6. **καὶ ζητήσειεν ἂν ἡδέως** 'would really be glad to investigate'—a hit at Menon, who, when *he* was 'numbed' (p. 177), complained and fell to doubting if knowledge was attainable (178,21). 7. **πρὸς πολλούς**: the very words of Menon (177,18). The *ἄν* (doubled) goes with *λέγειν*.

84 C 17. **ὤνητο**: 2nd aor. mid. (*ὀνίνημι*). 19. **ὅ τι καὶ ἀνευρήσει**: for the function of *καί* before a verb, see 72,1 n.

84 D 21. **φύλαττε**: note tense. 25. **τοῦτο**: haven't we 'here' the 4-ft. figure ABCD? 27. **τουτί**: BEKC.
187 30. **τόδε**: DCLG. 2. **τόδε**: CKFL.

84 E 13. **ἔστιν αὕτη γραμμή** 'here is a line.' 14. **τείνουσα,** viz. from D to B, B to K, K to L, L to D.

85 A 18. **περιέχουσαι** 'enclosing.' **τουτί**: DBKL. 27. **τηλικαῦτα,** viz. triangles of the size DBC. 29. **τῷδε**: ABCD.

188 **85 B** 5. **ταύτης**: DB. 10. **σοφισταί**: not here 'sophists' in the professional sense, but 'learned men.' 14. **ἔστιν ἥντινα** *κτλ.* 'is any opinion he has expressed in his answers not his own?'

85 C 17. **καὶ μὴν . . γε** ? adversat.; 157,18. 29. **ἀν-ερήσεται**: 9,23 n.

189 **85 E** 19. **ἄλλως τε** 'especially.'

190 **86 B** 16. **καὶ γὰρ ἐγώ**: *καί* c. *ἐγώ*. 17. **ὑπέρ** 'in behalf of.' 20. **ἃ μὴ ἐπιστάμεθα**: obj. of *εὑρεῖν*.

The student should turn to his Wordsworth, if he does not already know the poem by heart, and read his *Intimations of Immortality* beginning at: "Our birth is but a sleep and a forgetting: The Soul that rises with us (our life's Star) Hath had elsewhere its setting, And cometh from afar. Not in entire forgetfulness, And not in utter nakedness, But trailing clouds of glory, do we come From God, who is our home."

REPUBLIC I

On the occasion of a chance visit of Socrates and some friends at the house of an old acquaintance Cephalus in the Peiraeus, there comes up the question "What is Justice?" Various answers are offered, but none proves satisfactory. Socrates then proposes that they seek it first where it is writ large, viz. in the state, rather than in the individual. An ideal state, accordingly, is next presented with much detail — a state characterized by minute subdivision and specialization of labour, and by self-sufficiency in respect of daily needs, of defence, and of growth. And Justice, it is found, consists in the perfect working of each part (*τὰ ἑαυτοῦ πράττειν*). And this Justice writ large in the state may, they discover, become a quality of the individual also, if he will but discipline his parts. For each man's soul is a republic, where also either anarchy or law may reign.

That outer Republic is, of course, as Plato is the first to admit, a Utopia (*οὐτοπία* 'Nowhere') and one apt to remain so except by a divine hap (*ἐὰν μὴ θεία τις ξυμβῇ τύχη* 246,26), viz. if philosophers be kings, or kings philosophers. But for that smaller Republic, matters are not so hopeless. In a man's own soul, the perfect functioning of higher and lower *is* possible. And of that republic we must never despair. (See the extracts from the Ninth Book, especially p. 246.) The democracies in which we live may rage with madness like a storm, and we may be helpless. But the philosopher will stand aside under a wall (*ὑπὸ τειχίον ἀποστάς*) during that downpour, and himself at least remain pure from wickedness. (See the extracts from the Sixth Book, including that on page 268.)

The first extract is but a prelude, yet has especial interest for us in the picture it presents of the house and family of the aged Cephalus, father of the famous orator Lysias with his ill-fated brother Polemarchus, who was compelled by the Thirty to drink the hemlock.

327 A 1. **κατέβην,** viz. Socrates. 3. **ἑορτήν,** to the 191
Thracian goddess Bendis, identified with Artemis.

327 B 9. **ἀπῆμεν** 'going back'; a freq. sense. **ἄστυ**: Athens. 12. **ἕ**: Polemarchus. **μου**: with *λαβόμενος*, the special part added *τοῦ ἱματίου*. 15. **οὗτος** 'yonder.' 17. **ὅς** 'he,' viz. Glaucon (apposit.),

191 **327 C** 20. **ὡς** 'apparently.' 23. **οὐ γάρ** *κτλ.* 'certainly you are not a bad guesser.' 25. **τούτων . . κρείττους γένεσθε** 'prove yourselves stronger than these gentlemen'—a
192 playful challenge to combat. 26. **αὐτοῦ**: adv. 1. **ἕν,** *τὸ ἢν πείσωμεν* 'the (chance) of persuading.'

327 D 2. **καὶ δύναισθε**: *καί* precedes a word to be stressed, as *γε* follows it. Cf. the arrowhead (∧) over notes in music. 'Aye, *could* you?' 4. **ὡς,** c. gen. absol. (sometimes, as here, followed by a resumptive *οὕτω*), to be translated as an object-clause; 'then we shan't listen—make up your minds to *that*.' G. 1593,2. G. M. T. § 918. So 117,29.

328 A 6. **οὐδ' ἴστε** 'don't you know *either*?' **λαμπάς** 'torch-race.' L. & S. s.v. II, and cf. Arist. *Vesp.* 1203. **πρὸς ἑσπέραν**: *πρός* should be 'toward'—which will hardly do here. A torch-race would not be held before dark. 11. **καὶ πρός γε** 'and besides.' 12. **ἐξ-ανα-στησόμεθα**: lit. 'shall up and out'; 92,20. 107,22. 13. **ξυνεσόμεθα** *κτλ.*: a tempting thought for Socrates. 15. **μὴ ἄλλως ποιεῖτε**: 46,13. 48,10.

328 B 21. **καὶ δὴ καί** 'and so too'; 17,10. 25. **μάλα**: adv. c. subst.; 17,19. 175,22. **διὰ χρόνου** 'after some time' the regular sense. H. 795,1 e; G. 1206,1 c. *πολλοῦ* or *μακροῦ* are sometimes inserted.

328 C 26. **γὰρ καί**: does *καί* stress the foll. word as in li. 2, or is the group equiv. to *καὶ γάρ* at the head of a sent.? No Greek particle is more troublesome than *καί*. 28. **τεθυκὼς ἐτύγχανε** 'had been sacrificing, as it happened.' G. M. T. § 147.
193 30. **εὐθὺς ἰδών** 'as soon as he saw me'; 165,9. 1. **δέ**: for its posit., see 162,17 n. 'But Socrates —.' **θαμίζεις**: derived from the adv. (poetic) *θαμά* 156,29. 196,29. **ἡμῖν**: ethical dat.; 'we don't see you coming down often.' Cf. *αὐτῷ* 173,22. 2. **χρῆν μέντοι** 'you should, however.'

328 D 5. **νῦν δέ**: 6,6. 6. **ὡς**: causal. **ὅσον . . τοσοῦτον** (8) 'in proportion as—so,' 'the more . . the more'; properly, inner accus. 7. **κατὰ τὸ σῶμα** 'bodily.' 10. **ξύν-ισθι**: *-ειμι*. 12. **καὶ μήν** 'yes indeed'—used in hearty assent. *καί* is prob. not copulative, but intensive, as in *καὶ πάνυ, καὶ σφόδρα*. Cf. *καὶ μάλα* in 206,15. 208,9.

328 E 16. **τις** c. interrog.; 182,16 n. 19. **ἐνταῦθα** c. gen.; cf. *πόρρω* 36,21. 20. **ἐπὶ γήραος οὐδῷ** 'on the threshold of old age (i.e. the door of exit).' *Od.* 15,348. *Il.* 22,60. 24,487. 21. **χαλεπόν** goes back to *τοῦτο* (19); 'whether a hard part of life.'

329 A 25. **εἰς ταὐτόν,** 'together,' merely repeats *συν-*. For the neut. *ταὐτόν*, see H. 265, G. 400. 27. **παροιμίαν**:

ἦλιξ ἥλικα τέρπει. 29. **ποθοῦντες** 'missing,' 'regretting.' 193
31. **ἔχεται** 'connected with.'

329 B 4. **γήρως**: objective genit. of προπηλακίσεις. **ἐπὶ** 194
τούτῳ δή 'on *this* score,' δή giving stress to τούτῳ. 5. **τὸ γῆρας**: prolepsis; 'harp upon how many ills their (σφίσι) old age is the cause of.' 8. **κἂν**: καί c. ἐγώ. **ἕνεκα** 'so far as . . is concerned.' 10. **οὐχ οὕτως ἔχουσιν** 'not feeling so.' 11. **καὶ ἄλλοις, καὶ δὴ καί**: the second member ('and so too') freeing itself takes its own verb παρεγενόμην.

329 C 13. **πρὸς τἀφροδίσια** 'about love.' 15. **μέντοι** 'in very truth.' 21. **τὸ τοῦ Σοφοκλέους**: cf. 30,19. 138,28.

329 D 23. **ἀπηλλάχθαι** (perf. t. = pres. state) almost = ἐλευθερία above; 'release' 'freedom.' The clause, from δεσποτῶν on, is apposit. to τὸ τοῦ Σοφοκλέους. It is ἀπηλλάχθαι that 'comes true' (γίγνεται). 24. **καὶ τῶν γε πρός**— 'aye, and in (περί understood) their relations with their relatives.' 27. **εὔκολοι** 'of happy temperament.' Cf. the opposite δύσ-κολος, applied as a surname to the unhappy grammarian (and doubtless school-teacher) Apollonius Dyscolus. See L. & S. for the etymologic sense. **καὶ τὸ γῆρας** κτλ. 'even old age is but moderately painful.' 31. **ἀγασθεὶς αὐτοῦ εἰπόντος**: for 'delighted at *him* saying,' Engl. now prefers '*his* saying.' Cf.
56,15. 1. **ἐκίνουν** 'tried to draw him out' (lit. 'stir him 195
up')—this kinetic process being the one already known to us—that of the torpedo (p. 177), of the interested friend (107,29), of Antaeus the wrestler (103), of the cross-examiner (102), of the midwife (*Theaet.* 149 A).

329 E 8. **λέγουσι . . τι**: 23,12 n. 9. **οἴονται,** sc. λέγειν. 10. **εὖ ἔχει** 'holds good.' **Σεριφίῳ**: Serīphus was an insignificant little island even among the little Cyclades.

330 A 14. **τοῖς** carries to φέρουσιν. **δή** applies the witticism; '*now* to those too (καί) who —.' 16. **ἐπιεικής** 'reasonable,' 'temperate,' 'good.' **πάνυ τι ῥᾳδίως** 'entirely comfortably.' 18. **ἑαυτῷ**: dat. of interest; 'finds himself.' Plato is full of references to dissidence or concord with one's self. 20. **παρέλαβες**: 'to inherit.' **ἐπ**-εκτήσω: properly 'to *add* by acquisition.' **ποῖ' ἐπεκτησάμην**: to show that an assertion or question was nonsense, a Greek interlocutor would select the special word of offence for repetition with ποῖος. 'Acquired! forsooth,' 'What do you mean with your "acquired"?'

330 B 21. **μέσος τις,** c. gen.; 'a sort of midway money-maker between —' 23. **ὁμώνυμος ἐμοί**: grandsons quite regularly bore their grandfathers' names. 24. **οὐσίαν**:

195 incorporated into the relat. clause. Make it obj. of *παραλαβών*. 25. **πολλάκις** *κτλ.* 'doubled it many times over.' 27. **ἀγαπῶ** 'am content,' 'satisfied'; infra 30 'to set store by.' 28. **τούτοισιν,** viz. the three sons named in 192,18–20. Note the ending *-οισι*. 29. **οὗ τοι ἕνεκα** *κτλ.* 'why indeed I asked, said I, (was,) that you seemed —.' Lit. '(that) for the sake of which I asked (was this, viz.) that —.' See 3,20 App.

330 C 31. **ὡς τὸ πολύ** 'for the most part.' H. 719 b.
196 1. **διπλῇ ἤ** 'twice as much as.' 4. **ταύτῃ τε δή** *κτλ.*: *δή*, as in 195,14, applies the comparison; '*so* both in that way do (also—*καί*, superfluous in Engl.) those who have made a fortune make much ado about money, *and* also in the matter of its use.' 7. **καὶ ξυγγενέσθαι** 'even (or, also) to get along with.'

330 D 16. **εἰσέρχεται**: cf. 66,19 c. acc.; = *προσίσταται* 171,1 and *παρίσταται* 66,22. 20. **τέως**: 92,12.

330 E 23. **ἢ καί**: 19,4. **ὥσπερ**: better, I think, with *ἐγγυτέρω*, in the sense 'as it were,' than with *ὤν*, in the sense *ὡς*. 24. **δ' οὖν**: 1,3. 28. **καί** *κτλ.* 'even out of his sleep.' For the plur. of *ὕπνος*, see L. & S. s.v. 3. 30. **ἐλπίδος**: not alw. 'hope,' but oft. 'anticipation' or even 'foreboding' as here. 31. **γηροτρόφος** 'nurse of old age.'

197 **331 A** 1. **Πίνδαρος**: Cephalus is the typical old man. He is stocked with reflection, quotation, and jokes from the last generation. Again, he here quotes. 4. **οἷ**: dat. **ἀτάλλοισα** (= *-ουσα*) 'nourishing.' **συναορεῖ** 'accompanies'; c. dat. 5. **πολύστροφον** 'versatile' or (as others take it) 'capricious,' 'fickle.' 6. **θαυμαστῶς ὡς**: 79,21 n. **πρὸς δή** 'so, in view of.' 7. **τίθημι** 'hold,' as a thesis (*θέ-σις*, position). 8. **οὔ τι** 'not by any means.'

331 B 9. **τό** reaches to *ἀπιέναι*. The subj. of the infinitives is *τινα* modified by *ἄκοντα*, *ὀφείλοντα* and *δεδιότα*. **μηδέ**, 'not even,' is, of course, *not* correlat. to the second *μηδέ*. 10. **αὖ**, 'on the other hand,' adds his second article of faith; if a man would get through life *δικαίως* and *ὁσίως* (li. 2) he must 1st, tell no lies; 2nd, owe no debts. (The rendering *θυσίας θεῷ* is to live *ὁσίως*.) 11. **ἔπειτα** 'then,' like *οὕτω*, oft. follows a ptc. to stress the resulting state of affairs, *in which* the action of the main verb must take place. 12. **εἰς τοῦτο**, 'to *this* (result, I say),' picks up the long *τὸ . . ἀπιέναι* with a proper prepos. for the verb *ξυμβάλλεται*. Cf. 32,14. 14. **ἓν γε ἀνθ' ἑνός** is an apposit. to the sentence; '(weighing) one thing against another.' 15. **οὐκ ἐλάχιστον** (by litotes for *μάλιστα*) goes with *θείην ἄν*; 'most firmly should I hold.'

331 C 19. **δικαιοσύνην**: the theme of the dialogue is here

reached. Cephalus had set forth negatively his notion of a just 197
life—no lies, no debts. Socrates challenges this ideal of life. 'But this very matter of justice—are we to say so simply (*ἁπλῶς οὕτως*; or, simply in this fashion) that it consists (*αὐτὸ εἶναι*) in telling the truth and paying one's debts?' 23. **ἔστιν** = *ἔξεστιν*. 24. **οἷον** *κτλ.*: lit. 'like this, I mean.' 25. **εἴ τις . . εἰ ἀπαιτοῖ**: condition within condition; 2,17. 26. **ἀπαιτοῖ**, sc. *ὁ φίλος*. 28. **αὖ** turns to the second item in Cephalus's creed; supply *δίκαιος ἂν εἴη*. Take *ἐθέλων* as conditional ('if consenting'); or, possibly, supply *τις*.

331 D 2. **πάνυ μὲν οὖν** 'nay but it is.' See 121,2 n. 198
4. **καὶ μέντοι, καί** ('yes indeed; and —') marks hearty assent. Cf. *καὶ μήν* 193,12. See App. 8. **γελάσας** 'with a laugh'; coincident in time (24,7 App.). **ᾔει**: fittingly Cephalus here withdraws, not to reappear in the dialogue. Believing as he did that *δικαιοσύνη* consisted in telling the truth and paying your debts to God and man (not puzzling himself further about the definition of Truth and God), he typifies that older Athens, which had fought the Persians to be sure, and built the Empire, but had no head for dialectic or *γνῶθι σαυτόν*. Like his age, he had served his purpose, and retires for good.—Indeed, his *δικαιοσύνη* could have been as little pleasing to Plato as to the sophists. It was merely an inherited popular ('demotic') unreflected justice, and hence as bad as the false bravery and false temperance mentioned in the *Phaedo* 83,20 ff. And just as there Plato insists upon *ἀρετὴ μετὰ φρονήσεως* (84,30), so we shall find his final words in the *Republic* to be *δικαιοσύνην* **μετὰ φρονήσεως** *παντὶ τρόπῳ ἐπιτηδεύσομεν* (257,28).

343 C The sophist Thrasymachus happened to be present. With his views on Justice compare those on the right of might expressed by Callicles p. 135 ff. 9. **πόρρω** 'far off,' 'astray.'

343 D 1. **ἀπὸ τῶν ἴσων** 'upon equal properties.' 199

344 B 28. **κακουργημάτων**: causal genit.

344 C 8. **ἱκανῶς γιγνομένη**: conditional. 200

REPUBLIC II

In the construction of his ideal State, Socrates has discovered that, to protect his specialized population of farmers, builders, weavers, shoemakers, etc., against incursions there must be also a specialized body of warriors—the Guardians (*φύλακες*). What shall be their training, mental and physical? The following contains a warning in the matter of the mental.

200 **376 E** 15. **μουσική**, in its widest sense, included all schooling of the mind, as contrasted with *γυμναστική* the training of the body. 18. **μουσικῆς** '(as a part) of music do you reckon narratives?' 20. **ψεῦδος** 'fiction.'

201 **377 A** 1. **ὡς τὸ ὅλον εἰπεῖν** 'to speak generally' = *ὡς ἐπὶ τὸ πολύ* li. 13. **ἔνι** = *ἔνεστι*. 4. **ἔλεγον** 'I meant.'

377 B 8. **πλάττεται** (sc. *ὁ νέος*) 'is fashioned,' 'shaped.' **ἐνδύεται** 'sinks in,' viz. into the child, who is *ἁπαλός*. Cf. 270,25. 11. **ἐπιτυχόντας** 'chance,' 'hap-hazard.'

202 **377 E** 7. **εἰκάζῃ**: 'to give a description, represent.' 9. **ἐοικότα** (*τούτοις*), **οἷς ὅμοια.**

378 A 19. **μάλιστα μέν**: 29,19. 20. **δι' ἀπορρήτων** 'in a secret manner.' Cf. *διὰ βραχέων* 169,12. 21. **χοῖρον**: a cheap sacrifice—the usu. one at initiation into the Eleusinian mysteries. 22. **ὅπως . . συνέβη**: H. 884, G. 1371 for the indic.

203 **378 C** 3. **τοὺς μέλλοντας** *κτλ.*: i.e. the Guardians. With *ἡμῖν* cf. for translat. *αὐτῷ* 173,22. *ἡμῖν* 193,1. 5. **πολλοῦ δεῖ** *κτλ.*: the sent. returns to negat. recommendation as found in the first clause. See index under *Palindromia.* 6. **ποικιλτέον**: as they did, e.g. upon the famous Peplos, 'embroidered' quadrennially for the statue of Athene Polias and carried to the acropolis at the festival of the Panathenaea. 9. **οὐδεὶς . . πολίτης** *κτλ.*: it had been before agreed that the Guardians must be gentle within the state, though fierce without. 11. **εὐθύς** 'from the start.' 12. **γέρουσι** *κτλ.*: dat. of agent.

378 D 13. **γιγνομένοις**, viz. to the children 'when they grow older.' **καὶ τοὺς ποιητάς** 'also.' **ἐγγὺς τούτων** 'similarly.' 14. **δεσμούς**: 48,27 n. 15. **ὑέος**, viz. Hephaestus. The story is not in Homer, but may be read in Pausan. 1,20,3. **ῥίψεις**: *Il.* 1,590. 18. **ὑπονοίαις** 'allegories' (lit. 'underlying thought,' 'hidden sense'). Plato (Socrates) was no allegorizer or rationalist; see 259,11 ff. 22. **δυσ-έκ-νιπτα** 'hard to wash out,' 'indelible.'

378 E 23. **φιλεῖ** 'are apt.' 26. **ἀκούειν**: epexegetic; 59,29. 28. **αὐτά**, c. *ταῦτα*, in prolepsis; 'just what those subjects are.' For separation from *ταῦτα*, cf. 70,16.

204 **379 A** 1. **μὲν . . μήν** (3). 3. **αὐτοῖς** 'themselves.' 5. **θεολογίας**: theology is but an 'account (explanation) of God.' 7. **ἀποδοτέον** 'must ascribe' to him the quality (*οἷος*) that —. 8. **ἔπεσι, μέλεσι** 'epic, lyric, poems.'

379 B 11. **τί μήν;** 'what in truth (do you suppose)?' = 'of 204
course.' See *Theaet.* 162 B ἀλλὰ τί μὴν δοκεῖς;

379 C 20. **οὐδ' ἄρα** κτλ.: cf. the terrible trumpet-call of judgment 252,11.

379 D 1. **κατακείαται** κτλ.: *Il.* 24,527, though Plato 205
varies considerably, whether consciously or not. He was no more a professional rhapsode than he was lawyer. Why *should* he quote verbatim? 3. **ᾧ μέν**: resumed by ὅ γε (4). The antithesis is ᾧ δέ in 5. **ἀμφοτέρων**: partit. gen. 5. **τὰ ἕτερα**: euphemistic for κακά.

379 E 7. **οὐδ' ὡς** goes back to λέγοντος, li. 31 of last page. 9. **σύγχυσιν**: *Il.* 4,70 ff. 12. **ἔριν**: *Il.*, the twentieth book, entitled θεομαχία.

380 A 15. **θεός** κτλ.: a fragment; Dindorf 160. 17. **ποιῇ** 'composes,' 'treats in poetry'; obj. is τὰ πάθη κτλ. **ἐν οἷς**: the syntax is not clear. Perhaps ὡς Αἰσχύλος λέγει (13) has become misplaced, and should precede ἐν οἷς. Or is ἐν οἷς κτλ. a marginal note on Νιόβης? 21. **αὐτοῖς**, i.e. the poets.

380 B 23. **οἱ δέ**, i.e. the sufferers, Niobe, those of Pelops' line, etc. 24. **ὡς δὲ . . θεός** depends on λέγειν. The poet must not picture as miserable those who are paying penalty for wickedness. They are in the process of getting happy. They should even beg for punishment; cf. 118,8–14 and the head-
lines of pp. 127–133. 27. **ὡς**: causal. 4. **αὐτοῦ** refers 206
to τινά.

REPUBLIC III

THE subject is still the education of the Guardians.

401 B 16. **ἆρα**: the quest. concludes 207,13. 18. **ἀγαθοῦ**: separation from ἤθους emphasizes it.

401 C 3. **ἕν τι**: again emphasis marked by posit. The 207
contrast is between the many littles and the one large. 6. **εὐφυῶς** 'by native wit.' 10. **τι προσβάλῃ** 'any impression may strike upon.' 11. **χρηστῶν** 'wholesome.'

401 D 12. **ὁμοιότητα** κτλ. 'likeness, love, and harmony with fair reason.' 16. **ἐν μουσικῇ**: adject. to τροφή; 'musical education' (κυριωτάτη is predic.); cf. 170,31 and 1,16 App. 19. **φέροντα**: neut. nom., with 'rhythm and harmony.' **εὐσχημοσύνην** 'grace.'

402 A 28. **λόγον . . λαβεῖν** 'to apprehend (the) reason.'

The dialogue passes on to a discussion of the bodily training of the φύλακες—from which the following episode.

208 **405 C** 1. **τὸ . . δεῖσθαι . . ἀναγκάζειν** (7): subj. of *δοκεῖ* (8). **ὅτι μή** 'except.' 2. **τινων . . ἐπιπεσόντων** 'an attack of some summer or winter complaint.'

405 D 4. **δίαιταν οἵαν διήλθομεν**: they had just before 'gone over a living' which included sauces, Syracusan cookery and variety, and Corinthian damsels. 5. **ῥευμάτων τε καὶ πνευμάτων** 'flowings and blowings' (Purves); sarcastic assonance. 6. **ἐμπιμπλαμένους** 'by filling ourselves with —.' **φύσας** 'flatulencies.' 7. **ὀνόματα** '*as* names'; predic. acc. 8. **κομψούς** 'clever and complaisant'; sarcastic. 9. **καὶ μάλα**: hearty assent, as *καὶ μήν* 193,12. 12. **ὅτι κτλ.**: the curiously mixed syntax is: *ὅτι οὐκ ἐμέμψατο τῇ δούσῃ πιεῖν* Εὐρυπύλῳ *τετρωμένῳ ἄλφιτα κτλ. ἐπ' οἶνον* Πράμνειον, *ἃ δή κτλ.* But the citation is itself mixed, confusing *Il.* 11,638 ff. with 15,394 ff. **οἱ ὑεῖς**: Machāon and Podaleirius.

406 A 17. **καὶ μὲν δή** = *καὶ μάλα* above. 18. **οὐκ**, sc. *ἄτοπον ἦν*. 19. **παιδαγωγικῇ** 'coddling,' emphat. by posit. 23. **μείξας**: *μίγνυμι*. **ἀπέκναισε** 'teased,' 'fretted,' 'worried out.'

406 B 26. **παρ-ακολουθῶν** 'following close along,' 'dogging' (Warren). 27. **οὔτε . . τε** (28). 28. **ἐν ἀσχολίᾳ πάντων**
209 'with no-time for anything.' 2. **καλὸν ἄρα** 'fine surely.'

406 C 10. **ἐπί**, c. gen., 'in the case of.'

406 D 17. **ἀπηλλάχθαι** 'to *be* quit of'; perf. 20. **εἶπεν**: gnomic.

210 **407 A** 3. **Φωκυλίδου**: prolepsis; 'surely you haven't heard how Phocylides says.' For pres. of *ἀκούω, πυνθάνομαι, αἰσθάνομαι, λέγω*, etc. used of the past, see G. M. T. § 28. 4. **βίος** 'a living.' The verse (hexameter) ran: *Δίζησθαι βιοτήν, ἀρετὴν δ' ὅταν ᾖ βίος ἤδη*; prob. meant as a bit of sound worldly advice, like "Put money in your purse." But Plato wittily emphasizes the second part and twists out of it an exhortation to the rich man to seek virtue. The practice of virtue must be *his* necessary business, just as the poor man's is the getting a livelihood, *οὗ ἀναγκαζομένῳ ἀπέχεσθαι ἀβίωτον.* 5. **καὶ πρότερον**: supply *δεῖν ἀρετὴν ἀσκεῖν.* 8. **μελετητέον τοῦτο κτλ.**: the verbal is emphat. by posit.; 'whether the rich man *must* practise this business of his (viz. virtue)'—and, like the poor man, let his health take care of itself.

407 B 9. **ἡ νοσοτροφία** *κτλ.*: the sense is: or may he nurse his *νόσος* and still be unhindered in his virtue, although (*μέν*) for carpentering, etc. this *νόσος*-nursing *is* a hindrance. 14. **περαιτέρω γυμναστικῆς**: this excessive care of the body, going beyond *gymnastics* (emphat. by posit.), Glaucon disapproves of. With *ἐπιμέλεια* supply *ἐμποδίζει.* 15. **καὶ γάρ**:

first words in a response, as at 202,10,23. *καί* is prob. 'both.' 210
17. **δύσκολος**, sc. *ἡ νοσοτροφία.* **τὸ δὲ δὴ μέγιστον**: cf. 80,17 for syntax, and in a manner also for sense.

407 C 19. **κεφαλῆς διατάσεις**: plur. = '*spells* of racking headache.' 22. **ὅπῃ ταύτῃ** 'wherever in that way.' 26. **τοὺς μὲν . . ἔχοντας . . ἴσχοντας**: antithesis is *τὰ δὲ σώματα* li. 2 of next page. 28. **ἀποκεκριμένον** 'local' (Purves).

407 D 29. **τούτοις μέν** resumes *τοὺς . . ἴσχοντας*, but in altered case. 30. **τε** must serve here to connect the clauses of *καταδεῖξαι* and *προστάττειν*.

407 E 7. **καθεστηκυίᾳ περιόδῳ** 'regular round (course, 211
tenor)' of life (Purves). **μή**, not *οὐ*, because depending upon the deliberative *φῶμεν* in 26 of previous page.

408 A 14. **οὗ**: by attraction for a cognate accus. 16. **αἷμα** *κτλ.* : *Il.* 4,218 varied.

408 B 21. **κἄν** = *καί* 'even'; 218,6. L. & S. s.v. *κἄν*, I 2. 22. **κυκεῶνα**: from its ingredients (see 208,13) it must have been the ancient "welsh rabbit"—certainly most imprudent diet for any but Trojan heroes.

414 B 2. **τῶν ἐν δέοντι γιγνομένων** 'those that prove 212
expedient.' It had been agreed (389 B) that for the rulers of a state it was sometimes right to lie, deceiving even their own citizens, if for the common good—just as a physician may deceive his patient. 3. **γενναῖον**: in a double sense—'noble' and 'out and out' (genuine).

414 C 4. **μάλιστα μέν**: 29,19. 6. **μηδέν** deprecates. 8. **γεγονός** 'realized' (D. & V.). 9. **οἶδα εἰ**: as if *γένοιτο ἄν* were to follow; but just as *οἶδ' ὅτι* became a phrase absolved from syntax, so *οἶδα εἰ* here may be independent (= 'perhaps'), leaving *γενόμενον ἄν* to stand for an optat. 10. **πειθοῦς,** sc. *ὄν*; 'a tale requiring considerable powers of persuasion.' *πεῖσαι* is epexegetic.

414 D 17. **ἃ . . ἐτρέφομεν** 'the nurture we gave them' is resumed by *ταῦτα* (19). 19. **ἐδόκουν** 'they *fancied* merely that they were receiving all that, and that it was going on about them'—*ταῦτα* at once obj. of *πάσχειν* and subj. of *γίγνεσθαι*—'whereas in truth at that time, etc.' The idea is, that in the years of our youth and education we are not yet really born. 20. **ὑπὸ γῆς**: Plato could hardly have intended this in a purely local sense; immediately after we have *ἡ γῆ μήτηρ οὖσα*.

414 E 26. **τῆς χώρας**: supply *περί* from the comparison *ὡς περὶ μητρός*.

213 **415 A** 9. **ἐπίκουροι**: the Guardians were to be, some few, Rulers, but the great mass a standing army of Auxiliaries (ἐπίκουροι). 12. **τὸ μὲν πολύ** 'generally,' **ἔστι δ' ὅτε** 'but sometimes.'

415 B 17. **ὅπως . . ἔσονται**: instead of infin., after παραγγέλλειν. G. M. T. § 355. Cf. 68,21. 147,18. 'That they be of *nothing* such good guardians, or so thoroughly guard *anything* as —.' 19. **τούτων**, viz. metals. 20. **ἐάντε . . καὶ ἂν αὖ** (24).

415 C 28. **διαφθαρῆναι**: G. M. T. § 98 for the aor. infin. (not fut.) in oracular responses, on the analogy of verbs of *commanding* (κελεύω, τάττω, etc.).

214 **415 D** 6. **καὶ—μὲν δή**; 99,21 n. 7. **φήμη** 'the general voice,' *vox populi vox dei.*

416 A 24. **καὶ οὕτω** 'and in such a way'; correlat. of τοιούτους. 26. **ἐπιχειρῆσαι** 'to attack,' c. dat. κακουργεῖν (which governs the acc.) is probably a gloss upon ἐπιχειρῆσαι— or epexegetic.

215 **416 C** 15. **παύσοι . . ἐπαροῖ**: indir. disc. for the fut. indic. of purpose in a relat. clause. G. M. T. § 574.

416 D 26. **ταξαμένους . . δέχεσθαι** goes back to δεῖ, li. 18; 'must stipulate for all the necessaries (τὰ ἐπιτήδεια) from the other citizens, and receive them as wages (μισθόν) etc.'

216 **416 E** 31. **εἰπεῖν**, sc. δεῖ. 2. **ὅσια**: for ὅσιον (sc. εἶναι).

REPUBLIC V

GLAUCON has raised the objection to this highly organized state that it is impracticable. Socrates knows that well— *unless* philosophers be kings or kings become philosophers.

217 **472 C** 8. **πλεῖστα τῶν ἄλλων** = πλεῖστα πάντων; H. 755 b. 10. **αὐτό τε δικαιοσύνην**: H. 681 a.

472 D 17. **τὴν ἐκείνοις μοῖραν ὁμοιοτάτην** 'a lot most like to *them*'—instead of '*theirs*'; H. 773 b, G. 1178. 23. **ἀποδούς**: cf. 204,7.

472 E 26. **λόγῳ** 'in (word, reason) theory.' 31. **τοῦτο**
218 (viz. ἀποδεῖξαι), inner acc. c. προθυμηθῆναι. 1. **σὴν χάριν** 'for your sake.' 3. **διομολόγησαι**: imperat.

473 A 5. **ἢ φύσιν ἔχει** 'or is it natural?' Cf. λόγον ἔχει 72,21 and 25,4 App. **πρᾶξιν λέξεως** κτλ. 'that action realize (hit) truth less than speech'; i.e. 'are not things easier said than done?' 6. **κἂν**: 211,21 n. 8. **τοῦτο**, inner accus., resumed pleonastically by δεῖν in li. 10. The sense of

necessity is already in the main verb. See 47,24 App. 218
12. **φάναι**: infin. as imperat. G. M. T. § 784.

473 B 17. **τὸ δὲ δὴ μετὰ τοῦτο**: apposit. to the sent.; 'the next thing (is), let us try —.' Cf. 38,3.

473 C 29. **προῃκάζομεν κύματι**: Socrates had already surmounted two 'waves' of objection. 30. **εἰ καὶ μέλλει** 'though it *is* bound to —.' 31. **ἀτεχνῶς ὥσπερ**: 3,27. 24,9. **ἐκγελῶν** 'mocking.'

473 E 20. **ῥῆμα** *κτλ.* 'such utterance and doctrine have you 219
let fall, that in return (*ὃν εἰπών*) be sure (*ἡγοῦ* imperat.) —.' 21. **νῦν οὕτως** 'now, just as they are'; cf. 129,1. 22. **οἷον** 'as it were.' **ῥίψαντας**: to run the better.

474 A 22. **γυμνούς** 'in shirt sleeves' (Warren). 24. **διατεταμένους** 'with might and main'; 225,15. 25. **εἰ μὴ ἀμυνεῖ**: a warning fut. (20,11).

474 B 4. **μεγάλην ξυμμαχίαν**: of course all this last is jest, 220
satire, and seriousness in almost pathetic mixture.

REPUBLIC VI

492 A 11. **διαφθειρομένους** *κτλ.* 'that there are young men who are being corrupted.' See 93,12 App. 13. **ὅ τι καί** *κτλ.* 'worth mentioning at all.' On the thought, see Introd., § 33.

492 C 4. **ἂν . . ἀνθέξειν**: 62,2 n. and cf. 249,29. 7. 221
καὶ φήσειν: joined to *οἰχήσεσθαι*; hence *ἥν* (5) is properly subject; but mentally, it is *τὸν νέον.* 8. **τὰ αὐτὰ τούτοις** 'the same that they do'; 217,17 n.

492 E 23. **πρός** 'in its attitude toward.' Sense of the passage: a character of any other attitude toward virtue cannot, never has, and never will exist, that has been reared *by other than* (*παρά*) the training of these popular assemblies. For the thought, cf. 25,26 ff.

493 A 1. **ἕκαστος**, sc. *δοξάτω σοι.* 6. **οἱόνπερ ἂν εἰ** 222
= *ὥσπερ ἂν εἰ* 11,10.

493 B 11. **καὶ φωνὰς δή** 'and then its cries.' **ἐφ' οἷς**: dat. of cause with *φθέγγεσθαι*, as with *θορυβεῖν* and *βοήσεσθε* (23,19,22), *ἀγανακτεῖν* (32,15). 14. **καλέσειεν**: in the *εἰ*-clause along with *κατεμάνθανεν* (8), but with shifted mood. 15. **συστησάμενος** 'having *συ-στημα*-tized it (*τὴν σοφίαν*) into a sort of art (*ὡς τέχνην*).' 16. **εἰδώς**: the obj. is not *μηδέν* (merely a strong negat.), but *ὅ τι καλόν*, indir. quest.

222 **493 C** 19. **ὀνομάζοι . . ἐπί** 'should put all these names to (upon).' 27. **τούτου**: the great-beast server.

223 **493 D** 1. **ὁμιλῇ ἐπιδεικνύμενος**: in Engl. the ptc. becomes the main verb. The whole clause (*ὅ τι μὲν γάρ*—) is a sort of accus. of specif.; 'for, touching whatever profession a man may follow who consorts with the people.' 4. **ἡ Διομηδεία** *κτλ.*: supply *γίγνεται*. Just what 'the proverbial "*must*" of Diomedes' was, is not known; but clearly it was some ancient "Hobson's choice." 6. **ὡς δέ** *κτλ.* depends on *λόγον*. 9. **οὐδ' ἀκούσομαι** 'shall *not* hear *either*.'

499 B 11. **οὐδέ γ' ἀνὴρ ὁμοίως** 'nor individual either.' 15. **ἐπιμεληθῆναι** depends on *ἀνάγκη*; so too *γενέσθαι* in next line.

500 B 20. **τῷ ὡς ἀληθῶς . . ἔχοντι**: he has just been speaking of the spurious, quarrelsome, gossiping philosophers, who brought philosophy into ill-repute. 21. **πρὸς τοῖς οὖσι** 'toward the reality of things.'

500 C 23. **μαχόμενον**: note the freedom of syntax; first dat. (*τῷ ἔχοντι*), now acc., next plur. (*ὁρῶντας*). 25. **ἅττα** are the facts of abstractions, principles, 'orderly and ever the same.'

224 **500 D** 8. **διαβολή** *κτλ.*: cf. 45,24. 10. **ἐκεῖ**, viz. in the region of ideas. 11. **μελετῆσαι**: obj. is *τιθέναι*.

501 A 31. **ὑπογράψασθαι** 'to outline.' See 265,28 n.

225 1. **τί μήν;** 204,11.

501 B 9. **ἐγγιγνόμενον** 'when appearing in.'

501 C 16. **ἔφησθα**: in 219,24.

501 D 22. **μή** is the negat. to be expected aft. *ἀμφισβητεῖν*, *ἀρνεῖσθαι*, *ἐναντιοῦσθαι*, *ἀντιλέγειν*, *κωλύειν*, and like verbs—the inner accus. of which contains in fact *nothing but* subjective protest. L. & S. s.v. *μή*, B 5 b. 29. **φήσειν** repeats *ἀμφισβητῆσαι*. See 47,24 App. 30. **οὓς . . ἀφωρίσαμεν**: see 223,20 n.

226 **501 E** 5. **ἧττον**, sc. *ἀγριανοῦσι*.

REPUBLIC VII

THE famous opening of the Seventh Book concerning the masses that sit in darkness—concerning "those that know"—concerning the duty of these to those.

514 A 10. **τοιούτῳ**: as follows, namely. 13. **οἰκήσει**:

abstract for concrete, like our 'habitation.' 15. **παρά** 226
'along'; so in lines 22 and 26. 16. **δεσμοῖς**: 48,27 n. 17. **ὥστε**: with *ὁρᾶν*, the construct. of *ὥστε* ceases.

514 B 23. **θαυματο-ποιοῖς** 'jugglers,' Punch-and-Judy showmen. 24. **τῶν ἀνθρώπων** 'the audience.' **παραφράγματα** 'screens.'

515 A 3. **οἷον εἰκός**, 'as you might expect,' goes with what 227
follows. 9. **τὸ καταντικρύ** *κτλ.* 'that part of the cave opposite them.'

515 B 12. **τί δέ**: followed by a genit. In 14,13 and 84,7 a nomin. follows.

515 D 4. **μᾶλλον ὄντα** 'more real' (D. & V.). 5. 228
βλέποι: G. M. T. § 185 for mood. 9. **κἂν εἰ**: better taken as in 211,21. 218,6. It may, to be sure, anticipate the infin. *ἀλγεῖν* in li. 11 (which depends on *οἴει* in 7); but *ἀλγεῖν* has its own *ἄν*, and *κἂν εἰ* is too frequent as a fixed group to resuscitate its members on a bare possibility.

515 E 15. **τραχείας**: note predic. posit. (7,13).

516 A 28. **ἐκ δὲ τούτων**: whether temporal or 'in consequence of,' is not always easy to decide. Cf. 12,15.

516 B 30. **μεθ' ἡμέραν** 'by day'; lit. '*after* day,' i.e. 'day-break.' Cf. *ἅμα ἡμέρᾳ* 'at day-break.'

516 C 19. **αὐτῶν**, sc. *τῶν παριόντων*. 229

516 D 24. **τὸ τοῦ Ὁμήρου ἂν πεπονθέναι** 'would experience Homer's saying.' 25. **ἐπάρουρον** *κτλ.*: *Od.* 11,489.

516 E 1. **σχοίη** 'get'; 4,9. 5. **γνωματεύοντα δι-** 230
αμιλλᾶσθαι 'to enter a guessing-match on these shadows.'

517 A 6. **καταστῆναι** 'had got their focus' (lit. 'become settled'). 8. **τῆς συνηθείας**: c. *χρόνος*; 'the period for this habituation'—this focusing.

517 B 18. **ἕδραν**: mixing metaphor and simile as usual, he calls this visible world a 'seat,' because of his *seated* cave-dwellers. See 144,21 n. 21. **τὴν . . ἄνοδον** 'the ascent of the soul to the region of thought (intellect).' 26. **οὕτω**, viz., as follows. **τῷ γνωστῷ**: the same as *νοητὸς τόπος*. **ἡ τοῦ ἀγαθοῦ ἰδέα**: the 'idea' (lit. 'vision' *ἰδ-εῖν*) 'of the good' is the goal of Platonic philosophy. Supply *φαίνεται*.

517 C 30. **τὸν . . κύριον**: the sun.

517 D 7. **διατρίβειν**: epexegetic of purpose. 12. 231
ἀσχημονεῖ: cf. 172,10. 17. **ἀγαλμάτων** 'images,' sc. of justice; i.e. he is to contend about the shadows of the images of justice!

231 **518 A** 30. **φανότερον** and **λαμπροτέρου** are prob. neut., though at first reading we naturally supply *βίον*.

232 **519 C** 14. **ἑκόντες εἶναι**: 34,9. 15. **ἔτι**: c. *ζῶντες*. 17. **τῶν οἰκιστῶν**: apposit. to the *ἡμῶν* implied in *ἡμέτερον*; 'of us who are the founders.' The correlat. of **τε** is *καί* in 21. 19. **τὸ μάθημα,** viz. **ἰδεῖν τε . . καί** (20).

233 **519 E** 2. **τοῦτο**; sc. *τὸ εὖ πράττειν*. 6. **ὠφελεῖν** c. two acc.

520 B 17. **ἀκούσης** *κτλ*. 'with the government in each (city) antagonistic to them.' 18. **δίκην ἔχει** 'it is right'; cf. *λόγον ἔχει* (25,4 App.), *φύσιν ἔχει* (218,5). **τό γε αὐτοφυές** is subject of *προθυμεῖσθαι*. 21. **ἡμεῖς,** sc. we founders of this ideal State. 23. **ἐκείνων,** viz. than those *αὐτόματοι* in other states, contending with adverse circumstances.

520 C 24. **ἀμφοτέρων,** sc. modes of life—that of public life and that of philosophy. 25. **ἑκάστῳ**: dat. of agent with the verbal *-τέον*; 'each in turn must —.'

234 **520 D** 5. **ᾗ**: *ἐν ᾗ* (19,1). *ἐν πόλει* for *τὴν πόλιν*, by inverse attraction. 8. **σχοῦσαν**: 230,1 for sense of aorist. 10. **οἱ τρόφιμοι** 'our alumni' (Purves). 13. **ἐν τῷ καθαρῷ**: not in the dark cave but 'in the pure' outer and upper air of *νοητὸς τόπος*.

520 E 15. **ὡς ἐπ' ἀναγκαῖον** '(regarding it) as a necessity.'

539 B Plato is here dissuading from a too early schooling in dialectic. I give the passage for the benefit of those "educators" who introduce psychological laboratories and pedagogies and the like into the undergraduate curriculum. 18. **αὕτη** (viz. *τὸ μὴ . . γενέσθαι*) is predic., *εὐλάβεια* subject. He has been speaking of the 'precaution' to be taken against the despair that is apt to attack a good young mind in the process of education. 19. **αὐτῶν,** sc. *λόγων* 'logic.' 22. **ὡς** resumes *ὅτι* after *λεληθέναι*. 23. **μιμούμενοι**: cf. 11,26. 26. **ἀεί** 'for the moment.'

235 **539 C** 2. **τὸ ὅλον,** sc. *ἐπιτήδευμα*, as is expressed in li. 9. **εἰς τοὺς ἄλλους** *κτλ*. 'are damaged in the eyes of the world.' For *εἰς*, cf. 109,12. 5. **τὸν διαλέγεσθαι ἐθέλοντα καὶ σκοπεῖν**: e.g. a Socrates. 7. **τὸν παίζοντα**: e.g. a Euthydemus, p. 154.

539 D 10. **οὐκοῦν καί** 'then too'—adding, by way of a *second* 'precaution against this' *μηδὲν ἡγεῖσθαι*, something already said, viz. *τὸ τὰς φύσεις . . στασίμους*. The gen. *τούτου* is objective aft. *εὐλαβείᾳ*. Briefly put, "philosophy is a study, 1st for mature intelligences, 2nd for steadfast characters" (Bosanquet). 13. **καὶ μὴ ὡς νῦν** *κτλ*. 'and not like your Tom, Dick, and Harry who *now* —.' For this abbreviated form of comparison, see 144,22 App.

REPUBLIC VIII

THE Eighth Book enumerates and discusses the latter four of 235
the five possible forms of government, together with their corresponding forms of individual character. For each soul is a polity; and the commonwealth is but the sum of these, stamped with the character that predominates. The five forms in descending order are—aristocracy, timocracy, oligarchy, democracy, tyranny. Each is the origin of the next.

557 A 25. **οὗτοι . . ἡ τοιαύτη αὖ**: in contrast to those of the previous polities discussed.

557 E 3. **αὐτῷ**: to contrast *σοι* the individual with *νόμος*. 237
4. **ἐπίῃ**: cf. *προσίσταται* (171,1), *εἰσέρχεται* (66,19).

558 A 6. **ἡ πραότης** *κτλ*. 'the gentleness of some of the condemned—isn't it charming?' 7. **εἶδες,** sc. *αὐτήν*, the gentleness. We might have expected the foll. **αὐτῶν μενόντων** to be in the accus., as obj. of *εἶδες*. But the genit. seems to be that *in which* a quality is observed. Cf. *θαυμάζω τί σου*; see 1,7 n. 10. **καὶ ὡς** 'and how,' c. *περινοστεῖ*.

558 B 13. **οὐδ' ὁπωστιοῦν σμικρολογία** 'the anything but pettiness.' **αὐτῆς,** sc. democracy. **ἀλλά** 'on the contrary.' 15. **ὡς** depends on *ἐλέγομεν*. 17. **ἐν καλοῖς**: see p. 206.

562 B After describing the individual corresponding to this 'sweet polity' (li. 26), he here takes up its final end, showing how it too, like its predecessors in the cycle, by full attainment of the 'good' it set itself, is destroyed, and evolves the next in order—tyranny. 29. **προὔθεντο** refers to those who constituted the oligarchy. 30. **τοῦτο**: this establishment of oligarchy (described in 551 A B as taking place *βίᾳ μεθ' ὅπλων*).

562 C 8. **κάλλιστον**: adverb. 11. **ᾖα . . ἐρῶν** 'was 238
going to say.' 16. **ἐλευθερίας**: obj. of *διψήσασα*; **οἰνοχόων,** of *τύχῃ*.

562 D 18. **ἀκράτου αὐτῆς**: *ἐλευθερίας*.

562 E 27. **ἐπὶ πᾶν** 'to all lengths.' 28. **τὸ τῆς ἐλευθερίας** 'this freedom-business.' 29. **καταδύεσθαι**: the syntax of *ἀνάγκη* continues. 30. **τε . . καί**: at *καί* anacoluthon occurs. 31. **τὴν ἀναρχίαν**: an apposit., showing what this 'liberty-business' degenerates into.

563 A 9. **ἐν τῷ τοιούτῳ** 'in such a state of affairs.' 239

563 B 16. **ἵνα δή**: for the second time (see li. 5) a scornful *δή* 'you know.' So again in 20 and 31, and in 13 of next

239 page. 17. **τὸ δέ γε ἔσχατόν** (*ἐστιν*) **ὅταν** (20): see 80,17 and App. to 14,24.

563 C 27. **τὸ μὲν γάρ** *κτλ.* 'as for the domestic-animal question'—properly, of course, subject. The predicate *ἐλευθερώτερα* becomes plural *κατὰ σύνεσιν.* 29. **ἐν ἄλλῃ,** sc. *γῇ* or *πόλει.* 30. **παροιμίαν**: the proverb ran, according to the scholiast, in iambic trimeter: *οἵαπερ ἡ δέσποινα, τοία χὰ κύων.* 31. **γίγνονται . . ἐμβάλλοντες** 'get to running into.' L. & S. s.v. *γίγνομαι,* II 1.

240 **563 E** 23. **φιλεῖ** 'is apt' (203,23).

REPUBLIC IX

241 **588 B** 5. **ἦν . . λεγόμενον** 'there was an argument,' 'the argument was'; not equiv. to *ἐλέγετο* (93,12 App.). The reference is to the contention of Thrasymachus in the First Book. 8. **νῦν δή**: not here (at head of its clause) in the usu. sense of 'just now'; but '*now*, then.' **αὐτῷ,** sc. *τῷ ἐκεῖνα λέγοντι.*

588 C 15. **φύσεις** 'growths,' 'creatures.' 16. **καὶ ἄλλαι** *κτλ.* (supply *φύσεις*) 'and a good many other creatures are said to have arisen by many forms growing together in one.' The clause breaks away from what precedes, much as in 41,15. 137,7. 23. **πλάστου** 'modeller.'

242 **588 D** 3. **τρία**: these three creatures are to represent the three parts of the human soul as it had been previously analyzed (V 435 ff.). The many-headed monster corresponds to the appetitive (*τὸ ἐπιθυμητικόν*), the lion to the spirited (*τὸ θυμοειδές*), the man to reason (*τὸ λογιστικόν*).

589 A 16. **ὅπῃ . . ὁπότερον** 'wherever . . whichever'; cf. 253,15. 23. **τοῦ ἀνθρώπου,** i.e. the *ἔλυτρον* of the *tout ensemble,* is surely better taken as the genit. of the whole, not with *ἐγκρατέστατος,* as some take it.

243 **589 C** 6. **οὐδὲν ὑγιές**: with *ψέγει* 'has no soundness in the criticism he offers (*ὅ τι ψέγει*), or knowledge either (*οὐδ' εἰδώς*).' 7. **δοκεῖ,** sc. *ὑγιὲς ψέγειν.* 10. **τὰ . . αἰσχρά** *κτλ.* 'the fair and foul' (in ethical sense) **γεγονέναι νόμιμα** 'have come to be so regarded' **διὰ τὰ τοιαῦτα** 'for the following qualities,' **τὰ μὲν καλά** 'the fair, namely' **τὰ ποιοῦντα τὰ θηριώδη τῆς φύσεως** 'those that put the wild-beast part of his nature' **ὑπὸ τῷ ἀνθρώπῳ** 'under the man's control,' etc. 14. **αἰσχρὰ δέ**: symmetry would require *τὰ δὲ αἰσχρά.*

589 D 16. **ἔστιν ὅτῳ λυσιτελεῖ** 'is there any one whom it

pays?' 20. **ἢ εἰ μέν** *κτλ.* an *argumentum ex contrario*; see 243
49,2 App. We might preface it by: 'Or *can it be that*, if . ., it would not pay him, yet if . ., he is not forsooth wretched?' On *ἄρα*, see 30,11 App.

590 A 26. **πολύ,** c. *δεινοτέρῳ*; cf. 32,20. 39,9. 28. **ἐπί,** c. dat.; a condit. equiv. to price. Cf. 41,1. 1. **ἐν** 244
τῷ τοιούτῳ 'in a man like that.'

590 B 10. **τὸ αὐτόν**: 193,25 n. 11. **ὀχλῶδει** 'turbulent.' 12. **προπηλακιζόμενον** 'by abuse.'

590 D 29. **οἰκείως** (MSS. *οἰκεῖον*) **ἔχοντος,** sc. *τοῦ θείου.*

590 E 3. **ἀρχή,** sc. *δηλοῖ.* 245

591 A 7. **τοιούτῳ,** sc. *βελτίστῳ.* **ἀντι**-*καταστήσωμεν*: *ἀντί* perhaps 'in our stead.'

591 B 22. **μετὰ φρονήσεως**: 198,8 n. **ἢ** 'than' goes back to *τιμιωτέραν.* 23. **τοσούτῳ,** sc. *τιμιωτέραν.*

591 C 30. **τὴν . . τροφήν** 'as for his —.' This retains the Greek order. **οὐχ ὅπως . . ἀλλ' οὐδέ** (next page) 'not only
not . . but not even.' H. 1035. 1. **ζήσει**: with this main 246
verb go three circumstantial participles—1st *οὐκ ἐνταῦθα τετραμμένος*, 2nd *οὐδὲ βλέπων οὐδὲ πρεσβεύων*, 3rd **ἀλλ' ἀεὶ ἁρμοττόμενος.** Hence *φαίνηται* is unnecessary and of dubious syntax.

591 D 7. **μουσικός**: in a splendidly cosmic sense. A man of *νοῦς* must make his life harmonious music, like that of the spheres, through *δικαιοσύνη μετὰ φρονήσεως.* 8. **τὴν . . ξύνταξίν τε καὶ ξυμφωνίαν**: this acc. is like *τὴν ἐν τῷ σώματι ἁρμονίαν* above—an inner acc. c. *ἁρμοττόμενος.* 10. **οὐκ,** c. *αὐξήσει.* 11. **ἄπειρον . . ἀπέραντα**: assonance.

591 E 14. **παρακινῇ**: consult L. & S. 18. **τιμάς**: free accus. at head; later the sent. requires its change to gen. (*τῶν μέν*). Cf. 197,9 where the acc. must be picked up by *εἰς τοῦτο.* See also n. on 172,17.

592 B 31. **παράδειγμα**: the matter of the Platonic Ideas
this first book in Plato must not even enter upon. 3. **τὰ** 247
ταύτης μόνης *κτλ.* 'mind the affairs of that city only.'

REPUBLIC X

THE *Republic* closes with perhaps the greatest of Plato's *μῦθοι*, which are *λόγοι* (146,12).

614 A 9. **τοιαῦτα,** i.e. as just detailed. 12. **ἑκάτερον,** viz. both the just man and the unjust. 13. **ἀπειλήφῃ**:

247 note tense; 'may *be* in receipt (pres.) of what is due from the argument.' The argument is bound to furnish for hearing (*ἀκοῦσαι* epexegetic) a complete account to each of his fortune. 15. **ὡς . . ἀκούοντι**: cf. the gen. c. *ὡς* 192,4.

614 B 16. **οὐ . . Ἀλκίνου γε ἀπόλογον** 'not an Alcinoüs-tale'—for the tale told to Alcinoüs by Odysseus in the *Odyssey* is four books long. Suidas says the phrase was a proverb *ἐπὶ τῶν φλυαρούντων καὶ μακρὸν ἀποτεινόντων λόγον*. 17. **ἀλκίμου**: pun on *Ἀλκίνου*. Note **μέν**=*μήν*. **τοῦ Ἀρμενίου** 'the son of Armenius.' 23. **ἐκεῖ** 'in the other world'; 40,22 App. 24. **ἐπειδὴ . . ἐκβῆναι**: 94,6 n. for infin.

248 614 C 1. **ἐχομένω**: c. gen., 'adjoining.' 5. **τὴν εἰς δεξιὰν** (*ὁδόν*). 7. **τῶν δεδικασμένων** 'the judgments.'

614 D 11. **εἰπεῖν**, sc. *τοὺς δικαστάς*. 14. **κατά** 'by the way of.' 16. **κατὰ δὲ τὼ ἑτέρω** answers *ταύτῃ μέν* in 14. **ἐκ μὲν τοῦ**: demonstrat.; 'from the one.'

614 E 22. **οἷον**=*ὥσπερ*.

249 615 A 1. **πολλοῦ χρόνου**: predic. genit. H. 732, G. 1094. 5. **δεκάκις** 'tenfold.'

615 B 8. **οἷον** 'for example.' **καί** is awkward, and perhaps should be dropped.

615 C 16. **τῶν δὲ εὐθὺς γενομένων** *κτλ.*: this ought to mean 'concerning those who, as soon as born, died.' But the Greek surely does not warrant it. *ἀπογενομένων* has been suggested as a substitute, or *ἀποθανόντων* inserted after *γενομένων*. Of course *εὐθύς* does not belong to *γενομένων*. Though standing regularly before a ptc., it quite as regularly goes with some following verb. Cf. 165,9. 192,30. So *Phaedo* 75 C; and see G. M. T. § 858. 18. **ἀσεβείας** *κτλ.*: genit. of course. 19. **γονέας**: supply *εἰς*. 21. **παραγενέσθαι . . ἑτέρῳ**: cf. 194,12. 25. **ἤδη** *κτλ.*: i.e., a thousand years before.

615 D 29. **εἰπεῖν . . φάναι** 'said . . said he.' See L. & S. s.v. *φημί*, II 3, for the tautology. **οὐδ' ἂν ἥξει** 'and prob-
250 ably *won't* come'; 22,1 App. 4. **τῶν . . ἡμαρτηκότων**: predic.

615 E 7. **εἰς**: c. acc. of specific.; 22,17 App. 9. **ἰδεῖν** 'to look upon.' 10. **τὸ φθέγμα,** sc. *τοῦ στομίου*. 11. **διαλαβόντες** 'divided,' 'allotted' among themselves. Cf. Lysias 12,7 *διαλαβόντες τὰς οἰκίας*.

616 A 14. **παρὰ τὴν ὁδόν**: not '*down along* the road' (which is *κατά*; see n. on 1,16), but 'alongside and off' (*ἐκτός*) —where the *ἀσπάλαθος* was growing. 16. **τὸν τάρταρον** is prob. somebody's marginal note to show that *he* knew 'to what place' (*εἰς ὅ τι*). Note *ἐμπεσούμενοι* as the regular pass.

of *ἐμβάλλω*. 18. **τοῦτον,** sc. *τὸν φόβον*. 20. **σιγή-** 250
σαντος, sc. *τοῦ στομίου*.

616 B 25. **ἑκάστοις,** i.e. each band. 27. **ὅθεν καθορᾶν:** infin. in subord. clause of indir. discourse, as in 247,24. 28. **ἄνωθεν:** c. *τεταμένον*.—The description here becomes very puzzling. The student should consult the various editors. What explanation is here offered of the next dozen lines may be quite wrong,—very probably is wrong, since it differs, I believe, from some of the assumptions usually made. With this warning, I go on without discussion of other views. **διὰ παντὸς τοῦ οὐρανοῦ** *κτλ.*: if this band of light 'straight, like a pillar' lay like a *horizontal* pillar, then translate *διά* by 'across'; i.e. the *φῶς* lay 'across the earth' and out over the edges 'across the whole heaven' to the horizon or lower rim of heaven's vault. The *οὐρανός*, physicists taught in those days,
was like a *πνιγεύς* ('oven'). 1. **κατὰ μέσον τὸ φῶς** 'at the 251
middle point of this (horizontal pillar of) light'—just as *κατὰ μέσον* is used of the "centre" of an extended line of battle.

616 C 2. **τὰ ἄκρα αὐτοῦ** (sc. *τοῦ φωτὸς*) **τῶν δεσμῶν** 'the ends of its chains,' stretched from (the zenith of) heaven. Imagine, therefore, an inverted bowl as representing heaven, beneath it a disc for the earth, across the disc and reaching to the bowl's edges a bar, suspended at its middle point by a cord from middle of this *inverted* bowl. 4. **οἷον τὰ ὑποζώματα:** these were large ropes passed under the hull of a vessel weakened from age or threatened with storm, as is mentioned by Paul in *Acts* 27,17 (*ὑποζωννύντες τὸ πλοῖον*). It is to be supposed, of course, that they ran across deck, and so prevented a splitting apart of the vessel-walls. Like these tightly-stretched straight ropes, therefore, the *φῶς* also was a *ξύνδεσμος τοῦ οὐρανοῦ*, 'thus holding together all its circumference' (li. 5). 7. **δι' οὗ** *κτλ.* 'by means of which are turned all the orbits' (of the heavenly bodies); for the earth was the centre of the universe, and here we seem to have its very central point described. 8. **ἠλακάτην** 'shaft,' **ἄγκιστρον** 'hook,' **σφόνδυλον** 'whorl.' The student should look up these various parts of the spindle (*ἄτρακτος*) in some good dictionary of antiquities. 10. **μεικτόν:** *μίγνυμι*.—There follows a passage descriptive of the universe, which has been omitted as foreign to the elementary character of the present selections.

617 B 11. **αὐτόν,** sc. *τὸν ἄτρακτον*. **ἐν τοῖς τῆς Ἀνάγκης γόνασι:** cf. the Homeric phrase *ταῦτα θεῶν ἐν γούνασι κεῖται*. In Plato's time certainly the "scientific use of the imagination" was not underestimated. 12. **ἐπὶ δὲ τῶν κύκλων:** in the omitted passage the spindle (*ἄτρακτος*) is made to revolve by the whorl (*σφόνδυλος*) suspended from it consisting

251 of eight truncated spheres one within the other—let us say like a nest of porridge-bowls set one within another, each bowl having its separate rotary motion. The edges of these revolving bowls would represent the *κύκλοι* here referred to, described in the passage omitted as the orbits of the seven planets and the sphere of the fixed stars. 15. **ἁρμονίαν** in the ancient sense, is 'scale,' not the modern 'harmony.'—This is the famous music of the spheres,—a Pythagorean doctrine. There are eight tones in the diatonic scale—*εἷς τόνος* from each Siren. 16. **δι' ἴσου** 'at equal intervals.' Cf. *διὰ χρόνου* 'after an interval (apart-ness) of time.'

617 C 24. ***συν-επιστρέφειν*** : the spinner must touch up ('help turn') the whorl now and then (*διαλείπουσαν χρόνον*), to keep it going. **τὴν ἔξω περιφοράν** is the sphere or circle of the fixed stars—the edge of the largest porridge-bowl. There must be symbolism in all this detail. *Why* does Plato assign this duty to Clotho, that to Atropus? *Why* the right hand employed here, the left there? The student must consult the larger works on such matters.

252 **617 D** 5. **ψυχαὶ ἐφήμεροι** : hardly an item of rhetoric but is present in this brief but awful summons of the *προφήτης* of Fate. Note, there is no *ὦ* with the vocative; no article with *ἀρχή, γένους,* or *ἑλομένου* (11); no *αὕτη ἐστί* with *ἀρχή*; the 'death-bringing' adjective is at the end, separated from *περιόδου* its substantive; there is asyndeton at *οὐχ ὑμᾶς* and again in li. 11; there is chiasm of case in *ὑμᾶς δαίμων* as against *ὑμεῖς δαίμονα*; there is anaphora in *πρῶτος . . πρῶτος*; the word *ἀδέσποτον* is unfamiliar, and stands off coldly in the neuter gender; there is a balance (as if in the scales of Fate) between *τιμῶν καὶ ἀτιμάζων* and *πλέον καὶ ἔλαττον*.

617 E 7. **πρῶτος ὁ λαχὼν** *κτλ.* : the lots were numbered. The holder of number one would be entitled to first choice from the *βίοι*. 10. **πλέον καὶ ἔλαττον** : if *ἀρετή* is 'without a master,' then she brings us liberty, freedom of choice. The more we honour her, therefore, the greater freedom of choice we shall have. 14. **ἕ**, sc. Er, obj. of *ἐᾶν*. Subject of *ἐᾶν* is *τὸν προφήτην*. 15. **ὁπόστος** 'the how-many-eth'; H. 294.

618 A 21. **τυραννίδας** : many plural abstracts follow; see 48,27 n. 22. **διατελεῖς** 'lasting out' the tyrant's life, contrasted with those done away with in the midst. 25. **ἐπὶ εἴδεσιν**, with *δοκίμων*.

618 B 26. **ἄλλην** 'besides.' 29. **ψυχῆς τάξιν** 'soul-assignment,' 'soul-allotment'; *ψυχῆς* emphat. by posit., to be contrasted with *τὰ ἄλλα* (31). **ἐνεῖναι**, sc. *ἐν τοῖς βίοις*. No particular sort of soul was assigned to each life-pattern. *That*

was but a shell or husk; and whether a tyrant's or beggar's, 252
the chooser could display within it what soul he would—mean
or noble. 2. **μεσοῦν** c. gen.; cf. *μέσος* 195,21. 253

618 C 11. **ἐκ τῶν δυνατῶν**=*κατὰ τὸ δυνατόν* li. 7 of next page. 14. **τί**, with *κακὸν ἢ ἀγαθόν* (16); 'what in the way of bad or good.' **κάλλος**: subj. of *ἐργάζεται*.

618 D 15. **μετὰ ποίας**: quest. within quest. (*τί . . μετὰ ποίας*); cf. 242,16. 19. **φύσει, ἐπικτήτων** 'natural,' 'acquired.' 20. **τί**: repeated from li. 16.

618 E 27. **τὰ δὲ ἄλλα . . ἐάσει**: as so often, the appended *ἄλλα*-clause breaks away from the previous syntax (which had been acc. c. inf.), and takes a finite verb. See 241,16 n.

619 A 4. **τὸν μέσον βίον**: the *auream mediocritatem* of 254
Hor. *Odes* 2,10,5. So *medio tutissimus ibis* Ov. *Met.* 2,137.

619 B 10. **καὶ δὴ οὖν** 'and so as I was saying.' *οὖν* resumes the story after digression. **ὁ ἐκεῖθεν ἄγγελος**, sc. Er. 12. **καί** is perhaps 'even.' **ξὺν νῷ ἑλομένῳ**: fateful condition! 13. **συντόνως**: cf. *συντεταμένως* 12,13. *ξυντείνας* 245,26. 14. **μήτε** *κτλ.*: again, in this continuation of the speech of the *προφήτης* from p. 252,12, observe the rhetoric of asyndeton, balance, assonance (*ἀμελείτω, ἀθυμείτω*).

619 C 20. **εἱμαρμένην** 'a doom'; freq. as substantive. 21. **κατὰ σχολήν**: 27,15 n. 24. **τῶν κακῶν**: cause. **πάντα** *κτλ.* 'everything rather, instead of himself.' 27. **τεταγμένῃ** 'well-ordered,' 'sober.' 28. **ἔθει ἄνευ φιλοσοφίας**: for one who had 'partaken of virtue by habit, without philosophy' Plato had only contempt. Such virtue was merely *δημοτική* ('popular') and *ἀνδραποδώδης* ('slavish'; 85,4). Always his cry is: *μετὰ φρονήσεως*. See 198,8 n.

619 D 29. **ὡς . . εἰπεῖν**: *ὡς ἔπος εἰπεῖν*. 30. **εἶναι . . ἁλισκομένους** is not equiv. to *ἁλίσκεσθαι*. See 93,12 App.
6. **καὶ διὰ τὴν τοῦ κλήρου τύχην**: this 'luck of the lot' 255
comes in strangely. Many more *παραδείγματα* of lives had been set forth than there were choosers (252,17 ff.); and the *προφήτης* had said that the last comer need not despair (254,15). Where then is there room for 'luck'? Is it that, after all, the stern moralizer Plato had to admit a time-and-tide element in a man's fate along with the man's own soul? 7. **ἐνθάδε** 'here on earth.'

620 A 16. **ἐλεεινήν**: *τὴν θέαν*. 21. **μίσει**: dat. of cause. 24. **ἀηδόνος**, sc. *βίον*.

620 B 30. **ἐπί** 'after' (18,13).

620 D 15. **καὶ πρώτη** 'even though first.' *καί*=*καίπερ*. 256
20. **δ' οὖν**: 1,3 App., 3rd usage. 23. **ἑκάστῳ**: with

256 *ξυμπέμπειν*. **δαίμονα** ‘guardian spirit’—for good or bad. Hence the freq. *εὐδαίμων, κακοδαίμων*. 24. **τοῦτον** resumes *δαίμονα*.

620 E 25. **ὅν**, sc. *δαίμονα*, subj. of *ἄγειν*. 26. **αὐτήν**: the individual soul. 28. **κυροῦντα** ‘ratifying.’ 29. **ταύτης**, sc. Clotho. **ἐφαψάμενον**, like *λαχών*, is best referred, not to the *δαίμων* (although it is true that *δαίμονα* is the subject of *ἄγειν* and *ποιοῦντα*), but to the mortal man whose *ψυχή* is thus conducted. *ἐφάπτομαι* was also in 251,23. 31. **ἀμετάστροφα** ‘irreversible’—to be expected from *Ἄ-τροπος*.

257 **621 A** 9. **στέγειν**: here ‘to hold,’ ‘to keep in.’ *ἀγγεῖον* is subject.

621 B 11. **πλέον πίνειν τοῦ μέτρου**: fatal thirst! involving for their next life on earth all the weary labour of *ἀνάμνησις*. See p. 177. 15. **εἰς τήν** *κτλ.*: an iambic trimeter. Cf. 151,28 (and *Protag*. 320 E). 19. **ἀναβλέψας** ‘opening his eyes again’; so Xen. *Cyrop*. VIII 3,29, in contrast to *καταμύων*. 21. **μῦθος ἐσώθη**: a regular phrase, says Photius, “used at the end of stories told to children,” where we should say ‘the story’s ended.’ Perhaps it originated with the thought of the people *in* the story that were ‘saved’ (?). Plato plays on the phrase when he adds *καὶ ἡμᾶς ἂν σώσειεν*.

621 C 28. **δικαιοσύνην μετὰ φρονήσεως**: the keytone of Plato’s whole message; 198,8 n. and Introd., n. 45. 29. **ἡμῖν αὐτοῖς** does not stand here for *ἀλλήλοις*, as sometimes. It points rather to concord in a man’s inner Republic—his soul. 30. **αὐτοῦ . . ἐνθάδε**: a not infreq. combination; ‘*just* where we are.’

258 **621 D** 2. **καὶ ἐνθάδε**: this *καί* connects the two subjunctives *ὦμεν* and *πράττωμεν* in their dependence upon *ἵνα*. The scheme is:

ἵνα { *ὦμεν* . . { *αὐτοῦ τε* . . / *καὶ ἐπειδὰν* . . } / *καὶ* . . *εὖ πράττωμεν*. }

PHAEDRUS

The following extract gives us the attitude of Socrates towards the rationalists, and his passionate love of the study of man. He has met Phaedrus going for a walk outside the city-wall (*πρὸς περίπατον ἔξω τείχους*) with a book in his hand, viz. a speech of Lysias the orator. Phaedrus will read it to him, if he will go along. Socrates agrees.

229 A 9. **εἰς καιρόν**=*εἰς καλόν* 94,12. 156,22. *ἐν καιρῷ* 258
44,22.

229 B 20. **καθίζεσθαι**: an infin. after such adjectives as *δεινός, ἄξιος* etc. and after such substantives as *ὥρα, ἀνάγκη* and the like, is regular. The present extension of the usage is rarer. 24. **μέντοι** 'surely' from somewhere here; not often in questions (15 times in Plato).

229 C 6. **τὸ τῆς Ἄγρας**, sc. *ἱερόν*. 11. **ἀλλ' εἰ ἀπι-** 259
στοίην *κτλ*. 'well, if I were incredulous like your clever people, I wouldn't be absurd and then play the rationalist and say —.' For *εἶτα* 'and then,' see App. on 11,27. (This interpretation of the passage may be wrong, since it is, I believe, new.) There was much allegorizing of Homer in the sophistic period, discovering in him *ὑπόνοιαι* (203,18), and explaining away Zeus, Hera, Athene and the rest, as mere symbols of the elements.

229 D 17. **ἢ ἐξ Ἀρείου** *κτλ*.: very probably a learned note, crept in from the margin. 19. **ἄλλως μὲν . . δέ** 'besides regarding such explanations as clever, think them also to be —.' Cf. *καὶ ἄλλως . . καὶ δὴ καί* 90,18. Irony, of course. 21. **οὐ πάνυ εὐτυχοῦς**: litotes (4,13). 24. **ἐπανορθοῦσθαι** 'rehabilitate' (Jowett). 26. **ἀμηχάνων** *κτλ*.: the scheme is:

ἄλλων { *ἀμηχάνων πλήθει τε* / *καὶ ἀτοπίᾳ τερατολόγων* } *τινῶν φύσεων.*

φύσεων as 241,15.

229 E 27. **εἰ . . προσβιβᾷ** (fut.) 'if a man is going to bring each one into line according to probability.' 29. **ἀγροίκῳ σοφίᾳ** 'wooden-headed wisdom' (Purves)—that of Goethe's Wagner (?).

230 A 7. **ἐπιτεθυμμένον**:—*τύφομαι*; 'rabid,' 'furious.' For 260
πολυπλοκώτερον, see p. 241.

230 B 18. **ὡς ἀκμὴν ἔχει**: exclamatory; 'what a perfection of bloom it has (sc. *ἡ καταγωγή*), such as must make the spot most fragrant.' For the first *ὡς*, cf. *Prot.* 328 D *ὡς χάριν σοι ἔχω ὅτι*— 'how grateful I am to you that —.' For the second (relat.) *ὡς* followed by the potent. opt., see G. M. T. § 329,2. On the translat. of the potent opt. by 'must,' see 14,31 n. 20. **ὑπὸ τῆς πλατάνου**: the genit. here must be regarded as one of the no few marks of poetic flight (or certainly emotion) in this passage. (See 3,9 App.) Note the oath at the start, the poetic vocabulary, the strings of *τε*'s, the exclamatory *ὡς* (18 and 24), and the vocat. at end (29). 21. **ὡς . . τεκμήρασθαι** 'to judge by my foot'; absol. infin., as *ὡς ἔπος εἰπεῖν*. G. M. T. § 778. 22. **κορῶν** 'dolls.' Greek girls played with their dolls until just before marriage (which was early, to be sure),

260 when they dedicated them to Artemis. See the pretty little dedicatory verses in Anthol. Palat. 6,280.

230 C 25. **θερινόν**: inner acc. with *ὑπηχεῖ* (subject *ὁ τόπος*). 26. **τὸ τῆς πόας** 'this thing of the grass.' Cf. 238,28. 239,27. 27. **ὅτι** 'that' = 'because.' 28. **κατακλινέντι** *κτλ.*: lit. 'for a man to lie down and be quite comfortable with his head.' 29. **σοι**: dat. of agent. **ἐ-ξενάγηται**: *ξένος,*
261 *ἄγω.* 1. **οὕτως**: 1,4 App.

230 D 2. **οὔτ' . . ἀποδημεῖς**: on the fact, cf. 59,24. 8. **τῆς ἐξόδου τὸ φάρμακον** 'a physic to charm me out.' Such a genit. as this was the origin of the articular infin. in the genit. (e.g. *τοῦ ἐξελθεῖν*) to express purpose; G. M. T. § 798.

230 E 14. **μοι δοκῶ κατακεῖσθαι** 'I vote for lying down.' The infin. is not in indirect discourse ('I think I shall lie down'—which would require the future), but merely the object of thought. Cf. Aristoph. *Nub.* 1141 *δικάσασθαί φασί μοι* 'they talk of having the law of me.' See G. M. T. § 136.

MENEXENUS

The *Menexenus* was written probably as a parody on the ornate oratory of the day—to show that all that kind of thing was a mere empty play of juggling words, a trick easily caught, signifying nothing, *νοῦς* being not in it. Socrates tells Menexenus that anybody can compose off-hand one of these annual funeral orations (*ἐπιτάφιοι λόγοι*), such as were delivered over those who had fallen in battle during the year. You praise everybody and everything that is Athenian—rich man, poor man, beggarman, thief, the past, the present, and the future. That is all easy enough—among the Athenians (though it might require more oratory to win success, if your audience were Spartans). He will give a specimen himself—which is filled with the stock ornaments of epideictic oratory. Toward the close (here given) he tells what the dead themselves would say, had they the power, in exhortation of the living.

246 D 20. **καλῶς, καλῶς**: end-word and next beginning-word the same—anastrophe (*ἀνα-στροφή*); so next p., li. 2. 21. **καταστῆσαι . . αἰσχῦναι**: like endings—*ὁμοιοτέλευτον*. Cf. *εἶναι . . εἶναι* lines 24–26.

262 **246 E** 3. **λειπόμενα**, c. gen.; 'failing.'

247 A 14. **παντὸς πᾶσαν** *κτλ.*: with what sarcastic grin must Plato have penned this playful parody on the orator's pet

pride—the alliterated π. 17. **ἡμῖν,** sc. the dead fore- 262
fathers. As for the thought—that too is a mere cleverness, but has no depth. 21. **καταχρησόμενοι:** more freq. the fut. ptc. after *παρασκευάζομαι* takes *ὡς*.

247 B 25. **εἶναι:** its subj. is *τιμάς*; the whole clause is then subj. to an *ἐστί* understood. 31. **φίλοι παρὰ φίλους** is ornate. Cf. Soph. *Antig.* 73 *φίλη μετ' αὐτοῦ κείσομαι, φίλου μέτα.*

PROTAGORAS

An extract on Greek schooling.

325 C 1. **μέχρι οὗπερ:** *μέχρι*, like *ἕως*, is not alone 'up to,' 264
but sometimes 'as long as.' 3. **θᾶττον** after *ἐπειδή* is not common; rather *ἐπειδὴ τάχιστα* 'as soon as.'

325 D 11. **ἐὰν μὲν . . πείθηται:** apodosis ('good') omitted. See n. on 108,22. 14. **πληγαῖς:** memorize that fine old verse—the corner-stone of true pedagogy, *ὁ μὴ δαρεὶς ἄνθρωπος οὐ παιδεύεται.*

325 E 20. **τότε** refers to the time spoken of in li. 3. 22. **ἀναγιγνώσκειν:** inf. of purpose; 28,5. 20,29. **ποιητῶν:** especially Homer, Hesiod, Theognis, Phocylides were used. 23. **ἐκ-***μανθάνειν* 'to learn by heart.'

326 A 27. **ἕτερα τοιαῦτα:** inner acc.; 'take like care
again.' 3. **ποιητῶν . . μελοποιῶν:** for a picture of the 265
boys at school learning their 'lyric poets,' see by all means Arist. *Nub.* 966 ff.

326 B 4. **εἰς τὰ κιθαρίσματα ἐντείνοντες** (sc. *τὰ ποιήματα*) 'putting the poems (and their tunes) to the lyre-accompaniment'; cf. 69,27 for a different sense of *ἐντείνω*. 6. **ἁρμονίας:** 251,15 n. **οἰκειοῦσθαι:** cf. 207,16 *καταδύεται κτλ.* 10. **πᾶς γὰρ ὁ βίος:** for the thought, cf. 246,7. 14. **διανοίᾳ** 'mind,' 'intent.'

326 D 25. **αὐτοί** as in 17,27. 26. **ἐφ' αὐτῶν** 'by themselves.' L. & S. s.v. *ἐπί*, A I 1 d. 28. **ὑπο-γράψαντες:** *ὑπο-γράφω* is prob. 'to write the outlines'; e.g., when teaching the child to make the letter O, to write a small o within a larger one, leaving the pupil to fill in between the lines. (This explanation of Adam's I prefer to the usual one that straight lines were written by the teacher across the tablet, between which the pupil must remain.) 29. **οὕτω,** viz. as the participial clause has just indicated; 82,14. **γραμματεῖον** 'tablet.' 30. **ὑφήγησιν** 'lead.' **ὣς δέ** 'why, *so*.' *ὥς* accented is

demonstrat. = *οὕτως*. H. 120, G. 138,3. For *δέ* in apodosis,
266 see 35,29. 4. **παρ' ὑμῖν** 'with you Athenians'—Protagoras the speaker being a foreigner, from Abdēra.

REPUBLIC VI

495 C 11. **οὗτοι**, viz. those of fine qualities and many opportunities (wealth, birth, etc.) for a philosophic life, but who had been misled by flattery and the popular ideals—perhaps such as Alcibiades. **ἐκπίπτοντες**: a metaphorical use of its civil sense 'banished.' **οἷς μάλιστα προσήκει** 'to whom she (Philosophy) is nearest related.' Philosophy is here compared to an heiress (*ἐπίκληρος*), who properly was married by the nearest male relative. 12. **ἀτελῆ** 'inconsummate'—of unwedded state. 13. **τε . . δέ**: see Index. 17. **ὡς** 'namely, how that —.'

495 D 24. **εἰς τὰ ἱερά**: because a temple was an asylum
267 (*ἄ-συλον*). 2. **τεχνίον**: contemptuous diminutive, as *ἀνθρωπίσκοι* above. **ὅμως** goes past *καίπερ* c. partic. to the finite verb. **πρός**: of relation or comparison; L. & S., C III 4. 5. **ἐφιέμενοι**: transl. as main verb; 'this dignity (*ἀξίωμα*) they covet, although —.'

495 E 10. **δοκεῖς** 'think.' 11. **ἰδεῖν** 'in appearance.' 13. **λελυμένου . . λελουμένου**: intentional play on the words, of course.

496 A 23. **ἀκοῦσαι**: 175,22; fitting 'to be called.'

496 C 26. **τούτων . . οἱ γενόμενοι** 'those who have become members of this small band,' viz. of true philosophers—the
268 "remnant." 2. **οὐδ' ἔστι** depends on *ἰδόντες ὅτι*.

496 D 4. **ἀλλ' ὥσπερ** *κτλ.* 'but that he (sc. *τις* from above), like a man, etc. . . , would prove useless (*ἀνωφελὴς ἂν γένοιτο*) etc. . . , before (*πρίν*) etc.' 9. **λαβών**: a resumption, but in the sing. number, of *οἱ γενόμενοι* at the beginning of the sent. 10. **οἷον . . ἀγαπᾷ** 'the way he is content.'

REPUBLIC IX

586 A 25. **μέχρι** c. *πρός*. 26. **ταύτῃ** 'there,' viz.
269 between *μεταξύ* and *κάτω* 'mediocrity and lower.' 3. **δίκην**: adverb c. genit.; 'like.'

586 B 5. **τούτων**: objective genit. 8. **οὐχὶ τοῖς** 269
οὖσι 'not with realities' — that is (for Plato) 'spiritual things.' 9. **οὐδὲ τὸ ὄν** *κτλ.* 'nor yet the reality nor the containing (holding) part of themselves.' In *Gorg.* 493 B, Plato compares that part of the soul which desires (*οὗ αἱ ἐπιθυμίαι εἰσίν*) to a jar with a hole in it—it does not hold (*οὐ στεγανόν*). Cf. also 257,9.

SOPHISTES

For those who think they know when they do not, Plato believes *ἔλεγχος* ('refutation') by means of dialectic (*διαλέγομαι, ἡ διαλεκτικὴ τέχνη*) to be the best mode of education. He here reports the process of those who thus refute.

230 B 12. **διερωτῶσι**, i.e. the teachers; for the compound *δια-*, see 9,23 n. 13. **πέρι**: with *ὧν*. **τι . . λέγειν**: 23,12 n. **πλανωμένων**, sc. *τῶν οὐδὲν λεγόντων*. 14. **συνάγοντες**, viz. *τὰς δόξας* 'the opinions.' 15. **λόγοις** 'reason,' 'arguments.' **εἰς ταὐτόν** repeats *συν-* (193,25). 16. **αὐταῖς**: with *ἐναντίας*. 18. **ὁρῶντες**, viz. the contradiction or inconsistency.

230 C 21. **σκληρῶν**: 272,13. 22. **ἀκούειν τε ἡδίστην**, i.e. for the bystanders (cf. 11,25), not for the sufferer. *ἡδίστην* is cognate acc. (sc. *ἀπαλλαγήν*) with *ἀπαλλάττονται*. 23. **βεβαιότατα γιγνομένην** 'one that proves the surest.' Not many adverbs are common with *γίγνεσθαι* and *εἶναι*; e.g. *ἐγγύς, δίχα*. 25. **νενομίκασι**: "gnomic" perfect; G. M. T. § 154. **μή**:
note *μή* after *νομίζω*; 7,25 App. 1. **διενοήθησαν** is 270
anacoluthic, repeating *νομίζοντες* of li. 23.

230 D 6. **ἡγούμενον**, like *καθαρόν*, depends on *ἀποφήνῃ*. 10. **ἔλεγχον**: proleptic. 11. **τὸν ἀνέλεγκτον**: cf. 35,28.

230 E 15. **ἔπρεπε**, sc. *γεγονέναι*.

PHAEDO

We must not grow to hate reason.

89 D 24. **ἥ τε γὰρ μισανθρωπία**: the response to *τε*, bringing the application of the comparison, is here omitted. But the application is obvious.

THEAETETUS

272 **155 D** 5. **ὁ . . φήσας** is Hesiod; *Theogony* 265,780. Iris, as messenger of the gods, must have learned much.

155 E 8. **ἀμυήτων** 'uninitiated.' Those who had looked upon the Eleusinian mysteries must tell no tales. So in philosophy, the final truths were not for 'hard and repellant (impenetrable) souls' as he humorously calls them—applying to them the terms of their own materialistic doctrine. The reference is probably to Antisthenes and his school. See Zeller II 1, p. 297. 11. **οὐκ ἀποδεχόμενοι** *κτλ.* 'refusing to accept as belonging to the category of existence.' 13. **σκληρούς**: 269,21.

153 B 18. **ἐπὶ τὸ πολύ**: often *ὡς ἐπὶ τὸ πολύ*, as in 201,13.

273 **184 C** 7. **τὸ εὐχερές** 'easy use' (lit. 'handling'). **ὀνομάτων** *κτλ.*: 2,1 App. 10. **ἔστι δὲ ὅτε** = *ἐνίοτε δέ* (72,13). It may be added for the comfort of those who still regard the study of the grammar of a language as something not wholly unessential to its mastery, that Plato here proceeds to discuss the question whether we should say *ὀφθαλμὸν δι' οὗ ὁρῶμεν* or *ὀφθαλμὸν ᾧ ὁρῶμεν*.

POLITICUS

261 E 14. **πλουσιώτερος**: with genit., by the rule of "plenty and want."

PHAEDRUS

245 A 20. **ἠφανίσθη**: gnomic.

LAWS

274 **743 E** 10. **οὐχ ἅπαξ**: but often.

275 **732 B** 3. **μηδεμίαν** *κτλ.* 'allowing no shame for such a cause to stand in the way.'

APPENDIX

THE following is a list of books, and of the abbreviations used in citing them, to which reference is more or less frequent in the succeeding notes:

Aken: *Grundzüge der Lehre vom Tempus und Modus im Griechischen;* Rostock, 1861.

Alvin: *De usu praepositionis παρά apud Thucydidem;* Upsala, 1873.

A. J. P.: *American Journal of Philology.*

Bäumlein: *Untersuchungen über griech. Partikeln;* Stuttgart, 1861.

Birklein: *Entwickelungsgeschichte des substantivirten Infinitivs* (Schanz's *Beiträge*); Wurzburg, 1888.

Bl.-Kühn.: Kühner's *Grammatik der griech. Sprache,* revised by Blass; Hannover, 1890 and 1892.

Braun: *De Hyperbato Platonico;* Culm, 1847.

Dyroff: *Geschichte des Pronomen Reflexivum* (Schanz's *Beiträge*); Wurzburg, 1892.

Eibel: *De Vocativi usu apud decem oratores Atticos;* Würzburg, 1893.

Forman: *The Difference between the Genit. and Dative used with ἐπί to denote Superposition;* Baltimore, 1894.

Froh. Lys.: Frohberger's *Lysias,* 2nd and 3rd volumes; Leipsic, 1868 and 1871.

Geb.: Gebauer's *De hypotacticis et paratacticis Argumenti ex Contrario formis;* Zwickau, 1877.

Geb.-Froh. Lys.: Frohberger's *Lysias,* 1st volume revised by Gebauer; Leipsic, 1880.

G.-Kuhn.: Kuhner's *Grammatik der griech. Sprache, Zweiter Teil,* revised by Gerth; Hannover, 1898.

G. M. T.: Goodwin's *Greek Moods and Tenses;* Boston, 1890.

Hoefer: *De particulis Platonicis;* Bonn, 1882.

Kalinka: *De usu coniunctionum quarundam apud scriptores Atticos antiquissimos;* in *Dissertationes philologae Vindobonenses,* II (1890), p. 145 ff.

Krüger: *Griechische Sprachlehre;* Leipsic, 1875.

Kuhne: *Die Praepositionen bei Herodot;* Rostock, 1883.

Kuhn.: Kuhner's *Gram. d. gr. Sprache, Zweiter Teil* (cited so far as not yet revised by Gerth); Hannover, 1872.

Kugler: *De particulae τοι eiusque compositorum apud Platonem usu;* Trogen, 1886.

La Roche: *Beiträge zur griech. Grammatik;* Leipsic, 1893.

Lina: *De praepositionum usu Platonico;* Marburg, 1889.

Lutz: *Die Prapositionen bei den attischen Rednern;* Neustadt a. d. H., 1887.

Mommsen (T.): *Beiträge zu der Lehre von den griech. Prapositionen;* Berlin, 1895.

Monro: *Homeric Grammar;* Oxford, 1891.

Rehd. : Rehdantz's edition of Xenophon's *Anabasis* and of Lycurgus.
Rehd. *Ind. Dem.* : Rehdantz's *Indices* to his edition of the nine *Philippics* of Demosthenes, revised by Blass; Leipsic, 1886.
Rid *Dig.* : Riddell's edition of Plato's *Apology*, containing his *Digest of Platonic Idioms;* Oxford, 1877.
Schanz *Nov. Com.* : *Novae Commentationes Platonicae;* Wurzburg, 1871.
Schn. Isoc. : Schneider's *Ausgewählte Reden des Isokrates;* Leipsic, 1888 and 1886.
Schwab : *Historische Syntax der griech. Comparation* (Schanz's *Beiträge*); Würzburg, 1893.
Sobolewski : *De praepositionum usu Aristophaneo;* Moscow, 1890.
Sturm : *Geschichtliche Entwickelung der Construction mit πρίν* (Schanz's *Beiträge*); Würzburg, 1882.
Van Cleef : *De attractionis in enuntiationibus relativis usu Platonico;* Bonn, 1890.
Wähdel : *Ueber Gebrauch der Partikel οὖν bei Aristoph.;* Stralsund, 1869.
Westphal (F.) : *Die Präpositionen bei Xenophon;* Freienwald am Oder, 1888 and 1891.
Zycha : *Zum Gebrauch von περί bei den Historikern und Rednern;* Wien, 1887.

APOLOGY

1 **17 A** 1. **ὅ τι μὲν ὑμεῖς** : in responsion we should expect *ὅ τι δ' ἐγώ*, thus contrasting 'affect' with 'affect' (*ὅ τι*, inner acc. with *πεπόνθατε*). But after a mere hint at this contrast, Plato breaks off to obtain a second—that of *ὑμεῖς* and *ἐγώ*—by beginning the second clause with *ἐγώ*. This is the usual explanation. But I cannot help thinking it overnice. For why not take *μέν* with *ὑμεῖς*? Plato could not of course write it after *ὑμεῖς*, as that would leave *ὅ τι* common to both clauses *ὅ τι ὑμεῖς μὲν . .. ἐγὼ δέ*; nor again could he write *ὑμεῖς μὲν ὅ τι*, since the relative claims first place in the clause. *μέν* is therefore compelled to stand where it stands—*before* the word with which it belongs. But this is not impossible. See some 25 examples cited by Geb. *Argum. ex contrar.*, pp. 123–124.

17 A 3. **δ' οὖν** : distinguish carefully *γοῦν*, *γάρ*, *δ' ουν*.

γοῦν, i.e. *γε οὖν*, confirms a previous general statement by a special (*γε*) instance 'certainly' (*οὖν*) true. See Index for examples.

γάρ is a fusion of *γε ἄρα*, but older than *γοῦν* (which first emerges in Aeschylus). *γάρ* too confirms the previous statement, but not by offering a special instance, since *γε* is no longer a separate particle accentuating a special word. On the contrary, *γάρ* belongs to the sent. as a whole; e.g. *οἱ δὲ ἡδέως ἐπείθοντο· ἐπίστευον γὰρ αὐτῷ.*

δ' οὖν, like *γοῦν*, vouches for the truth of its own clause (*οὖν* 'certainly'), but stands in an adversative (*δέ*) relation to what has gone before, leaving it rather *un*-supported and even casting doubt upon it. Be that true or false, '*yet certainly*' the following is true. Hence the freq. use of δ' οὖν (1) after the report of 1 mere hearsay or of surmise; (2) after a digression, on returning to the main narrative or argument; (3) to cut the matter short and come to the point; (4) with imperatives, when you wish to drop a matter, or yield assent impatiently or unwillingly or listlessly with a 'well, well'—the feeling being 'I don't care,' 'at your own risk.' The formula **ἀλλ' οὖν . . γε** is but a stronger substitute, as ἀλλά is stronger than δέ; and contains also one element from γοῦν (the accentuating γε).

Under the first usage mentioned (dismissal of hearsay) fall many of the instances in Hdt. (I 140. II 49,125,167,181. III 115,116. IV 180. VI 82. VII 9 γ,35,153) and in Xen. (*An.* I 2,12,22,25. 3,5. 10,8. II 4,6. V 6,11. *Hell.* III 5,19. IV 1,38. 3,8. V 3,8. VI 4,8,31. In VII 4,12 δ' οὖν is certainly wrong). Under the second and third heads—resumptive and summary—fall (according to Kalinka, p. 177) all the Thucydidean examples save one (II 5,7), viz. I 3,4. 10,5. 63,1. II 16,1. 34,8. III 84,1. IV 82. VI 15,5. 56,1. VII 59,1. 82,1. VIII 24,6. 81,3 (is it resumptive?). 87,6. 94,3. 97,1. So Hdt. II 50. V 49. VI 76. II 40,70. IV 195. VII 145. With imperatives it is found in Aesch. *Prom.* 935. *Eum.* 217. Soph. *O.R.* 310 (but the reading must surely be wrong), 669. *El.* 891. *Tr.* 329,1157. *Aj.* 114,961. *O.C.* 1205. Arist. *Vesp.* 6,764,1154. *Lys.* 491. *Nub.* 39. *Av.* 56. *Thesm.* 612. *Ach.* 186. *Ran.* 31. (See Wähdel.) Genthe-Ellendt's remark (*Lex. Soph.*, s.v. δέ 12) that δ' οὖν is a conjunct. "*cum ratiocinatione*" I do not believe. See rather Bäumlein, p. 190 ("immerhin"). Also Paley's note on εἰ δ' οὖν Aesch. *Ag.* 1009 (=1042) seems to be wrong in taking δ' οὖν with the if-clause alone; whereas, it is the conjunct. for the whole sent., and as such should go rather with the main clause in its usu. sense 'anyhow,' 'be that as it may.' Kühn., p. 713 top, seems to have the same notion as Paley ("wenn aber wirklich"), but the example he cites does not bear him out. For exx. in this book, see Index.

17 A 4. **ὀλίγου ἐμαυτοῦ ἐπελαθόμην**: for ὀλίγου as prob. a gen. of time, see G.-Kühn. § 419,3.—Inasmuch as Socrates did not in fact forget himself but within a little would have done so, we might expect ἐπελαθόμην ἄν. But with ὀλίγου, μικροῦ, and the like, Greek uses the indic. aor. without ἄν (cf. Latin *paene*, *prope*, c. indic. perf.), as it does the imperfects χρῆν, ἔδει, καλὸν (κάλλιον, ἄξιον, κρεῖττον, ἀσφαλέστερον, etc.) ἦν. See G. M. T. § 416, G.-Kühn. § 391,4. For other examples with ὀλίγου in Plato, see *Menex.* 236 C (πληγὰς ἔλαβον), *Lysis* 210 E (ἐξήμαρτον), *Meno* 80 B (ἐξηπάτησας), *Euthyd.* 279 D, 303 B.

17 A 4. **οὕτω πιθανῶς ἔλεγον**: there is no asyndeton here. Conjunctions are needed when the discourse *proceeds.* But

1 when it does not proceed,—when rather it pauses to make some remark upon the preceding situation, picking it up with a demonstrat. pron. or adverb (a τοσοῦτος, τοιοῦτος, ἐνταῦθα, οὕτω, κτλ.), then there is really no place for a conjunct. E.g. "I could have shouted ; I was *so* glad." Here "so" (*οὕτω*) *is* the connecting link itself, and a demonstrat. pron., thus used, no more admits a conjunct. than does the relat. pron. ὅς. In such passages as the present, therefore, γάρ is only rarely present. See Geb.-Froh. on Lys. 12,1 Anh., for many examples, among them Dein. 1,81,82. Isoc. 4,141. Dem. 30,14. 61,29. Hdt. 3,85. Ar. *Nub.* 1125. *Eq.* 530. X. *Mem.* II 4,4. Lys. 3,13. 13,31. Cf. infra for οὕτω 59,30. 61,2. 155,28. 261,1 ; for τοιαῦτα 102,1 ; for τοσοῦτον 154,1.

17 A 7. **αὐτῶν ἓν ἐθαύμασα** : Stallb. and others take αὐτῶν with ἕν. The construction τοῦτό σου θαυμάζω (ἄγαμαι, ἐπαινῶ, μέμφομαι, etc.) is common, and σου at first glance seems to depend on τοῦτο ; 'this of you,' as H. 733 has it. But we should remember that τοῦτο *is here an inner accus.* with the verb, that hence it is not necessary to the construction, and as a matter of fact is very often absent, leaving the genit. alone with the verb, e.g. infra 43,14 ; X. *Mem.* II 6,33 ἄγασαι αὐτοῦ ; *Oec.* 4,21 ἄγαμαι τοῦ καταμετρήσαντος. Hence it is better with G.-Kühn. § 417, Anm. 10 b, to take the genit. as one *within which* the verb plays—a sort of genit. of the whole—and essentially the same as the genit. after verbs of *perception* (αἰσθάνομαι, ἀκούω, ὀσφραίνομαι, γεύομαι, ἅπτομαι). Cf. infra 1,13. 56,15. 147,18. 170,4. 172,13. 237,9. Also 101,12. (See, however, Krüg. 47,10, 8 and 9 ; Rehd. X. *An.* VI 2,4 ; Rehd. Lycurg. 135, Anh. ; Schn. Isoc. 4,1.)

17 B 10. **τὸ μὴ αἰσχυνθῆναι . . τοῦτο** : when οὗτος or ἐκεῖνος thus picks up again a word or phrase, it is called ἐπ-ανά-ληψις, epanalepsis. For exx., see Rehd. *Ind.* 1, s.v. οὗτος ; Schn. Isoc. 1,45 ; Geb. *Argum. ex contrar.*, p. 107. Cf. infra 4,9. 5,24. 27,9. 31,15. 70,19. 101,16. 132,19. 142,21. 148,21. 155,26. 175,5. 184,16. 210,29. 234,6. 236,24. 256,24. 261,16.

ἐκεῖνος and αὐτοῦ thus used are rare. For an ex. of ἐκεῖνος, see 224,6 ; for αὐτοῦ 102,16. 213,8.

17 B 16. **οὐ κατὰ τούτους . . ῥήτωρ** : οὐ κατὰ τούτους is an adjectival phrase-compound such as in "a never-to-be-forgotten day," "an afternoon walk." For many exx. from a freer period of Engl., see Abbott's *Shakespearian Gram.*, §§ 429–431 : "a that-way-accomplished courtier," "this so-never-needed help." Greek exx. Krüg. has collected at Thuc. IV 10,4 ἐν γῇ στρατός 'a land-army,' ἐν νυκτὶ φροντίδες Soph. *Tr.* 149, περὶ ταφὰς κόσμῳ X. *Hell.* VI 1,6. Cf. infra 170,31 σὺν αὐλητρίσιν κῶμοι ; 207,16 ἐν μουσικῇ τροφῇ ; 249,18 εἰς θεοὺς ἀσεβείας. For

a negat. compound, as in the present passage, see Thuc. I 141,6 1
μὴ πρὸς ὁμοίαν ἀντιπαρασκευήν. Note further in the present passage that if the negat. belonged to the whole clause rather than to the phrase-compound, we should expect rather *μή*, after *ὁμολογῶ*.

17 B 1. **ῥήμασί τε καὶ ὀνόμασιν**: these terms were used by 2
Plato (e.g. in *Sophist.* 262 f.) in a technical logical sense also—*ὄνομα* = 'subject,' *ῥῆμα* 'predicate,' 'that which is said' (*εἴ-ρηται*) of the subject. Later they became still narrower, and as grammatical terms mean 'noun' and 'verb.' In the present untechnical way, they are used in *Symp.* 198 B, 199 B, and infra 102,1. 273,7.

17 C 5. **μηδεὶς ὑμῶν προσδοκησάτω**: note what is rare in prohibitions—the aor. imperative. H. 874 b, G. 1347, G. M. T. § 260, G.-Kühn. § 397,3 b. In the Attic orators but six instances are to be found. See C. W. E. Miller in *A. J. P.* 13 (1892), p. 425. So infra 46,29.

17 C 9. **τοῦτο δέομαι . . μήτε θαυμάζειν** *κτλ.*: there is no asyndeton here. The infin. in explanatory apposition to *τοῦτο* happens to be postponed, but otherwise the case is similar to that in 73,21. 83,6, and often. See 10,14 App.

17 C 10. **διὰ τῶν αὐτῶν λόγων**: disting. *διά* c. gen. from *διά* c. acc. The *gen.* c. *διά* names the agent or instrument we purposely use to bring about a specific result. There is intention and foresight from the start. The *accus.* c. *διά* names that person, or thing, or state-of-things-already-existent, or act-already-done, that is beyond our control—a cause (often a blind one) working independently of us, sometimes *in spite of us*, though sometimes again we may avail ourselves of it (the "time and tide of affairs"), and appropriate its results as though our own. But *our* particular result was not *its* purpose at the start. Our result is only 'on account of (by reason of, owing to, thanks to)' its working. — See Frohb. on Lys. 12,58 (acc. "selbstthätig einwirkend"), Rehd. *Ind. Dem.*, s.v. *διά*. Exx. (1) of *διά* c. gen., in Dem. 2,3,26. 3,31. Lys. 10,11. (2) of *διά* c. acc. when the situation is made use of, Lys. 30,13. 12,58,77. 14,18. 7,5. 25,33. (3) of *διά* c. acc. that works adversely to our wish (= 'thanks to' spoken with bitterness), Lys. 13,46. 12,87. 25,27. (4) of *διά* with both gen. and acc. —the speaker choosing now one now the other point of view, Dem. 5,22. 6,6. 18,33 and 35. Cf. Lys. 12,87.

In *Theaet.* 184 C Plato distinguishes betw. the dat. and *διά* c. gen. It is the mind (*ψυχή*) *by* which (*ᾗ*), and the senses *through* which (*δι' ὧν*) we apprehend things. Again in *Rep.* X 609 E the line is drawn betw. *ὑπό* c. gen. and *διά* c. acc. The human body sickens and dies not *by* bad food (*ὑπό* c. gen.), but by its own

2 malady (ὑπό c. gen.) *on account of* bad food (διά c. acc.). See further G.-Kühn. § 434 Anm. (p. 485) for diff. betw. the dat. and διά c. acc.

For διά c. gen. of the instrument or agent, see infra 56,21. 77,25. 78,29. 79,2. 81,11. 96,17. 97,3. 102,5. 105,30. 150,2. 159,10. 202,20 (?). 205,10. 230,18. 235,23. 237,30. 273,8.

17 C 11. **ἐν ἀγορᾷ**: as regards the use or omission of the article, see G.-Kühn. § 462 b. Incidentally I have noted its omission with πρυτανεῖον (33,28), γῇ (257,6), ἄστυ (191,22; though *with* art. in 191,9. 193,3. 261,1), ἥλιος (17,2. 72,2. 90,9. 91,4. 100,4; but *with* art. in 17,4. 100,6). For the usage of Aristoph., see Starkie's *Vesp.* 492.

17 C 12. **ἐπὶ τῶν τραπεζῶν**: elsewhere in Plato and regularly in the orators, the dat. is used in this phrase. For an explanation of the genit., see my dissertation on ἐπί, p. 48.

17 D 15. **ἀναβέβηκα**: others think that ἀναβαίνω is used "on account of the position of the δικαστήρια, most of which were situated in the higher parts of the town" (Wagner); i.e. that ἀνα- refers to coming 'up' a hill. Possibly. But there seems to be no necessity for taking the word in other than its extremely freq. use in calling up to the βῆμα witnesses already present in court (ἀνάβηθι, ἀνάβητε). Cf. also καταβαίνειν in calling a speaker down; e.g. Ar. *Vesp.* 979 κατάβα, κατάβα, in the dog-trial. See Index.

17 D 16. **ἀτεχνῶς**: a word not to be found in epic, lyric, or tragic poetry, nor in the historians (X. *Mem.* III 11,7 ἀτέχνως), nor in the orators, but belonging to comedy and to Plato—15 times in Aristoph., 4 in the comic fragments, freq. in Plato (and thrice in Aristotle). It is used by Plato to assert (1) the literal, veritable truth of hyperbolic or metaphoric expressions; (2) the exactness of comparisons (ἀτεχνῶς ὥσπερ, ἀτεχνῶς οἷον); (3) the literal application of a proverb or quotation. Examples of (1) are in 3,19. 17,20. 32,7. 66,29. 141,8. 150,13. 155,12. 177,8. 260,31; of (2) are in 3,27. 24,9. 89,31. 218,31. 265,26; of (3) are in 239,29. *Euthyd.* 292 E, *Euthyphro* 3 A, *Lach.* 187 B, *Ion* 534 A, *Charm.* 154 B.—Other words used to corroborate hyperbole are ἀληθῶς, τῷ ὄντι, παν-τελῶς (177,9).

17 D 17. **ὥσπερ ἂν εἰ . . ξυνεγιγνώσκετε ἄν** is not a real case of repeated ἄν; for ἄν after ὥσπερ had lost its force and no longer anticipated a foll. optat. Often indeed no verb at all follows (e.g. 11,10. 17,27. 19,3. 121,4. 131,10,14) and ὡσπερανεί is merely 'just as if.' With the present case cf. 108,4. For another functionless ἄν, see κἄν 211,21 App. and οἷόνπερ ἂν εἰ 222,6.

18 A 19. **ἐτεθράμμην**: whenever a past tense of the indic. 2
—the mood of fact—is used of a situation *not* a fact, e.g. in unaccomplished wishes (εἰ γάρ με εἶδες), or in the protasis or apodosis of unreal conditional sentences (εἰ ἦλθες, καλῶς ἂν εἶχε), it attracts into indic. mood and secondary tense the verb of any dependent relative clause (as here), or temporal clause, or final clause, or (sometimes) causal clause. For exx. under the first three heads see G. M. T. §§ 559 (and 528); 613,2; 333, respectively; and also (in clear conspectus) G.-Kühn. § 399,6 B (p. 257).

18 A 25. **αὕτη ἀρετή** for τοῦτο ἀρετή: attraction of the demonstrat. in gender to that of the predicate noun is the rule —in Lysias, for instance, without exception. (Geb.-Froh. Lys. 25,13 cite from him 1,16. 7,23. 10,24. 12,37. 16,6. 24,10. 25,23,28.) So infra 12,28. 13,1. 84,21. 145,23. Yet the neut. is often used; cf. 21,17 τοῦτο πῶς οὐκ ἀμαθία ἐστί; 95,29. 130,6. 131,17. 142,21. 199,20. 217,3,6,21. See G.-Kühn. § 369, 1 and 2.

18 B 1. **καὶ πάλαι πολλὰ ἤδη ἔτη**: many exx. of this form 3
of pleonasm (called σχῆμα ἐκ παραλλήλου, using no καί to connect the words) are collected by Schanz *Nov. Comm.* § 4, and Rehd. *Ind. Dem.* 1, s.v. Pleonasmos. Among them are (1) temporal phrases: παραχρῆμα εὐθύς, ταχὺ (or ἤδη) παραχρῆμα, ἐκ τοῦ παραχρῆμα ἐξαίφνης (or εὐθύς), ἔπειτα μετὰ ταῦτα (or τοῦτο), ἔπειτα ὕστερον, διὰ τέλους ἀεί, διὰ τέλους τὸν ἅπαντα χρόνον, ἀεὶ διὰ βίου, ἀεὶ ξυνεχῶς, νῦν ἐν τῷ παρόντι.

(2) phrases of verification: ὡς ἀληθῶς τῷ ὄντι, τὸ δ' ἀληθὲς τῷ ὄντι, ἐν τῇ ἀληθείᾳ ὡς ἀληθῶς, τῷ ὄντι ἀληθινός, ἀτεχνῶς τῷ ὄντι, ἀλλὰ γὰρ τῷ ὄντι.

(3) of inference τοιγάρτοι διὰ ταῦτα, διὰ ταῦτα ἄρα, διὰ ταῦτα οὖν, ἐκ τούτου . . διὰ ταῦτα.

(4) of manner οὕτω δή, κατὰ ταὐτὰ ὡσαύτως.

(5) various; ἴσως τάχ' ἂν (very common), εἰς δύναμιν ὅτι μάλιστα (see Stallb. on *Rep.* 458 E), αὖ τοὐναντίον, αὖ πάλιν, αὖθις αὖ, ὀλίγου ὡς ἔπος εἰπεῖν, ἐν δίκῃ . . δικαίως, μάτην κενοῖς λόγοις (cf. 49,4), εἰκῇ ῥᾳδίως, μάτην ἄλλως, διὰ κενῆς ἄλλως, ἐνθάδε αὐτοῦ.

See infra αὖθις αὖ 13,5. αὖ πάλιν 18,29. 163,4. 167,7. 174,3. ἐξ ἀρχῆς εὐθύς 274,18. ἔτι πρὸς τούτοις 221,30. ἴσως τάχ' ἂν 24,19. οὕτω κατὰ τὸν αὐτὸν τρόπον 33,20. που ἴσως 37,31. συν- εἰς ταὐτόν 193,25. 269,13.

18 B 8. **φροντιστής** 'thinker,' 'speculator,' first appears in Aristophanes' *Clouds*, there too applied to Socrates. The word was perhaps coined by the poet and, striking the popular fancy, seems to have remained a nickname of the philosopher. But in the present passage it has been rejected by Bamberg and

3 Schanz as a mere marginal note of the Aristophanic term for one who investigated *τά τε μετέωρα καὶ τὰ ὑπὸ γῆς ἅπαντα.* For (1) if *μετέωρα* be taken as an acc. of specification with *φροντιστής*, only one other instance has been found of a *substantive* taking such acc., *Od.* 16,242 *χεῖρας αἰχμητήν* (G.-Kühn. p. 317, Monro *Hom. Gram.* § 139); or (2) if it be regarded as the object of the verb implicit in *φροντιστής*, as is the dat. in *τὴν ἐμὴν τῷ θεῷ ὑπηρεσίαν* (23,2), it should be observed that the *dative* with substantives is not so rare (G.-Kühn. § 424), while the only true parallel to *μετέωρα φροντιστής* would be, e.g. *Σωκράτη δικαστής*, *πόλιν προδότης*! (For dat. c. substantive, see 23,2. 24,7. 174,30. 223,2.)

18 B 8. **τὰ ὑπὸ γῆς**=*τὰ ὑπόγεια*, the phrase *ὑπὸ γῆς* having become a fixed one (cf. 212,20. 248,28. 261,26), in which *ὑπό* is no longer felt as a preposition, free to choose its case. For in Att. prose *ὑπό* in the literal sense of 'under' takes, not the genit., but the dat. (or, after verbs of motion, acc.; see Index). Its use c. gen. had become wholly metaphorical, equiv. to 'under the agency of.' See my dissertat. on *ἐπί*, App. C; and the note on 260,20 infra.

18 C 17. **ἐν ᾗ ἂν . . ἐπιστεύσατε**: G. M. T. § 244, G.-Kühn. § 392,5. The strong assertiveness of the mood of fact (indic.) is attacked and eroded, as it were, by such insect-words as *ἄν* and *ὀλίγου* (1,4).—The corresponding potent. for pres. or fut. time would be *ἂν πιστεύσαιτε.*

18 C 20. **ὃ δὲ πάντων ἀλογώτατον, ὅτι—**: such introductory relat. clauses (extremely common) are properly an assertion or predication concerning the sentence introduced,—the two together forming in fact a larger sentence, in which the introduced sent. is the subject, the introducing relat. clause the predicate. The copula *ἐστί*, however, is never found, I believe, except in the spurious Andoc. 4,16. The syntax following this omitted *ἐστί* may be much varied; e.g. (1) an independent sent.; (2) independ. sent. with a certifying *γάρ*; (3) a clause with *ὅτι*, as here; (4) *ὅτε γάρ*; (5) *ὅταν*, or *ὅταν γάρ*; (6) *εἰ*. Examples are found of (1) Lys. 30,29. Dem. 21,79. (2) Lys. 32,24. Isoc. 9,64. 17,14. (3) Isoc. 15,213. 4,176. (4) Isoc. 17,31. 21,11. (5) Isoc. 6,79. 5,52. (6) Isoc. 6,56. 14,45. 18,18.

For further information and many exx., see Rehd. Lyc. 56, Anh.; Sch. Isoc. 7,68; Froh. Lys. 32,24 and Anh.; but espec. Kvičala *Symbola Philologorum Bonnensium* (Leipsic, 1867), p. 656 ff., who connects with this syntax that seen, e.g. in X. *Anab.* VI 4,18 *ὡς γὰρ ἐγὼ . . ἤκουσά τινος ὅτι Κλέανδρος . . μέλλει ἥξειν* 'the way I heard (was), that —.' See also G.-Kühn, § 406, Anm. 9.

Examples in Plato are infra 99,6. 195,29. *Phaedr.* 248 B,

Lach. 184 B, *Euthyd.* 304 C, *Lys.* 204 D, *Rep.* 491 B. Cf. 14,24 App. 3

18 D 28. **σκιαμαχεῖν** *κτλ.* : any metaphorical or otherwise unusual expression apt to be misunderstood Plato at once parallels and explains by a subjoined (*καί* or *τε καί*) clause. Cf. 48,22. 112,18,31. 117,8. 169,17. 172,8. 234,2. So *Lach.* 194 C *χειμαζομένοις . . καὶ ἀποροῦσι.* For the reversed order of expression in Demos. (literal, then tropical), see Rehd. *Ind.* 1, s.v. Erweiterung, bot. of p. 14.

18 D 28. **σκιαμαχεῖν ἀπολογούμενόν τε**: we should expect *τε* to stand aft. *σκιαμ.* For even when words go closely together, as art. or prepos. with their noun, *τε* claims the second place, e.g. *ἥ τε μήτηρ, ἔν τε πόλει.* But this is by no means always its posit. Exx. of postponement are in 61,3. 65,21,29. 81,10. 169,14,28. 214,3. 228,30,31. 236,16. 240,24. 248,6,8,15. 250,16. 251,8. 258,13. 259,26. With the present passage cf. espec. 231,12 and also Lysias 19,23 *χαρίσασθαι ἐκείνῳ τε καὶ κομίσασθαι μὴ ἐλάττω* (if the text is sound), or X. *Mem.* II 1,9 *τοὺς μὲν βουλομένους πολλὰ πράγματα ἔχειν αὐτούς τε καὶ ἄλλοις παρέχειν.* See Geb. *Argum. ex contrar.* p. 359, and for Homer, Am.-Hentze on *Od.* 8,540 Anh.

18 E 6. **εἶεν** should perhaps be written with interior aspira- 4
tion *εἶἕν*, as also *ταὧς* 'peacock' and the interjection *εὐοἵ.* See Bl.-Kühn. I pp. 113 and 639. The etymology seems wholly uncertain. See Brugmann's *Greek Gram.* p. 225. Exx. are 4,19. 30,1. 33,1. 57,1. 88,11. 91,24. 108,19. 110,22. 118,1. 132,28 and elsewhere.

19 A 12. **πλέον τί με ποιῆσαι**: so the phrase stands in 64,4. 88,24. And. 1,150. 4,7. But usually it is *πλέον ἐστί μοι* or *γίγνεταί μοι* (negat. *οὐδὲν πλέον*—) as in Ant. 5,16,80,95. And. 1,7. Lys. 16,3. 19,4. Isoc. 4,2. 17,21. 21,7. Dem. 24,217. 35,31. 47,1. 55,6. Soph. *Ant.* 268. Eur. *Hel.* 322; *Heracl.* 466. Ar. *Eccl.* 1094. The sense: 'to make (gain) anything' by such and such a course—the latter expressed usu. by a ptc., sometimes by an *εἰ* (*ἐάν*)-clause (Isoc. 17,21. Dem. 47,1).

19 A 18. **ᾗ δὴ καί**: in subordinate clauses (relat., causal, final) a *καί* is often found, belonging to the whole clause, lifting it from its subordinate importance to equal rank with the main clause; = 'indeed,' 'in fact,' 'just.' The relat. in such clauses is often strengthened by *δή* (as here, and in 19,1. 25,20. 37,6) or by -*περ* (40,27). Here *ᾗ δὴ καὶ κτλ.* is about equiv. to *καὶ γὰρ ταύτῃ ἐπίστευε.* See Bäumlein, p. 152. Kühn. X. *Mem.* I 2,47 *ὧνπερ ἕνεκεν καὶ Σωκράτει προσῆλθον*, citing also I 2,31. III 8,2. Add Aesch. 3,189. (It must be remembered that not all *καί*'s in relat. clauses are to be thus taken. Sometimes,

4 as in 27,3. 85,19. 92,9. 135,26. 225,8, the *καί* attaches itself to the word that follows it, as usual.) For an *ἐπεὶ καί,* see 5,26. *ἐπειδὴ καί* 56,18. See further 19,1 App.

19 B 25. **τὰ αὐτὰ ταῦτα**: Schanz, *Nov. Comm.* p. 81, shows that in Plato whether with or without a foll. substant. *ὁ αὐτὸς οὗτος* is the almost invariable order of words (and not *οὗτος ὁ αὐτός*)—59 instances against 3.

19 C 31. **πέρι**: on anastrophe in general, see Mommsen, pp. 123 ff., 780–91. On that of *περί* c. gen. the foll. statistics may help to impress the quotation appended in regard to prose usage in Aristotle's time:

περί c. gen. follows its case (i.e. *πέρι*)

in Aesch.	in	13 of the	16	instances	
,, Soph.	,,	20 ,,	21	,,	
,, Eur.	,,	69 ,,	80	,,	
,, Aristoph.	,,	15 ,,	139	,,	(12 in iambic trimeter)
,, Herod.	,,	69 ,,	282	,,	
,, Thucyd.	,,	26 ,,	243	,,	
,, Plato	,,	338 ,,	1943	,,	
,, Xen.	,,	2(1?)	419	,,	
,, Att. Oratt.	,,	1 ,,	2897	,,	(viz. Ant. 1,21)

See Aristot. *Poetics* 1458 b *Ἀριφράδης τοὺς τραγῳδοὺς ἐκωμῴδει, ὅτι ἃ οὐδεὶς ἂν εἴποι ἐν τῇ διαλέκτῳ τούτοις χρῶνται, οἷον τὸ δωμάτων ἄπο ἀλλὰ μὴ ἀπὸ δωμάτων καὶ τὸ Ἀχιλλέως πέρι ἀλλὰ μὴ περὶ Ἀχιλλέως.*

In the large percentage reached by anastrophe in Plato as compared with its striking absence from the orators and Xen., Mommsen is inclined to see an evidence that Plato's style aimed at "Zierlichkeit" (p. 128). (For the statistics, see Dindorf's Lexicon for Aesch., Ellendt's for Soph. and the dissertations by Schumacher, Sobolewski, Zycha, Lina, Westphal, and Lutz.)

Examples of *πέρι* in this volume are in 7,26. 78,31. 80,16. 109,26. 173,28. 194,24. 216,23. 217,14. 226,12. 233,31. 235,2. 249,17. 269,13. 274,14.

5 **19 C** 2. **μή πως . . φύγοιμι** is taken by some as a wish. But I dislike this not only because the sense is not so good but also because from Homer to Aristotle inclusive, so far as I can learn from indexes, *μή πως is not used in wishes.* A glance at some of the Homeric instances of the combination (see Gehring's Index, s.v. *μή πως*) will show that its proper, and I think exclusive, seat is in final clauses and in those expressing fear. E.g. *η* 306. *π* 292. *δ* 396. *ε* 147. Γ 436. E 250,298. In the same way is *πῃ* sometimes added to *μή*, as in *Legg.* 652 B.

As for the irregularity of the optat. mood (*φύγοιμι*) following a pres. tense (*λέγω*), I think it amply protected by such parallels

as Ar. *Ran.* 23, *Av.* 1524. See G. M. T. § 323 and add to his 5
exx. Plato *Rep.* III 410 B ἆρ' οὖν . . οἱ καθιστάντες μουσικῇ καὶ γυμναστικῇ παιδεύειν οὐχ οὗ ἕνεκά τινες οἴονται καθιστᾶσιν, ἵνα τῇ μὲν τὸ σῶμα θεραπεύοιντο, τῇ δὲ τὴν ψυχήν;

19 C 3. **ἀλλὰ γάρ**: it is difficult for younger students to avoid thinking 'for,' whenever their eyes fall on γάρ, and 'but' if they hear ἀλλά. No habit can be worse. The logical conjunctions such as γάρ, οὖν, ἄρα, etc. did not originally serve to conjoin sentences in logical relation. Their earlier senses were broader. Only in course of time did each fall into its special narrow channel of usage. This tendency to narrowing is best seen in those conjunctions whose origins are patent—as καί-τοι, τοί-νυν, ἀλλά (from ἄλλος). As for the older conjunctions, their broader earlier senses are best studied in Homer and in such stereotyped phrases as the present—ἀλλὰ γάρ.

Attention, for example, to οὖν and ἄρα will soon discover that these were originally intensive particles, particles of corroboration, like ἦ, μήν, τοι, meaning 'truly,' 'surely,' 'indeed,' 'certainly'; that they looked neither backward nor forward to other sentences (i.e. were not conjunctions), but served merely the purposes of their own clause.

But if certification was the function of ἄρα, so it must have been of γάρ (from γ' ἄρα), indicating by its γε the specially important word. Very early, however, the two words parted company,[1] and the statement certified by γάρ came to be regarded as the ground or explanation of the statement immediately before or, as so frequently in Herodotus, after—as it were, an *a fortiori* argument; e.g. οὐκ εἶμι· ὕει γάρ (or ὕει γάρ· οὐκ εἶμι) 'I am not going; it's raining sure' (or 'Sure it's raining; I'll not go').

But because it happens that we can here give the equivalent of γάρ by our 'for,' is it not violent and unreasoning to force that translation upon it, or extort a causal sense from it, on all occasions? We have just seen that 'sure' answers as well.[2] Why then torture the Greek and supply endless ellipses in the following stereotyped usages of γάρ, in which plainly enough the old sense 'sure' survives? (1) εἰ γάρ in wishes. (2) ἦ γάρ at the end of a sent. = *n'est ce pas?* (3) γάρ introducing a question when the questioner can hardly believe his senses, and asks if the matter is 'really' true; e.g. X. *Anab.* I 7,9 οἴει γάρ σοι μαχεῖσθαι τὸν ἀδελφόν; Soph. *El.* 1221 and countless other passages. (4) γάρ in short answers, as οὐ γὰρ ουν, εἰκὸς γάρ, λέγω γάρ, εἴρηται γάρ, πῶς γάρ, πῶς γὰρ οὔ, πόθεν γάρ

[1] Already in Homer's time γ' ἄρα had become γάρ, and perhaps the origin forgotten, since over a score of times we find γάρ ῥα.

[2] Indeed the English prefers, in such short sentences, mere asyndetic juxtaposition; e.g. "Give me water; I am thirsty."

5 (these last being rhetorical questions used as answers). (5) γάρ epexegetic (see App. on 3,20. 7,2. 24,27). (6) τοίγαρ, τοιγαροῦν. (7) ἀλλὰ γάρ. Here ἀλλά is the conjunction and γάρ the primitive confirmatory adverb, as in all the above cases. The elaboration of an ellipsis can only be defended by rote, not by reason. We were many of us taught that way. For all this and much more, see Bäumlein, p. 68 ff. (whose treatment is praised by Kvičala *Zeitschr. f. d. oesterr. Gymn.* 1863, p. 312, and by Brugmann *Berichte üb. die Verhandl. der kön. sächs. Gesellsch. der Wiss.* 1883, p. 50); Kühn. § 509,8; Riddell's *Digest of Idioms* (in his edit. of Plato's *Apol.*) § 147; H. 1050,4; L. & S. s.v. ἀλλά, III 3. Cf. infra 5,13. 15,2. 16,10. 19,14. 42,17. 100,15. 104,24. 107,16. 150,31. 175,2. And see 14,14 App.

19 D 13. **οὔτε . . οὐδέ γε**: the combination rests on the affirmative one τε . . δέ, an anacoluthic shift from copulative to adversative conjunction that does not frequently occur without mitigating circumstances. For firstly the formula τε . . δὲ καί (e.g. σύ τε . . οἶμαι δὲ καὶ ἐμέ) is rather a strengthened form of the normal τε . . καί, since after all καί *does* appear. Exx. of this with ἔτι δὲ καί are in *Alc.* I 123 A, *Legg.* 641 C, Demos. 7,39; 50,25. ἔπειτα δὲ καί X. *Cyr.* IV 4,3; *Anab.* V 5,8. ὡσαύτως δὲ καί Plat. *Symp.* 186 E, *Legg.* 649 B. Other exx. are *Euthyph.* 3 E, *Alcib.* I 122 A, *Rep.* 394 C, 618 A, *Legg.* 823 B, 943 E, Thucyd. I 25,3, X. *Anab.* VII 8,11.—Secondly, when the first clause has become abnormally extended and τε has lost its carrying power, δέ quite naturally resumes the thread. E.g. infra 148,17 (see n.). 172,17. *Crat.* 406 C, *Polit.* 272 A, 310 D, *Alc.* I 121 B, *Rep.* 495 C, 611 D, *Tim.* 20 A, 44 A, 84 B, *Crit.* 113 E, *Legg.* 627 A, 715 A, 777 A, 834 C, 952 C; Lysias 2,17; Isoc. 12,136,144; Thucyd. VI 83,1; X. *Cyr.* II 1,22.—A third mitigation is where a fixed phrase has occurred to the writer which includes δέ but never καί, as ἔτι δέ, τί δέ, τὸ δὲ κεφάλαιον. Exx. are *Hipp. Maj.* 282 B, *Rep.* 367 C, 495 C, 568 D, 581 D, *Legg.* 664 B, 946 E, 967 D, *Polit.* 270 D, *Timae.* 58 C, *Eryx.* 392 D; Thucyd. I 11,1; Isoc. 9,15; 12,212; 15,232.—Quite without extenuation stands τε . . δέ in the following passages—many of them being emended and no longer read in the texts: Plat. *Timae.* 20 A, *Meno* 93 C, *Rep.* 611 D; Andoc. 1,5; X. *Hell.* I 1,34, IV 5,15, VI 5,30, VII 1,24 (the last four Gebauer would alter to μὲν . . δέ), VI 5,25; *Cyrop.* III 3,64, VI 2,4; *Symp.* 8,2; Lysias 25,34; Antiph. III β 6; Isoc. 3,32; 12,136; Isae. 4,4 (the last five changed by some to τε . . τε). So much for the simple τε . . δέ.

Schemes similar to the present οὔτε . . οὐδέ are: οὔτε . . οὐδ' αὖ (Plat. *Phil.* 22 E, 42 B, *Legg.* 840 A), οὔτε . . δέ (*Rep.* 388 E), τε . . οὐδέ (*Polit.* 271 E, *Tim.* 33 C), οὔτε . . οὐδὲ μήν

(*Parm.* 157 B), μήτε . . δέ (*Legg.* 627 E), εἴτε . . εἰ δέ (*Ap.* 33 D), 5
εἴτε . . εἰ δ' αὖ *Ap.* 40 C. (Not to be reckoned as anacoluthic are such groups as οὔτε . . οὔτε . . οὐδέ. For the two τε's supplement each other—their work is done—and οὐδέ merely tacks on a new negat. clause, as it may to any other preceding negat. clause.)

The matter is best treated in Geb.-Frohb. Lys. 25,34 Anh., and for Plato in Hoefer, p. 15 ff. Other notes are fugitive and sometimes misleading; Geb. *Argum. ex contrar.* p. 358 gives a list of them—Hartung, Bäumlein, Breitenbach on X. *Hell.* I 1,34, and others. Of little use also are Rehd. *Ind. Dem.*, Schneid. Isoc. 9,15, Kühn. Gram.

20 A 26. **ἐπεὶ καί** 'since indeed.' καί belongs to the sent. as a whole (a sent.-adverb), not to the word that follows it; hence it is about equiv. to καὶ γάρ, corroborating a general statement by offering a special instance. See Schn. Isoc. 4,131 and Geb. p. 267 f. for many exx., among them Isoc. 2,42. 4,139. 6,47. 7,62. Thuc. I 12,1. IV 80,3. VII 24,2. 67,3. Plat. *Prot.* 334 B.

καί is also a sentence-adverb in ὃς καί (n. on 4,18), ἐπειδὴ καί (56,18), ἵνα καί (9,15), εἰ καί (Stein Hdt. V 78), ὅπου καί and ὁπότε καί (Geb. p. 311).

20 A 27. **ὃν ἐγὼ ᾐσθόμην ἐπιδημοῦντα**: on this, Adam says: "Socrates implies that he has not himself met Evenus. With the construction contrast 22 C ᾐσθόμην αὐτῶν . . οἰομένων. There the gen. is used because Socrates *had* met them himself." This, I think, is over-interpretation. The Greeks do not seem to have observed a hard and fast distinction between acc. and gen. after verbs of perception. See G.-Kühn. § 417, Anm. 9 c. And from La Roche's exhaustive article on the Supplementary Participle, *Beiträge*, p. 57, note the following exx. of *accusative* part. after αἰσθάνομαι, when the context makes it clear that sensuous perception is meant: Isoc. 15,320 αἰσθάνομαι . . τὸ μὲν ὕδωρ ἡμᾶς ἐπιλεῖπον. Ar. *Plut.* 1010 εἰ λυπουμένην αἴσθοιτό με. X. *Cyr.* III 1,9 ἢν δὲ αἰσθάνωνταί σε ἄλλα ἢ τὰ γενόμενα λέγοντα. III 2,10 ᾐσθάνοντο φεύγοντας αὐτοὺς ἐκ τῶν ἐγγὺς οἰκήσεων. VII 1,21 ὁπόταν αἴσθησθε ἡμᾶς ἐπιτιθεμένους, yet in 22 ἐμοῦ ἐπιτιθεμένου. Plat. *Rep.* 439 E αἰσθανόμενος νεκροὺς παρὰ τῷ δημίῳ κειμένους. The most perhaps that can be said is that αἰσθάνομαι used of sensuous perception commonly takes, but does not require, the gen. participle. (For Lysias' usage, see Frohb. on 30,15 Anh.)

20 A 1. **ὑέε**: for the spelling and inflection of this Protean 6
word, see Bl.-Kuhn. I pp. 136,181,506 f. with the various authorities cited, espec. however Meisterhans *Gram. der att. Inschriften*[2] p. 47, and Schanz's *Plato* XII, p. viii.

6 **20 A** 4. **ἔμελλεν . . ποιήσειν**: G. M. T. § 76. But for the explanation that here there is but a periphrastic *past* future, see G. M. T. § 671, bot. of p. 261. Cf. infra 33,13. 36,3. 97,20. So too *Gorg.* 486 D, Isae. 2,25.

20 B 6. **νῦν δέ**: substitutes for *νῦν δέ* in introducing the true state of things after a false hypothesis are: *ἐπειδὴ δέ, ἐπεὶ δέ, ὅμως δ' ἐπειδή* (rare), *εἰ δέ, νυνὶ δέ*, etc. See Geb.-Frohb. Lys. 12,22 Anh., Geb. p. 252. Exx. of *νῦν δέ*: 25,4. 34,14. 45,29. 74,21. 152,29. 193,5. 194,10. See also *νῦν δὲ . . γάρ* 36,4 App.

20 B 14. **ὡς ἀληθῶς**: for the usu. explanation of the phrase, see Kühn. § 555 Anm. 15. But since the year 1831 another suggestion has been put forth independently, as it would seem, by three scholars, as follows.—From *ὁ αὐτός* 'the same (man)' comes, they say, *ὡς αὔτως* (aeolic accent) 'in the same way,' *ὡς* being the adverb of the article *ὁ*, or rather of *ὁ* when it had demonstrative force, as in Homer (*ὁ αὐτός* originally = *is ipse*). So perhaps is *ὡς* in *ὡς ἀληθῶς* the old adverb equivalent to the later strengthened *οὕτως*. The phrase *ὡς ἀληθῶς* therefore = 'thus truly,' 'so truly.' *ὡς ἄλλως* and *ὡς ἑτέρως* 'the (that) other way.'—Such is the explanation (1) of some anonymous scholar referred to by Schoemann in his Isaeus (1831), p. 368, and subscribed to by Kvičala in 1867 (*Symbola Phil. Bonnens.* p. 658); (2) of F. D. Allen *Transact. Amer. Philol. Assoc.* for 1877, p. 40; (3) of W. Fox *Zeitsch. f. d. oesterr. Gymn.* 1879, p. 321. Schanz *Rhein. Mus.* 1886, p. 309, heartily adopts Fox's view, and argues against all others. His proportion is *ἀληθῶς : ὡς ἀληθῶς : : ἀληθείᾳ : τῇ ἀληθείᾳ*. The objection, however, has been urged that not *ὡς* but *τώς* should be the adverb of *ὁ*. Exx. are: 21,7. 49,6. 52,22. 76,18. 77,13. 143,25. 144,5. 160,26. 223,21. 267,22.

20 C 18. **ἀλλ' οὐ γάρ**: see Kühn. § 509,8 (p. 725 mid.) for the transl. in the notes. He compares *νῦν δὲ οὐ γάρ* infra 36,4.

20 C 22. **οὐ γὰρ δήπου**: the Greeks were quick to see inconsistencies and much given, when arguing, to pointing them out. Their name for this form of argumentation was *ἐνθύμημα* (though this term had also a wider application); the Latin name was *argumentum ex contrario* (or *ex pugnantibus*). Its various formulae have been collected and classified by Gebauer in his book *De hypotacticis et paratacticis Argumenti ex Contrario Formis*, Zwickau, 1877. The hypotactic form is seen in the present instance, where one of the contradictories is expressed by a subordinate clause. The paratactic form presents two co-ordinate clauses set side by side, contrasted by *μὲν . . δέ*. See infra 20,27 App. *οὐ γὰρ δήπου* is one of the regular phrases used to introduce this *argum. ex contrar.* (Geb.

pp. xvi, xviii). So ἤ, for which see 49,2 App. For ἔπειτα as 6
here used after a partic. in this form of argum., Geb. cites infra 82,15; *Phaedo* 90 c; Ar. *Av.* 27 ff. Cf. the function of this ἔπειτα with that of ἄρα as explained infra 30,11 App.

20 D 2. **ἐρῶ**: disting. the fut. λέξω from ἐρῶ, the aor. 7
ἔλεξα from εἶπον. λέγω, λέξω, ἔλεξα are rather 'to narrate' in detail, 'to tell' a story (λόγος 146,8,14), or 'to make a speech' (λόγος), while φημί, ἐρῶ, εἶπον mean 'to say, state, speak'—with summary dispatch, even though the statement require some time. Recall ἔφη 'said he' inserted in a quotation, not ἔλεγε. Distinguish thus λέγε from εἰπέ.

20 D 2. **ἐγὼ γάρ** κτλ. is not a causal but an *object*-sent. after ἀκούετε δή (6,31)—the intervening sent. being parenthetic. γάρ in its old corroborating sense is often thus used, but in translat. must be dropped. So infra li. 30 (after διδάξειν). 9,16 (after ἐπιδεῖξαι). 13,5 (ἀπολογεῖσθαι). 23,24 (ἐρεῖν). 26,14 (ἐρῶ). 27,10 (ἔργῳ ἐνεδειξάμην). 38,8 (χρησμῳδῆσαι). 39,6 (ἐπιδεῖξαι). 39,21 (ἐρῶ). See 24,27 App. and L. & S. s.v. II. (See also 10,14 App. on asyndeton, 4.)

20 D 2. **οὐδὲν ἀλλ' ἤ**: see Kühn. § 535,6 with remarks, but espec. Bäumlein, pp. 1–7. The foll. passages are so arranged as to show the gradual death of a word (here, ἄλλο or ἄλλα) as an adject. and its gradual emergence as a conjunction:

(1) ἄλλο οὐδὲν ἢ ἐκ γῆς ἐναυμάχουν Thuc. IV 14,3.
(2) οὐδὲν ἄλλο γ' ἢ πτήξας δέμας παρεῖχε Aesch. *Pers.* 209.
(3) οὐδὲν γάρ ἐστ' ἀλλ' ἢ κοάξ Ar. *Ran.* 227.
(4) τίνα ἄλλον ἔχουσι λόγον . . ἀλλ' ἢ τὸν ὀρθόν; Infra 29,29.
(5) ἔστιν ὁ πόλεμος οὐχ ὅπλων τὸ πλέον ἀλλὰ δαπάνης Thuc. I 83,1.
(6) οὐχ οἱ πλούσιοι εὐδαίμονές εἰσιν, ἀλλ' οἱ ἀγαθοί.
(7) βουλοίμην ἄν· ἀλλὰ φοβοῦμαι.

Note that in ex. (3) ἀλλ' no longer stands near οὐδέν. Has it detached itself also in point of syntax? The ambiguous stage is reached. Is it a tadpole or a frog? I.e., is it ἄλλ' with some editors ('you are nothing *else* than Quack'), or ἀλλ' ἤ with others ('nothing but Quack')? Certainly in (4) ἀλλ' ἤ are fused, and ἀλλ' is so dead as an adject., that ἄλλον must be expressed afresh. In (5), 'war is not more (so much) a matter of arms, but of money,' the conjunctional stage is nearly reached, but negation (οὐχ) and comparison (τὸ πλέον) still precede it. In (6) comparison is dropped, in (7) negation, and at last ἀλλά stands forth a conjunction plenipotentiary. (A comparison of Bäumlein with the article on our own conjunct. "but" in Murray's Dictionary will be found most interesting. E.g.,

7 translate the first example above by 'they did *but* fight a naval battle on land.' Cf. "you have *but* to listen"; "this is *but* a dream"; "do *but* speak." Of course the Greeks felt no pleonasm in ἀλλ' ἤ. Children sometimes use the phrase "but 'cept.")

20 E 11. **μὴ θορυβήσητε**: in commands and prohibitions, as elsewhere, distinguish if possible between the present, which paints the act *in extenso*, in process, in evolution, and the aorist, which summarizes it from end to end, gives it concluded, with no process-notion whatever. But for many refinements in the application of the general distinction, one must look to G.-Kühn. § 389,6 c, or Blass *Rhein. Mus.* 44 (1889) p. 406 ff. (though at times he seems to be hair-splitting). Consult also Donovan *Class. Rev.* (1895) p. 145 ff., who sets side by side a list of pres. and aor. imperatives, which may well cause one to hesitate before dogmatizing. C. W. E. Miller *A. J. P.* 13 (1892) p. 424, after working through the imperatives in the Attic orators, declines to differentiate.

I have tried in the following lists to cite all the instances in this volume of imperatives pres. and aor., and of the aor. subjunctives in prohibition. By careful comparison of passages, attending always to the whole context, one may perhaps acquire a feeling for the difference between the two tenses, even though he find it sometimes difficult of expression. But younger students should first study the analysis of various passages given by G.-Kühn., l.c. (The forms ἄγε and φέρε are cited merely for completeness' sake. They are not of course true imperatives.)

I. Present Imperative in Commands and Prohibitions

ἄγε (-ετε) 90,31. 92,29.
ἄθρει 55,15. 272,7.
ἀθυμείτω, μή 254,15.
αἱρείσθω 252,8.
ἄκουε (-ετε) 6,31. 55,7. 146,11. 213,3. 261,17.
ἀμελείτω, μή 254,15.
ἀναγίγνωσκε 261,16.
ἀνάγκαζε, μή 218,9.
ἀξιοῦτε, μή 32,1. Cf. ἀξιώσατε 3,29.
ἀπαγέτω 69,1.
ἀποκρίνου 15,14. 56,17. 121,9. 124,2. 166,13. 184,17. -έσθω 18,6. Cf. ἀπόκριναι.
ἄσκει 141,12.
ἀφίετε 23,14. μὴ ἀφίετε 23,14.
ἄχθεσθε, μή 25,30. Cf. μηδὲν ἀχθεσθῇς 140,21.
βουλεύου 48,5.
διανοεῖσθε 192,5.
δίδασκε 55,6.
ἔα (-ᾶτε) 64,6. 75,16,20. 95,5,8. Cf. ἔασον.
ἐπείγου, μή 91,10.
ἐργάζου 70,14.
ἑστιᾶτε 95,10.
ἔστω 44,13. 242,1.
ἐχέτω 46,1. 124,18. Cf. παρασχέσθω 29,21.
ἡγοῦ 219,20.
θάρρει 107,26. 113,28. 157,13.

θαύμαζε μή 56,17. Cf. *μὴ θαυμάσῃς* 231,5.
θεραπεύετε 95,14.
θορυβείτω, μή 18,8. *-εῖτε, μή* 7,23. 23,17. Cf. *μὴ θορυβήσητε* 7,11.
ἴθι 13,24,29. 91,17. 231,3. *ἴτω* 4,14.
ἴσθι 48,24. 63,27. 64,2. 89,18. 196,15. *ἴττω* 72,18. *ἴστε* 7,1. 19,20. 22,31. 23,24. 25,26. 28,12. 74,22,25.
καρτερεῖτε 92,30.
κατακλίνου 94,25.
κέλευε, μή 120,11.
κινεῖτε, μή 95,7.
λέγε 6,26. 16,13. 55,6,9. 64,4. 70,4. 121,4. 182,31. 184,17. 186,24. 212,13. 219,1. *-έτω* 29,21. Cf. *εἰπέ.*
μέμνησθε 18,3. Cf. *ὑπόμνησον* 119,23.
μένετε 191,26. 192,15. Cf. *περιμένετε, ἐμμείνατε, παραμείνατε.*
ξύνισθι 193,10.
ὄκνει, μή 123,30.
ὀνειδίζετε 42,13.
ὅρα 48,3. 53,6,13. 54,23. 93,18. 103,16. 112,17. 120,20. 125,28. 183,5. 215,17. 226,26. Cf. *ἰδέ.*
παρασκευαζέτω 75,17.
παρατίθετε 95,10. Cf. *ἀπόθεσθον* 156,9.
πείθου 45,2. 46,13. 48,10. 141,11. *-εσθε* 23,14. Cf. *πιθοῦ* 91,18. 7
πειρῶ 53,15. 66,14. 90,24. 182,16. 184,24. 185,14. 220,2. Cf. *πείρασαι* 120,14.
περιμένετε 191,16. See *μένετε.*
πλάττε 241,18. Cf. *περίπλασον* 242,5.
ποίει 70,14. 264,11. *μὴ ποίει (-εῖτε)* 23,23. 46,13. 48,10. 91,18. 192,15. 193,9. 264,11. *οὐ-* 63,7. Cf. *ποιησάσθων* 214,15.
πρόσεχε 181,10.
σκόπει 49,18. 52,8. 54,29. 55,23. 58,12. 61,9. 82,19. 118,20. 124,31 etc. Cf. *σκέψαι.*
σύναπτε 242,3.
τρέπου 96,15.
τρέφε, μή 271,22.
φάθι, 124,2.
φέρε 15,17. 49,29. 51,5. 56,19. 74,14. 122,27. 162,20. 182,16.
φιλονικείτω 275,14.
φοβοῦ, μή 46,16. 212,13.
φοίτα 193,11.
φράζε (-ετε) 71,5. 5,8. Cf. *φράσον* 56,23.
φύλαττε 186,21.
χαῖρε 90,23,27.

II. Aorist Imperative in Commands and Prohibitions and Subjunctive in Prohibitions

ἀκολούθησον 153,17.
ἀκούσατε 26,9.
ἀμελήσητε, μή 93,16. Cf. *ἀμελείτω* 254,15.
ἀναβαλοῦ 94,14.
ἀξιώσατε 3,29. Cf. *ἀξιοῦτε* 32,1.
ἀπείκασον 226,10.
ἀπόδοτε 93,16.
ἀπόθεσθον 156,9. Cf. *παρατίθετε* 95,10.
ἀποκάμῃς, μή 46,28.
ἀπόκριναι 14,21. 15,9. 18,1,13. 60,15. 157,14. 162,20. 166,6. 168,14. 177,1. Cf. *ἀποκρίνου.*
ἀχθεσθῇς, μή 140,21. Cf. *ἄχθεσθε* 25,30.

7 γένεσθε 191,26. -έσθω, μή 46,29 (see App. on 2,5).
δεῖξον 185,16. Cf. ἔνδειξαι, ἐπίδειξον.
διαλέχθητον 156,24.
διομολόγησαι 218,3.
διόρισον 142,26.
δοξάτω 221,31. Cf. προσδοκησάτω.
ἔασον 46,9. 153,20. Cf. ἔα.
εἰπέ 13,21,24,29. 14,2. 15,7. 16,20. 46,2. 55,27. 70,3. 124,29. 135,3,8. 143,3,6. 159,27, etc. εἴπατον 164,19. μὴ εἴπῃς 143,12. Cf. λέγε.
εἰσάγγειλον 113,29.
ἐμμείνατε 23,18. See μένετε.
ἔνδειξαι 180,31. Cf. δεῖξον.
ἐνεγκάτω 91,1.
ἐννόησον 229,30.
ἐπίδειξον 162,18. -ατον 164,13,19. -ασθον 156,10. Cf. δεῖξον.
ἐροῦ 120,5.
θαυμάσῃς, μή 231,5. Cf. θαύμαζε 56,17.
θεασάσθων 214,10.
θορυβήσητε, μή 7,11. Cf. θορυβεῖτε.
ἰδέ 226,12,22. Cf. ὅρα.
λάβετον 156,23.
μήνυσον 13,29.
ξυνεπισκέψασθε 17,31. Cf. σκόπει, σκέψαι.
ξυνοιήθητι 231,4.
οἰήθητε 4,2.
πάραδος 120,14.
παραμείνατε 38,31. See μένετε.
παρασχέσθω 29,21.
παῦσαι 53,9. 141,11.
πείρασαι 120,14. Cf. πειρῶ.
πείσατον 156,11. πείσῃ, μή 63,25.
πέρανον 146,10.
περίπλασον 242,5. Cf. πλάττε 241,18.
πιθοῦ 91,18. Cf. πείθου.
ποιησάσθων 214,15. Cf. ποίει.
προθυμήθητι 66,6.
προσδοκησάτω, μή 2,5 ubi App.
πρόσελθε 181,6.
προσκάλεσον 181,3.
σκέψαι 76,29. 186,19. 233,10. -ασθε 7,28. Cf. σκόπει, ξυνεπισκέψασθε.
σώθητι 45,3.
τιμωρήσασθε 42,8.
τριψάτω 91,2.
ὑπόμνησον 119,23. Cf. μέμνησθε.
φθονήσῃς, μή 104,11.
φράσον 56,23. Cf. φράζε.

The imperative perfect is found 241,25 πεπλάσθω. 263,3 εἰρήσθω.

21 A 18. **ὑμῶν τῷ πλήθει**: according to Geb.-Frohb. Lys. 12,26, the regular phrase for 'your democracy' is *τὸ ὑμέτερον πλῆθος* (as infra 25,16), while *τὸ πλῆθος ὑμῶν* is 'the majority of you.'

21 A 25. **ἀνεῖλεν . . μηδένα σοφώτερον εἶναι**: why *μηδένα*, and not *οὐδένα*, seeing that the passage is one neither of command, condition, nor general statement? The serious student will save himself much time and vain brain-cudgelling in his future reading, if he acquires at once, (1) a general feeling for the "subjective" *μή* that is imperious or prayerful, that deprecates or hopes, that promises, guarantees and swears, that in brief shows all the human emotions,—and (2) a special sensitiveness to the use of this subjective *μή*, where

we, regarding the situation as one of fact rather than of feeling, 7
might expect the negative of fact, *οὐ*. To acquire this latter sensitiveness, let him study in their context not merely the cases cited in L. & S. and G. M. T. (see n.), but also those in *A. J. P.* 1 (1880) p. 48, and Bäumlein, p. 298 ff. Consult also *A. J. P.* 12 (1891) p. 387 ; 13 (1892) p. 259 ; Kühn. § 514,2 a. With the present passage, cf. X. *Apol. Soc.* 14 *ἀνεῖλεν ὁ 'Απόλλων μηδένα εἶναι ἀνθρώπων ἐμοῦ μήτε ἐλευθεριώτερον μήτε κτλ.* Hdt. VI 66 *ἡ Πυθίη . . ἔκρινε μὴ 'Αρίστωνος εἶναι Δημάρητον παῖδα.* Thuc. II 17,2 *ὃν* (*πόλεμον*) . . *τὸ μαντεῖον προῄδει μὴ ἐπ' ἀγαθῷ ποτε αὐτὸ κατοικισθησόμενον.* I 76,1 *εἰ τότε . . ἀπήχθησθε ἐν τῇ ἡγεμονίᾳ, ὥσπερ ἡμεῖς, εὖ ἴσμεν μὴ ἂν ἧσσον ὑμᾶς λυπηροὺς γενομένους τοῖς ξυμμάχοις.* Cf. Demos. 6,10. Soph. *Antig.* 1064. (It is strange that modern ingenuity has not yet seized on the present passage and that from Hdt. as examples of intentional oracular ambiguity, taking *μή* as that of "cautious assertion" ; 'maybe somebody is wiser' ; G. M. T. § 269.)

Cf. infra *μή* after *πέπεισμαι* 34,9,16 ; *νομίζω* 269,25 ; *διανοέομαι* 270,1.

21 D 26. **ὥσπερ οὖν** 'as indeed.' *Phaedr.* 252 E. *ὥσπ.* 8
οὖν καὶ Crat. 404 B, *Rep.* 564 C.

21 E 7. **νὴ τὸν κύνα**: against the widely-held explanation as 9
cited in the notes of the origin of at least some of these oaths, Geddes (*Phaedo,* Note S) says: "(*νὴ τὸν κύνα*) was in all probability derived from the mysticism of Egypt, and, like other oaths, was used long after any solemnity connected with it had disappeared." In oaths by the dog, the ram, and the goose, he would recognize respectively the Egyptian gods Anubis, Ammon, and the sacred goose of the Nile (*χηναλώπηξ* Hdt. II 72). Plato will find many pages of oaths to answer for, as catalogued in Schanz *Nov. Comm.* p. 18 ff. ; and the swearing of the orators is recorded against them in Rehd. *Ind. Dem.* s.v. *Schwurformeln.*

Cf. *μὰ Δία* 17,3. 110,26. 162,24,29. 217,24. 227,20. *μὰ τὸν Δία* 185,17. *οὐ μὰ Δία* 1,20. 17,16. 183,26. *οὐ μὰ τὸν Δία* 43,12. 180,28. 202,29. *ναὶ μὰ Δία* 107,6. 118,27. 137,9. 153,22. 164,7. *ναὶ μὰ τὸν Δία* 210,12. *νὴ Δία* 32,3. 38,10. 56,11. 78,26. 83,11. 161,29. 162,19. *νὴ τὸν Δία* 69,24. 76,7. 109,13. 193,23. *νὴ τὴν "Ηραν* 14,10. 260,14. *νὴ τὸν κύνα* 9,7. 246,24. *νὴ τοὺς θεούς* 106,14. 107,4. 135,8. 168,15. *ὦ Ζεῦ καὶ θεοί* 107,8. See also *πρὸς Διός* and others with *πρός* 15,7 App.

22 A 15. **ἵνα <μή> μοι καί** *κτλ.* : after careful study of each item in the situation—the usage of the language, the combinations *ἵνα καί* and *ἵνα μὴ καί*, the position of the words, the word *ἀνέλεγκτος*, the chances of haplography (infra 11,10),

9 and so on, it would seem that *μή must* be admitted. It should be further noted that its presence is *implied* in the Armenian version of the *Apology*. See Conybeare *Class. Rev.* for 1889, p. 341.

22 B 23. **διηρώτων ἄν**: for statistics on the use of ἄν iterative with the imperf. and aor. indic. see R. C. Seaton in *Class. Rev.* for 1889, p. 343; "Nearly fifty exx. in Aristophanes." For many citations, see Starkie on *Vesp.* 269.

10 **22 C** 1. **καὶ γὰρ οὗτοι** = *ἐπεὶ καὶ οὗτοι*. See Kühn. § 544, Anm. 2. Krüg. 69,32,21. Stress *καί* and hold it an instant, gliding over *γάρ* lightly. This will carry *καί* over to *οὗτοι* and distinguish it from the *καί* in the fused *καιγάρ* of 4,3. Cf. the vocal difference between "For he did not go" and "*For*, if what you say is true, he did not go."

Examples infra: 15,15 (?). 37,15. 66,10. 116,11. 138,17. 140,12. 167,31. 168,2. 177,12. 190,16. See Schn. Isoc. 1,16. Kühn. X. *Mem.* II 1,3.

22 C 3. **ἐφάνησαν**: in Attic prose distinguish sharply between *ἐφάνην* intrans. and *ἐφάνθην* a true passive. See Bl.-Kühn. II p. 558.

22 D 10. **τούτους δέ γε**: I cannot think that in this group *γε* emphasizes *δέ*, as sometimes held, e.g. by Marchant Andoc. 1,68. On the contrary, see Kühn. X. *Mem.* II 6,31 *τὰς δέ γε Σειρῆνας*: "*contra* (*δέ*) *Sirenes quidem* (*γε*). Particula adversativa *δέ* omnino indicat oppositionem, particula autem *γέ* cum vi effert id verbum, in quo potissimum oppositionis vis posita est." Hartung *Lehre von der Partikeln* I p. 382: "Der Nachdruck oder die Auszeichnung trifft immer dasjenige Wort, hinter welchem *γέ* entweder unmittelbar, oder durch *δέ* von ihm getrennt, steht." Let the student test the matter by asking himself in the foll. passages whether the sense calls for an emphatic '*but*,' or for emphasis on the contrasted object or action itself: X. *An.* III 1,35. IV 6,9. V 8,16. *Mem.* IV 6,4,14. *Cyr.* I 6,18. *Symp.* 4,13. Andoc. 1,68,136. Aesch. 3,28,117,246 (*ter*). Lyc. 93. Dem. 5,23. 19,90,279. 20,28. 21,27,95,220. 22,8. 24,129. 34,32. 43,27,39. 44,55. 46,6. 54,35. 60,36,37. *proem.* 47,1. Ant., Lys., Dein., Hyp. offer no examples.—I add further instances of the *ὁ δέ γε νόμος* type, which of course comes under the Hartung rule, although, owing to the presence of the article or for some other reason, *γε* must precede its substantive: X. *Mem.* IV 3,13 *ὅτι δέ γ' ἀληθῆ λέγω*. IV 4,6. *Cyr.* I 6,18 *τὸν δέ γε ἐργάτην στρατηγόν*. Dem. 19,299. 57,35. 58,44 (if the text of Blass is sound). The list is complete for the eight orators named and for Xen.'s *Anab.* and *Mem.*, when we add *An.* VII 6,36 *ὅπως δέ γε*, where possibly *γε* may seem to belong to *δέ*.

Observe when testing these passages that if indeed it is the adversative relation that is accentuated, it should make no difference in the sense, if an adversative expression of undisputed emphasis such as ἀλλά, δ' αὖ, τοὐναντίον, were substituted. But it will be seen at once that such substitution involves a material shift in the thought-accent. Finally, no argument for connecting the two particles can be found in such groups as εἴ γε, ὅτε γε, ἐπειδή γε. But this is too plain to need discussion. 10

Examples infra: 13,15. 78,14. 82,7. 118,8,17,30. 120,26. 123,27. 132,8. 133,4. 134,13 (δέ γε αὖ). 136,27. 137,16. 168,2. 173,21, etc.

22 D 11. **πολλὰ καὶ καλά**: on the καί that connects πολλοί with a second adj., see Kühn. § 523,1; or better yet Kvičala in *Zeitschr. f. d. oesterr. Gymn.* for 1863, p. 315, who explains, in brief, as follows: When *we* say, e.g. "many good men," our substant. is good-men (a unit) and "many" qualifies it as a whole. But in πολλοὶ καὶ ἀγαθοὶ ἄνθρωποι the Greek's substantive-thought is ἄνθρωποι alone, which he modifies by *two* adjectives.—Examples: 19,23. 37,6. 62,17. 101,11. 113,9. 144,23. 254,3.

22 D 14. **ταὐτόν μοι . . διὰ τό** κτλ.: the term *asyndeton* is variously applied. Perhaps it should be restricted to cases where there is *progress* in the thought (a new item added, a new consideration advanced), disallowing it altogether to cases of mere apposition, even when developed into whole clauses of epexegesis; for all such clauses indicate a pause and a re-flexion in the thought.

Thus no one would apply the term asyndeton to 164,8 ἦ καὶ τὰ τοιαῦτα, τοὺς ἀστέρας . . καὶ τὴν ἄμμον; The word τοιαῦτα is explained and gets its thought-contents in what follows. Though it is not always easy to tell whether the author adds his appositives, in such cases, as an afterthought, or whether he sets his demonstrative in the first place as a mere introductory word to the enlarged statement, yet in either case no new thought is taken up, as we pass the comma or colon: we pause rather for a clear marshalling and exposition of the thought already reached.

Now from this simple case of apposition it is impossible to separate the following instances of apposition, though the divergence becomes greater at each step, and at one point or another editors begin applying the term asyndeton:

(1) Infinitive and participial constructions prefaced by a οὗτος, οὕτως, ὅδε, τοιοῦτος or the like; e.g. infra 31,26. 73,21. 83,6. 120,1. 122,6. 136,22,25; also 2,9 where see App. With ptc. 105,20. 67,2 (οὕτω).

(2) Dependent clauses (ὅτι-, ὡς-, ἵνα-, ὅπως-clauses), likewise anticipated by a demonstrat. τοῦτο, etc.; e.g. ὅτι-clauses in

10 9,29. 101,27. 110,5. 135,14. 178,6. 197,2. 198,21 (*οὑτωσί*); *ὡς*-clause in 165,18; *ἵνα*-clause in 107,11; *ὅπως*-clause in 232,30.

(3) Independent clauses, yet as before, introduced by a demonstrat.; 8,7. 9,9. 36,25 (*τόδε*). 243,18 (*τοιόνδε τι*). 2,14 and 14,22 and 230,26 (*οὑτωσί* or *οὕτως*). 175,8 (*ὧδε*). Cf. 226,10–12.

(4) Independent clauses, no longer heralded by a demonstrat., yet added like the others in mere explanation or summary or comment to what has preceded; e.g. 10,16. 149,3. 174,4 (?). *Meno* 74 A, 95 C. *Euthyph.* 8 E; also infra 38,14 and even 136,18 (*λέγουσι* repeating *ψέγουσι*) and 137,11.—Indeed such clauses as these do not at all differ from the many *γάρ*-clauses of epexegesis such as in 7,2. 24,27. 26,14. 39,21.

(5) *ὥσπερ*-clauses of illustration, followed by a resumptive *οὕτω καί* or the like, which bring us *back* to the matter in hand, but do not advance us. (The punctuation is various and indifferent.) 70,17. 108,30. 158,27. 169,9. 236,12. *Meno* 71 A. *Rep.* 413 D, 432 D, and very frequent.

(6) Explanatory-clauses in a sort of partit. apposition, introduced by *μέν γε . . δέ* (as 97,3), on which see Geb.-Froh. Lys. 13,27 Anh.

(7) Clauses beginning with an epanaleptic *οὗτος, τοιοῦτος*, etc.; e.g. 10,2. 175,12. See 1,4 App.

By thus withdrawing from asyndeton all cases of mere epexegesis, and restricting the term to those cases where the conjunction is omitted though the thought *advances*, we shall reduce it—nearly—to its proper rhetorical function—that of indicating emotion, as infra 252,5. 254,14. (Note. The instances in 144,1. 155,12 seem to me to differ from all those mentioned above.)

11 **23 A** 3. **τὸ δέ** 'on the other hand,' 'whereas': Rid. *Dig.* § 19. (Krüg. 50,1,14 says nothing worth saying, and G.-Kühn. nothing at all.) Frequent in Plato; e.g. infra 34,7. 38,13. *Phaedo* 109 D. *Prot.* 344 E. *Meno* 97 C. *Theaet.* 157 B, 166 A, 183 A, 200 C, 207 B. *Rep.* 340 D. *Legg.* 803 D. *Soph.* 244 A. *Crat.* 404 C, 405 E, 439 C. Cf. *τὸ δέ γε Polit.* 263 D. *τὸ δέ γε ἀληθές Rep.* 443 C, *Tim.* 86 D.

23 B 10. **ὥσπερ ἂν εἰ εἴποι**: *εἰ* is not in the MSS., its omission being due to the merely graphical error called haplography—writing once (*ἁπλοῦς*=*simplex*) what we should write twice (*εἰ εἴ-ποι*). The opposite error is called ditto-graphy. Both are common.

23 B 13. **ταῦτ' οὖν . . ζητῶ** is properly an inner accus. ('that is my search')=*ταύτην τὴν ζήτησιν ζητῶ*. So infra 107,11 *αὐτὰ ταῦτα ἥκω* 'that is just my errand.' Cf. *quid rides?* (*τί γελᾷς;*) 'what is your laugh?' *illud glorior* 'that is my boast.' But since the fact or thing referred to by these pronouns is the *cause*

of the action or emotion expressed by the verb, modern languages 11
prefer to translate as if *διὰ ταῦτα, διὰ τί*, etc. G.-Kühn. § 410, Anm. 6.

So, in fact, the *ὅτι* that introduces a causal clause after *ἥδομαι, ἄχθομαι, θαυμάζω* and other verbs of *emotion*, is really 'that,' not a 'because.' For *that* fact *is* my joy, anger, wonder, and so on. See Rid. *Dig.* § 18 (p. 127); Monro *Hom. Gram.* § 133. Cf. *Symp.* 174 A. *Euthyph.* 4 D. Ar. *Nub.* 319,335,353; *Ach.* 90.

23 C 24. **αὐτόματοι**: for the interpretation given in the notes, see the ironical description given on p. 114 of Protagoras' well-drilled chorus of admirers, and on p. 158,8 ff. of that of Euthydemus.

23 C 27. **εἶτα** 'and then': for many exx. of this connecting *εἶτα* (not the indignant-question *εἶτα*, infra 19,26), see Frohb. Lys. 1,14 Anh. For both *εἶτα*'s, Rehd. *Ind. Dem.* s.v. Infra 24,22. 259,12.

23 D 11. **ἅτε . . φιλότιμοι ὄντες**: the student should endea- 12
vour to feel into *ἅτε* its accus. origin. Let him compare *καθ' ὅσον*. Here, e.g. *καθ' ὅσον φιλότιμοι, κατὰ τοῦτο ἐμπεπλήκασιν ὑμῶν τὰ ὦτα* 'in proportion as,' 'to the degree that, they were *φιλότιμοι*'; or, translating as a demonstrat., 'being that *φιλότιμοι*.' Compare, further, the two ways of translating the vulgar Engl. "she was that mad, she cried"; *ἅτε χαλεπαίνουσα, ἔκλαε*; or *ἔκλαε· οὕτως ἐχαλέπαινε*. Here *ἅτε* and *οὕτως* have the same function, viz. that of measuring the act or state spoken of in their respective clauses by reference to the other act or state in the other clause. Cf. App. on 1,4. See Kühn. § 489,2 and espec. Bäuml. p. 41.

Examples infra: 37,24,26. 86,29. 144,7. 150,10. 157,10. 172,12. 179,31. 180,6. 191,5. 213,11. 254,31. 255,2. 259,29. 269,8,13.

24 C 21. **ἄλλο τι (ἤ)**: so 55,28. 60,18,21. 76,21. 117,28. 13
123,22. 135,11. 157,30. 159,30. 161,14. 162,12. 167,1. 181,30. 182,3. 183,15. 187,4. Cf. also 177,5. See Kühn. § 587,18.

24 D 26. **μέλον γέ σοι**: cf. the now vulgar usage of 'being' in "being it's you." But see Murray's Dictionary s.v. *be*, B I 3, for exx. from earlier time, as: "being they are Churchmen" (Milton); "you loyter heere too long, being you are to take souldiers up" (2 *Henry IV*, II 1,200). Other accusatives absolute: 47,7,12,27. 48,1. 113,10. 142,11. 232,29. 244,27. 261,19.

24 D 2. **ὠγαθέ**: this crasis is found in the *Codex Clarkianus* 14
throughout except in *Ap.* 25 D (15,15), *Crito* 48 D (53,7), *Gorg.* 506 C, *Phaedr.* 260 D. Schanz *Nov. Comm.* § 22.

14 **25 A** 13. **τί δὲ οἱ βουλευταί;** see Kühn. § 587, Anm. 4. Also in 84,7 and perhaps 121,17 a nomin. is found with *τί δέ*; in 227,12 a genit. Elsewhere *τί δέ* stand alone: 54,14. 62,25. 67,23. 71,13,23. 77,5,6. 130,9. 159,10. 161,27. 163,14, etc.

25 A 14. **ἀλλ' ἄρα**: in searching for the original meaning of *ἄρα*, its two derivatives, *γάρ* and the interrog. *ἆρα*, must not be forgotten. No sense can be regarded as the original one, which does not also account for them. Evidently therefore the inferential sense is not the earliest. For if *ἄρα* marked the effect ('consequently'), it could hardly, in the form of *γάρ*, have come to mark the cause ('for'). Besides, the interrog. *ἆρα* shows no trace of such meaning. Indeed, *no* logical relation of clauses (causal, inferential, concessive, etc.) was expressed primitively by any language. This came only in course of time to be *felt into* words from which the proper sense was fading out. Hence *ἄρα* could not have signified originally 'therefore.'—But again, it could not well have indicated mere temporal sequence 'then' (*äussere Folge*), as a source of the later inferential sense. For here too the causal *γάρ* 'for,' indicating some fact that *precedes*, could not have sprung from a word properly introducing a fact that *succeeds*. And, as before, though temporal conjunctions appear in a language earlier than logical conjunctions, yet neither can *they* be looked for in the earliest stage. Hence the sequential 'then' is also rendered unlikely as the primitive sense of *ἄρα*.—Of course the really primitive sense is not discoverable, until the etymology of the word be made out. But as yet this is uncertain. Earlier guesses may be found in Kühn. § 509. The one connecting it with *ἀρ-αρ-ίσκω* seems probable to Bäumlein (p. 38), Kühn., and more recently to K. Brugmann (*Berichte üb. d. Verhandl. d. königl.-sächs. Gesellsch. der Wissensch.*, 1883, p. 37–70). H. Collitz (*Proceed. Amer. Philol. Assoc.* XXVI (1895), p. xxxix) proposes for its origin **ἀρί-ς*, an adj. supplanted by *ἀγαθός* in the posit. degree, but surviving in *ἀρείων*, *ἄριστος*, and in compounds like *ἀρί-γνωτος*, *ἀρί-ζηλος*. For accent and formation, he compares *τάχ-α* from *ταχ-ύ-ς*, *ὦκ-α* from *ὠκ-ύ-ς*, *ῥέ-α* (*ῥε-ῖ-α*) from **ῥη-ί-ς* *ῥη-ί-τερος* *ῥη-ί-διος*. The meaning of * *ἀρίς* he takes to be 'loyal,' 'brave,' 'true'; of *ἄρα* 'truly,' 'in truth,' 'forsooth'—herein agreeing with Bäumlein, who in 1861 worked out this meaning as the original one, though himself vainly attempting to extract it from *ἀρ-αρ-ίσκω*. Kühner also follows Bäumlein. It is true that Kvičala (*Zeitschr. f. d. oesterr. Gymn.* 1863, p. 309) and Brugmann (l.c.) dissent. But recalling the claims of *γάρ* and of interrog. *ἆρα*, it seems hardly possible to assume any other more definite meaning than this of 'verily,' 'sure enough,' 'in good sooth,' with no conjunctive power originally, but, like *οὖν* and *ἦ*, marking assurance as to the truth of its own clause. This original sense is not preserved alone in Homer, for examples of which see Bäumlein; it is found abundantly in Att. prose. For example 14

(1) in the post-Homeric interrog. ἆρα ('really and truly?'), which merely lengthens and holds the first syllable to recall its old force to a word whose force was fading.

(2) in the γάρ of such formulae as καὶ γάρ 'and i' faith,' ἀλλὰ γάρ 'but sure,' ἦ γάρ '*n'est-ce pas?*', εἰ γάρ in wishes; also in short answers, as οὐ γὰρ οὖν 'no *indeed*,' etc. See Kühn. § 509,8 a.

(3) in the use of ἄρα c. imperf. indic. (G. M. T. § 39) to mark that the statement was true 'sure enough,' though we had not realized it till now. E.g. 83,14. X. *Cyr.* I 6,31.

This ἄρα of *awakening*, however, is not restricted to use with the imperf. indic. See 53,26. 70,23. 160,28. X. *Cyr.* VII 2,24.

It is employed further when we discover to be true 'sure enough' what we had already suspected to be true, as in 115,5 (see n.).

(4) in the ἄρα that adds a 'sure' truth by way of confirmation of the preceding—a function usually filled by its derivative γάρ. See Kühn. § 509,5.

(5) in the freq. ironical ἄρα 'in good sooth.' E.g. in εἰ μὴ ἄρα 1,14; in the formula μὲν . . δὲ ἄρα of the *argumentum ex contrario,* for which see 30,11 App.

(6) in the formulae of quotation ὡς ἄρα, εἰ ἄρα ('whether indeed'), and εἰ ἄρα 'if indeed (as people say).' But here, espec. in ὡς ἄρα, the word may be used merely to note quotation. See Kühn. § 509,5. Rehd. *Ind. Dem.* s.v. ἄρα. For exx., see Index; of ὡς ἄρα, cf. also *Phaedo* 97 B. 107 D.

In course of time, among the many applications of this confirmatory ἄρα, that one became especially frequent which marked as 'surely' true the *result* of some other truth. This is its inferential use, 'then,' 'therefore,' so largely found in argument, e.g. in Euclid's demonstrations in geometry. For exx. in Plato, see Index. But the whole purpose of this note is to warn young students not to fall into the lazy and pernicious habit of translating all ἄρα's by 'therefore,' 'then.' Particularly to be borne in mind is the ἄρα of awakening ('after all,' 'sure enough') and the ἄρα ironical 'in good sooth,' 'forsooth.'

25 A 22. **περὶ ἵππους**: in the sense 'concerning,' shall περί take acc. or gen. in Att. prose? No fast line can be drawn. But an examination of the dissertations (see p. 409) including the one on the usage of Hdt. will show a preference for περί c. gen., after verbs relating to the mental world, as

14 those of perception, emotion, knowing, *thinking*, *saying* (asking, writing),

περί c. acc., after verbs of activity in the outer world, *except* those denoting strife—these latter preferring the genitive. But constantly the syntax is reversed and sometimes the case changes in close context, as *here* (li. 28 *περί* c. gen.).

Examples of *περί* c. acc.: 14,31. 24,6. 39,18. 47,8,17,25. 51,19. 56,26. 65,30. 77,2,6,10,15,27. 83,23. 85,16. 87,14,22,25. 104,10. 108,25. 111,31. 112,3,13. 130,2. 131,12. 145,21. 149,2. 153,13,14. 162,15. 179,8. 185,29. 193,8,30, etc.

25 B 24. **τοὐναντίον τούτου πᾶν**: cf. 29,22. 30,19. 38,3 =218,17. 41,9. 101,1. 163,5=167,22=221,3. These appositives to a sent., implying a predication about it, are often important enough actually to be made predicates—usually, however, with *ἐστί* omitted. Cf. 80,17 *τὸ δ' ἔσχατον πάντων* [*ἐστὶν*] *ὅτι*—. So 210,17. 239,17. Identical with these are also the relat. clauses treated at 3,20 App. Consult espec. G.-Kühn. § 406,6 with the remarks. (Rid. *Dig.* § 13, and Rehd. *Ind. Dem.* s.v. Accusativ, regard instances of the present kind as accus.—wrongly, if the explanation here and in 3,20 App. is right.)

25 B 30. **οὐ φῆτε**: *οὔ φημι* 'I deny' is so steady a collocation that *οὐ* does not yield to *μή* even after *εἰ* (*ἐάν*). (Cf. the Engl. "don't," used so much with *I*, *we*, *you*, *they*, that some say also "*he* don't.") H. 1028. G. 1383,2. L. & S. s.v. *οὐ*, A II 7 a. G. M. T. § 384. Kühn. § 513,4 (p. 748). Rehd. *Ind. Dem.* s. v. *οὐ*.

15 **25 C** 7. **ὦ πρὸς Διὸς Μέλητε**: for the word-order cf. *ὦ χαῖρ' Ἡράκλεις* Ar. *Av.* 1586 and the many such exx. collected ad loc. by Koch.

25 C 9. **ὦταν**: on etymology and writing, see, among much else, Rehd. *Ind. Dem.*, Voemel *Demos. Contiones*, Prolegg. § 14.

16 **26 A** 5. **παύσομαι ὅ γε ἄκων ποιῶ**: with *παύσομαι* supply *ποιῶν*. Otherwise *ὅ* should (by attract. of unexpressed *τούτου*) be *οὗ*, as in fact is edited by Schanz.

17 **26 D** 8. **ὥστε οὐκ εἰδέναι**: *μή* is regularly used c. infin. after *ὥστε*. But here the clause depends upon another infin. *in indir. disc.* (after *οἴει*), in which case *οὐ* is preferred—as if the original thought were *οὐκ ἴσασι*. G. 1451 end. L. & S. s.v. *οὐ*, A II 6 c end. G. M. T. § 594. Kühn. § 513,4 (p. 748). (In the citations on *ὥστε*, G. M. T. p. 220 footnote, the reference should be *A. J. P.* VII, not VI. Add *A. J. P.* for 1893, p. 240; and for the stylistic effect of the *ὥστε* construction consult Eckels *Proceed. Am. Philol. Assoc.* 1896, p. xxxv.)

26 E 12. **ἐκ τῆς ὀρχήστρας**: on the location of that 17
ὀρχήστρα near the market-place—*ἔνθα Ἁρμοδίου καὶ Ἀριστογείτονος εἰκόνες*, as Timaeus tells us—see Frazer's note on Pausan. I 8,6 (vol. II, p. 92), or Dörpfeld in *Mitteil. d. deutsch. archaeol. Instit.* for 1895, p. 185. And for a discussion of the present passage, see Adam's edit. of the *Apol.*

27 A 22. **ἔοικε . . ξυντιθέντι**, sc. *τινί*; for partic. used without article as a substantive, see G. M. T. § 827; G.-Kühn. § 462, 1. Cf. 2,3. 17,29. 75,12. 173,27. 174,12,17,18. 178,19. 192,3. 194,11. 252,11. 254,12,20. 260,28. *Rep.* 368 D, 595 C. *Soph.* 238 A. *Legg.* 795 B. *Meno* 97 A. *Lys.* 212 B, 213 C, 221 B. *Phaedo* 78 A. *Gorg.* 498 A. X. *Mem.* I 2,23. III 6,6. 9,14. *Oec.* 1,4 and 11.

Instances of such partic. after *ἔοικα*: 212,11. *Phaedo* 86 D, 104 B. *Rep.* 527 D. *Hipp. Maj.* 300 E. *Prot.* 361 C. *Crat.* 416 A. *Alc.* I 124 B. Cf. *ὅμοιος* c. ptc. 178,18. Yet sometimes *τινί* is present, as in 261,1.

27 A 27. **αὐτὸς ἑαυτῷ**: for many exx. of this strengthening of the nomin., see Dyroff I pp. 92,103,110,122; II pp. 36,39 for Aesch., Soph., Eurip., Arist., Antiph., Andoc., respectively. See also Kühn. § 455,2 mid., and Bl.-Kühn. § 168, Anm. 5.

Cf. infra 31,13. 34,18. 72,4,16. 73,1,18. 76,25,27. 78,17,23. 79,12,13. 132,31. 136,12. 139,3. 141,4. 142,12. 176,21. 180,27. 206,9. 229,3. 265,25, etc.

27 C 16. **οὐκοῦν**: that the word was not felt as a negative 18
is proved by the actual addition of a negat. when one was needed; e.g. 167,4. Examples of *οὐκοῦν* are on every page; as 49,23. 50,5. 72,31. 77,13. 78,21. 79,23. 81,18. 82,4,11. 83,12,21. 84,2. 110,5, etc., etc.

οὔκουν is very much rarer. In this volume I find only 31,29. 95,3. 121,1. 161,8. 180,13. 210,2.

27 C 18. **εἴτ' οὖν . . εἴτε**: *οὖν* ('indeed') stands usu. after the first *εἴτε* (*Prot.* 333 C, *Euthyph.* 3 D); but, since it is corroborative for the whole thought, it may stand also after the second (Soph. *Phil.* 345); and infra 31,1 and Aesch. *Cho.* 683 it is found after both.—The formula is not common: 4 times in Aesch. (*Ag.* 491,843, *Ch.* 683, *Frg.* 320); 4 times in Soph. (*O. R.* 1049, *El.* 199,560, *Ph.* 345); absent from Hom., Hes., Aristoph., Thuc., the Attic orators so far as indexed (all are indexed save Isoc. and Isaeus), and X. *Hell. Mem. Oec.* From Hdt. Kalinka (p. 177) cites VI 137 (*εἴτε ὦν δὴ . . εἴτε*) and VIII 54 (*εἴτε δὴ ὦν . . εἴτε καί*). Bäumlein, p. 184.

With this formula may be compared that in Hdt. VII 12 (and IX 18 and 26) *οὔτε ὦν . . οὔτε* or, as he has it in IV 96, *οὔτε . . οὔτε ὦν.* See also infra 221,22 *οὔτε . . οὔτε . . οὐδ' οὖν.* Observe too *τοι* in *ἤτοι . . ἤ.* See 18,24 App.

18 27 C 18. **ἀλλ' οὖν . . γε** = δ' οὖν, with the difference that ἀλλά is stronger than δέ. Exx.: infra 31,2. 185,23. *Phaedo* 91 B, 102 D, *Gorg.* 496 D, 506 B, *Prot.* 327 C, *Lys.* 221 A, *Soph.* 254 C. See also Rehd. *Ind. Dem.*; Schn. Isocr. 4,171; Blaydes Ar. *Nub.* 1002; Kalinka p. 175 (and Rehd. Lycurg. § 141 Anh. 2 for ἀλλ' οὖν γε). Cf. 224,26 ἀλλ' οὖν without γέ.

27 C 24. **ἤτοι . .** (γε) **. . ἤ**: see Kühn. § 540,5; Kugler, p. 14; Bäuml., p. 244. The formula is more freq. without γε. Examples are: 83,17. 121,21. 122,24. 189,10. 196,22. *Phaedo* 76 A, 103 A, 104 B. *Gorg.* 460 A, 467 E. *Prot.* 331 B. *Men.* 89 A. Examples of ἤτοι . . ἢ . . ἤ are 122,20. 123,1. 127,27. 129,21. X. *Mem.* IV 6,13 ἤτοι . . ἢ . . ἢ . . ἤ. Hence Classen's remark on Thuc. VI 34,2 "nur bei einer Zweitheilung" is to be corrected; also the statement sometimes made that τοι marks the more probable choice (for see 189,10). —On the whole, it is not a common formula, as compared with the simple ἢ . . ἤ; Aeschyl. 3 times, Soph. 2, Demos. and Thuc. 4 each, Andoc. 1, Dein. 1; but Ant., Lys., Hyp. not at all.

27 D 26. **εἰ μὲν . . εἰ δ' αὖ** (30): an example of δί-λημ-μα (λαβ-, λαμβάνω) 'double-catch' (Lat. *complexio*). So 39,29 ff. For a detailed discussion of its various forms, see Geb.-Frohb. Lys. 13, 75 Anh. The dilemma is here prefaced by the alternatives ἤτοι . . γε . . ἤ (24).

19 27 D 1. **ἔκ τινων ἄλλων, ὧν**: supply ἐξ with ὧν. The omission of the prepos. is quite regular. Cf. 159,10. 234,5. 244,22. See also 212,25 App. Krüg. 51,11,1; G.-Kühn. § 451,4. Rehd. *Ind. Dem.* s.v. Praeposition; and Schn. Isoc. 9,3 for a valuable note on the whole subject of prep.-omission. —But the prepos. *may* be repeated; see Krüg. Thuc. II 86,1 with over a dozen exx.

27 D 1. **ὧν δὴ καὶ λέγονται**: for καί see 4, 18 App. and cf. X. *Mem.* III 5,11 ὃ δὴ καὶ λέγονται πολὺ διενεγκεῖν—. II 1,21 ὅπερ δὴ καὶ πλείστοις ἐπιδείκνυται. 2,3 ἃ δὴ καὶ οὕτως ἡμῖν δοκεῖ παντὸς ἄξια εἶναι, ὥστε—. In II 6,36, however, καί belongs rather to the foll. word: ἃ δὴ καὶ ἐγὼ πεισθεὶς ὀρθῶς ἔχειν ἡγοῦμαι κτλ. (The similar clause in *Hellen.* VII 1,31 οὗ δὴ καὶ ἀπόγονος λέγεται is now thrown out as a later insertion.)

It is worth while to note that δή quite regularly accompanies the relat., when the verb of the clause is one of *naming* or *saying*; see 146,24. 174,12. 179,20. 180,9. 193,20. 222,1. 225,8. An equiv. -περ is used in 40,27 οἵπερ καὶ λέγονται.

27 E 6. **ὅπως σὺ ταῦτα οὐχί**: certainly, as the text stands, ταῦτα is awkward—either in posit. if it belongs to ἀποπειρώμενος, or in syntax if it goes with ἐγράψω. Many editors change. If this is to be done, I should prefer going back to οὐ for σύ, *as it really stands* (before correction) in Codex Clarkianus—see the

Facsimile—and then ejecting *οὐχί*, which was naturally inserted 19
after *οὐ* had become corrupted to *σύ*. The passage would then read: *οὐκ ἔστιν ὅπως οὐ ταῦτα ἀποπειρώμενος ἡμῶν ἐγράψω τὴν γραφὴν ταύτην.*

28 D 19. **παρὰ νηυσί**: what sign in this phrase is there 20
(besides the spelling of *νηυσί*) that it does not belong to Attic prose? *παρά* with the dat. of *an inanimate thing.* Since the prose limitation of *παρά*, whether with gen. or dat., to animate things only, is passed over in the grammars of Hadley and Goodwin, a note may not be amiss. The rule was known to the old Greek grammarians and has been entirely confirmed by Rau in Curtius' *Studien* III, p. 1 ff. His list of exceptions to the rule for Hdt., Thuc., Xen., Plato, the ten orators, and Aristoph. (in this matter practically prose)—a list very slightly augmented by more recent count—is as follows:

I *παρά c. dat. rei*: Hdt. IV 15,53,90 bis. VI 69. II 130. Thuc. II 43,2. 89,9. V 26,5. VIII 95,4. X. *An.* VI 2,2. VII 2,25. *Oec.* 20,18. Plat. *Phil.* 42 A, *Prot.* 337 B, *Ion* 535 B. Andoc. 1,116. Ar. *Pax* 1299, *Ran.* 1309, *Av.* 728.—To secure a rule for Attic prose, we (1) set aside Hdt.; (2) note that in two of the passages from Thuc. the phrase is the old Homeric *παρὰ ναυσί* (and Thuc. wrote old Attic at any rate); (3) recall that Xenophon's diction and syntax are both hopelessly un-Attic; (4) find that, as for Plato, it is Prodicus, the elegant stylist, who speaks the *Protag.* passage, and that in the *Ion* Socrates is describing an Homeric rhapsodist who 'gets out of himself,' imagines he is actually in Homeric action (*παρὰ τοῖς πράγμασι*) and may hence be excused if he uses Homeric syntax; (5) note finally that two of the Aristoph. passages are quotations from poets and the third (*Av.* 728) is in anapaestics rather than the iambic trimeter of dialogue. The rule to be deduced for Attic prose, *παρά c. dat. personae*, is consequently one of the most rigorous to be found.

II *παρά c. gen. rei* (see Rau, p. 12) is found only in Hdt. VII 182. Thuc. VIII 48,7. X. *Cyneget.* 13,4. Plat. *Rep.* 461 E, *Tim.* 85 E. Ant. 1,6. Isoc. 15,202,223; *epist.* 4,12. Aeschin. 1,129. Dem. 18,308. 20,15. (Not to be classified as thing-genitives are collective names of people, as *πόλις* Ar. *Eq.* 802; *ἀρχή* 'board of officials'; and *θέατρον* 'spectators' Plat. *Legg.* 659 A.) Even the above list should be reduced. For in some of the passages personification is either clearly or probably intended, as in *Rep.* 461 E *τοῦ λόγου* (see n. on 52,26 and cf. 154,2. 180,14), and in Thuc. VIII 48,7 *τῶν ἔργων* (ubi vid. Classen).—Setting these few instances against the whole use of *παρά*, we see how fixed the rule was: *παρά* c. gen. and dat. *of person only.* Consult the dissertations referred to on p. 409 by Kühne, Alvin, Westphal, Lutz.

20 Examples in this vol. of παρά c. dat. *of persons*: 57,25. 96,3. 106,13. 107,20. 139,23. 159,6. 170,20. 206,19,25. 216,6. 229,23,26. 232,26. 233,12. 245,6. 248,26. 266,4.

28 D 27. **δεινὰ ἂν εἴην εἰργασμένος** κτλ. : this is the first example in the *Apol.* of the paratactic *argumentum ex contrario* (see 6,22 App.). See Geb. pp. 80–103, and for this passage pp. 85 and 111. Perhaps the best introduction to the matter may be obtained by copying out and comparing in detail a few of the exx. in this book, as 20,17. 24,27–30. 25,12–17. 30,3–12. 34,31–35,6. 49,2–6. 57,9–21. 73,13. 82,27. 110,30.—A study might profitably be made here (1) of the corresponsions to the introductory clause δεινὰ ἂν εἴην εἰργασμένος (*if any*) ; (2) of the substitutes for εἰ ; (3) of the tenses and moods ; (4) of the form of sent. (declarative or interrogative).

Often the sent. is interrogative and variants for the introduct. clause are οὐκ οὖν δεινόν (or αἰσχρόν, σχέτλιον, ἄτοπον, γελοῖον, ἄδικον), εἰ—. πῶς οὖν οὐ δεινόν (αἰσχρόν, etc.), εἰ—. Substitutes for εἰ are ὅτι, ὅτε, ὅταν, ὅπου, etc. ; or an infin. construction (with or without article) takes its place. Examples are to be found on every page of Greek. A few from Lysias are offered for study : 10,8. 12,36,38,88. 14,18,36. 18,15. 24,13,23.

In the present passage there is a double μέν and a double δέ. Cf. Isoc. 17,48. Antiph. 6,9 ; and see Geb. p. 111. Schn. Isoc. 7,47. Rehd. X. *An.* VI 6,16. Fritzsche Plat. *Meno* 94 C.

28 E 31. (ἐν Ποτειδαίᾳ καὶ ἐν Ἀμφιπόλει καὶ) **ἐπὶ Δηλίῳ** : why the change of preposit. ? Because Delium was not a town *in which* or *in the district* of which, but a temple to Apollo *at* or *near* which the famous battle took place. See Kühn. X. *Mem.* III 5,4.

21 **29 B** 17. **ἀμαθία ἡ τοῦ οἴεσθαι εἰδέναι** : an apposit. gen. (Ἰλίου πόλις 'the city of Troy') is rare in prose ; G.-Kühn. § 402 d. Plato uses an *articular infin.* genit. rather freely. Cf. 142,27. 151,6,11. *Phil.* 11 D, 58 A. *Euthyd.* 289 D. *Legg.* 701 B. *Phaedo* 97 A. *Theaet.* 182 D. *Soph.* 242 C. See Birklein, p. 77.—An ex. of a *substantive* genit. in apposition stands in 142,16.

22 **29 C** 1. **ἤδη ἂν . . διαφθαρήσονται** : for ἄν c. fut. indic., c. fut. inf. (62,2. 221,4), and c. fut. ptc. (23,15), see G. M. T. § 197 with reff. The section does not look the battle-field that it is. I mention only a few of those who have fought upon it : Madvig *Adversaria Crit.* I 435. Cobet *Nov. Lect.* 693. Stahl *Quaestiones grammaticae ad Thucyd. pertinentes*, pp. 20–24. H. Richards *Class. Rev.* for 1892, p. 336 ff. See also G.-Kühn. § 392,1.

29 D 12. **οὐ μή** c. aor. subj. : on the origin of the construction, see G. M. T., App. II ; but also the more recent discus-

sions (with criticism of Professor Goodwin's theory) in the *Class.* 22
Rev. for 1896 (pp. 150, 239) and 1897 (p. 109) by Messrs. Chambers & Whitelaw. (Jannaris, *Hist. Greek Grammar* (London, 1897) § 1827, holds the remarkable view that *οὐ μή* is by corruption for *οὐ μήν*—the negat. of *ἦ μήν*.)

Examples in this vol.: 48,25. 79,31. 161,4. 166,10. 219,12. 221,23. 223,11. For many others, see Stallb. on *Rep.* 492 E. With fut. indic. *οὐ μή* is found in 45,6.

29 D 17. **εἰς σοφίαν**: see G.-Kühn. § 410, Anm. 18 (p. 317), and p. 471 c for *εἰς* c. acc. of specification. Cf. infra 31,13. 89,19. 250,7. See also *κατά* and *πρός* c. acc. in Index.

30 A 28. **ταῦτα . . νεωτέρῳ . . ποιήσω**: note dat. and acc. c. *ποιεῖν*, not two acc.: '*for*' a person, not '*to*' him. Exx. in G.-Kühn. § 411 Anm. 6, and Holden's *Hiero* 7,2 crit. note.

30 C 20. **καὶ γάρ**: note the *point* of reference for each of 23
the foll. *γάρ*'s. *καὶ γάρ* tells why they must listen (*ἀκούειν*, 20); *γὰρ οὖν* why he asked them not to make outcry (*μὴ θορυβεῖτε*, 17); *εὖ γὰρ ἴστε*, 'be assured *namely*,' is the object-clause of *ἐρεῖν* (7,2 App.) and the utterance against which he anticipated outcry.

30 C 21. **γὰρ οὖν** is freq. in answers either in the phrase *οὐ γὰρ οὖν* (e.g. *Phaedr.* 277 E, *Theaet.* 160 A, 171 B, 182 E), or with repetition of the interlocutor's main word (e.g. *λεκτέον γὰρ οὖν Phaedr.* 259 E, *φημὶ γὰρ οὖν Gorg.* 466 E). But as used here, it is not common; in Aesch. 4 times, Soph. 7, Aristoph. 3 (*Thesm.* 164, *Av.* 39, *Vesp.* 726), in the orators prob. not at all. For Hdt. Kalinka, p. 175, cites I 49. II 127. VIII 128,133; but adds that it is not rare. In Plato, cf. *Phaedr.* 247 C, *Crat.* 421 D and perhaps elsewhere. See also *καὶ γὰρ οὖν* 101,27.

30 D 30. **μέντοι . . ἀλλά**: Kugler, p. 25, compares *Phaedo* 76 B. *Theaet.* 151 E. *Soph.* 265 B. *Rep.* 348 E.

30 D 6. **μὴ ἐξαμάρτητε καταψηφισάμενοι** ('by condemn- 24
ing'): the action of the partic. cannot here be anterior to that of the verb *ἐξαμάρτητε*, since it is identical with it. In truth, the aor. partic. never, in itself, indicates past action, whether absolutely, or relatively to the main verb.—Why not?—Because without augment.—But no more has the aor. *infin.* augment.—True; and no more does it, of itself, indicate past time. Only by usage, probably arising from that of indirect discourse, does the action of the aor. partic. come to be understood as anterior to that of the main verb. Relics of its timelessness are found in such passages as the present (cf. also 69,25. 198,8. 209,27. G. M. T. § 150), and in its quite steady use with the aor. and fut. of *τυγχάνω* (e.g. 100,22. 157,21. 220,10), *φθάνω* (156,21), *λανθάνω* (199,24); G. M. T. § 144. For other instances of timeless aor. ptc., see G. M. T. § 148.

24 **30 E** 9. **γελοιότερον** 'rather ridiculous,' *νωθεστέρῳ* (12) 'rather sluggish.' Note in Engl. as in Greek the use of the comparative degree where we compare, not a higher degree of the quality with a lower, but the quality itself with its absence or its opposite, i.e. 'ridiculous rather [than serious],' 'rather sluggish [than active]' '—than not.' So *θᾶττον* 'quickly [and not slowly],' *ἡμέ-τερος* 'ours [, not yours].' See Monro *Hom. Gr.* § 122, and espec. Schwab I p. 107 ff. for a complete list of such comparatives.

Cf. infra 27,7. 35,4. 88,16. 96,18. 107,13. 141,9. 161,22. See also 37,22 App.

31 B 27. **οὐ γάρ** *κτλ.*: *γάρ* is not here causal, but rather introduces an appositive clause to *ἐνθένδε*—in such cases sometimes to be translated 'namely.' So in 39,25 (apposit. to *τεκμήριον*), 29 (*τῇδε*). 239,27, and very freq. Cf. *Prot.* 328 B, 349 D, 351 C. *Meno* 72 E. See Kühn. § 544,1. L. & S. s.v. *γάρ* II. Schn. Isoc. 7,68. Class. Thuc. I 8,1.

25 **31 B** 2. **καίτοι εἰ μέν τι**: MSS. read *καὶ εἰ μέντοι τι*—a logically impossible combination (see Kugler p. 29), which is usu. changed to *καὶ εἰ μέν τι*. The reading here adopted is Göbel's (taken from Adam). See however Geb.-Froh. Lys. p. 401 for retention of *μέντοι*.

31 B 4. **εἶχον ἄν τινα λόγον**: so infra 29,27. But usu. the phrase is used, not of a person, but of an action or course of action, as infra 72,21. 73,17. 241,2. 271,23. *Lach.* 196 B, *Alc.* II 142 B, *Legg.* 927 E. Dem. 44,54. 45,12. Lys. 3,31. 13,90 (ubi vid. Geb.-Froh., Anh.). Cf. also *ἔχει φύσιν* 218,5. *ἔχει δίκην* 233,18.

31 B 6. **ἀναισχύντως οὕτω**: *οὕτω* after the word it modifies. For this immediate postposition of *οὕτω* see Rehd. *Ind. Dem.* s.v. and Blaydes Ar. *Vesp.* 461; of *λίαν*, see Schn. Isoc. 9,48. 4,73. 7,77. 15,215; of *εὖ* Schn. Isoc. 9,58. 3,7. 4,80. 5,82. 6,4. For postponement in general, of an adverb (with much emphasis) entirely to the end, see Rehd. *Ind. Dem.* s.v. *Stellung*.

Examples of adverbs after their words: *οὕτω* 197,21. 201,11. 202,18. *μάλα* 54,30. 91,8. 160,18. *πάνυ* 76,10. 155,19. *τελέως* 225,28. *ὡς ἀληθῶς* 74,5.

31 D 29. **οὔτ' ἂν . . οὔτ' ἄν**: note doubled *ἄν*. Infra 124,7. *Symp.* 196 E. See Geb.-Froh. Lys. 12,98.

26 **32 A** 15. **ἀρχὴν οὐδεμίαν . . ἦρξα . ., ἐβούλευσα δέ**: the *βουλή as a body* was an *ἀρχή*, not the individuals composing it. Schanz cites Lys. 25,14 *οὐδείς με ἀποδείξει οὔτε βουλεύσαντα οὔτε ἀρχὴν οὐδεμίαν ἄρξαντα*.

27 **32 C** 3. **οἷα δὴ ἄλλοις . . πολλοῖς πολλά**: not only is the chiastic (crosswise X) arrangement to be noted (cf. 15,20 *σὺ*

ἐμοῦ . . τηλικούτου ὄντος τηλικόσδε ὤν), but the juxtaposition of 27
different forms of the same word (one of the forms of paronomasia)—extremely common from Homer down; *Od.* 3,272 ἐθέλων ἐθέλουσαν; Dem. 37,24 πολίτης πολίτην; so πολλῶν πολλά, πολλῶν πολλάκις, ἄλλος ἄλλα, etc. A nomin. usu. claims first position, even thrusting itself between prepos. and noun, as ἐπ' αὐτὸς αὐτῷ. See Kühn. § 607,2; Rehd. *Ind. Dem.* s.v. Paronomasia; Schn. Isoc. 1,19. For Plato, see 17,27 (αὐτὸς ἑαυτῳ, ubi v. n.); 35,8 (ἄλλην ἐξ ἄλλης πόλεως); 262,31 (φίλοι παρὰ φίλους, ubi v. n.).

33 A 31. **εἰ . . τις . . ἐπιθυμεῖ, . . οὐδενὶ . . ἐφθόνησα**: is the 28
present ἐπιθυμεῖ to be taken as a past (either as inclusive of it, or as a quasi-historic)? Or is the past ἐφθόνησα to be translated as a present; i.e. one of those *timeless* aorists that ignore their augment and, when negatived, deny the very *notion* of the act for all time, including present? Editors differ.

33 C 22. **τινί ποτε καὶ ἄλλῳ** is implied by the Armenian version (see supra on 9, 15) and would seem to be expected in contrast to the strong ἐμοί at the head of the sent. τίς ποτε καὶ ἄλλη, going with θεία μοῖρα, is the reading of the MSS. and of most editors.

33 D 4. **πάρεισιν . . ἐνταυθοῖ**: on "pregnant construc- 29
tion," see G.-Kühn. § 447, Anm. 4 b and cf. infra 33,12. 64,17. 89,25. 96,23. 107,28. 153,18. 155,1. 231,5. Cf. further 17,12 and see n. on 26,19 and on 114,3. But apart from this explanation it should be remembered that ἐνταυθοῖ was sometimes used in Attic prose for ἐνταῦθα. See Geb.-Froh. Lys. 12,50. Andoc. 1,89. Dem. 41,20.

33 E 13. **οὐκ ἂν . . καταδεηθείη**: for the translation 'cannot,' see Gildersleeve in *Am. Journ. Phil.* 1893, p. 499; also for the translat. of the affirmative potential by 'must' in 14,31. Cf. 34,30. 40,7. 260,19.

34 C 5. **εἰ ὁ μὲν . ., ἐγὼ δέ** (10): an *argum. ex contrar.* 30
(20,27). Here the εἰ is equiv. to ἐπεί for the first clause, to ὅτι for the second. Geb. (pp. 156,162–64) cites *inter alia*: Dem. 27,28. Lys. 29,4. 10,13. 20,19. And. 1,102.

34 C 11. **οὐδέν** here stands in an εἰ-clause, where μή is the rule. But an εἰ-clause after verbs of emotion (here ἀγανακτήσειεν, 4) = a ὅτι-clause. In such cases, οὐ is frequent. Kühn. § 513,5. Krüg. 67,4,1. But if one would go to the bottom of the matter, he should study Gebauer's book, or at least pp. 154–163. Cf. infra 72,12.

34 C 11. **ἄρα** serves a recognized incisive purpose in the *argum. ex contrar.* (Geb. p. 323). It marks the place where there *ought* to stand a logical conclusion. But of course there

30 is none, since the conclusion of the *arg. ex contr.* is an absurdity. Hence *ἄρα* proves to be not a 'therefore' but a derisive 'in good sooth.' It stands (as one would expect) usually in the second member as here, and infra 35,6. 49,4. 82,31. 243,26. *Phaedo* 80 D, *Meno* 91 E, *Rep.* 445 B, *Phil.* 30 B. Lysias 10,22. 12,36. 31,28.—Rarely it is found in both clauses, as infra 57,9 and 15. *Phaedo* 97 A, *Prot.* 325 B, *Rep.* 600 C; or in the first clause as *Legg.* 840 B. Lysias 3,30. See also Bäuml. p. 26.

31 **35 A** 8. **ὡς δεινόν τι οἰομένους πείσεσθαι**: more briefly *ὡς δεινόν τι πεισομένους*, since *ὡς* c. ptc. implies *οἰομένους* (1,10).

35 B 14. **ἔν τε ταῖς ἀρχαῖς καὶ ταῖς ἄλλαις**: *τε* comes apparently too early. We should expect

ἐν { *ταῖς τε ἀρχαῖς*
{ *καὶ ταῖς ἄλλαις.*

But this is one of the very many passages where the prepos. is to be supplied with the second noun, as in 19,1 it was to be understood with the relative. For many exx. of this kind, and also of true pre-position of *τε* (e.g. *Rep.* 348 B *ἅμα αὐτοί τε δικασταὶ καὶ ῥήτορες ἐσόμεθα*), see Geb. p. 356. Cf. infra 43,13. 52,21. 270,27. *Phaedo* 94 D, *Prot.* 325 B, 336 C, 338 B.

35 B 20. **τὰ ἐλεεινὰ ταῦτα δράματα**: *οὗτος* in attribut. position: 83,2. 111,12. 153,23. 210,15. So *ἐκεῖνος* 174,2. See Rehd. *Ind. Dem.* s.v. *οὗτος*.

32 **36 A** 20. **οὕτω παρ' ὀλίγον**: cf. infra 39,9. 243,26. *Euthyd.* 305 C *πάνυ παρὰ πολλοῖς*. *Phaedo* 110 C *πολὺ ἔτι ἐκ λαμπροτέρων*. *Euthyph.* 14 B *πολὺ διὰ βραχυτέρων*. *Crat.* 413 C *πολὺ ἐν πλείονι ἀπορίᾳ*. Cf. further 52,25 *οὐδενὶ ξὺν νῷ*; and Frohb. Lys. 1,42 *ὡς μετὰ πλείστων* (i.e. *ὡς ἂν δύνωμαι μετὰ πλείστων*).

36 A 22. Five hundred is the number now usu. assumed for the dicasts that tried Socrates. See Rid. *Introd. Ap.*, p. xii. As for the remarks of Diogenes Laertius, a writer of uncertain value living six or seven hundred years after the event, Schanz (ad loc.) seems to show that he had no more data on the matter than we. It may be safer, therefore, to say that the number is not known.

33 **36 B** 5. **ὅ τι μαθών**: cf. infra 161,23. 168,19. *Prot.* 353 D. Kühn. § 587, Anm. 6, explains by what he regards as a parallel: *ὅ τι μαθών* is for *διὰ τοῦτο ὅ τι μαθών* just as in *Phaedo* 117 C *ἀπέκλαιον οἵου ἀνδρὸς ἑταίρου ἐστερημένος εἴην* stands (as he says) for *ἀπέκλαιον ὅτι τοιούτου ἀνδρός κτλ.* But where is the parallel in

{ *ὅ τι μαθών = διὰ τοῦτο ὅ τι μαθών*
{ *οἵου ἀνδρός = ὅτι τοιούτου ἀνδρός* ! !

Adam (*Apol.*, App. II, note on 17 A) explains τί παθών 33
(practically equiv. to τί μαθών) as follows: "τί = 'what': therefore τί παθών = 'why' in direct and ὅ τι παθὼν = 'why' (ὅ τι) in indirect; but as ὅ τι and ὅτι are the same word, and as ὅτι means not only 'why,' but also 'because,' ὅ τι παθών also comes to mean 'because.'" Involuntarily I exclaim with poor idiotic Strepsiades (*Nub.* 153) ὦ Ζεῦ βασιλεῦ τῆς λεπτότητος τῶν φρενῶν.—For myself, I can offer no explanation beyond the translation given in the notes.

It should be noted further that G. Hermann (Ar. *Nub.* p. xlvi), followed by Cobet (*Misc. Crit.* pp. 38,150, and elsewhere) and by Sauppe (*Prot.* 353 D) would everywhere alter μαθών to παθών. (Again I feel obfuscated like Strepsiades with his genders, and wonder why then they do not alter the old proverb to παθήματα παθήματα.) Few editors make the alteration. Schanz varies, safely. In 1874 (*Euthyd.*) he prints μαθών, in 1880 παθών, in 1893 (*Apol.*) μαθών.—Exx. of the direct quest. τί μαθών, as found in the best MSS.: Ar. *Ach.* 826, *Nub.* 1506, *Vesp.* 251, *Lys.* 599, *Plut.* 908. Demosth. 10,39. 20,127. See Schmid's *Atticismus*, Registerband s.v. τίς, for exx. in later Greek.

36 C 14. **[ἰών]**: on this Adam says: "it is probably what Plato wrote. If instead of ἐνταῦθα ᾖα Plato had written τοιόνδε τι ἔπραττον, all would be clear: as it is, in spite of the preceding ἰών, he chooses ἐνταῦθα ᾖα to balance ἐνταῦθα μὲν οὐκ ᾖα."

36 D 23. **καὶ ταῦτά γε**: Schanz brackets γε because he does not find it elsewhere attached to this phrase. Yet it stands in *Rep.* 420 A and *Soph.* 238 A; and we may compare καὶ ταῦτα μέντοι supra 17,17. καὶ ταῦτα without γε is found at 30,11. 55,17. 142,18. 153,31. 243,22.

37 A 9. **ἑκὼν εἶναι**: see G. M. T. § 780; Grünenwald (as 34
cited by Goodwin, p. 310). The latter finds 34 exx. of ἑκὼν εἶναι in classic Greek (16 of them in Plato), all but two in negative sentences—for which fact he offers explanation. Gildersleeve reviews the book in *Am. Jour. Philol.* 1889, p. 381. Some exx.: infra 71,13. 232,14. *Euthyph.* 15 C, *Phaedo* 61 C, 80 E, *Prot.* 335 B, *Gorg.* 499 C.

37 A 11. **ἐγᾦμαι**: the *Codex Clarkianus* thus writes ἐγὼ οἶμαι throughout, with but two exceptions: in *Ap.* 28 C (20,11), *Crito* 45 B (46,21).

37 B 16. **πολλοῦ δέω . . ἀδικήσειν**: for the tense, see G. M. T. § 113.

37 B 22. **ὧν εὖ οἶδ' ὅτι κακῶν ὄντων**: for the construct., see Kühn. § 550, Anm. 3. Cf. *Gorg.* 481 D.

37 C 25. **τῇ ἀεὶ καθισταμένῃ ἀρχῇ**: Uhle suggests that this

34 may not refer to the prison-magistrates at all (*τοῖς ἕνδεκα*), but to the various fickle changes of the general government, such as the Athenians had had in the previous twelve years.

36 **38 B** 4. **νῦν δὲ . . γάρ**: for this formula, c. exx., see Geb.-Froh. Lys. 13,62 Anh. p. 397; Kühn. p. 725 mid. citing Plat. *Charm.* 175 A, B. *Lach.* 184 D, 200 E. *Euthyph.* 11 C. *Symp.* 180 C.

38 C 14. **ἕξετε . . αἰτίαν**: *Rep.* 565 B, *Lach.* 186 B. Antiphon 5,67,85. 6,26. Lys. 13,62. X. *Oec.* 11,24, and frequently. See Schn. Isoc. 7,58 for exx. in Isoc.

37 **39 A** 22. **πολὺ χαλεπώτερον πονηρίαν**: to say that one thing is 'far more difficult' than another implies that that other is also difficult. But it has just been said that that other, viz. escape from death, was *not* difficult. This means, not that the Greeks were here illogical, as is sometimes said, but that their notion of the comparative did not wholly coincide with ours. Translate 'much *rather* is it difficult to escape wickedness,' and see Schwab I 64 for many similar passages and a clear explanation. See supra 24,9 App.

39 A 23. **καί** 'and so,' 'namely,' 'for example.' Kühn. p. 791 mid. Rehd. on X. *An.* VII 1,33. Cf. X. *An.* I 9,6,14. 8,23. III 3,5. It must not be understood that *καί means* the above translations; rather, that the Greeks merely connected, where we use a specialized, logical, connection.

38 **39 C** 8. **ἀπεκτόνατε**: the use of the perf. or aor. tense of something not yet come to pass is often merely rhetorical. G.-Kühn. §§ 384,5 and 386,12 (G. M. T. § 51 is inadequate). Note Soph. *Aj.* 1127, where, when Menelaus refers to Ajax as his slayer (*κτείναντά με*), Teucros twits him scornfully—

κτείναντα; δεινόν γ' εἶπας, εἰ καὶ ζῇς θανών.

But see also Mahlow's article in Kuhn's *Zeitschr.* 26,580, as cited and approved by Brugm. *Gr. Gram.* § 159 end. Mahlow shows that the connotation of many Greek words is not the same as of those by which we translate them. E.g. 'to kill' *de*-notes the act of one man, and *con*-notes its effect upon another. But in Greek such connotation was not attached to *ἀποκτείνω*. You may *ἀποκτείνειν* a man, but he need not, as a result, die. Such his explanation of (e.g.) Eur. *Ion* 1291=1500. *ἔκτεινά σε.*

39 **40 A** 7. [**ἡ τοῦ δαιμονίου**] is bracketed by Schleiermacher, Schanz, and Uhle-Cron, as inconsistent with Platonic usage. The monitor of Socrates is named by him *τὸ δαιμόνιον, δαιμόνιόν τι, τὸ σημεῖον, ἡ φωνή, ἡ μαντική*; but nowhere does he use *τὸ δαιμόνιον* in so substantival and concrete a way as to put it into an oblique case. See Schanz.

40 A 11. **ἅ γε δή** *κτλ.*: for the double function of ἅ (nom. 39
and acc.), cf. infra 212,19 *ταῦτα*. *Charm.* 156 C *ταῦτα οὕτω λέγουσί τε καὶ ἔχει*. X. *Cyr.* II 1,24 *ταῦτα . . προείρητό τε καὶ ἠσκεῖτο ἡ στρατιά*. So Thuc. IV 17,1 *ὅ τι*. See further 41,17 App.

40 A 13. **ἕωθεν** 'from morn,' i.e. '*at* dawn.' So X. *An.* IV 4,8. Cf. *ἀφ' ἑσπέρας* 'in the evening' X. *An.* VI 3,23. *ἐκ νυκτός* (*νυκτῶν*) 'in the night' *Cyrop.* I 4,2. VIII 5,12.

Not alone temporal, but also local designations oft. employ the preposıtt. *whence* rather than *where*. Cf. *ἐκ δεξιᾶς* etc. 114,3. 154,18. 155,1. 166,1.

40 B 16. **καίτοι . . νῦν δέ**: observe that the *νῦν-δέ*-clause is merely a restatement of the sent. preceding *καίτοι*. Such run-around (*περιοδικά*) clauses after *καίτοι* are extremely common —introduced now by *δέ* (as here and infra 177,19. *Gorg.* 499 C. *Rep.* 332 A, etc.), now by *ἀλλά* (*Phaedo* 77 A. *Lach.* 186 C, 194 A, 195 B, etc.), or again by *ἀλλ' ὅμως* (84,10,16. *Charm.* 175 C, etc.). See Kugler, p. 18 f. For palindromic clauses of various kinds, see *Palindromia* in Index.

40 C 29. **δυοῖν γὰρ θάτερον**: many exx. in Geb.-Froh. Lys., p. 440. Infra 59,9 (*θάτερα*). 80,30. 122,18.

40 C 31. **αἴσθησιν**: the supposition (but no more) that *αἴσθησις* continues after death is found in other passages, as *Menex.* 248 B, and in the orators, as Lys. 12,100 (where *οἶμαι*, as usual, is merely 'I fancy'), Isoc. 19,42, etc. See Rehd. Lycurg. § 136, Anh. 2; or for full treatment H. Meuss *Jahrb. f. Philol.*, vol. 139, p. 801.

40 E 22. **ἐκεῖ**: a freq. designation of the other world; as 40
infra 27. 41,17,19. 63,10. 71,29 (*ἐκεῖσε*). 150,14. 153,3 (*ἐκεῖσε*). 196,19,24. 247,23. *Symp.* 192 E. Arist. *Ran.* 82. Lycurg. 136. Eurip. *Med.* 1073.

41 C 17. **οἷς . . διαλέγεσθαι . . καὶ ἐξετάζειν**: the case of 41
an object common to two verbs is usu. that required by the nearer (Krüg. 60,5). See infra 94,8. *Lach.* 187 A *τίνων . . ἐπιμεληθέντες . . ἀγαθοὺς ἐποιήσατε*. *Legg.* 689 A, 856 E. *Phaedr.* 240 C. *Gorg.* 460 D.

But there are exceptions; and the rule is sometimes laid down (as by Hickie on Andoc. 1,30 and 37) that if one of the verbs is in participial form, the case of the object is determined by that verb rather than by the other; e.g. Ar. *Ach.* 191 *τασδὶ τὰς δεκέτεις γεῦσαι λαβών*. Yet this is contravened by such exx. as X. *An.* I 8,11 *καλέσας παρεκελεύετο τοῖς Ἕλλησι* (which reverts to the main rule), and Thuc. II 39,2 *τοὺς . . ἀμυνομένους μαχόμενοι τὰ πλείω κρατοῦμεν* (which contravenes both rules).

41 C 18. **ἀμήχανον . . εὐδαιμονίας** is not quite the same

41 thing as ἀμήχανος εὐδαιμονία. For to substantivize an attributive adjective, throwing the noun into the genit., is to shift the emphasis upon the adjective. Cf. "the height of folly" with "the highest folly"; "a monster of a ship" with "a monstrous ship." See G.-Kühn. § 405,5 b. Cf. infra 173,9 ἄτοπα τῆς σμικρολογίας. 176,11 τὴν ὁμοιότητα τῆς διαγωγῆς = τὴν ὁμοίαν διαγωγήν.

42 **41 E** 14. **τι εἶναι**: for the enclisis of τι, see G.-Kühn. § 470, Anm. 1. Infra 116,19. 153,30. 262,22.

CRITO

43 **43 A** 1. **πηνίκα μάλιστα**: for μάλιστα, see L. & S. s.v. μάλα, III 5. G.-Kühn., p. 469 footnote.

43 A 6. **εὐεργέτηται** with the MSS., not εὐ-ηργ. See Bl.-Kühn. § 204, p. 33, with Meisterhans' testimony.

43 B 19. **ὡς ῥᾳδίως αὐτὴν . . φέρεις**: often is such a ὡς "explained" in notes by the brief equation ὡς = ὅτι οὕτως '*that* you *so* lightly bear it.' But why insert a ὅτι? Why not give an accent to ὡς at once, and say that here too ὡς is an old demonstrative equiv. to οὕτως, as in the phrases οὐδ' ὥς 'not even *so*,' καὶ ὥς 'even *thus*'? We should then transl. here '*so* lightly do you bear it.' It is true that οὕτως often replaces ὡς, as e.g. in 1,4 'I almost forgot myself, so (οὕτω) persuasively were they talking' (where see App.). But, if rightly interpreted, is not the demonstrat. function still retained in the following uses of the so-called relative ὡς?

1. ὡς *in exclamations:* e.g. ὡς ψυχρός ἐστι 'he is so cold' (not '*how* cold he is!'). ὡς ἥδομαι 'I am so glad' (not '*how* glad I am!'). ὥς μοι δοκεῖς πιστεύειν κτλ. (143,21) 'you seem to be so sure' (not '*how* sure you seem to be!'). οἴμοι, ταλαίνης, ὡς ὑπερδέδοικά σου (Soph. *Ant.* 82) 'I do so fear for thee' (not '*how* I fear for thee!'); the ὡς-clause tells why Ismēne had used οἴμοι ταλαίνης, viz. she was 'that' afraid for her sister. Exactly this *measuring* function of ὡς will be found in all so-called exclamatory passages with ὡς, e.g. Soph. *O.R.* 439, *Ant.* 320,572, Ar. *Ach.* 333, *Av.* 338, etc. etc.

2. ὡς *causal:* e.g. οὐκ ἔχω φθέγγεσθαι· ὡς φοβοῦμαι 'I can't utter a sound, I am so afraid,' or vulgarly '*that* afraid' (not 'since'—or 'because,' or 'as—I am afraid'). As above, the second statement is measured by the first; my fear and my inability to speak are equal. ὡς merely points back to, is resumptive of, what has gone before, to get a measure. It does not in itself express any logical relation, such as cause.

For observe that the order of clauses may be reversed, the same 43
ὡs used to connect them, and *then* we are taught that ὡs introduces result! *φοβοῦμαι, ὡs οὐκ ἔχω φθέγγεσθαι* 'I am afraid, so that I can't speak.' It is true that *ὥστε* is regular here, rather than ὡs; but see G. M. T. §§ 608–609.—Cf., further, such passages as Soph. *O.R.* 319, where some find a causal ὡs, others an exclamatory: *τί δ' ἔστιν; ὡs ἄθυμος εἰσελήλυθας* 'what is it? so dejected art thou come.' Of course the ὡs-clause does give a reason—the reason, namely, for the question; I ask 'what is it?' *because* thou art come dejected. But 'because' is not in ὡs. ὡs merely points back, and the cause for asking the question, viz. the dejected look of Teiresias, is said to be adequate to its result, viz. the question. So *Ant.* 997 and frequently.

3. ὡs *final:* e.g. Ar. *Av.* 1508 'Hold this shade over me, so the gods won't see me' *ὡs ἂν μή μ' ὁρῶσιν οἱ θεοί.* Of course, taking ὡs as relative, we may supply a *οὕτως* in the main clause ('hold it in *such a way οὕτως, as that ὡs*'). But what is the need, if ὡs be taken at once as a resumptive, back-pointing 'to'?

4. ὡs *before which "supply ἴσθι,"* as we are usually told, e.g. at Soph. *Aj.* 39. Odysseus asks Athene if he labours to any purpose. Athene's response is: *ὡs ἔστιν ἀνδρὸς τοῦδε τἄργα ταῦτά σοι* 'aye, so sure have you here the deeds of yonder man.' Cf. Ar. *Vesp.* 416. Eur. *Phoen.* 720, *Hec.* 400, and frequently.

5. *ὡs δή in ironical comparison:* e.g. Aesch. *Ag.* 1633 *ὡs δὴ σύ μοι τύραννος Ἀργείων ἔσει* 'so then *you* will be etc.' (not 'as if'; for there is no 'if'). Cf. Soph. *O.C.* 809. Eur. *H.F.* 1407, *Cycl.* 674, *Androm.* 235. Plato *Gorg.* 468 E, 499 B.

6. ὡs in ὡs ἀληθῶs, for which see 6,14 App.; ὡs c. partic., which needs no words.

Cf., further, *ἅτε* c. ptc. 12,11 App.; and such so-called relatives as that in *Od.* 4,611 *αἵματός εἰς ἀγαθοῖο, φίλον τέκος, οἷ' ἀγορεύεις* 'thou art of good blood, dear boy, *such* is thy speech' (viz. 'good').

Returning to the present passage, cf. infra 66,20. 114,19. 160,21. That a *τοῦτο* introduces the ὡs-clause sometimes (e.g. *Phaedo* 89 A) does not affect the argument. It is merely preparatory, while ὡs, as usual, is resumptive.

43 C 2. **ἐν τοῖς βαρύτατα**: see G.-Kühn. § 349 b, Anm. 4, 44
and L. Herbst in *Philol.* 16, p. 346 (10 times in Thucyd.). Infra 59,14,16.

43 D 6. **οὔτοι . . ἀλλὰ . . μέν**: for *ἀλλὰ . . μέν* aft. a negat. clause, see Kühn. p. 692 near top, Bäumlein, p. 162. So infra 166,17. *Prot.* 344 A, *Meno* 87 A, *Soph.* 240 B, *Theaet.* 197 C, 201 B.

43 D 9. **ἐκ τούτων τῶν ἀγγέλων**: i.e. from their *report.*

44 Later editors either alter the text or resort to questionable interpretation (e.g. ἐκ = ὑπό c. gen. agentis). But I cannot see why the brachylogy is more impossible than in κόμαι χαρίτεσσιν ὁμοῖαι (*Il.* 17,51) 'hair like to [that of] the graces.' A glance at Kühner's paragraphs on brachylogy will discover far more incredible instances.

44 A 18. **γέ τοι δή**: *Phaedr.* 264 B, *Rep.* 476 E, 504 A. Soph. *O.R.* 1171. Ar. *Ran.* 1047, *Nub.* 372 (γέ τοι). See Kugler, p. 12.

44 A 19. **τῆς ἐπιούσης ἡμέρας**: distinguish the temporal uses of genit. and dative, respectively the *period within which* and the *point at which* an act occurs. Any time-word (day, night, year, etc.) may be taken now as a period, now as a point (in a larger period). In the present passage ἡμέρα is a period, within which, at any one of a thousand points the boat may arrive: but in line 16 (4 lines above), ἡμέρα is a point in Socrates' life; hence the dative. (The temporal usage has sprung from the space-usage in both cases. Thus, Μαραθῶνι (locat.) τῆς Ἀττικῆς '*at* Marathon *in* Attica.)

Distinguish further the temporal genit. from the temporal accusative. In negative sentences, if you deny the occurrence of the verb at all, the extent of time of that non-occurrence is put in the genitive. You sweep the act out of that whole sphere of time (genit. of the whole). Therefore in the sent.: "We were not in Thrace for a long time," if you mean you were not there at all during that time, it is πολλοῦ χρόνου οὐκ ἦμεν ἐν Θρᾴκῃ. If, however, you *were* there, but not for long, it is πολὺν χρόνον, as it stands in Ar. *Ach.* 136. Cf. the genitives in Ar. *Eq.* 944, *Vesp.* 91,490,1478, *Pax* 151, *Lys.* 280, *Thesm.* 806, *Plut.* 98 with the accus. in *Ach.* 136, *Av.* 635, *Lys.* 881, *Ran.* 160,707; but espec. cf. *Vesp.* 91 with 93.

44 B 27. **ἤματί κεν τριτάτῳ Φθίην ἐρίβωλον ἵκοιο**: Philosophy has been defined "a sort of homesickness." To the old philosopher Socrates, no dream could have come of happier omen. At last he was to see Truth face to face.

45 **44 B** 8. **ὡς οἷόστ' ὢν σε σῴζειν**: if *not* able to save, Crito could not of course be thought guilty of neglect. But '*because*' able to save (as many supposed) he etc. To express this, ὡς seems to be the only proper word. I cannot understand why Schanz should propose ὅμως.

44 C 10. **αἰσχίων . . ταύτης δόξα—ἢ δοκεῖν**: for other exx. of genit. and ἤ-clause combined after a comparat., see Schwab II 123,—among them infra 270,21. *Gorg.* 500 C, *Theag.* 127 B, *Legg.* 738 D, 811 D. Lysias 2,73. 10,28. Isae. 1,20. Demos. 15, 4. On δόξα foll. by δοκεῖν, see Rehd. *Ind. Dem.* s.v. δόξα, and cf. infra 61,22.

44 D 22. **δῆλα** [ἐστιν] **ὅτι**: so a ὅτι-clause after the personal 45
δῆλος infra 101,5. 164,3. *Rep.* 348 E. Thuc. I 93,1. X. *Cyr.* I 4,2. Lys. 12,50. 31,6. Ar. *Pax* 1048.

44 D 24. **ἐν αὐτοῖς**: see Lutz, p. 28, for ἐν as *coram* in the orators; also Rehd. *Ind. Dem.* s.v. Cf. 96,9. 144,14,16. 224,9.

44 D 27. **ἐργάζεσθαι** repeats ἐξ-εργάζεσθαι from li. 23, but drops the prepos. This use of the simple for the compound verb on its second occurrence is regular, though sometimes (but rarely) it is reversed. Cf. 67,13 παρῆν . . ἦν. 69,5 ἐξ-έτριψε . . τρίβων. 151,4 ἐγ-γίγνεσθαι . . γιγνομένων. *Rep.* 336 E ἐξ-αμαρτάνομεν. *Crat.* 399 A ἐπ-εμβάλλομεν. *Theaet.* 157 D ξυν-εξαγάγω. *Euthyd.* 281 C ἐξαμαρτάνοι. (*Euthyph.* 14 A ἀπ-εργασίας.) *Phaedo* 71 E, 104 D. *Legg.* 944 A. *Theaet.* 178 A. Andoc. 1,4. See 212,14 App. on ὁποίᾳ . . ποίους. Cf. the French *lorsque* . . *que*. See also my dissertat. on ἐπί, p. 52 for a shift, on repetition, from ἐπὶ τῇ κεφαλῇ to ἐπὶ τῆς κεφαλῆς, with the same lightening of touch as in the case of the compound verbs. Further, one may consult Abbott's *Shakespearian Grammar* § 475, for the reduction in metrical value of a word when it is used for the second time in a verse.

44 D 30. **ποιοῦσι δὲ τοῦτο**: I have followed Adam in interpreting ποιοῦσι.

45 B 22. **εἰ . . οὐκ οἴει** κτλ.: why οὐ after εἰ, and not μή? 46
Because the εἰ-clause does not really express a condition without which the conclusion would not be true. The ξένοι were quite ready to spend their money, no matter what Socrates thought about accepting Crito's. If μή were used, it would mean that the ξένοι would, in case Socrates refused Crito's money, be willing to spend theirs, but not otherwise.

45 B 23. **ξένοι αὖ τοι**: MSS. ξένοι οὗτοι. The source of the reading adopted I have unfortunately lost. I might suggest, is a second choice for οὗτοι, οὑμοί, since in 47,2 and 62,6 it is Crito's ξένοι that are referred to, and not those of Socrates. Indeed it is hardly likely that *he*, poor man as he was, had any guest-friends abroad. He never went abroad, nor would many care on visiting Athens to lodge under Xanthippe's roof.

45 B 25. **ἐπ' αὐτὸ τοῦτο**: ἐπί c. *accus.* of purpose, while in 7,10. 31,26. 33,26, it stood c. dat. The difference? Comparing the exx. collected by Classen, Stein, and Rehdantz on Thuc. (IV 3,2), Hdt. (V 44,14), X. *An.* (I 6,10) and also those in G.-Kühn. pp. 502 bot. and 504 bot., the difference seems to be that hinted at by Stein, viz.: Where the purpose involves for its accomplishment actual bodily motion *to* it, *or where it is thus pictured,* the accus. is used; where it may be reached by merely mental activity exerted *for* it (i.e. where the *idea* of

46 purpose and not its realization is more prominent), the dative. Exx. of acc. : as in Hdt. v 12 ἐπ' ὕδωρ ἔπεμπον, so in vii 131 οἱ ἀποπεμφθέντες . . ἐπὶ γῆς αἴτησιν. Thuc. iv 3,2 ἐπὶ τοῦτο γὰρ ξυνέπλευσε ; i 59,2 ἐφ' ὅπερ . . ἐξεπέμποντο ; iii 111,1 ἐπὶ λαχανισμὸν . . ἐξελθόντες ; v 87 ἐπὶ τοῦτο (sc. ἥκετε from the context).—Exx. of dat. Hdt. i 60,10 μηχανῶνται ἐπὶ τῇ κατόδῳ ; 66,6 ἐχρηστηριάζοντο . . ἐπὶ πάσῃ τῇ . . χώρῃ. X. *An.* vi 4,9 ἐπ' ἐξόδῳ ἐθύετο.

Examples of ἐπί c. acc. of purpose: 59,24. 134,2. (Cf. also 170,30. 171,23. With χρήσιμος 133,14,19. 134,28.) Examples of ἐπί c. dat. : 7,10. 31,26. 33,26. 109,19,20. 114,10. 200,14. 211,24. 244,25.

45 B 25. **Σιμμίας**: Schanz writes Σιμίας, appealing to inscriptions, but citing none. For Σιμμίας, see Collitz *Sammlung der Dial. Inschr.* i 706,1 (a Theban inscript.).

45 B 27. **μήτε . . ἀποκάμῃς** (in the sense of ἀπαγορεύω) c. infin. is not the same as c. ptc. See G. M. T. § 903,3.

45 B 31. **ἄλλοσε ὅποι ἂν ἀφίκῃ** for ἄλλου ὅποι. Kühn. § 555, Anm. 14. Cf. X. *Hiero* 7,2 τοιαῦτα ποιοῦσι τοῖς τυράννοις οἱ ἀρχόμενοι καὶ ἄλλον ὅντινα ἀεὶ τιμῶντες τυγχάνουσι. It is quite regular indeed that any form of ἄλλο- (pronoun or adverb) should be attracted by the case or form of the following relative, as ἄλλον (for ἄλλος) ὅντινα ; ἄλλοθεν (for ἄλλου) ὁπόθεν. See Rehd. X. *An.* v 5,12 and *An.* i 4,15. *Cyr.* i 3,14. 6,43. vi 1,27. 2,13. Thuc. i 53,2. ii 72,4.

47 **45 E** 24. **μὴ δόξῃ . . πεπρᾶχθαι . . δοκεῖν**: for this anacoluthic resumption by δοκεῖν of the main verb in sense and a dependent infin. in syntax cf. *Prot.* 341 d οἶμαι . . Πρόδικον . . παίζειν καὶ σοῦ δοκεῖν ἀποπειρᾶσθαι. X. *Hell.* vii 4,35 ἐνόμιζον . . ποιεῖν καὶ . . οἴεσθαι . . χαρίζεσθαι.

More frequently, however, the idea of the main verb is resumed in infin. form *without* the excuse of some comrade infin., but rather because of the amount of intervening matter ; e.g. infra 218,10 μή ἀνάγκαζέ με . . (9 words) . . δεῖν . . ἀποφαίνειν ; supra 21,2 τοῦ δὲ θεοῦ τάττοντος . . (7 words) . . με δεῖν ζῆν ; infra 225,29 φήσειν resumes ἀμφισβητῆσαι 7 lines distant. So *Soph.* 267 c προθυμεῖσθαι resumes ἐπιχειροῦσι ; Aeschin. 2,35 οἴεσθαι resumes νομίζειν. Cf. also 58,18 τῳ ἐξουσίαν πεποιηκέναι resumed in li. 22 by ἐξεῖναι.

46 A 31. **οἵτινες**=*quippe qui.* For the causal usage, with many exx., see Schn. Isoc. 7,9 and 9,49. Ellendt's *Lex. Soph.* (e.g. Soph. *El.* 187, *Tr.* 6). Kühn. § 554, Anm. 1. See also Holden X. *Oec.* 19,2. Rauchenstein Lys. 13,77. Kühn. X. *Mem.* ii 1,30. Eur. *Or.* 286. Andoc. 1,31,67,150. Antiph. 6,47.—Disting. betw. ὅστις and ὅς γε in the *quippe qui* sense. In assigning the cause with ὅστις you relegate the man

to the *class* of people who do that sort of thing; with ὅς γε you 47
have in mind only the man himself and his deed—you have him ἐπ' αὐτοφώρῳ.

46 A 1. οἷόντε καὶ δυνατόν: like pleonastic groups with καί 48
are: πάντως καὶ πάντῃ, ὅπῃ κ. ὅπως, ὅλῳ κ. παντί, οὕτω κ. ταύτῃ, *Phaedo* 68 D τῷ δεδιέναι κ. δέει, 77 D ἐκ θανάτου κ. τοῦ τεθνάναι, Demos. 23,103 φόβον κ. δέος. See Rehd. *Ind. Dem.* s.v. *Erweiterung* and cf. the similar groups (but *without* καί) noted on 3,1 App.; also those consisting of metaphor and interpretation (3,28 App.).

Schanz has pointed out (*Philol.* 28, p. 724) that the *Crito* has an unus. number of these doublets—a fact that perhaps strikes every one and that may be due to the rhetorical character of the piece. Note, for instance, the duplication aft. ἐμοὶ πείθου 46,13. τρέφοντα 47,18. πρεσβεύω 48,22. παιδιά 49,5. ἐμμένω 55,8. οἱ νόμοι 55,25. εἶναι 56,1. τοὺς νόμους 57,18. ξυνθήκας 60,12. φεύγειν 61,13. τὰ νόμιμα 62,1. ὑπερχόμενος 62,18.

46 C 27. δεσμοὺς καὶ θανάτους καὶ ἀφαιρέσεις: for full treatment of pluralized abstract substantives, see G.-Kühn. § 348,3 c. Cf. infra 99,10. 175,28. (196,28.) 210,20. 252,21 ff.

46 D 2. ἦ: one of the freq. particles for turning into an 49
argum. ex contrar. (Geb. pp. xi and 81). So infra 57,9. 82,27. 110,30. 243,20. Cf. οὐ γὰρ δήπου 6,22 App.

47 B 30. τοῦτο πράττων 'making this his business': the phrase in Hdt. is τοῦτο μελετῶν VI 105. III 115.

47 B 10. καὶ . . γε turns with some emphasis to a new 50
class of things in a series. So *Gorg.* 450 D ἀριθμητικὴ καὶ λογιστικὴ καὶ γεωμετρικὴ καὶ πεττευτική γε καί . . In strengthened form *Gorg.* 508 E καὶ . . γε ἅμα. *Theaet.* 156 B καὶ . . γε δή.

More frequently it *closes* the series with an important item. So *Rep.* 598 E καὶ τά γε θεῖα. X. *Mem.* I 2,53 where Kühn. cites III 5,10. 8,6. 11,10. 14,3. X. *Symp.* 2,5. The stronger form here is καὶ . . γε πρός ('besides'); e.g. *Gorg.* 469 B, 513 B, *Meno* 90 E, *Euthyd.* 294 A (see Stallb. for other exx. at *Gorg.* 469 B). A variant of this again is καὶ πρός γε, with the item following it, as infra 192,11. *Soph.* 234 A, *Rep.* 466 E.—The same γε also closes a negat. series (οὔτε . . οὔτε . . οὐδέ γε), or marks a change in an alternate series (ἤ . . ἤ . . ἤ γε), e.g. *Hipp. Maj.* 301 A γενναῖοι ἢ σοφοὶ ἢ τίμιοι ἢ γέροντές γε ἢ νέοι.

Without classification, the foll. exx. of καὶ . . γε are given from this vol.: 52,24. 65,2. 66,4. 76,15. 77,21. 78,26. 91,8. 98,4. 100,14. 103,1. 111,29. 120,29. 122,12. 137,9. 151,4. 152,26. 159,3. 162,3. 163,24. 165,3. 167,28,30. 168,13. 192,11, etc.

50 47 C 25. **δικαίων καὶ ἀδίκων** κτλ. in chiastic order—good bad, bad good, good bad. See 27,3. 146,25. Schanz cites *Gorg.* 459 D, 474 C, *Lach.* 190 A ὄψις ἀκοὴ ἀκοὴν ὄψιν, *Phaedo* 80 A δουλεύειν ἄρχεσθαι ἄρχειν δεσπόζειν, *Prot.* 314 A σιτία ποτὰ πιόντα φαγόντα.

51 47 D 7. **διολέσωμεν**: the verb is frequently found in tragedy and in Plato. Elsewhere I can find it (by the indexes) only as follows: Hom. 1 (β 64), Aristoph. 1 (*Ach.* 1192, a highly tragic passage), Thucyd. 3 (III 40,6. 59,4. VIII 26,3), Isae. 3 (5,43. 6,18. Frg. 17,2)—in all, 8 times. As for its appearance in Plato, it need not surprise us. But for Isaeus, it should be added to the list of his poetic words made up by Blass *Att. Beredsamkeit* II², p. 504.

47 E 16. **τὸ ἄδικον μὲν . . τὸ δὲ δίκαιον**: for variation in the posit. of μὲν . . δέ, see many instances in Geb. p. 114; e.g. ὑπὸ μὲν τούτων . . ἐν ὑμῖν δέ. περὶ αὐτῶν μὲν . . περὶ δὲ τῶν δεσποτῶν. Also Schn. Isoc. 7,44.

48 A 25. **τί . . ὅ τι**: two indirect questt., the one asked by an interrog., the other by the indef. relative pronoun. This is very frequent. See infra 212,14 App. Cf. *Phil.* 17 B πόσα . . ὁποῖα. *Gorg.* 500 A ποῖα . . ὁποῖα. 448 E τίς . . ὅντινα. *Phaedr.* 271 A ὅτῳ . . τί. *Rep.* 400 A, 578 E.

48 A 31. **ἀλλὰ μὲν δή**: this anticipation of your enemy's objection is called ὑποφορά. See Rehd. *Ind. Dem.* s.v. for the many diff. formulae of its introduction. ἀλλὰ μὲν δή (with μέν) is not commonly used thus, but rather like καὶ μὲν δή as a mere transition-phrase. See Geb.-Froh. on Lys. 12,35, Anh. Cf. infra 156,28.

52 48 C 20. **ἃς δὲ σὺ λέγεις τὰς σκέψεις**: usually the name "incorporation" is reserved for those cases where the subst., in passing into the relat. clause, loses its article—the relat. clause itself serving the purpose of the defining art.; e.g. *Rep.* 456 D τυχόντας ἧς διήλθομεν παιδείας (see Van Cleef, pp. 14 and 34, for all Platonic instances). But no fast line can be drawn between those and passages like the present, which retain the article and give the feeling rather of explanatory apposition—though the addition is a necessary one. See Rid. *Dig.* § 216, Kühn. § 556, Anm. 2. Cf. 40,28 Μίνως nomin. where we expect acc.; 80,27 φρονήσεως where we expect nomin.; *Prot.* 342 B οὓς Πρωταγόρας ἔλεγε τοὺς σοφιστάς for nomin. *Hipp. Maj.* 281 C Πιττακοῦ for nomin. *Rep.* 402 C οὔτε αὐτοὶ οὔτε οὕς φαμεν ἡμῖν παιδευτέον εἶναι τοὺς φύλακας. 533 C γεωμετρίαν for nomin.

53 48 E 13. **ὅρα . . τὴν ἀρχήν, ἐὰν . . λέγηται**: the object-clause (ἐάν κτλ.) happens here to stand as apposit. to a noun (ἀρχήν); but such noun is not necessary. Cf. 76, 29 σκέψαι ἐὰν

ξυνδοκῇ. *Rep.* 432 c. See Monro *Hom. Gr.* § 294 ; G. M. T. 53
§ 491.

49 A 26. **γέροντες ἄνδρες**: so 62,13. 249,26. Ar. *Ach.* 679. *Plut.* 258,628,1066. Cf. *Nub.* 1457. G.-Kühn. § 405,1. See also 77,1 *φιλοσόφου ἀνδρός.* 88,5. 92,18. 109,28. 215,25. 256,3,12. Cf. 102,2 *σατύρου ὑβριστοῦ.* 165,29 *καρκίνῳ σοφιστῇ.*

49 B 29. **παντὸς μᾶλλον**: freq. in Plato; infra 81,17. 153,7. 178,14. *Phaedo* 106 E, *Phaedr.* 228 D, *Symp.* 223 A, *Hipp. Maj.* 295 E, *Prot.* 344 B, etc. etc. See Schwab II p. 33.

49 B 7. **οὐδὲ ἀδικούμενον ἄρα ἀνταδικεῖν**: some are inclined 54
to doubt whether Socrates ever came so far as this beyond the ethics of his age, anticipating the Christian teaching. They base their doubt on a passage in X. *Mem.* II 6,35. But there, I think, Socrates is merely running over the points that are recognized by most men as desirable qualities in a friend. He does not himself subscribe to them.

49 C 23. **καθομολογῶν** seems to be a rare word—by the indexes, found only four times (Plato *Crito* 49 C, *Gorg.* 499 B; Andoc. 1,42; Dem. 56,14). The sense given to it in the notes is in accord with the most freq. force of *κατα-* in composit. and fits the four passages far better than that assigned it by Adam ('gradual piecemeal admission').

49 D 1. **ὀρθῶς ἔχοντος . . τοῦ ἀδικεῖν**: for the articular 55
infin. in genit. absolute, see Spieker *Am. Journ. of Philol.* 6, p. 326.

50 A 23. **ἡμῖν . . ἐλθόντες**: the dat. of *person to whom* with verbs of motion is properly a dat. *commodi aut incommodi*, not merely a locative. See G.-Kühn. § 423,17. For such dat. c. *ἐλθεῖν* in Thuc., Classen cites (at the first passage) I 13,4. 27,1. 61,1. 107,7. III 70,1. VI 46,3. VIII 96,1. Add V 50,3. Sauppe on Plat. *Prot.* 321 C cites (from prose) *Rep.* 596 E, X. *Symp.* 2,1, for *ἔρχομαι*. Cf. supra 38,9 for *ἥκω*.

50 C 15. **αὐτῶν θαυμάζοιμεν λεγόντων**: the substantive 56
thought lies in the participle, not in the word with which the partic. agrees. It is the *speaking* of the laws, not the laws themselves, that cause wonder. So in 11,25 the young disciples of Socrates find pleasure in hearing the *examination* of men (*ἀκούοντες ἐξεταζομένων τῶν ἀνθρώπων*), not in hearing the men. Cf. 82,26. 194,31. To call these participles supplementary may be grammatically correct, but in sense they are substantive participles, i.e. they stand for the abstract substantives by which we are often compelled to translate them.

The construction is sometimes called the *ab urbe condita* construction ('from the *founding* of the city'), as if peculiar to

56 Latin. But the Greek is full of it from Homer down. For Homer, see Monro *Hom. Gram.* § 245. In Herod., besides the many temporal phrases such as I 9 μετὰ δ' ἐμὲ ἐσελθόντα 'after my entrance,' I 34 μετὰ δὲ Σόλωνα οἰχόμενον 'after Solon's departure,' II 22 ἐπὶ χιόνι πεσούσῃ 'after a snow-fall,' I 170 ἐπὶ διεφθαρμένοισι Ἴωσι 'after the destruction of the Ionians,' I 15 ἐπὶ τούτου τυραννεύοντος, I 51 ὑπὸ τὸν νηὸν κατακαέντα 'about the time of the burning of the temple,' etc. (see Kühn. § 486, Anm. 3) — besides these, note espec. those passages where we are driven to a substantive transl.; as I 23 Ἀρίονα ἐξενειχθέντα 'the rescue of Arīon,' I 46 ἡ ἡγεμονίη καταιρεθεῖσα 'the overthrow of the government,' II 129 τὴν θυγατέρα ἀποθανοῦσαν 'the death of his daughter.'—Thucyd. is even yet bolder (or more awkward ?) in his use of the construction. In addition to the simple temporal phrases such as III 1,1 ἅμα τῷ σίτῳ ἀκμάζοντι; II 2,1 ἅμα ἦρι ἀρχομένῳ; VI 3,3 μετὰ Συρακούσας οἰκισθείσας 'after the founding of Syracuse'; II 49,4 μετὰ ταῦτα λωφήσαντα; and in addition to I 100,3 τὸ χωρίον κτιζόμενον 'the founding of the place'; IV 29,3 ἡ νῆσος ἐμπρησθεῖσα; IV 47,2 τοὺς ἄνδρας κομισθέντας; we have still higher value (if that is possible) in the participles προειπόντες IV 26,5 (the passage must be studied in context); ὑποτιθεῖσα IV 65,4; εἰδότες VIII 9,3; and finally in those passages where a τό is placed before the whole phrase, as in IV 63,1; V 7,2; VIII 105,2. But for all this, see Classen on IV 63,1 Anh.; Haupt in *Hermes* 3, p. 150. Consult further Gildersleeve in *A. J. P.* 13 (1892), p. 258; 19 (1898), p. 463; 20, p. 258. and for Engl. usage, Whitney's *Essentials of Engl. Gram.* §§ 446–47, 459–60, where he compares "Pardon *me* blushing" (Greek syntax) with "Pardon *my* blushing" (modern Engl.); "I saw *him* getting down from his horse" with "I saw *his* getting down."

57 **51 A** 20. **ποιῶν . . πράττειν** 'do . . act.' These verbs are often said to be without difference. But if so, they should be interchangeable; and at that all would probably hesitate, as we should in English before interchanging 'do' and 'act.' To prove indifference, Schanz cites X. *Cyr.* V 5,35. IV 1,3. *Hell.* III 4,9. II 3,49. Add *An.* VII 1,1; and cf. *Oec.* 7,2 with 7,3. Yet ποιεῖν seems to present the deed aoristically (i.e. with a swift end-to-end view), πράττειν rather as in process. Cf. ποίημα 'a thing done' 'a creation' with πρᾶγμα 'business,' 'profession.' See Rehd. *Ind. Dem.* s.v. πράττειν.

51 A 21. **οὕτως εἶ σοφός**: this postponement of the word to which οὕτως belongs, suspending the attention, was much practised by Isocrates. See Schneider on 9,39 (οὕτω περὶ αὑτοῦ θρασέως), who cites *inter alia* 5,12. 7,25,37,67. 9,6,58,67. See Rehd. *Ind. Dem.* s.v. οὕτως for exx. from other orators. See infra 61,2. 104,9. For οὕτως *after* its word, see 25,6 App.

51 D 26. **εἰ μὴ ἀρέσκοιμεν** : a purely ideal case—"remotely 58
probable"; 'should we not please.' G. M. T. §§ 501, 510.

52 A 11. **σέ, Σώκρατες** : for the various emotions (indigna- 59
tion, contempt, etc.) occasioning the omission of ὦ with vocat., see G.-Kühn. § 357,4. For exx. from the orators, see Eibel pp. 13–14. In Plato ὦ is omitted with proper names, *Lach.* 197 E, *Menon* 98 A, *Phaedr.* 264 A, *Phil.* 12 A, 21 A, *Gorg.* 489 A, 521 A, C, *Theag.* 127 B, 129 C, *Euthyd.* 294 B, *Theaet.* 144 D, *Symp.* 172 A, 173 E, 175 A, C, 213 C, D, 216 A, 217 B, 218 C. (In *Prot.* 358 A, E, 359 A, *Euthyd.* 293 D, since ἐγώ precedes, ὦ may have dropped out by haplography. In *Ap.* 25 C, *Meno* 71 D, where ὦ πρὸς Διός precedes, the ὦ may belong to the vocat., but in 164,2 ὦ πρὸς τῶν θεῶν seems to be a unit in itself.) Further, ὦ is oft. omitted in addressing slaves; παῖ, e.g. *Theaet.* 143 C, *Symp.* 175 A; παῖδες *Symp.* 212 D; but it is ὦ παῖ infra 181,14. 183,29. 188,11. Finally, ἄνδρες *Symp.* 176 A, 212 E; ἄνδρες Ἀθηναῖοι *Ap.* 30 C. This list is prob. incomplete. Schanz's *Comm. Platonicae* has not been at hand.

52 D 21. **ἄλλο τι οὖν ἂν φαῖεν** : no punct. seems advisable, 60
separating ἄλλο τι οὖν of the quotation from ἂν φαῖεν introducing it, for the reason that ἄν when c. opt. does not head its clause. Cf. *Phaedo* 87 A τί οὖν ἂν φαίη ὁ λόγος ἔτι ἀπιστεῖς. *Hipp. Maj.* 299 A μανθάνω ἂν ἴσως φαίη καὶ ἐγώ. Dem. 1,19 τί οὖν ἄν τις εἴποι σὺ γράφεις—.

52 D 22. **ἡμᾶς αὐτούς** : for the non-reflexive combination of personal pronoun and intensive, Dyroff II 92 f. cites, for Plato, *Phaedo* 79 B, *Theaet.* 160 B, *Lach.* 186 B, and others. The Greeks might have been expected to distinguish by order of words the reflexive, e.g. 'yourselves' from the differentiating 'you yourselves' (sc. and no other)—ὑμᾶς αὐτούς perhaps for the first, αὐτοὺς ὑμᾶς for the second. But they did not. From Dyroff's several reports on the Attic orators may be gathered 55 instances of the non-reflexive combination, 31 of which are in the order ὑμᾶς αὐτούς, 24 αὐτοὺς ὑμᾶς. On the other hand however, the *reflexive* order was usually steady, viz. ὑμᾶς αὐτούς. Dyroff cites but three instances of the reversed order (all from Demosthenes).

53 A 4. **δῆλον ὅτι· τίνι γὰρ ἂν πόλις ἀρέσκοι ἄνευ νόμων;** 61
the temptation is very strong to bracket this. See Cobet *Mnemos.* 2 (1874), p. 245.

53 D 3. **οἴεσθαί γε χρή** : so 63,4. 83,5. 144,28. *Prot.* 62
325 C. *Gorg.* 522 B. For other formulae used in the same logical situation, see Geb. p. 315.

53 E 18. **ὑπερχόμενος** : students cannot be too often reminded that *in Attic prose* the simple verb ἔρχομαι in the literal

62 sense 'to go (come) is confined to the present indicative. Its imperf. is not ἠρχόμην (from ἄρχομαι), but ᾖα; its subj. etc. ἴω, ἴοιμι or ἰοίην, ἴθι, ἰέναι, ἰών. But compounds in a metaphorical sense, as ὑπέρχομαι, are not so bound.

54 A 29. **θρέψονται καὶ παιδεύσονται**: mid. for passive. The passive fut. is a post-Homeric formation—the only one that occurs in Hom. being found in the late book *Il.* 10,365. Elsewhere the mid. fut. served, as it very frequently continued to serve even in the classic period. See Bl.-Kühn. § 229,2; G.-Kühn. § 378,3–4. La Roche, *Beiträge* I pp. 227–29, has collected many exx. from the heart of Att. prose. For Aristoph. see Starkie on *Vesp.* 893.

63 **54 A** 1. **ἐπιμελήσονται . . οὐχὶ ἐπιμελήσονται**: for the repetition of the word (οὔ would have sufficed), see Geb. p. 135. Exx. *Charm.* 168 A. Antiph. 5,92. Isae. 5,25. 7,20. 10,22. Dem. 9,5. Cf. supra 22,21.

PHAEDO

64 **57 A** 16. **Φλειασίων** may perhaps be allowed to stand, as an apposit. See G.-Kühn. § 463 Anm. and cf. *Meno* 70 B οἱ τοῦ σοῦ ἑταίρου Ἀριστίππου πολῖται Λαρισαίου.

66 **58 D** 16. **καὶ μήν**: in answer to a request (introduced by ἀλλά), καὶ μήν here accedes, and begins the story. So, frequently, in the debates (ἀγῶνες) of Aristophanes' comedies—the request there too being regularly prefaced by ἀλλά; e.g. *Eq.* 335, *Vesp.* 548, *Nub.* 1036,1353, *Ran.* 907, *Lys.* 486, *Eccles.* 583. Cf. infra 86,3. *Rep.* 544 B.—This is, of course, but one of the uses of the group. See Kühn. § 502,4 c; and infra 157,18. 122,5.

67 **59 C** 23. A less violent and perhaps better correction than that of inserting οὐ is the one suggested by Couvreur, viz. the insertion of ἆρ' before Ἀρίστιππος (omitted by haplography), recalling that questions with ἆρα are not infreq. where ἆρ' οὐ might be expected, e.g. *Rep.* 566 A, *Charm.* 159 B; and see Ellendt-Genthe *Lex. Soph.* s.v. ἆρα.

59 C 28. **σχεδόν τι οἶμαι τούτους** κτλ.: cf. for σχεδόν τι, *Prot.* 348 C τοῦ Καλλίου δεομένου καὶ τῶν ἄλλων σχεδόν τι τῶν παρόντων (sc. δεομένων)—where we should expect an ἁπάντων.

68 **59 E** 21. **παραγγέλλουσιν ὅπως ἂν . . τελευτήσῃ**: such an object-clause as this should, I think, be included in G. M. T. § 355. So infra 147,18 and (c. fut. ind.) 213,17. Add Isae. 7,27 and see Aken, § 151.—The same ὅπως ἄν-clause may stand as *subject*, e.g. X. *An.* VI 1,17 εἰσῄει αὐτοὺς ὅπως ἂν καὶ ἔχοντές τι οἴκαδε ἀφίκωνται. Why not, then, as object?

60 D 4. **αὐτῷ . . ἐκείνῳ**: referring to the same person. 70
This use of *ἐκεῖνος* on second mention is freq. Cf. infra 107,7. *Euthyph.* 14 D, *Phaedo* 106 B, 111 B. X. *Cyr.* IV 5,20; V 2,37. Thuc. I 132,5; 138,6. Sometimes the order is reversed (*ἐκείνῳ . . αὐτῷ*). See in general Rehd. X. *An.* VII 3,4. Frohb. Lys. 14,28 and Anh. Schn. Isoc. 1,25.

60 E 9. **εἰ πολλάκις**: not infreq. after *εἰ, μή, ἵνα μή*, the word *πολλάκις* is said to be equival. to 'perhaps.' Ast says: "*quia quod frequenter fit, id facile iterum fieri suspicamur.*" He cites (with added *ἄρα*) infra li. 23. *Phaedr.* 238 C, *Polit.* 264 B, 283 B, *Lach.* 179 B, 194 A; without *ἄρα Prot.* 361 C, *Rep.* 424 C, 584 B, etc. So too Ar. *Eccl.* 791,1105. Thuc. II 13,1.

61 C 15. **ἐθελήσει Εὔηνος καὶ πᾶς**: after the verb is uttered, 71
the subject is often thus amplified into plurality; cf. 100,24. 101,8,22. 196,16. 207,17, and prob. many other instances in the book. Sometimes indeed the verb is in the sing. though two subjects have *preceded*, as in 194,28. 244,6; espec. if both subjects are under one article, as in 239,23. 244,4,5. Not so striking are those passages where a postscript subject is added to the original one after the verb, as in 114,21. 191,18. 194,19. 196,31.

62 B 20. **οὐ μέντοι ἀλλὰ . . γε**: so li. 26. *Symp.* 173 B, 72
199 B, *Meno* 86 C; without *γε Crat.* 436 D. See Kugler, p. 26.

62 B 21. **ὁ ἐν ἀπορρήτοις λόγος**: Zeller, *Philosophie* etc. I 1[5], p. 59, refers this *λόγος* and that of 85,12 and 179,12 ff. ultimately to the Orphic theologists.

62 C 6. **πρὶν . . ἐπιπέμψῃ** without *ἄν*. So 102,19. 104,1. 73
Sturm, pp. 352,368, would insert *ἄν*; and so many editors.

63 C 24. **ὅτι . . ἥξειν**: Kühn. § 550, Anm. 3 b, for infin. 74
aft. *ὅτι* or *ὡς*. The construct. is very freq. in the MSS. But Cobet *Nov. Lect.* p. 432 would alter in every case and even Rehdantz would follow him. See his notes on Lycurg. § 90 Anh. and X. *An.* VII 5,8. Examples are: X. *Cyr.* I 6,18 *ὅτι . . εἶναι.* II 4,15 *ὅτι . . γενέσθαι.* VIII 1,25 *ὡς . . ἐθέλειν.* *Hell.* II 2,2. VI 5,42. But by all means see Geb.-Froh. Lys. 13,9 Anh.

65 B 4. **αὗται τῶν αἰσθήσεων**: the genit. of the whole (so- 78
called "partitive") is not common, I think, in dependence on a demonstrat. pronoun. I have noted Andoc. 1,82 *τούτους τῶν νόμων.* Hdt. VII 12 *ταύτην τῶν ὁδῶν.* Thuc. I 71,1. IV 119,2. V 24. Plat. *Eryx.* 393 E.

66 E 27. **φρονήσεως**: we might have expected a nomin. in 80
apposit. to the unexpressed subject of *ἔσται*; but the *οὗ*-clause intervenes and attracts. See 52,20 App.

81 **67 A** 5. **ὅτι μή** = πλὴν εἰ 42,20. So infra 208,1. The origin is of course ὅ τι μή 'what not.' Cf. ὅσον μὴ ἀνάγκη *Phaedo* 83 A. See Kühn. § 512,4 b. Cf. *Phaedr.* 274 A, *Rep.* 581 D. Hdt. I 18,143,181; II 13; III 155; Thuc. IV 26,2; sometimes with words between as Hdt. II 50 ὅτι γὰρ δὴ μή; III 125.

84 **68 E** 9. **καίτοι . . ἀλλ' ὅμως**: 39,16 App.

85 **69 D** 19. **ὧν . . οὐδέν**: Braun, I p. 26, finds that in Plato a pronoun, whether genit. or governed by a genit., *fere semper seiungitur* from its regimen. He cites, *inter alia, Phaedo* 113 B, *Lys.* 209 B. *Gorg.* 469 D (τινὰ . . αὐτῶν). *Rep.* 526 C (ὅσον . . αὐτοῦ).

87 **114 E** 24. **θάτερον** as a euphemism for τὸ κακόν originated in the dualistic system of Pythagoras (Odd Even, One Many, Right Left, Male Female, Rest Motion, Good Bad). See the brief good note *ad loc.* by Geddes. Cf. infra 166,4.

93 **118 A** 10. **πρὸς τῇ καρδίᾳ γένηται**: after γίγνεσθαι in the sense 'to reach,' 'arrive at,' 'get to,' the dative, not accus., is regularly used with the prepositions ἐπί, ὑπό, πρός, and (of course) ἐν. Cf. 94,6. 113,11. See Rehd. X. *An.* I 5,17.

118 A 11. **ἤδη . . καί** 'already . . *when*': so infra 99,26. Cf. X. *An.* II 1,7. IV 6,2. VI 4,26. VII 4,16. The same 'when' καί after a simple τε, e.g. X. *An.* IV 2,12. *Cyr.* II 1,10; after οὔπω infra 159,23. *Euthyd.* 273 A. But instead of καί, a relat. such as ἡνίκα *may* be used; so X. *An.* I 8,1.

118 A 12. **ἦν . . ψυχόμενα**: wherein the periphrasis here differs from ἐψύχετο, I do not see. On the whole matter of periphrases by means of partic. c. εἶναι or γίγνεσθαι, see Alexander, *A. J. P.* 4 (1883), p. 291. The justification and special significance is often plain (e.g. in 39,9 and 96,8 because of the preceding adject.; in 146,26. 181,18,22. 185,20. 241,5. 254,30 because εἶναι is not a mere copula, but predicates existence—the partic. being more or less circumstantial or supplementary. So too perhaps 220,11,12). But here I fail to follow Alexander's transl. 'was actually growing cold' (as foreseen).

The theoretic difference between verb and periphrasis is simple. The verb asserts that the act is taking place, that its subject is manifesting that activity; e.g. πίνει 'he is drinking.' The periphrasis πίνων ἐστί asserts that the subject has a certain quality which *may* manifest itself in action—that he belongs to a certain class. Cf. any adjectival predicate, as πονηρός ἐστι. If the habit becomes fixed upon the man, we say ποτικός ἐστι, using the adjective. Should he become a confirmed tippler, we use the noun and say πότης ἐστί. Thus does the single act of the verb become by repetition characteristic, and finally harden into concrete substantivism. —The partic. characterizes, but (theoretically) does not assert the particular act. And it should be noted that certain participles have gone further than others toward adjectival or even substantival equivalence; e.g. προσήκων, συμφέρων, διαφέρων. See the article.

SYMPOSIUM

175 E 19. **καλῶς γε ποιῶν** (*ἥκεις*): cf. 69,25 *εὖ γ' ἐποίησας* 94
ἀναμνήσας με—a more emphatic form of approval, inasmuch as *ποιῶν* is here made the principal verb. See Sandys on Dem. *First Olynthiac* § 28.

175 B 10. **πάντως παρατίθετε**: what *πάντως* signifies, I do 95
not see. It is used in intelligible fashion with imperatives elsewhere, e.g. X. *Oec.* 3,12. 12,11. 17,7 (c. subj. hortat.). *Cyr.* VII 1,18. VIII 3,27. It is found in the answer-formula *πάντως* (*δή*)*που*. It sometimes seems to mean 'anyhow,' 'be that as it may' (*δ' οὖν*). But here I cannot find its logical connection.—The word is little used outside of comic poetry and Plato—but 4 times in the orators (so far as they have been indexed), viz. Andoc. 1,102. [4,7.] Lys. 12,6. Demos. 18,256. In Thuc. 3 times (V 41,3. VI 20,1. VII 87,6). In Xenoph. here and there, e.g. in *Hell.* but once (II 3,47). Examples in this vol.: 14,29. 29,4. 41,18. 83,21. 111,18. 118,10.

175 C 24. **ἵνα καί** 'just to —'; the adverb *καί* is often our Engl. 'just,' when it *evens up* one thing with another, e.g. fact with requirement or expectation, cause with effect (or vice versa). Of course, *καί* after *ἵνα* may sometimes belong to the following word (e.g. 271,22), but in these instances it seems to mean, with *ἵνα*, 'just to —': *Gorg.* 467 C *ἵνα καὶ εἰδῶ ὅ τι λέγεις* 'just to see what you'll say.' 501 C. *Lys.* 204 A *ἵνα καὶ ἴδῃς*. *Rep.* 346 A *ἵνα τι καὶ περαίνωμεν*. 351 A. 445 C. *Alc.* I 106 C. *Menon* 75 A. *Symp.* 174 B. 186 B. *Crat.* 407 E. Xen. *Oec.* 11,2. Lys. 21,9. 25,13. In the same way *ἵνα καὶ μή* *Lach.* 194 A. But N.B. *ἵνα μὴ καί* is probably *not* to be so taken. Cf. *Theaet.* 145 C. 173 B. *Apol.* 22 A (supra 9,15).

175 D 30. **κενότερον**, not *κενώτερον*, because originally *κενϝός*. So *στενότερος*, not *στενώτερος*, because *στενϝός*. Bl.-Kühn. § 154, Anm. 2.

215 B 3. **ὁ μέν γε . . σὺ δέ** (10): what is the function of 97
γε? By all means see Geb.-Froh. Lys. 13,27 Anh., where it is maintained (contrary to Kuhn. § 503,3 d) "das *γε* bezieht sich nicht auf das Wort vor *μέν*, auch nicht blos auf das erste Glied, sondern (wie das *τοί* in *ἤτοι . . ἤ*) auf den Gesamtinhalt des Satzes, der dadurch als etwas Unzweifelhaftes oder allgemein Anerkanntes gekennzeichnet wird. Im Deutschen lässt sich die Partikel in der Regel durch *ja* oder *doch* übersetzen." There follow endless examples.

215 C 8. **μόνα κατέχεσθαι**: *μόνος* is a favourite hyperbole. So 102,9. Froh. Lys. 14,7 cites instances from Lyc. 143; Lys. 10,3; 30,5; 31,33. Demos. 21,195. 26,13.

97 **215 E** 25. **τῶν λόγων τούτου**: on the predic. posit. of *τούτου*, see G.-Kühn. § 464,4 end. Cf. Ar. *Pax* 890, *Lys.* 360, *Av.* 922, *Plut.* 1110; also the manuscript readings for Dein. 1,79,92,111. Isae. 9,10,36. 10,4. Demos. 43,15. 53,7. See Rehd. *Ind. Dem.* s.v. *οὗτος*; he would excuse the predic. posit. only if another attribute be present, as in Demos. 4,3 *τῇ νῦν ὕβρει τούτου* (so 21,80,158. 54,2). Consult espec. Sobolewski p. 111.

98 **216 B** 17. **τιμῆς τῆς ὑπὸ τῶν πολλῶν**: agent c. *ὑπό*, as if *τιμῆς* were *τοῦ τιμᾶσθαι*. So with *θεραπεία* *Prot.* 354 A. *δυναστεία* *Polit.* 291 D. *ἐπίταγμα* *Rep.* 359 A. *δεσμός* *Rep.* 390 C. *παίδευσις* X. *Mem.* II 1,34. *τιμή* *Hiero* 7,6 (*παρά*). *Cyr.* III 3,2. *γραφή* *Mem.* IV 4,4. *ἀξίωμα* Thuc. I 130,1. VI 15,3. *δόξασμα* I 141,7. *ἀρχή* II 65,9.

Cf. infra c. *πάθη* 202,17. *δεσμοί* 203,15. *θάνατος* 255 22. And with adjectives: 149,17. 172,23. 226,19. 253,31.

219 E 26. **τοῖς πόνοις . . περιῆν**: surely the *ἐν* inserted by some editors is unnecessary. Cf. the simple dat. with *περίειμι* 'to excel' in Thuc. I 121,4. II 13,8. III 45,1. VI 22,1. X. *Hell.* III 4,2. *An.* I 8,13. 9,24.

99 **220 B** 12. **οἵου δεινοτάτου**: Kühn. § 555,3. 14. **θαυμαστὰ ὅσα**: Kühn. § 555, Anm. 15.

220 C 28. **θαυμάζοντες ἄλλος ἄλλῳ ἔλεγεν**: Rehd. X. *An.* VII 3,47 and *Ind. Dem.* s.v. Apposition, for many exx. of the predic. verb taking the number of the distributive appositives *ἄλλος* and *ἕκαστος*.

101 **221 C** 13. **ἐπιτηδευμάτων**: on this free genit. (*quod attinet ad*—), see Krüg. 47,3,3; slightly different is G.-Kühn. § 417, Anm. 11. Cf. Thuc. V 18,8. X. *Oec.* 3,11 (ubi v. Holden). 11,11. Plat. *Rep.* 576 D; and also the genit. following *τί δέ* without verb; e.g. 227,12. *Phaedo* 78 D. *Gorg.* 509 D, and freq.

221 D 24. **εἰ μὴ . . εἰ**, 'unless.' So infra 133,18. *Rep.* 581 D. *Symp.* 205 E. *Lach.* 196 A. Thuc. I 17. Kühn. § 577,8. Krüg. 65,5,11.

221 D 27. **καὶ γὰρ οὖν**: a rather rare strengthening of the familiar *καὶ γάρ*, just as we found *γὰρ οὖν* was sometimes used for *γάρ* (23,21 App.). It is found once in Aesch. (*Ag.* 524), once in Soph. (*Ant.* 489), 6 times in X. *An.*, twice in *Hellen.*, not once in *Cyrop.* (I quote Joost on Xen.'s usage). Cf. Plato *Lach.* 184 B, and perhaps elsewhere. Not in Aristoph., and prob. not in the orators.

102 **222 A** 8. **ἰδὼν δή**: others retain the MSS. reading *ἰδὼν ἄν*, the *αν* going with the fut. indic. *εὑρήσει*, as implied in 22,1. 23,15. 62,2.

REPUBLIC

487 C 10. **ἐπεί** κτλ. : this is one of the many passages where **105**
for convenience *ἐπεί* is often translated 'although' (see L. & S. s.v. B 4; G. M. T. § 719,2). But the student should bear in mind that *ἐπεί* never really means 'although.' Perhaps it is but mental sloth that can tolerate such a wide divergence from the Greek. For as a matter of fact *ἐπεί* is always 'since' causal,—when it is not purely temporal. Certainly it cannot mean *both* 'since' and 'although.'

The confusion arises from failing to see that the *ἐπεί*-clauses which we are tempted to translate by 'although' give the reason, not for the previous fact, but for the statement of that fact or for some part of that statement. The speaker suddenly drops objective discourse and becomes parenthetic, diving as it were to swim a moment in subjectivity. Always we may supply: '(I say this and not the opposite) *for*'; or '(I make use of this particular word or phrase rather than any other) *for*.' In *Gorg.* 471 E, for instance, Socrates says: "I don't admit a single thing you say," to which Polus replies *οὐ γὰρ ἐθέλεις, ἐπεὶ δοκεῖ γέ σοι ὡς ἐγὼ λέγω* 'that's because you *won't*; for you do *believe* (*γε*) what I say.' Now of course if Socrates believed Polus's words, that would be, not a reason for refusing assent, but rather the best of reasons for being willing to assent. The *ἐπεί*-clause consequently does not belong to the objective context. Rather, Polus adds it to explain why he had used 'won't'; I say that 'won't,' and nothing else, is the reason for your refusal to agree with me, *because* etc. (Let it be carefully noted that *γε* is almost the constant attendant on this *ἐπεί*, indicating very delicately the logical accent—offering the key to the unexpressed thought in the speaker's mind.) Again in *Theaet.* 142 C 'But how is it he would not stop here at Megara?' —'He was in a hurry to get home. Since, for myself, *I* begged him to stop; but he wouldn't' *ἠπείγετο οἴκαδε· ἐπεὶ ἔγωγ' ἐδεόμην . . ἀλλ' οὐκ ἤθελεν.* That is, it must have been his home-sickness, and no coldness on *my* part, that was the reason for his refusing to stop; for as far as I was concerned (*ἔγωγε*) etc.—So would *ἐπεί* be proper, e.g. in: "You may thank *him* for your fall; for *I* should have prevented it." "You will not be pleased; for as for myself, it makes no difference."

The following passages offer more or less difficulty, but always the *ἐπεί . . γε* clause will prove to contain a subjective explanation or justification: *Euthyph.* 9 B. *Ap.* 19 E, 37 A. *Prot.* 317 A, 333 C, 335 C (*bis*), 336 D, 338 C, 353 A. *Theaet.* 150 A, 150 C, 158 B, 167 A, 167 C (cf. 5,17 n.). *Symp.* 187 A.

105 *Rep.* 358 C, 368 B, 619 D. *Crat.* 410 A. *Cleit.* 410 C. *Theag.* 128 B (*bis*). *Legg.* 769 B. Thucyd. VI 89,6. VII 30,2. Andoc. 1,94. Lys. 26,18. Demos. 9,29,40. 18,49.

This kind of ἐπεί-clause is but one of the many threads of subjective woof that we find woven into the objective warp of Greek discourse. For example, (1) great numbers of γάρ-clauses can be only so explained; see 36,1 n.; (2) little qualifying phrases such as ὡς ἔπος εἰπεῖν, that betray the speaker's consciousness of self (see Grünenwald, p. 21); (3) the corrective ἤ, where a question is withdrawn and a more fitting one substituted (= 'or rather let me ask'; see 16,14 n.); (4) all confirmative adverbs such as μήν, τοι, δήπου, which are personal and intrusive; (5) μή, whether deprecating, cautious, prayerful, or swearful; (6) all instances of (ἐπι)διόρθωσις, προδιόρθωσις, *simm.*, for which see Geb.-Froh. Lys. 12,62 Anh.; (7) espec. ἀναδίπλωσις (διπλασιασμός) such as μέγας γὰρ ὁ ἀγών, ὦ φίλε Γλαύκων, μέγας; or *Eheu fugaces Posthume, Posthume, labuntur anni* (Hor.). On this see Kolster *Philol.* 5, p. 601: "Das erste Posthume ist einfache Anrede, während das zweite andeutet, dass die Persönlichkeit des Posthumus zu dem Satze in einem näheren Verhältnisse stehe. . . Wo nur immer sich die Anadiplosis findet, da sind gleichsam zwei Personen in dem Redenden,—Verstand und Gefühl, welche zugleich das Wort ergreifen, so dass das letztere die Worte des ersteren bestätigt." (8) *any* clause, indeed, may desert the objective surface of the sentence to be justified only by searching the hidden emotions of the speaker. See the beautiful example of a ἵνα-clause in *Od.* 8,461 where Nausicaa bids goodbye to Odysseus: χαῖρε, ξεῖν', ἵνα καί ποτ' ἐὼν ἐν πατρίδι γαίῃ | μνήσῃ ἐμεῖο. That is: I *say* χαῖρε, that you may etc.

Style is the man. Perhaps one of the best ways to measure a writer's individualism would be to note how often and in how many forms he allows his personality to emerge from his objective discourse.

PROTAGORAS

107 **310 D** 9. **ἐν τούτῳ**: for ἐν cf. 111,6. *Prot.* 319 C, 354 E, 356 D, 357 A. A long list is given by Rehd. Lyc. 52, Anh.

108 **311 C** 10. **τί ἂν ἀπεκρίνω**: other exx. of aor. where we should expect imperf. are: *Symp.* 199 D εἶπες, *Euthyph.* 12 D εἶπον, *Ion* 540 D ἔγνως, *Theag.* 123 B ἀπεκρίνω, *Meno* 72 B, 86 D, *Gorg.* 447 D, 514 D.

109 **312 B** 26. **μέλλεις . . παρασχεῖν**: for aor. inf. after μέλλω, see G. M. T. § 74. Schanz, *Proleg. ad Symp.* p. vii, cites about a score of instances from Plato.

312 E 26. **οὐκέτι** not infrequently must be translated 'not 110
now,' 'not likewise (as before).' Cf., e.g., infra 123,13. Thuc. I 126,6. II 93,4. VIII 23,4. Xen. *Cyr.* I 5,8. 6,27. IV 3,4. VII 5,76. Herod. VI 17. Plato *Euthyd.* 280 A; *Prot.* 321 D; *Rep.* 468 B, 430 D; *Meno* 93 A.

313 A 5. **ὃ δὲ . . περὶ δὲ τούτου**: for this special form of 111
resumption in *argument. ex contrar.*, see Geb. p. 110.

313 C 29. **ὅπως μή** with "sigmatic" aor. subjunct. *ἐξαπατήσῃ*. For the matter of "Dawes' Canon," see G. M. T. § 364 (and § 283); Weber pp. 261–62; Stallb. on *Gorg.* 480 A; Kühn. § 553, Anm. 5; Krüg. 54,8,5. For X. *Mem.* see Gilbert's *Praefat.* (Teubner text) on I 2,37.

315 C 4. **καὶ μὲν δὴ . . γε**: this is a more emphatic form 115
of transition than *καὶ μὴν . . γε* (see 122,5 App.) or *καὶ δή* 'yes indeed, and.' In *Gorg.* 507 A B, after two important points are won by *καὶ μήν*, a third and last is added as a climax by *καὶ μὲν δή*. So *Rep.* 464 B, *Symp.* 197 A.—For Lysias, see Geb.-Frohb. on 12,35 who cite *inter alia* 12,30,49. 7,36. 10,5,29. 14,12,32,34,43; and the Lysias-passage in *Phaedr.* 231 D, 232 B E, 233 A. For Isoc., who preferred *καὶ μὲν δὴ καί*, see Schn. on 7,66 (e.g. 3,36. 4,40. 8,24. 11,21,36,39).

On *καὶ μὲν δή* to mark assent, see 208,17 App.

315 C 5. **γὰρ ἄρα**: infra 180,12. *Gorg.* 469 D. *Symp.* 205 B. *Rep.* 438 A. *Legg.* 698 D. Kühn. § 509,8 b.

GORGIAS

472 A 2. **ἐν Πυθοῖ**: for prepos. c. locat., see Bl.-Kühn. 117
§ 336,4 δ; Frohb. Lys. 19,28 ("die Hinzufügung von *ἐν* ist nirgends ausgeschlossen"), Krüg. § 46,1,3. But perhaps those are right who alter to *ἐν* Πυθίου (sc. *τεμένει*), making it refer to the precinct of the temple to the Pythian Apollo in Athens.

473 C 9. **τυραννίδι ἐπιβουλεύων**, 'with a view to tyranny,' 119
not 'against' it. So *Menex.* 241 E. *Epist.* 7,329 C. Lysias 28,8. Herod. *passim.* L. & S., s.v., 2.

474 E 5. **καὶ μὴν . . γε** is not a formula of transition, that 122
merely itemizes like *ἔτι δέ*. It marks ascending importance. See 132,5. *Gorg.* 487 D, 504 B, 507 A. *Phaedo* 71 A, 72 E. *Meno* 87 D, 98 C. *Erast.* 138 B. *Alc.* I 130 A. II 139 B.—For many instances from the orators, see Geb.-Froh. Lys. 12,27 Anh.; Schn. Isoc. 9,36 (e.g. 4,115,145,185. 5,96,97,103). For the yet more emphatic *καὶ μὲν δή*, see 115,4 App.

124 **475 D** 1. **παρέχων** without reflex., 'submitting *yourself*.' So 133,25. *Gorg.* 456 B. *Charm.* 176 B, etc. See Stallb.; Ar. *Nub.* 422. Soph. *Aj.* 1146.

131 **479 C** 25. **πᾶν ποιοῦσιν ὥστε δίκην μὴ διδόναι**: a *purposed* result—but one in which we feel the purpose so much more strongly than the result, that we should have expected a *ἵνα*-clause. G. M. T. § 587,3. Cf. supra 36,28. 37,19.

134 **481 A** 19. **ὅπως μὴ δῷ** *κτλ.*: note the varying syntax of *ὅπως*—with simple subjunct., subjunct. with *ἄν* (li. 21), fut. indic. (26 and 28). Whatever the difference may be, it must be slight. Kühn. § 552, Anm. 4. But Lodge's note *ad loc.* is better.

137 **484 A** 21. **ἀνεφάνη**: "gnomic" aor. The Greek present tense in vivid situation is too slow. It unrols a panorama (action in process), when we want a flash. *ἀναφαίνεται* says 'he . . is . . rising . . to . . view,' whereas we wish a meteoric rush. But the Greek had no such timeless, swift, aoristic present (barring a *φημί* or so). What did it do? It shut its eye to the augment, and used the *aorist*! Examples are: 149,13,21,22. 151,20,28. 209,20,27. 268,27,28. 269,1.

144 **521 E** 13. **κρινοῦμαι**: Blass distinguishes this pres. (durative) fut. pass. from *κριθήσομαι* the aoristic fut. pass. See Bl.-Kühn. II pp. 466,585.

522 A 22. **οὐχ ὥσπερ ἐγώ** *κτλ.*: this (for us abbreviated) form of comparison also in *Prot.* 341 A. *Symp.* 179 E, 189 C. *Epist.* I 333 A. Demos. 21,218; *prooim.* 35,3. Ar. *Eq.* 784. Eur. *Bacch.* 929. *Eubul.* 44 (Koch). Paul II *Corinth.* 3,13. See Kuhn. § 600,2. Rehd. *Ind. Dem.* 2, s.v. Ellipse. Infra 235,13.

522 A 27. **ὁπόσον οἴει** *κτλ.*: such indirect questions, with *εἰπέ μοι* or *ἡδέως ἂν ἀκούσαιμι* understood, are found infra 154,16 (*ὁπότερον*). *Charm.* 170 C (*ὅ τι*). *Meno* 74 D. *Lysis* 212 C. *Rep.* 348 B. 578 E. *Alcib.* I 110 C. Lysias 30,4. Many editors change, needlessly. Cf. *ὅπως* c. fut. indic. with the dominating *σκόπει* omitted; Aristotle's *μή* (*ποτε*) with a *ζητητέον* or the like omitted. For later usage, see Schmid's *Atticismus* IV p. 73; Gregory in Tischendorf's *N. T.* III^{8}, p. 125, or Blass's *Gram. des Neutestam. Griechisch.* § 77,2.

148 **524 B** 17. **τό τε σῶμα τὴν φύσιν τὴν αὐτοῦ** (*ἔχει*): this is not a random fancy of Plato's, but the superstition of all primitive folk. Hence arose, in Greece, the murderers' terrible custom of cutting off the extremities of their victims, that thus maimed they should be powerless for vengeance. So was Agamemnon's body treated by his murderous wife. See L. & S.

s.v. *μασχαλίζω*; Kittredge in *A.J.P.* 6 (1885), p. 151; Rohde's *Psyche* p. 253.

525 C 14. **τοῖς τῶν ἀδίκων ἀφικνουμένοις**: the attributive posit. of a partit. genit. is rare. Stahl, on Thuc. VI 62,5, denying it altogether between art. and true substantive, rejects *τῶν Σικελῶν* of that passage, and will admit it only betw. art. and substantivized adject. or (as here) substantivized partic. He cites Thuc. I 126,11. III 22,5. 65,3. See G.-Kuhn. § 464, Anm. 1 end. 150

525 E 1. **καί**: I am not sure that *καί* has the right reference in my translat., but prefer that to Cron's explanation, who says: *καί* "hat seine Beziehung in *δυναμένων*: wie sie *δυνάμενοι* sind, so sind sie *auch σφόδρα πονηροί*." Cope translates *εἰσὶ καί* 'actually belong.' But that would surely be *καί εἰσι*. 151

EUTHYDEMUS

275 E 18. **καὶ μήν** 'and (yet) surely'—adversative; so *Gorg.* 452 C, 511 C. *Phaedo* 92 C. *Meno* 98 B. *Hipparch.* 231 D. It is about equiv. to *καίτοι*, *καὶ μὲν δή* (in its adversat. use), *ἀλλὰ μήν*; see Geb. p. 272; Schn. Isoc. 4,33. Cf. infra 188,17. 221,12. 157

276 C 19. **οὐκ εὖ**: the MSS. have *οὐκ εὐθύς*. May they not be right? Is not Dionysodorus so hopelessly sunk in frivolity that he closes with a pun on his brother's name—*οὐκ εὐθὺς ἄρτι Εὐθυ-δήμῳ ἀπεκρίνω*? See L. & S. s.v. *εὐθύς*, B II 3 for the sense 'simply,' 'straight,' of manner. 158

276 E 5. **τοιγάρτοι**: so 159,5. 172,2. Kugler, p. 38, cites *Phaedo* 82 D; *Symp.* 179 D; *Lach.* 183 A; *Gorg.* 471 C, 494 D; *Rep.* 409 B, 454 C, 568 B. The word is not common—Demos. 5 times, Lys. 2, Andoc. 4 times, etc. 159

277 A 17. **ἆρα οὐ μανθάνεις**: for the sake of the contrast between 'you' and *ὁ μὴ ἐπιστάμενος* in the foll. line, we might have expected a *σὺ μέν* before *οὐ μανθάνεις*. But sometimes the contrast does not seem to be foreseen. Cf. 165,17–18. Stallb. cites X. *Cyr.* IV 5,31 and other places.

283 A 19. **ὅπερ οὖν καὶ συνέβη**: a freq. formula; cf. equivalent phrases in *Charm.* 155 B. *Euthyph.* 4 D. *Crat.* 404 B. 160

293 E 15. **τοῦτο τὸ αὐτὸ πάθος**: a rare order. Almost invariably in Plato it is *τὸ αὐτὸ τοῦτο*, whether with or without foll. substantive. Schanz *Nov. Comm.* p. 81. 163

MENON

178 **80 D** 24. **εἰ ὅτι μάλιστα**— 'no matter how much —.' Ast cites *Crat.* 435 A. *Euthyph.* 4 D, 9 C. *Alc.* I 106 A, 113 D. *Charm.* 160 C.

REPUBLIC

192 **327 D** 4. **ὡς . . μὴ ἀκουσομένων, οὕτω**: just such a genit. absol. c. ὡς, followed by an epanaleptic οὕτω as here, is found in X. *Cyr.* I 6,11 (οὕτως ἔχε τὴν γνώμην); II 3,15 (οὕτως . . γίγνωσκε); VIII 7,10 (οὕτως ἀποδέχεσθε); *Anab.* I 3,6 (οὕτω τὴν γνώμην ἔχετε). Isoc. 2,12 (οὕτω διάκεισο τὴν γνώμην). Thuc. VII 15,1 (οὕτω τὴν γνώμην ἔχετε). Cf. *Phaedr.* 244 C. *Rep.* 523 C. *Crat.* 439 C, and freq. Cf. supra 117,29.

328 B 25. **διὰ χρόνου**: the phrase is freq., and the sense fixed. Cf. *Phaedr.* 247 D. Xen. *Cyr.* I 4,28. V 5,41. Thuc. II 94,3. Ar. *Vesp.* 1252,1476. *Pax* 570,710. *Lys.* 904. *Plut.* 1045,1055. Aesch. *Pers.* 741. Soph. *Phil.* 758.

328 C 31. **ὦ Σώκρατες, οὐ δέ**: for this pre-position of vocat., ignored by the foll. conjunct., cf. 162,17. *Phil.* 48 D. *Legg.* 890 D. 963 B. (*Theag.* 127 C.) X. *Mem.* I 3,13. II 1,26. 9,2. Stein on Hdt. VII 141,23.

193 **328 D** 12. **καὶ μήν** in hearty assent. Cf. *Phaedo* 92 A. *Hipp. Maj.* 300 C. *Hipp. Min.* 363 A. See Index for other uses.

196 **330 E** 23. **ὥσπερ** is taken with the partic ὤν in G. M. T. § 874.

197 **331 A** 8. **οὔ τι . . ἀλλά**: a freq. formula. Stallb. cites *Hipp. Maj.* 297 E. *Phaedo* 81 D. *Theaet.* 156 E. *Crat.* 393 B. *Alc.* I 135 E. *Tim.* 19 D. *Rep.* 373 E, 438 E.

198 **331 D** 4. **καὶ μέντοι καί**: the first καί is perhaps adverb; 'yes indeed, and.' Cf. καὶ μήν 193,12. Other instances are: 2,8. *Theaet.* 144 C. *Rep.* 588 A. *Lys.* 216 A. *Phaedr.* 266 B. *Alc.* I 113 C. *Theag.* 127 B. *Eryx.* 397 D. Kugler, p. 24, is incomplete.

203 **378 C** 6. **ποικιλτέον**: regarding the Peplos of Athene Polias and her temple, see Frazer's *Pausanias* II, p. 574.

208 **406 A** 17. **καὶ μὲν δὴ . . γε** marks entire assent. So 272,13. *Rep.* 526 B, 528 D. *Crat.* 396 D. For its use in marked transition, see 115,4 App.—Like καὶ μήν (157,18 App.), it is sometimes used in adversat. sense = καίτοι; e.g. *Polit.* 287 D. *Hipp. Maj.* 290 A. *Crat.* 428 A. See espec. Thuc. III 113,4.

407 A 4. **ἀκούεις**: on the tense, see G.-Kühn. § 382,4. 210

408 B 21. **κἄν** = *καί*. So 218,6. 228,9. *Polit.* 308 C. 211
Soph. 267 D. *Phil.* 58 C. *Phaedo* 71 B. *Prot.* 328 B. *Rep.* 477 A. 579 D. *Theag.* 121 A. *Meno* 72 C. Cf. 2,17 App. on *ὥσπερ ἂν εἰ*. See G.-Kühn. § 398, Anm. 2.

414 D 14. **ὁποίᾳ . . ποίοις**: shift in indir. quest. from 212
indef. relat. to interrog. So X. *Mem.* IV 4,13 *ὁποῖον . . ποῖον*. *Cyr.* I 6,43 *ὅπως . . πῶς*. VII 3,10 *ὅ τι . . τί*, and freq.; also the reversed order sometimes, as supra 51,25 *τί . . ὅ τι*. *Gorg.* 500 A *ποῖα . . ὁποῖα*.

414 E 25. **ὡς περὶ μητρός, τῆς χώρας**: the prepos. is not repeated with the main substantive (here *χώρας*), when already used in a *ὡς*-clause of comparison. So 234,15. *Prot.* 337 E. *Rep.* 545 E. *Theaet.* 170 A. Yet cf. supra 82,3. 88,21. G.-Kühn. § 451,6. (See 19,1 App. for omission of prep. with relat.)

472 C 8. **πλεῖστα τῶν ἄλλων** : for a complete list of super- 217
latives c. genit. of comparison (i.e. those of the *τῶν ἄλλων*, *τῶν πρότερον* type) for classic Greek, see Schwab II, p. 34 ff. In the *Republic*, for instance, 472 C, 578 B, 603 E.

492 E 24. **παρὰ τὴν τούτων παιδείαν**: Stallb. translates 221
παρά by *iuxta*; Davies and Vaughan, 'in close contact with.' The context as well as the *usus loquendi* is against them.

493 C 19. **ὀνομάζοι ταῦτα ἐπὶ ταῖς** *κτλ*. 'put these names 222
to —.' So *ἐπί* c. dat. after *ὀνομάζω* *Alc.* I 108 A, 135 C; after *καλέω* *Rep.* 470 B, *Parm.* 147 D, 164 B, *Euthyd.* 277 E, *Soph.* 218 C.

515 B 12. **τί δὲ τῶν παραφερομένων**; so the genit. *Rep.* 227
470 A, 582 C. *Gorg.* 509 D. *Phaedo* 78 D. G.-Kuhn. § 417, Anm. 11.

539 B 20. **σε λεληθέναι ὅτι . . ὡς**: not infrequently is a 234
conjunct., after intervening matter, repeated, or as here an equivalent given. So *Legg.* 736 C. *Hipp. Maj.* 281 C. *Rep.* 470 D. *Epist.* 7,335. Herod. III 71, IX 6. X. *Cyr.* V 3,30. VI 4,5. *Anab.* V 6,19. VII 4,5. *Hell.* VI 4,37. 5,13. Andoc. 1,29 (*ὡς . . οἷα*). (Soph. *Ant.* 2 *ὅ τι . . ὁποῖον*?)

558 A 8. **ἀνθρώπων καταψηφισθέντων θανάτου ἢ φυγῆς**: 237
Adam alters to *θάνατον ἢ φυγήν*. But why not let the text stand, and (if one dislikes the usual interpretation) make *θανάτου* the genit. absol. c. partic., taking *ἀνθρώπων* as the object after *κατα-*? (That the ptc. is plural makes, of course, no difference.) At all events, in the ten orators so far as indexed, I can find no instance of the *personal* passive use of this verb (e.g. *ὁ ἄνθρωπος κατεψηφίσθη*).

558 A 9. **εἶδες . . αὐτῶν μενόντων**: some scholars construe

237 the genit. here directly with the verb, comparing the genit. after the general verbs of perception such as αἰσθάνομαι (e.g. 10,4) and γιγνώσκω (17,24).

238 **562 C** 11. **ᾖα . . ἐρῶν**: so *Theaet.* 180 C, 198 E. *Rep.* 449 A. For Herod., see Stein on I 5,11, who cites I 122,11. 194,3. II 11,4. 35,1. 40,4. 99,3. III 6,2. IV 82,9. V 62,4.

244 **590 A** 2. **τὸ δεινὸν τὸ μέγα ἐκεῖνο θρέμμα**: for the duplicated art., see G.-Kühn. § 464,7 c. Cf. 193,6. 210,13. *Rep.* 368 B, 565 D. *Symp.* 213 E. *Hipp. Maj.* 281 D, etc.

245 **591 C** 26. **ξυντείνας βιώσεται**: an example probably of the timeless aor. partic., whose action is contemporary and identical with that of the main verb; 'a life of strain and tension.' See 24,6 App.

257 **621 B** 13. **γενέσθαι . . γενέσθαι**: the repetition after so short an interval may be, for us, unpleasing. But cf. ἐλέγετο 49,3. ἐλέσθαι 254,17. γίγνοιτο *Phaedr.* 245 D. ἐγένετο . . γίγνεται X. *Hell.* IV 3,8. ἐπὶ τὸ ἄκρον X. *An.* III 4,44. See Rehd. X. *An.* VII 5,7 and *Ind. Dem.* s.v. Antistrophe; Geb.-Froh. Lys. 13,49 Anh.

621 B 21. **μῦθος ἐσώθη**: for an opinion on the phrase differing from that of Photius, as cited, see Badham *Phileb.* 14 A.

PHAEDRUS

258 **229 A** 14. **πρόαγε δή**: the sure and final test of one's knowledge of Greek is to be applied to his knowledge of the particles. Any man can remember the words for 'horse,' 'stone,' and other visibles, and also the rules for their syntax. But a feeling for, and control of, these little airy *form*-words—meaning nothing in particular, but everything to the ultimate sense and character of the sentence—is to be acquired only by closest observation, comparison, and wide reading. Let the student tabulate other particles such as δή, a scheme of which is here given:—

I δή with Conjunctions; e.g. ἀλλὰ δή, ἀλλὰ μὲν δ., γὰρ δ., δὲ δ., καὶ δ.—for which see the Index; cf. also οὖν δή 132,28. οὔκουν δή 210,2. γὰρ οὖν δή 249,30. Further, with subordinating conjunctions, as εἰ δή 7,15. 21,20. 127,25. 135,1; ἵνα δή 180,26. 239,5,16. 240,13; ὅταν δή 239,20; ὅτι δή 25,12; ὡς δή 163,7.

II δή itself a Quasi-Conjunction; e.g. 4,6. 9,14. 13,11. 30,1. 34,16. 46,1. 62,18. 149,2. 156,19. 218,8. 250,9,17, etc. Cf. also its use after demonstrat. pronouns at head of sent.

III δή with Pronouns; e.g. (1) with demonstrat. 10,27.

34,22. 35,18. 55,15. 59,11. 66,6,25. 70,28. 88,11. 258
100,27. 126,1. 136,25. 147,13, etc. (2) with relat. 4,18.
14,1. 19,1,22. 25,20. 37,6. 39,11. 60,29. 62,10. 65,16.
68,28. 85,19. 93,13. 97,21. 99,2, etc. (3) with interrog.
—often δὲ δή, δὴ οὖν or οὖν δή 4,20. 7,4. 14,12. 28,14. 30,25.
41,13. 43,28. 54,11. 59,15. 64,13. 75,27, etc.

IV δή with Imperatives: 6,31. 13,24. 15,17. 17,31. 26,9. 49,18,29. 51,5. 54,29. 74,14. 76,29. 90,31. 110,2. 121,4. 122,27. 146,11, etc.

V δή in combination with Single Words: 7,20. 16,14. 17,24. 25,5. 39,17. 40,19. 44,10. 45,20. 47,29. 68,30. 69,22. 72,23. 75,21. 82,28. 89,3,6. 98,1. 99,14. 101,1. 145,12. 195,14. 196,4,20. 204,4. 207,24. 218,28. 222,11,31. 224,17 (in apodosis), etc. See also γε δή in Index.

Other and rarer uses are omitted.

229 D 25. **καὶ . . δέ,** thus beginning a clause, is in Plato 259
extremely rare. Xenophon is fond of the formula, and Demos.
uses it freely; the other orators seldom. See Froh. Lys. 19,5n.
and Anh. So too is it rare in tragedy, not a dozen times in
Aristoph., nor a dozen in Thucydides.

230 B 18. **ὡς ἀκμὴν ἔχει:** other examples of ὡς exclam. 260
with a verb are: 143,21 ὥς μοι δοκεῖς πιστεύειν—. 212,10 ὡς
ἔοικας ὀκνοῦντι λέγειν. *Gorg.* 490 E ὡς ἀεὶ ταὐτὰ λέγεις. *Hipp.
Maj.* 281 A ὡς διὰ χρόνου ἡμῖν κατῆρας εἰς τὰς Ἀθήνας.

INDEX OF PROPER NAMES

᾿Αγάθων, *-ωνος*, *Agăthon*, Athenian tragic poet of some originality, but wholly rhetorical; so that, as he himself said, if you remove his antitheses, *λέληθας σαυτὸν τὸν ᾿Αγάθωνα ἐκ τοῦ Αγάθωνος ἀφανίζων.* A few fragments of his dramas remain. He was a close friend of Euripides, and is the ridiculous hero of Aristophanes' comedy, the *Thesmophoriazousae*. See Introd. to *Symposium*, p. 350. Cf. also 115,17.

᾿Αγαμέμνων, *-ωνος*, *Agamemnon*, leader of the Greek host against Troy. 255,30.

῎Αγρα, *-ας*, *Agra*, a suburb of Athens on the left bank of the Ilissus, where was a temple to Artemis (Pausan. I 19,6; where see Frazer). 259,6.

᾿Αδείμαντος, *-ου*, *Adeimantus*; (1) the son of Ariston, a (probably elder) brother of Plato, one of the interlocutors in the *Republic*. 29,15. 191,19, etc. (2) the son of Leucolophides, a prominent general at the close of the Peloponnesian War, one of the traitors at Aegospotamoi (X. *Hell.* II 1,32. Lys. 14,38. Ar. *Ran.* 1513). 115,20.

᾿Αθηνᾶ, *-ᾶς*, *Athēna*, daughter of Zeus. 205,10.

Αἰακός, *-οῦ*, *Aeăcus*, son of Zeus and Aegīna, born in the island Aegīna; famous for his justice, he became, after his death, one of the judges in the lower world. 40,28. 147,30. 151,29. 152,19.

Αἰαντάδωρος, *-ου*, *Aeantadōrus*; unknown. 29,16.

Αἰγίνη, *-ης*, *Aegīna*; (1) a daughter of the river-god Asōpus, who became by Zeus mother of Aeăcus. From her the island took its name. 152,19. (2) the island in the Sarōnic gulf, about 100 stades from Athens. 67,25.

῞Αιδης, *-ου* (i.e. *ἀ- ἴδης* from *ἀ-* and *ἰδ-εῖν*), *Hades*, the god of the invisible world. From the beginning of the 5th cent. B.C. he was often called **Πλούτων** *the Giver of Wealth* (from the nether earth come crops and metals),—a euphemistic name and with the intent, perhaps, to rob Death of his terrors.

Αἴας, *-αντος*, *Ajax*, the son of Telămon, after Achilles the bravest Greek before Troy. On the death of Achilles, a contest was held for his arms. The award was made to Odysseus. This drove Ajax to madness, and he killed himself. 41,6. 255,28.

Αἰσχίνης, -ου, *Aeschĭnes*, a very poor but devoted follower of Socrates, and writer of Socratic dialogues. 29,8. 67,16.

Αἰσχύλος, -ου, *Aeschy̆lus*, the earliest of the three great tragic poets of Greece (525–456 B.C.). Seven of his tragedies are yet extant. 205,13. 239,25.

Αἴσωπος, -ου, *Aesop*, the famous narrator (in prose) of fables, said by Herod., II 134, to have been a slave in Samos at the time of Croesus, middle of 6th cent. B.C. 69,15,28. 71,3.

Ἀκαρνάν, -ᾶνος, *an inhabitant of Acarnania*, the most westerly province of Greece. 155,15.

Ἀκουμενός, -οῦ, *Acumĕnus*, a physician, and friend of Socrates. 114,28. X. *Mem.* III 13,2.

Ἀλκιβιάδης, -ου, *Alcibiădes*; (1) ὁ παλαιός (156,17), grandfather of (2) the great Alcibiădes (450–404 B.C.), of great beauty, wealth, birth, and genius—Athens' darling, but without principle and a traitor. Aristophanes gives Athens' feeling towards him thus: ποθεῖ μέν, ἐχθαίρει δέ, βούλεται δ' ἔχειν. See notes to *Symposium*.

Ἀλκίνους, -ου, *Alcinoüs*, the mythical king of the mythical Phaeacians; entertainer of Odysseus. 247,16.

Ἀμέλης, -ητος (ποταμός), *the River of Indifference*. 257,8.

Ἀμφίπολις, -εως, *Amphipŏlis*, a town of Macedonia, an important colony of Athens, scene of a battle in 422 B.C. between Athenians and Spartans, in which both leaders, Cleon and Brasĭdas, were slain. 20,30.

Ἀμφιτρύων, -ωνος, *Amphitry̆on*, husband of Alcmēne the mother, by Zeus, of Herăcles. 173,9.

Ἀμφίων, -ωνος, *Amphīon*, son of Antiŏpe, by Zeus; twin brother of Zethus. See n. on 140,14.

Ἀνάγκη, -ης, *Necessity*, a personification of Orphic theology (post-Homeric). 251,6. *Symp.* 195 C, 197 B. Aesch. *Prom.* 514. Hor. *Odes* I 35,17. She had a temple at Corinth (Pausan. II 4,6).

Ἀναξαγόρας, -ου, *Anaxagŏras*, Ionian philosopher born c. 500 B.C., friend of Pericles and Euripides, accused in Athens of impiety, but saved from sentence of death by Pericles. 17,5,8; Introd. § 22.

Ἀνδροτίων, -ωνος, *Androtĭon*; unknown. 114,30.

Ἄνδρων, -ωνος, *Andron*; unknown. 114,29.

Ἀνταῖος, -ου, *Antaeus*, son of Poseidon and Earth, a Libyan giant and wrestler, invincible as long as his feet touched the mother-earth. But Herăcles lifted him, and so destroyed him. 103,25.

Ἀντήνωρ, -ορος, *Antēnor*, one of the wisest of the Trojan Elders. 101,19; *Il.* 3,148 and often.

itself, aiming at the practice of life, not its theory. In agreement with Protagoras, he taught that we can know only our sensations, not their causes ; of sensations some are pleasurable, others painful. The rational end of our effort should be therefore to obtain as many of the one kind and avoid as many of the other as possible. *ἡδονή* is good, *ἄλγος* is bad, the rest is indifferent (*ἀδιάφορον*). We must use *φρόνησις*, however, in balancing and choosing our pleasures.—This led to Epicureanism, as the Cynic philosophy of Antisthenes led to Stoicism. 67,23.

Ἀριστόδημος, -*ου*, *Aristodēmus* "the Little" (*ὁ μικρός*). See Introd. to *Symp.* p. 350.

Ἀριστοκράτης, -*ου*, *Aristocrătes*, a prominent member of the oligarchic party, one of the six generals executed after the battle of Arginūsae (n. on 26,18). 117,1. X. *Hell.* I 7,2 ; Ar. *Av.* 125 ; Thuc. VIII 89.

Ἀριστοφάνης, -*ους*, *Aristophănes*, the greatest comic poet of Greece (c. 450–385 B.C.). Eleven plays are extant. 4,27. 101,1. Introd. § 6.

Ἀρίστων, -*ωνος*, *Ariston*, father of Plato, Adeimantus, Glaucon ; otherwise without fame. 29,15.

Ἀριστώνυμος, -*ου*, *Aristonȳmus* ; an unknown. 192,23.

Ἀρμένιος, -*ου*, *Armenius* ; unknown. 247,17.

Ἀρχέλαος, -*ου*, *Archelāus*, king of Macedonia 413–399 B.C. ; murdered his half-brother to obtain the throne ; patron of art and literature, inducing Euripides, Agathon, and others to come to his court. 117,27. 131,6. 132,15,18. 150,16.

Ἀσκληπιάδης, -*ου*, *an Asclepiad* ; a name given properly to those practitioners of medicine who traced descent as well as art to Asclepius. But the term was applied more widely, not merely to the priests in the temples of Asclepius, but to any learned physician. 108,6. 208,8.

Ἀσκληπιός, -*ου*, *Asclepius* or *Aesculapius*, mentioned in Homer as a "blameless physician" (*ἀμύμων ἰατρός*), *Il.* 4,194 ; 11,518 ; also 2,731. Later he is made the son of Apollo, is taught the healing art by the centaur Cheiron, and comes to be worshipped as a god. 93,15. 208,11 ff.

Ἀταλάντη, -*ης*, *Atalanta*, the swift maid who would marry no one but him who could outrun her. The successful suitor won her by dropping during the race three golden apples, that tempted her to delay to pick them up. 256,2.

Ἄτροπος, -*ου*, *Atropus*, the post-Homeric name for one of the Fates (*Μοῖραι*). 251,20. Cf. *Il.* 24,49 and *Od.* 7,197 with Hes. *Theog.* 217.

Ἀττική, -*ῆς* (sc. *γῆ*), *Attica*, a district of Greece. 261,12.

Ἀχελῷος, -*ου*, *Achelōüs*, the great river-god, worshipped in all parts of Greece. 260,22. *Il.* 21,194 ; 24,616.

Ἀχιλλεύς, -*έως*, *Achilles*, the hero of the *Iliad.* 101,17.

Ἐπειός, -οῦ, *Epēus*, maker of the wooden horse. 256,5. *Od.* 8,493; 11,522. Virg. *Aen.* 2,264. (*Il.* 23,665 ff.)

Ἐπιγένης, -ους, *Epigĕnes*, pupil of Socrates. 29,9. 67,15.

Ἑρμογένης, -ους, *Hermogĕnes*, a poor brother of the rich Callias, an interlocutor in the *Cratylus*; unknown. 67,15.

Ἐρυξίμαχος, -ου, *Eryximăchus*, a physician, one of the guests in the *Symposium*. 94,25. 114,28.

Εὔηνος, -ου, *Evēnus*, the sophist, a poet and rhetorician of some note. 6,13. 69,30 ff. *Phaedr.* 276 A.

Εὐθύδημος, -ου, *Euthydēmus*; (1) the sophist known only from Plato's pages (154,25 etc.); (2) the brother of Lysias (192,20).

Εὐκλείδης, -ου, *Eucleides* or *Euclid*, a pupil of Socrates, who later taught and wrote dialogues at Megara; not to be confounded with the mathematician who lived at Alexandria in the time of the first Ptolemy (323–285 B.C.). 67,21.

Εὐριπίδης, -ου, *Euripides*, the third great tragic poet of Greece (480–406 B.C.), many of whose tragedies (18 or 19) still exist. Especially was he the poet of the Sophistic Movement, greatly admired by Socrates. 138,28. 140,11.

Εὐρύπυλος, -ου, *Eurypўlus*, a Greek chieftain in the Trojan War. 208,12. 211,18.

Εὐρώπη, -ης, *Europe*. 147,29. 148,4.

Ἐχεκράτης, -ους, *Echecrătes*; unknown. 64,8.

Ζεύς, Διός, *Zeus*, the supreme Olympian god, son of Cronus and Rhea, along with Hades, Poseidon, Hera, Demēter, and Hestia. 146,16. 202,17. 203,15. 205,3, etc. Hes. *Theog.* 453 ff.

Ζῆθος, -ου, *Zethus*. See Ἀμφίων, and n. on 140,14. 140,11.

Ἠλεῖος, *an Elēan, of Elis* (Ἦλις, -ιδος), a district on the West coast of Peloponnēsus, within whose borders lay Olympia, the seat of the Olympic games. 5,20. 113,8.

Ἤρ, -ός, *Er*; unknown. 247,17.

Ἥρα, -ας, *Hera*, sister and wife of Zeus. 203,14.

Ἡρακλῆς, -έους, *Herăcles* or *Hercules*, son of Zeus and Alcmēne, greatest of the Greek heroes. Among the labours imposed upon him by Eurystheus was that of destroying the many-headed water-serpent (ὕδρα) of Lerna near Argos (Hes. *Theog.* 313 ff.). See also Γηρυόνης supra. 104,6. 137,31. 165,25. 166,8 ff. 173,9.

Ἡρόδικος, -ου, *Herodicus*, a physician of the 5th cent. B.C. from Selymbria in Thrace, tutor of the great Hippocrates. 208,21.

Ἡσίοδος, -ου, *Hesiod*, the early Greek poet of Boeotia. Of his works (composed in dactylic hexameter) there remain the Θεογονία, the Ἔργα καὶ Ἡμέραι, with a third bearing his name, the Ἀσπὶς Ἡρακλέους. 41,1. 201,31.

Ἰλισσός, -οῦ, *Ilissus*, a small river of Attica, flowing past Athens on the South. 258,6,24. Pausan. I 19,5 (Frazer).

Ἰόλεως=Ἰόλαος, Iolāus, son of Iphĭcles (who was the half-brother of Herăcles), the trusty charioteer and attendant of his uncle. 166,2,4,7,15. (See Hes. ἀσπὶς Ἡρακλέους.)

Ἱππίας, -ου, *Hippias* of Elis, ridiculed by Plato as a sophist of many accomplishments, but vain and ostentatious. His roster of instruction included astronomy, geometry, arithmetic, philology, poetry, mythology, history and archaeology. He displayed himself at Olympia with everything about him self-made —the engraved finger-ring, flesh-scraper, shoes, cloak, belt, poems of all sorts, and prose speeches besides. 5,20. 113,8. 114,26. Introd. § 29. *Hipp. Maj.* 285 B, *Hipp. Min.* 368 B.

Ἱπποκένταυρος, -ου, *Hippocentaur*; these were mythical creatures of Thessaly, half-man and half-horse. See L. & S. s.v. Κένταυρος. 259,23.

Ἱπποκράτης, -ους, *Hippocrătes;* (1) an Asclepiad of the island Cos, the famous "father of medicine," resident in many places, writer of many treatises in the Ionic dialect concerning his art. But most of the extant works under his name are said to be spurious. 108,6. (2) an unknown one, but for Plato. 106,2 ff.

Ἱππόνικος, -ου, *Hipponīcus*, father of Callias, himself the son of a Callias, a link in the long family of Hipponīcus-Callias, extending from Solon's time with alternating names. The present one fell in the battle of Delium 424 B.C. 5,30. 107,20. Andoc. 1,130. 4,13.

Ἶρις, -ιδος, *Iris*, in the *Iliad*, the messenger of the gods; in the *Odyssey* she is not mentioned. 272,5.

Ἰφικλῆς, -έους, Iphĭcles, half-brother of Herăcles. 166,18. (See Hes. ἀσπ. Ἡρακ. 54.)

Καλλίας, -ου, *Callias*, scion of a very old Athenian family (see supra Ἱππόνικος) and one of the richest—an extravagant patron of sophists and high living. He died in want. Alcibiades married his sister. 5,30 ff. 107,20 ff. Andoc. 1,130; X. *Hell.* VI 4; Athen. 12,52.

Καλλικλῆς, -έους, *Callĭcles*, unknown but for Plato,—perhaps indeed a fictitious name for Charicles one of the Thirty (Bergk, *Griech. Literaturgesch.* IV, p. 447). 135,5 ff.

Καλχηδόνιος, *of Chalcēdon*, a Greek city across the Bosporus from Byzantium. 192,22.

Κέβης, -ητος, *Cebes*, a Theban, disciple of Socrates, former pupil of Philolāus. 46,26. 67,21 ff.

Κεῖος, *a Cēan, of the island Ceos* (Κέως), one of the Cyclădes. 5,20. 113,9. 115,5.

Κεραμῆς, -έων, *the Potters*, a deme of the tribe Acamantis. 115,14.

Κέρβερος, -*ου*, *Cerbĕrus*, according to Hesiod, the 50-headed dog of Hades (*Theog.* 311 ff.). He is not mentioned in Homer. Later he is given but three heads. 241,16.

Κέφαλος, -*ου*, *Cephalus*, of Syracuse, a wealthy man induced by Pericles to come to Athens. He lived as a metic in the Peiraeus. 191,11 ff. Lys. 12,4.

Κῆπις, -*ιδος*, *Cepis* ; unknown. 115,20.

Κηφισιεύς, -*έως*. See 29,9 n.

Κλαζομένιος, *of Clazomĕnae*, one of the twelve Ionian cities of Asia Minor. 17,9.

Κλεινίας, -*ου*, *Cleinĭas* ; of no note. 156,18.

Κλειτοφῶν, -*ῶντος*, *Cleitophon* ; unknown, though a dialogue is named after him. 192,23.

Κλεόμβροτος, -*ου*, *Cleombrotus* ; unknown, though some identify with the Ambraciot spoken of on p. 335. 67,23.

Κλωθώ, -*οῦς*, *Clotho*, one of the three Fates. See Ἄτροπος. 251,19 ff. 256,26.

Κρήτη, -*ης*, *Crete*, one of the large islands of the Mediterranean, in control of the Dorians. 60,28. 65,12.

Κριτίας, -*ου*, *Critias*, a quondam pupil of Socrates, but not for philosophy's sake ; an extreme oligarch, pre-eminent among the Thirty for cruelty. 275,8. For his murder of Theramĕnes and his own death at the battle of Munychia, see X. *Hell.* II 3,2,15–56. 4,1–19.

Κριτόβουλος, -*ου*, *Critobūlus*, son of Crito, and pupil of Socrates. 29,7. 36,9. 67,13. 154,22.

Κρίτων, -*ωνος*, *Crito*. See Introd. to *Crito*, pp. 320,321. 29,6. 36,8. 69,1, etc.

Κρόνος, -*ου*, *Cronus*, son of Urănus (Οὐρανός), whom he dethroned, and father of Zeus, who in turn dethroned him. 146,18. 202,15.

Κτήσιππος, -*ου*, *Ktesippus* ; unknown. 67,16. 161,20 ff.

Κῷος, *a Coan, of Cos*, an island lying opposite to Halicarnassus, sacred to Asclepius, birthplace of Hippocrătes. 108,6.

Λακεδαιμόνιοι, *the Lacedaemonians*. 103,23.

Λακεδαίμων, -*ονος*, *Lacedaemon* = Sparta. 60,28.

Λάχεσις, -*εως*, *Lachĕsis*, one of the three Fates. See Ἄτροπος. 251,19 ff. 252,1 ff. 256,22.

Λάχης, -*ητος*, *Laches*, an Athenian general, active in the first half of the Peloponnesian War. He fell in the battle of Mantinēa, 418 B.C. (Thuc. V 74). 100,25,30. 102.

Λεοντῖνος, *of Leontīni*, a Sicilian town near Syracuse. 5,19.

Λευκολοφίδης, -*ου*, *Leucolophĭdes* ; unknown. 115,21.

Λέων, -*οντος*, *Leon*, a rich Salaminian, arrested and put to death by the Thirty without a trial. 27,2. X. *Hell.* II 3,39. Andoc. 1,94.

Λήθη, -*ης*, *Lethe*, the river of Oblivion. 257,4,24.

Λύκειον, *-ου*, *the Lycēum*, a famous gymnasium and temple in Athens, sacred to *Ἀπόλλων Λύκειος* (the Wolfish); favourite haunt of Socrates, and the regular place later for Aristotle's peripatetic (*περιπατητικός*) instruction (Pausan. I 19,3; Frazer). 154,10.

Λύκων, *-ωνος*, *Lycon*, one of Socrates' accusers, otherwise unidentified. There is a Lycon, father of Autolȳcus, in X. *Symp.*, and also one in Ar. *Vesp.* 1301. 12,16,18. 32,26.

Λυσανίας, *-ου*, *Lysanias*; unknown. 29,7.

Λυσίας, *-ου*, *Lysias*, son of Cephalus, one of Athens' ten great orators; some 34 speeches of his are still extant. 192,19.

Λυσίμαχος, *-ου*, *Lysimăchus*; (1) father of Aristīdes (151,14); (2) son of Aristīdes (103,2).

Μαρσύας, *-ου*, *Marsȳas*, a satyr of Phrygia, who with the flute contended against Apollo with the lyre. Apollo was victor, and flayed Marsȳas alive (X. *Anab.* I 2,8). 96,25. 97,6. 98,1.

Μέγαράδε, Μεγαρόθεν, *to (from) Megăra* a town on the Isthmus about 30 miles from Athens. 61,16. 67,21.

Μέλητος, *-ου*, *Melētus*, described by Plato (*Euthyph.* 2 B) as *νέος καὶ ἀγνώς, ἔστι δὲ δῆμον Πιτθεύς*. Identification is doubtful. He may be the son of the tragic poet ridiculed by Aristoph. in *Ran.* 1302, but is hardly the one concerned in the mock celebration of the Mysteries in 415 B.C. (Andoc. 1,12,35,63,94). 4,18 ff.

Μενδαῖος, *a Mendēan, of Mende*, a town in Chalcidĭce. 114,9.

Μενέλεως, *-ω*, *Menelāus*, brother of Agamemnon, husband of Helen. 211,14.

Μενέξενος, *-ου*, *Menexĕnus*; unknown, but giving his title to the dialogue *Menexenus*. 67,17. 261.

Μένων, *-ωνος*, *Menon*, a Thessalian pupil of Gorgias, one of the Greek generals under Cyrus. For his treachery, and death by torture, see X. *Anab.* II 4,15. 5,28. 6,29. Plato names a dialogue from him (p. 177).

Μίδας, *-ου*, *Midas*, the mythical king of Phrygia, of fabulous wealth. He obtained his desire that all he touched might be turned to gold, unhappily even his food. For his ass's ears, see the dictionaries of mythology. 211,26.

Μίνως, *-ωος*, *Minos*, a son of Zeus and brother of Rhadamanthus, king and lawgiver of Crete (*Il.* 13,450. 14,322. *Od.* 11,568). 40,28. 147,28. 148,4. 151,30.

Μνήμη, *-ης* = *Μνημοσύνη*, *Mnemosȳne*, mother of the 9 Muses (Hes. *Theog.* 915). 157,6.

Μοῖραι, *-ῶν*, *the Fates*, 3 daughters of Zeus and Themis (Hes. *Theog.* 901). 251,17.

Μοῦσαι, *-ῶν*, *the Muses*, 9 daughters of Zeus and Mnemosȳne

(Hes. *Theog.* 52 ff. *Od.* 24,60). Pausan. IX 29,2 makes them originally three in number, with the significant names Μελέτη, Μνήμη, Ἀοιδή. 157,6. 273,16.

Μουσαῖος, -*ου*, *Musaeus*, one of those poets of Greece so ancient, that even for the ancients themselves they had become mythical. Such were Orpheus, Eumolpus, Thamўras, Linus and others. Musaeus was said to have been the pupil of Orpheus. 41,1.

Μυρρινούσιος, *of the deme* Μυρρινοῦς, tribe Πανδιονίς. 114,29.

Μυσός, -*οῦ*, *a Mysian*, Mysia lay in the N.W. corner of Asia Minor. 143,10.

Μῶμος, -*ου*, *Momus*, the god of Faultfinding, offspring of Night (Hes. *Theog.* 214). 104,18.

Νέστωρ, -*ορος*, *Nestor*, the oldest Greek leader before Troy, his most active fighting days long since past. But he was strong (and long) in counsel. 101,19.

Νικήρατος, -*ου*, *Nicerătus*; (1) father of Nicias, of no note (116,24); (2) son of Nicias (191,20), put to death by the Thirty utterly without cause (Lys. 18,6). He could recite the whole *Iliad and Odyssey* by heart (X. *Symp.* 3,5).

Νικίας, -*ου*, *Nicias*, a famous but unfortunate (or incompetent) Athenian general, who in Sicily 413 B.C. sacrificed an Athenian army and his own life to his religious scruples. 116,23.

Νικόστρατος, -*ου*, *Nicostrătus*; unknown. 29,11.

Νιόβη, -*ης*, *Niŏbe*, daughter of Tantalus and wife of Amphīon, slain with her 7 sons and 7 daughters by the shafts of Apollo and Artemis, because of her boast of numerous progeny over their mother Leto, who had borne but two. 205,18.

Νύμφαι, -*ῶν*, *the Nymphs*, female divinities that peopled ocean, river, mountain, and wood—Nereids, Naiads, Oreads, Dryads (Hes. *Theog.* 130). 260,21.

Ξανθίππη, -*ης*, *Xanthippe*, the unhappy mate of Socrates, whose name the world has chosen to stand for the scolding wife. If she were indeed a scold, perhaps the world's final debt is to her for Socratic philosophy. 68,27.

Ξάνθιππος, -*ου*, *Xanthippus*, son of Pericles, who with his brother Parălus died in the great plague of 430 B.C. (Plut. *Life of Pericles*, ch. 36). 114,8.

Ξέρξης, -*ου*, *Xerxes*, son of Darīus, invader of Greece. 137,5.

Ὀδυσσεύς, -*έως*, *Odysseus* (*Ulysses*), the hero of the *Odyssey*, a man who had suffered much and wandered far. 41,15. 152,1. 256,8.

Οἰνόη, -*ης*, *Oenöe*, a deme of the tribe Ἱπποθωντίς, near Boeotia. 106,18.

Ὀλυμπίασι, *at Olympia,* the seat of the great games in Elis, western Peloponnēsus. 33,30.

Ὄλυμπος, -*ου*, *Olympus,* earliest semi-mythical master of the ancient flute (a quasi-clarinet). It is said there were two of this name. 97,6.

Ὅμηρος, -*ου*, *Homer* "the poet," now dissolved by many scholars into mythic mist. Cf. the fate of Ὄλυμπος, Ὀρφεύς, Μουσαῖος.

Ὀρφεύς, -*έως*, *Orpheus,* most famous of the mythic bards of Greece, drawing stones and trees by the power of his lyre. He descended into Hades to bring back Eurydĭce, but failed at the moment of success. He was torn to pieces by Bacchanalian women. 40,31. 255,20.

Οὐρανός, -*οῦ*, *Urănus,* son of Earth (Γῆ), and, by her, father of many primeval gods (Hes. *Theog.* 126 ff.). 202,14.

Παιανιεύς, -*έως*, *of the deme* Παιανία, of the tribe Πανδιονίς. 67,17. 192,22.

Παλαμήδης, -*ου*, *Palamēdes,* a Greek hero of the Trojan War, stoned to death for treachery, when there was found in his tent a letter signed with Priam's name, though in fact a forgery by Odysseus. The story is not found in Homer. 41,5.

Παμφυλία, -*ας*, *Pamphylia,* a narrow district on the S. coast of Asia Minor, seat of a mixed race (*πάμ-φυλοι*). 249,24. Πάμφυλος ; 247,18.

Πάνδαρος, -*ου*, *Pandărus,* a Trojan ally famous for his bowmanship. 205,10. 211,15.

Πανοπεύς, -*έως*, *Panopeus* ; unknown. 256,5.

Πάραλος, -*ου*, *Parălus* ; (1) an unknown (29,14) ; (2) a son of Pericles (114,5).

Πάριος, *a Parian, of the island Paros,* one of the Cyclădes, famous and important for its marble. 5,27.

Πατροκλῆς, -*έους*, *Patrŏcles,* an unknown brother of Socrates. 166,16.

Πάτροκλος, -*ου*, *Patroclus,* the friend of Achilles, slain by Hector, and avenged by Achilles. 20,11. 208,16.

Παυσανίας, -*ου*, *Pausanias,* known only from Plato ; he is a guest in the *Symposium.* 115,13.

Πειραιεύς, -*ῶς*, *Peiraeus,* the port-town of Athens, about 4 miles distant. 191,1.

Πελοπίδαι, -*ῶν*, *the Pelopĭdae,* descendants of Pelops, who came from Asia Minor and gave his name to Pelopon-nēsus. 205,18.

Περικλῆς, -*έους*, *Pericles,* the great aristocratic leader of the democracy of Athens when at the height of her glory. He died 429 B.C. 97,27. 101,19.

Πήγασος, -*ου*, *Pegăsus,* the winged horse of Bellerŏphon and the Muses, springing from the blood of Medūsa when Perseus cut off her head (Hes. *Theog.* 280,325). 259,26.

Σιμωνίδης, -*ου*, *Simonĭdes* of Ceos, like Pindar, one of the great lyric poets of Greece (556–468 B.C.) Many fragments of his poems are extant. 198,3.

Σίσυφος, -*ου*, *Sisyphus*, a wicked king of Corinth (or Ephȳra), whom Odysseus saw punished in the lower world, by being made to roll uphill a stone that ever shamelessly ran down again (*Il.* 6,153. *Od.* 11,593). 41,15. 150,27.

Σκέλλιος, -*ου*, *Scellius*; unknown. 117,1.

Σκίρων, -*ωνος*, *Sciron*, the noted highwayman near Megara, who robbed wayfarers and then kicked or shoved them off the cliff-road into the sea—slain at last by Theseus. 103,23.

Σκύθης, -*ου*, *a Scythian.* 137,6.

Σκύλλα, -*ης*, *Scylla*, a she-monster with 12 feet, 6 necks and heads, and 3 rows of teeth in each head, apt to catch all sailors that were trying to avoid the whirlpool Charybdis that lay on the opposite side of the strait (*Od.* 12,85). 241,15.

Σόλων, -*ωνος*, *Solon*, most famous of the ἑπτὰ Σοφοί, Athenian lawgiver and poet for the first half of the 6th cent. B.C. (archon c. 594 B.C.). Many fragments of his poems are extant. 103,7.

Σούνιον, -*ου*, *Sunium*, the southern promontory of Attica, upon which stood a temple to Athēna c. 300 feet above the sea. 44,8.

Σοφοκλῆς, -*έους*, *Sophocles*, the second great tragic poet of Greece (496–406 B.C.). Seven tragedies still remain. He marks the culminating glory of the Athenian drama. 194,13 ff. Introd. § 4.

Σφήττιος. See 29,8 n.

Σωκράτης. See Introd.

Σωφρονίσκος, -*ου*, *Sophroniscus*, the father of Socrates, 166,24.

Τάνταλος, -*ου*, *Tantălus*, son of Zeus and father of Pelops and Niŏbe, punished after death for whatever his sins were (accounts differ), by being placed in a lake of water up to his chin, from which he might never quench his thirst (the water receding as he stooped), while over his head waved branches of fruit that blew out of his reach whenever he would satisfy his hunger (*Od.* 11,582). 115,4. 150,27.

Τάρταρος, -*ου*, *Tartarus* (*Il.* 8,13–16) is the deepest pit under the earth, as far below Hades as earth is below heaven. 146,24.

Τελαμών, -*ῶνος*, *Telămon*, son of Aeăcus, was brother of Peleus, and father of Ajax. He was king of Salamis and a friend of Heracles. 41,6. Τελαμώνιος 255,28.

Τερψίων, -*ωνος*, *Terpsion*; unknown. 67,22.

Τιτυός, -*οῦ*, *Tityus*, son of Earth (Γῆ), who in the under world of punishment lay stretched upon the ground over 9 plethra, with two vultures feeding upon his liver, for he could

Χαιρέδημος, -ου, *Chaeredēmus*; unknown. 166,25.

Χαιρεφῶν, -ῶντος, *Chaerephon*, a devoted, cadaverous, barefooted, impetuous admirer of Socrates, the butt of Aristophanic wit in *Nub.* 104,144–56,503,831,1465; *Vesp.* 1408–12; *Av.* 1296,1564. 7,17 ff.; 135,3.

Χαρμαντίδης, -ου, *Charmantĭdes*; unknown. 192,22.

Χαρμίδης, -ου *Charmĭdes*, Plato's uncle, giving his name to one of the dialogues; he was prominent in the oligarchical party, and fell with Critias in the battle with the returning democratic party at Munychia, 404 B.C. (X. *Hell.* II 4,19). 114,6.

Χίμαιρα, -ας, *the Chimaera*, a she-monster of Lycia described in *Il.* 6,180 as *θεῖον γένος, οὐδ' ἀνθρώπων, | πρόσθε λέων, ὄπισθεν δὲ δράκων, μέσση δὲ χίμαιρα, | δεινὸν ἀποπνείουσα πυρὸς μένος αἰθομένοιο.* It was slain by Bellerŏphon (Hes. *Theog.* 325). 241,15. 259,24.

Χίος, -ου, *Chios*, one of the large and important islands of the Aegēan sea. 155,8.

Ὠρείθυια, -ας, *Oreithyia*, daughter of King Erechtheus of Athens. See 258,25.

GREEK INDEX

The figures give the page and line; "n" refers to the notes, "A" to the Appendix. There is usually a note on the first passage cited, even though not indicated by "n."

INDEX—ENGLISH

THE figures give the page and line; "n" refers to the notes, "A" to the Appendix. Usually there is a note on the first citation, even though not indicated by "n."

THE END

Printed by R. & R. CLARK, LIMITED, *Edinburgh*.